Learn to
Program
with Visual Basic 2010 Express

D1429749

John Smiley

Smiley Publishing
Philadelphia

Smiley Publishing

PO Box 2062

Riverton, NJ 08077

U.S.A.

smileypublishing@johnsmiley.com

Learn to Program with Visual Basic 2010 Express™

ISBN: 978-0-9827349-0-2

Learn to Program with Visual Basic 6

Learn to Program with Visual Basic 6 Examples

Learn to Program am with Visual Basic 6 Objects

Learn to Program with Visual Basic 6 Databases

Learn to Program with VB.Net 2002/2003

Learn to Program with VB.Net 2005 Express

Learn to Program with VB.Net 2008 Express

Learn to Program with Visual Basic 2010 Express

Learn to Program with Java

Learn to Program with C#

Learn to Program with C++

Learn to Program with JavaScript

Learn to Program with Visual C# 2005 Express™

Learn to Program with Visual C# 2008 Express™

Learn to Program with Visual C# 2010 Express™

10 9 8 7 6 5 4 3 2 1

Trademark Acknowledgements

Smiley Publishing has endeavored to provide trademark information about all the companies and products mentioned in this book by the appropriate use of capitals. However, Smiley Publishing cannot guarantee the accuracy of this information.

Credits

Author John Smiley	**Layout and Proof** John Smiley
Development Editor John Smiley	**Cover** John Smiley
Technical Editor John Smiley	**Index** John Smiley
Technical Reviewers John Smiley	

Printing History:

May 2010: First Printing

This book is dedicated to my wife Linda

About the Author

John Smiley, a Microsoft Certified Professional (MCP) and Microsoft Certified Solutions Developer (MCSD) in Visual Basic, has been programming and teaching for more than 20 years. He is the President of John Smiley and Associates, a computer consulting firm serving clients both large and small in the Philadelphia Metropolitan area. John is an adjunct professor of Computer Science at Penn State University, Philadelphia University, and Holy Family College, and also teaches in a variety of Internet venues including SmartPlanet and ElementK.

On the writing front, John is the author of the immensely popular **Learn to Program with Visual Basic 6**, along with Learn to Program with Visual Basic Examples, Learn to Program Databases with Visual Basic 6, Learn to Program Objects with Visual Basic 6, Learn to Program with Java, Learn to Program with VB.Net 2002/2003, Learn to Program with VB.Net 2005 Express, Learn to Program with VB.Net 2008 Express, Learn to Program with Visual Basic 2010 Express, Learn to Program with C#, Learn to Program with Visual C# 2005 Express, Learn to Program with Visual C# 2008 Express, Learn to Program with Visual C# 2010 Express, Learn to Program with C++ and Learn to Program with JavaScript..

Feel free to visit John's Web Site at

http://www.johnsmiley.com

or contact him via email at johnsmiley@johnsmiley.com. He religiously answers all of his emails, although not necessarily instantaneously!

Contents

Acknowledgments

I want to thank first and foremost my wife Linda for her love and support.

Many thanks also go to the thousands of students I've taught over the years for your tireless dedication to learning the art and science of computer programming. Your great questions and demanding persistence in getting the most out of your learning experience truly inspired me, and has contributed greatly to my books. Many of you dragged yourself to class after a long hard day of work, or rose early on your Saturday day off to learn Visual Basic and the other programming languages I have taught. You have my greatest respect and admiration.

I also want to thank the many readers of my books who took the time to write or email me about the books. Most of the time, the correspondence is incredibly glowing---I truly appreciate hearing from each of you, and I want you to know that I read and respond to each email I receive.

Particular thanks go to Mike Webb, who provided valuable feedback of previous editions of this book.

I want to thank all the members of my family for their continued belief in and support of me over the years, in particular my mother, who continues to say several hundred novenas for the success of my books, and who has probably said just as many for this one I'm sure.

Finally, I want to acknowledge my father, who although not physically here to see this book, is surely flipping through the pages of it now. It's been over twenty five years since I last saw you---and your role in the writing of this and my others books can never be understated---you and mother have been a great inspiration and role model for me. I know that the God who made us all will someday permit us to be together again.

Organizations/Conventions Used in the Book

Each chapter of the book follows in a session in a make-believe college classroom. Read along and learn the material with the rest of the students.

Every chapter has example programs and practical exercises for you to complete. I encourage you to follow along with the example programs---and by all means complete the exercises in the book as well. If typing is not your strong suit, you can download both the completed examples and exercises via this link

http://www.johnsmiley.com/main/books.htm

Care to take a quiz to test your knowledge? Follow this link and you can take a series of multiple choice quizzes drawn from the book

http://www.johnsmiley.com/tester/login.asp

Finally, if the book isn't enough for you to get going with Visual Basic, consider joining me in an Internet-based Visual Basic class. My introductory classes are held several times throughout the year---and I'll be teaching these classes for as long as I'm sojourning in this dimension. For more information, follow this link...

http://www.johnsmiley.com/main/training.htm

Chapter 1---Where Do I Begin?

"Where do I begin?" is a question I am frequently asked by my students, and this seems like a good question to tackle right at the beginning of this book. In this first chapter, we'll look at the development process of an actual working program through the eyes and ears of my university programming class and you will also be introduced to our 'class project'. By the end of the book, we'll have taken a real-life application through from the concept all the way to the finished product!

> **NOTE: Occasionally, my students get disillusioned when they hear that we won't be diving straight in and coding our application. However, when I remind them that programming is much the same as writing a report (or in other words, it is a two stage process of planning and then producing) they tend to settle down.**

Where Do We Begin

As part of answering the question, "Where do we begin?" this chapter looks at the Systems Development Life Cycle, which is a methodology that has been developed to ensure that systems are developed in a methodical, logical and step-by-step approach. We'll be looking at the Systems Development Life Cycle in quite a bit of detail, since the majority of this book will be spent in developing a real-world application. In this chapter we'll meet with a prospective client and conduct a preliminary interview with him. From that interview (and a subsequent one!) we'll develop a Requirements Statement, which provides details as to what the program should do. This Requirements Statement will form the basis of the application that we will develop throughout the rest of the book

> **NOTE: From this point on, you will follow me as I lead a group of my university students in an actual class on Visual Basic. If I do my job right, you will be a part of the class, learning along with them as we complete a fifteen-week course about programming in Visual Basic.**

Many books on computer programming have the reader, perhaps as early as the first chapter, code a program which 'cutely' displays a message box that says 'Hello World'. Then the author will point to the fact that within the first few minutes of reading their book, the reader has already written a working program. I'm not so naive as to believe that writing such a program makes you a programmer. Therefore, we'll opt for a slower approach. Simple programs, although great for the ego, are not the programs that are found in the real world. Real-world programs are written to meet someone's needs. These needs are frequently complex and difficult to verbalize. In this book, you and I will embark on a journey together that will see us complete the prototyping stage of a real-world project. I believe that this is the best way to learn programming.

In my university classes, I don't usually introduce the class project until several weeks into the semester. When I finally do introduce the class project, I give the students in my class a Requirements Statement. Since the class project is to develop a Windows application, with an event-driven paradigm (look that one up in the dictionary), I never tell my students exactly *how* the application should look, or how to program it. I tell them only what is required. In other words, I complete the hard part for them - gathering the user requirements.

Programming the Easy Way

When I first began to teach programming, some of my students would tell me that they just didn't know where to start when they first began to work on their programming assignments. They would start to program the application, then stop. Some of them would find themselves re-writing their code and re-designing their application several times. Then they would change it again. Face to face I could usually clear things up for them by giving them a gentle nudge or hint in the right direction. However, their work would show a definite lack of direction. Why the problem? They lacked a plan.

As soon as I realized this, I began to teach them more than just programming. I began to teach them the Systems Development Life Cycle (SDLC), the methodology I mentioned earlier. You see, people need blueprints or maps. They need something tangible, usually in writing, before they can begin a project. Just about all of my students agree that having a blueprint of some kind makes the development process that much easier.

Sometimes I'll meet former students of mine at the university, and I'll ask them how their other programming classes are coming along. Occasionally, they'll tell me that they're working on a great *real-world* assignment of some kind, but they just don't know where to begin. At that point, I'll remind them of what I told them in class - that they should begin with the design of the user interface, observe the default behavior of the design and then add code to fill in the gaps. That's not the problem, they tell me. The problem is that they don't know how to gather the user requirements for the system. They don't really know what the system should do.

Often the real problem is that the client isn't prepared to give the programmers a detailed enough Requirements Statement. In class the professor gives out a well-defined Requirements Statement but in the real world, programmers need to develop this themselves. Unfortunately, they may not know how to sit down with the prospective user of their system to determine what is required to satisfy the user's needs.

That skill, to listen to the user and determine their needs, is something that I now teach to some extent in all of my computer classes - whether they are programming courses, courses on Systems Analysis and Design, or Database Management.

Planning a Program is Like Planning a House

A friend of mine is a general contractor and home-builder. His job is similar to that of a programmer or system designer. He recently built an addition to a customer's house. He wouldn't think of beginning that work without first meeting with the owner of the house to determine their needs. He couldn't possibly presume to know what the owner wants or needs. The builder's role, in meeting with the owner, is largely to listen and then to advise.

My friend the home builder tells me that certain home owners may want a design that is architecturally unsound - either because their ideas and design are unsafe and would violate accepted building code regulations, or because they would violate local zoning regulations for their neighborhood. In some cases, he tells me, owners ask for features that he is certain they will later regret - and probably hold him responsible for. His role as an advisor demands that he inform the homeowner of these problems.

As soon as my friend believes that he understands what the owner wants, then he prepares a set of blueprints to be reviewed by the homeowner. Frequently the owner, after seeing his own vision on paper, will decide to change something, such as the location of a window or the size of a closet. The *concrete* characteristics of the blueprints make an agreement between the builder and owner easier to arrive at. The same can be said of a concrete plan for the writing of a program or the development of a system.

The big advantage of developing a plan on paper is that, while the project is still on paper, it's relatively painless to change it. Once the house has been assembled and bolted together, it becomes much more of a problem to change something.

The same is true of a computer program. Although it's not physically nailed or bolted together, once a programmer has started to write a program, changing it becomes very labor-intensive. It's much easier to change the design of a system prior to writing the first line of code.

In the world of software development, you would be surprised how many programmers begin work on an application without really having listened to the user. I know some programmers who get a call from a user, take some quick notes over the phone, and deliver an application without ever having met them! It could be that the user's requirements sound *similar* to something the programmer wrote last year, so the developer feels that will be good enough for the new client.

Other developers go a step further, and may actually meet with the client to discuss the user's needs. Nevertheless, sometimes the developer may not be a good listener, or just as likely, the user may communicate their needs poorly. The result may be that the user receives a program that doesn't come close to doing what they wanted it to do.

In this course, we'll develop a prototype for a real-world application called the China Shop Project, and then take it through to the complete product. As we progress through the course together, we will work through one possible solution, but I want you to know that in

Visual Basic programming, the number of solutions are almost infinite. As I tell my students all the time, there are many ways to paint a picture. One of the things I love about teaching Visual Basic is that I have never received the same solution to a project twice. Everyone brings his or her own unique qualities to the project.

I want you to feel free to take the China Shop Project and make your solution different from mine. In fact, I encourage it, but you should stick close to the Requirements Statement that we are going to develop in this chapter.

We Receive a Call from the China Shop

One Monday morning I received a call from a prospective client, Mr. Joe Bullina. Having seen my ad in the Western Suburban Times he wanted a computer program. By saying the magic word "program" Mr. Bullina had now got my complete attention.

Mr. Bullina owned a store that sold fine china. The dish variety. I know next to nothing about china. Writing programs about something that you know nothing about is not unusual for a programmer. That's why the Systems Development Life Cycle (SDLC) was introduced many years ago. At a minimum, the SDLC will result in the creation of a Requirements Statement, which will form the basis of an agreement between the programmer and the user as to what the program should do.

Mr. Bullina told me that he had spoken to other software developers in the area, but at their rates ($50 an hour and up), he didn't think he could afford them. Like so many people these days, he was on a tight budget, and I agreed with him, custom software development is not cheap.

"Have you checked out your local computer store for software that might meet your needs?" I asked him.

He told me he had, but with no luck.

"What about trade magazines?" I suggested.

He told me he'd checked them, but the programs advertised seemed too complicated for his needs. He wanted something simple.

"Why computerize?" I asked Mr. Bullina.

He told me it seemed like a good idea. That may sound like a good motive, but it's not usually the best reason to computerize.

We agreed to meet on Tuesday afternoon as I had another client in the area that needed some assistance with a DOS program that I had written. I told Mr. Bullina I'd stop by the China store after I finished up there.

We Meet with Our Client

I arrived at the Bullina China Shop at around 2 p.m. on Tuesday afternoon. Going into the store, a small brick building, I saw that there were around ten or fifteen customers and three neatly dressed sales clerks serving the customers at a counter. A display area took up most of the store. There were glass display counters along the walls and behind the counters were shelves of dishes… I mean fine china. It's always best to try and get into the client's mindset. I got the attention of one of the sales clerks.

"Hi, I'm John Smiley, I'm here to meet with the owner of the store."

"Just a minute Mr. Smiley, Joe is expecting you."

Good, I thought. The sales clerk called the owner by his first name. I prefer an informal atmosphere. It usually makes for better business. A few moments later, Mr. Bullina appeared from behind a curtain separating the front of the store from the back.

"Sorry to keep you waiting," he said, warmly extending his hand. "I was on the phone with one of my overseas china suppliers."

He led me past the counters into the back of store, past shelves of china, and into a small office where we took a seat before getting down to business.

"Mr. Bullina," I said, "in our conversation on the telephone, you said that you were interested in me writing a program for you."

"Please, call me Joe," he said smiling. "Yes, as you probably saw when you came into the shop, I had a number of customers waiting for my sales clerks to serve them. At any given time, I have about ten or more customers in the store, but only three sales clerks to wait on them. Some of those customers will grow impatient and leave. Some of my sales clerks, sensing this, may rush the customers they're helping. The thing about this is that I'm lucky if three out of those ten customers actually purchase something. Most of them are just browsing and checking prices, they have no real intention of buying anything. Still, they're consuming the time and resources of my sales clerks. This is where the program comes in."

I was starting to get interested in this. I love projects with a positive payback for my client, and it was obvious that this had one.

"I'd like to place a computer in the middle of the sales floor," he said, "on a table top or counter. Like the kind I've seen in some of the shopping malls. You've probably seen them. They give directions to shoppers, advertise sales, some even print coupons!"

"You mean kiosks," I said.

"Yes, exactly," he continued. "I'd like to place a kiosk computer in the middle of my sales floor, and have it compute a price for a customer based on the selections they make. That way, my sales clerks can concentrate on the customers who actually want to purchase something."

"Do you have any details in your mind as to what you want the program to look like?" I said.

"Not really," Joe said. "I was really hoping you could take care of those details. Don't get me wrong. I know what I want the program to do, that is, calculate a quote for some china. Beyond that, my biggest requirement is that the program be simple. I don't want to intimidate any of my customers. I'm just guessing, but I don't think many of my customers have used a computer before."

"I like my clients to give me as much detail as they can," I said. "That way I can do my best to write a program which really does what they want it to."

"I don't think the program will be very complex," Joe said. "Let me tell you a little bit about the China Shop. Basically, we're a specialty store. We only sell three brands of china, and only one pattern of each brand. Our inventory includes plates, butter plates, soup bowls, cups, saucers and platters. We sell either complete place settings or."

"Excuse me," I interrupted as I started to take notes. "What's a complete place setting?"

"A complete place setting," he explained, "is one each of a plate, a butter plate, a soup bowl, a cup and a saucer, all of the same brand." He looked at me sensing the confusion on my face. "I guess the business of a software developer is a constant learning process for you," Joe said. "Each new program you write requires that you learn new terms and new rules. It must be difficult."

I nodded in agreement and said, "It's a challenge, but I do enjoy it, almost as much as I enjoy teaching."

"I didn't know you were also a teacher," Joe said. "Where do you teach?"

After I told him, he told me that he would like to take a class with me some day.

"That would be great," I said, "then you'll have an opportunity to learn some of my terms!" We both laughed. "By the way," I said, "what's a butter plate?"

"A butter plate is a 6-inch plate," Joe said. "There are also salad plates and dessert plates, but we don't stock them. Did I tell you that we also sell individual pieces of china?"

"Such as one plate, or two cups?" I replied.

"Yes, exactly," he said. "But we only sell them in quantities of one, two, four or eight."

"Quantities of one, two, four, or eight what?" I asked. "Complete place settings or individual pieces?"

"Both," Joe said. I was beginning to get horribly confused.

"Let me get this straight," I said. "You sell complete place settings in any quantity, but individual pieces only in quantities of one, two, four or eight?"

"No," he said. "The quantity restrictions apply to both complete place settings and individual pieces. Over the years we have found that selling in quantities other than those can really wreak havoc with our inventory."

"I don't know much about china," I said, "but I think my wife and I have an eight piece place setting of Mikasa china at home, plus a platter and some big bowls."

"Yes," he said, "but in my shop, a complete place setting does not include a platter. A complete place setting includes only a plate, a butter plate, a soup bowl, a cup and a saucer. Of course, we do offer platters for sale, although we don't carry the big bowls - most likely those are serving bowls."

"In what quantities," I asked, "do you sell the platters - quantities of one, two, four and eight also?"

"That's a good question," Joe said. "I'm glad you asked that, because I probably would have forgotten to tell you. Because platters are a specialty item, they're very expensive, we only sell platters in quantities of one. In other words, only one to a customer." Joe could see that I was puzzled. "It's confusing I know," he said. "Of course, we can always special order any item in the store if the customer wants it," he said, "but I want the program to restrict the quantity of a platter on the sales quotation to one. Maybe the program could display a message telling the customer they can only purchase one. Is that possible?"

"Sure," I said, "that's possible, that's why I'm here. To give you exactly what you want. You're doing an excellent job of explaining your requirements. A lot of my clients can't express their needs as well as you have. The better you communicate them to me, the closer the program I write for you will come to meeting those needs."

"Let me summarize my understanding of what we have so far," I continued. "The customer can select from three brands of china. You only sell one pattern of each brand. The customer can select either a complete place setting, which consists of one each of a plate, a butter plate, a soup bowl, a cup and a saucer of the same brand. Alternatively, the customer can also select any individual piece they wish. The customer can select complete place settings and individual pieces only in quantities of one, two, four or eight. Platter quantities are limited to one. If the customer attempts to select more than one platter, you want a message displayed telling them that sales of platters are limited to just one."

"That's right so far," Joe said.

"Your china inventory includes plates, butter plates, soup bowls, cups, saucers and platters. A complete place setting is made up of a plate, a butter plate, a soup bowl, a cup and a saucer, all of the same brand," I added and looked up from my notes, somewhat proud of my requirements gathering abilities.

"Yes, that's about it," Joe said, "but did I make it clear that the customer must order the same quantity of everything? In other words, the customer cannot order four cups and two saucers. Again, it wreaks havoc on my inventory."

Fumbling through my notes, I realized I hadn't recorded that. Neither could I remember Joe mentioning this before.

"So," I said, "the customer can't order two cups and four soup bowls, is that correct? Only two cups and two soup bowls, or four cups and four soup bowls?"

Joe nodded approvingly. "Exactly," he said smiling, apparently happy with our progress.

"I just thought of something," I said. "Can the customer order items from different brands? Such as two cups from Brand X, and four saucers from Brand Y?"

Joe thought for a moment. "It's pretty rare for a customer to request a combination like that. If it's OK with you," he continued, "I'd rather restrict the sales quotation to a single brand at one time. If the customer needs to replace pieces from more than one brand, they'll need to get two separate quotes."

That was fine with me, I thought. Ultimately, that one little restriction would make the system easier to program.

"One more thing," I said. "In my notes, I've mentioned the word 'order' several times. You want the program to provide only a price quotation, not to initiate an actual sales order. Is that correct?"

"Yes, only a quotation," Joe said. "I want the program to display the price of the customer's selected china pieces. At that point, if they like the price quoted, then they can come to the counter to finalize the sale."

"Can you think of anything else?" I asked.

"No, I don't think so," he said. He hesitated for a moment and then added hopefully. "What do you think? The program doesn't sound too difficult, does it?"

Famous last words, I thought to myself.

"Mr. Bullina…Joe," I said, "it's very hard to say at this point. No, it doesn't seem terribly complex. This has just been a preliminary investigation of your requirements though. I still need a few more things from you, in order to get a better idea of the complexity of the project. For instance, we haven't even discussed how the price of the sales quotations should be calculated. I need to know the prices of the individual items."

"Rules," he said obligingly. "Oh yes, that shouldn't be a problem."

"How often do the prices of your china inventory change?" I asked.

"Not very often," he said, but then I detected a look of worry appearing on his face. "But they do change occasionally. If I need to change the price of an item, will you have to rewrite the program?"

"Not if I design it properly," I said. "You could use a software package such as Microsoft Access to maintain the prices of your china inventory, which I could program your system to use. That way, if your inventory prices change, or if you decide to sell a new brand of china, or discontinue an old one, then all you need to do is use Access to update the inventory record."

I could see that I was beginning to lose him.

"I really don't know much about computers," Joe said, "and I don't know what Microsoft Access is. In fact, only one of my sales clerks, Midge, has even used a computer. Incidentally, she was the one who saw your ad. She tells me the only program she knows how to use is something called Notepad."

"That would work," I said. "You, or Midge I should say, could use Notepad to record your inventory prices in a file stored on the computer's hard drive. If the prices change, Midge could then use Notepad to update the prices in the file. We wouldn't need to use Microsoft Access after all."

"That sounds better to me," Joe said. "Would you show Midge how to do that?"

I explained that training is part of my fee. Joe paused for a moment. "How much do you think the program will cost?" he asked.

I hesitated and then said, "Again, Joe, at this point it's difficult for me to say because we're really just in the preliminary investigation phase of what is known as the Systems Development Life Cycle. Every program is different...but I can tell you I have designed and programmed systems, similar in scope to this one, which have cost the client somewhere in the neighborhood of $2,500, not including the price of the computer. With the computer, I would guess somewhere between $3500 and $4000." I was surprised to see a look of disappointment come over his face.

"I really wasn't looking to spend more than a few hundred dollars for the program," he said. "When I was looking through the software aisle at my local computer store, most of those programs were selling for under $50."

I explained to Joe that custom software development is more expensive than purchasing software 'off the shelf'. This is because 'off the shelf' software is sold in large quantities to many people; the development costs can be divided among many purchasers.

I looked up at the clock on his wall and realized that I was nearly late for my Tuesday evening university computer class.

"Joe, I've got to be heading out," I said as I started to gather my notes and place them into my briefcase. "I have a class to get to at 6 p.m."

As I packed up, I explained to Joe that I charged by the hour. With my travel time, and this initial meeting, we were already well over two hours. To design and program the system we had been discussing for just a few hundred dollars would be impossible.

"Here's my card," I said as I took one out of my wallet and handed it to him. "Think it over, and if you're interested, just give me a call."

"How much do you charge per hour?" he asked hesitantly. I told him, and he did some quick mental calculations.

"Isn't there anything we could do to cut the cost?" Joe said. "I'm really excited by the possibility of this project, and I would be disappointed not to proceed with it."

I pondered the possibility for a moment, and then an idea hit me. I explained to Joe that on Saturday I would be meeting with my 'Introduction to Programming' Spring Semester class for the first time. I then went on to explain to Joe that for the last year, I'd been thinking about assigning, as a class project, some kind of project just like his, a real-world programming project. I had put out some feelers with some local organizations, but most of them had 'shied' away from having a programming class write a program for them.

NOTE: This project, though 'real world' has been toned down a bit for learning purposes.

"Perhaps," I said, "instead of a formal class project, I can have the class adopt your program as their class project."

Joe looked excited and nervous at the same time. "How would that work?" he asked.

"Well," I said, "each semester I give my programming students a project to develop. Ideally, it's something they can really sink their teeth into. Usually, I just make something up. For instance, last semester, they wrote a program for an imaginary store that sells sneakers. Your project excites me, and I think it will excite them. It's better than anything I could ever dream up, because it's real, with a real customer, you, expecting real results. And your requirements have a few 'quirks' that will make it a little more challenging than anything I could throw at them."

I looked at Joe for a reaction. I saw a look of unease on his face. "I can take these notes," I continued, "distribute them to my students on Saturday, and over the course of our semester, they can program the entire system for you.

In eight weeks, you'll have a prototype of the program. Seven weeks after that, you'll have the program running in your store! Unless of course, you're in a huge hurry..."

"No," Joe said, "I can live with fifteen weeks. Of course, I'm guessing that the program won't be as sophisticated as one that you would write. After all, your students are just beginners."

"Not at all," I said. "I'll be working with them every step of the way. You can expect a top-notch program, and I have no doubt that we can do it at a price you can afford."

"What would that be?" Joe said.

"You were willing to pay me a few hundred dollars," I said. "I have eighteen students in my class. How about $450 to be shared equally among the members of the class?"

I must have said the magic words; at this Joe smiled, extended his hand and said, "That sounds like a deal to me."

As I prepared to leave, I warned Joe that what we had done this afternoon merely represented the first step, the tip of the iceberg, so to speak, in a six step process known as the Systems Development Life Cycle (SDLC). The first phase, the Preliminary Investigation, had begun and ended with our initial interview. Five phases of the SDLC remained.

As I walked to the door, Joe and I mutually agreed that I would fax him several items within a day or so:

- A letter confirming my agreement to 'take on' the project

- A Requirements Statement that will take shape from the notes I have taken at today's meeting

- The specifications for the computer hardware that he will need to purchase

We agreed that Joe would pay me the sum of $450 for the program, to be equally distributed among the students in my class. For just about all of them, I guessed, this would be their first 'professional' programming job.

I warned Joe that when he read the Requirements Statement that I would send him, the possibility existed that he would find some things about his business that I had misinterpreted, and perhaps some things that he was sure he had mentioned that wouldn't appear at all. I told him that the Requirements Statement would act as a starting point for the project. Until I received a signed copy of the Requirements Statement from him, acknowledging his agreement to its terms, neither my student team nor I would proceed with the development of his system.

Joe agreed that he would fax me a letter by the end of the week with details concerning china brands and item prices so that we could begin building a text file of brands and prices for inclusion in his program.

Mr. Bullina told me about a nephew of his who sold computers at a local computer superstore, who, he assured me could get him a deep discount on a new system. I told him that it would be fine with me as long as the system met my minimum systems requirements.

As I walked out the door of the Bullina China Shop, we both said warm 'good byes'. Joe was a genuinely likable man, and I hoped this experience would be a rewarding one for both him and the students in my class. I left Joe attending to a customer in the front of his store, and I headed off to teach my evening class at the university.

The Systems Development Life Cycle (SDLC)

During the drive to my evening class, I gave a lot of thought to Joe's program. The more I thought about it, the more I believed that having my students program the system was a great idea, and I was sure they would think so too. Working on a real-world application would be a great practical assignment for them. Even more so than something I made up, this project would give each of them a chance to become deeply involved in the various aspects of the SDLC. For instance:

- Someone in the class would need to work on the user requirements

- Someone else would be involved in a detailed analysis of the China Shop

- Everyone would be involved in coding the program

- Some students would work on installing the software

- Some students would be involved in training and implementation

Four days later, on Saturday morning, I met my 'Introductory Programming' class for the first time. For the last few semesters, my university has been using Visual Basic as our introductory programming language.

As is my custom during my first class, I took roll, and asked each of the students to write a brief biography on a sheet of paper. Doing this gives me a chance to get to know them, without the pressure of having to open themselves up to a room full of strangers, although many of them will become good friends during the course of the class.

I only called out their first names as I like to personalize the class as much as possible. Usually, I have some duplicated first names, but this semester, that wasn't a problem.

"Valerie, Peter, Linda, Steve, Katherine Rose."

"If you don't mind, just call me Rose," she said.

"Rhonda, Joe, John."

"Jack, if you don't mind."

"Barbara, Kathy, Dave, Ward, Blaine, Kate, Mary, Chuck, Lou, Bob."

That makes eighteen students.

I began reading over their biographies. A few had some programming experience, using languages that were a bit dated. A number were looking to get into the exciting world of computer programming, either because they had an opportunity at work, or believed one would open up shortly. A couple of them were people looking to get into the work force after years away from it. One of the students, Chuck, was just fifteen, a local high school student. Another student, Lou, was permanently disabled, and although he didn't look it, he wrote that his disability would probably end up restricting him to a wheelchair.

My classroom is about 40 feet by 20 feet and there are three rows of tables containing PCs. Each student has their own PC, and at the front of the room I have my own, cabled to a projector that enables me to display the contents of my video display.

My first lecture usually involves bringing the class up to a common level so that they feel comfortable with both the terminology and methodology of using the Windows environment. This time, however, instead of waiting a few weeks before introducing the class project, I could hardly wait to tell them. In the first few minutes of class, I introduced the students to the China Shop Project. Just about everyone in the class seemed genuinely excited at the prospect of developing a real-world application. They were even more excited after I offered to split the profits with them. In only their first Visual Basic course, they would all be paid as professionals, with a legitimate project to add to their resumes.

"You mean this course isn't going to be the usual 'read the textbook, and code the examples' course," Ward said.

"Exactly," I said, "we'll be developing a real world application, and getting paid for it!"

"How will we know what to do?" Rose asked nervously.

I explained that in today's class, we'd actually develop a Requirements Statement.

"A Requirements Statement," I said, "is just an agreement between the contractor (in this case us) and the customer (in this case Mr. Bullina) that specifies in detail exactly what work will be performed, when it will be completed, and how much it will cost."

I continued by explaining that at this point, all we had were my notes from the initial interview. This was hardly enough to begin anything more than a quick sketch of the program. While we might very well have produced a quick sketch of the user interface in the following hour or so, we still did not know how to write a single line of code in Visual Basic. There was still much to learn! Furthermore, we still did not have the processing rules (e.g. the price of the various items) which Mr. Bullina had promised to fax to me by that day's class.

NOTE: Processing rules are known either as Business Rules or Work Rules.

"Can you give us an example of a business rule?" Peter asked.

"Sure Peter," I answered. "A good example would be a web-based ticket purchasing Web site, where customers are typically restricted from ordering large quantities of tickets. The Web site might have a business rule that prohibits the same customer from purchasing more than 4 tickets to the same event."

"That very thing happened to me just last week," Valerie said. "I tried to purchase an entire row of tickets to the upcoming Elton John concert, but the Web site restricted me to just 4."

And I also pointed out that we still needed to fax him a Requirements Statement and the specifications for the computer itself. I told them that there was the possibility that the Requirements Statement would have some mistakes in it, and even some missing items. I cautioned them not to be too hasty at this point in the project. There was still a lot of planning left to do!

"Such hastiness," I said, "is exactly why the Systems Development Life Cycle was developed."

> **NOTE: The SDLC was developed because many systems projects were developed which did not satisfy user requirements and the projects that did satisfy user requirements were being developed over budget or over time.**

I saw some puzzled looks. I explained that the Systems Development Life Cycle (SDLC) is a methodology that was developed to ensure that systems are developed in a methodical, logical and step-by-step approach. There are six steps, known as phases, in the Systems Development Life Cycle.

Different companies may have different 'versions' of the SDLC. The point is that just about everyone who does program development can benefit from one form or other of a structured development process such as this one.

- The Preliminary Investigation Phase

- The Analysis Phase

- The Design Phase

- The Development Phase

- The Implementation Phase

- The Maintenance Phase

> **NOTE: Different companies may have different versions of the SDLC. The point is nearly everyone who does program development can benefit from one form or other of a structured development process such as this one.**

I continued by explaining that out of each phase of the SDLC, a tangible product, or deliverable, is produced. This deliverable may consist of a Requirements Statement, or it may be a letter informing the customer that the project cannot be completed within their time and financial constraints. An important component of the SDLC is that at each phase in the SDLC, a conscious decision is made to continue development of the project, or to drop it. In the past, projects developed without the guidance of the SDLC were continued well after 'common sense' dictated that it made no sense to proceed further.

"Many people say that the SDLC is just common sense," I said. "Let's examine the elements of the SDLC here. You can then judge for yourself."

Phase 1: The Preliminary Investigation

I told my class about my meeting with Joe Bullina, which essentially constituted the Preliminary Investigation Phase of the SDLC.

"This phase of the SDLC," I said, "may begin with a phone call from a customer, a memorandum from a Vice President to the director of Systems Development, or a letter from a customer to discuss a perceived problem or deficiency, or to express a requirement for something new in an existing system. In the case of the China Shop, it was a desire on the part of Mr. Bullina to develop a 'program' to provide price quotations to customers in his China Shop."

I continued by explaining that the purpose of the Preliminary Investigation is not to develop a system, but to verify that a problem or deficiency really exists, or to pass judgment on the new requirement.

The duration of the preliminary investigation is typically very short, usually not more than a day or two for a big project, and in the instance of the China Shop Project, about two hours.

The end result, or deliverable, from the Preliminary Investigation phase is either a willingness to proceed further, or the decision to 'call it quits'. What influences the decision to abandon a potential project at this point? There are three factors, typically called constraints, which result in a go or no-go decision.

- **Technical**. The project can't be completed with the technology currently in existence. This constraint is typified by Leonardo Da Vinci's inability to build a helicopter even though he is credited with designing one in the 16th century. Technological constraints made the construction of the helicopter impossible.

- **Time**. The project can be completed, but not in time to satisfy the user's requirements. This is a frequent reason for the abandonment of the project after the Preliminary Investigation phase.

- **Budgetary**. The project can be completed, and completed on time to satisfy the user's requirements, but the cost is prohibitive.

"In the case of the China Shop Project," I told my students, "Mr. Bullina and I came close to dropping the project." I explained that budgetary constraints on the part of Mr. Bullina were the chief reason. Technically, the project was not very complex, and there was no doubt in my mind that together we could easily complete the project. Neither was time a constraint here, as we could easily complete the project during the course of the semester. The limiting factor had been Mr. Bullina's desire to spend no more than a few hundred dollars for the program.

With the assistance of my students, we decided to take on the project, and proceed with the second phase of the SDLC.

Phase 2: Analysis

The second phase of the SDLC, the Analysis phase, is sometimes called the Data Gathering phase.

> **NOTE: In this phase we study the problem, deficiency or new requirement in detail. Depending upon the size of the project being undertaken, this phase could be as short as the Preliminary Investigation, or it could take months.**

I explained that what this meant for my class was another trip to the China Shop to meet with Mr. Bullina, to spend more time talking with him and observing his operation.

> **WARNING: As a developer, you might be inclined to believe that you know everything you need to know about the project from your preliminary investigation. However, you would be surprised to find out how much additional information you can glean if you spend just a little more time with the user.**

You might be inclined to skip portions of what the SDLC calls for, but it forces you to follow a standardized methodology for developing programs and systems. As we'll see shortly, skipping parts of the SDLC can be a big mistake, whereas adhering to it ensures that you give the project the greatest chance for success.

I told them that while some developers would make the case that we have gathered enough information in Phase 1 of the SDLC to begin programming, the SDLC dictates that Phase 2 should be completed before actual writing of the program begins.

"The biggest mistake we could make at this point would be to begin coding the program. Why is that? As we'll see shortly, we need to gather more information about the business from the owner. There are still some questions that have to be asked."

In discussing the SDLC with the class, I discovered that one of my students, Linda Schwartzer, actually lived about half a mile from the Bullina China Shop. Linda was a full time Network Administrator who was interested in learning to program using Visual Basic. Linda offered to contact Mr. Bullina, and set up an appointment to spend part of the day with him in the China Shop. This meeting would fulfill the data-gathering component of the Analysis Phase. In the short time I had spent with Linda, I sensed a great communicative ability about her, and so I felt very comfortable with Linda tackling the Analysis phase of the SDLC.

Typically, our first class meeting is abbreviated, and since we were basically frozen in time until we could complete Phase 2 of the SDLC, I dismissed the class for the day. Prior to Linda's meeting with Mr. Bullina, I faxed the following letter to him.

> Dear Mr. Bullina,
>
> I want to thank you for taking the time to meet with me last Tuesday afternoon. As I discussed with you at that time, it is my desire to work with you in developing a "kiosk" style computer system to be deployed in the middle of your sales floor.
>
> The system will be developed as part of my *Introduction to Programming* computer class at the

university. As such, your costs will be $450, payable upon final delivery of the program. In return, you agree to allow me to use your contract to provide my students with a valuable learning experience in developing a real-world application.

Sometime during the coming week, one of my students, Linda Schwartzer, will be contacting you to arrange to spend part of the day observing your business. Although you may not see the necessity in this additional meeting, it will satisfy the next phase of the Systems Development Life Cycle I discussed with you at our meeting. Adhering strictly to the SDLC will result in the best possible system we can develop for you.

I'd like to take this opportunity to highlight the major points we discussed last week. We will develop a Windows-based system for you. Here are the major functions that the developed system will perform:

1. This system will provide a customer with a user-friendly interface for requesting a price quote of fine china.

2. The customer may choose a complete place setting, or may choose individual components for their quotation.

3. The component pieces are: plate, soup bowl, butter plate, cup and saucer.

4. The customer may also select a platter, but the program is to 'assume' a quantity of one whenever the customer selects a platter.

5. The customer may not 'mix and match' brands for the price quote. All of the components must be of the same brand.

6. The customer may only choose a quantity of one, two, four or eight for both place settings and individual components.

7. The customer may not 'mix and match' quantities. For example, the customer may not choose four cups and two saucers.

I think I've covered everything that we discussed last Tuesday. If I have missed anything, please let Linda know when she arrives to observe your operation.

Regards,

John Smiley

This letter, in essence, will become the Requirements Statement that we will formally develop shortly. The next day I received the following fax from Mr. Bullina.

Dear Mr. Smiley,

Here is a price matrix of the prices for the 3 brands of China we sell in our China Shop.

I had a chance to review the fax you sent me yesterday, and everything looks fine. I'm really excited about the project.

One thing I forgot to mention last Tuesday is that we offer a discount for a complete place setting. I hope that this will not complicate the program too much.

BRAND	PLATE	BUTTER PLATE	SOUP BOWL	CUP	SAUCER	PLACE SETTING	PLATTER
CORELLE	$4	$1	$2	$1	$1	$8	$5
FABERWARE	$10	$3	$5	$3	$3	$21	$13
MIKASA	$25	$10	$10	$5	$5	$50	$50

Regards,

Joe Bullina

Complicate the program? Sure, a bit. I was sure Linda would more than likely find other surprises as well. This new 'requirement' was about par for the course. I checked my notes, and Joe was right, he never mentioned it. Of course, a good developer can anticipate requirements such as these. I just missed it.

Linda called me on Monday morning to tell me that she had arranged to meet with Joe Bullina on Thursday morning. That evening Linda called to tell me that the observation had gone well. Contrary to what I expected, she saw nothing in the day-to-day operation that contradicted the notes that I took during my preliminary investigation. For instance, it wouldn't have surprised me to find that someone in the shop was selling china in quantities of three!

However, Linda reported that nothing out of the usual occurred. She did tell me that from her observations, it was obvious that the program would pay for itself in no time. She noticed a number of people who spoke with the sales clerks only to get price quotations, and then immediately left the shop. A 'kiosk' type program would be perfect.

Linda also told me that she assisted Mr. Bullina in developing the computer hardware requirements for his nephew. Because of her background in computer hardware and Network Administration, I had no problem with her doing this. Although ordinarily these specifications aren't developed until Phase 3 of the SDLC, I had promised these specs to Joe, and so I was happy that Linda had assisted him with them.

That Saturday, I again met with our class. After ensuring that I hadn't lost anyone in the intervening week (yes, everyone came back), we began to discuss the third phase of the SDLC.

Phase 3: Design

"Phase 3 of the SDLC is the Design phase," I said.

I explained that design in the SDLC encompasses many different elements. Here is a list of the different components that are 'designed' in this phase:

- Input
- Output
- Processing
- File

"Typically," I said, "too little time is spent on the design phase. Programmers love to start programming." I continued by saying that you can hardly blame them, with some of the marvelous modern application tools such as Visual Basic to work with. Unfortunately, jumping immediately into coding is a huge mistake.

"After all," I said, "you wouldn't start building a house without a blueprint, would you? You simply cannot and should not start programming without a good solid design."

I pointed out that critics of the SDLC agree that it can take months to complete a house, and making a mistake in the building of a house can be devastating; writing a Visual Basic program, on the other hand, can be accomplished in a matter of hours, if not minutes. If there's a mistake, it can be corrected quickly.

> **NOTE: Even though at this point the class knew very little about Visual Basic Express, they were already familiar with Windows programs (a requirement for the course). Designing and developing the 'look' of a Windows program is really independent of the tool that you'll use to program it.**

I should point out here that my role in the Design Phase was to act as a guide for my students. Mr. Bullina had told us what he wanted the program to do. Like any 'client', he described his program requirements in functional terms that he understood.

My students were already familiar with Windows, but at this point in our course, they were not Visual Basic experts. However, knowing Windows was not sufficient for them to know how Mr. Bullina's requirements translated into the terms of a Windows program. Ultimately, it was my job to help them translate those requirements into Visual Basic terms.

Critics of the SDLC further argue that time constraints and deadlines can make taking the 'extra' time necessary to properly complete the Design Phase a luxury that many programmers can't afford.

"I answer in this way," I said, citing a familiar phrase that you have probably heard before. "It seems there is never time to do it right the first time, but there's always time to do it over."

The exceptional (and foolish) programmer can begin coding without a good design. Programmers who do so may find themselves going back to modify pieces of code they've already written as they move through the project. They may discover a technique halfway through the project that they wish they had incorporated in the beginning, and then go back and change code. Worse yet, they may find themselves with a program that 'runs' but doesn't really work, with the result that they must go back and start virtually from the beginning.

"With a good design," I said, "the likelihood of this happening will be reduced dramatically. The end result is a program that will behave in the way it was intended, and generally with a shorter overall program development time."

Armed with our notes from the Preliminary Investigation, Linda's notes from the Detailed Analysis, and Joe Bullina's concurrence of our preliminary Requirements Statement, my students and I began the Design Phase in earnest. By the end of the design phase, we hoped to have a formal Requirements Statement for the program, and perhaps even a rough sketch of what the user interface will look like.

I reminded them that the Requirements Statement would form the basis of our agreement with the Bullina China Shop. For some developers, the Requirements Statement becomes the formal contract to which both they and the customer agree, and sign.

Linda began the design phase by giving the class a summary of the three or four hours she spent in the Bullina China Shop on Thursday. Linda said that she felt comfortable in stating that nothing she had observed that day contradicted the view expressed in my notes, and in my letter to Mr. Bullina.

Not everyone in the class had had the benefit of seeing my notes or the letter, so I distributed to the class copies of my notes, my letter to Mr. Bullina, and his letter to me. I gave them a few minutes to review and digest the material.

We began to discuss the program requirements. I could see there was some hesitation as to where to begin, so I began the process with a question. "Let's begin by making a statement as to what we are trying to accomplish here," I said.

"We need to write a program to display a price quotation," Dave said.

"Excellent," I said. Dave had hit the nail squarely on the head. The primary purpose of the program was to produce a price quotation. To be sure, there would be more to the program than that, but from Mr. Bullina's point of view, all he needed the program to do was to display a price quotation.

Frequently, new programmers are unable to come to grips as to where they should begin in the Design Phase. I suggested to them that most programs are designed by first determining the output of the program. The reasoning here is that if you know what the output of the program should be, you can determine the input needed to produce that output pretty easily. Once you know both the output from, and the input to the program, you can then determine what processing needs to be performed to convert the input to output.

Output Design

I told them that we were fortunate, in that the class's first project was one where the output requirements could be stated so simply: a price quotation.

"Where will the price quotation go?" I asked.

"To a printer?" Jack suggested. "On the computer screen," Rose countered.

"I agree with Rose," I said, "probably to the computer screen."

Some of the students seemed perplexed by my answer. "Probably?" Dave asked.

I explained that Mr. Bullina and I had never formally agreed where the price quotation would be displayed. The issue had never really come up. A kiosk-style program certainly implied the display of the price quotation on a computer screen. However, there was always the chance that Joe would want a price quotation printed to a printer.

"Let's be sure," I said, "to explicitly specify a display of the price quotation in the Requirements Statement. Speaking of which…is there a volunteer to begin to write up the specifications for it?" Dave volunteered to begin writing our Requirements Statement, so he loaded up Microsoft Word and started typing away.

Rhonda made a suggestion for the color and font size for the program's price display, but Peter said that it was probably a bit premature to be talking about colors and font sizes at this point in our design. I agreed, and told them that I never include that amount of detail on a Requirements Statement.

"Is there any other output from the program?" I asked and several moments went by.

"I'd like to suggest that we display the date and time on the computer screen," Valerie suggested. I was pleased with this suggestion, because I knew this would give us a chance to work with a Visual Basic Timer control, which would be good experience. Of course, at this point the students didn't know what a Timer control was, but they would learn about them shortly.

"Good idea," Mary said.

However, Linda disagreed, arguing that the display of the date and time was unnecessary considering the fact that most versions of Windows display the current time on the Windows TaskBar anyway. I countered by saying that in a kiosk-style program like this, Mr. Bullina might choose to turn off the display of the TaskBar. By not displaying the TaskBar, we would lessen the temptation on the part of customers to change important Windows settings that can be accessed via the TaskBar. The majority of the class agreed that this would be our recommendation to Mr. Bullina. Once we decided not to display the TaskBar, we further agreed that displaying the date and time on the program's screen was a good idea.

Taking a moment to summarize, I said, "We now have three output requirements, a price calculation, a displayed date and a displayed time. This is sufficient information to proceed to the next step. Which is?"

Barbara suggested that since we seemed to have the output requirements identified, we should move onto a discussion of processing.

"As I explained earlier, it will be easier for us if we discuss input into the program prior to discussing processing," I said. "It's just about impossible to determine processing requirements if we don't know our input requirements."

Input Design

"So does anyone have any suggestions as to what input requirements we need?" I asked the class.

Dave quickly rattled off several input requirements: a brand of china, one or more component pieces of china and a desired quantity.

"Excellent," I said. "Those certainly appear to be the input to the program. Anything else?"

Kate pointed out that we hadn't yet taken into account the discount for a complete place setting. "The discount for a complete place setting," I said, "is a processing rule, which we will discuss shortly." However, Kate's point about the complete place setting discount was an excellent one. We decided to include a formal definition of a 'complete place setting' in our Requirements Statement.

"Anything else?" I repeated. "How will input be entered into the program? How will the customer let the program know their choice for a china brand, for instance?"

Choosing the Brand

Several students suggested that the user could type the china brand using the computer's keyboard.

"How many brands do we have?" I asked. A quick peek at the handouts revealed that at the present moment, the Bullina China Shop carried only three brands of China. "My motto is to have the user do as little typing as possible," I said. "In fact, I envisioned that absolutely no typing on the part of the user would be necessary."

I could see that some of the students were surprised at my statement. You must remember that a number of them had come from the DOS world, and were accustomed to writing programs where there was a great deal of typing required of the user.

I explained that typically in Windows programs, when there are a finite number of choices, it's best to display a list of choices for the user to choose from.

"Does anyone know of anything they've seen in Windows that displays a list of choices for the user to choose from?" I asked. Mary said she recalled seeing a list of Font names and Font sizes to choose from on the Microsoft Word toolbar.

"That's a list of choices," she said. "Excellent, Mary," I said.

I said this list was actually a Windows ListBox object. Such a ListBox would be perfect to display the available china brands in our program. After all, it would be senseless to have the user type the brand name of the china when our program could display it for them in a neat ListBox.

"Then the user," I said, "need only use their mouse to click on the brand in the ListBox. No typing required! Let's add that to the Requirements Statements, Dave."

"What else?" I asked.

Choosing the Items

Our discussion then moved on to how the customer would select the individual component china pieces. Some students, obviously liking the idea of a ListBox, also suggested using one to display the six possible component china pieces. Although this certainly was a workable solution, this situation didn't quite match the previous one for brands.

"If you'll recall my initial meeting with Joe Bullina," I said, "only one brand of china can be selected per quotation. However, more than one item can be selected per quotation." I asked them if they knew of anything in Microsoft Word that displayed a series of choices to the user, where more than one selection could be chosen at a time.

Ward said that he recalled seeing boxes on the Options submenu of the Tools menu that permitted him to specify 'settings' for saving documents in Word. I asked all of the students to take a look at this menu, and sure enough, there were several boxes, which the user can click with their mouse to select settings for saving documents in Word.

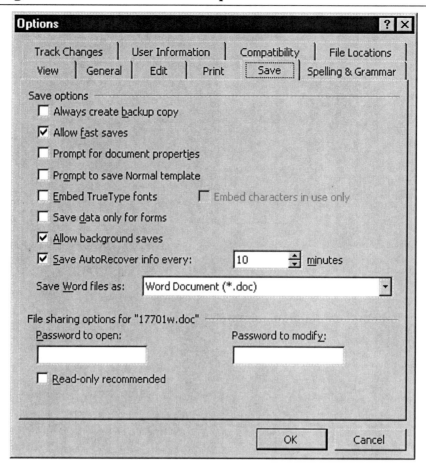

Note: I pointed out that there was one disadvantage of using the CheckBox that we don't have with the ListBox. China brands in the ListBox are displayed as a 'scrollable' list of items. If we need to add more brands, the screen 'real estate' occupied by the ListBox control doesn't need to change. CheckBoxes, on the other hand, occupy definite real estate on the screen.

I told the students that these boxes were actually the Windows CheckBox objects or controls.

"In Windows," I said, "a CheckBox is either selected or not selected. Windows CheckBoxes enable the user to make a selection by clicking on the box with their mouse. The user can then de-select it by clicking on the CheckBox again with their mouse."

We agreed that CheckBoxes would be perfect to permit the customer to make a selection of one or more component china pieces.

"Suppose," I said, "Mr. Bullina calls tomorrow to say that in addition to the six china pieces he is already selling, he wishes to offer salad plates for sale as well. Then our form would need to be redesigned."

It was just about time for a break, and so at break time I called Mr. Bullina at the store and asked him about the likelihood that another component piece might be added to his inventory. He told me it was very unlikely, and so after we returned from break, we decided to use the CheckBox to allow the user to specify their china items. Again, I asked Dave to add this to our Requirements Statement.

Selecting a Quantity

That left us with the quantity to deal with, which caused a great deal of discussion. Several students were in favor of having the user type the quantity into the program somehow. I asked the students to come up with an example in Word where a quantity of some type is specified. Joe immediately cited the Print submenu, where the user can specify the number of copies to be sent to the printer.

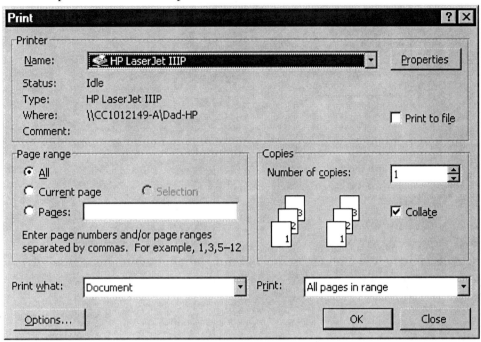

"Excellent, Joe!" I said.

Word uses a combination of something called a Text Box and a vertical scrollbar in this Print dialog box. If the user desires, they can type the quantity directly into the text box, or if they wish, they can click on the scrollbar to adjust the quantity. There was only one problem with using this technique in the China Shop Project, and that was the fact that the user could only select quantities of 1,2, 4 or 8.

"That constraint complicates the project a bit," I said.

Several students favored using a ListBox to display quantities, with the items labeled eight, four, two and one. A ListBox would be fine for quantity, I thought, but I wanted to give them an opportunity to use another technique. Just then Ward asked about using the 'circles' he saw on the Print submenu to designate Page Range. I told them that those 'circles' were Windows RadioButtons.

"Unlike the CheckBox," I said, "where more than one selection can be made at one time, with RadioButtons, only one selection can be made at any one time." I asked the class to go into the Print menu and the Page Range frame of Word to prove this for themselves. I explained that we could display four buttons representing the four possible permissible quantities, and have the customer make a selection from one of the RadioButtons to designate their quantity selection.

"Don't we need an RadioButton set for each piece of china that the customer selects?" Bob asked.

Peter reminded everyone that there could only be one choice of quantity. That is, the customer could not ask for two plates and four saucers. The customer could only obtain a price quotation for four saucers and four plates, or two plates and two saucers. In addition, there was a limit of one platter per customer. If the customer selected a platter in their order, then the program would 'assume' a quantity of one. Therefore, Bob's concern over how to allow the customer to select a quantity for each piece was unwarranted. There could be but one quantity selected per price quotation.

Everyone agreed that using RadioButtons to represent the customer's quantity selection was a good idea, so Dave added this to the Requirements Statement.

The First Screen Design

So far, so good. We had identified all of the input into the system (or so we thought), and had decided how best to input them. During the course of the discussion, Barbara had begun sketching a preliminary form design. She offered to show it to the class, and I displayed it on the classroom projector. This is the preliminary sketch of the input design that she showed to the class.

CORELLE FARBERWARE MIKASA	☐ PLATE	○ 8
	☐ BUTTER PLATE	○ 4
	☐ SOUP BOWL	○ 2
	☐ CUP	○ 1
	☐ SAUCER	
	☐ PLATTER	

The class was pleased with the sketch, and in general, with all that we had accomplished so far.

Mary, after seeing the sketch, suggested that since we had used Microsoft Word as our guideline up to this point, that our interface should also have a menu, just like Word. Everyone agreed, and this prompted a discussion as to what should appear on our menu.

> **Note: As is typical, I found that a discussion of the menu quite naturally turned into a discussion of processing requirements. I wasn't sure that this was the direction in which I wanted the class to move, but on the other hand, I didn't want to stifle their creativity either. There was no harm in it, since we were under no obligation to include everything in the Requirements Statement.**

- Every Windows application requires a File submenu, and a Help submenu. File always contains an Exit command. The File menu can be accessed by pressing the Alt *and* F combination. The Exit command can be accessed by pressing the Alt *and* X combination.

- Help, which can be accessed by pressing the Alt *and* H combination, always contains some basic help, and an About command, which can be accessed by pressing the Alt *and* H combination and then the letter A.

No one in the class was aware of the difficulty and tediousness of writing Visual Basic help files. I cautioned them that creating a Help menu would complicate our project quite a bit, and that we might want to consider it as a possible enhancement in the future. After some discussion, we decided to drop Help as a requirement of the menu.

Everyone agreed that there was no need for the typical Windows Edit submenu, since there wouldn't be any editing of any kind occurring.

Blaine suddenly had an idea. He suggested that many users like to customize their environment to some degree or other.

"Customize their environment?" Barbara responded. He explained that he had used other Windows programs where you could specify preferences such as colors, font size, and other options.

"Any ideas on what we should do here?" I asked. "Colors!" was the almost unanimous response. Changing colors seems to hold more of an attraction for beginners than nearly anything else. In practice I don't advise providing a means for the user to change colors. I prefer instead to have the user change colors through the Color settings in the Windows Control Panel. However, the will of the majority prevailed and we agreed to add a menu item to change the background color for the quotation form. I asked Dave to add this to the Requirements Statement as well.

Lou questioned exactly how we would do this. I cautioned him that at this point in the SDLC it wasn't necessary to discuss the 'how' of what the program would do, but to get the requirements on paper.

FILE   COLOR
EXIT

```
┌─────────────────┐     □ PLATE          ○ 8
│ CORELLE         │     □ BUTTER PLATE   ○ 4
│ FARBERWARE      │     □ SOUP BOWL      ○ 2
│ MIKASA          │     □ CUP            ○ 1
│  │              │     □ SAUCER
│  ▼              │     □ PLATTER
└─────────────────┘
```

At this point, we agreed on File and Color as menu items for our menu. Dave added these specifications to the Requirements Statement, and Barbara redrew the sketch of the form.

Everyone seemed to notice at the same time that our sketch still didn't show the most important piece of output we had identified! The price quotation. After all, it wasn't like we hadn't discussed it. In fact, we discussed output first. This goes to show you how easy it is to leave something important out.

Note: I have received projects from students in the past where they accepted input into a program, performed processing of some kind, but have forgotten the output!

Having noticed the error of our ways, we had a brief discussion as to where and how to display the price. We finally agreed to place it somewhere toward the bottom of the form, although the exact location wouldn't be determined until we actually began to develop the interface in Visual Basic. Again, Barbara redrew the proposed interface.

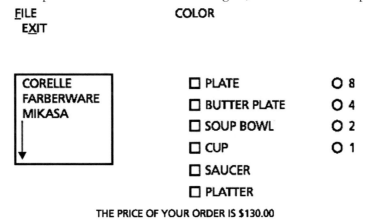

FILE   COLOR
EXIT

```
┌─────────────────┐     □ PLATE          ○ 8
│ CORELLE         │     □ BUTTER PLATE   ○ 4
│ FARBERWARE      │     □ SOUP BOWL      ○ 2
│ MIKASA          │     □ CUP            ○ 1
│  │              │     □ SAUCER
│  ▼              │     □ PLATTER
└─────────────────┘
```

THE PRICE OF YOUR ORDER IS $130.00

Rhonda suggested some changes to the menu layout. We all agreed that these ideas were good ones, so we incorporated them into the project. I particularly liked the changes, because I knew that the programming behind these ideas would prove to be a challenge for them. Here are the changes she proposed:

• Change the name of the Color menu to Preferences menu.

• Add a submenu called Colors, with two choices: Customize and Default (in order to set the colors back to a default color).

• Add two submenu items to the Preferences menu called 'Date and Time On' and 'Date and Time Off'. The idea was to be able to turn the display of the date and time on and off.

After we had added these changes to the Requirements Statement, Ward suggested that we place a border around the CheckBoxes and RadioButtons, to make them 'stand out'. "Those are called GroupBoxes," I said.

We agreed, and Barbara adjusted the sketch of the user interface again.

FILE   PREFERENCES
  EX̲IT   DATE AND TIME ON
                        DATE AND TIME OFF
                        COLORS
                          CUSTOMIZE
                          DEFAULT

```
┌─────────────────┐   ┌──────────────────────┐   ┌─────────┐
│ CORELLE         │   │ ☐ PLATE              │   │ ○ 8     │
│ FARBERWARE      │   │ ☐ BUTTER PLATE       │   │ ○ 4     │
│ MIKASA          │   │ ☐ SOUP BOWL          │   │ ○ 2     │
│                 │   │ ☐ CUP                │   │ ○ 1     │
│ ↓               │   │ ☐ SAUCER             │   └─────────┘
│                 │   │ ☐ PLATTER            │
└─────────────────┘   └──────────────────────┘
```

THE PRICE OF YOUR ORDER IS $130.00

The Requirements Statement

We were working hard, and making excellent progress, and so it was time for another break. Before adjourning, I asked Dave, the student who was developing the Requirements Statement, to let us see what he had developed so far. I made copies of his work, and after break, handed these out to the rest of the class for discussion. Here is the copy of the Requirements Statement I gave to them.

<u>REQUIREMENTS STATEMENT</u>

Bullina China Shop

GENERAL DESCRIPTION

The program will consist of a main screen, on which there will be:

- A ListBox containing china brands.

- 6 CheckBoxes for china piece components.

- 4 RadioButtons representing quantities.

- A menu with submenu items for File and Preferences.

- The File submenu will display only an Exit command. The File menu will be alternatively accessible by pressing the Alt and F combination. The Exit command will be alternatively accessible by pressing the Alt and X combination.

- The Preferences submenu will display a submenu called Colors and a command called Display Date and Time.

- The Colors submenu will consist of two commands called Customize and Default. The Customize command will permit the customer to set the color of the main form to any color they desire through the use of a ColorDialog box. The Default command will set the color of the main form back to a predetermined color.

- The Display Date and Time command will permit the user to turn the displayed date and time off and on.

OUTPUT FROM THE SYSTEM

- A price quotation displayed on the main form.

- Current Date and Time displayed prominently on the form.

INPUT TO THE SYSTEM

- The customer will specify:

- A single china brand (to be selected using a Visual Basic ListBox control).

- One or more component pieces (to be selected using a Visual Basic CheckBox control).

- A quantity for the component pieces (to be selected using a Visual Basic RadioButton).

BUSINESS RULES

- No more than one platter may be selected.

- Quantities may not be mixed and matched in an order. Only one quantity selection per order.

- Brands may not be mixed and matched in an order. Only one brand per order.

DEFINITIONS

- Complete Place Setting: A user's selection composed of a plate, butter plate, soup bowl, cup and saucer of the same brand.

As you can see, the Requirements Statement can easily form the basis of a contract between the customer and the developer. The Requirements Statement should list all of the major details of the program. You should take care not to paint yourself into any unnecessary programming corners by including any 'window dressing'. These can just get you into trouble later.

For instance, notice here that we didn't specify precisely where we would display the Date and Time. Suppose we had specified the upper right hand corner of the main form, and then later changed our mind and wanted to place it in the lower left-hand corner? Theoretically, deviating from the Requirements Statement could be construed as a violation of contractual terms.

I asked for comments on the Requirements Statement and everyone seemed to think that it was just fine. However, several students turned their attention to the sketch of the user interface, and indicated that they believed there were still some problems with it.

Rhonda apologized for being picky, but pointed out that we had not drawn on where the date and time would be placed. She was right. We had entirely left the date and time display off our latest sketch. Details, details, details! We quickly agreed that we would display it in the upper right hand portion of the form. Because this type of detail was considered 'window dressing', no change to the Requirements Statement was required.

"Anything else?" I asked.

Blaine suggested that our sketch didn't have identifying captions for the CheckBoxes, RadioButtons, or ListBox. The rest of the class agreed that the interface would be less confusing to the customer if we provided identifying captions.

"Good point," I said. We decided to place captions on the interface reading Brands, China Pieces and Quantity. Barbara began to make the changes to the sketch.

"Barbara, wait a minute," I said. I told them that displaying a caption with the CheckBoxes and RadioButton frames was easy. However, there was no built-in way of displaying a caption for a ListBox. "Besides," I said, "the ListBox items are pretty self-explanatory. Let's drop the caption on the ListBox."

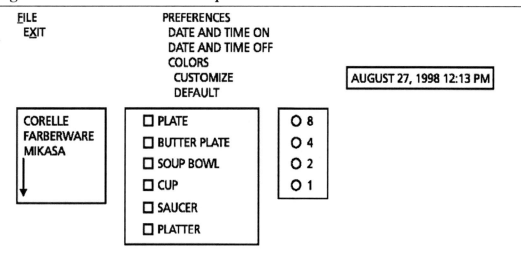

THE PRICE OF YOUR ORDER IS $130.00

Barbara quickly made the changes to the sketch. Neither one of these changes were detailed enough to warrant mentioning them on the Requirements Statement, so Dave made no changes there.

Everyone thought that the interface was coming along quite nicely, but as they say, 'the proof is in the pudding.' It's only the customer's opinion that counts. With no more comments or suggestions on the user interface or the Requirements Statement, we set about completing the Design Phase of the SDLC by looking at Processing.

Processing Design

"Processing is the conversion of inputs to outputs, the conversion of Data to Information," I said. "At this point in the Design phase of the SDLC, we should have now identified all of the output from the program, and all of the input necessary to produce that output."

I explained that just as a good novel will typically have several subplots; a Visual Basic application is no exception. It contains several processing 'subplots' as well.

We have the main 'plot', that is the calculation of the sales quotation, but we also have 'subplots' such as:

- Changing the colors of the main form
- Turning off and on the display of the date and time
- Exiting the application

Here, it's important to note that in Processing Design, we don't actually write the program. That's done later. In Processing Design, we specify the processes that need to be performed to convert input into output.

Looking at Processing in Detail

"Let's look at a simple example which isn't part of the China Shop Project," I said, "that most of you are probably familiar with, the calculation of your paycheck."

I continued by saying that if you want to calculate your net pay, you need to perform several steps. Here are the steps or functions necessary to calculate your net pay:

1. Calculate gross pay

2. Calculate tax deductions

3. Calculate net pay

> **NOTE: Programming is done in the next phase of the SDLC, the Development Phase. Specifying how processing is to occur is not as important in this phase as specifying what is to occur. For instance, this sequence identifies the 'what' of processing, not the how. The 'how' is a part of the Development phase.**

These functions can be broken down even further. For instance, the calculation of your gross pay will vary depending upon whether you are a salaried employee or an hourly employee. If you are an hourly employee, your gross pay is equal to your hourly pay rate multiplied by the number of hours worked in the pay period. The specification of these functions is exactly what the designer must detail in the Processing Design phase of the SDLC.

When it comes to processing design, documenting the processing rules is crucial because translating processing rules into a narrative form can sometimes result in confusion or misinterpretation. Over the years, systems designers have used various 'tools' to aid them in documenting the design of their systems.

Some designers have used tools called flowcharts. Flowcharts use symbols to graphically document the system's processing rules. Here are the net pay processing rules we discussed earlier depicted using a flowchart. (My apologies to any accountants reading this; these calculations have been simplified for illustration purposes.)

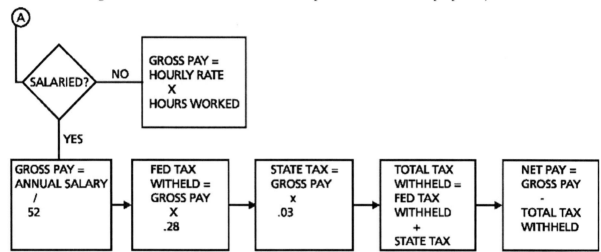

Other designers favor pseudo-code. **Pseudo-code** is an English-like language that describes in non-graphical form how a program should execute. Here are the same net pay processing rules depicted using pseudo-code.

Assumption: Pay is calculated on a weekly basis (52 pay periods per year).

Assumption: Salaried employee pay is Annual Salary divided by 52.

Assumption: Hourly employee pay is Hourly Rate multiplied by hours worked.

1. If employee is salaried, then go to Step 4

2. Employee is hourly, then calculate gross pay equal to hourly wage rate multiplied by hours worked in pay period

3. Go to Step 5

4. Employee is salaried, so calculate Gross Pay equal to Annual Salary divided by 52

5. Calculate Federal Tax withheld equal to Gross Pay multiplied by 0.28

6. Calculate State Tax withheld equal to Gross pay multiplied by 0.03

7. Calculate Total Tax withheld equal to Federal Tax withheld + State Tax withheld

8. Calculate Net Pay equal to Gross Pay less Total Tax withheld

NOTE: Both of these techniques found favor in the era of the Procedural Program.

A Procedural Program is one that executes from top to bottom virtually without interruption. A procedural program ordains to the user exactly how they will interact with your program. For instance, in the China Shop Project, the customer will select a brand of china, then select one or more china items, and then select a quantity.

I frequently find students who have a strong programming background writing procedural programs. Procedural Programming (using languages like Basic, Fortran and COBOL) is like taking a ride on a tour bus, where all of the destination stops are pre-determined, and pre-ordered.

Windows programs are Event-Driven programs. Event-Driven programs (using languages

such as Visual Basic, C++ and JavaScript) don't force the user to behave in a certain way, but rather react to the user.

An event-driven program does not attempt to 'dictate' to the user what they should do in the program, and when they should do it. Instead an event-driven program presents the user with a visual interface that permits them to interact with the program. This is more like choosing the rides at a carnival.

Once entry has been gained, the rides they go on and the order in which they ride them is entirely up to the user. An event-driven program must be able to work and respond to any eventuality.

"In my classes," I said, "I don't require the use of either flowcharting or pseudo-code. All that I ask from you is that you give careful thought to the processing that is necessary to solve the problem before beginning to code in Visual Basic."

I could see some happy faces and I continued by saying that invariably, this means working out a solution on a piece of paper prior to coding it. Some students are more 'visual' than others, and they prefer to design their solution in graphical terms. Others are less 'visual' and their solutions look very much like the pseudo-code we saw earlier. The point is, without some written plan, the programming process can go awry.

I cited this example. Several years ago, I was teaching a class on another language called COBOL, and I gave my students the following programming problem.

Write a program to calculate the net wage of a laborer who works 40 hours at a pay rate of $5 per hour. Income tax at the rate of 20% of the gross pay will be deducted. What is the net pay?

The correct answer is $160. Forty hours multiplied by $5 per hour results in a gross pay of $200. The income tax deduction is 20% of $200, which is $40. $200 less the $40 income tax deduction results in a net pay of $160.

A number of students calculated the net pay as $240. Instead of deducting the income tax deduction of $40 from the gross pay, they *added* it instead. When I questioned the methodology behind their incorrect answer, most of them told me they thought the problem had been so simple, that they hadn't bothered to work out the solution on a piece of paper ahead of time. They just started coding. Had they taken the time to work out the solution on paper first, they would have known what the answer should be and they wouldn't have submitted a program to me that calculated the results incorrectly.

"This is what I'm suggesting to you," I said. "Take the time to work out the solution on paper. You'll be happy that you did."

Back to the Bullina China Shop

We continued by discussing processing design. I reminded them that, in general, design is an iterative process. It's rare that the designer or programmer hits the nail perfectly on the head the first time. It's very possible that after going through processing design, you will discover that you are missing some crucial piece of input necessary to produce a piece of output. In this case, you would need to look at your input processing again. For instance, with the China Project, we could have forgotten to ask the user to specify the quantity of china that they wished to purchase. That omission would make it impossible to calculate a sales quotation.

As a starting point in our processing discussion, we agreed to begin with our primary goal: *To calculate a sales quotation*. We had already determined that in order to calculate a sales quotation, we needed to know the customer's desired brand of china, one or more component china pieces, and the quantity the customer wants.

We started with a hypothetical customer. How would we calculate a sales quotation if the customer selected Mikasa as the brand, a cup and a saucer as the component pieces, and wanted two of each?

"I'd take the price for a Mikasa cup, the price for a Mikasa saucer, add them together, and then multiply by two," Ward said.

"Good," I replied.

Dave suggested, "You could also take the price for a Mikasa cup, multiply it by two, then take the price for a Mikasa saucer, multiply that by two. Then add the two subtotals, and display the result."

"Both would work. What would the sales quotation be?" I asked.

The students turned to the page in their handouts where the prices were written. "Twenty dollars," Joe said. The other students agreed.

"I think we've got a problem here," Chuck said. "We're looking up prices from a sheet of paper. Where is the program going to get these prices?"

"You're right," I said. "So far, we haven't considered how the program will obtain these prices."

Kathy suggested that the prices could be entered every day by one of the sales clerks in the China Shop. I proposed that this would not be very palatable to the China Shop staff. China prices don't change every day. Why force a sales clerk to enter the same prices each day? The system was supposed to permit the sales clerks to have more time serving customers.

Who would want to deal with a system that requires inventory prices to be re-entered each day?

"We'll probably save the prices in a file of some kind," I suggested.

Valerie thought of another problem. "Where will the list of china in the ListBox come from?" she asked. "We never discussed that either."

Ward said that he felt this process seemed to be 'ego deflating'. We all had thought that our design process was coming along so well, and here were two new problems to contend with. I reminded them that this was exactly what I meant when I said that the design process was an iterative one. We were doing well! Just because we had missed some details, and had to go back and make some changes to our original design, didn't mean that we weren't progressing.

"What data needs to be saved from day to day?" I asked. Mary volunteered; china brands for the ListBox and china prices for calculations. Blaine suggested that colors, once changed by the user, would also need to be saved from day to day. Nothing frustrates a user more than having to re-select their preferences every time they start up the program.

"What about the other preferences the user can select?" Mary said. "The choice to display the date and time, we should save that as well." I agreed. Anything that alters the user's environment needs to be saved when the program ends, and 'read' when the program starts up again.

"Saved preferences are output, aren't they?" Dave added. "But then when the program starts up again, the preferences are input."

"An excellent observation," I said. "Anything else?"

Ward said, "There's something here I don't understand. How are we going to save these preferences, and then retrieve them later? I understand how the user will interact with our program. But getting prices into our program without the user's interaction … and saving colors … I just don't understand that."

As for prices, I explained that eventually we would create a data file with 'fields' for both brands and prices. When the program starts up, it would 'read' this file, and load up the ListBox control with the brand names and the prices into something called an array.

An **_array_** is like a data file on a disk, but it is contained in the computer's RAM. As the file is in the memory it means that any activity relating to the array occurs more quickly. We'll be talking about this in more detail next chapter.

> **NOTE: However, for the purposes of the prototype, we will 'hardcode' the information into the program. This will make the information much harder to change, but will get the prototype working as quickly and painlessly as possible.**

When the user selects a brand, one or more component pieces, and a quantity, then the program will 'look up' the price of the items in the array, much like we had manually done using a piece of paper earlier.

Once obtained, these prices will be used to calculate a sales quotation.

I further explained that when we advanced the prototype towards the production-ready application, we would save the user's color and date/time preferences to the Windows Registry using a Visual Basic function or command. When the program starts up, it will read these preferences from the Windows Registry, and adjust the color of the form and the visibility of the data/time label accordingly.

One of my students expressed concern about the prospect of working with the Windows Registry. She explained that she heard that 'fooling around' with the Windows registry was dangerous. I explained that Visual Basic's functions for reading from and writing to the Windows Registry was easy and also very safe.

"Why don't we store the prices in the Windows Registry instead of a disk file?" Linda asked.

I explained that this would not be a good idea since the China Shop's sales clerks would be updating inventory prices periodically. Updating a disk file is something the sales staff could easily do using Notepad. However, updating the Windows Registry is not something we could permit them to do.

"Have we missed anything with the price calculation?" I asked. "Suppose," I added, "the customer clicks on a brand, selects a component piece or pieces, but forgets to select a quantity. What should the program do?"

Everyone agreed that we needed to display some sort of error message if we didn't have all of the ingredients necessary to arrive at a valid price calculation. An error message is another form of output.

"How and when should the calculation take place?" I asked.

Mary suggested that we could trigger a price calculation when the user clicked on one of the CheckBoxes to select an item. Barbara said, "Suppose the user clicks on the soup bowl CheckBox, but hasn't yet selected a brand or a quantity. They'll just see an error message telling them to select a brand and a quantity. Aren't you pre-supposing that they've made a selection of brand and quantity first?"

Mary admitted that she was. I agreed. "You've got to be careful not to try to anticipate the order in which you think the user or customer will make their selections," I said. "Brands, Quantity, and Items. That's probably the order that you would make your selections. But that's not going to be the case with every customer."

I explained that expecting customers to perform actions in a particular order sounded very much like procedural programming. Like a trip to the Automated Teller Machine:

- Insert card

- Enter PIN number

- Select withdrawal or deposit

- Specify an amount

- Deposit your cash or take your cash

- Take your receipt

- Take your card

I explained that procedural programming is something we want to avoid. Procedural programming often gives the user the feeling that they are being pushed or rushed and that they are not in control. When we write Windows programs, it's a great idea to give the user the impression that they are in control.

I suggested the use of a button captioned Calculate to allow the user to tell the program when they are ready for a price quotation. This way they won't get the impression that the program is waiting for them to do something.

The students thought about this for a moment, and agreed with the notion. We agreed that we would place a button on the form captioned Calculate. We further agreed that we would not perform a price calculation until a brand, a quantity, and at least one component piece had been selected. We added this to the business rules section of our Requirements Statement.

Dave made a great suggestion concerning the selection of a 'complete place setting'. Why not have a CheckBox captioned Complete Place Setting which, when selected, would check off the five component pieces that made up a complete place setting? This would save the customer the trouble of checking off all of the five pieces individually. We added that to the Requirements Statement as well.

Now it seemed as though we were gaining momentum. Another student suggested a Reset button that would set all of the components on the form back to their default values. This was another great idea. Again, we added this to the Requirements Statement.

As I mentioned earlier, during the course of processing design, we may uncover 'holes' in the input or output design. That had been the case here. While it's certain that we eventually would have noticed these holes when we were coding the program, fixing these flaws while you are still in the design phase of the SDLC is easier and cheaper than fixing them in the midst of programming the application.

In large projects particularly, portions of the project may be given to different programmers or even different teams of programmers for coding. It could be some time before flaws in the design are uncovered, in some cases weeks or even months. The longer it takes to discover these flaws, the more likely it is that some coding will have to be scrapped and re-done. A well thought out design phase can eliminate many problems down the line.

We'd plugged the holes in the Price Calculation processing, so now it was time to turn our attention to our 'subplot' processing design. Namely:

- Changing the colors of the main form

- Turning off and on the display of the date and time

- Exiting from the application

We didn't get into a lot of detail with these requirements. You must remember that at this point, I still hadn't taught them anything about Visual Basic. All I could do at this point was to assure them that these requirements were indeed feasible. I reminded them that during the design phase, it's not as important to itemize the 'how' of something, as it is to identify the requirement on paper. We had done that, and in the coming weeks they would learn the Visual Basic 'how' of the requirements.

At this point, one of the students suggested that we couldn't allow the customer to exit the program. Only a sales clerk should be able to exit the program. This presented a dilemma. How could we permit a sales clerk to exit from the program, but not a customer?

Another student suggested prompting for a password before permitting the program to 'end'. Again, the details as to 'how' this would be accomplished we would put off for a bit. We agreed that after the user had selected the Exit submenu, the program would prompt for a password and if it was correct, the program would end. If not, the program would continue to run.

Here is the final sketch of the user interface that the class agreed upon.

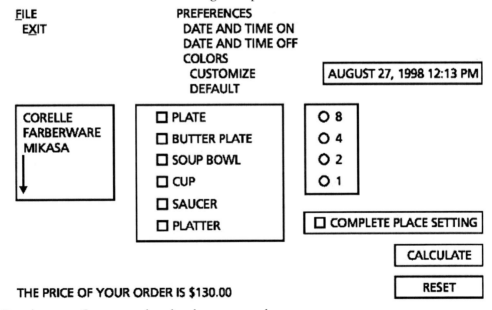

And here is the final Requirements Statement that the class approved.

REQUIREMENTS STATEMENT

Bullina China Shop

GENERAL DESCRIPTION

The program will consist of a main form, on which there will be:

- A ListBox containing brands of china

- 6 CheckBoxes for china piece components

- A single CheckBox to permit the customer to select a Complete Place Setting

- 4 RadioButtons representing quantities

- A button, which when clicked, would perform the price calculation

- A button, captioned Reset, which when clicked would clear the selections in the ListBox, CheckBoxes, and RadioButtons

- A menu with submenu items for File and Preferences

- The File submenu will display only an Exit command. The File menu will be accessible by pressing the Alt and F combination. The Exit command will be accessible by pressing the Alt and X combination.

- The Preferences submenu will display a submenu called Colors and a command called Display Date and Time.

- The Colors submenu will consist of two commands called Customize and Default. The Customize command will permit the customer to set the color of the main form to any color they desire using a ColorDialog box. The Default command will set the color of the main form back to a predetermined color.

- The Display Date and Time command will permit the user to switch the displayed date and time off and on.

- A password will be required to exit the system via the Exit command of the File submenu.

OUTPUT FROM THE SYSTEM

- A price quotation displayed on the main form

- Current Date and Time displayed prominently on the form

INPUT TO THE SYSTEM

The customer will specify:

- A single china brand (to be selected from a ListBox)

- One or more component pieces (to be selected using CheckBoxes)

- A quantity for the component pieces (to be selected using an RadioButton)

This is not customer input, but:

- The program will read china brands and prices from a text file. The sales clerk using Microsoft Notepad can update the inventory and prices when necessary.

- Any changes made to the user's color preferences will be saved to the Windows Registry and read by the program at startup.

- Any changes made to the user's preference for date and time display will be saved to the Windows Registry and read by the program at startup.

BUSINESS RULES

- No more than one platter may be selected

- Quantities may not be mixed and matched in an order, only one quantity selection per order

- Brands may not be mixed and matched in an order, only one brand per order

DEFINITIONS

> • Complete Place Setting: A user's selection composed of a plate, butter plate, soup bowl, cup and saucer of the same brand.

I checked to see if everyone agreed with the statement, and then revealed that we were now done with the Design Phase of the SDLC. I once again reminded them that the Design Phase of the SDLC tends to be an iterative process, and that we might find ourselves back here at some point. We then moved on to a discussion of the fourth phase of the SDLC.

Phase 4: Development

I told them that we wouldn't spend a great deal of time discussing the Development Phase here since the rest of the course would be spent in developing the China Shop Project, in which they would play an active role!

"The Development phase is," I said, "in many ways the most exciting time of the SDLC. During this phase, computer hardware is purchased and the software is developed. Yes, that means we actually start coding the program during the Development phase. We'll be using the standard edition of Visual Basic as our development tool."

I explained that during the Development Phase, we'd constantly examine and re-examine the Requirements Statement to ensure that we were following it to the letter, and I encourage them to do the same. I explained to them that any deviations (and there may be a surprise or two down the road), would have to be approved either by the project leader (me) or by the customer.

I also explained that the Development Phase can be split into two sections, that of Prototyping and Production Ready Application Creation. Prototyping is the stage of the Development Phase that produces a pseudo-complete application, which for all intents and purposes appears to be fully functional.

Developers use this stage to demo the application to the customer as another check that the final software solution answers the problem posed. When they are given the okay from the customer at that point, the final version code is written into this shell to complete the phase.

The class was anxious to begin, but they promised me they would remain patient while I explained the final two phases of the SDLC.

Phase 5: Implementation

The Implementation Phase is the phase in the SDLC when the project reaches fruition. I explained to them that after the Development phase of the SDLC is complete, we begin to implement the system. Any hardware that has been purchased will be delivered and installed in the China Shop. In the instance of the China Shop, this means that Mr. Bullina's nephew will deliver and install the PC in the China Shop.

Software, which we designed in Phase 3, and programmed in Phase 4 of the SDLC, will be installed on the PC in the China Shop. Not surprisingly, everyone in the class wanted to be there for that exciting day.

Barbara raised the issue of testing. During the Implementation phase, both hardware and software is tested. Because Mr. Bullina was purchasing the hardware from a reputable computer superstore, the class was fairly certain of hardware integrity. However, the class was confused over the issue of software testing.

We agreed that students in the class would perform most of the testing of the software, as everyone agreed that it would be unreasonable and unfair to expect the customer to test the software we had developed in a 'live' situation. We decided that when the software was installed on the China Shop's PC, the program should be bug (problem) free.

On the other hand, I cautioned them, almost invariably, the user will uncover problems that the developer has been unable to generate. I told them we would discuss handling these types of problems in more detail in our class on Exception Handling.

"I've heard the term 'debugging' used among the programmers at work," Valerie said. 'Is that something we'll be doing?"

"Most definitely Valerie," I said. "**Debugging** is a process in which we run the program, thoroughly test it, and systematically eliminate all of the errors that we can uncover. We'll be doing this prior to delivering the program to the China Shop."

I then explained that during the Implementation phase, we would also be training the China Shop staff. Again, everyone in the class wanted to participate in user training. One of my students noted that she thought that there needed to be two levels of training performed:

- The first level of training would be aimed directly at the staff of the China Shop. It would involve demonstrating how to turn the computer on each morning and how to shut it down gracefully each night. The staff would also be trained in how to make changes to the two text files necessary to add china brands to the system inventory, and for updating inventory prices. This would require someone training them in the use of Notepad.

- The second level of training would also be aimed at the staff of the China Shop, but this would be more from the customer perspective. Like it or not, the sales staff would be the primary point of contact for customers who were having trouble using the system. Therefore, quite naturally, they would need to know how to operate the system from the customer's perspective.

Several students thought that it would be a good idea to have a student present in the China Shop during the first week of operation, in order to assist customers in the use of the system, and to ease any 'computer' anxiety that the sales staff might have. I thought this was a great idea, and also pointed out that this would provide invaluable feedback on the operation of the system from the most important people in the loop, the end users.

In fact, this feedback led quite naturally into a discussion of the final phase of the SDLC.

Phase 6: Audit and Maintenance

Phase 6 of the SDLC is the Audit and Maintenance Phase. In this phase, someone, usually the client, but sometimes a third party such as an auditor, studies the implemented system to ensure that it actually fulfills the Requirements Statement. Most important, the system should have solved the problem or deficiency, or satisfied the desire that was identified in Phase 1 of the SDLC - the preliminary investigation.

More than a few programs and systems have been fully developed that, for one reason or another simply never met the original requirements. The Maintenance portion of this phase deals with any changes that need to be made to the system.

Changes are sometimes the result of the system not completely fulfilling its original requirements, but it could also be the result of customer satisfaction. Sometimes the customer is so happy with what they have got that they want more. Changes can also be forced upon the system because of governmental regulations, such as changing tax laws, while at other times changes come about due to alterations in the business rules of the customer.

As I mentioned in the previous section, we intended to have one or more members of the class in the China Shop during the first week of system operation. That opportunity for the customer to provide direct feedback to a member of the development team would more than satisfy the Audit portion of Phase 6.

In the future, we hoped that Mr. Bullina would be so happy with the program that we had written for him, that he would think of even more challenging requirements to request of the class.

Where To From Here?

It had been a long and productive session for everyone. I said that in our next meeting we would start to discuss how a computer works, and we would actually begin to work with Visual Basic.

Ward asked me how the progression of the project would work, that is, would we finish the project during our last class meeting, or would we be working on it each week? I said that I thought it was important that we develop the program incrementally. Each week we met, we would finish some portion of the project. Developing the project in steps like this would hold everyone's interest, and give us a chance to catch problems before the last week of class.

Summary

The aim of this chapter was to tackle the question "Where do I begin?" We saw that the design of an application is best done systematically, with a definite plan of action. That way, you know that everything has been taken into account.

A good place to begin is with a requirements statement, which is a list of what the program has to be able to do. Usually, you get the information for this from whoever is asking you to write the program. It's a good idea to keep in continuous contact with this person, so that any changes they want can be tackled before it becomes too much of a problem.

A good systematic approach is embodied in the systems development life cycle (SDLC), which consists of six phases:

- The Preliminary Investigation: Considering the technical, time, and budgetary constraints and deciding on the viability of continuing development of the application.

- The Analysis Phase: Gathering the information needed to continue.

- The Design Phase: Creating a blueprint of the program's appearance and program structure without actually starting any programming.

- The Development Phase: Creating the application, including all interface and code.

- The Implementation Phase: Using and testing the program.

- The Maintenance Phase: Making refinements to the product to eliminate any problems or to cover new needs that have developed.

Using the SDLC method can make any problems you encounter in your design more obvious, making it easier for you to tackle them at a more favorable point in your design, rather than changing existing code.

As you'll see as we progress, it can also be a good idea to go through a prototype stage of the development phase, in which the application contains all the core functionality, but in a more limited fashion. Our China Shop Project prototype (in Chapter 8) will perform the necessary calculations, but have no facility for updating prices or customizing the environment, for example.

Chapter 2---What Is a Computer Program?

In this chapter, we follow my computer class as they learn what a computer program is and what it does. Along the way, you learn what happens when you turn your computer on and we' demystify the behind-the-scenes workings of the computer. Why learn this, you might ask? Although you don't need an intimate knowledge of the inner workings of your computer to write Windows programs, the more you know, the better the programs you can write.

What Is a Computer?

At the conclusion of our last class, I warned my students that during this class meeting we'd need to discuss some of the nitty-gritty of computer hardware and software before we could get on with the fun part—looking at and learning Visual Basic.

"Can anyone give me a definition of a computer?" I asked my class. For whatever reason, everyone seemed a little reluctant to volunteer, so I gave my definition, as follows.

> **A computer is a machine, made primarily of metal and plastic. It has few moving parts and is mostly electrical in nature. It accepts data in some form of input with which it then performs calculations and other types of operations on the data with tremendous speed and accuracy. It then generates information in some form of output.**

"We'll look at some of the terms I use here in a little more detail shortly," I said. I continued by explaining that a computer performs its calculations and operations through instructions provided by a human being. Collectively, these instructions are called a computer program, and the person who writes the program is called a programmer.

"You'll be doing exactly that," I said, "when you write programs in Visual Basic."

Data

Linda noted I used the word "data" in my definition of a computer. She asked me to clarify exactly what I meant by data. I thought for a moment, and said data is anything the computer uses to produce information. Data, for example, can be numbers, letters, symbols, names, addresses, student grades, pictures, or charts.

"But the computer doesn't understand the language of human beings," I said. "For that reason, data must first be translated into a language the computer does understand. Its native language is sometimes known as machine language and takes the form of ones and zeroes. It's also called binary language or binary code."

> **Note: It's not only data that must be translated into binary code. Programs submitted to the computer to run must also be translated.**

Several students told me they recognized the word "binary." I asked if anyone could tell me exactly what binary meant.

"Two," Dave answered.

"Good," I said. "Binary means two, and both data and programs are represented in the computer by a series of ones and zeroes."

"Why only ones and zeroes?" Ward asked.

"The reason for this is the computer is electrical," I answered. "It's relatively easy for the computer to represent data and programs as a series of on or off switches, where on is a one, and off is a zero."

I said most of my students are overwhelmed at first by the notion that the computer uses ones and zeroes to represent data and programs, but it's absolutely true. Because of the miniaturized state of the electronic components in the computer, the computer can contain millions and millions of these on/off switches.

"Each one of these on/off switches has a special name—a bit," I said.

Bits

Nearly everyone told me they had heard the word "bit" somewhere.

"A bit sounds like something small and it is," I said. "A bit is the smallest unit of data in the computer. You can think of a bit as the light switch on your wall. It can either be on or off. When a computer bit is on, it has a value of 1. When a computer bit is off, it has a value of 0."

I displayed the following sketch on the classroom projector.

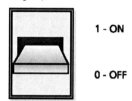

"One bit can represent only two values: 1 or 0. Suppose we add a second bit. With two bits, we can represent four possible values."

- Both bits can be off

- Both bits can be on

- The first bit can be on and the second bit can be off

- The first bit can be off and the second bit can be on

I displayed the following sketch on the classroom projector.

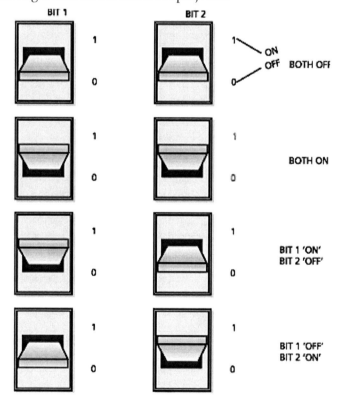

"With 3 bits, we can represent 8 possible values. With 4 bits, 16 values. With 5 bits, 32 values. With 6 bits, 64. With 7 bits, 128 values. And, with 8 bits, 256 values."

I displayed the following sketch of eight light switches on the classroom projector, with some of the switches set to on and some set to off.

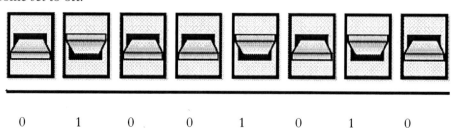

"This bit pattern, as it's called," I said, "is the binary form of the capital letter J."

"You're kidding," Ward said. "So my name could be represented in the computer by a pattern of these light switches—I mean ones and zeroes?"

Bytes

"Exactly right," I replied. "A unique bit pattern exists for every letter of the alphabet (both uppercase and lowercase), each number and each punctuation key on the computer's keyboard."

I asked the students to take a quick look at their keyboard. The keyboard has 26 letters. Counting both lowercase and uppercase letters, there are 52. Count the numbers and we're up to 62. Now count the punctuation keys. "On my keyboard, I count another 32," Rose said.

"That gives us a total of 94," Jack said.

I explained that to represent any one of those 94 characters on the keyboard requires 7 bits, because 7 bits can represent 128 characters. To represent the not-printable characters as well requires 8 bits.

"A collection of 8 bits is called a byte," I said, "and the standardized bit pattern is known as the ASCII Code. ASCII stands for the American Standard Code for Information Interchange."

"Where can we find the ASCII Code?" Barbara asked.

"Sure. When we start up Visual Basic, you'll find the ASCII Code can easily be found in Visual Basic's Online Help by searching for the keyword ASCII."

I told the class not to be intimidated by all this talk of bits and bytes because memorizing the ASCII code isn't necessary to be a good programmer. However, knowledge of what goes on behind the scenes can be invaluable.

"A Visual Basic programmer should be aware of binary," I said, "because Visual Basic, like all other programming languages, acts as a translator. The programmer writes in a language—in our case Visual Basic—which is similar to English. Then something known as the Visual Basic compiler converts this English-like writing to binary code which the machine can understand."

Memory

"OK," I said. "We've looked at the most basic form of data in the computer. Now let's examine how and where that data is stored in the computer."

I continued by saying that something that always seems to confuse students is the concept of computer memory. I reminded them of my definition of a computer: it accepts data, and performs calculations and other types of operations on that input in to generate information.

"These calculations and operations are performed in the computer's memory," I said. "Computer memory is also called RAM, which is an acronym for random access memory. Bits and bytes are recorded electrically in the computer's RAM. The computer uses RAM just like you would use a piece of scratch paper. RAM holds not only data, but every program currently running."

I displayed the following sketch on the classroom projector.

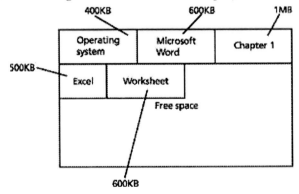

"Here's a sketch of RAM use in a typical computer," I said.

"Do we need to memorize this?" Rhonda asked.

"Goodness, no!" I exclaimed. "I'm not discussing RAM for that reason. What's important here is for you to understand how the computer uses it—that's what can make you a better programmer." I continued by explaining that RAM temporarily holds programs currently running and any data these programs require.

"How temporary is temporary?" Mary asked.

"A fraction of a second," I said. "The ones and zeroes stored in RAM are there only as long as the computer is on. When you turn your computer off, the contents of RAM, the bits and bytes, are lost."

"If you're using your computer," I said, "and a thunderstorm suddenly knocks your power out, the contents of RAM are lost in an instant. The term volatility is used to describe the temporary and fragile nature of RAM."

"What do KB and MB mean?" asked Rhonda.

"KB is an acronym for kilobyte, which is the term for approximately one thousand bytes. A megabyte—MB is its acronym—is approximately a million bytes," I replied. "We'll look more at these terms when we discuss computer storage."

"Something that confuses beginners," I said, "is the notion of RAM capacity and the speed at which data can be accessed from it. When you buy a computer, it comes with a certain amount or capacity of RAM, which is also rated with a length of time. The capacity tells you the total number of bytes the computer's RAM can hold and the rating indicates the time it takes the computer to get to or access a particular piece of data in RAM."

"I've taken a look inside my computer at home and I know I have 512MB of RAM and it s rated at 60 nanoseconds," Peter said.

"Thank you, Peter," I said. "A nanosecond is one billionth of a second. This means Peter's computer can access a particular piece of data in RAM in 60 billionths of a second."

I continued by saying that in addition to RAM, other devices in the computer also have ratings. For instance, floppy disks and hard disk drives are rated in the millisecond range. Because 1,000,000 nanoseconds are in a millisecond, accessing data from a floppy disk or hard disk drive takes a much longer time than accessing the same data from RAM.

"Relatively speaking then, RAM is very fast," Dave said.

"Yes it is," I agreed.

"My computer has 4 gigabytes of RAM," Ward said proudly.

"Actually," I replied, "that'll be the storage capacity of your hard disk drive, which is also measured in bytes. Your hard drive has 4 billion bytes of storage space, as a gigabyte, whose acronym is GB, is approximately one billion bytes. I told you these terms could be confusing. Your computer has a certain amount of RAM and a certain amount of storage. We'll look at the concept of storage in a minute or so."

Linda observed that RAM capacity is always less than the capacity of the computer's hard drive.

"Excellent observation, Linda," I said. "RAM, as I mentioned, uses electricity to store bits and bytes, and is much more expensive than disk drives, which use magnetism to permanently store bits and bytes. At home, my computer contains 512MB of RAM, while my hard disk drive contains 120GB. Therefore, the capacity of my disk drive is about 200 times as large as my RAM."

I displayed the following slide on the classroom projector.

To Summarize THEN, RAM:

- Uses electricity to store ones and zeroes
- Holds programs and data for execution
- Is temporary in nature, sometimes called volatile
- Has less capacity than a hard disk drive
- Is faster than a hard disk drive
- Is more expensive than a hard disk drive

Computer Storage

"Let's address Ward's confusion concerning RAM and storage," I said. "Beginners frequently confuse the terms 'memory' and 'storage.' This confusion arises because both RAM and hard drive storage capacity are measured in bytes. Here's a chart that shows you some of the common terms of capacity measurement, along with a real-world application of the term."

I displayed the following chart on the classroom projector.

Term	Approx.	Other terms used	Real World
Byte	1 character		A letter or number
Kilobyte	1 thousand characters	K, KB	One double-spaced typewritten page
Megabyte	1 million characters	Meg, MB	50 pages of a textbook, including graphics and illustrations
Gigabyte	1 billion characters	Gig, GB	An encyclopedia with graphics, audio and video

"Although they may seem large at first," I said, "some of these storage terms aren't that big when you consider how much capacity is required to store some common, everyday pieces of data. For instance, one chapter of a textbook, including the diagrams and formatting information, may use about 1MB of RAM and storage. An encyclopedia consumes about one third of the storage capacity of one of our classroom hard disk drives.

"Think of memory as being like a desk. You work with items on your desk, but you store them elsewhere, in a filing cabinet. When you need to work with items, you retrieve them from the cabinet. A computer's filing cabinet is storage. Memory, as we just saw, is RAM, which is electrical and very much a temporary commodity. Sooner or later, you'll turn off the computer but, because RAM is temporary, when you do that, any data in the RAM will be lost. The user of the computer must have a way of saving data contained in RAM permanently. So, storage is where the data that was held temporarily in the RAM is stored permanently."

I continued by saying that computer storage today is either magnetic (hard disk drives and floppy drives) or optical (CD-ROMs and writeable CDs).

"How do disk drives work?" Blaine asked.

"In a nutshell," I said, "where RAM uses electricity to record ones and zeroes, disk drives use magnetism to record magnetic ones and zeroes permanently on spinning disks coated with a magnetic oxide. Magnetic oxides can hold information without power. When you switch the computer back on again, the information is still there. This is the key idea to storage."

I pointed out that floppy disks and hard disk drives are actually the slow link in the computer's strong speed chain. Both these devices introduce us to something we haven't seen yet in the computer—physical movement. Forcing a computer that operates at the speed of electricity to interact with a device that needs to move to operate is like driving a racing car in bumper-to-bumper traffic. RAM performs operations on billions of bits in a matter of seconds. By comparison, disk drives are incredibly slow.

> **TIP: Anything you, the programmer, can do to reduce or eliminate reading or writing data to a disk drive makes the programs you write in Visual Basic much faster.**

"The RAM in our classroom computers is rated at 60 nanoseconds, our hard disk drive is rated at 9 milliseconds, and our floppy disk drive at 70 milliseconds," I said. "If you do some quick math, you can see accessing a piece of data in RAM is about 150,000 times faster than accessing that same piece of data on the hard disk drive. Accessing that data on the hard disk drive is about eight times faster than accessing it from the floppy disk drive."

The operation of floppy and hard disk drives is virtually identical. The main differences are speed of access and storage capacity. Whereas the hard disk drive on my computer holds 3.1GB, the floppy disk currently sitting in my floppy disk drive holds a little over 1MB. CD-ROM drives are closer in speed and capacity to a hard disk drive than a floppy disk drive.

To summarize, then, storage

- Uses magnetism or optics to store ones and zeroes

- Permanently stores programs and data

- Has more capacity than RAM

- Is slower than RAM

- Is cheaper than RAM

RAM versus Storage

"Let's summarize our discussion of RAM and storage," I said.

"Two kinds of information are held in a computer," I said. "The programs you're using and the documents you're working on. The computer treats these bits of data differently. When you finish with a program, it's simply cleared out of RAM and never gets sent back to storage. After all, you got it from RAM in the first place, so you can do that again whenever you want to. When you finish with a document, it's usually saved to the hard disk, so it can be recovered after the computer is turned off and the RAM is 'flushed.'"

Prior to our first break of the day, I displayed the following chart on the classroom projector.

	RAM	Storage
How data is recorded	Electricity	Magnetism or Optics
Temporary or Permanent?	Volatile, disappearing when the computer is turned off	Permanent, until you ask the computer to delete the file
Cost	More expensive than storage	Less expensive than RAM
Time taken to access data	Faster than storage, in the nanosecond range	Slower than RAM, in the millisecond range

What Makes a Computer Program Run?

After a ten-minute break, I asked if anyone could tell me what running a computer program means. No anxious volunteers raised their hands.

"Sometimes," I said, "you hear the terms 'execute,' 'load,' or 'start' in place of the word 'run.' These terms are frequently used interchangeably."

"I've also heard other terms for 'program,'" Linda said. "That's right," I agreed. "You'll probably hear me use terms such as 'project,' 'application,' or 'app' quite a bit during this course."

"Did you say app?" Ward asked. "Yes, app is short for application," I said.

I reminded them that most computer programs are written to convert data into information or to convert information to data, for storage and later processing. The program is written by a programmer and sold or distributed to end users.

"Like the China Shop program," Mary said. "Exactly," I answered.

For a program to run on a computer, it must first be written with the aid of an editor (such as Notepad) or a program development tool, such as Visual Basic. After the program is written, the program is either compiled, or run in an interpreted mode. I displayed the following explanation on the classroom projector.

> A <u>compiled</u> program is a program that's translated into machine language instructions (ones and zeroes). The compiled program is saved, usually as a file ending with a file extension of .EXE. The compiled program is then run on a computer, where the ones and zeroes are read directly by the operating system.

> An <u>interpreted</u> program is a program that isn't translated ahead of time, but is translated line by line as the program is run. Interpreted programs run more slowly than compiled programs.

I continued by saying programs that run on a computer are either Operating Systems or Application Programs. Operating Systems, a term often abbreviated as OS, take care of work within the computer, often complex and repetitive work, which allows the applications to run. For instance, the OS is responsible for finding the letter you wrote to Aunt Sarah or Uncle Bill last winter.

> **NOTE: Visual Basic is one programming language among many that can be used to create Application Programs. Most System Programs are written in languages such as Assembler, C, and C++, although many apps are written using these languages as well.**

"Few, if any, people would buy a computer just for the operating system," I said. "It's the apps you can run that makes the computer a useful tool." I cited word processing, electronic spreadsheet programs, and game programs as common examples of apps.

"Application programs can't run without the assistance of operating systems, can they?" Valerie asked.

"That's right," I said. "Apps couldn't work without an OS to take care of internal chores. On the other hand, an OS would have no purpose if there weren't any applications people wanted to use."

I displayed this chart illustrating some uses for each type of program.

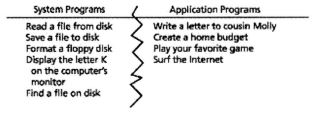

"Why should we be so concerned about our OS?" Valerie asked. I answered by saying that, at this point in their programming careers, the understanding of the OS might not seem significant. In my opinion, though, you can't be a great programmer without understanding how your programs interact with the OS controlling your computer.

"Is Windows the Operating System?" Ward asked.

"Windows is one of many Operating Systems for the PC," I said. "A PC is capable of running any number of different Operating Systems. You could even run them simultaneously but, frankly, you're unlikely to ever want to do that."

"Is an OS written for a specific brand of computer?" Joe asked.

"No," I said, "an OS is written to work with a specific microprocessor, such as the Intel Pentium microprocessor some of you may have heard of. The Intel family of microprocessors is so popular that many different operating systems have been written to run on it, including DOS, UNIX, and the various versions of Windows. The OS is the workhorse of the PC. Virtually from the time the computer is turned on, the OS is in nearly full control. Any app that runs on the PC runs under the control of the OS. It's important to our understanding of programming to know a little bit more about how the OS operates."

I paused before continuing.

"At this point," I said, "our lesson can go in many different directions because many different operating systems can run on a PC. Today we're going to examine two of the most popular operating systems: DOS and Windows."

A Little Computer History

"Why waste time talking about DOS?" Linda asked. "Hasn't that gone by the wayside? I would think everyone here is running Windows at home or at work." Several students disagreed, however. Some of them were still running DOS on their PCs at work.

"My purpose here is not to explain how to use DOS," I said. "I want to place Windows in a historical perspective, so you can appreciate it for what it is, an OS developed to correct the deficiencies of DOS. For those of you who have never seen DOS in action, today will give you a clearer vision of why Windows was developed."

DOS

"In the next few moments," I continued, "I'll present an overview of DOS, how it boots, how programs run under DOS, RAM use under DOS, and, finally, the limitations of DOS that led to the development of Windows."

I noted that DOS (disk operating system), sometimes known as MS-DOS or PC-DOS, was introduced in 1981 for the original IBM PC.

"The original IBM PC was primitive compared to the computers we're using today in this classroom," I said. "The original version of DOS (Version 1.0) didn't need to be terribly complicated. Today's versions of DOS are much more complicated than their predecessors, reflecting the great advances in hardware that have transformed the computer industry."

Booting DOS

"Most, if not all of the PCs sold these days are running a version of Windows," I continued, "which is one of the reasons you're all here. Worldwide, though, plenty of PCs are still only running DOS." I thought it would help the class if I gave them a historical perspective of Microsoft DOS.

"When DOS was being developed, two technological limitations had to be dealt with:"

- First, the original IBM PC was slow

- Second, it didn't have much RAM (64KB)

"We know how important RAM is to the operation of the PC," I said. "Because the size of RAM was restricted to only 64KB and, to run an application, the OS, the application, and the data had to be in memory at the same time, you can appreciate why the OS had to be pretty lean.

I continued by explaining that no design could be lean enough. Considering everything an OS is called on to do, there was no way to load all of DOS into RAM at the same time and still leave room for anything else. For this reason, DOS was divided into a series of smaller programs. Three programs were designated intrinsic programs and the rest were designated as extrinsic programs.

These three intrinsic programs were designed to remain permanently in RAM (at least while the PC was running). Together, these three files—IO.SYS, MSDOS.SYS, and COMMAND.COM—were small enough (about 45KB) so they could all squeeze into RAM, leaving about 19KB for apps and data.

"But what about those other files," Ward asked, "the extrinsic files you spoke about? What are they used for?"

I explained the extrinsic files are typically found in a subdirectory of your hard disk drive. Without exception, these files execute commands that aren't necessary for the PC to operate. Instead, they offered the user some additional tools.

"For instance," I said, "in Windows 95, if you insert an unformatted floppy disk into your PC's floppy disk drive, you're asked if you want to format the floppy disk. In DOS, to format a floppy disk, you must run the extrinsic FORMAT program, which is located on the PC's hard disk drive. When you run the FORMAT program, FORMAT.COM is found, and then loaded into RAM by the intrinsic portion of DOS, the program is run, and when the floppy disk is formatted, the extrinsic FORMAT program is removed from RAM."

Running Programs in DOS

I then asked the class to consider a computer booting DOS as its OS. I had preconfigured a PC to run DOS, and I took a moment to connect it to our classroom projector.

This screenshot is what everyone saw on the classroom projector after the computer had finished booting up.

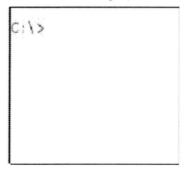

"What is that?" Rhonda asked. "It looks like a random collection of characters. Did you press the keys by mistake?" Many of the students had never seen a DOS prompt and it was a shock to them.

"Where's the interface?" Rose asked. "This is it!" I said. "At this point, the computer is now just sitting there waiting for us to give it something to do."

I noticed some obvious grins. "Yes, this is the DOS prompt," I said. "In DOS, this prompt is displayed to let the users know the computer is ready and willing to do something for them. A flashing underline, called the cursor, blinks to the right of the greater than (>) sign to let the user know the PC is awaiting instructions."

I continued by saying that, at this point, the users can either type in a DOS command or the name of a program they want to run.

"In DOS," I said, "only files with extensions ending in .EXE, .COM, or .BAT can be run, although the user doesn't have to type the extension of the filename to run it."

> **NOTE: Filenames in DOS followed an 8.3 naming convention. That is, the name of the file can contain anywhere from one to eight characters, followed by an optional period (.), followed by an optional file extension, containing anywhere from one to three characters. The latest version of DOS, Version 7, supports longer filenames.**

"After the user enters the name of a command at the DOS prompt," I continued, "DOS takes a quick look in RAM to see if the name of the program the user typed is an intrinsic command, in which case it is found there. If DOS finds it, the command is executed. If DOS doesn't find the name of the command there, DOS continues its search by looking in the current directory and, if that fails, DOS looks in the directories specified in something called the DOS Path."

> **NOTE: The DOS Path is a list of directories contained in a special startup file called AUTOEXEC.BAT. The DOS Path tells DOS where to search for the command or program the user wants. If DOS finds the appropriate file, it loads it into RAM and starts the program running. Of course, the program could either be an extrinsic DOS command or an executable program written by someone other than Microsoft.**

"That's to keep DOS from having to search the entire hard disk, isn't it?" Linda asked. "Exactly," I agreed.

I went on to say that the DOS prompt is an example of a character-based interface, which means the only way users can tell the OS what they want to do is to type a command or a filename using the keyboard.

"In other words, there's no mouse," Dave said.

"Right you are," I replied. "The character-based interface has some inherent weaknesses. First, typing is slow. Second, you need to remember all the commands. And, third, making mistakes is much easier."

I informed my class that I had installed a copy of WordPerfect for DOS on my PC prior to the beginning of this class this morning. I could tell from their expressions that several of them had never heard of WordPerfect, so I explained WordPerfect is a word processing program, much like Microsoft Word.

"Unlike the version of Word we have in the classroom," I said, "the DOS version of WordPerfect doesn't require Microsoft Windows to run."

I wanted to illustrate how an app runs under DOS. I said all I needed to do to run the program was to type the name WP at the DOS prompt, and then press ENTER. Like this.

C:\>WP

I did so and, a few seconds later, WordPerfect was running on the PC. I quickly exited the program and we were back to the DOS prompt.

"How did you know to type WP?" Ward asked.

"Good point," I replied. "First, you have to know, and second, you have to remember. But, suppose instead of typing **WP**, I type **WO** instead? Like this."

C:\>WO

I typed that and this message was displayed on the classroom projector.

Bad Command or File name

"What happened?" Bob asked.

I told them that when I typed the command WP at the DOS prompt, DOS looked in RAM to see if this was an intrinsic DOS command. It wasn't, so DOS checked the current directory, and then checked each directory in the DOS Path, looking for a file called WP.EXE, WP.COM, or WP.BAT. It finally found a file called WP.EXE in the \WP51 directory, which I had placed in the DOS path of the PC's AUTOEXEC.BAT file.

"And what about WO?" Joe asked.

"DOS," I said, "followed the same procedure looking for a file called WO.EXE, WO.COM, or WO.BAT, but couldn't find them anywhere in its path. At that point, it displayed the error message."

"One of those user-friendly error messages I've grown to love," Lou said sarcastically.

RAM Use in DOS

"How much RAM do we have on these PCs?" I asked.

"I believe you said 512MB!" Dave replied.

"That's right," I said. "I bet most of you think that right now, DOS is using this PC's RAM pretty efficiently."

There were a number of affirmative nods. I pointed out that our assumption had a slight problem. Back in 1981, when DOS was being written, the programmers working on it were worried about squeezing programs into RAM. Although they anticipated the larger amounts of RAM that would be available in PCs today, they didn't plan for it in their design of DOS. With the 64KB of RAM in the original IBM PC, an upper limit of 1MB of RAM seemed pretty reasonable. I could see some puzzled looks.

"What do you mean an upper limit?" Linda asked.

"I mean DOS can't load a program into RAM beyond the first megabyte because it simply can't count beyond one million—and that's regardless of the total amount of RAM on the PC. With 512MB of RAM on this PC, by running DOS with only a single program running, we're actually wasting the remaining 511MB of RAM. Only the first megabyte of RAM can be accessed by DOS!"

"Eventually," I said, "third-party software vendors and Microsoft itself came up with software to use all the RAM on DOS-based PCs more fully, but these attempts were basically a patchwork until Windows came along. Shortly, you'll see that Windows overcame this RAM limitation, which is another reason why it was immediately popular with microcomputer owners."

Valerie noted that the DOS programs she had used in the past seemed rudimentary in comparison to the Windows version of the same program.

"That's an excellent point," said. "The RAM limitation severely limits the functionality of DOS programs. To a large degree, the number of bells and whistles a program has is dependent on the number of program instructions it contains. In effect, this prevents DOS programs from being as large as their Windows counterparts. For instance, the executable file for the DOS version of WordPerfect is about 300,000 bytes. The executable file for the version of Microsoft Word in our classroom is about 3.5MB."

I explained that as users begin to use WordPerfect, it makes various requests of DOS (remember, apps work with the OS, not directly with the computer). "For instance," I said, "the user may ask the app to save a document. The app passes the request to the OS, which uses one or more of its commands to achieve the required result, using registers and stacks to process the commands at the right time."

Registers

"Registers and stacks?" Linda asked. I explained registers are high-speed memory devices contained within the microprocessor. Each microprocessor contains varying numbers of registers.

"The microprocessor uses registers to perform calculations," I said, "and to keep track of the next program instruction to be performed. If the OS needs to perform an addition, for example, the microprocessor uses two registers to hold each number, placing the calculated result in a third register."

"It sounds like registers are part of RAM," Rhonda said.

"No, but that's a common misconception. The registers are contained within the microprocessor."

The Stack

"A stack is a different story," I said. "A stack is a data structure contained in RAM that holds information about running applications. Whereas registers are manipulated by the microprocessor, stacks are manipulated either by the app or the OS."

"What's a data structure?" Chuck asked.

I explained that in the world of computer science, data structures are logical entities. They don't physically exist, but they're created to aid the OS to do its job.

"We'll be creating data structures of our own later in the course," I said, "when we create files for the China Shop Project. Files are data structures."

"I understand the concept of a register," Jack said, "but I'm having trouble understanding stacks."

"Suppose," I said, "you go into your favorite diner or restaurant tonight, and sit at the counter.

You're bound to see a pile of dishes placed into a plate 'stack,' which is a mechanical device with a cylindrical compartment and a spring on the bottom. The spring pushes upward on the plates so, when you take one out, the next one pops to the top."

"Yes, I've seen those," Rose said.

"Just like the plate stack is used to store dishes neatly, while providing easy access to the next dish, the data structure stack is used by the OS and app to store program instructions, results of calculations, and other data, ready for when they're needed."

I continued by explaining that when the OS places something on to the stack, it's called a ***push operation***. Accessing and, subsequently, removing an entry from the stack is called a ***pop operation***. Keeping the details straight as to what on the stack belongs to the OS and what belongs to one or more apps can be complex.

"Fortunately," I said, "that's something we don't have to worry about because the OS takes care of all those details. When we discuss Windows, which permits more than one app to run at the same time, you'll see that each Windows application has an internal stack of its own."

Problems with DOS

Ward (obviously a DOS fan) remarked that from his experience, DOS does more than an admirable job of running programs.

"Why do we need Windows?" he said.

In reply, I posed this question, "Suppose the users, while working in WordPerfect, needs to work on their Lotus 1-2-3 spreadsheet files? In DOS, it isn't possible to work on more than one app at the same time unless you use special software. To be on the safe side, DOS should only be used for single tasking. This means users should work with only one program at a time. Users should finish working in WordPerfect, save whatever document they're working with, and then exit. DOS clears RAM of WordPerfect and any documents it was using. The user then stares at the DOS prompt, remembers the command for Lotus 1-2-3, types it in, and waits as DOS locates and loads Lotus 1-2-3 into RAM."

"So," Ward replied half-heartedly, "what's wrong with that?"

We all agreed that clicking an icon on your desktop is certainly a lot easier.

"And then, suppose," I continued, "users need to incorporate some data from their Lotus 1-2-3 spreadsheet into the WordPerfect document they're working on. In DOS, there's simply no way to take that data and place it in the spreadsheet."

I asked if everyone considered these limitations as severe. Everyone, including my stalwart DOS fans, agreed these were pretty severe. I pointed out that, although many people in the world are still using DOS, I think most of them, given the choice, would be Windows converts.

I displayed the following list of DOS limitations on the classroom projector:

- DOS Uses a Character-based Interface. The user has to type arcane, hard-to-remember instructions at a DOS prompt to tell the PC what it should do. Giving the computer instructions in this way is by nature error-prone. Typing a command at a DOS prompt will never be as easy as clicking an icon with a mouse.

- RAM Limitations. DOS cannot take advantage of the modern PC's abundant RAM without the use of additional applications. As we have seen, DOS, even on a PC with 512MB of RAM, only initially uses the first megabyte.

- DOS Is Single Tasking. A DOS user cannot work with more than one application at a time.

- DOS Lacks a Common User Interface. Every DOS program looks different from the other. A uniform interface greatly reduces training time. In DOS, you would have to learn different commands to perform the same function in different applications.

- Information Transfer in DOS from one application to another is impossible. In DOS, no way exists to transfer data from one program to another. Windows introduced a "clipboard," which gives Windows programs a way to share data easily.

I suggested a die-hard DOS fan might say, "Problem with DOS? DOS doesn't have any problems. The character-based interface never bothered me. My DOS programs run perfectly fine in 1MB. Besides, who in their right mind would want to run more than one program anyway?"

This statement elicited quite a few chuckles.

"I've heard this argument for years," I said. "To me, this is like saying that airplanes flew better with propellers instead of jet engines. It's time to realize the five limitations I previously stated are the reasons Microsoft Windows is the OS of choice for PCs today."

I continued with our minihistory lesson. I said that eventually, as PCs became more and more popular, users heard about another microcomputer that had a graphical user interface (called a GUI—pronounced GOO-ey), which took full advantage of the increasing power of microprocessors and permitted the user to run more than one program simultaneously.

> **NOTE: To clear up a few things: Windows is the registered trademark for the OS we're discussing. A window is a rectangular space on the screen in which you do work. And Window is a menu choice, which gives the user options about how to arrange the windows (workspaces) on the screen.**

"That microcomputer was the Macintosh," I said, "and the users weren't the only ones to see the potential of this. Microsoft did, as well, and the company began work on Windows."

Microsoft Windows

I could see some relieved looks on the faces of my students. Finally, they were thinking, we're going to look at Windows. Again, I emphasized the reason I'd devoted so much time to discussing DOS was to place Windows in the correct historical perspective.

"Now, I want to move our discussion to Windows, which right now is the dominant GUI interface in the world," I said. "I must warn you, though, any discussion of Windows is complicated because multiple distinct versions of Windows are currently available: Windows XP, Windows Vista, and Windows 7. For the most part, I'm going to discuss Windows as if it were a single entity. Where differences exist between the various versions of Windows, I'll point those out."

"Before we get into the nuts and bolts of Windows," I said, "let's take a quick peek at a typical Windows application, the Windows Calculator. Every Windows program has a similar look and feel, so looking at the Calculator is a great way to discuss the features common to them all."

I instructed everyone in the class to press the Windows START button, and then to select Programs | Accessories | Calculator. This screen was displayed on the classroom projector.

"As you can see, the Calculator exemplifies a Windows program," I said. "It's graphical!"

"As you can see, the calculator contains a title bar, a menu bar, and some of the objects we discussed during our last class. For instance, each of the number keys is a button control. The box at the top of the Calculator, that currently displays the number zero, is a text box."

"Are there any radio buttons and check boxes?" Blaine asked.

I asked them to select View | Scientific from the Calculator's menu. When they did, the scientific view of the Calculator was displayed.

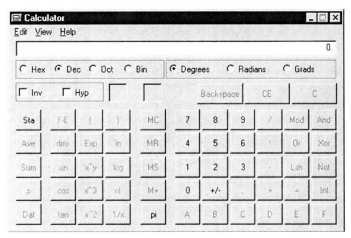

"The scientific view of the Calculator," I said, "has more than its fair share of radio buttons and check boxes."

"Notice the radio button group with the labels Hex, Dec, Oct, and Bin," I said. "Only one radio button can be selected at a time. In this case, Dec, an abbreviation of decimal, is selected. With check boxes, more than one check box can be selected in a group, such as Inv and Hyp." I saw a few puzzled looks, but I assured everyone they would have ample opportunity to experiment with both radio buttons and check boxes before the end of the course.

"The Windows Calculator is just a Windows program," I said. "It was written by a programmer using the same types of tools available in Visual Basic." I told them that in previous classes, one of the class projects had been for the students to write their own Windows Calculator program using Visual Basic.

"Will we be doing that in this class?" Steve asked.

"No," I replied. "All our energies will be devoted to writing the China Shop Project. But, by the end of the course, you'll certainly be able to write such a program if you want to. Let's use the Windows Calculator to discuss the characteristics it shares with every other Windows program, including those you'll write yourselves."

The Title Bar

I explained that the title bar in a Windows program contains the name of the program. But that's not all it contains. To the left of the program name is an icon that usually represents what the program does. In the case of the Calculator, it's a picture of a calculator.

"The programs we write," I said, "including the China Shop Project, will contain such an icon. But this icon is more than only window dressing. This icon is called a Control menu bar."

I asked the class to click their mouse on the icon and, when they did, the Control menu bar was revealed.

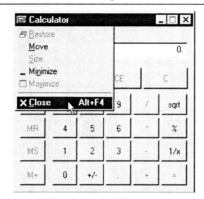

I explained the Control menu bar gives users options for minimizing, maximizing, or closing their windows. "When we design the China Shop Project interface," I said, "you'll see there's a way to tell Visual Basic either to display or not to display the Control menu bar. As you see a little later, we'll choose not to display it."

I asked the students to look to the right-hand side of the title bar. Three buttons are located there: the Minimize, Maximize, and Close buttons. "In fact, these buttons are shortcuts for the Control menu bar. Clicking the Minimize button reduces the Calculator to an icon on the Windows task bar," I said.

"Why is the second button dull?" Rhonda asked.

"The second button is the Maximize button," I replied. "Ordinarily, clicking it would enlarge the Calculator to the full size of the monitor. However, the designers of the Calculator 'disabled' the Maximize button, so the Calculator couldn't be maximized. We're able to do the same thing for programs we design in Visual Basic."

I also mentioned you could usually move your mouse pointer to the borders of a Windows program, and click-and-drag to change the size and shape of the window. However, just as the designers of the Calculator had chosen to disable the Maximize button, they had decided the user shouldn't be able to resize the window. "Again," I said, "this is something you can specify for the programs you design in Visual Basic."

I concluded my discussion of the Control menu bar by saying that clicking the Close button closes, and then ends, the Calculator program.

"When we design the China Shop Project interface," I said, "we'll see that in Visual Basic options or properties determine which, if any, of these buttons will be displayed when the user runs our program."

I reminded them we'd already decided the user could only exit the China Shop Program via the menu. "For that reason," I said, "we'll disable the Control menu bar itself, so the user won't even see it."

Some people were looking tired after all the things we'd covered—from bits and bytes all the way to Windows—so I asked everyone to take a quick break.

The Menu Bar

When everyone returned from break, we turned our attention to the menu bar of the Calculator. I didn't have to remind the class that we'd discussed the China Shop Project's menu at great length during the design phase of the SDLC.

"The Calculator's menu," I said, "deviates slightly from the Windows standard menu in that it doesn't contain a File command. Aside from that, though, it operates in a typical Windows way. Notice the Edit command can also be accessed by pressing the ALT and E keys." I also told them you can do the same with many menus—just press ALT and the underlined letter.

Windows Behavior

"I don't want to leave you with the impression that the main difference between DOS programs and Windows programs is graphical quality," I said. "That's part, but not all of it." I said some DOS programs have existed with pretty impressive graphical appearances.

"I think, though," Linda said, "that to someone coming from the DOS world, the most impressive aspect of a Windows program is the beautiful graphical interface." I agreed. Viewing the Calculator for the first time and seeing it actually looks like a calculator is certainly startling. The buttons are so lifelike, your first inclination is to reach out and press them with your fingers (in fact, if you had a touch screen, you could). Without the benefit of a touch screen, you have to use the next best thing, a mouse.

"A Windows program is also different from a DOS program," I said, "in that it can accept input and responses from a user in lots of ways a DOS program can't."

"As an illustration," I said, "I want you to consider exactly what happens when you use your mouse to move the pointer over the number 6 on the calculator, and then click the left mouse button. In fact, several things happen":

- First, the mouse pointer moves in response to the mouse being dragged on the mouse pad.

- Second, after the mouse pointer has been placed over the number 6, when the user presses and holds the left mouse button, the appearance of the button changes. It appears to have been pressed. I asked them to click the number 6.

"Notice how the button for the number 6 now looks as if it's being pressed down," I said. "This is the default behavior of the button."

- Third, after the user releases the left mouse button, the button reverts to its previous appearance. It no longer appears to be pressed. At the same time, the number 6 appears in the box at the top of the window.

"Will we have to program this kind of behavior into the button controls we use in the China Shop Project?" Lou asked.

"We won't have to program the button to change its look and feel," I said, "because it's built into the button already. That's one of the things that makes programming in Visual Basic so easy!"

"What's going on behind the scenes here?" Linda asked. "What makes the button change in response to the mouse click?"

"That's a great question," I replied. "Windows is constantly on the alert for events taking place in the Windows environment and has been programmed to react in a predetermined manner to these events."

"An event?" asked Ward. "I don't exactly know what you mean by that. Can you give us an example?"

"For instance," I continued, "when users drag the mouse on their mouse pads, this movement generates a MouseMove event, which Windows detects and reacts to. Likewise, when users press the left mouse button, that action generates a MouseDown event, which Windows detects."

"Most important, Windows has been programmed so it can detect where on the desktop the mouse has been clicked. In this case, over a button control displaying the number 6. Windows takes this as a cue to change the display of the number to 6 to make it appear as if it's been pressed down. Finally, when the user releases the mouse button, a MouseUp event is generated. Windows detects two things: the button has been released and this action took place over the button control displaying the number 6. Windows responds by changing the display of the number 6 back to its original appearance."

"We'll be able to take advantage of these same events," I said, "as well as predetermined behavior when we write the China Shop Project."

I continued by saying that an important feature of Windows is its capability to run more than one program simultaneously. "For instance," I said, "while we're running the Calculator, we can also be creating or editing a document in Microsoft Word. Another important feature of Windows is its capability to copy-and-paste data between applications. For instance, we can use the Calculator to perform a calculation, select Edit | Copy from the Calculator's menu, copy the number in the Calculator's text box into something called the Windows Clipboard, switch to Microsoft Word, and then select Paste from its menu to copy the result into the document."

A More In-depth Look at Windows

"Are we going to go behind the scenes of Windows, like we did with DOS?" Dave asked. I asked the rest of the class what they thought and nearly everyone agreed we should.

"Okay then, but before we go any further," I said, "I'm afraid we have to return to our discussion of memory because Windows uses something called virtual memory and I don't want you to become confused."

Virtual Memory

I reminded them that, while they're running, RAM is used to storing the active programs and any data the user is working on temporarily. You might think, that for a computer with 512MB of RAM, running out of memory would be next to impossible but, unfortunately, that isn't so. Because Windows enables you to run many programs at the same time, it's easy to use it all up.

"Because you can't run a program without first loading it into RAM," I said, "running out of RAM means you can't run another program. Windows gets around this problem by using virtual memory."

I continued by explaining that using virtual memory means removing a portion of a running program from RAM, and placing the program, and, perhaps, some of its data, onto the computer's hard disk drive in something called a swap file. This action frees up some RAM, into which a new program can be loaded. This process, known as swapping or paging, can be repeated every few milliseconds, enabling the computer to run many more programs than the RAM alone could cope with.

NOTE: Only portions of programs or data, not entire programs, are swapped.

I displayed this illustration of virtual memory on the classroom projector.

Operating System	Microsoft Word	Chapter1
Chapter 2	Chapter 3	Chapter 4
Chapter 5	Chapter 6	Chapter 7
Excel	Worksheet	Access

"The big problem with virtual memory is this: because you have to use the hard disk drive, you're effectively reducing the performance of any paged applications down to that of the storage," I explained.

"Thus the main improvements Windows makes over DOS are"

- ***Windows replaced the character-based interface with a graphical user interface.*** The GUI effectively eliminated the user's need to interact with a DOS prompt ever again. Programs are represented by symbols called icons. The user clicks the icon with the mouse. The program represented by the icon is then run.

- ***The memory constraints of DOS don't effect Windows.*** Windows uses all the PC's RAM. Not only that, but Windows can simulate more memory than the computer actually contains through the use of virtual memory.

- ***Windows uses virtual memory.*** Virtual memory comes in handy when the users are running their umpteenth simultaneous application and not enough memory is left to load one more into RAM.

- ***Windows overcomes the DOS limitation of single tasking.*** Windows is multitasking. This means it can run more than one application program simultaneously.

Multitasking

"Multitasking?" Ward asked. "I don't remember discussing that."

"We haven't really," I said. "Although we did discuss that DOS is single tasking and, therefore, capable of running only one program at one time. Remember, I said if we were running WordPerfect for DOS and needed to run Lotus 1-2-3, we first had to exit WordPerfect because we can't run the programs simultaneously."

I pointed out that Windows is a multitasking operating system, but the type of multitasking varies with the version of Windows you're running. Multitasking in Windows 3.1 is vastly different from multitasking in Windows 95 and above. The differences are significant enough to spend a few moments discussing.

"With a single microprocessor," I said, "it's not possible for the PC to do anything simultaneously. For instance, when the microprocessor is asked to add a column of ten numbers, it performs the addition step by step. When the Calculator is running alongside Microsoft Word, multitasking makes it appear as if programs are being executed simultaneously because computers are so fast these days. The programs appear to be running uninterrupted, even though the PC is only giving each program a small percentage of its time."

"Two types of multitasking exist," I explained. "Namely, preemptive multitasking and nonpreemptive multitasking."

Nonpreemptive Multitasking

"With ***nonpreemptive multitasking***," I said, "it's up to the application to implement the multitasking. In other words, the OS isn't in charge." I said programs running under a nonpreemptive multitasking operating system must be specially written to cooperate together, yielding control of the microprocessor every so often. Because the OS can't physically wrestle control away from an application, one program can hog the processor, and so the computer can appear to lock-up. "You see later that a Visual Basic function called DoEvents does exactly that—it allows the program to do events while something else is happening," I said.

Worse yet is the case where the unyielding app manages to freeze itself. Because the running program never relinquishes control to the microprocessor, the entire system remains frozen. The user's only choice is to reboot the PC (or shut down the offending program, using the CTRL | ALT | DELETE key combination).

Preemptive Multitasking

"With ***preemptive multitasking***," I said, "the OS decides when an application no longer has control of the microprocessor and simply takes it away. The program itself has no control over when it gains control of the microprocessor. This means if you forget to code a DoEvents function, the OS can still find a way for other program to get their fair share of the microprocessor's time."

Running Programs in Windows

I told the class that running programs in Windows is vastly different from running them in DOS. The main similarity is in the boot process whereby Windows is loaded into the RAM and the GUI is launched.

"Knowing how a program runs in the Windows environment," I said, "can have an impact on how you code your Visual Basic programs in the future. For that reason, we need to take a close look at how programs run in the Windows environment. Let's divide the process into two parts."

- Preparing the Windows program to run

- Running the Windows program

Preparing the Windows Program to Run

"Before we can discuss running a Windows program," I said, "I need to introduce you to some new terms. In the world of DOS, programs execute as . . . well, as programs. In the Windows world, programs are subdivided into processes and threads."

NOTE: A process is nothing more than a program, and a thread is a piece of a Windows program.

I continued by saying that when a user double-clicks an icon representing a Windows program, five distinct steps occur

1. Windows creates a new process and an initial thread for the program.

2. The Application Program code is loaded into RAM, just as it is in a DOS program.

3. If the application uses any dynamic-link libraries, they're also loaded into RAM.

4. Space for items such as data and stacks is allocated in RAM.

5. The application program begins to execute.

"Let's discuss each of these in detail," I said.

1. Windows Creates a New Process and an Initial Thread for the Program

In multitasking environments, you frequently see the term "process" in place of the term "program." Under Windows 95 and above, applications can ask the microprocessor to do work in threads. Theoretically, this can make the entire process run faster.

"That almost sounds like multitasking," Dave said. "That's true," I replied. "Except this time, it's occurring in the same application. There's a kicker, though."

"For instance," I continued, "a program might need three tasks performed to accomplish a function, such as updating an inventory record. Task A might take 16 milliseconds, task B might take 484 milliseconds, and Task C 3 seconds. If you ran the tasks on the same process (with one thread), the job would take three and a half seconds to accomplish."

Then I continued, "But, if we multithreaded the job, allocating one thread to each task, the job would take closer to four seconds to complete."

"But that's longer than a single thread. I thought multithreading was supposed to speed things up?" Dave asked.

"Good spot, Dave. Unfortunately, multithreading isn't as easy to master as it could be. The extra time is generated directly by the use of the additional threads. You see, when the OS decides one thread has had enough time to execute, it frees up the processor registers by saving the current contents to RAM and loads in the next thread's data. This takes some time and, with long threads, this means the process as a whole takes longer."

"So, why bother with threads at all?" asked Ward.

"Because on two occasions, threads can speed up the time required to perform a job. The first is when you have multiple processors. The number of threads allocated to a processor is reduced. Each thread is given more time to execute, so it's accomplished quicker. Most of the time, you'll be working on a single processor machine, though, so you can only rely on the second occasion, which is what I call downtime."

"Downtime," I continued, " is the collection of occasions when the user is (or, rather, isn't) interacting with the computer. Suppose you have those same three tasks to perform and, this time, the long three seconds' task is user-dependent or, in other words, it should be three seconds, but could take longer if the user needs typing practice. Now, instead of the job requiring half a second, plus the long task time, the job only takes the long task time as the threads allow the other tasks to complete while the user is messing around. The user also doesn't notice any delay because the swapping between threads is so quick. The moral of the story is this: background calculations should always be given their own threads or at least separate threads to the user interface control tasks."

2. The Application Program Code Is Loaded into RAM, Just as It Is in a DOS program

"The difference between a Windows and a DOS application is each process is assigned its own address space in RAM, including its own stack which, if you recall, is a data structure contained in RAM. Stacks are used by the operating system and your applications to store program instructions and other data, so they can be easily accessed when needed."

By assigning each process its own address space and stack, Windows isolates each process. This is the reason (theoretically) one renegade, out-of-control process shouldn't be able to cause the entire PC to crash."

3. If the Application Uses Any Dynamic-Link Libraries, They Are Also loaded into RAM

"Dynamic-link libraries?" Mary asked. "I'm checking my notes, but I don't think we've seen those today."

"That's right," I said. "We haven't—yet." I continued by saying that to explain a dynamic-link library (DLL) fully, I needed to go back and explain static-link libraries. Both types of libraries are special files used to store prewritten and pretested program instructions, or code. This code has been written so it can be incorporated in someone else's program."

I continued by explaining the major difference between the two types of libraries is when they're actually loaded into memory. "Static-link libraries are physically combined into each program that uses the instructions they contain," I remarked. "This means the resulting executable is the size of your code, plus the entire static-link library."

"Does that mean if the size of your program is 5KB and the library code is 3KB, the final size of your executable is 8KB?" Steve asked.

"Yes, but that's not all!" I exclaimed. "If you write two separate programs, the static-link library is used twice but, instead of simply being referenced (as you would expect the term 'library' to mean), the whole thing is copied and combined with each separate application."

"So if you have a 5KB program, a 6KB program and a 10KB library, you would generate 31KB of executable in total?" Steve asked.

"That's exactly right, Steve," I said. "A very inefficient process, don't you think?"

"And, unfortunately, there's more bad news!" I said. "Because a copy of the library is made whenever you build an executable out of your program, if you find a mistake in the library and fix it, that's only the beginning of your problems! All the programs using that library are going to be affected and all must be rebuilt before they can work correctly!"

"Wow, that seems like a lot of hard work," said Rose. "And you have to put up with that inefficient use of hard disk space!"

"Is this where DLLs come in?" asked Jack.

"Yes," I replied, "with Windows and the introduction of DLLs, programmers now had an alternative that retained the benefits of static link libraries, but cut out most of the drawbacks. Now, programmers didn't physically have to include the library in their code. They only referenced the instructions contained in them."

"I don't understand how this referencing works," said Barbara, "How does the executable get hold of the library's instructions when it needs them?"

"Well, this is the really innovative part and why we needed a new operating system to be invented before the idea of DLLs would work," I said. "You see, when a DLL is created, it's registered with Windows. This means Windows knows where the DLL is on your hard drive, what information it contains, and what name a calling program will use to reference it.

"So when a program is being run in Windows and it gets to a reference to some code held in a DLL, Windows knows exactly what to do. It goes off to the appropriate part of the hard drive, loads up the DLL, looks up the required set of instructions, and then runs them," I continued.

"That is clever! And doesn't that mean you only ever need one copy of the DLL?" asked Steve. "I mean, once Windows knows where it is, any number of programs can use it, if they know its name, right?"

"You're really getting the hang of this, Steve! That's perfectly correct, but there's some more good news!" I replied. "Because Windows is essentially controlling the existence of the DLL in RAM, it knows once the library has been loaded, the hard disk step can be skipped if another application wants the same DLL. And, in fact, if all the applications using the DLL are closed down, Windows automatically unloads the DLL from RAM to save space!"

"That is a terrific feature, but what about the bad code problem? Did DLLs solve that as well?" asked Linda.

"Yes, they did, Linda!" I said. "If you think about what's happening with a DLL, you can see why! Suppose you do find a problem with a DLL, fix it, and reconstruct the library. If you keep the library's appearance (by which I mean its name, location, and so on) the same, Windows simply uses the new code whenever a application calls it. You don't have to rebuild any of your programs. You just use a DLL for any code that might need to change in the first place and your future maintenance problems are drastically minimized.

4. Space for Items Such as Data and Stacks Is Allocated in RAM

In Windows, each process has its own protected area in RAM and its own copy of a stack. When one application hangs, it doesn't hang the entire system.

5. The Application Program Begins to Execute

As was the case in the DOS world, the program begins to execute. "There's certainly a lot more work to get to that stage, though," Ward said.

Running the Windows Program

"You're right about that," I said. "Now let's see how running a Windows program is different from running a DOS program."

"Now that the Windows program and everything it requires has been loaded into RAM," I said, "execution can begin. You can see in a moment, though, that running a Windows program is more complicated than executing a DOS program. The reason is the windows. I don't mean the OS in this case, but the window objects that occupy the user's desktop."

I asked the students to look at their Windows desktop, as I displayed mine on the classroom projector.

"Virtually everything you see in Windows is a window," I said. "Let's take a quick look at my desktop":

- The desktop itself is a window (one window)
- Each icon on the desktop is a window (three windows)
- The caption beneath each icon is a window (three windows)
- The Start bar is a window (one window)
- Each button on the Start bar is a window (two windows)
- Each one of the Microsoft Office icons is a window (nine windows)

"By my count, 19 windows are on my desktop," I said. "Most beginners don't realize nearly everything you see in the Windows environment is a window and Windows must maintain visibility of these windows like an air-traffic controller keeps track of planes in the sky. Let's look at a Windows application, Microsoft Word."

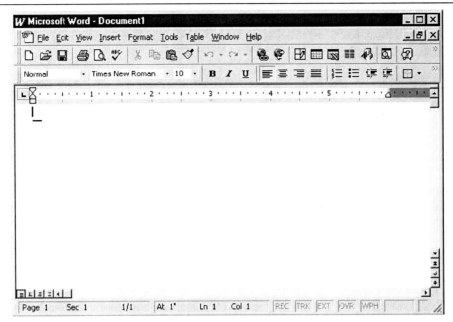

I explained that Microsoft Word is also made up of many windows, but most people don't think of the program in that way. The document window is an obvious window, but what about the menu bar at the top of Word? Or the buttons on the toolbar just beneath that? Or the scroll bars running vertically down the side and horizontally across the bottom? These are all windows.

In Windows, each window has characteristics and behaviors associated with it. For instance, a window has a height and width, it's displayed in a maximized, normal, or minimized state, and it has a location on the screen.

Plus, different types of windows exist. There are windows we all recognize as windows, and then there are the windows that appear as buttons, icons, lists, scroll bars, and even menus. Each of these different types of windows has different behaviors associated with it. For instance, if you click a menu, the behavior is different from clicking a scroll bar.

"That all sounds terribly chaotic," Linda said. "How can Windows keep track of all these windows and, better yet, know what to do with them?"

I told Linda the answer is through the use of Windows handles, messages, and a whole bunch of default behavior that's already built in for you.

"Don't worry," I said. "I'll explain exactly what these items mean and show you how they're used by Windows to make sense out of chaos, just like an air-traffic controller uses radar to coordinate the movement and behavior of planes."

The Windows Handle

A **Windows handle** uniquely identifies each window in the Windows environment. When a window is loaded, the OS assigns it a Windows handle, and each of these numbers is stored in a Windows handle table. This table keeps track of the handle number, as well as any other properties that describe the window, such as its height, width, and location on the desktop for later reference.

Without a Windows handle to track each of all the individual windows on the desktop, the OS would become hopelessly confused. Suppose the user moved a window? How would the OS know where the window was located? The very process of moving the window updates the appropriate property of that window in the Windows handle table.

Windows Messages

"I want to compare the Windows environment," I said, "to someone working in front of a very fast conveyor belt that contains boxes and packages bound for delivery all over the world. The person's job is to identify destinations for these packages by markings on them, as the boxes fly by them on the conveyor belt. As soon as that person identifies the destination, she pushes a button that reroutes the packages to other conveyor belts in the system."

"Now pretend the person working in front of the conveyor belt is actually the Windows OS. The conveyor belt is the Windows message queue, and the packages moving along the conveyor belt contain Windows Messages, and are marked with a Windows handle number."

"You're not talking about e-mail messages, are you?" Ward asked. "No," I said. "I'm talking about internal Windows messages generated when a user clicks the button of the mouse or types an entry into a text box, or when a window is resized."

I explained that Windows messages are constantly flowing from apps to Windows, and vice versa. "This process may sound chaotic," I said, "but with the Windows handle, the OS can easily determine where the message came from and where it should go."

"Even more amazing," I continued, "is that in the space of a few seconds, a user can generate hundreds of different events, all of which generate Windows messages. When these messages are generated, they're placed in the Windows message queue to await processing. The message queue is only a repository where all pending messages, along with their Windows handle numbers, are stored. If the system is running well, however, the messages don't have long to wait before they're processed."

I displayed the following graphic on the classroom projector.

Windows Message Queue

Windows handler	Event
1	Click
2	MouseDown
1	Double Click
2	MouseUp
2	GotFocus
2	LostFocus
1	MouseMove
1	Load

"Windows is continuously checking the message queue for pending messages," I said. "In fact, when we discuss the Visual Basic DoEvents method, we see Microsoft recommends we code this function into our program to allow Windows to process pending events on the Windows message queue."

"How does Windows know what to do when it reads the Windows message?" Barbara asked.

I explained that because the message contains the Windows handle, Windows knows from which window the message came. Cross-referencing the Windows handle to the Windows handle table, Windows also knows the type of window from which the message originated. Depending on the type of window, different messages generate different behavior. This behavior is built-in behavior, sometimes known as default behavior. For instance, when you click a radio button, the default behavior for that type of window is different than if you click a check box.

"Programmers can enhance the default behavior of these windows," I said, "thereby providing additional functionality to their programs."

"I'm confused," Ward said. "Can you give me an example of how Windows uses messages and handles?"

"Sure," I said. "How about this? You have both Word and Excel open on your desktop. You type the number 22. How does Windows know whether to enter the number into Excel or to place it in your Word document? It all comes down to the Windows handle that accompanies the request to display the number. And this is dependent on something called the focus."

The Focus

I knew it had been an intensive class and my students were getting a little restless.

"The final subject I want to discuss today," I said, "is the focus. In Windows, only one window can have the focus at any given time. You can't have two windows with the focus at the same time."

> **NOTE: Just because only one object in Windows can have the focus at any one time, doesn't prevent multitasking from happening behind the scenes.**

"Let's look at the Excel-Word example I used a minute ago," I said. "Here we have two apps, but only one keyboard. How does Windows know which window is to receive the keystrokes you type at the keyboard? Where do the keystrokes go? Do they go to the Excel spreadsheet or to the Word document? The answer is the keystrokes go to the window that has the focus, the active window."

"How can you determine the active window?" Rhonda asked.

"The title bar of the active window has a different color from the title bars of your other windows," I said. "The exact color depends on the settings in your control panel."

I waited for additional questions, but there were none. I could see the class was getting a little tired after all the material we'd covered, but I wanted to bring together everything we'd learned in this lesson to arrive at a final definition of what a computer program is.

What Is a Computer Program?

I looked around the class: pencils were tapping, heads were down. This had been a tough morning. I took a deep breath, chose my moment carefully, and threw out a simple question: "So, what's a computer program?"

No one said anything. I could see many furrowed brows.

"Do you mean a DOS program or a Windows program?" asked Steve. "Any type of computer program," I said.

"How about," Ward said uncertainly, "computer programs are how we make computers do what we want them to do."

"That's a good start, Ward," I said, "but how exactly does a computer perform the tasks we want?"

"By manipulating the data stored inside the computer," Dave offered. I was impressed. The class had obviously understood that everything we see computers do involves the processing of huge amounts of data held inside the computer itself.

"But you haven't told us how we actually write computer programs yet," Linda pointed out.

"I've been waiting for someone to mention that all through the lesson," I said. "The rest of the course is going to explain how to write computer programs in detail, but all you need to know now is computer programs are made up of a series of commands and operations that manipulate data. We write specific commands, which you learn all about in the coming weeks, to manipulate that data exactly how we want. Is this clear to everyone?"

"So, you mean we write out specific commands in a program to tell the computer what to do?" asked Valerie, who had been sitting quietly.

"That's basically it!" I said.

I knew my class wanted to know more about those commands to manipulate data and how those commands would make up real computer programs, but I cautioned them all to take one step at a time. I explained they all had plenty to think about, and said we'd be seeing lots of computer programs and how they worked in the lessons to come.

I dismissed class and told my students that next week, we would start up Visual Basic, and begin to get comfortable with it.

Summary

The aim of this chapter was to help you understand computers at a fundamental level, to make it easier for you to see how the programs you write fit into the Windows environment. You learned that a computer program is a set of instructions used to control something or to cause something to happen.

During the running of a program, information known as data is used or stored. Data, at its lowest level, consists of a series of bits, each of which is either on or off. A group of eight bits is called a *byte*. Data exists both in memory and storage, and these work in different ways. Random access memory (RAM) is temporary and very fast. Storage, on the other hand, is semi permanent, but has longer access times. That's why programs are loaded into RAM to be run, which speeds up their operation. Both memory and storage have their capacity measured in bytes.

Operating systems include DOS and Windows, and are used to control how the computer interacts with hardware, input devices, output devices, programs, and so forth.

Windows has a ***graphical user interface*** (GUI), which is a user-friendly interface in which the user clicks buttons, icons, and menus instead of typing commands at a command line. GUI is also capable of ***multitasking***, which is the capability to run more than one program at the same time.

The use of dynamic-link library (DLL) files reduces the size of programs by keeping procedures used by more than one program in separate files. It also means the procedure can be updated once, without the need to update each program.

Chapter 3---Getting Comfortable With Visual Basic

In this chapter, we follow my computer class as they take their first look at the Visual Basic Integrated Development Environment (IDE). The purpose of the chapter is to give you an overview of the Visual Basic environment. Giving you anything more than a "comfort level" feeling about the IDE is impossible. I know the material in this chapter is a tremendous amount for you to process, but you needn't memorize it. I simply want to introduce you to the material. If you ever become confused about any aspect of the IDE, come back to this chapter and refresh your memory. Depending on the version you're using, some of the screen shots might differ slightly from yours, but most should match exactly what's displayed on your machine.

The great news about the chapter is, by its end, we'll be ready to start developing the China Shop Project!

The Visual Basic Environment

I began this class by apologizing to my students for making them wait until now before formally beginning our discussion of Visual Basic. I reminded them, first and foremost, our class had concentrated on good fundamental programming techniques. I told them a thorough understanding of the Systems Development Life Cycle and what goes on behind the scenes in a computer would provide benefits further down the road, and make them better program writers.

"We'll be examining the Visual Basic Integrated Development Environment, or IDE for short," I said. "We'll begin to develop the China Shop Project within this environment in next week's class. I've often found the sheer volume of menu items and toolbar buttons in the IDE can be a bit overwhelming for beginners. Don't worry if you can't remember what all the items do and where they're located. Learning to use the IDE is a gradual process that takes time. I promise you that by the time you finish this course, you'll be feeling much more confident. The IDE isn't difficult or, at least, it's no more so than finding your way around an amusement park for the first time."

Preparing the Way for Programming

"Before we charge into the Visual Basic IDE, we have one last preparation to complete. Beginner programmers sometimes lose their programs because they don't know where they saved them. I want to ensure that once you save your projects, you know where they're saved, so you can always find them," I began.

"To do that, I'd like you to create the same directory structure on your computer that I have on mine. This way, we'll both be 'singing from the same song-sheet.' If the term 'directory' or 'folder' is foreign to you, you probably need to read through your Windows documentation for a refresher.

"I save all my Visual Basic projects in a directory named VBFiles. Underneath this directory, I create subdirectories, each appropriately named for the project I'm working on. Let's create a directory structure for the China Shop Project now."

Exercise 3-1 Using Microsoft Explorer to Make a Home for Our China Shop Project

1. Find the Windows Start button and right-click it. You should see a pop-up menu appear. One of the choices is Explore.

2. Select this option and the Explorer window should appear. It should look similar to this screen shot, although because this is a screen shot of my PC, what you're seeing won't be identical. Notice the Explorer window itself has two windows. The window on the left side is the directory tree window, which displays all the directories on your hard drive. The window on the right side is the files window, which shows you subdirectories and files contained within the selected directory in the directory tree window.

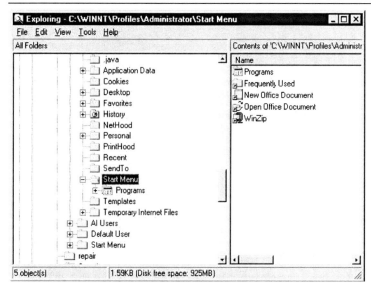

3. Use your mouse to scroll upward in the directory tree window, so you can see the C: drive of your computer. Your C: drive is your computer's hard drive.

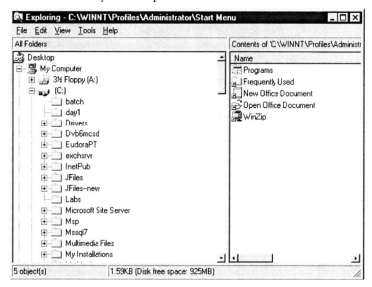

4. Select the C: drive in the directory tree window by clicking the mouse on it. The Files window's content should change to reflect what's contained in the root of your hard drive.

5. Select File | New | Folder from the menu of the Explorer window. As you can see from the following screen shot, Explorer creates a new folder called New Folder in the right-hand file window.

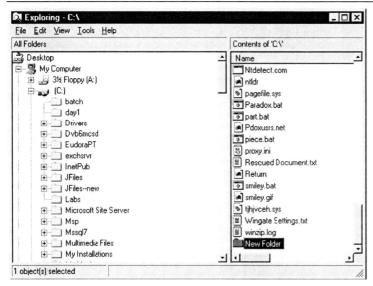

6. We don't want to name our folder New Folder. Instead, we want to name it VBFiles. To give the new folder this name, type the word VBFiles, and then press the Enter key. You should now see a new folder called VBFiles.

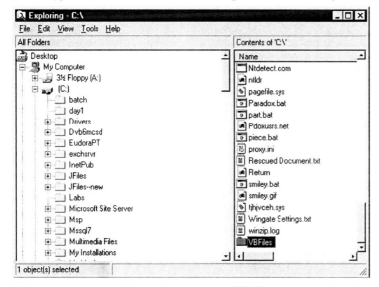

When you press the Enter key, you see VBFiles has taken its place in the directory tree of your hard disk drive, while the files window is empty. Remember, a new folder is empty and we haven't saved anything in it yet. We have a little bit more to do now.

7. Now, we want to create a subdirectory of VBFiles. As I mentioned, I create a subdirectory for each project I work on in Visual Basic. Because we'll be working on the China Shop Project throughout the rest of the course, let's create a subdirectory called China. We need to repeat Steps 4, 5, and 6, but with a slight variation. Instead of selecting the C drive as we did in Step 4, this time select VBFiles in the directory tree window, and then select File | New | Folder from the menu of the Explorer window. As Explorer did the last time, it creates a new folder called New Folder in the right-hand window.

8. As before, creating a directory called New Folder doesn't makes any sense. We want to name it China instead. As we did in Step 6, change the name New Folder by typing over it, this time with the word "China," and then press the Enter key. Now, you should see a new folder called China, as a subdirectory of VBFiles.

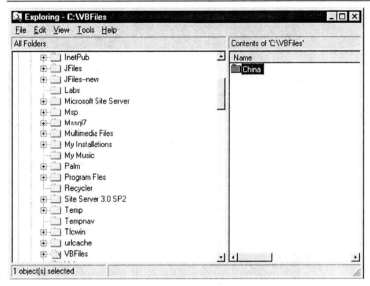

9. Repeat these steps to create another directory called Practice. We want to save all our non-China Shop practice programs in this directory, in case we need them later.

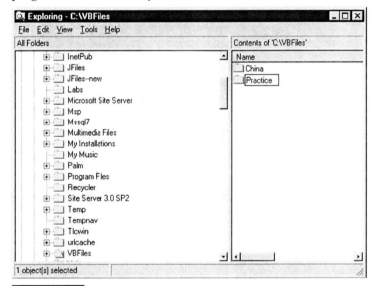

Discussion

That's it! You now have a directory created for your China Shop Project. Make sure you save all your work to this directory as you build your version of the China Shop Project.

Let's Start Up Visual Basic!

"Visual Basic isn't the only Windows development tool on the market," I said, "but, in my opinion, it's the easiest for beginners to use. Let's start it now."

The exact manner in which you start up your copy of Visual Basic will vary depending on the version and how you installed it. Also, don't worry if your screen doesn't exactly match the screen shots you see throughout this workbook. As you use Visual Basic more and more, it "remembers" changes you make to the IDE. The more you work in the IDE, the less likely your screen will exactly match mine.

The following window was displayed, indicating Visual Basic is alive.

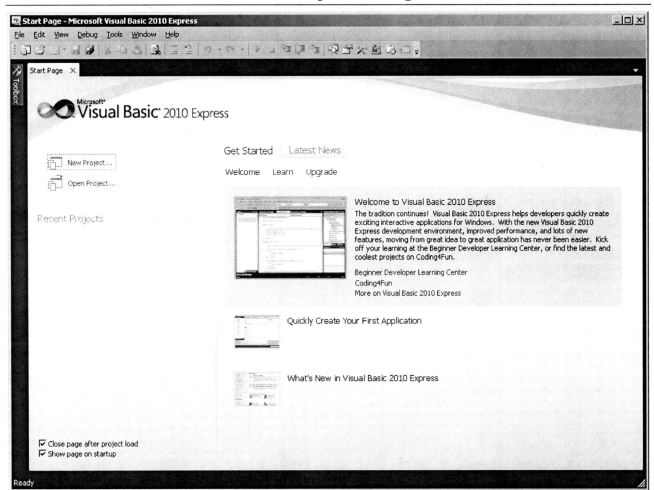

"When you first start Visual Basic," I said, "this Start Page is the first screen you'll see. This screen, or window, is part of the Visual Basic IDE, which where you'll write your programs and where, together, we'll write the China Shop Project."

The Visual Basic Project

"Take a good look at this initial window, called the Start Page," I said.

I pointed out that the Start Page enables us to create a new project, open an existing project for modification, or select from a list of recently worked on projects. For now, I'm going to click the link that says Create Project---it's in the Recent Projects tab."

> **NOTE: Depending on the exact version of Visual Basic you're using, you may or may not see all the folders in this window.**

"What's a project?" Steve asked.

"Good question. A project is simply another name for a program. In Visual Basic, projects are made up of component pieces," I said. "The China Shop Project we'll create in the coming weeks will be made up of a single window—called a Form—which makes it a pretty simple project in Visual Basic terms. For the duration of this course, we'll work exclusively with the Windows Application Project, which is the kind of project the China Shop application will be. In other courses here at the university, you can learn how to create the other types of Visual Basic Projects."

"You've mentioned the term 'Form' before, but what exactly do you mean?" asked Dave.

"A form is simply a window on to which we 'draw' the program's interface. When our program runs, the form becomes the window the user sees," I explained. I continued by saying that when we first start up Visual Basic, it wants to know if we'll be working with a new project or opening an existing project. We indicate our choice here."

"That's pretty similar to other Windows programs," Linda said. "Generally, you either create something new or use an existing one."

"That's right," I agreed. "From the Start Page, selecting the Create Project link indicates we want to create a new project. After that, we must also indicate the type of project we want to create."

"You said all our projects would be Windows Application Projects. Is that right?" Barbara asked.

"Exactly," I said, pausing a moment before going on. "Selecting the Open Project button indicates that we'll be working with a project that's been created already. Notice a list of recently accessed projects at the top of the window. This is a convenient feature, particularly if you're working on a project for an extended time period."

At this point, I asked everyone to select the Create Project link by double-clicking on it.. This window appeared.

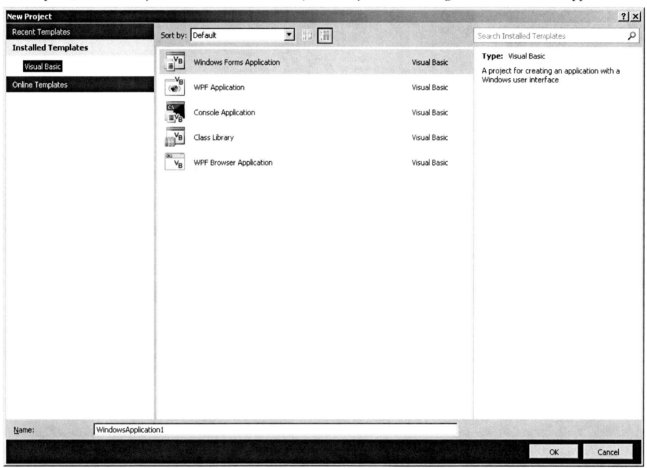

"Notice," I said, "that the default project type is Windows Application, and that the default name for the Project is WindowsApplication1. If you want to give the project a more meaningful name, now is the time to do so. For now, let's just click on the OK button to create our first Windows Application project."

I did exactly that, and the following screen was displayed on the classroom projector.

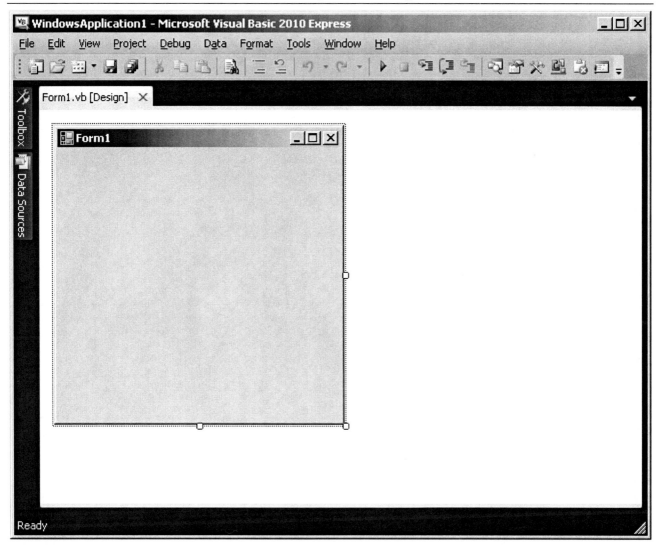

The IDE

"Finally, here we are, right in the middle of the IDE!" I exclaimed. "I remember the first time I saw the IDE, many versions of Visual Basic ago. I know it can look confusing—so many new menus to get familiar with—but, believe me, by the end of our course, you'll feel pretty comfortable navigating through the IDE."

I directed everyone's attention to the window, located roughly in the middle of the IDE, labeled Form1.

"For a new Windows Application project," I said, "Visual Basic automatically creates a form for you right in the middle of the IDE. Notice the form 'is labeled Form1."

I explained we would place the controls we'd discussed during the design phase of the SDLC on Form1.

"You mean we place check boxes and radio buttons on that tiny thing?" Joe asked.

"That's right, Joe," I said. "You'll see a little later that we can enlarge the size of the form within the IDE."

I looked for signs of confusion in their faces, but everyone seemed to be hanging in there. "Let's look at the Visual Basic Toolbox now," I said. "We can bring it into view using two different methods. If you check the IDE, to the left of Form 1, there is a tab entitled Toolbox. If you click on it, the Visual Basic Toolbox will appear. You can also select View | Other Windows | Toolbox from the Visual Basic Menu Bar. Either way, the Toolbox appears. I select the menu item."

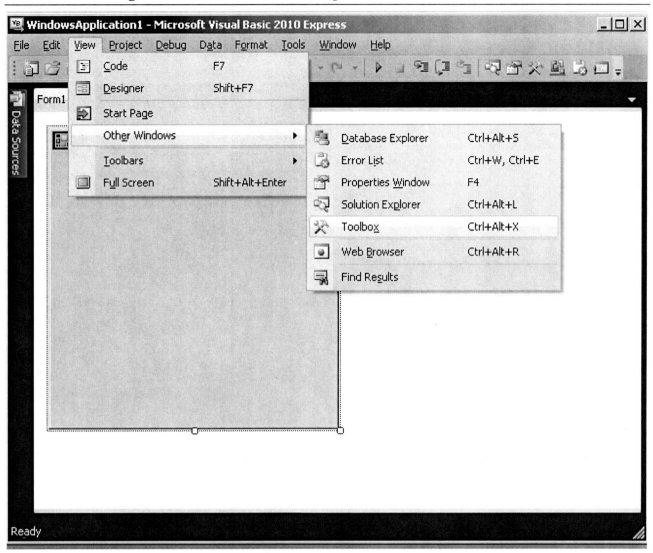

...and the Visual Basic Toolbox appeared.

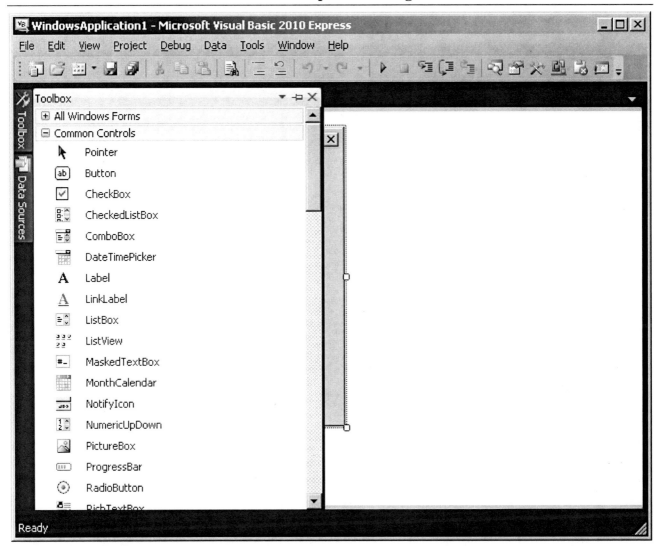

"This is the Visual Basic toolbox," I said. "The icons you see inside the toolbox represent the major categories of the controls we discussed during the design phase of the SDLC: labels, check boxes, and radio buttons, to name a few. If I click on the + sign next to 'All Windows Forms', you'll see every control that can be placed on a Form."

I did so and the following screenshot appeared...

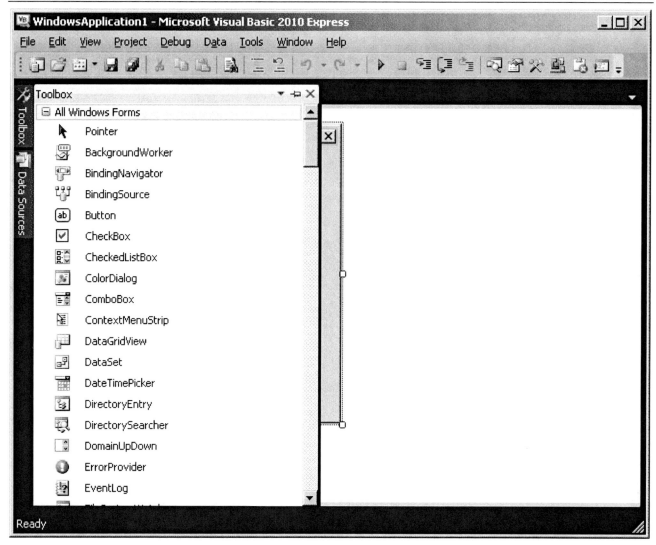

Again, I paused to give everyone a chance to take this in. "Although the IDE is unfamiliar to you, it's made up of windows, and you should be familiar with those by now," I said. "For instance, at the top of the IDE is a title bar. Right now, its caption tells us we're designing a Windows application called WindowsApplication1, which is the default name assigned to this project."

The Modes of Visual Basic

"Let me explain something at this point: we'll be in two distinct modes of operation while we develop programs in Visual Basic," I said. "The first is Design mode and the second is Run mode. Design mode occurs when you are designing your program (or project). Run mode occurs when you tell Visual Basic to execute or run the program you designed. When you're in run mode the title bar of the IDE displays (running)---otherwise, you know you're in Design mode."

"Is there a way to change the project name?" Rhonda asked. "WindowsApplication1 isn't very meaningful."

"Yes, you can change the project name," I said, "and we will do that later in the course."

I continued by directing everyone's attention to the upper left-hand corner of the title bar of the IDE. "Do you see the Control Menu icon?" I asked. "Clicking it enables you to move, resize, minimize, maximize, and close Visual Basic." I also pointed out that the Minimize, Maximize/Restore, and Close buttons are in the upper right-hand corner of the IDE.

The Visual Basic Menu Bar

At this point, everyone seemed pretty comfortable with the notion that the IDE was nothing more than an ordinary Windows window. I suggested we now turn our attention to the Visual Basic menu bar.

File	Edit	View	Project	Build	Debug	Data	Format	Tools	Window	Community	Help

"The Visual Basic menu bar," I said, "contains the File, Edit, Window, and Help menu items, which appear in virtually all Windows applications, plus some others that are unique to Visual Basic. We won't discuss some of these menu items in this class. Depending on the version of Visual Basic you're using, some of the items you see here in this class might be unavailable to you at home."

The File Menu

Before I had a chance to begin discussing the File menu, Rose, jumping ahead of me, remarked that the File menu looked familiar to her. I agreed, but also noted that, despite its similarity to the File menus of other Windows programs, several submenus would be foreign to her and everyone else.

"For instance," I said, "because Visual Basic manages everything by project and form, several menu items here pertain to projects and forms."

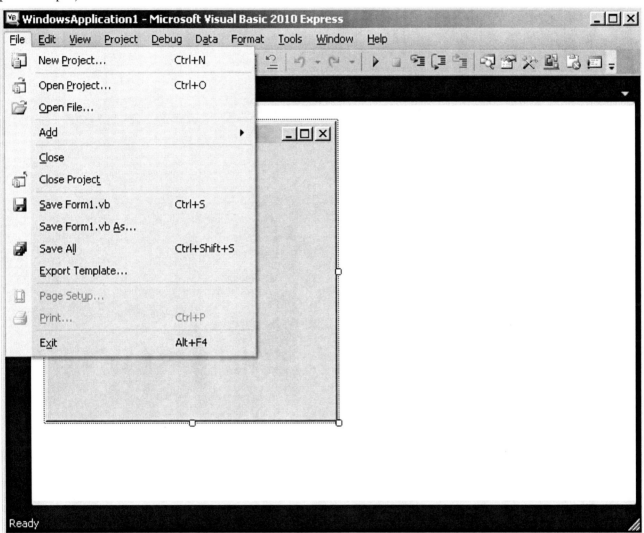

"We'll have an opportunity to work with some of these menu items later in the course," I promised, "and I'll discuss them quickly today."

Continuing, I said, "The next item in the File menu I want to discuss is related to printing, and is the Print item."

The Print Menu

The Print menu isn't active unless you have the Visual Basic code window open—I wasn't quite ready to discuss that with the class yet. I opened up the Visual Basic Code window by double-clicking on the Form, then selected Print from the File Menu...

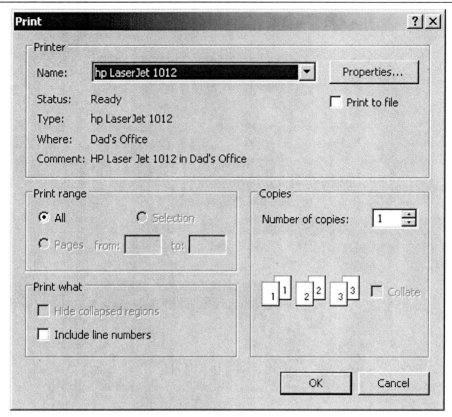

"This looks similar to other Print dialog boxes I've seen," Steve said. "But what exactly is being printed here—it's not like we're operating in a word processing document?"

"Good question, Steve," I said. I explained that a Visual Basic program is made up of two parts: the Visual part, which is the form and the controls sitting on it, and the Code part. As we'll see in a few weeks, the code part of a Visual Basic program is the instructions we write to make the program do something meaningful."

"So when we select Print here," Linda asked, "are we telling Visual Basic to print the code we've written?"

"Exactly, Linda," I said.

The Edit Menu

Having finished with the File menu, I predicted my students would feel pretty comfortable with the Edit menu, once they'd seen it.

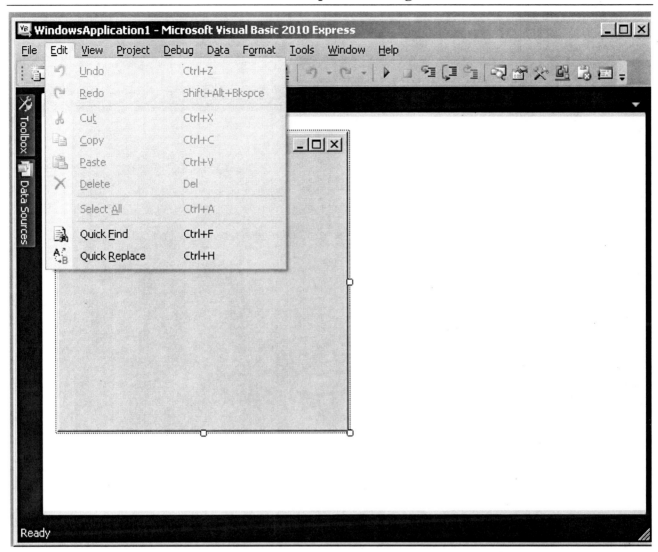

"I hesitate to use the word 'standard' when describing a menu," I said, "but I think I'm pretty safe in describing the Visual Basic Edit menu as fairly standard."

After seeing the Edit menu, nearly everyone in the class agreed with me. Included on it were the usual Undo and Redo items, along with Cut, Copy, Paste, Delete, and Select All. Also included are Find and Replace.

"Once you open the Visual Basic code window, there are more items for the Edit menu than you see here," I said. "We're not quite ready to discuss the code window yet—but when we get there, you'll notice additional Edit menu items that can give you powerful editing capabilities in the code window."

I asked the class if I needed to discuss any of these options in more detail. Dave said he was familiar with these Edit menu items from his experience with other Windows programs, and everyone else nodded affirmatively.

The View Menu

"With the View menu," I said, "we're definitely starting to move into some specific Visual Basic material."

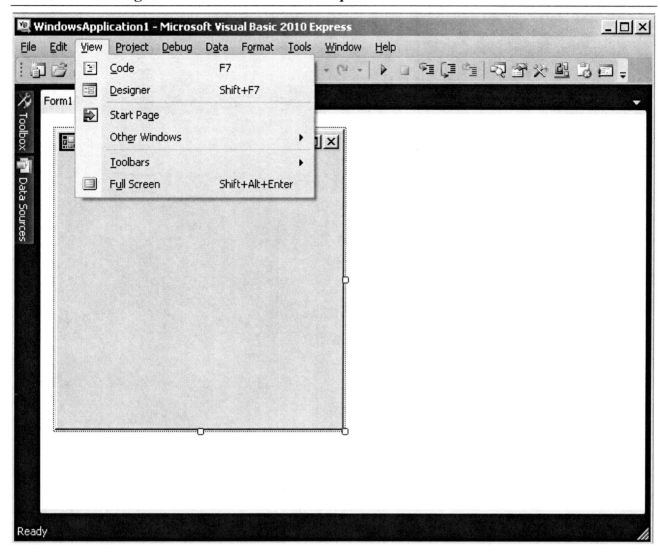

"Most of the items you see in the View menu that we'll be concerned with in this class enable you to open other windows in the Visual Basic IDE," I said. "For instance, earlier in the class, we selected View | Other Windows | Toolbox, and we saw this opened the Visual Basic Toolbox, which is just another window. Later on in this course, we'll work quite a bit with the Visual Basic Toolbox, the Solution Explorer, and the Properties Window—all of which can be 'opened' by selecting them here. Notice also shortcut keystrokes can open these windows—for instance, I use F4 all the time to open the Properties window."

The Project Menu

No one had any questions about the View menu, so I displayed the Project menu on the classroom projector.

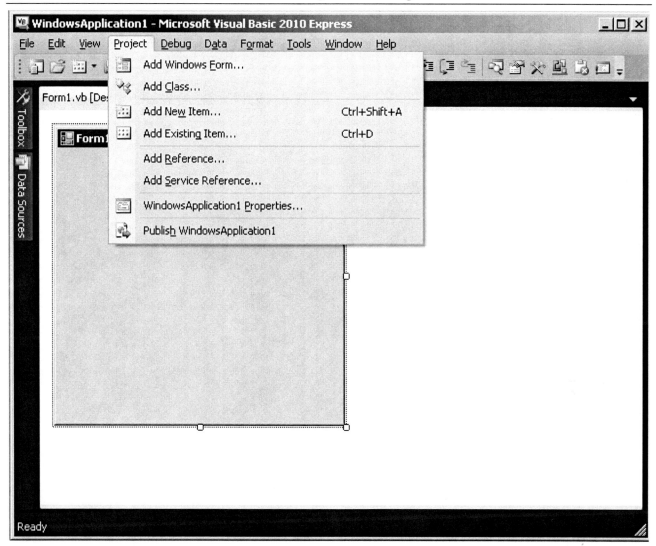

"The Project menu deals with the management of a Visual Basic project," I said. "In this course, our project will be pretty simple—just a single form. But there are other component pieces to a Visual Basic Project—and you see them here. Items such as User Controls, Modules, and Classes to name a few, but those are beyond the scope of this introductory Visual Basic class."

"'Did you say you can't rename a Project once you start it?", Linda asked.

"Good question Linda," I said, "In previous versions of Visual Basic, it was pretty easy to rename a Project. Renaming Projects is not nearly as easy in Visual Basic---the best thing to do is to carefully name the project when you select the Create Project link. Let's take a look at the Build Menu now."

The Build Menu

"The Build menu lets us build our project," I said. "Previous versions of Visual Basic, and other programming languages call this compiling. The Build Menu is only available if you select Expert Settings from the Tools | Settings Menu."

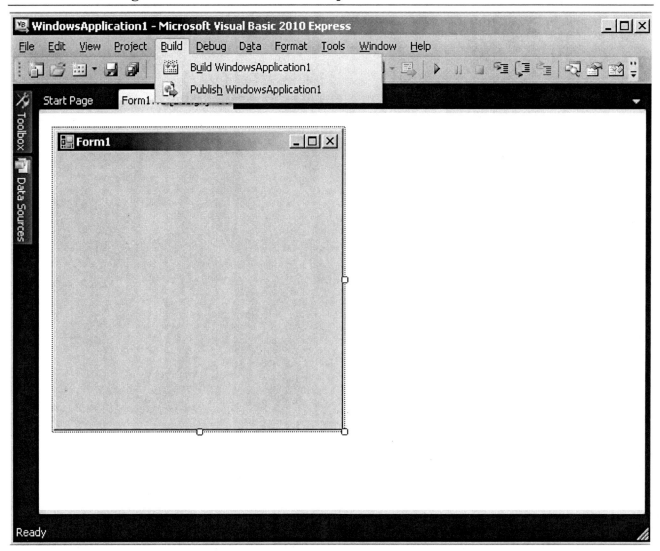

"Building our project creates an executable file, which is a program that can be run outside the Visual Basic environment. For example, the executable file for Microsoft Word is winword.exe, for Visual Basic it's devenv.exe. If you were trying to view these executables using something like Notepad, it would appear as gibberish, because the code can only be read and interpreted by the computer. Not all versions of Visual Basic enable you to generate an executable file. The options here can be pretty complex. We discuss compiling our finished China Shop program into an executable toward the end of this class."

The Debug Menu

Debug is the next menu," I said.

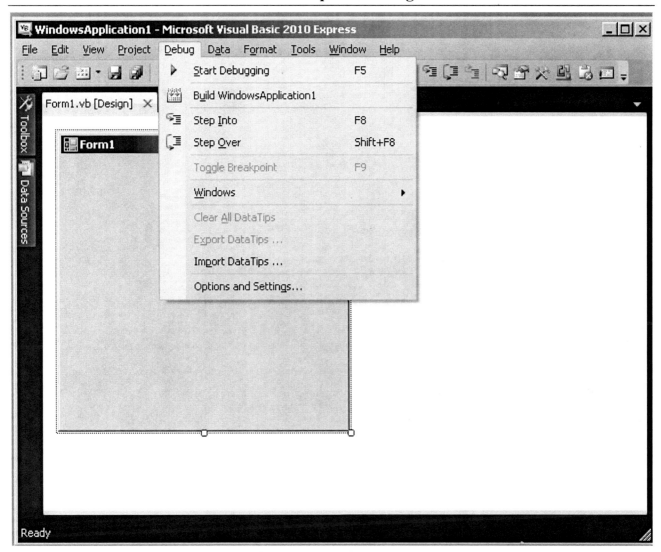

"We'll cover this pretty thoroughly in a few weeks, though, so let's hold off on a detailed discussion of the Debug menu until then."

The Data Menu

"The Data menu is something we discuss in our Visual Basic Database class," I said. "We won't be dealing with it at all in this Introductory class—so hold on until then."

The Format Menu

Our look at the Build and the Debug menu had been quick because we had simply glossed over most of the menu items on it. The Format menu, however, would be a different story. I directed everyone's attention to the dots on the form, called the Form Grid.

"In two weeks," I said, "we'll begin to place controls on the China Shop form. Most of you are going to be concerned with the exact placement of the controls on your form. Remember the Format menu at that time, because it, in conjunction with the Form Grid, will play an important role in you placing your controls exactly where you want them."

"I'm sorry," Ward said, "I know you've used that term several times, but I forgot. Exactly what is a control?"

I thought I'd mentioned it already but, just in case. . . .

"A control is any one of the objects found in the Visual Basic toolbox," I explained, "such as a check box or a radio button."

There were no other questions.

"Let's look at the Format menu now."

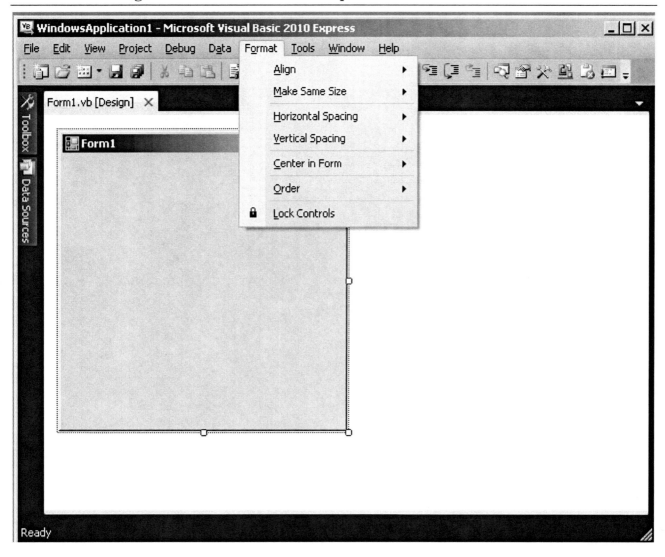

Align

The Align Submenu itself contains submenus that let you align your controls by some constant, such as the leftmost edge of all the selected controls. As a demonstration, I placed two label controls from the Visual Basic toolbox on a form and displayed the form on the classroom projector.

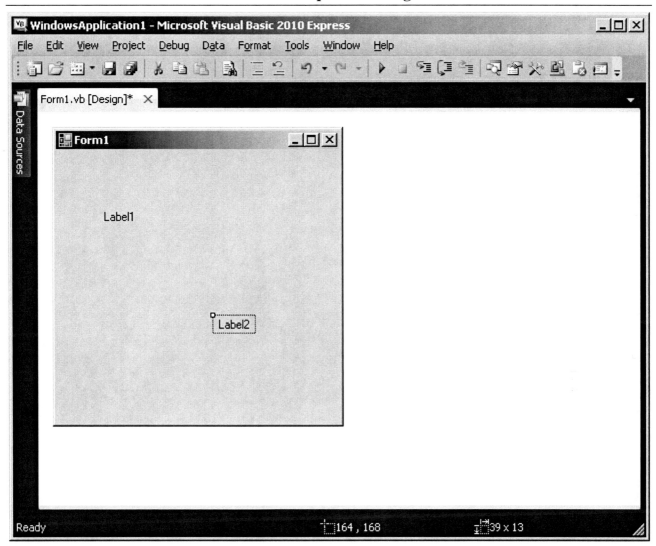

"Don't worry about how to add controls to the form at the moment. We cover that in detail later. I'm more interested in you understanding how to align them right now," I told the class. I continued by noting that these label controls weren't aligned in any meaningful way, neither vertically nor horizontally.

"Suppose," I asked, "I want to align these controls? Let's say horizontally. I can select a control, and click-and-drag it to move it. That's the slow way. To align these controls quickly, all I need to do is select both of these controls on the form."

"Hang on a minute," Ward said. "How do you do that?"

"Oops," I said. "Sorry! Sometimes I take these things for granted. You can select a group of controls by two methods. One method is to select one control by clicking it with the mouse, press and hold the CTRL key, and then select the second control. Now both controls are selected. Both controls selected will have 'resize' handles around them."

I then demonstrated this technique on the classroom projector.

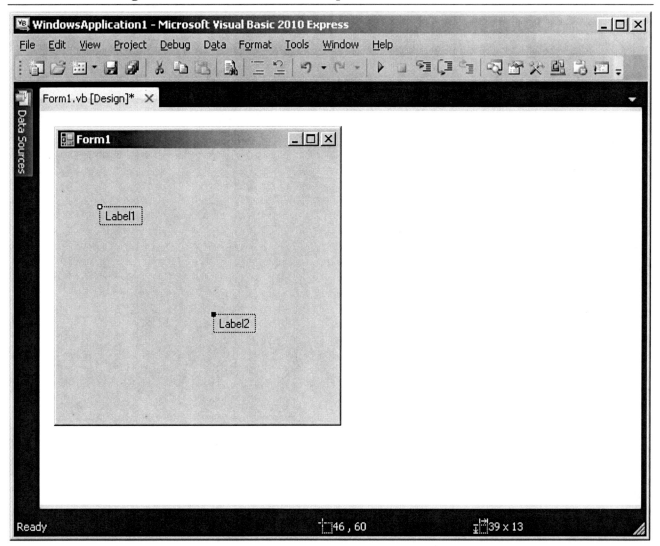

"One of the controls has a dark outline," Kate said, "and the other has a white outline. What's the difference?"

"Remember focus and the active window?" I asked. "When you multiselect controls in the Visual Basic IDE, one of the controls is considered to have the focus and is known as the active control. That's the one with the dark outline. By the way, that outline is technically known as grab handles. The other control lets us know it's also selected because it has white grab handles. By the way, the second method I mentioned to select more than one control at once is to lasso the controls by clicking-and-dragging your mouse pointer around them. It's much faster." I then demonstrated this technique for the class.

"So now that we have more than one control selected, now what?" Ward asked. These are selected for what reason?"

"Selected for whatever action we want—in this case, for alignment," I replied. "In fact, you can select six alignment commands once you have multiselected controls."

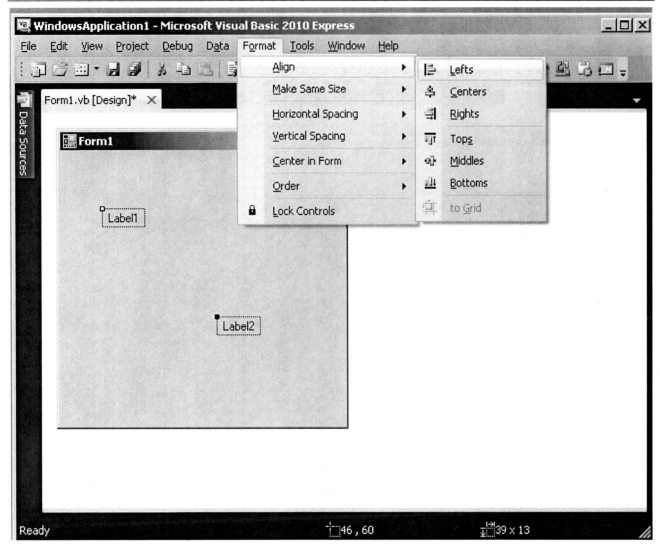

- **Lefts** Aligns the horizontal position of the selected controls, putting the leftmost edges in line with that of the last selected control, which is the one with the blue grab handles.

- **Centers** Aligns the horizontal position of the selected controls, putting the centers of the controls in line with the center of the active control.

- **Rights** Aligns the horizontal position of the selected controls, putting the rightmost edges in line with that of the active control.

- **Tops** Aligns the vertical position of the selected controls, putting the tops in line with that of the active control.

- **Middles** Aligns the vertical position of selected controls, putting the middles in line with the vertical middle of the active control.

- **Bottoms** Aligns the vertical position of the selected controls, putting the bottoms in line with that of the active control.

- **To Grid** Aligns the top left of the selected objects to the closest grid point (or dot).

I then clicked the Lefts option and the two controls were aligned on their leftmost borders.

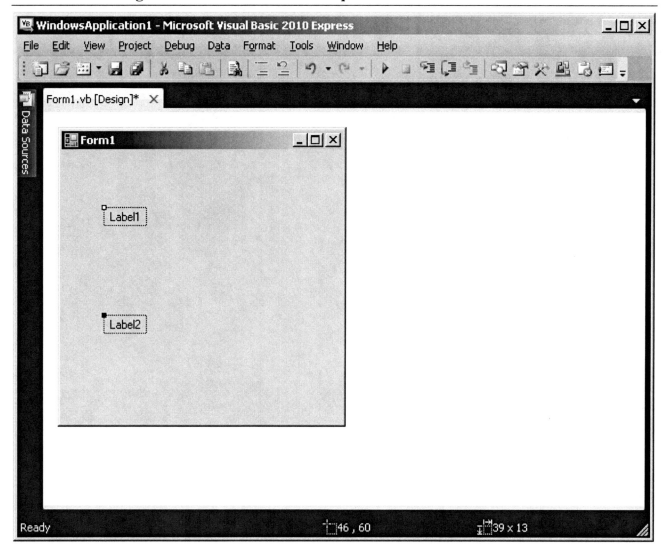

"You won't believe how much time these format options can save you," I said, "if you remember to use them."

Make Same Size

"Make Same Size contains submenus for Both, Height, Width, and Size to Grid. These items give you the capability to make selected controls the same size quickly," I said. "The way to make controls the same size is similar to the process we use to align them. Multiselect them by selecting one control, press and hold the CTRL key, and then select the next control. Then select the appropriate menu item."

"Can you select more than two controls at the same time?" Ward asked.

"Yes, you can," I said. "Sorry if I didn't make that clear. You can select as many controls simultaneously as you want."

"I presume," Linda asked, "these controls are sized the same as the last control selected? Is that right?"

"That's right," I said. "These commands give you the choice of making all the selected controls the same width, height, or both of the last control selected."

"And that would be the one with the dark grab handles," Kate said.

"Excellent, Kate," I said. "You have it!"

"I pretty much understand the alignment and size items," Rose said, "but why isn't 'Align to Grid' active---and what does it do?"

"The Grid is a series of dots that you can have appear on your form in Design Mode," I said. "The Grid can make it easier for you to design your form. Let me show you how to turn it on---once you do, it appears when you create a new Project or add a form to your project. You select it via the Tools-Options menu--select General under Windows Forms Designer. Once it appears, select 'SnaptoGrid' as the LayoutMode, and set ShowGrid to True."

I did exactly that...

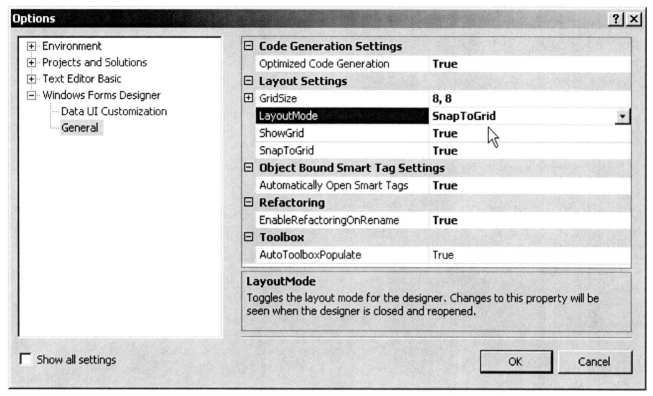

and then exited Visual Basic and started it up again. The Grid then appeared on the form---and 'Align to Grid' was now an option.

I saw Jack whispering to Rose. When they saw me watching them, Jack told me he'd discovered how to turn on Align to Grid adjusts the control's height and width, so its border aligns with the grid.

"And the grid is the dots," Kate said. "That's right," I answered.

Horizontal Spacing

Horizontal Spacing contains submenus for Make Equal, Increase, Decrease, and Remove. These options give you the capability to vary the horizontal spacing quickly between selected controls. The method to adjust horizontal spacing between controls is similar to the method to align them. Multiselect them, and then select a menu item.

- **Make Equal** moves the selected controls, so equal space is between them using the outermost objects as endpoints. The outermost controls don't move.

- **Increase** increases the horizontal spacing by one grid unit based on the control with focus (which, of course, is the one with the blue grab handles).

- **Decrease** decreases horizontal spacing by one grid unit based on the control with focus.

- **Remove** removes the horizontal space between controls, so the controls are aligned with their edges touching based on the control with focus.

"Speaking of grid units," Linda said, "can you change the spacing between the dots on the grid?"

"Good question," I said. "Yes, I call that the grid granularity. You can change the distance between your grid units by selecting the General tab of the .Windows Forms Designer Folder of the Options menu, something we'll look at soon."

Vertical Spacing

Vertical Spacing contains submenus for Make Equal, Increase, Decrease, and Remove.

"This menu is identical to the Horizontal Spacing menu, except it affects the vertical spacing of your selected controls," I said. "So, I'll leave you to experiment on your own with this."

Center In Form

Center In Form contains submenus for Horizontally and Vertically. Selecting this command centers (either horizontally or vertically) selected controls on the central axes of the form.

"Will selecting this command center a single control on the form?" Dave asked.

"No," I said. "In fact, if only one control is selected, the Center In Form command is disabled."

- **Horizontally** Aligns the middle of the selected controls to an imaginary horizontal line in the middle of the form.

- **Vertically** Aligns the centers of the selected controls to an imaginary vertical line in the center of the form.

Order

"Order contains two submenus: Bring to Front and Send to Back. The Order menu affects the Z-order of the selected controls on a form," I told my class.

I didn't even need to look at Ward to know his question. "Z-Order is the third dimension of controls on a form," I said. "It's pretty easy to place one control on top of another. Using Bring to Front you can place a selected control 'on top' of other selected controls. Using Send to Back, you can place a selected control 'underneath' other selected controls."

"Why not just click-and-drag?" Joe asked.

"Using Order can save you a little work," I said, "particularly if you have a number of controls and you want only one to be at the top."

"I still don't see the point," Linda said. "Perhaps it's just something I need to work with."

Lock Controls

"Lock Controls," I said, "is the final menu on the Format menu. This command "locks" or freezes all the controls on the form, so you don't accidentally move them. A great idea once you have the controls positioned on the form the way you want them."

The Tools Menu

The Tools menu contains a number of menu options—the one we want to concentrate on here is the Options menu.

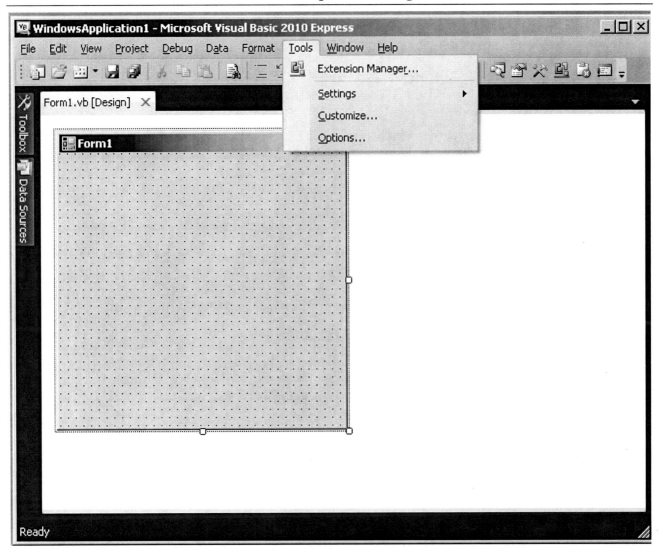

"Everything you see here except the Options submenu is an advanced topic that we'll deal with after we create our prototype, so I won't cover any of them except that one today. Also, depending on the version of Visual Basic you're running, you might not see all of these options."

I glanced at the clock in the classroom.

"We should probably take a break," I told everyone, "because the discussion of the Options submenu could take some time."

Options

When the class returned from its break a few minutes later, I told them all that the Options menu lets us change a variety of default settings in the Visual Basic IDE.

"Options you select in the Options menu," I said, "will still be in force when you start up Visual Basic the next time. The Options menu contains a dialog box with a number of different options. We'll talk about the most important ones here today. Many of the others pertain to advanced features that you won't see in this course."

The Environment-Startup Tab

"The Environment Tab," I began, "gives you the opportunity to make some general changes to your Visual Basic environment. When you first select the Options menu, you might not notice it, but not all of the possible option settings are showing---only General, Fonts and Colors and Keyboard are available."

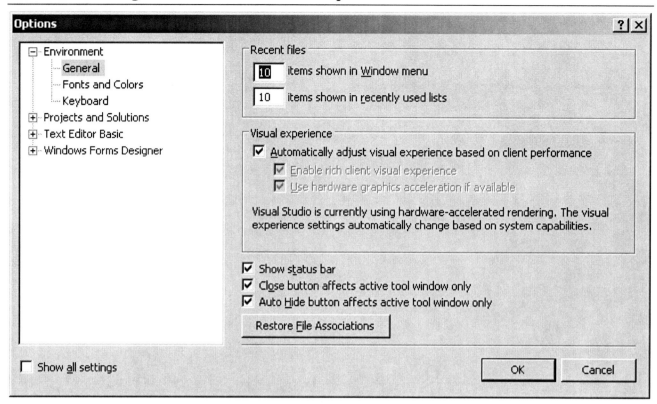

"...Select 'Show all settings' to see them all."

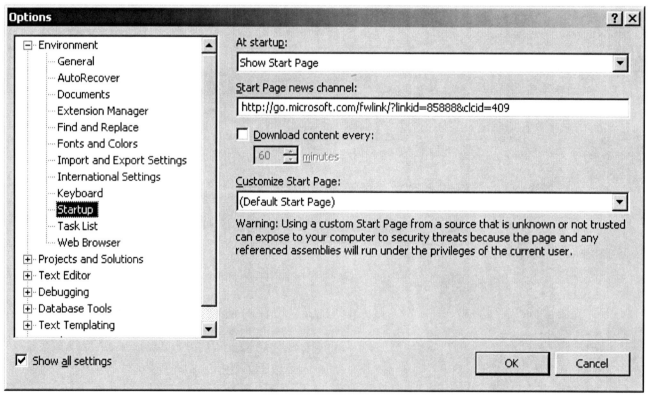

"Now, if you look at the 'At startup' drop-down ListBox, you can see this is where you specify whether to display the Start Page when Visual Basic first starts up. You can customize this to display a New Project dialog box or even to load up the last recently worked on project if you want."

The Environment-Fonts and Colors Tab

"The Environment-Fonts and Colors Tab," I said, "lets you specify various fonts and colors for the displayed text in the Visual Basic environment—primarily in the code window."

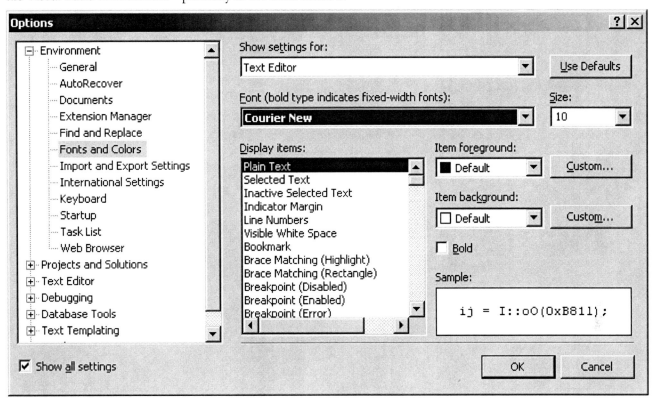

The Projects and Solutions Tab

"The Projects and Solutions Tab," I said, "contains one of the more important settings you can adjust—the default location of your Visual Basic Projects. You'll recall that earlier in the class we made a 'home' folder for our Visual Basic projects. You can specify a default location for your Visual Basic projects using this Tab—and it's a great idea to do so. Another important feature to select here is the Build and Run Options. Be sure this is set to Prompt to save changes. What this means is prior to running a program you have coded, Visual Basic prompts (or reminds you) to save your changes. Although this is unlikely, it's always possible that, somehow, the program you wrote could cause your PC to hang—which is why a gentle reminder from Visual Basic to save the program first, before running it, can be a life saver."

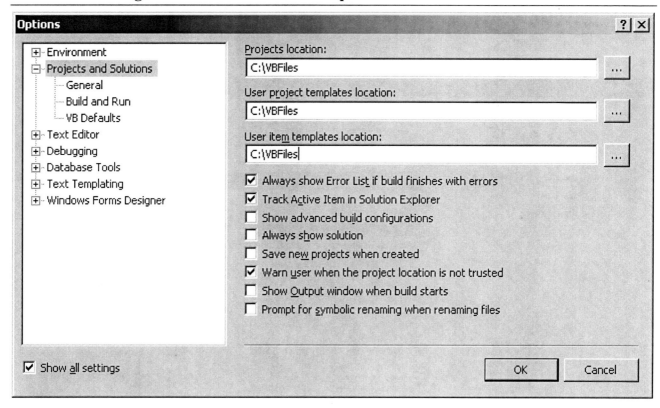

The Text Editor-Basic-General Tab

"The Text Editor-Basic-General Tab," I said, "contains several settings I want to mention. In general, the settings on this tab affect the Visual Basic code window we examine in a week or so. The two settings I want to mention here are Auto List Members and Line Numbers. Checking 'on' for Auto List Members is important, especially for beginners. In Visual Basic, members refer to an Object's Properties, Methods, or Events, which are crucial to writing Visual Basic programs. With this check box selected, Visual Basic automatically displays a list of an Object's Properties, Methods, and Events for you in a drop-down ListBox. This can be useful for a beginner programmer. The final feature—Line Numbers—affects whether line numbers are displayed in Visual Basic's code window. This is largely a personal choice for programmers—some programmers feel that line numbers clutter the code window, while others find them useful. My feeling is beginners should probably have this option turned on—I think this can make following my instructions easier for you."

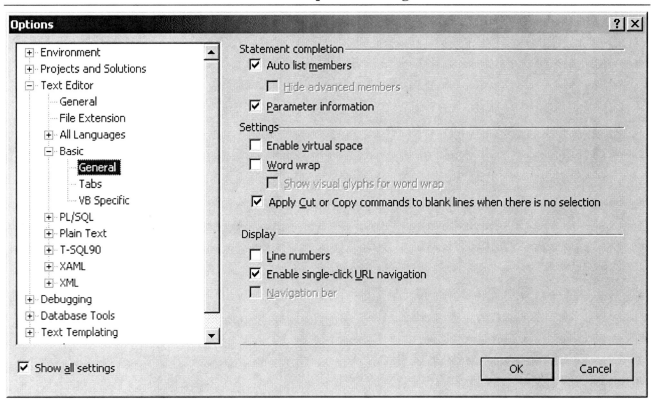

The Windows Forms Designer-General Tab

"A few minutes earlier," I said, "I mentioned the Visual Basic Grid—the Windows Forms Designer-General Tab is where you can change settings that impact the granularity of the Grid or whether it's displayed. If you choose not to display the Grid, set the ShowGrid value to False."

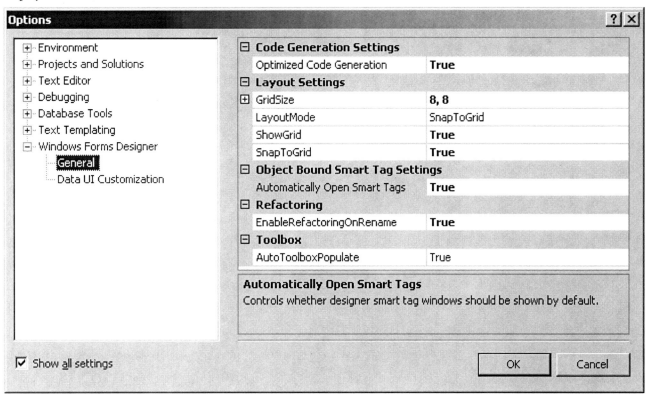

The Window Menu

"Again, I hate to say things like this, but the Window menu is pretty much standard," I said. "One thing I should point out, is the Split option is only available when you're working in the Code window."

The Help Menu

"The Help menu," I said, "is full featured. Feel free to experiment with Help on your own. The level of Help you have depends on the version of Visual Basic you're running."

The Visual Basic Toolbar

"Nearly every toolbar button," I said, "has a corresponding menu item, so it shouldn't take us too long to get through this."

I reminded everyone that when you first start Visual Basic, only the Standard toolbar is visible.

"You can select View | Toolbars from the Visual Basic main menu to see the others," I said. "By default, the Standard toolbar is docked at the top of the IDE."

Several of my students were surprised to find that you could move the Standard toolbar anywhere you want by dragging-and-dropping. This is true of the other toolbars as well.

"You can also customize your own toolbar," I said, "with the Customize command of the Tools menu." I then displayed the Standard toolbar on the classroom projector.

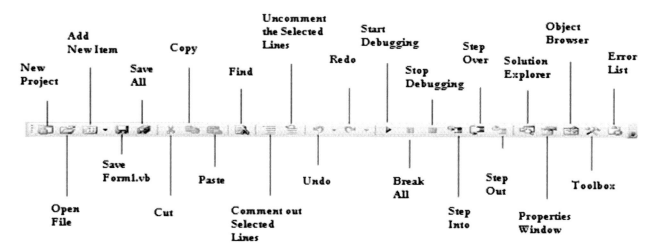

"What does the arrow after the Add New Item button mean?" Ward asked. I directed everyone's attention to the pull-down arrow on the toolbar.

"Good question, Ward," I said. "Whenever you see an arrow like this, that means there's a submenu with more options available."

I clicked the arrow and a pull-down list was displayed, exposing the rest of the items available when you click this button.

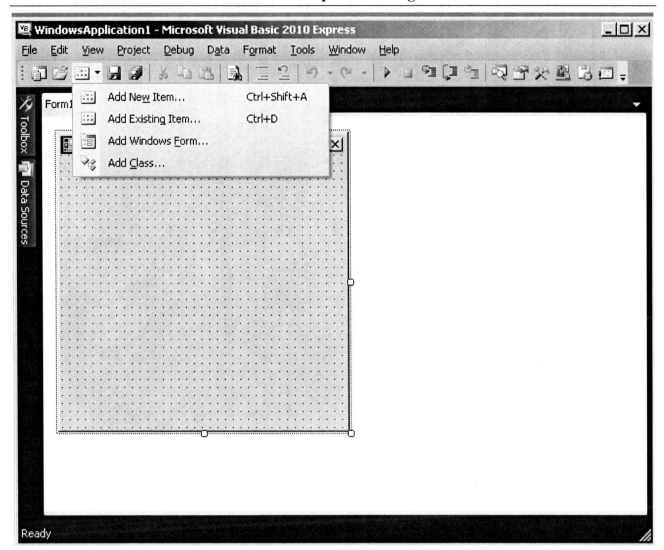

"Don't worry about most of these items because we won't be using them," I said.

The Visual Basic Toolbox

I told the class the Visual Basic Toolbox is a window that contains controls we would use to design our programs.

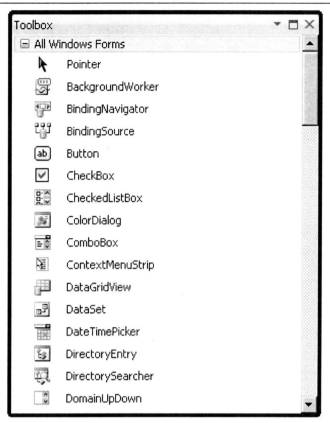

"The Visual Basic default Toolbox contains controls that we can then place on our form," I said. "Depending on the version of Visual Basic you're using, you might see more controls---or you might see less."

"That's pretty overwhelming," Ward said, "there must be over fifty of them."

"There are a lot of them, Ward," I answered. "If you want, you can click on the 'minus sign' next to 'All Windows Forms'--look what happens."

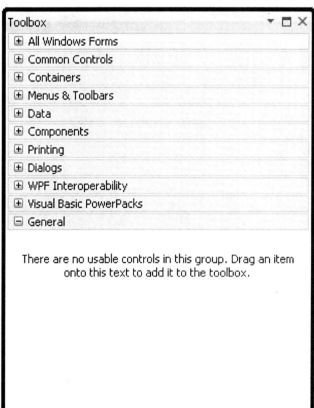

"Now there are no controls," Rhonda said.

"That's right Rhonda," I answered, "all we have now are categories of Controls that we can use to build our VB program---virtually all of the Controls that we will use in this course can be found in the Common Controls category---let's click on its 'plus' sign and this time, we'll be presented with a more manageable list of controls."

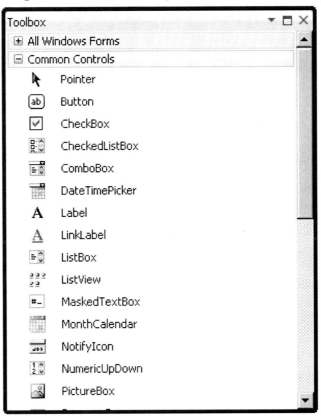

"That's a little better," Linda said, scrolling through the list, "there are only about 20 here."

"Hold on," said Linda. "Is there any rhyme or reason to the order of these controls?"

"You can sort them alphabetically," I said. "Right-click your mouse on the toolbox and select Sort Items Alphabetically."

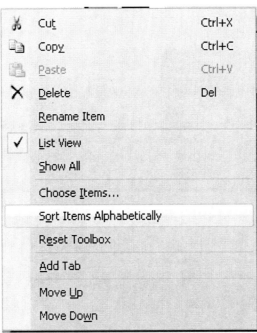

"Something I like to do to make the toolbox a bit less cluttered," I said, "is to list the controls by their icons. To do that, right-click the mouse and check 'off' List View."

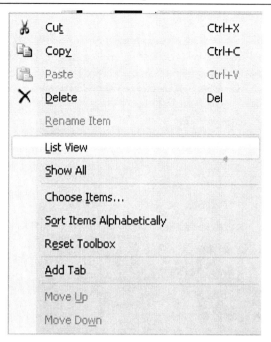

"Now the controls will be listed by their icons," I continued. "I personally prefer that look and feel to the toolbox."

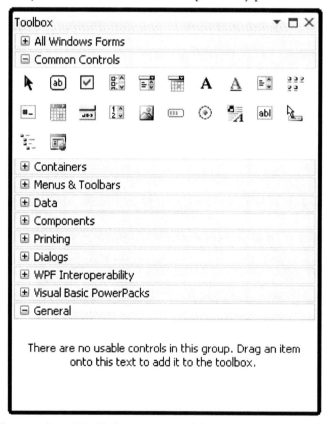

I paused to see if anyone had a question. "We'll discuss most of these controls, but not all of them, over the course of the next two weeks. You'll find in the beginning of your Visual Basic programming career, you use about 20 percent of these controls 80 percent of the time."

"The old 20–80 rule," Ward muttered.

"Exactly, Ward," I said. "You'll find the same rule generally holds with code—you use 20 percent of the syntax 80 percent of the time."

The Properties Window

We were nearly finished for the day. I just wanted to show the class a Properties window. We would leave the details of the Properties window for our next session. I displayed the Properties window associated with the form loaded in the IDE by selecting Properties window from the View menu.

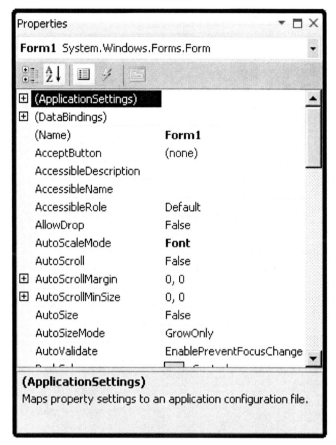

"The Properties window," I said, "displays properties associated with the form or a control. Properties are attributes that determine the look and behavior of a form or a control on the form. For instance, the caption for each of the two labels on the form is determined by one of its properties—the Text property. The caption in the title bar of the form is determined by its Text property. We'll spend the next few weeks looking at properties of the form and its controls in detail."

I dismissed class, telling everyone that next week we would begin to develop the China Shop Project by examining Visual Basic properties, methods and events.

Summary

In this chapter, you were exposed to the nitty-gritty of the Visual Basic IDE, covering the Visual Basic menu, toolbar, and toolbox. Again, I know there was a tremendous amount of material to assimilate here, but we couldn't move on until I took you on a tour of the IDE. Next chapter, we'll be ready to begin coding the China Shop Project.

We saw that, in Visual Basic, a project consists of all the components that make up your program.

We looked through the Visual Basic menus, which have some similarities with other Microsoft applications, and some items specific to Visual Basic. We also looked at the windows scattered around the IDE.

The View menu brings up the various additional toolbars and windows, for example, the Object Browser, which enable you to work with your project.

The Project menu enables you to add forms or modules to your project and to alter the project properties.

The Format menu enables you to size and align the controls on your form to make its appearance more uniform and tidy.

The Options menu item in the Tools menu lets you change various options to suit you. For example, whether the Auto Help Info pop-ups are enabled. Certain options in this menu are best left untouched, such as Require Variable Declaration, which can lead to hard-to-spot errors if it's disabled.

The Toolbox contains the more commonly used controls you place on your forms.

The Properties window displays the properties for the selected item or control, enabling you to change them for the best operation.

Chapter 4---Programming Is Easy

In this chapter, follow my computer class as I show them just how easy programming can be in Visual Basic. In today's class, we begin working with Visual Basic in earnest, with a specific focus on the built-in, or default, behavior of forms and some controls. We begin the chapter by starting the Integrated Development Environment (IDE) and learning about Visual Basic properties and methods by examining the Visual Basic form—the starting point for the China Shop Project. By the end of today's class, we'll have created and modified the one and only form required for the program.

Less Is Best

I began this class with a simple statement: "Less is best."

Not surprisingly, my statement elicited some strange looks from the students assembled in the computer lab. When you teach programming, though, you become used to this kind of response quickly.

"Visual Basic programming can be easy," I continued, "provided you don't overprogram. Many beginners overprogram their projects, just like new drivers tend to over steer their cars. Whenever you program in Visual Basic, especially when you're just starting out, remember my motto."

"What exactly do you mean by 'overprogram'?" Kate asked. "Don't you need to program for your project to do something?"

"That's exactly my point," I replied. "Beginners always want to begin coding, but it's important to understand what your project does with no additional code from you."

"Well, I wouldn't think it could do anything," Ward said. "How can it with no code?"

"Actually, a Visual Basic program with no code can do quite a lot," I said. "Remember, Visual Basic programming is a two-part process. First, we design the visual part of our program, called the User Interface. Then we write code."

> **NOTE: Visual Basic programming is a two-part process. First, we design the visual part, and then we write code.**

"Isn't the design of the User Interface just a matter of placing controls on the form?" Linda asked.

"Yes and no," I said. "That's true, but that's not all there is to it. After placing controls on the form, you should pat yourself on the back, and then observe the default behavior of the form and the controls on it."

"What do you mean by default behavior?" Steve asked.

"The form itself, and each control we place on the form," I said, "comes complete with built-in behavior. You'd be amazed at the number of beginners who write code that duplicates, or even defeats this built-in behavior."

"Okay," Joe said, "so after observing the default behavior of the form and controls, then we write code?"

"Not quite," I replied. "Then we modify the properties of the form and controls to get them exactly the way we want them to look."

"And then we write code?" Valerie asked.

"Yes, then we write code," I said. "In today's class, we begin the China Shop Project and examine the default behavior of its form. Then we adjust some of its properties according to the design we came up with during the design phase of the Systems Development Life Cycle."

Visual Basic Properties, Methods, and Events

I could sense some excitement building in the class when I announced we would begin working on the China Shop Project.

"First things first," I said. "Let's start Visual Basic."

I asked everyone to start Visual Basic, to select Create a New Project from the Start window, and then to select a new Windows Application from the New Project dialog box.

I waited a few minutes, and then . . .

"Everyone at this point," I said, "should have Visual Basic running, with a form displayed. Is everyone okay so far?"

"You've mentioned properties several times so far in this class," Ward said. "Before we get much further, can you give us a definition of a property?"

Visual Basic Properties

"A property is an attribute or characteristic of a Visual Basic object," I said. "An object in Visual Basic is most often a form or a control. Properties are to objects what characteristics are to a person. For example, a person has a name, and each object in Visual Basic has a Name property. A person can be described by their height, and some objects, such as the form or a button control, have a Height property."

NOTE: A property is an attribute or characteristic of a Visual Basic object.

"I'm expecting to see the Properties window here," Barbara said, "but I don't see it."

I explained the Properties window can be displayed in four ways, all of which require you to select the form first. To select the form, all the user must do is click it, preferably on the form's title bar:

- Select Form1 and press the F4 key.

- Select Form1 and select View | Properties window from the main menu.

- Select Form1 and select the Properties window button on the standard toolbar.

- Select Form1 in the Project window, right-click the mouse, and then select Properties.

I opened the Properties window on my PC, and the following screen was displayed on the classroom projector.

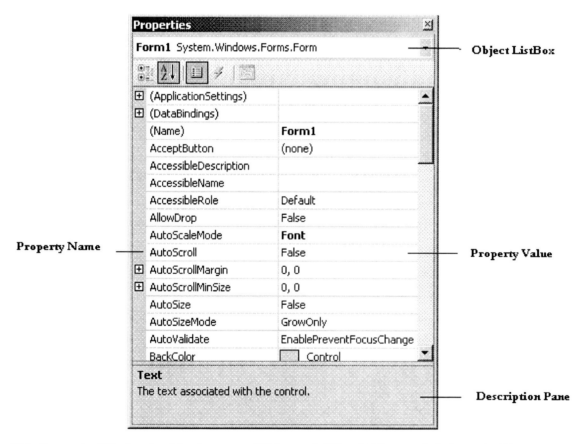

"My Properties Window is wider than yours," Mary said. "Should I be worried about that?"

"No," I said. "The Properties window is a standard window—that means you can resize it just like any other window to look the way mine does. Notice it also contains a Close button in the upper right-hand corner."

I directed everyone's attention to the most important part of the Properties window, the properties themselves.

"Those are properties of what?" Ward asked.

"In this case, Properties of the form," I said. "For the moment, don't concern yourselves with the individual property names and values. We'll get to those in a few minutes. Let's take a moment to get comfortable with the layout of the Properties window."

I pointed out the Object ListBox, directly underneath the title bar.

"The Object ListBox," I said, "lists all the objects that 'belong' to the selected form, including the form itself, and any controls placed on it."

NOTE: The Object ListBox lists all the objects situated on the form, including the form itself.

"I don't see any other objects besides Form1 in the Object ListBox," Rhonda said.

"That's because we haven't placed any controls on the form yet," I replied. "We'll do that during our next class."

"What does 'System.Windows.Forms.Form' mean?" Linda asked.

"Visual Basic tries to emphasize object-oriented principles more so than previous versions of Visual Basic did," I answered. "In this case, System.Windows.Forms.Form indicates our Form1 is 'inherited' from that family of objects. Try not to concern yourself too much with objects and inheritance in this class—we cover those in other classes here at the University."

After pausing to see if I'd thoroughly confused anyone with this slight digression into the Object Orientation of Visual Basic, I continued by saying that directly under the Object ListBox are five buttons: Categorized, Alphabetized, Properties, Events and Property Pages.

"These buttons," I said, "affect the way the Properties window displays the Properties. By default, when you open the Properties window, the Properties are displayed alphabetically. If you select the Categorized button, then the properties are sorted according to categories, such as Appearance and Behavior."

I then clicked the Categorized button (the first button, the one with the plus (+) and minus (–) symbols), and the following screen was displayed.

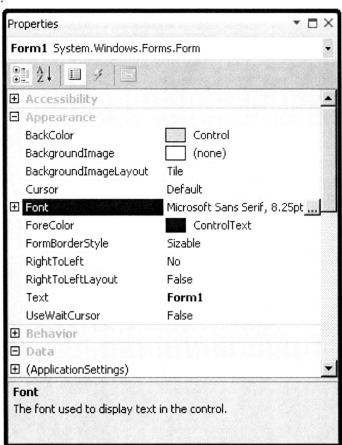

"What do the plus and minus signs mean?" asked Rose. "There's one in front of the Font property."

"The plus sign means the category is collapsed," I said. "This means additional properties are there that you can view, if you expand it by clicking the plus sign."

I clicked the plus sign next to the Font category and the following screen was displayed.

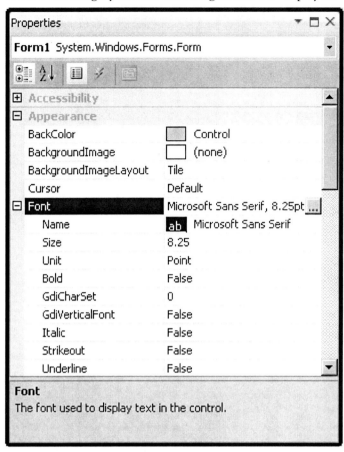

"As you can see," I said, "now we can see the properties that make up the Font category. The minus sign you now see next to the word 'Font' indicates the category has already been expanded. In the same way, you can click the minus sign to collapse the category."

"Do you have a preference for how the properties are displayed?" Peter asked.

"Personally, I prefer to display the list alphabetically," I replied, "but that's because I'm familiar with the Properties and generally can find what I'm looking for. I think if I were a beginner, I'd prefer to see them categorized."

"Do we have to memorize these property names?" Chuck asked.

"No," I said, "I wouldn't want you to try. You'll see, as you develop your skills in Visual Basic, that most of the time you need to work with only a few of these properties. Besides, most of the others have names that convey what they do—and there's always Visual Basic Help to help us when we're stuck. By no means should you waste your time memorizing anything in Visual Basic. You'll learn by practice."

"The two columns," Ward said, "are those the property names and their values?"

> **NOTE: The Properties window has two columns: one for the Name of the property and the other for its Value.**

"Yes, that's right, Ward," I said. "The left column is the name of the property and the right column is the value."

Before moving on, I pointed out that at the bottom of the Properties window is a Description Pane, which displays a brief description of the property. I told the class I was going to perform a small demonstration now.

"I'm going to change properties of the form in the Properties window," I said, "so you can see how changing properties will have an immediate effect on the form."

I collapsed every category in the Properties window except for Layout and displayed the Properties window on the classroom projector.

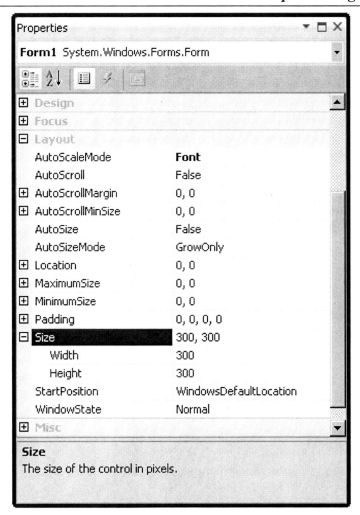

"Several properties are in the Layout category," I said. "All of these affect the size and position of the form relative to the screen. Pay particular attention to the Size property, which I've expanded."

"What's that number—300—in the Height property?" Mary asked.

"That's the height of the form in pixels," I said. "300 means the form is 300 pixels high."

"How many inches would that be?"

"That depends on the resolution of the monitor displaying this form," I said. "In this case, it looks about 3 inches high × 3 inches wide."

"I'm looking at the Location Property," Rhonda said. "What do the X and Y properties mean?"

I explained the X property specifies the distance, in pixels, of the form's left border from the left edge of the screen.

"Then the Y property specifies the distance, in pixels, of the form's top border from the top of the screen," Barbara said.

"That's right," I replied. "Right now, with X and Y both specified as 0, if we click the Start button, we would display this form in the upper left-hand corner of the screen. We can change the location and dimensions of the form by changing these properties—X, Y, Height, and Width. One, important point, though—the StartPosition property must be set to Manual for changes to the X and Y properties to have an effect."

To illustrate, I changed the StartPosition property to Manual, the X and Y properties from 0 to 100, and changed the Height and Width properties from 300 to 450, and then 'ran' the program by clicking the Start button. The form appeared in the upper left-hand portion of the screen, smaller in size than it appeared in the design-time environment. I then stopped the program by clicking the form's Close button (you can also select Debug | Stop Debugging from the Visual Basic Menu Bar) and changed the Left property from 100 to 0. The form moved to the left edge of the screen.

"I like this," Ward said. "This looks like fun. How many properties of the form can we play with?"

NOTE: Not every property of an object is displayed in the Properties window. Some properties are only available at run time.

"A bunch," I said, "but before you start experimenting, I also want to show you another way to change the position and size of the form. As you would with any window, click-and-drag the form to move it or drag the resize handles to resize it."

Everyone seemed to be having a good time modifying the properties of the form, so I gave them a few minutes to experiment.

"I want you to know," I said, "that you're all programming now."

A few students looked up—stunned—when I said that.

"I wouldn't exactly call this programming," Lou said.

"Sure it is," I said. "It's just not what you thought programming in Visual Basic would be.

What you spent the last few minutes doing is 'programming' the visual interface to your application. This is the first step in the development of any great Visual Basic program—and, in some other languages, such as C++ or Java, this all would have to be done manually."

"Can't property values be modified through program code?" Dave asked.

"You've been reading ahead, Dave," I said, "but, yes, you're right. What you're doing now by modifying values in the Properties window can also be done while your program is running in code."

"When we begin to develop the China Shop Project," Joe asked, "will we need to change all the properties of the form?"

"No," I said. "That won't be necessary. As you can see, each property in the Properties window has a default value. In most cases, we simply accept that default value. We only need to change the properties that are important to us where the default isn't acceptable."

NOTE: When you write a Visual Basic program, most of your objects' properties can be left at their default values.

"This seems too easy," Chuck said.

"So our next step," Joe said, "is to place controls on the form, and then adjust their properties."

"Yes, that's right," I agreed.

"Can I ask a question before we go on?" Linda said. "I was experimenting with some of the other form properties. When I click some of them, a ListBox appears."

"An excellent point, Linda," I said. I displayed the Properties window on the classroom projector and clicked the Alphabetic button. Then I clicked the arrow in the Enabled property next to True.

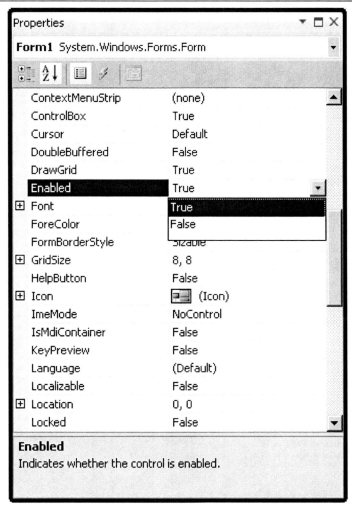

"Some properties," I said, "have a limited range of acceptable values. In those cases, when you select the property to change it, a ListBox of valid values is displayed. For instance, the Enabled property can have one of two values, either True or False."

I asked everyone to select the StartPosition property. "That has five possible values," I said.

"What about the BackColor property?" Valerie asked. "What does that colored panel mean?"

"Good question," I said. I asked everyone to select the BackColor property. I did the same, and the following screen was displayed.

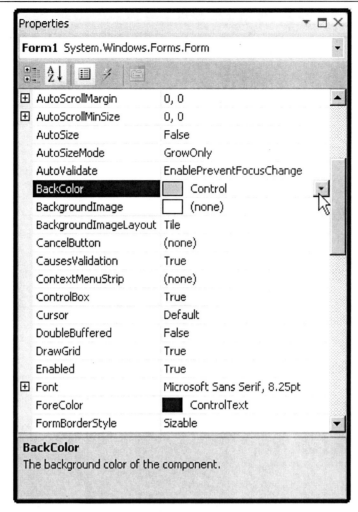

"The BackColor property," I said, "sets the background color of the form. I have to warn you the color properties are probably the most complicated of all the properties to explain. Fortunately, changing them is pretty easy. Just click the drop-down ListBox."

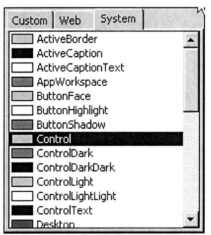

"By default," I said, "the System tab is selected, and the default setting for BackColor is already selected. For the BackColor property, a system-defined color has been assigned."

"What does Control refer to?" Linda asked.

"That's Visual Basic's attempt to 'map' a selection from the user's choice of a color in the control panel to the BackColor of the form," I answered. "In this case, Control refers to a selection the user made in the control panel. Selecting a color from the list you see on the System tab is 'safe' because if the user changes his mind about his preferred color selections, if we've selected Control or ControlLight here, our form automatically picks up on the user's color change because his change impacts the color displayed in Control or ControlLight."

"So the color associated with Control or ControlLight on one PC isn't necessarily the same color on another PC?" Mary asked.

"That's right," I said. "If you want to set an absolute color for BackColor, select the Custom tab instead."

I invited the class to do that now. I did the same, and the following screen was displayed.

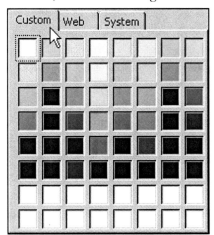

"You can select a color from the palette," I said, "and the BackColor of the form changes to the exact color you specify."

"But those aren't all the available colors, are they?" Valerie asked. "What if you want a color that isn't displayed?"

"If you **right-click** the mouse in one of the 'empty' color boxes at the bottom of the Custom tab," I said, "you open the Define ColorDialog box."

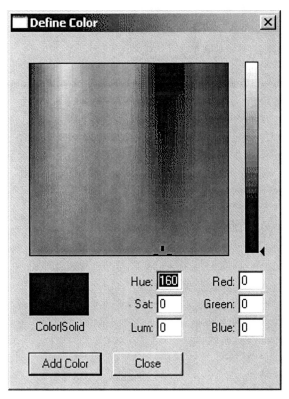

"From there, you can add a new color to the Custom Color tab."

"I just selected Red from the Custom tab," Rhonda said, "and the BackColor of my form changed to red. Also, now the value for the BackColor property reads Red. Could I just type the word 'red' into the BackColor property of the form?"

"Yes, you can," I said, "if it's a valid color. Let me demonstrate by typing the word 'Cyan' directly into the BackColor property."

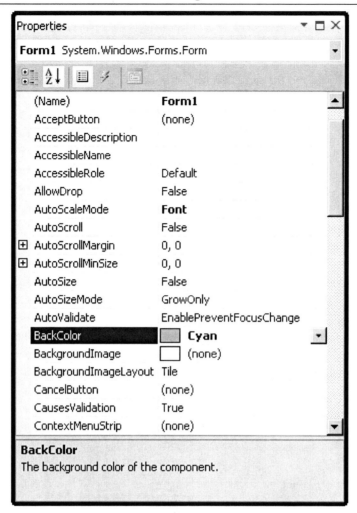

I did so and, immediately, the BackColor of the form changed to Cyan.

"Notice the change is immediate," I said. "Most of the properties you change in the design-time environment of Visual Basic take effect immediately, but not all."

"How do we know the valid colors for the BackColor property?" Linda asked.

"Check out Visual Basic Help," I answered. "If you search for the word "Color," followed by a period, you see a listing of all the valid colors for this property."

"I have another question," Linda said. "Why does the BackgroundImage property contain the value (None)?"

"That's another good question," I said. "The BackgroundImage property enables us to display a graphic as background on the form. (None) indicates that no image will be displayed."

I displayed the Properties window on the classroom projector and directed everyone's attention to the BackgroundImage property.

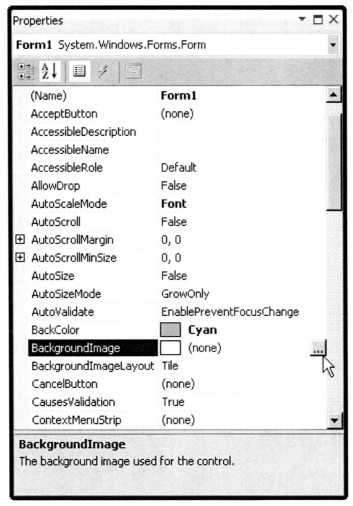

"As you can see," I said, "the default value for this property is (None). Do you see those two dots on the button? Whenever you see those three dots, called an ellipsis, that means a dialog box is available to help make a selection for us. I call the ellipsis an expression builder. Sometimes, a property value is long and complicated like a directory path and filename, for example. By including the expression builder with that property, Microsoft provides us with a way to avoid typing mistakes or plain simple errors."

> **NOTE: Whenever you see three dots, or an ellipsis, in a property value, this means a dialog box is available to help you make a selection.**

"What do you mean?" Ward asked.

"Well," I said, "the BackgroundImage property of the form requires us to designate a graphic file to display as background for the form. Visual Basic needs to know exactly where this file is located. Rather than have us type in a directory and a filename, Visual Basic 'builds' it for us with the expression builder."

I clicked the ellipsis and the following screen was displayed. Remember, your display might show a different directory structure from mine.

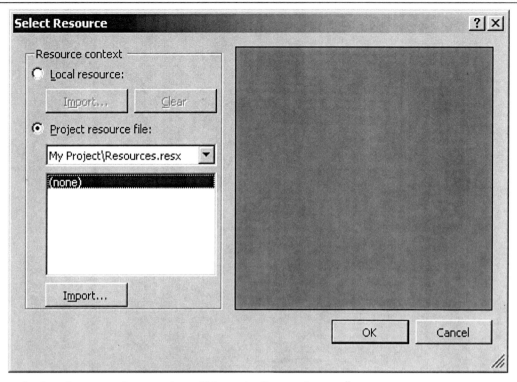

"Let's click on the Local resource button, then click on the Import button."

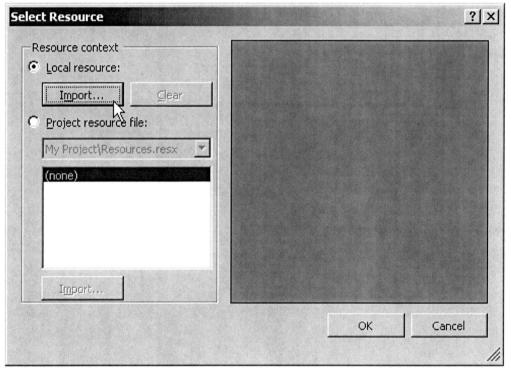

"Now you can use the Open dialog box to locate and specify a graphics file," I said. "On my PC, I have some bitmaps in the Windows folder."

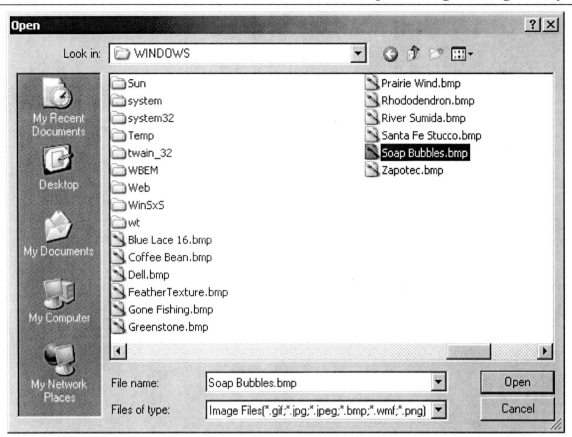

".....let's select Soap Bubbles"

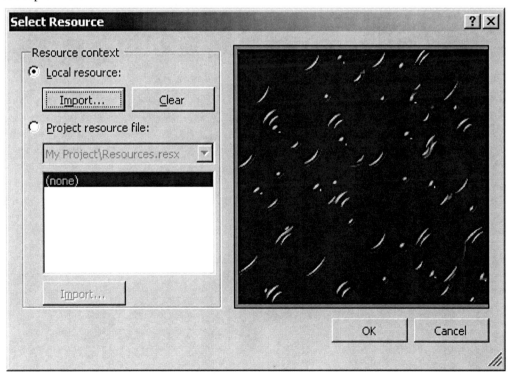

. . . and the following screen, depicting our Visual Basic form, was displayed on the classroom projector.

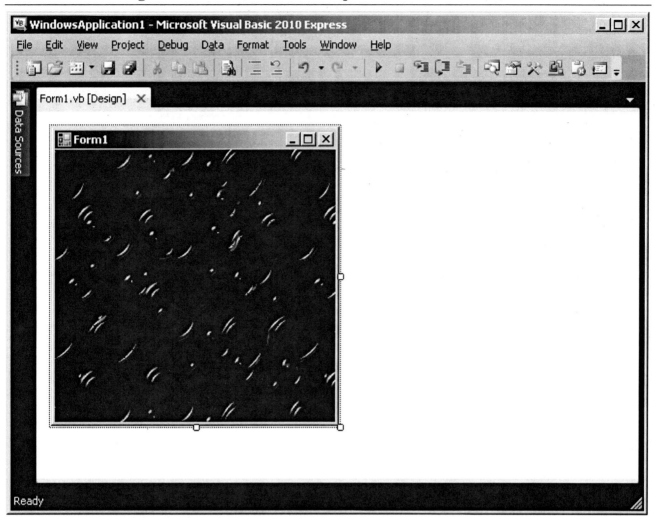

I pointed out that the **BackgroundImage** property now reads System.Drawing.Bitmap.

"That's Visual Basic's way of designating the bitmap being used as the Background Image," I said. "Unfortunately, the Properties window doesn't tell you the exact name of the Image—although you can see the image displayed in the property value. To determine the name, click the ellipsis again. By the way, one of the questions I'm asked most is how to set the value of the BackgroundImage property back to (None). Right-click the image in the value column…"

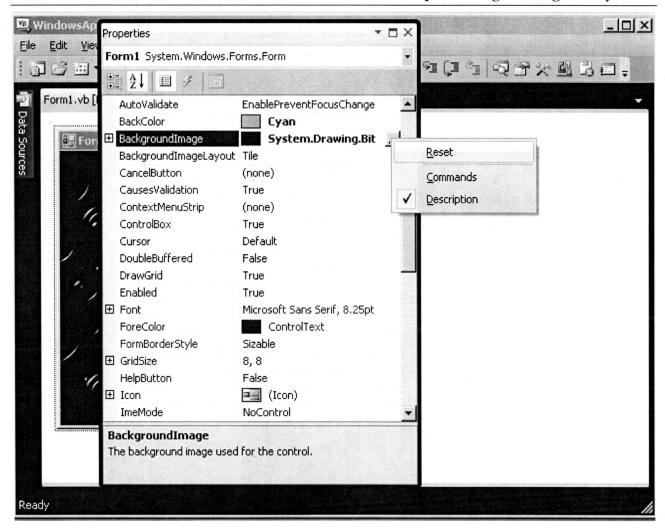

"…and then select Reset. The BackgroundImage will be cleared."

I asked if anyone had any questions. For the moment, no one did. I thought this would be a good opportunity to let everyone in the class do a formal exercise on their own.

"In this exercise," I said, "we'll do some naming housekeeping, which is important in keeping things tidy in our program. We'll create a new Visual Basic project, change both the name of the project and the form, and then you have a chance to explore the Visual Basic Properties window."

Exercise 4-1 Displaying and Modifying the Properties of the Form

1. Start a new Visual Basic Windows Application project. At the New Project window, specify the Name of the Project as 'China'. Use the following screenshot as your guide.

2. By default, a new Windows Application contains a single form named Form1. It's always a good idea to give our forms meaningful names, therefore, we want to change the name of the form. When the Visual Basic IDE appears, select the form by clicking it with your mouse.

3. Once the form is selected, select the Solution Explorer by selecting View | Other Windows | Solution Explorer from the Visual Basic Menu Bar.

4. We want to rename Form1 as Main.vb. Select Form1.vb in the Solution Explorer window, right-click your mouse on the name of the form, and when the pop-up menu appears, select Rename.

5. Change the name of the form from Form1.vb to Main.vb and press the ENTER key (make sure you include the extension .vb in the name).

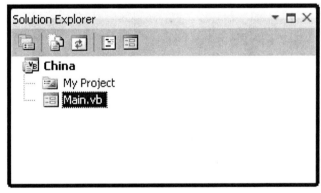

6. Select Tools-Options-Projects and Solutions, and be sure that C:\VBFiles appears as the 'home' for your VB Projects---use the Screenshot below as your guide..

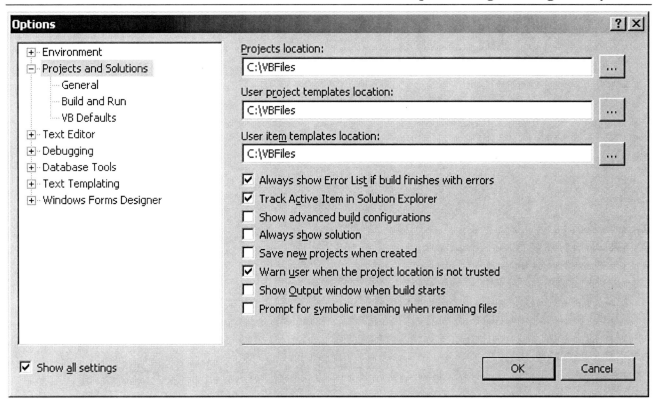

7. Select Tools-Options-Environment-Projects and Solutions-Build and Run. Be sure that 'Prompt to save all changes' is specified in the Before building listbox. Use the Screenshot below as your guide.

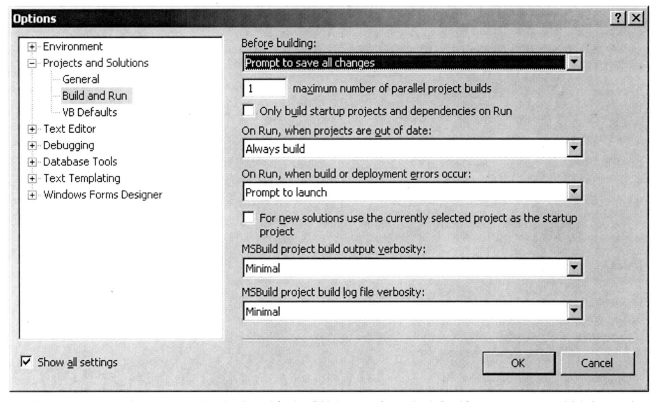

8. Click on the SaveAll button on the Toolbar (it's the fifth button from the left---if you are unsure which button it is, let your mouse pointer hover over it, and Tooltip Text will tell you what it is. You should see the following Screenshot.

Save Project		?| X
Name:	China	
Location:	C:\VBFiles	▼ Browse...
Solution Name:	China	☑ Create directory for solution
		Save Cancel

9. Be sure that your dialog box is completed as the Screenshot above shows---then click on the Save button to save your project.

Discussion

The majority of the class seemed to have no problem with our first exercise. Of course, there's always a certain amount of uneasiness the first time you begin working with Visual Basic on your own. But, as I told everyone, you can't hurt anything! If you make a mistake, you can always start again from the beginning.

"In Visual Basic," I said, "saving your work is easy. The work we did in the previous exercise has already resulted in several files being saved to our folder C:\VBFiles\China. When we selected New Project in our previous exercise, we gave our Project a name---when we clicked the Save All button on the Toolbar, provided we specified 'Create a directory for solution', a folder with the name China will be created within the China folder of our hard drive."

"What happened when we renamed our form from Form1 to Main?" Linda asked.

"Visual Basic automatically renamed the file for us on our hard drive," I said. "This is a big advance over previous versions of Visual Basic, believe me, where I'd have needed to spend five minutes or so discussing how to save your project. As you saw, all we needed to do to save any changes we made to your project was to click the Save All button on the Visual Basic Toolbar."

I gave everyone a chance to catch their breath, to verify that they indeed did have a folder called C:\VBFiles\China on their hard drive, and waited to see if there were any additional questions—there were none. Now, it was time to run the China Shop Project for the first time.

Running the China Shop Project for the First Time

"Okay then," I said, "if there are no more questions, let's run the China Shop Project."

I asked everyone to click the Start button on the toolbar, the button that resembled a right arrow.

"This isn't much of a program," Ward blurted out.

"Actually, there's quite a bit to our program, Ward," I replied, "although I can see your point. It might appear that we have only a single form, with no controls on it, but there's a lot of built-in, default behavior."

"Is that all we need to do to run the program?" Chuck asked. "Just click the Start button? Shouldn't we compile the program or something?"

"That's a good question. Visual Basic lets us quickly test our application within the IDE before we compile it into an executable. A handy feature, as you will see!" I replied. I then clicked the Start Button on my PC.

"When you start your program," I continued, "a number of things happen in the IDE to let us know our program is running. First, the caption of Visual Basic's Title Bar changes; it should display the word [Running] somewhere. Second, when your program starts to run, the Start button on the toolbar is dimmed. Finally, a run-time version of the form appears 'over' the design time form."

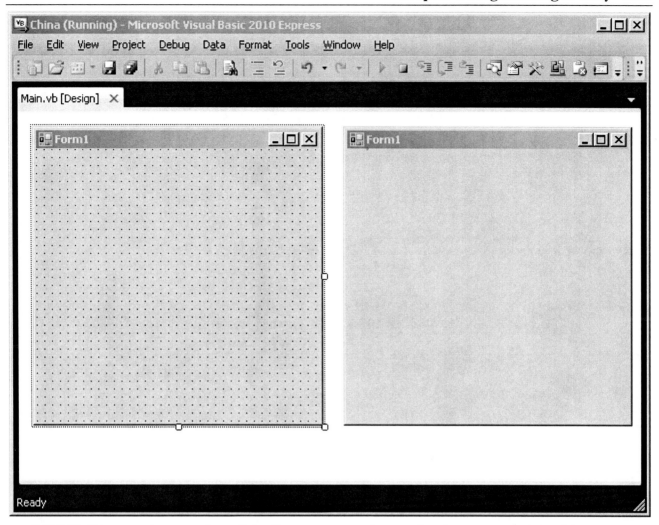

NOTE: The run-time version of the form may not sit exactly where you see it in this screenshot. It's been formatted to lie next to the design time form---it may be above it or below it.

"I can see evidence that my program is running," Linda said, "but I wouldn't say it's doing anything. Just about all I can do is minimize, maximize, and close it."

"You can also drag and resize the form, can't you?" I replied.

"OK," Linda said, "I'll give you that. Is that the default behavior you were talking about?"

"Exactly," I said. "That's my point. In a matter of a few minutes, and with next to nothing in terms of effort, we've designed a working Windows application. Granted, it doesn't do much, but the same application, written in C++ (another programming language) might have taken us a week to do!"

"You're kidding," Dave said. "A week to create a program with a single window?"

"Maybe I'm exaggerating a little bit," I said smiling, "but it might have taken us that long the first time around counting lecture and instruction time. Visual Basic is a great tool for rapid development."

"How come my title bar still reads Form1?" Chuck asked. "I know I changed the name of the form."

"Good question, Chuck," I replied. "Even though we changed the name of the form, the caption in the title bar comes from the form's Text property—and that we didn't change—yet."

I looked around the classroom and noticed Rhonda seemed to be having some difficulty.

"I have some kind of error," she said. "Something about Build Errors. What did I do wrong?"

I explained to the class that Rhonda's Error Message about Build Errors occurs when Visual Basic evaluates your project and its code prior to running the program. In this instance, something was wrong. I took a quick walk to Rhonda's PC and, sure enough, there was the dialog box every Visual Basic programmer dreads.

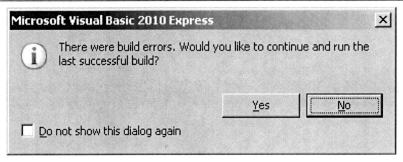

"Should I continue?" she asked.

"It doesn't make sense to answer Yes here," I said. "Let's click the No button and see what's wrong."

I clicked No and another window appeared.

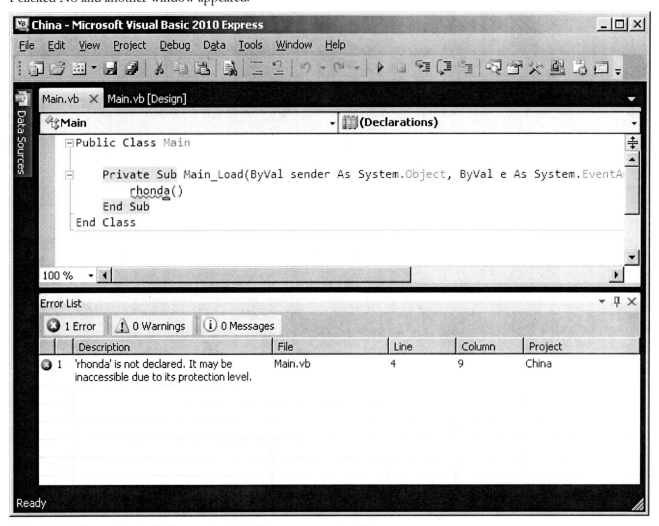

"What's the Error List for?" Steve asked, looking over our shoulders.

"In this case, Steve," I said, "it's telling us what's wrong with the project. This error message— Name 'rhonda' not declared---means Rhonda accidentally typed something into the 'code' portion of her Form."

"I thought I would type my name in there," Rhonda chimed in, "was that wrong?"

"Not wrong Rhonda," I said, "it's a good idea to identify your project with your name----but you need to use a special syntax called a comment to do that, and we haven't learned how to do that yet. For now, I'll just delete the line of code with your name in it."

I did so, then clicked on the Start button again, and Rhonda's program ran swimmingly.

"I've noticed how you seem to start and stop the program so easily," Valerie said. "I've been having problems myself. How are you doing it?"

"To start the program," I said, "I click the Start button on the toolbar. To stop the program, I can either select Debug | Stop Debugging from the Visual Basic Menu Bar or click the Stop button on the Toolbar----it appears as a solid square"

I waited a moment to see if there were any other problems, but everyone seemed to be doing fine.

"I'd like to give you an exercise," I said, "to ensure that you know how to find your project after exiting, and then restarting Visual Basic."

"Is that a problem?" Valerie asked. "It can't be that difficult."

"Well, it is different working with an existing project than creating a new one," I said. "You'd be surprised at the number of calls I get from students who can't find the project they're working on!"

I then distributed this exercise to my students.

Exercise 4-2 Exit and Restart Visual Basic and Find the China Shop Project

In this exercise, you exit Visual Basic, restart it, and then find the China Project you just created.

1. Exit Visual Basic by selecting File | Exit from the Visual Basic Main Menu.
2. Restart Visual Basic.
3. When the Start window appears, instead of selecting Create New Project as you did before, you have two choices. You should see the China Project you just created at the top of the Start window

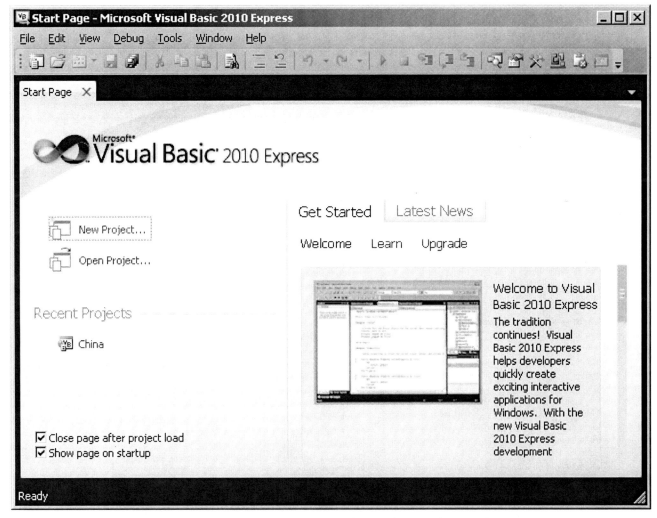

You can double-click the China Project and it will be opened for you in the Visual Basic IDE.
4. Or, you can find and open the China Project by clicking the Open Project link, navigating to the appropriate folder on your PC (C:\VBFILES\CHINA), and double-clicking the China.sln file. This, too, will open the China Project for you in the Visual Basic IDE.

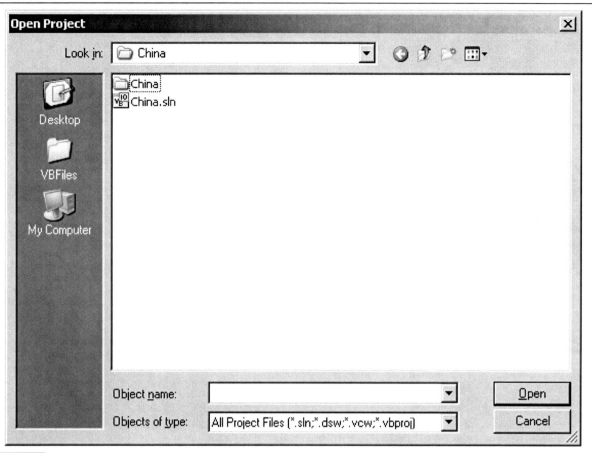

Discussion

"This was an exercise that was either going to work or not," I said. "Either you were going to find your China Project listed on the Start window or you wouldn't, in which case, that would mean something had gone wrong in the Save exercise we did before."

Ward immediately had a problem. When he exited Visual Basic and restarted it, the Start window didn't appear. After some quick detective work, we discovered Ward had mistakenly selected the "Show Empty Environment" CheckBox in the At startup listbox in the Tools-Options-Environment-Startup tab the last time he used Visual Basic. As a result, Ward was unable to open the China Shop Project in the same manner everyone else did.

We found the project by selecting the Open Existing project link. Then we corrected the Option setting that caused the Start window not to be displayed in the first place by selecting the Environment | Startup tab of the Tools | Options menu item, and then selecting Show Start Page in the At Startup drop-down ListBox.

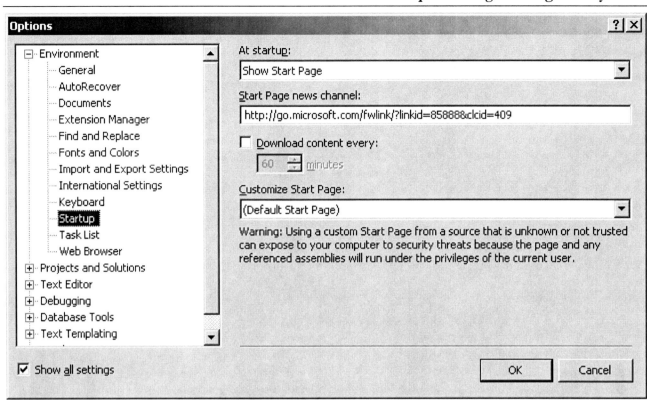

I was pleased to find no one else had any difficulty finding his or her China Shop Project. Time for a well-deserved break. I told my students that when we returned from break, we would discuss some of the properties of the form and also make changes to the properties of the Main form of the China Project that would begin to shape the look and feel of our program.

"By the way," I said, as they began to file out of the classroom, "next week when we discuss Visual Basic Controls and their properties, you'll see most of the form properties we examine after break are also found in those controls. That should give us a good head start in getting comfortable with the properties of controls."

Properties of the Form

When we returned from break, I informed everyone they would soon complete an exercise that would have them changing the properties of the one and only form of the China Shop Project. I then displayed the following table on the classroom projector, so they could have a preview of the changes to come.

Property	Value	Comment
Name	Main	Technically not a property. Included for documentation purposes only.
ControlBox	False	No control box will appear, and neither will minimize, maximize, close. or restore buttons.
FormBorderStyle	FixedSingle	Prevents the user from resizing the form.
Height	456	Your value may be different, but don't worry about it. If you can't find this property, look under Size.
StartPosition	Center Screen	Centers the form within the screen
Text	The Bullina China Shop	Appears in the Title Bar of the form.
Width	600	Your value might be different, but don't worry about it. If you can't find this property, look under Size.

"Before we make these changes," I said, "I want to spend a few minutes discussing these properties. Notice that of the approximately 50 or so properties associated with a form, we are only going to change 7."

"Less is best," Linda said.

"You took the words right out of my mouth," I replied.

Name of the Form

"I know we've already discussed the Name of the form," I said, "otherwise known as the Class Name."

"What's a class?" Linda asked.

"We'll discuss classes a bit later on," I said, "For now, suffice to say that a class is an object—either a form or a control."

I continued by explaining the Class Name, which I also termed the internal name, is the name by which we would refer to the form when we write code that refers to it.

"We've already changed the default name of the form from Form1 to Main," I said. "Now, it's almost standard practice to name your form and controls according to a convention called Hungarian Notation, named after the Hungarian computer scientist Charles Simonyi who developed it."

Naming Conventions

I then distributed a handout with suggestions for naming the common controls that appear in Visual Basic. The first section provided a list of prefixes for all the basic controls that come with Visual Basic.

Control	Prefix
Button	btn
CheckBox	chk
ComboBox	cbo
ColorDialog	dlg
Form	frm
GroupBox	gbx
Label	lbl
ListBox	lst
Menu	mnu
PictureBox	pic
RadioButton	rad
TextBox	txt
Timer	tmr

The second section of the handout covered the different variable types used in our Visual Basic code. Although we haven't discussed variables yet, these will come in useful later.

Variable	Prefix
Boolean	bln
Date	dat
Double	dbl
Integer	int

Long	lng
Short	sht
Single	sng
String	str

"In Hungarian Notation," I said, "the name of the object begins with a prefix (usually three characters) that describes the object (in the case of our form, frm) and the rest of the name should meaningfully describe it. For that reason, all my form names begin with frm. Typically, I give my first form the name Main. Therefore, Main is the name of the main form of the China Shop Project—in our case, the one and only form."

NOTE: Not all programmers use three-character prefixes like we do here. Some programmers prefer one-character prefixes, but I think three characters enable you to describe your object more specifically.

"Can a form's Name contain spaces?" Mary asked.

"That's a good question, Mary, and the answer is No," I replied. "In Visual Basic, the Name of a form and, for that matter, the name of a variable, may not contain spaces. Remember, though, the Class Name for the form and the external disk file form names are different. In Windows 95 and above, it's permissible to create a filename with spaces in it, but the Class name and the name of our variables cannot have spaces."

Height and Width Properties

We previously discussed both the Height and Width properties. They affect the dimensions of the form.

"The values for these properties are displayed in the table as 450 pixels (about 4 inches, depending on your monitor's resolution) × 600 (about 6 inches, depending on your monitor's resolution), respectively," I said. "I want you to feel free to deviate from these exact dimensions if you feel the need. I'm not necessarily out to get carbon-copy projects from everyone at the end of the course. Those values are only guidelines. The important thing is to design your form, so the controls we're going to place on it next week all fit."

The FormBorderStyle and ControlBox Properties

"We're going to change some properties of the form," I said, "that prevent the user (or the customer) from doing three things:"

- Changing the size of the form

- Maximizing the form

- Minimizing or closing the form

Everyone agreed that preventing these actions was important because we wanted a stable, uniform look to our project.

"We don't want a customer accidentally minimizing a form," Ward said, "or worse yet, closing it so the next customer can't use our program."

"Right you are, Ward," I agreed. "Fortunately, Visual Basic makes building these safeguards into our program easy just by adjusting some properties of the form. To prevent the user from resizing the form, we'll set the FormBorderStyle property of the form to FixedSingle."

"What about minimizing, maximizing, and closing the form?" Linda asked.

"That requires an update to another property," I answered.

I continued by explaining two form properties exist—MaxButton and MinButton—that can be set to False to prevent the user from maximizing or minimizing the form. And, if you try these properties for yourself, you can see the Maximize and Minimize options are also removed from the Control Box menu. However, we're still left with the problem of the Close button. There is no Close property.

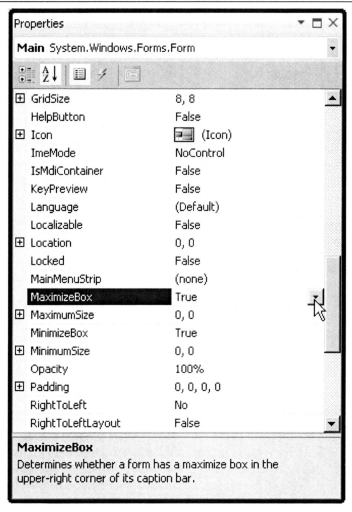

There is, however, the ControlBox property, which when set to False, not only removes the Control Box icon from the form, but causes the Maximize, Minimize, and Close buttons to disappear from the form as well. Therefore, if we change the ControlBox property to False, we can take care of all three requirements at one time.

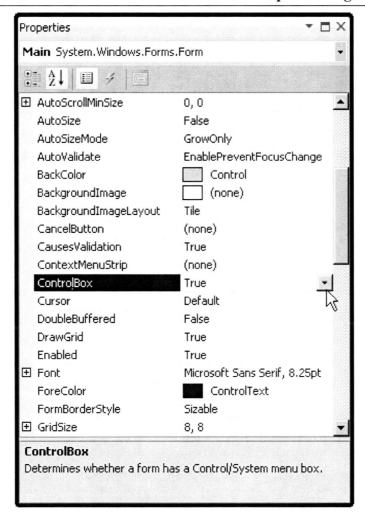

The StartPosition Property

"Why didn't you include values for the Left and Top properties?" Blaine asked. "They weren't in your table."

"We don't need to worry about those, Blaine," I said, "and I'll tell you why."

I explained we needn't concern ourselves with the Left and Top properties of the form.

There's a Visual Basic property called StartPosition, which we'll use to center the form right in the middle of the screen. To do this, we simply select CenterScreen from the drop-down ListBox.

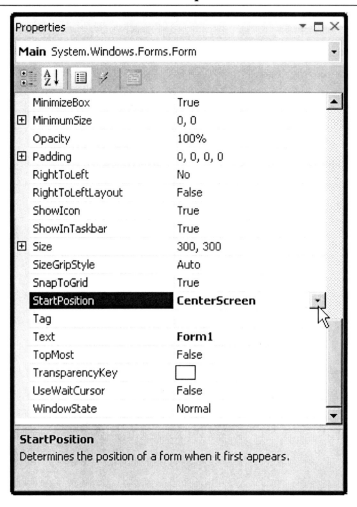

The Text Property

"Finally," I said, "we'll change the form's title bar to display the name of the China Shop by setting the Text property. This will be displayed in the form's title bar."

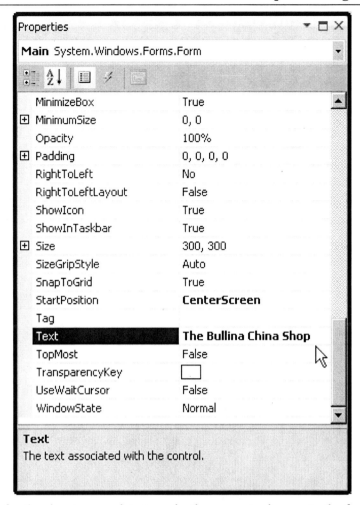

I distributed this exercise for the class to complete to make the property changes to the form.

Exercise 4-3 Change the Properties of the China Shop's Form

1. Select your form by clicking it with the mouse.
2. View the Properties window by using one of the four methods discussed in today's class.
3. Find the FormBorderStyle property in the Properties window, and click once on the value side of the property. A ListBox appears, offering seven possible values for the FormBorderStyle property. Select FixedDialog. (Another technique you can use with a property that contains a drop-down ListBox of multiple values is to double-click the value side of the Properties window, and the next value in the list is then displayed. Continue to double-click until the desired value appears.)
4. Change the remainder of the properties according to the following table. Remember, if you make a mistake, just go back and correct the property.

Property	Value	Comment
FormBorderStyle	FixedDialog	Prevents the user from resizing or maximizing the form.
ControlBox	False	No control box will appear, and neither will minimize, maximize, close, or restore buttons.
Height	450	Your value may be different, but don't worry about it.
StartPosition	Center Screen	Centers the form within the screen,
Text	The Bullina China Shop	Appears in the title bar of the form.

Width	600	Your value may be different, but don't worry about it.

5. When you've made the remainder of the changes, test the changes you made to your project by running the project. Click the Start button on the toolbar or select Debug | Start from the Visual Basic Menu Bar. If Prompt To Save Changes has been selected in Tools | Options | Environment, you should be prompted to save the changes to your Solution, Project, and form.

6. Verify the form is centered within the screen when the program begins to run.

7. Verify there's no control box, and no Maximize, Minimize, or Close buttons.

8. Verify the form cannot be resized.

9. Verify the title bar of the form reads The Bullina China Shop.

10. Stop the program by clicking the Stop button on the Visual Basic Toolbar, or select Debug | Stop Debugging.

Discussion

I gave the class about ten minutes to complete this exercise. Everyone agreed this was the most complicated of our exercises so far, but they also agreed they felt pretty comfortable doing it and, besides, it was fun! Steve remarked he hadn't received a prompt to save his project and associated files when he ran the program after changing his form properties. A quick trip to his PC, along with a check of Tools | Options | Projects and Solutions | Build and Run revealed Don't Save Changes was selected as a preference for when his project runs.

I must admit I was glad to see the students in the class were so obviously pleased with themselves. Although all they had done was change some properties of the form, I could see they now began to see where all this was leading. Programming in Visual Basic is easy and, better yet, they were beginning to realize it was also great fun. They were catching the programming bug!

"It isn't practical or productive," I said after they had finished the exercise, "to go through every property of the form in detail. Besides, many of the properties wouldn't mean much to you now anyway. I recommend you browse through online help or any other Visual Basic reference guides you might have and read about all the properties of the form and of the other controls we'll study."

"What's next on the agenda?" Peter asked. "Are we going to start placing controls on the form now?"

"No," I said, glancing at the clock. "That's a topic for next week. In our closing minutes today, I want to introduce you to Visual Basic Methods and Events, which form the basis of the code we'll write in the coming weeks."

Visual Basic Methods

"Properties," I said, "are attributes or characteristics of a Visual Basic object. Methods are actions that you, the programmer, perform on those objects."

I saw some puzzled looks.

"Let's take a real-world example. Color, number of doors, and horsepower are attributes or properties of an automobile. Forward, Stop, and Reverse are methods. To perform some kind of action on an object, a programmer uses methods. For instance, there's a method of the form called Hide, which makes the form invisible. Interestingly enough, there's also a property of the form called Visible, which, when set to False, also makes the form invisible."

Visual Basic Events

"If we continue with our analogy of Visual Basic objects to automobiles," I said, "then approaching a red light at an intersection could be thought of as an event. The ApproachingRedLight event happens to the vehicle and, in response, the driver (or programmer) executes the Stop Method. In a similar way, the form, and the objects on it, can also recognize and respond to events. Each object has a range of events to which it can respond. For instance, ListBoxes are designed in such a way that an item in the ListBox is selected. Not surprisingly then, the ListBox reacts to an event called SelectedIndexChanged (more on this later). Not surprisingly, the button control doesn't react to this event—you wouldn't expect it to because the button control is designed to be clicked up—therefore, it reacts to a Click Event."

> NOTE: Methods are something a programmer does to an object in code. Events are triggered by the user doing something to a program while it's running.

I waited to see if I had lost anyone—I hadn't, and so I continued.

"For every event to which an object can respond, there is a corresponding event procedure that will appear in the Visual Basic Code window. An event procedure is a fragment of code that relates to a particular object and a particular event. For instance, if you have a button control called Command1 and a button control called Command2, each one would have its own event procedure. Depending on the requirements of your program, you can place code in these event procedures to have your program 'do something' when the event takes place."

"Who decides what events an object responds to?" Barbara asked.

"Microsoft, when it developed Visual Basic—really, it's a function of the operating system—decided the events to which an object would respond." I said. "For example, most objects in Windows respond to being clicked by a user, but not all. This behavior is a function of the Windows environment."

"So you're saying that to make our program do something," Jack said, "we need to place code into an event procedure that will be triggered when the user performs an action on that object—is that right?"

"That's perfect, Jack," I said. "That's exactly what you would do. Now, if this isn't perfectly clear yet for the rest of you, don't worry, it will be soon."

I then started a new Visual Basic project and double-clicked my mouse on the form. This opened the Visual Basic Code window, which I then displayed on the classroom projector.

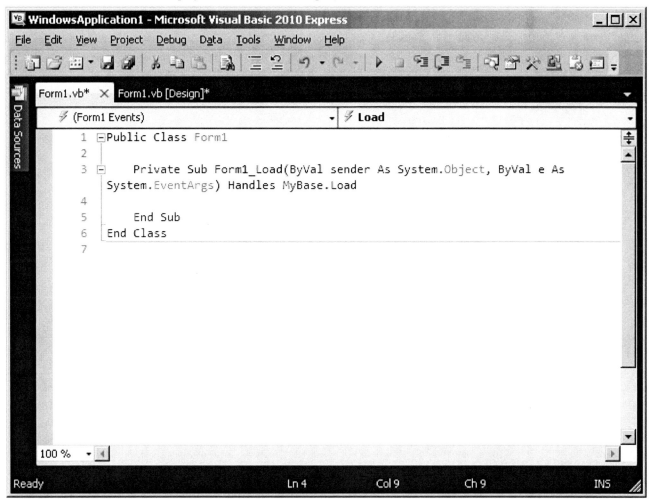

NOTE: Your code window may not look exactly like this one---I've turned 'Word Wrap' on in my screenshot, and also have Line Numbers enabled. Read on to learn how to turn these features of the Code Window off and on.

"So that's the Code window you've been talking about," Joe said.

"Yes, this is the Visual Basic Code window," I said, "which lets us place code in an event procedure. As I said, an event procedure is associated with both an object and an event."

I directed everyone's attention to the two ListBoxes at the top of the Code window.

"The ListBox on the left," I said, "is called the **Class Name** ListBox, and the ListBox on the right is known as the **Method Name** ListBox, although I prefer to call it the Event ListBox. The Class Name ListBox shows our form, plus every control that appears on the form. The Method Name ListBox shows every event to which the object selected in the Class ListBox can respond. Notice the event procedure name is the name of the selected object, plus the name of the event, separated by an underscore (_)."

I then pointed out the line of code reading Private Sub Form1_Load.

"That's the Procedure Header for the Load event procedure of Form1," I said. "Whenever this form is loaded—in other words, when it's created in the run-time environment—this event procedure is triggered, and any code appearing between this line of code and the End Sub, which you see after that, will be executed.

"This Code window is confusing," Linda said. "I've used other versions of Visual Basic and I didn't see all this clutter. What are those numbers? And what are those plus and minus symbols?"

"You're right, Linda," I said, "the Code window can be confusing, particularly in this version of Visual Basic. The numbers you see are line numbers assigned automatically to each line of code. You needn't use them—in fact, if you select Tools | Options | Text Editor | Basic from the Visual Basic Menu Bar, you can turn the line numbers 'off.'

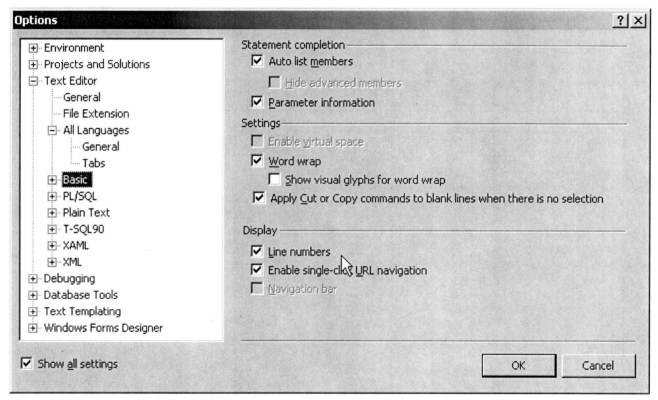

"...As far as the plus and minus symbols, certain portions of the Code window have sections, which can be expanded by clicking the plus sign, and contracted, in which case they have the minus symbol next to them. Like me, you may find this useful as the amount of code in your Code Window increases."

"Why does it appear that your code is word wrapped?" Kate asked.

"That's another option you can set in Tools | Options | Text Editor | Basic | General," I said. "That comes in handy when you have long lines of code."

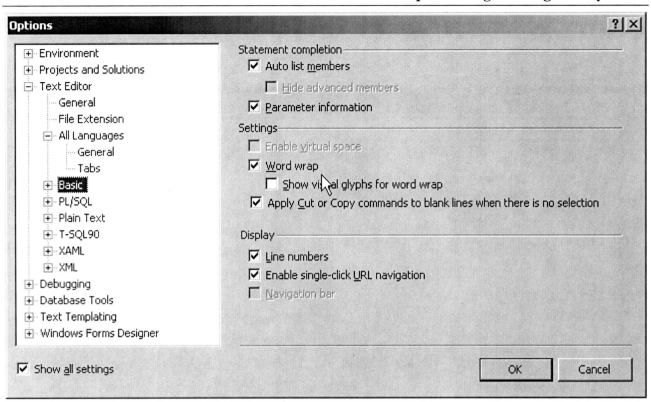

"How can you see all the event procedures for an object," Dave asked, "or for other objects, for that matter?"

"To see other event procedures for which we can write code," I said, "we need to do two things: first, click the Class ListBox and select (Main Events). Next, click the Method Name ListBox, and a full list of the event procedures to which the form will react are displayed." I did so to let everyone see the full range of events to which the form can respond. The following screen was displayed on the classroom projector.

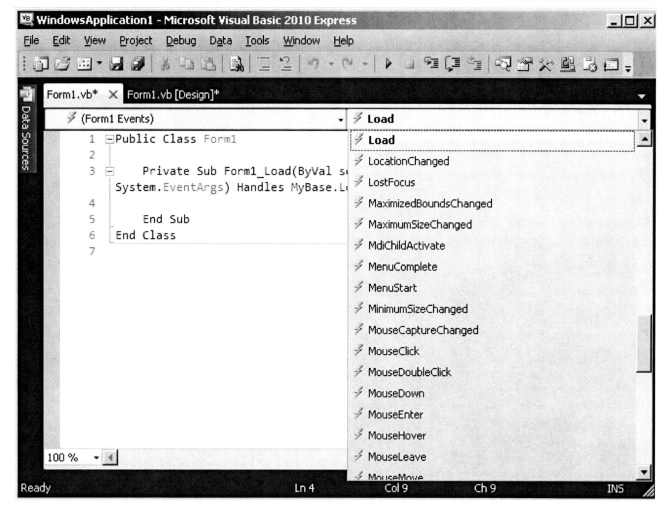

"To see event procedures for other objects, you need to select them first in the Class Name ListBox."

"Why aren't all the event procedures already in the Code window?" Linda asked.

"The event procedures don't appear in the Code window until after you select them, " I answered. "At that point, Visual Basic builds the event procedure stub—the header and the End Sub line for you."

"Can we write some code for the Click event procedure of the form?" Dave asked.

"Good idea, Dave," I responded. "Let's do that now."

I found the Click event procedure for the form by scrolling through the list in the Method Name ListBox. This action placed the Code window's cursor right at the Procedure Header of the Click event procedure.

"It's important to place your cursor within the body of the event procedure," I said, as I did exactly that. "We'll discuss writing code later in the class. Right now, before we finish for the day, I want to give you a demonstration on what can be done using code. I'll show you how you can change the caption in the form's title bar by writing code in the Click event procedure of the form."

"Can't we also do that by setting the Text property?" Valerie asked.

"That's an excellent question," I said, "and you're absolutely right. We can also change the title bar of the caption by changing the Text property of the form in the Properties Widow. By the way, this won't be the first time we'll see there's a way to achieve the same result by executing a method or setting properties."

I then typed this code into the event procedure for the Click event of the form.

```
Me.Text = "I Love Visual Basic"
```

"Me?" Rhonda asked.

"Working in the event procedures of the form can be a bit tricky," I said. "Me is a special Visual Basic keyword that lets you refer to the form itself without using its name—Form1. In fact, if we use the name Form1 here, our program generates an error when we run it. By the way, we could also write this code to do the same thing."

```
MyBase.Text = "I Love Visual Basic"
```

"If you're really confused now, this has something to do with the 'hidden' code that lies behind the scenes of a Visual Basic project. When Visual Basic was first introduced, programmers would see this code---and unfortunately, sometimes beginners would modify it, leading to problems with the program. In Visual Basic Express, you can't see this 'hidden' code---but if you know what you are doing, you can still work with it like this. You need to trust me on this—most of the code we write won't be nearly this confusing."

I noticed someone who seemed to be working on her own, writing code in the China Project.

"By the way, " I said, "if you're following along with me here in the classroom, remember, I started a new project— don't do this to the China Shop Project!"

I then ran the program by clicking the Start button of the toolbar. With the program running, I then clicked the form, and the form's title bar was changed from Form1 to I Love Visual Basic. I waited a few minutes as I gave the class a chance to experiment with this on their own.

"When I entered the code and ran the program," Rhonda said, "the title bar of the form was immediately changed— and I hadn't even clicked it."

"Most likely," I said, "that's because you accidentally entered the code into the Load event procedure of the form, or perhaps the Activated Event, but not the Click event. The Activated event procedure is first in the list of Event Procedures in the Methods Listbox—so it's easy to do that. It's also an event that's triggered when the program starts, unlike the Click event procedure, which is triggered when the user clicks the form. That's easy to fix Rhonda—just cut-and-copy the code out of the Activated event procedure and place it in the Click event procedure."

"Oh, I see, that's exactly what I did," Rhonda said. A few moments later, her little program was behaving as advertised.

"I don't know about anyone else," Chuck said, "but I'm excited about this. I took a C++ class last year and it was a lot harder than this. We're actually programming!"

I could tell Chuck wasn't the only one in the class excited at the prospect. Still, I sensed some nervous souls were still in the audience, so I assured everyone that we'd be discuss methods of the form and controls as they arose during the development of the China Shop project. I asked if there were any questions—there were none, and I advised everyone in the class to make sure they had a good night's sleep next Friday night.

"In next week's class," I said, "we'll complete the China Shop User interface. You'll need to be fresh!"

Summary

In this chapter, you followed my class on a tour of Visual Basic properties and methods. You had your first look at the exercises that will guide you through the China Shop Project.

Along the way, we discussed the default behavior of the Visual Basic form and, at the end of the class, you had a chance to see a Visual Basic method in action.

Two basic stages create a program: designing the user interface, which involves placing controls on to your form and modifying their properties, and writing and checking the code.

Forms and controls are types of objects. Objects have properties, which are characteristics we can modify, such as their name or their appearance.

Objects also have methods, which are actions we can perform on them. Methods differ from events, which are user-initiated actions to which an object will respond. An event procedure is code that's triggered, and then executed, when an event occurs.

Chapter 5---Building the User Interface

In this chapter, follow my computer class as we complete the interface of the China Shop Project. Along the way, we learn more about some of the other Visual Basic controls and their properties.

Completing the User Interface

I began this week by reminding everyone of the tremendous progress we made during our last class. "In today's class," I told everyone, "we'll complete the user interface for the China Shop." I reminded everyone that during the design phase of the Systems Development Life Cycle (SDLC), we developed a sketch of the China Shop Project User Interface.

"This isn't to say our sketch is the only way we can do it," I said. "In fact, I want to encourage you all to incorporate some of your own ideas into your program's interface. You can paint a picture in many. In designing a Visual Basic interface, don't let yourself believe there's only one 'right' design or a single 'best' way to code something."

"So are you giving us free reign to deviate from the design sketch?" Linda asked.

"By the end of today's class," I said, "I know we'll design at least one interface that matches the sketch exactly, because that's what I'm going to do. So, if you feel comfortable with the idea, feel free to impart your own style and ideas into the interface, provided the functionality we agreed on in the design phase remains intact. In other words, you don't have to match the sketch pixel for pixel. If you want to place a button on the opposite side of the screen, feel free."

The visual aspect of your program is what the user is going to remember most about your program. This is the most obvious manifestation of your program. It doesn't matter how beautiful, eloquent, or brilliant your program code is. If the user can't interact with the interface you design, then, ultimately, the program is considered a failure.

John Smiley's Ten-Step Guide to Successful Interface Development

To give everyone a perspective on where we were in the development of the China Shop Project, I displayed my ten-step guide for successful Visual Basic development on the classroom projector.

1. Develop a Requirements Statement.

2. Sketch the user interface on paper.

3. Use the Visual Basic IDE to develop the user interface.

4. Run the program in Visual Basic.

5. Admire your work.

6. Observe the default behavior of the interface.

7. Modify the interface, if necessary, by changing the properties of the form or controls.

8. Run the program in Visual Basic.

9. Admire your work.

10. Begin coding to enhance the default behavior of the interface.

"Looks like we're about halfway through Step 3," Lou said.

"That's right," I said. "And, by the end of today's class, we'll have completed Steps 3 through 9."

I took a few moments to emphasize how important it is to work with the default behavior of the Visual Basic forms and controls. Taking a steady, measured approach to developing the project is equally important.

"Even though it seems frivolous," I said, "Steps 4, 5, 8, and 9 are crucial to the development of a successful project. You can't have too much positive reinforcement!"

At this point, I asked everyone to start up Visual Basic. This wasn't necessary because almost everyone had Visual Basic started with the China Shop Project visible in the IDE.

"Now it's time to look at the objects in the Visual Basic Toolbox that we'll add to our form to complete the user interface. The word "toolbox" sounds funny to beginners, but that's exactly what it is. The toolbox contains controls we'll use to build our interface. Remember my analogy of creating a program with building a house? We already have a blueprint for the form—the sketch we created during the design phase of the Systems Development Life Cycle (SDLC)—so all we need to do is use the contents of the toolbox to block out the form in Visual Basic."

I displayed the Visual Basic Toolbox on the classroom projector.

The Visual Basic Toolbox

"This is the Visual Basic default Toolbox," I said.

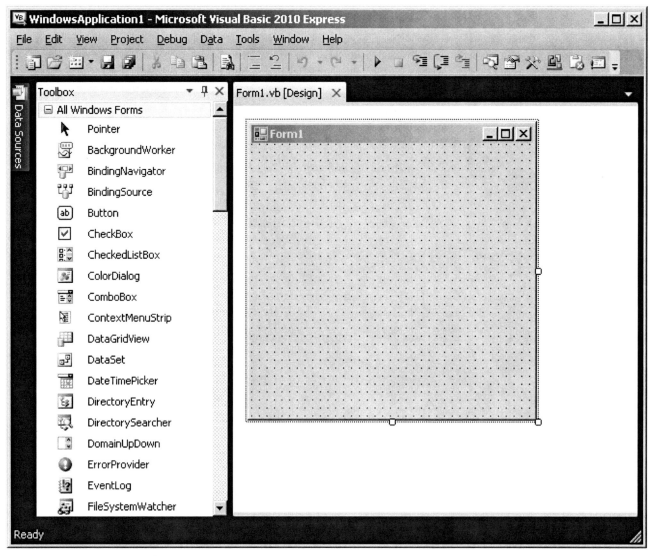

"Why do you call it the default?" Barbara asked.

"Well," I said, "this is the appearance of the toolbox when you first install Visual Basic. It doesn't necessarily look like this each time you see it, because you can add other controls to the Visual Basic Toolbox."

"The toolbox contains a bunch of controls," I said, "this excludes the Pointer (the arrow), which isn't a control."

> **NOTE: The Visual Basic Toolbox can be configured to hold hundreds of controls. The controls that appear in the toolbox are known as the Visual Basic Intrinsic Controls and form the basic building blocks of your user interface. As your Visual Basic programming prowess develops, you'll add additional controls to the toolbox.**

"I know we've covered this before," Kate said, "but you've used the term "control" several times. What's the difference between a control and an object?"

"The terms are often used interchangeably because controls are a type of object. In Visual Basic, a control is an object you place and position on a form, such as a button or a check box. Controls are a visible object—at least at design time. Some controls aren't visible at run time, however. Some objects have no visual interface. Those we discuss in another Visual Basic course here at the university."

"I'm glad you said 'most' controls are visible," Ward said. "During the week, I was experimenting and I placed one of the controls from the toolbox on my form. When I ran the program, I didn't see it."

> **NOTE: Not all controls are visible on the form at run time. Some controls, like the Timer control and a group of Controls known as Dialog controls, are visible at design time, but are invisible at run time.**

"That's right," I agreed. "Most controls are visible when you run your program, but not all. For instance, today we place two controls on the China Shop form—the Timer control and the ColorDialog Control—which aren't visible when we run the program." I continued by saying that controls have properties, just like the form we examined the previous week. These properties affect the appearance and behavior of controls.

The China Shop Controls

"You'll recall," I said, "that I indicated earlier that creating a Visual Basic program is a two step process. First we create the user interface, and then we write code. It's time to pursue Step 1—the creation of the user interface."

Creation of the China Shop Form

"Let's look at the design sketch for the China Shop interface," I said, as I displayed it on the classroom projector.

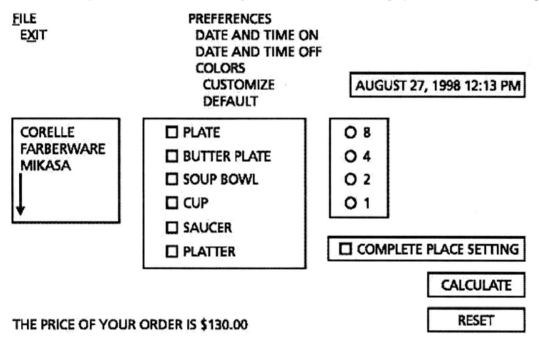

"As you can see, the sketch includes the following Visual Basic components"

- 1 Form
- 1 Menu
- 1 ListBox control
- 2 Label controls
- 2 Button controls
- 3 GroupBox controls
- 4 RadioButton controls
- 7 CheckBox controls

"All the controls you see on the sketch," I said, "including the menu, are contained in the default toolbox."

"What about the menu?" Dave asked.

"We'll talk about the Menu control later on in the course," I said. "For today, I want to restrict our discussion to controls that impact the core functionality of the project—calculating the customer's price."

"What's the ColorDialog Control used for?" Ward asked.

"The ColorDialog Control," I said, "displays a dialog box that prompts the user to make a selection from a color palette, so the user can change the color of the form." I paused before adding, "I think it's time we start adding controls from the toolbox. The logical first step is to add the GroupBox controls to the interface of the China Shop Project."

The GroupBox Control

"The GroupBox control?" Blaine asked. "Isn't that the border we drew on the sketch?"

"That's right," I said, "but the GroupBox control is much more than a border. The GroupBox control is known as a Visual Basic Container control because it can 'contain' other controls, much as the Form contains other controls."

"I'm not sure what that means," Ward said.

I explained that experienced programmers place controls within GroupBoxes because adjusting the properties of the GroupBox affects all the controls contained within it.

"For instance," I said, "suppose you place ten CheckBoxes within a GroupBox control, and then you decide to make all the CheckBoxes invisible? The CheckBox has a property called Visible, which, if set to False, makes the CheckBox invisible. Setting ten CheckBox properties in this way can be pretty tedious—and it's easy to miss one. If all the CheckBoxes are contained within a GroupBox control, however, all you need to do is set the Visible property of the GroupBox control to False and, voila, all the CheckBoxes are now invisible."

My students seemed happy with that explanation, so I continued by saying that in the China Shop Project, we'd use three GroupBox controls: one GroupBox for the china items, another for the customer's selected quantity and, finally, one for the Complete Place Setting option.

I asked everyone to open their saved copy of the China Shop Project from the previous week's class and, after verifying they'd successfully retrieved it form the correct folder on their hard drive, I distributed this exercise for them to complete.

Exercise 5-1 Add GroupBox Controls to the China Shop Form

In this exercise, we add our first control to the China Shop's form. Because the GroupBox control contains other controls, it makes sense to start our interface design by placing the GroupBox controls identified in our design sketch on to the form first.

1. Start Visual Basic and open the China Shop Project you first saved in Chapter 4.

2. Let's begin by placing the GroupBox that will contain the china items on the form. You can use three methods to place a control on the form: the first is by double-clicking the GroupBox control icon (the one with XY displayed on a gray square) in the Visual Basic Toolbox. If you're ever unsure what a control in the toolbox is, hold your mouse over it and Visual Basic will display ToolTips showing you the name of the control. The second way is to select the GroupBox control icon by clicking it with your mouse, releasing your mouse, and then clicking-and-dragging on the form to draw the GroupBox. The third method is to click-and-drag the control directly from the toolbox to the form. For this exercise, I presume you double-clicked the control onto the form.

3. After you double-click the GroupBox control, Visual Basic places it in the upper left-hand corner of your form, with an arbitrary size. As well as deciding the size for you, Visual Basic also assigns a name to the control, in this case GroupBox1, because this is the first GroupBox control on your form. Don't worry about its placement or size because controls are easy to move once they're on the form. Click the border of the control and, when your mouse pointer turns into a four-sided arrow, drag it to the desired location. Changing the dimensions of the control is also easy by clicking the size handles that appear along the edges of the control—when the mouse pointer turns into a double-headed arrow, drag it and the control changes size.

4. Move the GroupBox to the location specified on our design sketch by clicking-and-dragging on the border of the control until the mouse pointer becomes four-sided.

5. Resize the GroupBox's dimensions according to our design sketch by clicking-and-dragging the control's grab handles. When you place your mouse pointer on the grab handles, your mouse pointer changes shape and becomes a double-headed arrow, as the following illustration shows.

6. Let's use the second technique to add another GroupBox control, for the quantity, to the form. Select the GroupBox control in the toolbox by clicking it once. Now, position your mouse pointer over the form, at which point it changes shape to cross-hairs. Now click-and-drag the mouse over the area of the form where you want the control placed. As you do so, an outline of the control appears. When the outline is the size you want, release your mouse button, and there it is! Again, notice a name for the control is assigned for you—this time GroupBox2— because this is the second GroupBox control placed on the form.

7. The China Shop project requires one last GroupBox control, the one to contain the Complete Place Setting option. Use the third technique, directly dragging the GroupBox control to your form. Your form should look similar to this illustration.

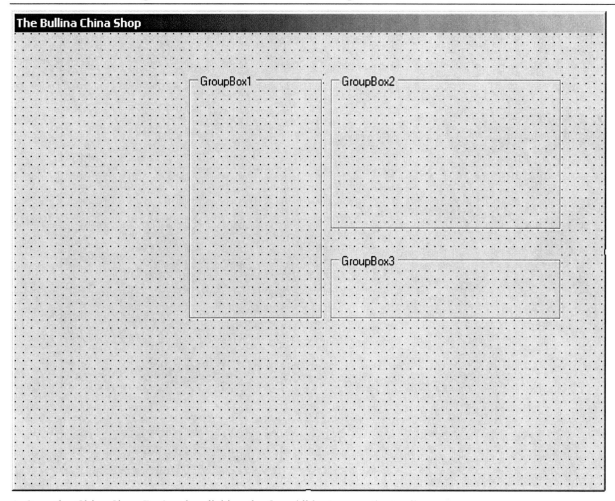

8. Save the China Shop Project by clicking the SaveAll button on the toolbar.

Discussion

I took a quick walk around the computer lab and everyone seemed to being doing fine. I asked members of the class which method of control placement they preferred. Almost universally, they said the double-click method.

"What's your preference?" Linda asked.

"None of the three methods is right or wrong," I said. "Most beginners feel more comfortable with the double-click method. You should practice the other methods as well, though, particularly the method where you select the control, release the mouse, and then click-and-drag on the form—you need to use that method when you place controls within the GroupBoxes we just placed on the form."

I asked if anyone had trouble moving or resizing the controls after they were placed on the form. No one had reports of trouble.

"There's a keyboard alternative to moving and resizing the control using a mouse," I said. "You can 'nudge' a control by selecting it with your mouse, and then using a combination of CTRL plus an arrow key to move it in one direction or another."

"You said you can also use the keyboard to resize controls?" Lou asked. "Yes," I said. "Again, select the control with your mouse, and then use a combination of SHIFT plus an arrow key either to expand or shrink the control." I also pointed out an important piece of information: if you want to get rid of a control added on to a form, select it, and then press DEL on the keyboard.

The ListBox Control

There were no more questions about the GroupBox control, so we moved on to the ListBox control.

"We'll use the ListBox control," I said, "to display the brands of china available for sale in the China Shop. A ListBox control eliminates the need for users to type and its inherent functionality means the user is prevented from making an invalid selection or a spelling mistake. When the user wants to make a selection from the ListBox, he or she clicks it with the mouse, which results in the selection being highlighted."

"How are items placed in the ListBox?" Dave asked.

"Items can be placed in the ListBox by the programmer either at design time or at run time. In the production version of the China Shop Project, we'll add the items at run time," I replied. "But, for speed, we'll add them at design time in the prototype."

"Will we do that by invoking a method?" Barbara asked.

"In the production version, yes," I said. "That's exactly how we'll do it, but we still have some things to learn before we see how that method works."

I continued by explaining that ListBox controls occupy a fixed amount of space on the form. Some thought needs to be given in determining how high and how wide to make the ListBox. "But it's not a big deal," I continued. "If the number of items in the ListBox exceeds its size, a scrollbar appears automatically, which enables the user to scroll through the items in the list. This means you can use the ListBox to display hundreds of items, without using all the screen."

"Is there a limit to the number of items you can display?" Joe asked.

"Yes," I replied, "but the capacity of the ListBox is so large that, in almost all cases, we needn't worry about it."

"So, how do you decide how tall and how wide a list box should be?" asked Kate.

"Well," I replied, "initially, we know only three items will be in the ListBox and none of these items is more than ten characters in length, so I think we can display all of them at the same time. And, even if the number of items increases later, a ListBox automatically scrolls. From a design point of view, I don't recommend making a list box too small, even if it is scrollable. After all, we want the user to be able to see it! For that reason, I always size my list boxes so they display at least three items."

"To summarize," I said, "here are some features of the ListBox that also make it a popular control with the user as"

- The user needn't scroll through every item in a list box to make a selection. Although the ListBox doesn't accept direct keyboard input, the user can type the first letter of an item in the List Box and it then automatically scrolls to the first item beginning with that letter. If the user types that letter again, the List Box scrolls to the next item beginning with that letter, and so on. For instance, we could have a list box containing the 50 states in the United States. If a user types the letter N, Nevada would appear at the top of the list, as it is the first item in the list beginning with N. If the user types N again, then the highlighted entry would change to New Jersey, the second item in the list beginning with N.

- The items in a list box can be sorted alphabetically, by setting the Sorted property to True.

There were no other questions about the ListBox, so I distributed the next exercise.

Exercise 5-2 Add a List Box Control to the China Shop Form

In this exercise, we add a list box to the China Shop's form.

1. Use one of the three techniques from the previous exercise to place a list box on the form. Be careful because the list box and the combo box look similar in the toolbox. If you are unsure which control is which, hold your mouse pointer over the control and Visual Basic will display a ToolTip. Notice, when you place a list box on the form, Visual Basic assigns it the name ListBox1. This name appears as an item in the list box itself. Don't worry about this for the moment because we'll update the properties of this control later.
2. Make sure the list box is correctly placed and properly sized according to our design sketch, remembering to take into account the contents it'll display.
3. Your form should now look similar to this illustration. Again, don't worry if it doesn't match mine exactly.

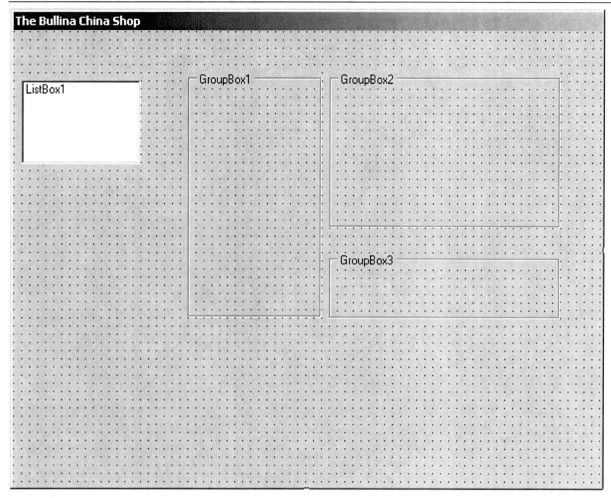

4. Finally, save the China Shop Project by clicking the SaveAll button on the toolbar.

Discussion

Again, no one had major problems. One student had resized his toolbox, so only a few controls were displayed. We corrected this problem easily by expanding the Toolbox exactly as we would a normal window, and then everything was fine.

The Label Control

"We'll use the Label control to display information to the user," I said, "The Label control is ideal for displaying information to the user—and there's no way for the user to change the information displayed in one."

We reviewed the sketch of the China Shop interface and determined we would need two labels: one to display the date and time, and another to display the actual sales quotation.

"How does the information get into a label?" Barbara asked. "The Label control," I said, "contains a property called "Text," which determines what's displayed in the label. Like most properties, that property can be set either at design time or at run time."

No one else had a question, so I distributed this exercise.

Exercise 5-3 Add Label Controls to the China Shop Form

In this exercise, we'll add two labels to the China Shop's form.

1. Place two labels on the form, using our sketch as a guideline for their location and dimensions. The first label needs to be placed in the upper right-hand corner of the form to display the date and time. The second label needs to be placed in the bottom portion of the form to display the sales quotation. Notice Visual Basic assigns the names of Label1 and Label2 to these controls.

2. Your form should look similar to this illustration.

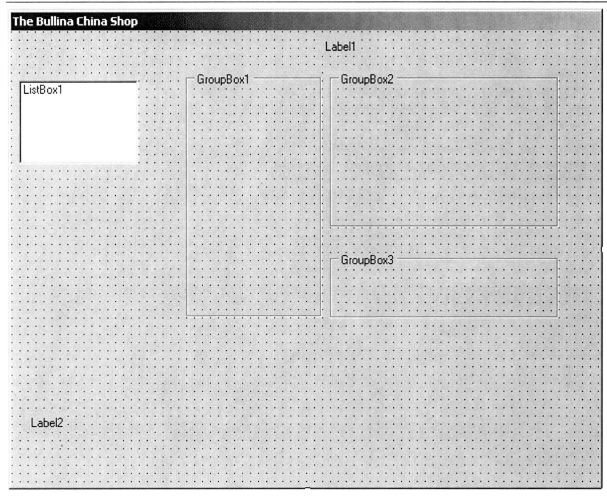

3. Don't forget to save the China Shop Project by clicking the SaveAll button on the toolbar.

The Button Control

"What's next?" Dave asked. "I'm really enjoying this."

I suggested we place the Button controls on the form next. "In previous versions of Visual Basic, Button controls were called Command buttons," I said. "Button controls are used to initiate some sort of action and, because of that, lots of code is usually in their Click event procedures."

I pointed out that when a user clicks a button, the button changes appearance slightly and appears to have been pressed down. When the user releases the mouse button, the Button control reverts to its normal appearance.

"I noticed the Button control also displays text," Rhonda said. "Does that mean it has a Text property?"

"Yes, it does," I replied.

I told everyone that by the end of today's class, we would adjust one of the properties of the Button control—the Text property—and two properties of the form that related to the Button controls—the AcceptButton and CancelButton properties of the form.

"What do those properties have to do with the Button control?" Linda asked.

"Interesting you should ask, Linda," I replied. "In previous versions of Visual Basic, each Button control had a Default and a Cancel property. If the Default property of the Button control was set to True, then when the user pressed ENTER, Visual Basic behaved as if the user had clicked the Button control designated as the default. Another property, the Cancel property, works in a similar way except it uses the ESCAPE key. If the user presses ESC, Visual Basic behaves as if the user has clicked the Button control designated as the Cancel button."

"And now this has changed?" Linda persisted.

"That's right, Linda," I said. "Now the form has two properties—AcceptButton and CancelButton—in which we specify the Button controls on the form we want as the AcceptButton and CancelButton buttons."

"Makes sense to me," Dave said.

No one seemed to have any problems dealing with the Button control and so, once again, we reviewed the sketch of our interface, and determined we would need two Button controls: one captioned Calculate and the other Reset. We had a brief discussion concerning the AcceptButton and CancelButton buttons, finally deciding that if the user presses ENTER, this should be equivalent to clicking the Calculate button. We also agreed that if the user presses ESC, this should be equivalent to clicking the Reset button. I promised we would make the appropriate property changes before the end of today's class.

With no other questions, I distributed this exercise.

Exercise 5-4 Add Button Controls to the China Shop Form

In this exercise, we add two Button controls to the China Shop's form.

1. Place two Button controls on the form, using our sketch as a guideline for their location and dimensions. As was the case with the other controls we've placed on the form, Visual Basic assigns the names of the controls for us—in this case, Button1 and Button2.

2. Your form should now look similar to the following illustration.

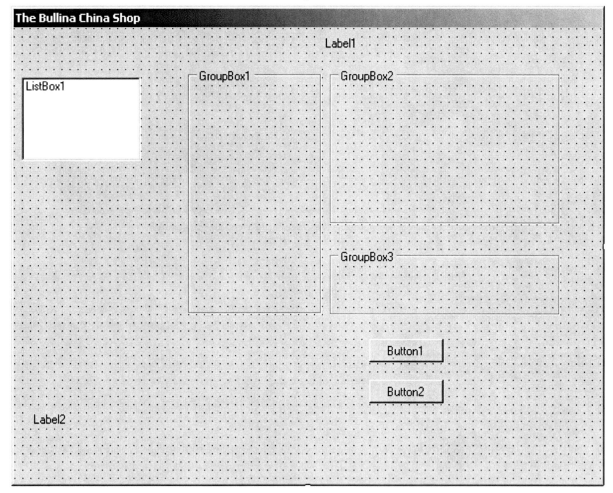

3. Save the China Shop Project by clicking the SaveAll button on the toolbar.

The CheckBox Control

I suggested we next work on the CheckBox control.

"I've been experimenting with this control a little bit," Ward said, "and it confuses me."

I explained I didn't think the CheckBox control itself was confusing as much as how CheckBoxes work in unison.

"The CheckBox control," I said, "enables the user to give a True/False, Yes/No, or On/Off answer. The CheckBox either displays a check mark or not. If the CheckBox has a check mark, this indicates a True, Yes, or On answer. If the CheckBox doesn't have a mark, this indicates a False, No, or Off answer."

I continued by saying that in Visual Basic terms, when a check mark is present, the CheckBox control's Checked property is set to True; otherwise, it's set to False.

"So when the user clicks a CheckBox," Linda said, " the check mark appears. If the user clicks it again, the check mark disappears?"

"That's right," I replied, "I call it a Toggle control. Click it once and it's checked on. Click it again and it's checked off."

"Suppose we have more than one CheckBox?" Ward asked. "Do I remember hearing or seeing something about the user not being able to select more than one CheckBox at once?"

"No Ward," I replied. "I believe you're thinking of the radio button—and we'll examine that in a moment. Any number of CheckBox controls can be selected at one time."

As an example, I displayed a CheckBox group containing four categories of sports on the classroom projector.

"As you can see," I said, "three of the CheckBoxes are selected."

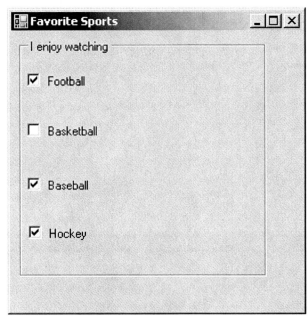

I continued by stating that I thought the CheckBox control was also an ideal way for the customer to select china items in the China Shop Project. The customer needs to make six separate Yes/No decisions about items. If the customer wants to include an item of china in the price quotation, all he or she needs to do is click the CheckBox and that item of china is selected and our program then knows the customer answered 'Yes' to that china item. If the customer changes his or her mind, clicking the CheckBox again deselects that item.

"How will our program know if a check mark is in the CheckBox?" Bob asked.

"Later on," I said, "when we start writing code, we'll see that we can examine properties of Visual Basic controls while the program is running. All we need to do is examine the Checked property of the CheckBox."

"We have quite a few CheckBoxes," Kate said, "so how will the program know which CheckBox we're examining?"

"Good question," I said. "We need to identify each CheckBox uniquely by assigning each CheckBox a different name—and we'll do that by specifying the Name property of each of our CheckBoxes."

I then explained we were going to place the CheckBox indicating a Complete Place Setting on our form first. I also cautioned everyone that they were about to see one of the few 'picky' attributes of Visual Basic. Whenever you place a control inside a container control, such as a GroupBox, you absolutely must use the click-and-drag technique for control placement because the double-click method doesn't work and it results in the control being placed 'underneath' the GroupBox.

Exercise 5-5 Add a CheckBox Control to the China Shop Form

In this exercise, we add one CheckBox to the China Shop's form.

1. Place a CheckBox control on the form within GroupBox3, sizing it roughly according to the following screenshot. It's important that you don't use the double-click method here (use either of the other two methods) because the

CheckBox must be explicitly drawn within the GroupBox. You should notice that Visual Basic has automatically given the CheckBox a name of CheckBox1, but the name CheckBox1 only appears if you draw the control large enough. . (If you have trouble re-sizing the CheckBox, it may be because its AutoSize Property is set to True--set it to False.)

2. It is vitally important that the CheckBox is contained within the GroupBox. To verify this, select the GroupBox and drag it. If the CheckBox is contained within the GroupBox, the CheckBox will move with it.

3. Save the China Shop Project by clicking the SaveAll button.

Discussion

I took a quick look around the computer lab to see how everyone was doing. Because most of the students had been double-clicking controls on to the form in the previous exercises, they were a bit unsure using one of the other two techniques. All in all, though, they were doing fine.

"That technique for ensuring the CheckBox is contained within the GroupBox is a life saver," Linda said. "I was certain I'd placed my CheckBox within the GroupBox, but when I moved the GroupBox, the CheckBox didn't move at all!"

I had to agree. Whenever you're working with container controls, such as the GroupBox, it's important to make sure that any controls you place within the container control are really contained in there.

"I wanted to let everyone know," Dave said, "that, just for the heck of it, I set the GroupBox's Visible property to False and not only did the GroupBox disappear when I ran the program, so did the CheckBox, just the way you said it would!"

I knew our next exercise, adding the remainder of the CheckBoxes to our form, would be a tedious one, so I called for a break. When everyone returned, I handed out the following exercise.

Exercise 5-6 Add the Remainder of the Checkboxes to the China Shop Form

In this exercise, we place the six CheckBox controls to represent china items on the China Shop's form.

1. Either select the CheckBox control in the toolbox and carefully draw it within GroupBox1, or click-and-drag the CheckBox control into GroupBox1. Visual Basic automatically assigns it the name CheckBox2. Make sure you resize it, so you can fit five other CheckBoxes within the GroupBox as well, and ensure that the CheckBox is truly contained by the GroupBox. (If you have trouble re-sizing the CheckBox, it may be because its AutoSize Property is set to True--set it to False.)

2. Use the same method you used in Step 1 to add the remaining five CheckBoxes to GroupBox1. These CheckBoxes will be named CheckBox3 through CheckBox7. Don't worry about their names—we rename them later. Remember to use the Format | Align menu item to align the controls along its left borders. You can also use the Format | Vertical Spacing menu item to space them an equal vertical distance apart. When you finish, your form should look similar to this screenshot.

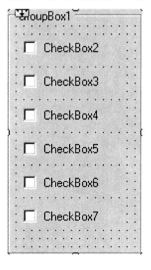

3. Save the China Shop Project by clicking the SaveAll button on the Visual Basic Toolbar.

Discussion

Despite my fear that some students would misplace their CheckBox controls outside the GroupBox, no one in the class had any problems, so we moved on to the RadioButton control.

The RadioButton Control

"Like the CheckBox control," I said, "the RadioButton control enables the user to give a True/False, a Yes/No, or an On/Off answer. In previous versions of Visual Basic, option buttons were called radio buttons. They're called radio buttons because they mimic the behavior of old-time radios, where you pushed a button to select a channel. On a radio with five buttons, one button was always selected, but never more than one."

"The radio button is displayed on a form with a caption and a circle next to it, and the radio button is selected when the user clicks their mouse on it. Once selected, the radio button displays a small, black circle in it. The difference between a radio button and a CheckBox control is its group behavior. The user can select only one radio button in any one group, whereas, as we saw previously with the CheckBox control, the user can select any number of CheckBoxes within a group."

"I'm not certain what you mean by a group?" Rhonda said.

"Good question, Rhonda. A CheckBox Group or a RadioButton Group," I said, "is a set of check boxes or radio buttons bounded by a container, such as a form or a GroupBox. If, on your form, you have three RadioButtons in a single GroupBox, you have only one group of RadioButtons and the user can select only one RadioButton within them."

"Is it possible to have more than one group?" Linda asked.

"Yes, it is," I said. "For instance, suppose you have six radio buttons on your form, but three are contained in GroupBox1 and three are in GroupBox2—therefore, you have two RadioButton groups."

"I see," Ward said. "Now does that mean the user can select one radio button from within GroupBox1 and one radio button from within GroupBox2?"

"Exactly, Ward," I said, as I displayed the following example on the classroom projector.

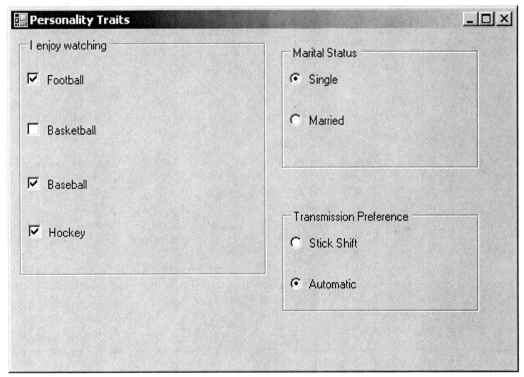

"Here we have a form with three GroupBoxes," I continued, "with two RadioButton groups and one CheckBox group. Notice the difference in the behavior of the CheckBoxes and the RadioButtons; more than one CheckBox can be selected at once, but only one RadioButton per group can be selected."

I said that I thought the RadioButton control was a perfect way for the user to specify a quantity selection in the China Shop project. The customer may only select a single quantity selection from four possible values.

"Does the radio button have a Checked property," Linda asked, "like the CheckBox control does?"

"Good question," I said. "Yes it does—like the CheckBox control, it the radio button is selected, its Checked property is True—if it isn't selected, its Checked property is False."

I then distributed this exercise to the class.

Exercise 5-7 Add a Radio Button to the China Shop Form

Add a Radio Button to the China Shop Form

In this exercise, we place four radio buttons to represent possible quantity selections on the China Shop's form.

1. Either select the RadioButton control in the toolbox and carefully draw it within GroupBox2, or click-and-drag the RadioButton control intro GroupBox2. Visual Basic automatically assigns it the name RadioButton1. Make sure you resize the RadioButton control, so you can also fit three other radio buttons within the GroupBox and ensure the radio button is truly contained within the GroupBox. (If you have trouble re-sizing the RadioButton, it may be because its AutoSize Property is set to True--set it to False.)

2. Use the same method you used in Step 1 to add the remaining three radio buttons to GroupBox2. These radio buttons will be named RadioButton2 through RadioButton4. Don't worry about their names—we'll rename them later. Remember to use the Format | Align menu item to align the controls along its left borders. You can also use the Format | Vertical Spacing menu item to space them an equal vertical distance apart. When you finish, your form should look similar to this screenshot.

3. Save the China Shop Project by clicking the SaveAll button on the Visual Basic Toolbar.

Discussion

We'd been doing pretty well, but quite a few students failed to hit the mark with this exercise. As sharp as they had been in placing CheckBoxes in the various GroupBoxes, this seemed to be just the opposite. Several students totally failed to follow the instructions for the radio buttons and, for whatever reason, 'double-clicked' four controls directly from the toolbox on to the form.

As you can imagine, this took some time to straighten out. As I'm fond of saying, though, true learning sometimes comes at the expense of frustration. Everyone who had problems understood immediately where they'd gone wrong and, now, they were confident.

"What should we do now?" I asked.

"Take a break," Linda said, smiling.

"That's not quite what I was thinking," I said, "although that is a good idea. Even better, let's take a moment to admire your work. You're all doing well and this interface is shaping up quite nicely. In fact, it won't be long before we're finished."

I asked everyone to take a well-earned break. "When you return from break," I said, "I'll have a surprise for you."

The PictureBox Control

When the class returned from break, I told everyone I'd wanted to give them a chance to work with graphics of some kind, but nothing in our initial interface design had warranted using them anywhere.

"But, during the week," I said, "I called Mr. Bullina and ran this idea by him. I told him I thought it would be a great idea to display a picture of the china pattern after the customer made his or her brand selection."

This possibility elicited a positive response from everyone in the classroom—graphics are fun, after all—and we quickly decided to add this feature to our interface.

"Where will we display the china pattern?" Barbara asked. "On the form—or within a PictureBox control?"

"Let's discuss that," I replied. "As we saw in an earlier class, we can display graphics on the form, but we can also display them in a PictureBox control."

"What kinds of graphic files can we display on the form or in a PictureBox control?" Dave asked.

I pulled out my Visual Basic reference manual to double-check.

"Graphic sources include bitmaps, icons, or metafiles, as well as enhanced metafiles, JPEG, or GIF files. These terms might not mean much to you at the moment, but these cover nearly every kind of graphic you might want to put into a project," I said.

I warned everyone that my programming abilities far outweighed my artistic ones, but I assured them that, in the right hands, Visual Basic is capable of displaying outstanding and powerful graphics.

"There must be disadvantages to using the form to display graphics," Ward said, "otherwise, there wouldn't be a PictureBox control."

"You're right, Ward," I replied. "The PictureBox is a powerful control—perhaps second only to the form itself in functionality. But, the biggest advantage to using the PictureBox control is the capability to fine-tune exactly where your graphics will appear on the form. This should come in handy when we display an image of the customer's china selection."

I then distributed this exercise for the class to complete.

Exercise 5-8 Add a PictureBox Control to the China Shop Form

In this exercise, we place a single PictureBox control on the China Shop's form.

1. Place a PictureBox control on the form (it appears as a mountain and sun icon in the Visual Basic Toolbox). Because this control didn't appear on our original sketch, my suggestion is to place it somewhere under the ListBox. Unlike the other controls you placed on the form, no obvious hint will exist as to what Visual Basic has named the PictureBox control. If you check out the control's properties, however, you'll see it has been named PictureBox1.
2. Your form should look similar to this screenshot. Again, it needn't match mine exactly.

3. Save the China Shop Project by clicking the SaveAll button on the toolbar.

Discussion

The class didn't have any problems with the exercise and no one had any questions after they completed it.

"Only two more controls," I said, "and we'll be done placing controls on our form."

The ColorDialog Control

"The next two controls," I said, "the ColorDialog Control and the Timer control, are both invisible to the user at run time. However, they're both vitally important to the operation of the China Shop program. We need to include the ColorDialog Control to enable the user to change their preferred colors, while the Timer control will be used to display the date and time."

No one had any questions.

"Great," I said, "now let's add the ColorDialog Control to the form."

"Will the user of the program see the ColorDialog Control?" Linda asked.

"That's a great question, Linda," I said. "In previous versions of Visual Basic, so-called invisible controls like the ColorDialog Control and the Timer control would appear on the design-time form, but be invisible at run time. The latest version of Visual Basic enables you to place these invisible controls on the form but, instead of the controls appearing on the form, they appear in a window pane called the Component Tray, beneath the design-time form in the IDE. You'll have a chance to see for yourself when you complete the next exercise."

I then distributed this exercise for the class to complete.

Exercise 5-9 Add a ColorDialog Control to the China Shop Form

In this exercise, we add a ColorDialog Control to the China Shop's form.

1. Add a ColorDialog Control to the form. The placement of the ColorDialog Control on the form isn't at all important because Visual Basic will place the control on the Component Tray (a window pane beneath the design-time form), as shown in the following illustration. Although it's not obvious, Visual Basic will name the control ColorDialog1.

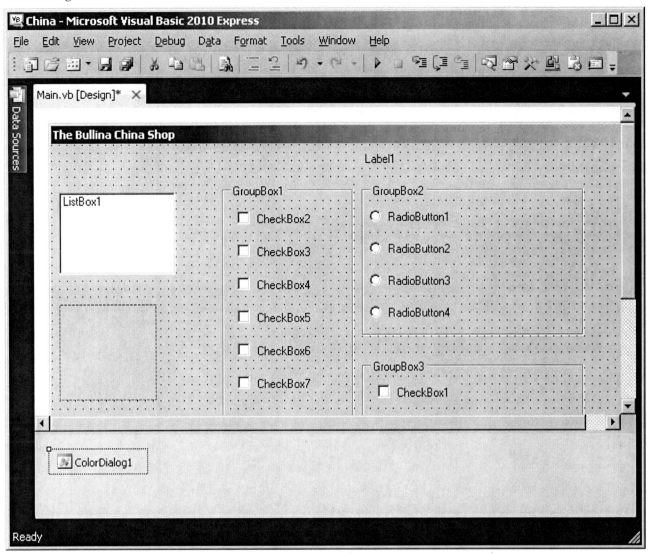

2. Save the China Shop Project by clicking the SaveAll button on the toolbar.

The Timer Control

No one had any major problems placing the ColorDialog Control on the form—although one or two students did have trouble locating the ColorDialog Control in the Visual Basic Toolbox, and one student forgot the control wouldn't 'show up' on the design-time form. Once we solved these minor problems, it was time to move on to the Timer control.

"Just like the ColorDialog Control," I said, "the Timer control is invisible both at design time and at run time."

"What's the purpose of the Timer control?" Chuck asked.

"The Timer control," I replied, "is used to execute code placed in its Tick event procedure. This execution takes place at regular intervals, based on the value of its Interval property. The Interval property value is expressed in milliseconds, so a value of 1,000 is equal to 1 second. If you want to trigger the Tick event every tenth of a second, you would set the Interval property equal to 100—to trigger it every ten seconds, set the Interval property to 10,000."

I looked for signs of confusion, but there were none. I continued by saying the uses for the Timer control are virtually limitless.

"The Timer control," I said, "is a popular control with programmers who write game programs. In the China Shop Project, we use the Timer control to display a running display of the date and time."

"What do you mean by a *running display*?" Peter asked.

"I mean a date and time that continuously changes," I said. "Or, I should say, changes every second or so. Eventually, we'll place code in the Tick event procedure to display the date and time. Because the Tick event procedure will be triggered every second; the minutes and seconds on the display will appear to continuously change."

No one else had a question, so I distributed this exercise.

Exercise 5-10 Add a Timer Control to the China Shop Form

In this exercise, we add a Timer control to the China Shop's form.

1. Add a Timer control to the form. The placement of the Timer control on the form isn't important because Visual Basic places the control on the Component Tray (a window pane beneath the design-time form), as shown in the following illustration. Although it's not obvious, Visual Basic will name the control Timer1.
2. Your form should now look similar to this screen.

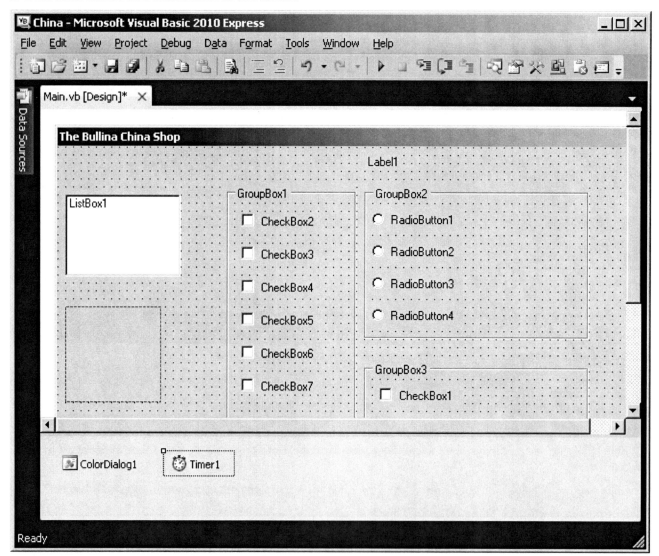

3. Click the SaveAll button on the toolbar to save the project.

Discussion

"Congratulations," I said to the class, "you've just completed the China Shop interface. You definitely deserve a pat on the back and a well-earned break. But we're not done yet—we haven't completed Steps 4, 5, and 6 of my ten-step plan for a successful Visual Basic development project."

I reminded everyone of my ten steps for successful Visual Basic development, which we examined earlier in the class. So far, we'd completed the first three steps. We had developed a Requirements Statement and sketched the user interface during our second class meeting. We had just completed Step 3, which is to use the Visual Basic IDE to create the user interface. Now it was time for Steps 4, 5, and 6. These are to run the program, admire our work (always important!), and observe the default behavior of the user interface.

Let's Run the China Shop Project!

"There's quite a bit of life in this program already," I explained. "Even though we haven't coded anything yet, the form and the controls on it come complete with a lot of built-in behavior. I have an exercise here for you, which asks you to run the program and observe the default behavior of the controls. Then, after that, we'll begin to adjust some of the properties of the interface."

Exercise 5-11 Run the China Shop Project

1. Test the changes you made to the China Shop form by running the project. Click the Start button on the toolbar or select Debug | Start from the Visual Basic Menu Bar.
2. Let's take some time now to examine the China Shop program in action. Visual Basic gives you some clues that you're now in the run-time environment. First, the run-time form should appear and its caption should read Bullina China Shop. Second, if you look on the toolbar, you'll notice the Start button has been disabled. Finally, notice the IDE's title bar now says [run] instead of [design].
3. When your project is running, notice the ListBox is now empty. The name of the control, which appears as an item of the ListBox in the design-time environment, has now disappeared.
4. Click the CheckBox in GroupBox3. When you first click it, a check mark appears but, if you click again, it disappears. Notice also that you can click the caption of a CheckBox to select it, as well as the CheckBox itself.
5. Click several of the CheckBoxes in GroupBox1. Notice that any number of them can be selected at one time.
6. Click the radio buttons in GroupBox2. Notice when the form is first displayed, none of the radio buttons are selected but, as soon as you click one of them, it becomes selected. Click another radio button and it becomes selected, in the process 'deselecting' the previous one. Once a radio button that's part of a RadioButton group has been selected, there is no way to 'deselect' all of them. As was the case with the CheckBoxes on the form, you can also click a radio button's caption to select it.
7. Click the Button controls. Notice, when you click either one of the two buttons, the button appears pressed. When you release the mouse button, it reverts to its 'unpressed' look.
8. Notice no evidence exists of a ColorDialog Control or a Timer control in the run-time environment.
9. Stop the program by selecting Debug | Stop Debugging on the Visual Basic Menu Bar.

Discussion

My students took some time observe the default behavior of the form and the controls on it—and I believe I detected some obvious pride in what they had done. No one had any major problems—they had taken their time completing the exercises and had paid careful attention to the details that reduce problems down the road. A few students took this opportunity to resize some of their controls—to expand or contract the size of the GroupBoxes. Quite a few students—even Lou, who earlier in the class had been pretty skeptical about the default behavior I had been harping on—expressed some surprise as to how functional the program was already. I asked if anyone thought any changes needed to be made to their interfaces. Barbara reminded us all that we still needed to develop a menu.

"You're right, Barbara," I said, "and we'll do that later in the class. But, for now, the absence of a menu won't impact our ability to calculate a sales quotation for our customer—and that'll be our primary focus during the next few weeks of class. Anything else?"

There were no other suggestions.

"In that case," I said, "we have now completed the first six steps of my ten-step plan for the successful development of a Visual Basic Project. Now it's time to discuss and complete Step 7, which is to enhance the interface, if necessary, by modifying the properties of the form or its controls. But first, we need to take another break."

Common Properties of the Controls in the China Shop Project

"Okay," I said after we all returned, "it's time to start adjusting some of those properties I was referring to earlier as we placed our controls on the form. Before we start changing properties, though, I think discussing them first is a good idea. Let's begin our discussion by looking at the properties every control in the China Shop Project possesses. Then, we'll look at the unique properties of each control. Let's start with the most basic of properties, the Name property."

The Name Property

"Every object in Visual Basic has a Name property," I said. "The Name property is the way Visual Basic identifies an object."

"I know we've gone over this before," Rhonda said, "but the Name property isn't the same name we specify when we save our project, is it?"

"No, it's not, Rhonda," I said. "In Visual Basic, the Name property is the internal name by which Visual Basic identifies our controls. When you save your Visual Basic program, you're saving a solution, a project, and any form files you created—and these are saved as external disk files on your hard drive. The names of those files, although they might be the same as the Project's Name or the form's Class Name, aren't related."

I cautioned my students never to change the name of a control after writing code for any of the control's event procedures. "If you do that," I said, "the code you wrote for the event procedure with that combination of control name and event will no longer be executed when the event is triggered because the control now has a different name. In effect, you'll orphan the code, although you can fix it pretty easily by cutting-and-pasting the code from the old event procedure to the new one."

"Are there any rules for naming the Name property?" Bob asked.

"Good question Bob, and, yes, there are," I said. "The Name property can be up to 40 characters. It must begin with a letter. The Name property can contain letters, numbers, and the underline character, but it cannot contain any other punctuation characters."

"Can the Name Property contain a space?" Linda asked.

"No, the Name property cannot contain a space character," I replied. "Use the underscore to break up long names."

I reminded the class about the Hungarian notation we had discussed the previous week. "According to Hungarian notation," I said, "each control should be named with a character prefix—I prefer three characters—that describes the object's type, followed by a reasonable description of the object. That's why we named the China Shop's Class Name as Main. We'll be naming the controls of the China Shop project in a similar manner."

There were no more questions about the Name property, so we moved on to the Text property.

The Text Property

"Nearly every control on the China Shop form has a Text property," I said. "The form, CheckBox, Button control, GroupBox, Label, Menu, and RadioButton all have a Text property. In previous versions of Visual Basic, the Text property was called the Caption property and, frequently, you'll hear the identifying text in the Text property referred to as the control's Caption. The Text property identifies the object to the user of your program by showing some text on the form to identify it."

> **NOTE: The Label control's Text size is unlimited. For all other controls that have a Text property, the limit is 255 characters.**

"Some students get the Name and Text properties confused," I said. "The Name property is used to identify the object for Visual Basic and, for the Name property, we use Hungarian notation. The Text property, on the other hand, is used to identify the object to the user and can contain virtually anything that makes it useful to the user—including spaces."

I then displayed the design-time China Shop form on the classroom projector and noted the default captions Visual Basic had assigned our controls—captions we'd change shortly to make them more descriptive.

"As you can see," I said, "each object's caption is displayed in a slightly different way. For instance, the form's caption is displayed in its title bar—the Button control's caption is displayed in the middle of the button."

I reminded everyone that in our second class meeting, we discussed the concept of access key, sometimes known as hot keys for controls. "You can create an access key for a control," I said, "by using a special feature of the Text property. To create an Access Key, you need to place an ampersand (&) character immediately before the character in the caption you want to identify as the access key. For example, to assign the letter O as the Access key in the caption of a Button control, you enter &OK into its Text property."

I suggested that at this point, we had exhausted the coverage of the common properties of the Form and controls.

CheckBox Properties

"We've already discussed the Checked property of the CheckBox," I said. "That property, plus the Name and Text properties, are the only properties of the CheckBox we'll work with today. For that reason, I'm going to ask you to complete this exercise."

"Do you mean with all those properties in the Properties window," Linda asked, "we'll only be modifying three properties?"

"That's right, Linda," I said. "In general, you needn't change a lot of the properties of the controls to get the behavior you want."

I then distributed the following exercise.

> **CAUTION: Because your user interface is just the way you want it, prior to starting this exercise, a good idea would be to lock your controls, so you don't accidentally move them out of their desired location. Remember, to do this, select Format | Lock Controls from the Visual Basic Menu Bar or right-click your form and select Lock Controls.**

Exercise 5-12 Change the Properties of the CheckBox Controls

In this exercise, you will change the Name and Text properties for the seven CheckBoxes contained on the China Shop form.

1. Bring up the Properties window, by selecting the control and pressing F4.

2. Use the following table to make changes to the CheckBox currently named CheckBox1, which appears inside GroupBox3.

Property	Value	Comment
Name	chkCompletePlaceSetting	Hungarian Notation
Text	Complete Place Setting	Provides an identifying caption for the CheckBox

3. Use the following table to make changes to the CheckBox currently named CheckBox2, which appears inside GroupBox1.

Property	Value	Comment
Name	chkPlate	Hungarian Notation
Text	Plate	Provides an identifying caption for the CheckBox

4. Use the following table to make changes to the CheckBox currently named CheckBox3, which appears inside GroupBox1.

Property	Value	Comment
Name	chkButterPlate	Hungarian Notation
Text	Butter Plate	Provides an identifying caption for the CheckBox

5. Use the following table to make changes to the CheckBox currently named CheckBox4, which appears inside GroupBox1.

Property	Value	Comment
Name	chkSoupBowl	Hungarian Notation
Text	Soup Bowl	Provides an identifying caption for the CheckBox

6. Use the following table to make changes to the CheckBox currently named CheckBox5, which appears inside GroupBox1.

Property	Value	Comment
Name	chkCup	Hungarian Notation
Text	Cup	Provides an identifying caption for the CheckBox

7. Use the following table to make changes to the CheckBox currently named CheckBox6, which appears inside GroupBox1.

Property	Value	Comment
Name	chkSaucer	Hungarian Notation
Text	Saucer	Provides an identifying caption for the CheckBox

8. Use the following table to make changes to the CheckBox currently named CheckBox7, which appears inside GroupBox1.

Property	Value	Comment
Name	chkPlatter	Hungarian Notation
Text	Platter	Provides an identifying caption for the CheckBox

9. Save the China Shop Project by clicking the SaveAll button on the toolbar.

10. Run the program and pay particular attention to the captions of the CheckBox controls. Here is a run-time illustration of how the China Shop form should look with the changes you've made to your CheckBox controls.

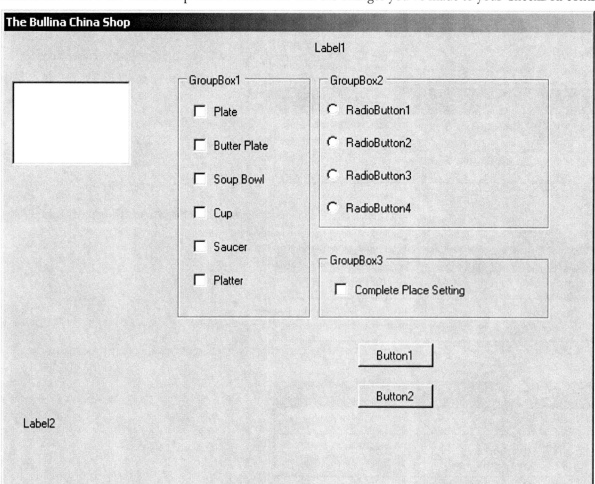

Discussion

The exercise to modify our CheckBox properties was fairly long, so I gave my students about 15 minutes to complete it. As they were completing it, a number of them told me they were having trouble changing the properties of the correct control—something I hadn't anticipated.

"How can I find the Properties window for the correct control?" Linda asked.

"You can do that in a number of ways," I said. "Probably the easiest way, and the method I use all the time, is to select the control with your mouse, then bring up the Properties window by pressing F4. Another method, although probably more confusing to beginners, is to select the control from the Properties window itself by finding it in the Object drop-down ListBox."

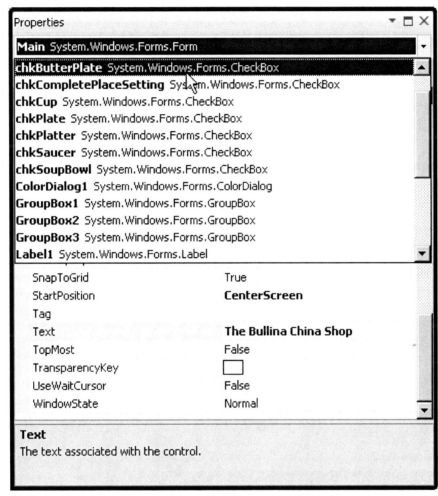

Aside from these minor problems, eventually everyone was able to change the CheckBox properties. Now, it was time to move on to the Button controls.

Button Control Properties

"The Button controls," I said, "have only two properties that we'll change—the Name and Text properties. But, if you recall our discussion of the AcceptButton and CancelButton properties of the form, we'll also be making changes to those two properties of the form as soon as we change the Name properties of our two Button controls. Although they're no longer properties of the Button control, this is the appropriate place to discuss the AcceptButton and CancelButton properties of the Form a little more."

The AcceptButton Property of the Form

"The only control in Visual Basic with a AcceptButton property is the form," I said.

"Is that the property of the form that designates a Button control on the form as the AcceptButton button?" Dave asked. "That is to say, it causes Visual Basic to treat the press of the ENTER key the same as if the user clicked that Button control?"

"That's perfect, Dave," I said. "I couldn't have said it better myself!"

"Can you explain to me again why we would want to do this?" Ward asked. "What's the big deal about the ENTER key. Why can't the user simply click the button?"

I explained that many users of Windows programs are still very much keyboard-oriented—in the past, many DOS programs made the press of ENTER a central part of their functionality. Designating a AcceptButton Button control can provide a 'comfort level' to the customers of the China Shop who are more familiar with DOS programs than they are with Windows program.

"Also," Lou pointed out, "some users are physically impaired and might be unable to use a mouse—yet they can still press ENTER on the keyboard!"

"That's an excellent point, Lou," I said. "In fact, Microsoft's recommendations have always been to design your program so it can be used without a mouse—and the China Shop program will be no different. If the user needs to, our program can be used without a mouse—all of the controls on our form can be reached via the TAB key and selected using the SPACEBAR."

"That's amazing," Valerie said. "I didn't realize that."

I continued by noting that only one Button control on a form can be designated as the AcceptButton button. Earlier in the day, we had suggested the CalculateButton control should be the default—the customer could then initiate a price calculation by either clicking the Calculate button or pressing ENTER.

"Are there any guidelines," Valerie asked, "as to which button on the form should be the AcceptButton button?"

"Let common sense be your guide," I replied. "Never make the AcceptButton button something associated with an irretrievable or noncorrectable action, such as deleting files. Given a choice, make the AcceptButton button the most intuitive, safe operation available."

The CancelButton Property of the Form

"The only control in Visual Basic with a CancelButton property is the form," I said. "The CancelButton property is similar to the AcceptButton property of the form. Designating a Button control as the CancelButton equates the press of ESC to the click of that button. Again, the reasoning behind designating a Button control as the CancelButton is the same as that for the AcceptButton property—having one provides a comfort level to those users who are either more comfortable using keys on the keyboard or who, for physical reasons, cannot use a mouse."

I pointed out that, as was the case with the AcceptButton property, only one Button control on the form can be designated as the CancelButton. Previously in the class, we decided that the ResetButton control should be designated as the CancelButton—whose purpose it would be to reset the controls on the China Shop form, so they'd be ready for a fresh price calculation.

No one had any more questions, so I distributed this exercise.

Exercise 5-13 Change the Properties of the Button Controls

In this exercise, we change some of the properties for the two Button controls on the China Shop form.

1. Use the following table to make changes to the Button control currently named Button1. At this point, without code in the click events of the btnCalculate or btnReset Button controls, it's impossible to verify either their AcceptButton or CancelButton behavior.

Property	Value	Comment
Name	btnCalculate	Hungarian Notation
Text	Calculate	Provides an identifying caption for the Button

2. Use the following table to make changes to the Button control currently named Button2.

Property	Value	Comment
Name	btnReset	Hungarian Notation
Text	Reset	Provides an identifying

		caption for the Button

3. Click the SaveAll button on the toolbar to save the project.

4. Run the program, paying particular attention to the captions of the Button controls.

5. Here's a run-time illustration of how the China Shop form should look now with the changes you just made to the Button controls.

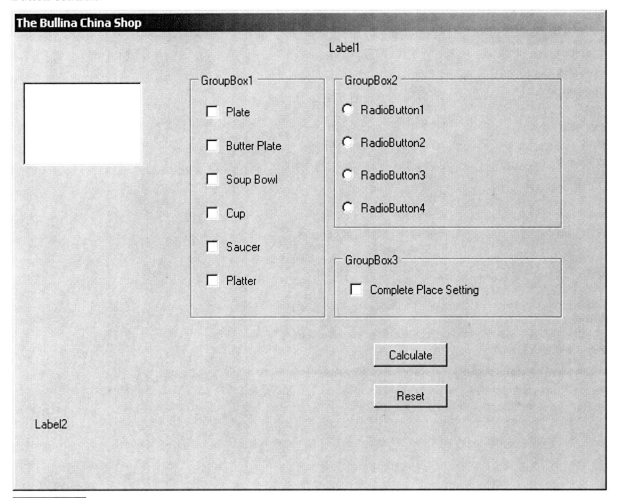

Discussion

No one had any problem changing properties of the Button controls—by now, everyone was getting pretty comfortable changing properties.

"We still need to designate the AcceptButton and CancelButton buttons for the form," I said. "Here's an exercise to do that."

Exercise 5-14 Change the AcceptButton and CancelButton Properties of the Form

In this exercise, you change the AcceptButton and CancelButton properties of the form.

1. Bring up the Properties window for the form and designate its AcceptButton property as *btnCalculate*. Be sure to choose the Button control from the drop-own ListBox.

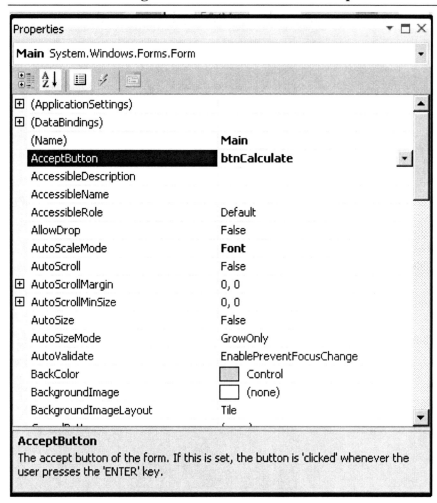

2. Bring up the Properties window for the form and designate its CancelButton property as ***btnReset***. Be sure to choose the Button control from the drop-down ListBox.

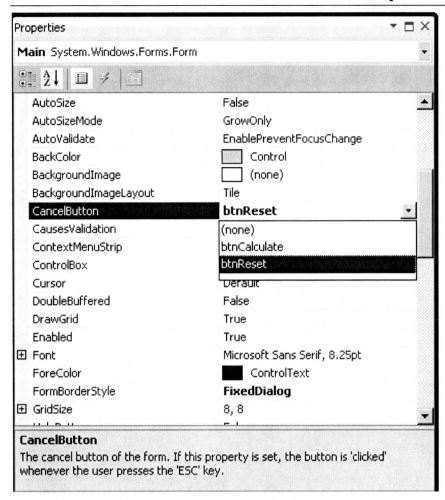

NOTE: At this point, without code in the Click event procedures of the btnCalculate or btnReset Button controls, it's impossible to verify either their AcceptButton or CancelButton behavior. We'll do that later in the course.

3. Click the SaveAll button on the toolbar to save the project.

Discussion

Again, no one had any major problems completing this exercise—although I did spy a student or two attempting to type the names of the two Button controls into the AcceptButton and CancelButton properties—a bad idea when the drop-down ListBox can ease that task. We then moved on to a discussion of the ColorDialog Control.

ColorDialog Properties

"Most beginner programmers," I said, "when they first start working with the ColorDialog Control believe it does a lot more for them than it really does. The ColorDialog Control does a nice job of enabling the user to make a choice from a wide range of color selections but, after that, it's up to you—the programmer—to do something with that color selection. We learn more about that when we start to look at Visual Basic coding."

"Should we be aware of any properties of the ColorDialog Control?" Linda asked.

"Good question, Linda," I said. "In prior versions of Visual Basic, working with the ColorDialog Control was a lot more difficult than it is now—for one thing, it performed a bunch of different functions. But the Visual Basic version of this control is simple to work with and the only property we need to change is the Name property."

"What about the AnyColor property?" Chuck asked. "What does that do for us?"

"If you set the AnyColor property of the ColorDialog control to True," I replied, "the user can then create a custom color of their own. If the AnyColor property is set to False, then they can choose a color only from a standard palette of colors. I don't mind if you folks want to set the AnyColor property to True—but I'd advise against it."

No one had more questions, so I distributed this exercise.

Exercise 5-15 Change the Properties of the ColorDialog Control

1. Use the following table to make changes to the ColorDialog Control currently named CommonDialog1.

Property	Value	Comment
Name	dlgChina	Hungarian Notation

2. Save the China Shop Project by clicking the SaveAll button on the toolbar.

Discussion

This was about as easy an exercise as we would have the entire course. I pointed out to my students that it would be some time before we had a chance to see the ColorDialog Box in action. No one had any questions, so we moved on to a discussion of the properties of the GroupBox.

GroupBox Properties

"We have a little work to do with our GroupBoxes, but not much," I said. "All we need to do is change their captions—I should say their Text properties—from their default values to something a little more meaningful." I then distributed the following exercise for my students to complete.

Exercise 5-16 Change the Properties of the GroupBoxes

In this exercise, we change two properties of the three GroupBoxes on the China Shop form—the Name and Text properties. Be careful you selected the GroupBox control and not one of the controls within it.

1. Use the following table to make changes to the GroupBox currently named GroupBox1.

Property	Value	Comment
Name	grpItems	Hungarian Notation
Text	China Items	Provides an identifying caption for the GroupBox

2. Use the following table to make changes to the GroupBox currently named GroupBox2.

Property	Value	Comment
Name	grpQuantity	Hungarian Notation
Text	Quantity	Provides an identifying caption for the GroupBox

3. Use the following table to make changes to the GroupBox currently named GroupBox3.

Property	Value	Comment
Name	grpCompletePlaceSetting	Hungarian Notation
Text	Complete Place Setting?	Provides an identifying caption for the GroupBox

4. Save the China Shop Project by clicking the SaveAll button on the toolbar.

5. Run the program, paying particular attention to the captions of the GroupBoxes. Here's a run-time illustration of how the China Shop form should look now with the changes you just made to the GroupBox controls.

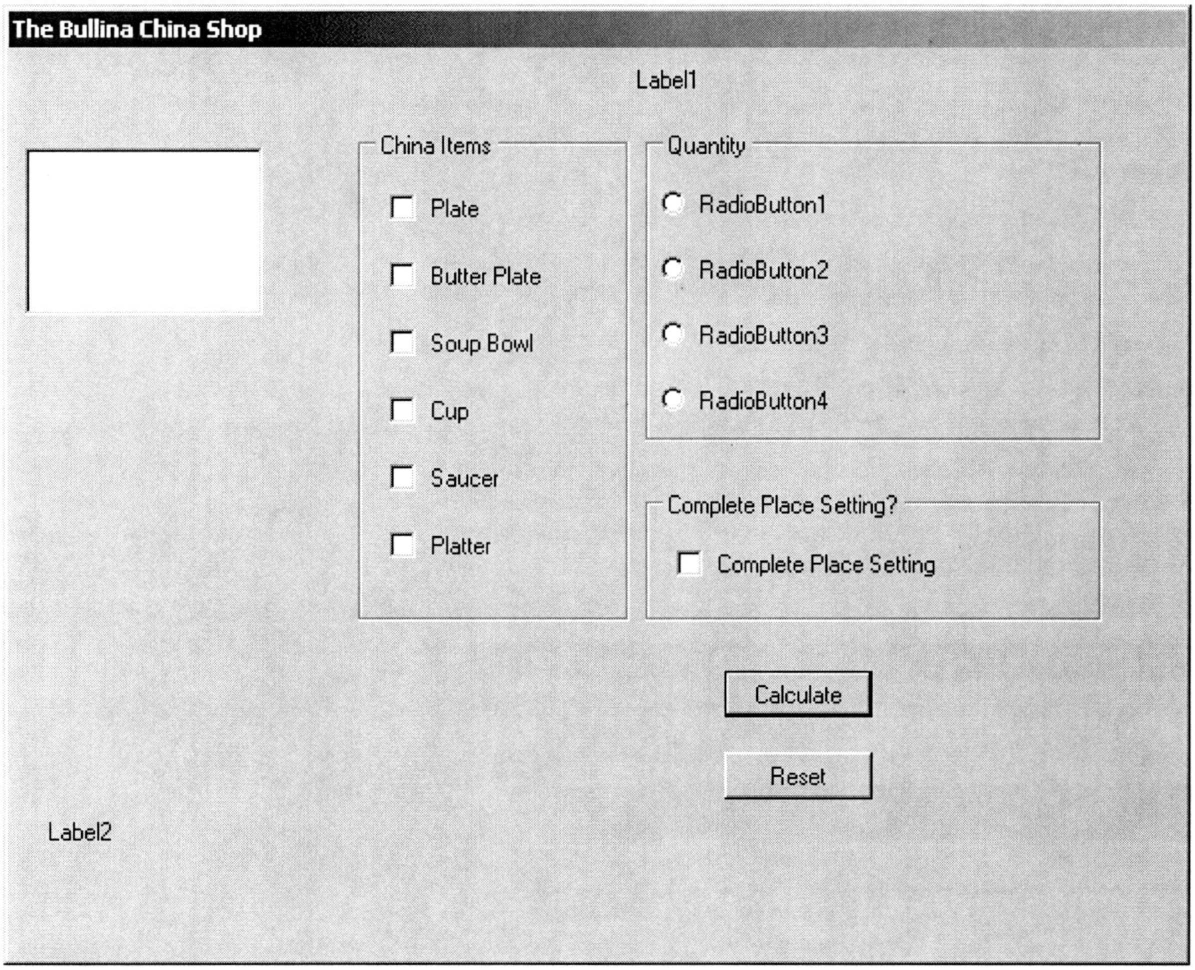

The Bullina China Shop

Label1

China Items
- ☐ Plate
- ☐ Butter Plate
- ☐ Soup Bowl
- ☐ Cup
- ☐ Saucer
- ☐ Platter

Quantity
- ○ RadioButton1
- ○ RadioButton2
- ○ RadioButton3
- ○ RadioButton4

Complete Place Setting?
- ☐ Complete Place Setting

Calculate

Reset

Label2

Discussion

"I had some difficulty," Rhonda said, "selecting the GroupBox controls to change their properties. I kept selecting one of the controls within the GroupBox."

"I know the feeling," I replied. "Selecting GroupBoxes can be a problem. I've had good success by clicking the borders of the GroupBox. In other words, stay away from the inside portion of the GroupBox. Another method you can use is to display the Properties window by pressing the F4 Function key, and then select the appropriate GroupBox from the object drop-down ListBox."

There were no questions, so we moved on to a discussion of the PictureBox control.

PictureBox Control Properties

"We'll only change two properties of the PictureBox control," I said, "the Name property and the SizeMode property."

The SizeMode Property

"When the customer makes a selection of a brand of china from the ListBox," I said, "we'll use the PictureBox control to display an image of the china pattern from a graphics file contained on our PC's hard disk drive. By default, when an image is displayed in a PictureBox control, the image is placed in the upper-left corner of the PictureBox, and any part of the image that's too large for the PictureBox control is cut off, or what's known in graphics' circles as cropped."

"That's not good," Chuck said. "Can we do anything about that?"

"You're right, Chuck," I replied, "that's not what we want to happen to the image of the customer's china pattern. We have several alternatives to this, however. We can set the SizeMode property of the PictureBox control from its default value of Normal to AutoSize, in which case the PictureBox control is resized to fit the image."

"I'd think that could wreak havoc on your interface design," Barbara said. "Do you mean the PictureBox control will change shape to accommodate the graphic?"

"Yes, that's exactly what happens" I said, "and we don't want that behavior either. I'm not sure what the dimensions of Mr. Bullina's graphics files are, but we can't afford to have our PictureBox control changing shape to accommodate them."

"Do we have another alternative?" Linda asked.

"Fortunately, we do, Linda," I replied. "We can set the SizeMode property of the PictureBox to StretchImage—in that case, the image changes its shape to accommodate the dimensions of the PictureBox control."

Everyone seemed to agree this behavior was ideal.

"To display an image on the form last week, we changed its Image property," Rhonda said after a moment or two. "Will we also change the Image property of the PictureBox control?"

"We will," I said, "but not at design time. Because the image we want to display in the PictureBox varies according to the customer's selected brand of china, we need to make the determination of the graphics file to load into the Image property of the PictureBox at run time and use a method called FromFile to load the Image property of the PictureBox dynamically at run time. For now, we'll leave the Image property of the PictureBox as is."

No one had other questions or comments, so I distributed this exercise for the class to complete.

Exercise 5-17 Change the Properties of the PictureBox Control

In this exercise, we change the Name and SizeMode properties of the PictureBox control on the China Shop form.

1. Use the following table to make changes to the PictureBox control currently named PictureBox1.

Property	Value	Comment
Name	picChina	Hungarian Notation
SizeMode	StretchImage	Resizes the graphic to fit the size of the PictureBox control; otherwise, the PictureBox control resizes to fit the size of the graphic.

2. Save the China Shop Project by clicking the SaveAll button on the toolbar. Until we write code to load a graphics file into the PictureBox control, there are no obvious changes to the PictureBox control. So, at this time, we're unable to check its behavior.

Label Properties

There were no questions or problems completing the PictureBox control exercise, so we moved on to a discussion of the Label control.

"We'll change three properties of our Label controls," I said, "the Name, Text, and AutoSize properties."

"What kind of caption are we setting for the Label controls?" Chuck asked. "I thought the captions for the Label controls would be displayed only when the program is running."

"You're right, Chuck," I said. "We won't specify a value for the Text property of the Label controls—we'll erase the default value that's already there. Remember, when the form is first displayed, we don't want anything displayed in either of the two label's captions."

"I thought we were using the Text property of Label1 to display the price quotation," Rhonda said, "and the Text property of Label2 to display the current date and time. How can we do that if the caption is empty?"

"We'll assign a caption to the Label controls at run time," I said, "but, first, we need to erase what's there."

The AutoSize Property

"AutoSize?" Dave asked. "That sounds suspiciously like the SizeMode property of the PictureBox control. Is it?"

"You're on the right trail, Dave," I said.

I then explained that the AutoSize property tells Visual Basic to resize the label based on the width of its Text property.

"That means the size of the Label control is determined solely by what's displayed in it. Is that right?" Linda asked.

"That's perfect, Linda," I said. "And because we don't know exactly what captions will be displayed in the Label controls at design time—because one label will display a price quotation and the other a changing date and time—setting the AutoSize property to True can ensure we don't accidentally 'chop off' some of the caption."

"Can you hit me with that again?" Ward asked.

"Sure thing, Ward," I answered. "For example, when our program is running, we assign a date and time to Label1's Text property, and a price quotation to Label2's Text property. Depending on the day of the year and the time of day, the number of characters in Label1's Text property can vary by several characters—the same is true of the number of characters in the price quotation."

"So, this is a formatting nicety?" Blaine asked.

"Not entirely," I said. "If we misjudge the size of the Label controls at design time, if the number of characters in the caption exceed the width of the Label control, some of the caption won't be displayed."

"I see now," Ward said. "That makes sense."

I warned everyone that as soon as they set the AutoSize property of the Label control to True, on the form, the Label control would immediately shrink to apparently nothing. "When you see your Label control shrink like that," I said. "Don't worry about it. Once a value is assigned to its Text property, the Label control automatically adjusts its size, and it looks fine."

"How do we assign a blank value to the label's Text property?" Bob said.

"Good question, Bob," I replied. "All we need to do is select the Text property in the Properties window by double-clicking it, and then press BACKSPACE. That clears the default entry."

No one had other questions, so I distributed this exercise.

Exercise 5-18 Change the Properties of the Label Controls

In this exercise, we change the Name, Text, and AutoSize properties for the two Label controls on the China Shop form.

1. Use the following table to make changes to the control currently named Label1.

Property	Value	Comment
Name	lblDateAndTime	Hungarian Notation
AutoSize	True	To accommodate a date and time that can have different sizes
Text		Null caption (select all the text in the Text property, and then press the BACKSPACE key---not the SPACEBAR

2. Use the following table to make changes to the control currently named Label2.

Property	Value	Comment
Name	lblPrice	Hungarian Notation
AutoSize	True	To accommodate a date and time that can have different sizes
Text		Null caption (select all the text in the Text property, and then press the

		BACKSPACE key---not the SPACEBAR

3. Save the China Shop Project by clicking the SaveAll button on the toolbar.

4. Run your project and ensure the captions for both labels are now both Null. Here's a run-time illustration of how the form should look after you've made these changes to the Label controls—notice the Label controls seem to have disappeared!

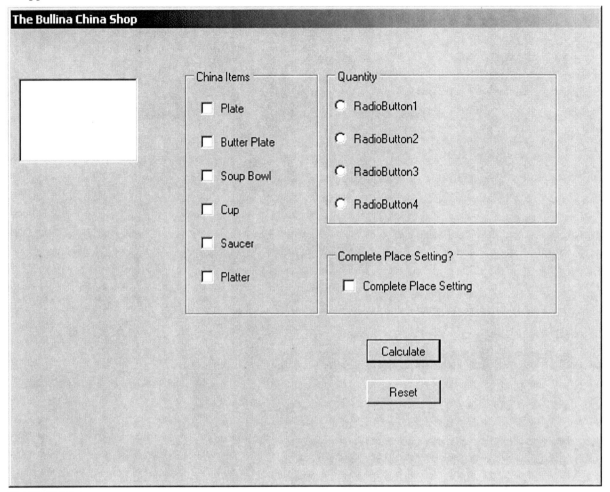

Discussion

Almost immediately on making changes to the properties of their Label controls, several students were in a panic—apparently they missed my comments about the Label controls shrinking after we set the AutoSize property to True. As a result, they thought something had gone horribly wrong after setting the property. Thank goodness, I caught them before they did something drastic that students are apt to do—start the project from scratch!

"Because we set the Text property of the Label controls to null," I said, "and because the AutoSize property was set to True, Visual Basic automatically resized the Label control to a zero width—so they both seemingly disappeared. But don't worry—they're fine."

No one else had problems completing this exercise, so we moved on to a discussion of the ListBox control.

ListBox Properties

"We'll only change one property of the ListBox;" I said, "the Name property."

"What about the items in the ListBox?" Bob asked. "Shouldn't we add the china brands to the Items property of the ListBox?"

"Good for you, Bob," I said, "I see you've been reading ahead. You're right—there is an Item property and we could add the china brands to the ListBox using that property. But, as is the case with the PictureBox control, we'll add items to the ListBox dynamically at run time. For now, we'll leave that property alone."

"Can you be a little more specific?" Linda pressed. "How will items be added to the ListBox?"

"When our program first starts up," I said, "we'll use the AddItem method of the ListBox to add each of the brands to the ListBox as an item. Eventually, toward the end of the course, we'll read the items from a disk file maintained by the staff of the China Shop and load them into the ListBox that way."

No one else had a question, so I distributed this exercise for the class to complete.

Exercise 5-19 Change the Properties of the ListBox Control

In this exercise, we change the Name property of the ListBox control on the China Shop form.

1. Use the following table to make changes to the ListBox control currently named List1.

Property	Value	Comment
Name	lstBrands (begins with the lowercase Letter L— NOT the number ONE)	Hungarian Notation

2. Save the China Shop Project by clicking the SaveAll button on the toolbar.

Discussion

Only one person had a problem with this exercise—he tried to type the numeral 1 as the first character of the name of the ListBox, instead of the letter l. Dave immediately pointed out that as soon as he changed the name of the List Box from List1 to lstBrands, the default item displayed in the ListBox changed in the same way. With no further questions or comments, we moved on to a discussion of radio buttons.

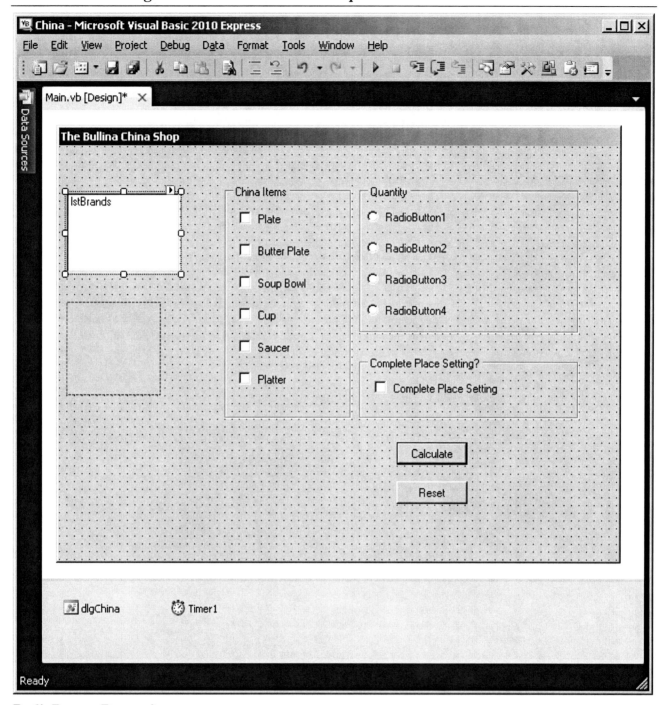

RadioButton Properties

"We'll change two properties of the RadioButton controls," I said, "the Name and Text properties." I then distributed the following exercise and asked everyone to complete it.

Exercise 5-20 Change the Properties of the Radio Buttons

In this exercise, we change the Name and Text properties of the four RadioButton controls on the China Shop form.

1. Use the following table to make changes to the radio button currently namedfRadioButton1, which appears inside the Quantity GroupBox.

Property	Value	Comment
Name	rad8	Hungarian Notation
Text	8	Quantity of 8

2. Use the following table to make changes to the radio button currently named RadioButton2, which appears inside the Quantity GroupBox.

Property	Value	Comment
Name	rad4	Hungarian Notation
Text	4	Quantity of 4

3. Use the following table to make changes to the radio button currently named RadioButton3, which appears inside the Quantity GroupBox.

Property	Value	Comment
Name	rad2	Hungarian Notation
Text	2	Quantity of 2

4. Use the following table to make changes to the radio button currently named RadioButton4, which appears inside the Quantity GroupBox.

Property	Value	Comment
Name	rad1	Hungarian Notation
Text	1	Quantity of 1

5. Save the China Shop Project by clicking the SaveAll button on the toolbar.
6. Here's a run time illustration of how the main form should look with the changes you've made to the RadioButton controls.

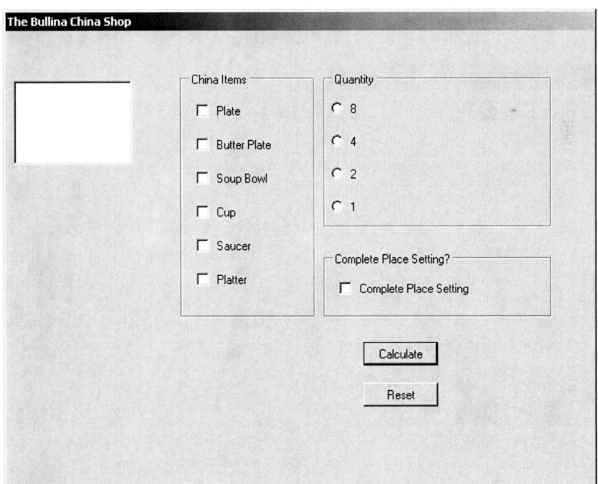

Discussion

The class had quite a few problems with this exercise—I think the naming conventions caused some students to become confused, and several questioned the wisdom of naming our controls rad8, rad4, rad2, and rad1, respectively— suggesting it might be better to name them radEight, radFour, radTwo, and radOne instead. I reminded the class that, in most cases, the names we select for our controls must be typed in to the Visual Basic code window in one way or other—ending the RadioButton controls with a number as opposed to the written number, which, to me, is much easier to type. With no more questions, now it was time to move on to the Timer control.

Timer Properties

I looked at the clock and said, "We're almost done, in fact, the Timer control is the last control we'll discuss today—in fact, aside from the Menu control that we'll examine in a few weeks, it's the last control we'll place on the form. We'll change just two properties of the Timer control—the Name and the Interval properties."

The Interval Property

"As you might recall from our earlier discussion," I began, "the Timer control executes code contained in its Tick event procedure at regular intervals according to a value found in its Interval property. In other words, the Interval property determines how often the Tick event procedure is triggered, ranging from one millisecond (a thousandth of a second) to the upper limit for an Integer data type, which is somewhere around 2.1 billion. Remember, the value in the Interval property is expressed in milliseconds, so an Interval value of 1,000 is equal to one second. Somewhere later in the class, we'll place code in the Tick event procedure to display the current date and time in the Text property of lblDateAndTime—with an Interval property of 1,000, the date and time will appear to be updated continuously."

There were no questions about the Timer control, so I distributed this exercise.

Exercise 5-21 Change the Properties of the Timer Control

In this exercise, we change the Name and Interval properties of the Timer control on the China Shop form.

1. Make the following changes to the Timer control.

Property	Value	Comment
Name	tmrChina	Hungarian Notation
Enabled	True	Enable the Timer Control
Interval	1000	Causes the Tick event to trigger every second.

2. Click the SaveAll button to save the China Shop Project. Until we write code and place it in the Tick event procedure of the Timer control, we won't be able to verify the changes we just made.

Discussion

Rhonda said it looked like we were nearly finished with the China Shop user interface.

"I agree, Rhonda," I said. "We're very close, almost to the point where we can pat ourselves on the back and admire our work. But, there is just one more thing to consider—the Tab Order of the controls on the form."

"Tab Order?" Mary asked.

Tab Order and the TabIndex Property

"Yes," I said. "Do you remember our discussion a few minutes ago when I said each control on our form can be accessed via the TAB key? Well, the Tab Order determines the order in which the controls on the form are accessed when the user presses TAB. The order of this access, also called focus, is determined by the TabIndex property of each control."

I saw some puzzled looks and decided to take another shot at my explanation.

"Only one control can have focus at one time," I said. "In Visual Basic, if the user presses TAB, focus moves from the control currently having it to the control next in the Tab Order—in other words, the control with the next highest value for its TabIndex property. If no control has a higher value for its TabIndex property, then the control with the lowest value of all the controls on the form receives the focus."

"What controls on the China Shop form have a TabIndex property?" Kate asked.

"The CheckBox, Button, GroupBox, Label, ListBox, and RadioButtons all have a TabIndex property," I said.

"How important is Tab Order?" Steve asked.

"Some users never press TAB," I answered, "but others, such as those who expect a certain kind of behavior from the ENTER and ESCAPE keys, probably will use TAB to move from control to control. If the Tab Order of the program isn't in a logical sequence, we'll end up with a few frustrated users."

I waited a few moment before continuing. "Another interesting point is the control with the lowest TabIndex value is the control that first receives the focus when the form is displayed at run time."

"A little earlier you mentioned that it's important for the Tab Order be in a logical sequence," Rose said. "What do you mean by that?"

"What I mean is this: the designer of the program should probably sit down with a user or a group of users and, together, determine what the logical sequence of controls the user is likely to select," I said. "For instance, will the customer select a brand of china first or first select a quantity? Once the quantity is selected, would he or she next select an item of china? That's what I mean."

"How does the TabIndex property originally get assigned?" Linda asked. "Does it have something to do with the order in which we place controls on the form?"

"That's right, Linda," I said, "The TabIndex property is determined by the order in which the controls are placed on the form. Additionally, by default, a GroupBox control has its own TabIndex value, which is a whole number."

"Can a GroupBox receive focus?" Dave asked.

"A GroupBox control itself cannot have focus at run time," I replied. "Therefore, each control within a GroupBox has its own decimal TabIndex value, beginning with .0. In fact, if you check the TabIndex values of the controls on the China Shop form, you can see chkPlate in the grpItems GroupBox has a Tab Index of 0.0 and rad8 in the grpQuantity GroupBox has a Tab Index of 1.0."

"I'm getting confused," Rhonda said. "Is there any way to see all of this?"

"You can check the individual TabIndex values for each of the controls," I answered. "Or, if you have Expert Settings enabled, you can select View | Tab Order from the Visual Basic Menu Bar . . ."

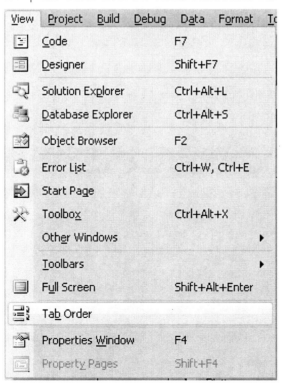

". . . which displays this window, showing you the Tab Order of all the controls on your form."

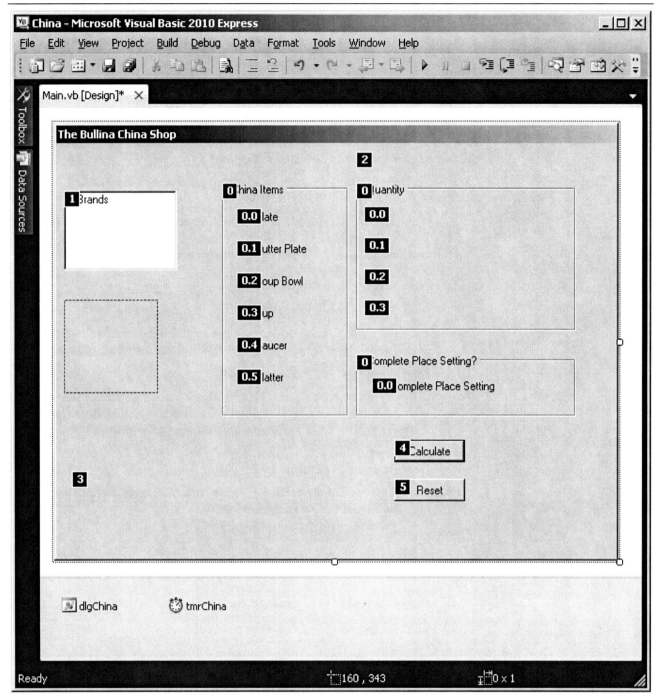

"So, in theory," Mary said, "this window is telling us the current Tab Order of the controls on our form?"

"That's right, Mary," I answered.

A Surprise Visit

While glancing toward the door of the classroom, I noticed a special guest had just arrived. No, it wasn't Bill Gates (maybe next class!), but it was the next best person—Joe Bullina. After I introduced him to the class, Joe thanked my students for the magnificent work he'd heard they were doing on his China Shop system—the class was thrilled to hear his praise.

"Joe," I said, "it's great to have you here. You're just in time to see the final stages of the China Shop User Interface development. In fact, your timing is perfect—we can really use your help here. We just began to work on determining what the logical Tab Order sequence for the program should be."

Everyone in the class seemed pretty surprised to find that Joe actually knew what we were talking about. What they didn't know was that Joe had been outside the classroom for the last 20 minutes or so, intently listening while we discussed the concepts of Tab Order. I asked Joe if he wouldn't mind sitting down at my classroom PC and putting the China Shop Interface we'd developed so far through its paces. I started the program—warning Joe that, at the moment, it was more of a prototype than anything else—and asked him to tab through the controls on the form.

"Hey, I love what I see here!" Joe said excitedly. As he worked with the interface, the students and I noted that the current Tab Order for the controls on the form was exactly as the Tab Order window had predicted.

1. The Plate CheckBox, chkPlate

2. The Butter Plate CheckBox, chkButterPlate

3. The Soup Bowl CheckBox, chkSoupBowl

4. The Cup CheckBox, chkCup

5. The Saucer CheckBox, chkSaucer

6. The Platter CheckBox, chkPlatter

7. The Complete Place Setting CheckBox, chkCompletePlaceSetting

8. The ListBox containing the china brands, lstBrands

9. The CalculateButton control, btnCalculate

10. The ResetButton control, btnReset

"What happened to the radio buttons?" Ward asked. "None of them received focus."

"Good observation, Ward," I answered. "The reason is none of the radio buttons were selected. Radio buttons behave in a funny manner when it comes to receiving the focus. In actuality, if one of the radio buttons in the group is selected, then that radio button will be active in the Tab Order. If none of the radio buttons is selected, the entire RadioButton group is skipped."

"Joe," I said, turning to Mr. Bullina, "can you come up with an ideal Tab Order for us?"

We gave Joe a minute or two to think about it, and this is what he came up with:

1. The ListBox containing the China brands, lstBrands

2. The Complete Place Setting CheckBox, chkCompletePlaceSetting

3. The Plate CheckBox, chkPlate

4. The Butter Plate CheckBox, chkButterPlate

5. The Soup Bowl CheckBox, chkSoupBowl

6. The Cup CheckBox, chkCup

7. The Saucer CheckBox, chkSaucer

8. The Platter CheckBox, chkPlatter

9. The quantity 8 RadioButton, rad8

10. The CalculateButton control, btnCalculate

"That's great, Joe," I said, as I turned to the class. "I hope you can all see the benefit of getting the user directly involved in this process. Of course, in hindsight, it makes perfect sense for the Calculate button to receive the focus after the china brand—one or more items of china and a quantity have been selected. Without Joe's help, though, we might have missed this altogether!"

"What about the Label controls?" Chuck asked.

"Those are inconsequential," I said. "Label controls themselves cannot receive focus."

"How can we change the Tab Order?" Linda asked. "Should we change the values of the TabIndex properties?"

"That's one way to do it," I said, "but the easiest way to change the Tab Order is to bring up the Tab Order window I displayed earlier—and click the controls in the order in which you want them to receive the focus."

"This I have to see," Ward said.

I then distributed the final exercise of the day to implement changes to the current TabIndex properties of our controls.

Exercise 5-22 Change the TabIndex Properties

In this exercise, you modify the TabIndex properties of the controls on the China Shop form.

1. Use the following table to make changes to the TabIndex properties of the controls on the China Shop form. In order to change the TabIndex properties of these controls, it may first be necessary to 'unlock' them if you followed my suggestion to lock them earlier.

Object	TabIndex Value
lstBrands	0
grpItems	1
chkPlate	1.0
chkButterPlate	1.1
chkSoupBowl	1.2
chkCup	1.3
chkSaucer	1.4
chkPlatter	1.5
grpCompletePlaceSetting	2
chkCompletePlaceSetting	2.0
grpQuantity	3
rad8	3.0
rad4	3.1
rad2	3.2
rad1	3.3
btnCalculate	4
btnReset	5
lblDateAndTime	6
lblPrice	7

You can either update the TabIndex properties by using the Properties window or, if you prefer, use the TabOrder window. Just click on the number with your mouse to advance it. When you finish, your Tab Order window should look like this.

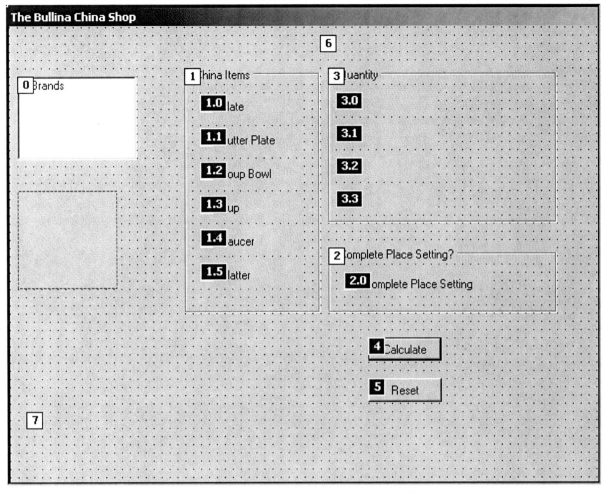

2. Save the China Shop Project by clicking the SaveAll button on the toolbar.

3. Run the program and observe the Tab Order of the controls by clicking on the Tab button on your keyboard.

Discussion

"Once you get used to it," Ward said, "that Tab Order window is great."

A few minutes later, Rhonda raised her hand.

"I have a question," Rhonda said. "These tabs are giving me problems. Every time I try to tab through the radio buttons, the only one I can tab 'to' is the quantity 8 button. What am I doing wrong?"

"That's the behavior of the radio buttons I mentioned earlier," I said. "In a RadioButton group, Visual Basic tabs to the radio button with the lowest TabIndex value in the RadioButton group. When you press TAB again, Visual Basic moves to the next control in the Tab Order outside the RadioButton group."

As the class wound down, Joe Bullina spoke.

"I want to thank everyone," Joe said, "for the fine job you're doing with this program. I can't tell you how excited I am to have such a fine group of people working on it, and I can't wait to get this up and running in my shop." With that, Joe excused himself. He had a meeting with an import dealer concerning a delivery of fine china. Before dismissing class for the day, I couldn't help but congratulate everyone myself. After only six weeks, we had completed the China Shop interface. We had come a long way and the fun was just beginning.

"Next week," I said, "we begin to write code!"

Summary

Believe it or not, we now have a working user interface. We've come a long way! We've looked at the Visual Basic Toolbox and placed all the necessary controls on the form of the China Shop Project. We then adjusted the properties of those controls and, like all good developers, we ran the program, admired our work, and prepared to code our program.

We've seen how to add controls to the form and change their properties. We also examined the most commonly used controls, such as the GroupBox, CheckBox, RadioButton and Label controls, and, one of the most important, the Button control.

Some users are more keyboard-oriented, so it's a good idea to assign common keys—such as ENTER and ESC—to often-used Button controls, using the AcceptButton and CancelButton properties, respectively. Also, consider the order the program cycles through the controls when you press TAB to make it more intuitive. This is done by setting the TabIndex property of each control and using the Tab Order window. Changing the TabIndex values for every control on the form is a fairly easy process.

Chapter 6---A First Look at Coding

In this chapter, we'll examine Visual Basic events in more detail and I'll introduce you to the Visual Basic Debugger. Most courses (and books) treat the Debugger as a tool to correct errors in your program instead of treating it as the great learning tool it can be. In my mind, the Debugger is like an MRI or CAT scan—it can allow a programmer (especially the beginner) to see and understand what's going on behind the scenes of their program. Today we'll also write our first piece of code for the China Shop Project.

"I think that you all now have an appreciation," I said, "for the fact that programming in Visual Basic is more than just writing code. After all, we've just spent two weeks working on our visual interface. For those of you who have been waiting anxiously to begin learning how to write code, today is that day."

Events and Event-Driven Programming

"When we write Visual Basic code," I said, "we place that code in event procedures, which are executed when Windows events are triggered. Although we've previously discussed Windows events, I want to take just a little more time to reinforce the concept of an event before we begin writing code."

In the Old Days...

Peter had a comment: "For those of us who programmed in the old days of DOS, it might be a good idea, prior to talking about Windows events, to talk about 'old time' programming."

Everyone agreed, and so I began to tell this story: "When I first started programming way back in 1974, procedural programming was really the only way to write a program."

"What's a procedural program?" Jack asked.

"A procedural program," I said "tells the computer exactly how to solve a problem, in a step-by-step manner. From the programmer's point of view, things were pretty simple. You knew what data to expect, where it would be found (usually a file on a mainframe computer), its exact format, and so on. With procedural programming, there were very few surprises—and very little user interaction."

I suggested that we analogize a procedural program to an old-time grocery store. If a customer wants to buy a pound of bacon, a dozen eggs, and two bananas, he or she might walk up to the counter, and hand a note to the grocery clerk with those items written on it. While the customer waits at the counter, the grocery clerk walks up and down the aisles of the grocery store, selecting items and putting them in a bag.

Having located all of the customer's desired items, the clerk places them on the counter for a quick examination and then rings them up. Suppose the customer didn't like the quality of the bacon or the color of the bananas? Then the clerk would obtain replacements, and the sales would be finalized. The chain of events for the purchase of the groceries, from the grocery clerk's perspective, would look something like this:

1. Obtain customer's note.

2. Walk down aisle 3.

3. Locate freezer compartment.

4. Obtain bacon from refrigerator compartment.

5. Walk up aisle 5.

6. Locate egg rack.

7. Obtain eggs from egg rack.

8. Walk down aisle 6.

9. Locate fruit bin.

10. Obtain two bananas from fruit bin.

11. Carry items back to front counter.

12. Place items on counter for customer's approval.

13. If anything is wrong with the items, find replacements, repeating appropriate steps above.

14. Ring up sale.

15. Collect customer's payment.

"As you can see," I said, "this method of purchasing groceries was very much a procedurally oriented approach, with very little room for flexibility. Most customers, given the choice, would prefer to roam the aisles of the grocery store on their own, taking as little or as much time as they need, judging the quality of the items for themselves. The grocery clerk, on the other hand, very much enjoyed the predictability of the procedural approach. With no customers permitted in the aisles of the store, the shelves were always in perfect order. There was less spillage and no pilferage. But in the end, this way of purchasing groceries went by the wayside. Customers simply prefer to shop their own way."

The Modern Approach

Just like the grocery clerk in the old-time grocery store, most programmers liked the predictability of procedural programming. From their point of view, it was easy to write programs when they knew what input their program would receive, where it was located, and what its format would be. As time passed, procedural programming languages allowed users to interact with them via terminals. But it was always on the terms of the program. Only certain data could be input by the user, and it always had to be input into predetermine locations or fields on the user's monitor. Just as was the case with the old-time grocery store customer, the user in the case of a procedural program wasn't fully satisfied.

I suggested that we compare the modern, event-driven approach of Windows programming to a modern self-service grocery store. Today, the customer might enter the grocery store with that same note listing bacon, eggs, and fruit, but instead of handing that note to a grocery clerk, the customer heads toward the groceries, walking the aisles of the store in any order they desire. If they meet a friend, they can chat for a while, unhurried by anyone. Some customers enjoy the freedom of making up their minds about their purchases as they go along. Instead of writing a list, they just drive up, grab a shopping cart, and begin walking up and down aisles, selecting items as they see them.

With the modern approach, the only thing the owner of the grocery store knows for certain is that the customer will eventually appear at one of the check-out lines with some items to ring up. Everything else in between is a big unknown, and quite honestly, of no concern to the owner of the store, provided the customer buys something. For instance, there's no way of knowing what aisle the customer started with, or whether they walked up and down each and every one. With this modern approach to grocery shopping, more customers are served in less time, and for the most part, they are much happier with the experience.

"So the bottom line," Linda said, "is that removing the procedural restrictions on the way the customer had to shop resulted in greater customer satisfaction."

"That's right," I agreed. "Of course, the modern approach makes managing the grocery store more difficult. Items on shelves may be in disarray shortly after they're placed there, and there's always the danger of pilferage. Removing tight control is not without its risks, but there's no argument that the customer is much happier this way—and that's the name of the game."

"How does this relate to programming?" Kathy asked.

"The theory behind event-driven programming, Kathy," I said, "is the same as the modern self-service grocery store. We don't force the user to perform functions in a predefined sequence of our choice. Instead, event-driven programs react to what the user wants to do and in the order that they wish to do it."

"Isn't that harder to program?" Chuck asked.

"Yes, it is, Chuck," I said. "Just like procedural programs, event-driven programs need to ensure that all the data they require is input, and that can be more difficult in an event-driven program. But if the user wants to choose an item of china before they select the brand, who are we to tell them they are wrong?"

What's an Event?

"I'm still a bit confused over this concept of events," Ward said. "How and when do events occur?"

"Events in a Windows program," I said, "occur as the result of one of three things:"

- The user does something to trigger an event.

- The operating system triggers an event.

- An event is triggered through Visual Basic code.

"There are many Windows events," I said, "and many of them are common to each of Visual Basic's objects. For instance, the Button control responds to a Click event procedure, as does the Form, the RadioButton, and the CheckBox. But not every object responds to every possible event. For instance, while virtually every object in Visual Basic does respond to a click by the user, the ListBox does not respond to the Click event. In today's class, we'll discuss the most common events in the Windows environment, and of course, we'll start coding the China Shop Project."

An Event or an Event Procedure?

"Is an event the same as an event procedure?" Rhonda asked.

"Not quite," I said. "An event is something that occurs in the Windows environment, and an event procedure is the code that executes when that event takes place. For instance, the Click event of a Button control named Button1 occurs when the user clicks on it with their mouse. This event in turn triggers the Button1_Click event procedure which is triggered as a result of the event happening. I know it sounds like I'm splitting hairs, but the distinction can be important."

I continued by explaining that every object in Visual Basic is preprogrammed to detect and respond to events. For every event to which these objects can react, there is an event procedure stub sitting behind the scenes into which the programmer can place code.

"So if the event occurs," Blaine said, "and the programmer hasn't placed any code in the event procedure, what happens? Nothing?"

"That's what most people think," I said, "but the correct answer is that the default behavior of the object occurs regardless of whether or not the programmer has inserted code into the event procedure."

An Example of an Event Procedure Stub

"I think this would make more sense to me if we could look at one of these event procedure stubs," Ward said. "Can we see one?"

I thought that was a good idea, and so I displayed the China Shop Project on the classroom projector, then double-clicked on the Calculate Button control and opened the Visual Basic code window.

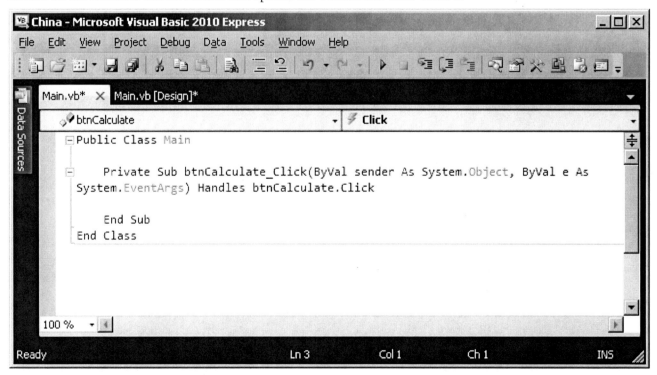

"Wow, is that confusing," Linda said.

"You're right, Linda," I replied, "the Visual Basic code window can be confusing. It wasn't always like this—previous versions of Visual Basic had a much cleaner look to the code window than Visual Basic does. But don't worry too much. Once you get used to it, you'll be fine. It's just a matter of concentrating on the parts of the code window that you should be writing in, and ignoring the parts that Visual Basic creates for you."

"What parts can we write in?" Chuck asked.

"Usually we write code only within event procedures," I said. "That would be the part between the lines of code that read Private Sub btnCalculate_Click and End Sub. Those lines of code comprise what is known as a procedure stub. As you can see, there's a blank line between them. That's where we write code of our own."

"When did that procedure stub get created?" Dave asked. "Was it when you double-clicked the button on the form?"

"That's right, Dave," I said. "When I double-clicked the Calculate button, Visual Basic assumed I wanted to create a procedure stub for the Click event procedure of the button. That's not the only way to create a procedure stub—for instance, I could have brought up the Visual Basic code window by selecting View | Code from the Visual Basic menu bar, and then selected the button in the Class Name drop-down list box, and then the Click event in the Method Name drop-down list box. Doing so would have created the same procedure stub you see here, but you'll see that in a moment when we create the procedure stub for the btnReset button."

I paused a moment before continuing.

"Let's get back to examining the procedure stub for the btnCalculate Click event procedure," I said. "Notice that the event procedure header consists of the words 'Private Sub' followed by the event procedure name, btnCalculate_Click. Notice also that there are a pair of parentheses following the event procedure name, and within the parentheses are what are known as arguments—pieces of information that are passed or sent to this Click event procedure when the user clicks the button. The Click event procedure of the Button control is passed two arguments, as you can see, named **sender** and **e**. We'll be talking about these arguments in a little more detail in our Intermediate Visual Basic class."

"It appears that your code window is wrapping your header line," Linda said. "Mine isn't. What am I doing wrong?"

"You're right, Linda," I said. "I narrowed the width of my code window, and when I did, the lines of code wrapped. Otherwise they would have scrolled beyond the right margin of the code window. This behavior is an optional setting. To turn it on, select Tools | Options | Text Editor | All Language | General, and specify Word Wrap there." I gave Linda and the rest of the class a chance to change that setting.

"So an event procedure stub is just an empty event procedure?" Ward asked.

"You can think of it that way. Notice that there is also a Click event procedure for the Reset Button control," I said as I selected btnReset from the Class Name drop-down list box and displayed its Click event procedure.

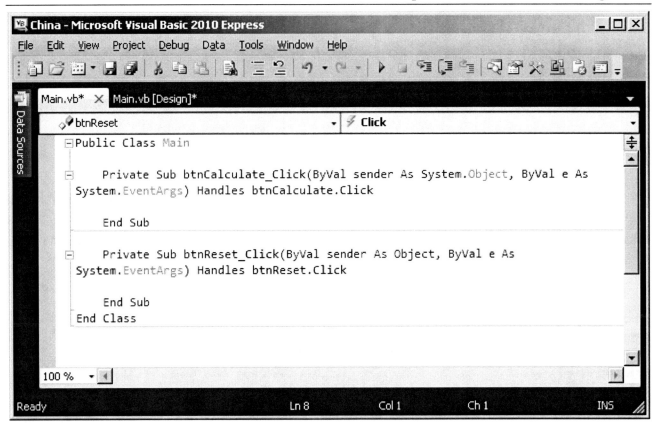

"I'm not sure I see any difference in this procedure stub from the previous one, other than its name," Rhonda said. "What is the difference?"

"The name is the difference, Rhonda," I said. "The code that we place in this event procedure will be executed whenever the user clicks the Reset button. The code in the other event procedure will be executed whenever the user clicks the Calculate button."

"Is that what the phrase 'Handles btnReset.Click' following the closing parenthesis of the procedure header means?" Chuck asked.

"Exactly, Chuck," I replied. "Visual Basic has automatically set this event procedure to handle the Click event for the Reset button. The Handles keyword is actually optional, although Visual Basic decided to add it to the end of the procedure headers for both buttons. Later on in the course you'll learn that you can create procedures of your own that don't necessarily belong to a particular event. If you wish, you'll be able to associate those procedures with a Visual Basic event. There's also an added benefit in that you can have the code in one event procedure handle the events of multiple controls."

"What do you mean?" Peter asked.

"For instance," I said, "we have six CheckBox controls on the China Shop form that represent different items of china. We might want to execute the same code whenever any one of those six check boxes is clicked. Rather than write the same code for six different Click event procedures, we could write code in just one of the CheckBox Click event procedures, and then modify the Handles clause of that event procedure to tell Visual Basic that it will be handling the events for the other five check boxes as well."

I gave everyone a chance to think about this. From the smiles on their faces I could tell I might be getting a bit ahead of myself.

"Can you go over the naming convention for a procedure header?" Kathy asked.

"I'd be glad to, Kathy," I said, as I displayed this code on the classroom projector.

```
Private Sub btnReset_Click(ByVal sender As System.Object, _
    ByVal e As System.EventArgs) Handles btnReset.Click
```

"The name of an event procedure is automatically created by Visual Basic. It is formed by combining the name of the object (in this case, btnReset), an underscore character (_), and then the name of the event (in this case, Click)."

"What does the word Private mean in the code?" Rhonda asked.

"Private refers to the event procedure's scope," I said. "Scope means the extent to which the procedure can be seen within your program. In Visual Basic, you can create a procedure with Private, Public, or Protected scope. In this course, all of our procedures will be created with Private scope."

I then asked everyone to be patient about scope. "We'll be discussing the scope of variables and procedures a little later in the class."

"How many event procedures will we be writing code for in the China Shop Project?" Linda asked.

The Events in the China Shop Project

"Linda, you must have read my mind," I said. "I was just about to say that I thought it would be a good idea if we briefly discussed the event procedures for which we will write code in the China Shop Project. Then we can actually begin to write some code."

I went on to explain that many beginner programmers feel the need to place code in every event procedure in their program and that simply isn't necessary.

"For each event in your program," I said, "there is set of built-in, default behaviors associated with it. It's only necessary to write code when you need to enhance the default behavior of the form or the controls on the form."

I then displayed this chart on the classroom projector.

Object or Control	Name	Event Procedures We Will Code	Comments
Form	Main	Load	Displays the china brands in ListBox
CheckBoxes	chkPlate, chkCup, etc.	Click	More on this later
	chkCompletePlaceSetting	Click	Will initiate selection of all china items except for Platter
Buttons	btnCalculate	Click	Initiates price calculation
	btnReset	Click	Resets controls to their startup state
ColorDialog	dlgChina	None	
GroupBox	grpPieces	None	
	grpQuantity	None	
	grpCompletePlaceSetting	None	
PictureBox	picChina	None	
Labels	lblDateAndTime	None	
	lblPrice	None	
ListBox	lstBrands	SelectedIndexChanged	Will initiate loading of china pattern graphic into PictureBox control
Menu	More on this later	Click	More on this later
RadioButtons	rad8, rad4, rad2,rad1	Click	More on this later
Time	tmrChina	Tick	Used to display date and time

"This is a list of all of the controls in the China Shop Project," I said, "and a list of the event procedures for those objects which I believe we will need to write code for. My guess, at this point, is that we'll be writing code for about 20 event procedures."

"I don't know about anyone else," Valerie said, "but that low number somehow surprises me. I thought we would be writing a lot more code."

"See what I mean?" I said. "That's the beginner's inclination. Believe me, if this were a C++ class or a Java class, you would be writing a bunch of code. But with Visual Basic, we need to write code only when it's necessary."

"Something else that I find interesting," Rhonda said, "is that it looks like we'll only be writing code that primarily responds to the Click events."

"That's a good observation, Rhonda," I said. "If you think about it, that makes a lot of sense. Since we are writing an event-driven program, and since it's the user who triggers the majority of events via a click of the mouse, it makes sense that the code we write will need to react to those clicks."

I waited a moment, and then suggested that now would be a great time to examine the events for which we would write code: the Click event, the Load event, the Timer event, and the SelectedIndexChanged event.

The Click Event

"In the China Shop Project, four different objects will react to the Click event: the Menu, the CheckBox, the Button control, and the RadioButton. Regardless of the object, the Click event is triggered when the user presses and then releases a mouse button over that object."

"Suppose you have a form that contains a Button control," Joe said, "and the user clicks the button. Are there two Click events triggered, one for the button and one for the form?"

"That's a good question, Joe" I said. "The answer is that there is only one Click event triggered. If the user clicks the button, the Click event procedure of the Button control is triggered. If the user clicks on the form itself, the Click event procedure of the form is triggered."

The Load Event

"In the China Shop Project," I said, "only the form reacts to a Load event, and it only occurs when a form first appears."

"Does the Load event happen when we first run our project?" Valerie asked.

"That's right, Valerie," I answered. "The form's Load event occurs when the project is first run."

"What kind of code will we place in the Load event procedure?" Dave asked.

"Typically, any code that is used to set up the display or the environment before the user first sees your interface," I answered. "Programmers call this housekeeping code. In the China Shop Project, we'll place code in the form's Load event procedure that will initialize the list box with the names of the brands of china for sale. We want those brands to be visible in the list box when the user first sees the China Shop Project's user interface."

"So the Load event procedure takes place before the form becomes visible," Rhonda said.

"Technically, that's right," I agreed, "although the whole process happens so fast you can't notice." I waited to see if anyone had any problems, but no one had any, so I continued on.

The SelectedIndexChanged Event

"Only the list box reacts to the SelectedIndexChanged event," I said, "and it occurs whenever the user clicks and selects an item in the list box. As you'll see a little later, we'll be able to easily determine which item in the list box has been selected, once this event triggers to alert us that the user has made a selection. I should point out that in previous versions of Visual Basic, the ListBox supported a Click event, but in Visual Basic, the event that tells us the user has made a selection in the list box is the SelectedIndexChanged event." We then moved on to the Timer control.

The Tick Event

"Only the Timer control reacts to the Tick event," I said. "The Tick event is triggered periodically, based on the Timer control's Interval property. We've already discussed how we'll use this event in the China Shop Project to display a running date and time."

I paused to see if any of the students had any questions about the controls we had discussed. No one did, and so I said, "I think at this point, it makes sense to begin to write some code!"

Writing Code

"The Visual Basic code window is really nothing more than an editor," I said, "just like Windows Notepad or Word. In the code window, we write code that becomes part of a procedure, usually (but not always) an event procedure."

I asked my students to verify that they had all properly retrieved the China Shop Project from their hard drive, as I distributed this exercise for them to complete.

Exercise 6-1 Add Code to the Load Event Procedure of the Form

In this exercise, you'll add code to the Load event procedure of the China Shop form to add china brands to the lstBrands list box.

1. Start up Visual Basic and open the China Shop Project you first saved in Chapter 5.
2. Double-click on the China Shop form, making sure you don't select one of the controls by accident. The Visual Basic code window will then appear.

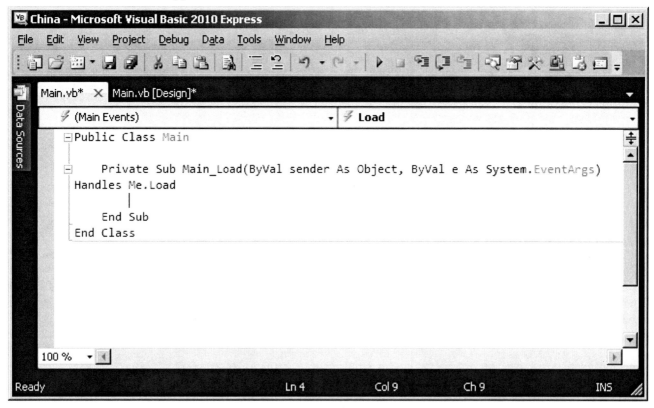

3. We want to insert some code into the Form's Load event procedure. Look for the empty line in the Load event procedure.

4. We'll use the Add method of the Items Collection of the ListBox (that's a mouthful, isn't it!) to add brands of china to the list box. Placing that code in the Form's Load event procedure ensures that when the China Shop program starts up the china brands will appear in the list box. To invoke a method in Visual Basic, we type the object name (in this case, lstBrands), followed by a period and then the method name. The Add method is a bit more complex than usual in that the Add method is actually a method not of the ListBox itself, but of a Collection called Items that belongs to the ListBox.

5. Click your mouse pointer on the blank line following the Load event procedure header and type **lstBrands** followed by a period in the code window. As soon as you type the period, Visual Basic should display a drop-down list box containing members (methods, properties, and events) of the ListBox control. This drop-down list box is called the AutoList Members window.

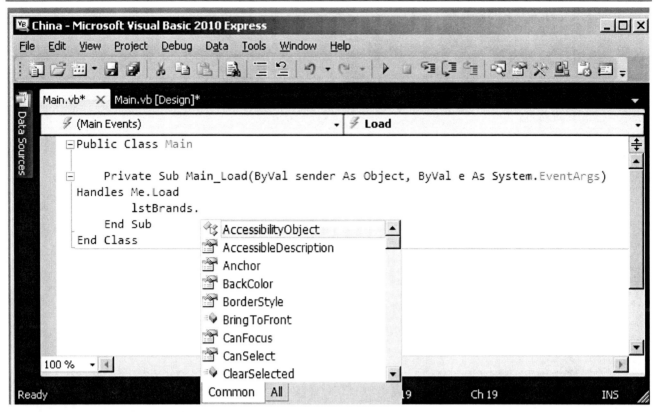

TIP: If you don't see the AutoList Members window, select Tools | Options | Text Editor | Basic | General. AutoList Members must be checked on in order for Visual Basic to display this list of properties, methods, and events.

6. The AutoList Members window (sometimes called Intellisense) can make our work much easier. Scroll down the AutoList Member window until you see Items.

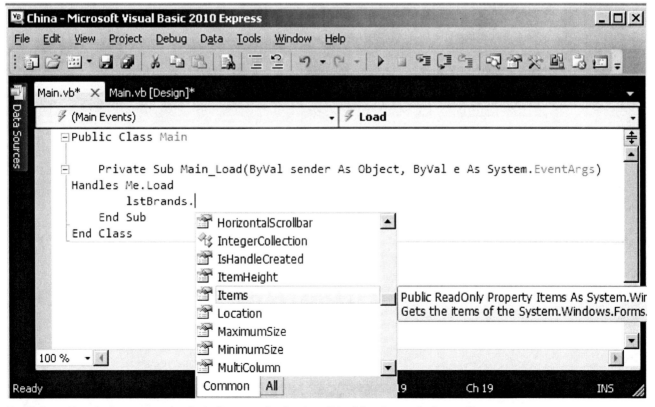

7. Click on Items, then type a period. Once again the AutoList Members window will appear.

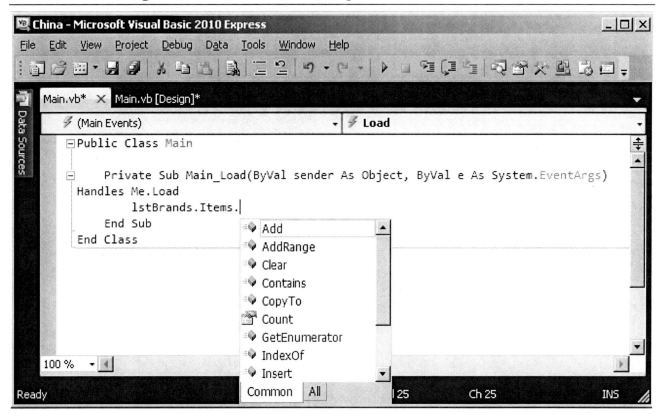

8. The Add method appears at the top of the AutoList Members window. At this point, you can type the method name yourself, use your mouse to select it, or press the TAB key and the word "Add" will be typed for you automatically in the code window.

9. We're not done yet. The Add method requires a single argument that tells Visual Basic what it is we want to add to the list box. In our case, it's the names of the three brands of china for sale in the China Shop program, and we'll need to code a separate Add method for each brand of china to be added to the list box. Complete the line of code by typing a space and Corelle, like this.

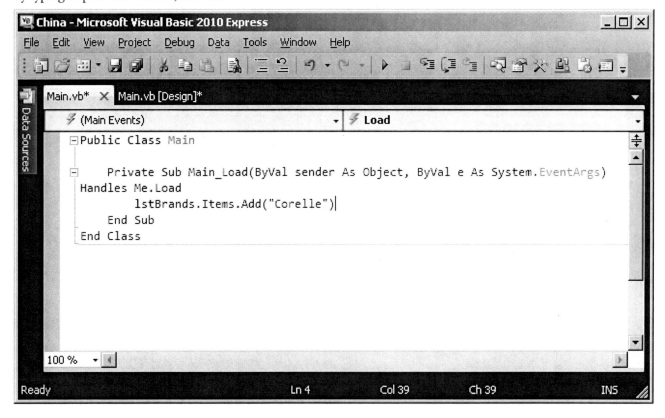

10. You'll notice that Visual Basic automatically places parentheses around the word "Corelle." This is fine (you could type it directly like that if you wish). Now repeat the process for Farberware and Mikasa so that it looks like this.

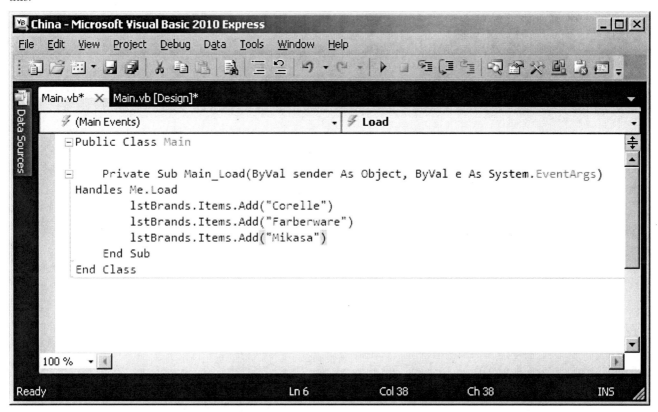

11. Save the China Shop Project by clicking SaveAll on the Visual Basic toolbar.
12. Run the program now. The China Shop form should appear with three brands in the list box.

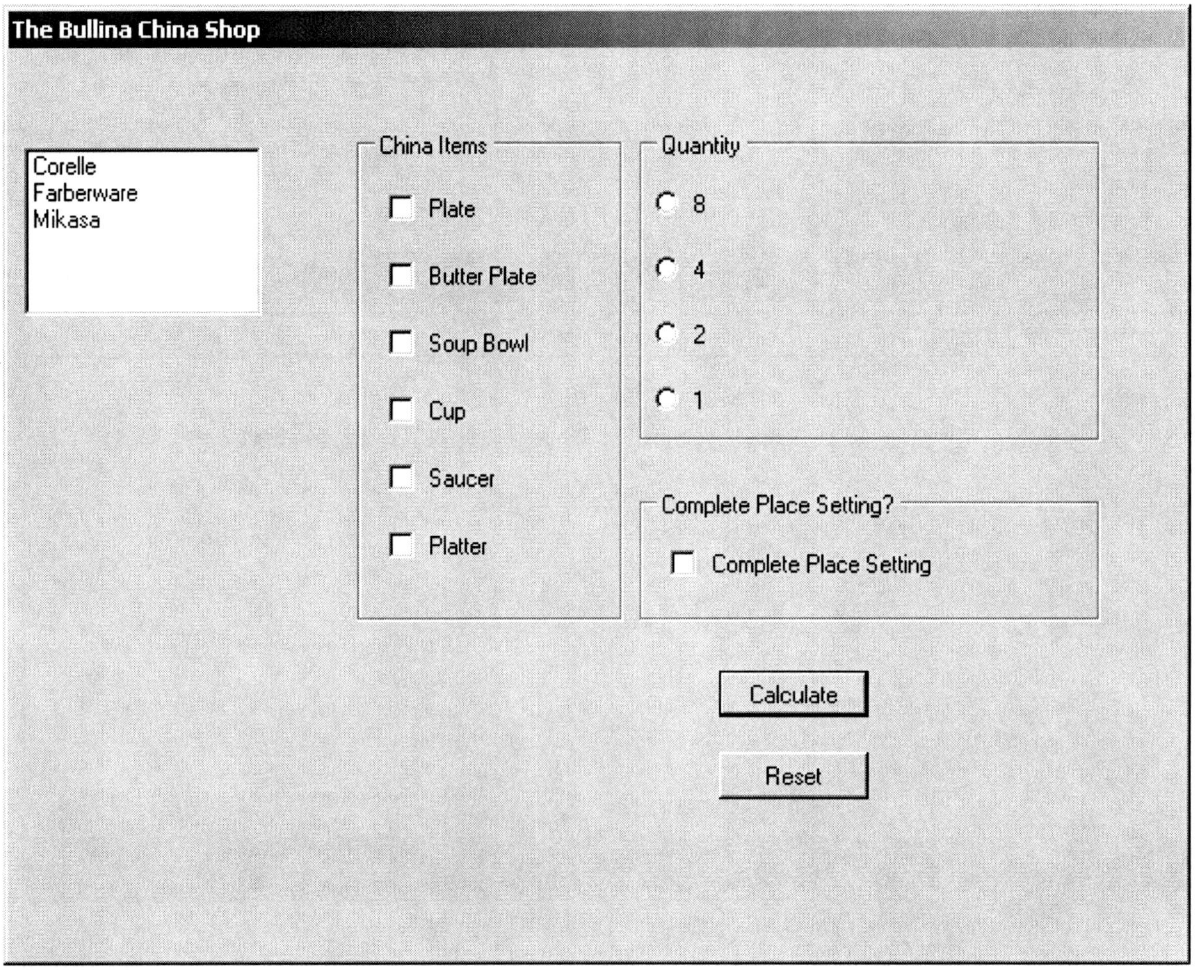

Discussion

The exercise went slowly, but all in all, the class completed this exercise with very few problems. I sensed that my students were more than a little proud of themselves—particularly when they ran their copy of the China Shop program for the first time and saw the items in the list box loaded. That's not to say there weren't some anxious moments. After all, this was the first time anyone in the class had coded even a single Visual Basic statement before.

For instance, one student had mistakenly believed that the Add method would appear after typing **lstBrands** and a period. Of course, he now knows that the Add method is a method of the Items Collection of lstBrands. A few people forgot to enclose the brand of china within quotation marks. A few students kept erasing the parentheses that Visual Basic put around the brand name. Still another put a space between lstBrands and Add. All of these mistakes were quickly and easily resolved.

When everyone had finished the exercise, I displayed the following screen on the classroom projector.

Class Name ListBox **Method Name ListBox**

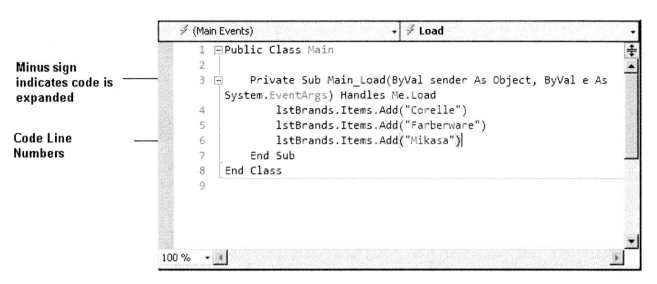

Minus sign indicates code is expanded

Code Line Numbers

"The code window," I said, "like any ordinary window, has a title bar which displays the name of the form. It also has buttons to minimize, maximize, and close itself, and like any other window, the code window can be resized."

"How long can a line of code be?" Valerie asked. "I noticed that none of the lines of code we've written so far have been very long."

"Good question, Valerie" I said. "In Visual Basic, a single line of code can be up to 1,023 characters, and the total number of lines in a procedure is virtually unlimited. That's why the code window can contain both horizontal and vertical scrollbars."

I directed everyone's attention to the two drop-down list boxes directly under the code window's title bar. "The code window contains two drop-down list boxes," I said, "the Class Name list box on the left and the Method Name list box on the right."

"I think we examined these a few weeks ago," Ward said, "and at that time I think you referred to the Method Name list box as the Event list box."

"That's right," I said. "I tend to use the two terms interchangeably. Depending on your perspective, the Method Name list box also displays all the events to which the object in the Class Name list box will respond."

I continued by explaining that when you double-click a control, the code window's Class Name list box will display the name of the control you double-clicked on. "And if it doesn't?" Chuck asked.

"That probably means you didn't double-click the control you thought you did," I said. "That's an important point, because if you double-click the wrong control, you could accidentally place code in the wrong event procedure. Beginners frequently make that mistake."

I then clicked on the Class Name list box.

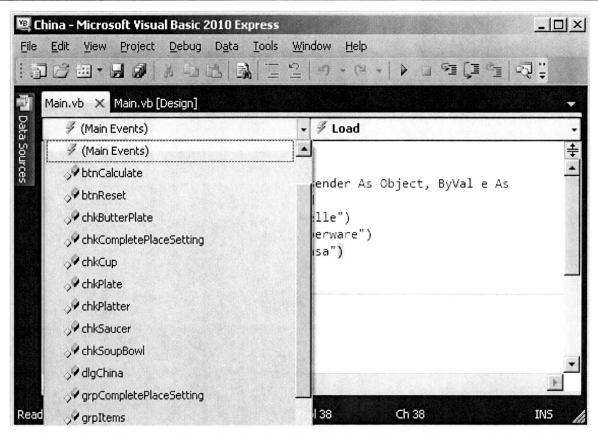

"As you can see, if you click on the Class Name list box, Visual Basic will list all of the controls contained on your form." I then clicked on the Method Name list box.

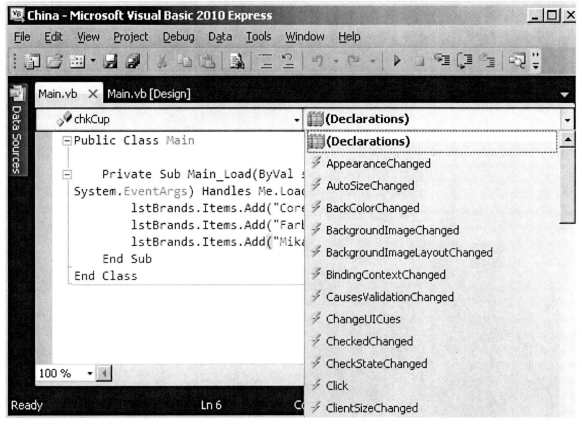

"In a similar way," I said, "if you click on the Class Name list box, Visual Basic will list all of the events recognized by that object."

"So that means there's an event procedure stub associated with every event in the Procedure list box, is that correct?" Lou asked.

"That's right," I answered. "As you can see, there are a great many events listed here. Don't worry too much about what they all mean now, as we'll only be using a handful of them in the China Shop Project."

Pausing for a moment, I said. "Before I move on to a discussion of Visual Basic comments, there's one more thing in the Method Name drop-down list box that I need to show you."

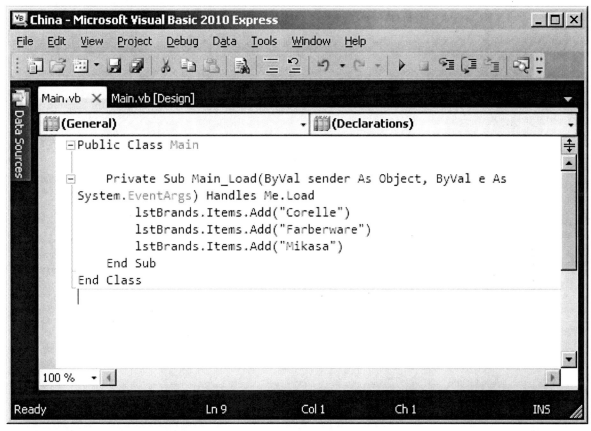

"At the top of the Method Name drop-down list box," I said, "you will always see something called Declarations displayed."

"I'm a little confused," Ward said. "Is Declarations the name of an event procedure, and if so, what object is it associated with?"

"Actually," I replied, "it's pretty much the opposite. The Declarations section is where you place code that is not associated with a particular object."

"Where is the Declarations section?" Linda asked. "Is it at the top of the code window, or is it in between the event procedures?"

"You're right on both counts, Linda," I answered. "The Declarations section is any section of code not contained within an event procedure—although by convention, we'll place code that belongs in the Declaration section at the top of the code window. That makes it easier to find it later."

"Will we be placing any code in the Declarations section?" Dave asked.

"Yes, we will," I said, "but not until the latter half of the course."

"I have a question about something you did earlier," Valerie said. "I noticed that when you typed the name of the list box, lstBrands, you typed it in lowercase. I did the same and Visual Basic automatically changed the b in lstBrands to uppercase. That was pretty cool."

"That's an excellent point," I said. "You probably noticed that when we named our controls in the China Shop Project, we named them in what is called "mixed case," a mixture of upper- and lowercase letters. Visual Basic maintains a list of all the objects in our program and when it sees an object referenced in code, it looks up the name and changes it in code to match the exact spelling of the object."

"That's nice," Mary said, "but does it serve any other purpose?"

"It's a great check of your code," I said.

"What do you mean?" Chuck asked.

"Well, since we know that each of our objects has been named in mixed case," I said, "if you type the name of an object in an event procedure in lowercase, Visual Basic should change it to mixed case. If, however, the object name remains in lowercase, you know something is wrong: either you misspelled the object name in the code window, or the name of the object isn't what you think it is."

I waited a moment while this sank in. No one seemed to have any problems, and so we moved on to a discussion of inserting comments into our code.

Program Comments

"Program comments are explanatory statements that we include in the code we write," I said. "Comments are a useful addition to our code for three reasons:"

- For ourselves when we come back at a later time to maintain or debug the code

- For other programmers who may read our code or need to modify it

- To tell Visual Basic to ignore a line of code without having to delete it from the code window

"All programming languages allow for some version of commenting," I said. "Exactly how they implement it varies from language to language. The trick is how to signal to Visual Basic that something you are entering into the code window is a comment, and not a line of code that you want Visual Basic to execute. In Visual Basic, you indicate a comment by using the special comment character, the apostrophe ('). Everything that follows the apostrophe is ignored by Visual Basic."

"Didn't we notice that Visual Basic had inserted a comment line in the code window for us earlier?" Dave asked.

"Absolutely right, Dave," I said. "In addition to the comments that Visual Basic inserts, we can include comment lines of our own." I then displayed the form's Load event procedure we had just written on the classroom projector, this time with comments included.

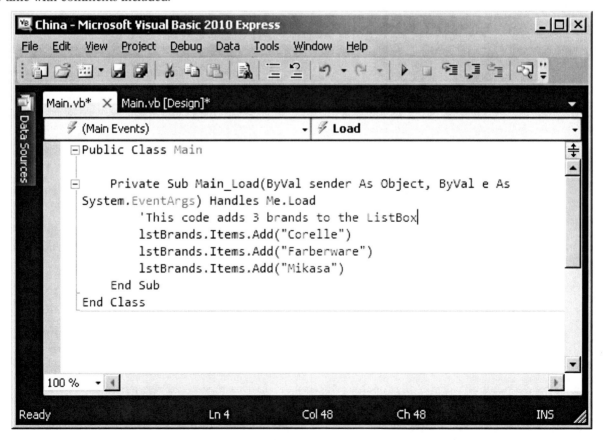

"Notice that our comment is displayed in green," I said. "That's a function of the selections that are set in the Tools | Options | Environment | Fonts And Colors menu."

"Where should we place our comments?" Rose asked.

"To some degree," I answered, "that may depend upon your employer. Some companies require their programmers to include a comment or two at the top of the code window indicating the author of the code, the date the code was written, and anything else that might be useful. It might also be required that each event procedure be similarly commented. Some programmers never write a single comment."

"What about you?" Steve asked.

"My rule of thumb is never to comment the obvious," I answered. "I specifically use comments whenever the code I'm writing is something I've never done before or that took a lot of effort to get to work. That's the kind of code you might come back to in a week or two and totally forget what it's doing or how it works. That type of code definitely needs to be commented—not only for me, but for other programmers who may be looking at it down the road. Some programmers, by the way, really go to town, making their comments very elaborate, drawing something programmers call a flower box."

I then modified the code we had written earlier to include a flower box and displayed it on the classroom projector.

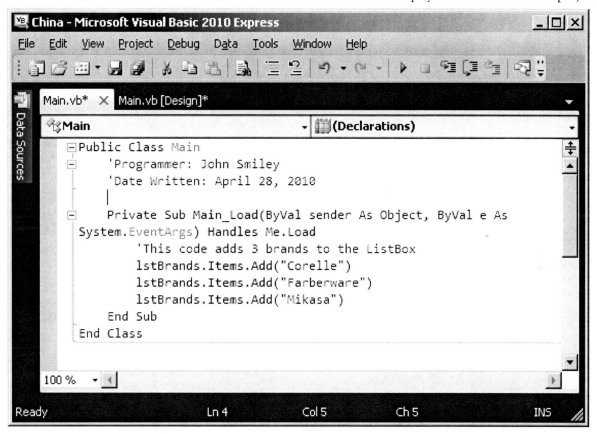

You can also comment a program with the REM statement, which is short for Remark. Begin a line of code with REM and Visual Basic will ignore the rest of the line. I prefer the use of the apostrophe to the REM statement as it is quicker. However, many programmers who programmed in the old DOS Basic language still prefer to use REM, so be prepared to come across it.

"Can a comment only appear on a line by itself or can it come after a Visual Basic statement?" Dave asked.

"Another good question, Dave," I said. "The answer is yes, you can place a comment after a Visual Basic statement. Let me show you."

Once again, I modified the code and displayed it on the classroom projector.

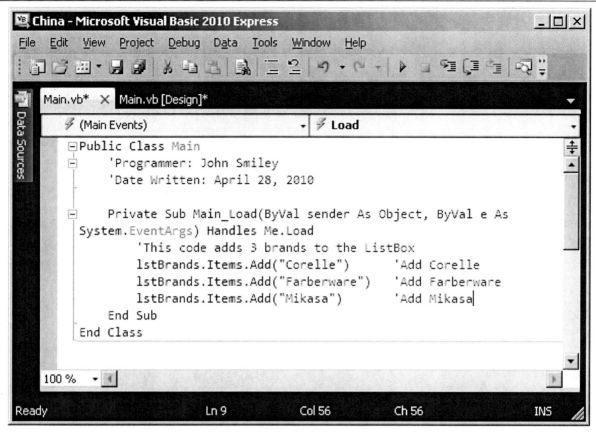

"Will we be adding comments in the exercises we do?" Kathy asked.

"I won't be including any explicit instructions in the exercise to add comments," I said. "But feel free to include comments of your own."

The Line Continuation Character (_)

As there were no other questions, we moved on to a discussion of the Visual Basic line continuation character.

"As I mentioned earlier," I said, "a single line of Visual Basic code can be as many as 1,023 characters long, but for readability purposes, I wouldn't advise you to type beyond the width of the code window. Otherwise, you or someone reading your code will have to use the horizontal scroll bar to see all of the code. However, as you'll see a little later, some of the code that we need to enter into the code window will routinely exceed even that width. When that happens, we have two choices: continue typing and create a long line of code, or use the Visual Basic line continuation character to split the line in two. Also, as we saw earlier, with this latest version of Visual Basic, the code window has an option to wrap long lines of code."

"So you just can't break the code up into two lines?" Linda said.

"For the most part that's true, " I said. "Visual Basic 2010 is a bit more intelligent than previous versions of Visual Basic, and in some cases will manage to figure out what it thinks you mean if you break code into multiple lines. But I'm uncomfortable with that. Most programming languages are pretty strict as to the format of their code statements and I prefer not to have it 'guess' as to what I really mean. For instance, if you split a Visual Basic statement into two separate lines and then run the program, it will display an error message."

I then split the line of code in two that adds "Corelle" to the list box and displayed the code on the classroom projector. "Notice how I've split the line into two," I said.

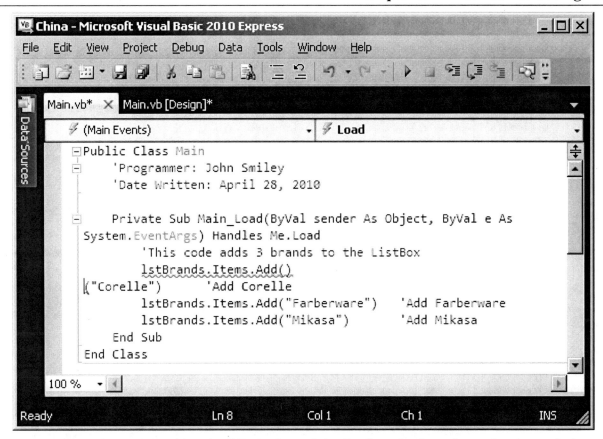

"When you split the line," Linda said, "Visual Basic changed the first line of code, and now there's a squiggly character in the front of the second line."

"That's right, Linda," I answered. "By splitting the line of code into two, we've confused Visual Basic. That squiggly character is a clue that Visual Basic doesn't know how to deal with the syntax. If you see that squiggly character in the code window while you are typing, you should know that something's wrong. On the other hand, if you miss that signal, and then try to run the program, you'll receive a message that there was a build error."

I ran the program, and the following error message was displayed.

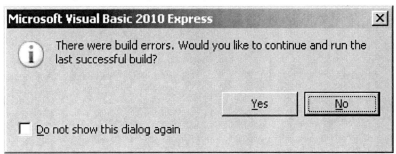

"What is that?" Rose asked.

"Visual Basic is telling us that our program has errors," I said. "We have two choices. We can tell VB to run the last version of the program--the one before the changes we just made--- or click No to display a window that will tell us the lines of code that have errors."

"What's the point of running the older version?" Kate asked.

"Exactly Kate," I answered, "there's really no point to it--we made changes to the program---obviously, we'd like to know what VB doesn't like about them. To find out, just click the 'No' button."

I clicked No and this window was displayed.

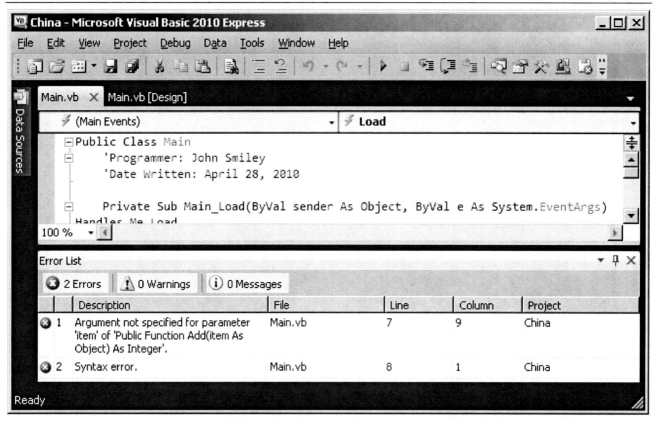

"What does all of that that mean?" Linda asked. "Is this Visual Basic's way of telling us what's wrong with our code? Those error messages don't seem very helpful. The first one I don't understand, and the second one about a syntax error is pretty generic."

"The usefulness of the error messages varies," I answered. "Sometimes Visual Basic is so confused, it can only guess at what's wrong—and that's the case here. But what is useful is the line number referenced. Those are the lines of code that Visual Basic is having trouble deciphering. And in this case, those happen to be the two lines of code we split in the code window. In fact, if we click on the line number, Visual Basic will take us right there in the code window."

I did, and the Visual Basic code window appeared—with my cursor positioned at the line of code with the error.

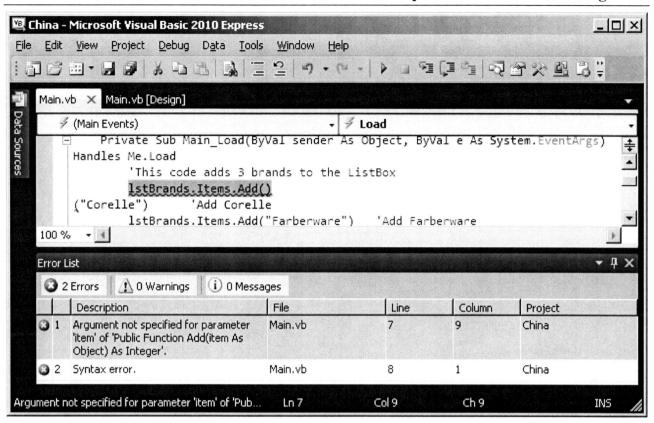

I then explained that the answer to our dilemma was to use the Visual Basic line continuation character, which is the underscore character (_).

By using the line continuation character, you can split a Visual Basic statement onto two or more lines. This code won't cause any problems," I said, as I displayed it on the classroom projector.

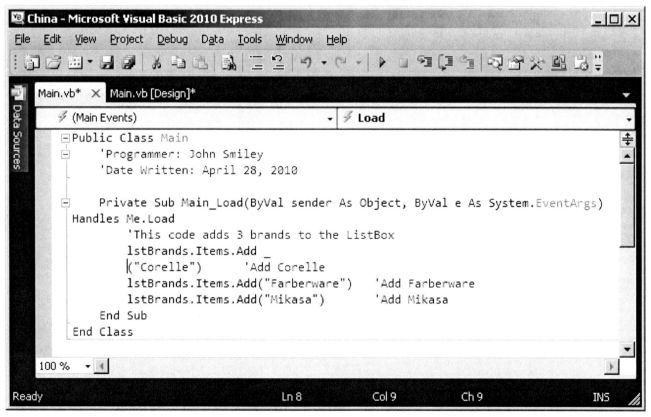

"Is that space between Add and the line continuation character required?" Rhonda asked.

"Excellent question, Rhonda," I said. "The line continuation character must be separated from the last word on the line by a space, and nothing else—not even a comment—can follow the underscore."

"Are there any situations where you can't use the line continuation character?" Dave asked. "Just one," I said. "You can't use a line continuation character in the middle of what is known in programming circles as a string literal, or in the middle of the names of objects or variables."

"What's a string literal?" Chuck asked. "A string literal is a series of characters sandwiched by quotation marks," I answered.

"Like the names Corelle, Farberware, and Mikasa, which are arguments of the Add method?"

Chuck asked. "Are those string literals?"

"Exactly right, Chuck," I said. "Since they are enclosed within quotation marks, they are string literals. You can't place a line continuation character in the middle of them to split a line."

No one had any more questions or comments, and so I gave the class a ten-minute break.

A Visual Basic Code Overview

When we resumed after break, I told my students that for the remainder of the class, I would present an overview of the three types of programming structures that form the building blocks of all computer programs.

"Structure?" Ward said. "That sounds like a house."

"The building analogy is a good one, Ward," I said. "We've already seen how the first step in developing a program is to create a 'blueprint' in the form of a Requirements Statement. Many years ago, computer scientists discovered that any program can be written using a combination of three structures, much like a house can be constructed using a series of standard components. These three structures—the sequence structure, the selection structure, and the loop structure—will form the basis of our discussion over the next few weeks."

"Will we be writing code ourselves today?" Rhonda asked. "Are we ready for that?"

"I think it's a great time to start writing code," I answered, "and today I'll give you some practice exercises for you to complete. Ordinarily, the exercises we complete here in class will ultimately lead to the completion of the China Shop Project. However, from time to time we'll complete some exercises just for practice. So we don't get confused, if you want to save your practice exercises, you should save those in the Practice folder you created earlier. Let's take a look at the Visual Basic sequence structure now."

The Sequence Structure—Falling Rock

"Unlike the selection and loop structures," I said, "which require special syntax to implement, any code that we write—like the code we wrote to add three items to our list box—is automatically a sequence structure. I like to analogize a sequence structure to the behavior of a falling rock."

"Falling rock? What do you mean by that?" Steve said, obviously amused.

"Have you seen signs warning you of falling rock on the highway?" I said. "If you've ever seen rock fall, you know that once it gets rolling there's no stopping it. The same way with our code. In the code we wrote earlier today, we wrote three separate Visual Basic lines of code to add items to our list box. And I believe that everyone took it for granted that the first line of code would execute to add Corelle to the list box, then the second line of code to add Farberware, and then finally the line of code to add Mikasa. In other words, our code was executed one line after another, in sequence."

"Oh, I see where the term comes from now," Valerie said. "But what else could happen? Doesn't every line of code get evaluated by Visual Basic?"

"Yes, every line of code is evaluated by Visual Basic," I said, "but not every line of code will necessarily be executed once. That's where the selection structures and loop structures come into play. In order to implement intelligence into our program in the form of decision-making capabilities, the falling rock behavior of a sequence structure just won't do. The selection structure allows us to selectively execute lines of code based on certain conditions our program finds, and the loop structure allows us to execute a line of code repetitively."

I paused a moment before adding. "In order to illustrate the alternatives to falling rock behavior, I'd like you to complete a series of exercises based on a fictitious collection of seven restaurants in New York City. Pretend, for a few moments, that you have been hired by these seven restaurants to write a program to display their ads on a giant display screen in Times Square. In our case, we're going to use the Visual Basic Output Window as our giant display screen."

"The Output Window?" Valerie asked. "Isn't that where the messages appear that our program is being built when we start it?"

"That's right, Valerie," I said. "When we start our program, messages appear in the Output Window indicating that it's being built. We can insert lines of code in order to write messages to the Output window. These will aid us as we experiment with the three different types of Visual Basic programming structures. In the upcoming exercises, we'll use the WriteLine method of the Console object in order to display messages in the Output Window."

"Console object?" Ward said. "Do we need to add a control to our form to do that?"

"Think of the Console object as an invisible control," I answered. "You don't need to do anything special in order to be able to execute its methods—and its WriteLine method can be used to write messages in the Output window."

"This I have to see," I heard Blaine say, as I handed out this exercise for the class to complete.

Exercise 6-2 Eat at Joe's—the Selection Structure---Falling Rock Behavior

In this exercise, you'll create a new Windows application, add a Button control to your form, and write code using the WriteLine method of the Console object to display information in the Visual Basic Output window. The WriteLine method is a great learning tool. Pretend that the Output window is actually a giant display screen.

1. Start a new Windows application project.
2. Find the Button control in your toolbox, and place it on your form.
3. Using the Properties window, change the name of the Button control to btnSequence and change its caption (via the Text property) to Sequence Structure.
4. Double-click on the Button control to open the Visual Basic code window and place the following code in its Click event procedure.

```
Private Sub btnSequence_Click(ByVal sender As System.Object, _
   ByVal e As System.EventArgs) Handles btnSequence.Click

Console.WriteLine("Eat at Joe's")
Console.WriteLine("Eat at Tom's")
Console.WriteLine("Eat at Kevin's")
Console.WriteLine("Eat at Rich's")
Console.WriteLine("Eat at Rose's")
Console.WriteLine("Eat at Ken's")
Console.WriteLine("Eat at Melissa's")

End Sub
```

5. Save your program—you'll be modifying it in Exercise 6-3.
6. Run the program, and click on the Button control to trigger its Click event. The code that you have just placed in the Click event procedure of the Button control will execute, one line after another. You should see the restaurant advertisements appear in the Output window. (You may need to select View-Other Windows-Output from the VB Menu Bar to see the Output Window.) Your Output window should look similar to the illustration below.

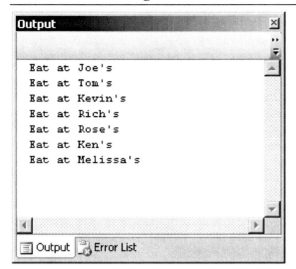

TIP: You may need to select View-Other Windows-Output from the VB Menu Bar to see the
Output Window

Discussion

Aside from some obvious nervousness with working in the code window, no one seemed to have any major
problems with this exercise. I noticed that the students were very careful to place their code into the correct event
procedure—something I hoped they would do each and every time they wrote code in the code window. I then
began to explain what we had done. A couple of students managed to "lose" their Output window, but once we
found it (View | Other Windows | Output from the Visual Basic menu bar), I think they were pretty impressed with
it.

"The seven lines of code that we wrote in this exercise," I said, "represent something known as a sequence structure.
All that means is that the second line of code executes after the first, the third after the second and so on."

"The falling rock behavior," Ward chimed in.

"Exactly right, Ward," I said. "Is everyone okay with the WriteLine method of the Console object?"

"Sure," Rhonda said. "It just prints text in the Output window, isn't that right?"

"That's basically it," I said.

There were no other questions, and so I continued. "Suppose," I said, "that the proprietor of Joe's restaurant takes a
semi-retirement and decides to open the restaurant only on Sundays. Tom, of Tom's restaurant, hears about Joe, and
decides to open his restaurant only on Mondays. Kevin follows suit and opens only on Tuesday. Soon the rest of the
bunch hear about this, figure that one day of work a week is great, and the next thing we know Rich is open only on
Wednesday, Rose only on Thursday, Ken only on Friday, and Melissa only on Saturdays. To save advertising costs,
each owner contacts us to tell us they want to advertise on our giant display screen only on the days that their
restaurant is actually open. How can we deal with this in our program?"

I gave everyone a moment or two to think about this. "I suppose," Ward said, "we could write separate programs
for different days of the week— although if you tell me there isn't a better way than that, I may need to drop out of
the class!"

"You're right, Ward," I said. "We could write a program for each day of the week, but don't drop out of the course
over this. There is a way to make our program smart enough to know what day of the week it is and, with that
knowledge, to make a decision as to which restaurant to advertise. Armed with the day of the week (something that
Visual Basic can easily determine), and by using the selection structure to which I alluded a little earlier, we can make
our program intelligent."

The Selection Structure

"Selection structures," I continued, "can alter the default (falling rock) behavior of Visual Basic, but they are a little
more complicated to code. We'll be taking a closer look at these in the weeks to come, but for now, let me just say
that the programmer needs to specify conditions that Visual Basic needs to evaluate or analyze. Based on those
conditions, Visual Basic will make a decision. In the exercise that you'll complete in just a few minutes, the condition

that we'll ask Visual Basic to evaluate will be the day of the week. Then, based on Visual Basic's analysis of that condition, various decisions to display advertising in the Output window will be made. Coding selection structures requires a little more up-front thought than merely coding a plain sequence structure." With that, I distributed this exercise for the class to complete.

Exercise 6-3 The If Statement (or Which Restaurant is Open Today?)

In this exercise, we'll add code to our project to use an If…Then statement to evaluate the day of the week, and based on that analysis, selectively display an advertisement in the Output window.

1. Continue working with the project from Exercise 6-2.
2. Add a second Button control to your form. Name it btnSelection, and change its caption to Selection Structure.
3. Double-click on the Button control to open the Visual Basic code window and place the following code in its Click event procedure.

```
Private Sub btnSelection_Click(ByVal sender As System.Object, _
    ByVal e As System.EventArgs) Handles btnSelection.Click

If WeekDay(Now) = FirstDayOfWeek.Sunday Then
    Console.Writeline("Eat at Joe's")
End If

If WeekDay(Now) = FirstDayOfWeek.Monday Then
    Console.Writeline("Eat at Tom's")
End If

If WeekDay(Now) = FirstDayOfWeek.Tuesday Then
    Console.Writeline("Eat at Kevin's")
End If

If WeekDay(Now) = FirstDayOfWeek.Wednesday Then
    Console.Writeline("Eat at Rich's")
End If

If WeekDay(Now) = FirstDayOfWeek.Thursday Then
    Console.Writeline("Eat at Rose's")
End If

If WeekDay(Now) = FirstDayOfWeek.Friday Then
    Console.Writeline("Eat at Ken's")
End If

If WeekDay(Now) = FirstDayOfWeek.Saturday Then
    Console.Writeline("Eat at Melissa's")
End If

End Sub
```

4. Save your program—you'll be modifying it in Exercise 6-4.
5. Run the program, and click on the Selection Structure Button control to trigger its Click event. The code that you have just placed in the Click event procedure of the Selection Button control will execute. Depending upon the day of the week, you should see one restaurant ad (and only one) in the Output window. Your Output window should look similar to the illustration below.

Discussion

Although no one had any trouble completing the exercise, there were still a number of puzzled looks in the classroom.

"That's really cool, I had no idea you could do something like this," Steve said, "although I must confess I don't think I understand half of the code I just wrote."

I explained that the code we had placed in the btnSelection Button control had used the Visual Basic If statement to alter Visual Basic's default "falling rock" behavior. Instead of displaying all seven advertisements in the Output window, this code first determines the day of the week from the system date maintained on the user's PC and then prints the advertisement appropriate for that day.

"Is that what that WeekDay statement is?" Dave asked.

"That's right," I said. "WeekDay is an example of something called a Visual Basic function. Functions perform an action, then return a result of some kind—in this case, the WeekDay function returns a number from 1 to 7 indicating the day of the week. Since today is Saturday (at least it is in our simulated classroom) Visual Basic returns a value of 7."

"So Saturday is considered the seventh day of the week, is that right?" Linda asked.

"Yes, by default that's true," I said.

Let's take a look at the code used to display Melissa's ad.

```
If WeekDay(Now) = FirstDayOfWeek.Saturday Then
   Console.Writeline("Eat at Melissa's")
End If
```

"The key to the code," I said, "is the ability of our program to know what day of the week it is. Fortunately, there is a Visual Basic function called Now which interrogates the system date and time on the user's PC, and returns the date. We then used this return value as an argument to the WeekDay function, which examines a date and returns a number equal to the day of the week."

"I'm okay with that," Peter said, "but why are we comparing it to FirstDayOfWeek.Saturday? What exactly is that about?"

"FirstDayOfWeek in this case is a System object," I said, "and Saturday is a property of that object which in this instance has a value of 7. In fact, we could have written this line of code to look like this, and it would have worked fine…"

```
If WeekDay(Now) = 7 Then
   Console.Writeline("Eat at Melissa's")
End If
```

"Why not use the number then?" Kate asked. "It seems easier to me."

"Two reasons, Kate," I said, "The first is that the code is not as easy to read. Here you see the word 'Saturday,' and right away you can recognize what the programmer is trying to do. The second reason is that Saturday is not always the seventh day of the week. On some computers, and on some systems that Visual Basic may find itself running on, Saturday might be the sixth day of the week. So you see, we don't want to compare the return value of WeekDay to a number. And that's where the FirstDayOfWeek object comes in. It ensures that no matter what the first day of the week is, as determined by the user's PC, FirstDayOfWeek.Saturday will always equate to what WeekDay believes to be Saturday."

I waited a moment.

"You may be confused at this point," I said, "and that's understandable—this is all pretty new to you. Hang in there, though, because in next week's class, we're going to spend all of it talking about nothing but selection structures."

The third and last programming structure we examined was the loop structure.

The Loop Structure

"Loop structures," I said, "allow you to execute portions of your code repetitively without having to write the code more than once."

"Why would we want to do that?" Rhonda asked. "What types of programming instructions need to be repeated over and over again?"

I thought for a moment and then said, "Let's consider an automated teller machine (ATM). When I visit my neighborhood ATM, I almost always find it up and running, and the first thing it prompts me to do is insert my card and enter my PIN number. If you think about it, after the previous customer finishes using the ATM, the ATM program doesn't end—it just loops back to the beginning, prompting the next customer to insert their ATM card to begin a new transaction."

"You're right," Ward agreed. "After I'm done with my transaction, the ATM prompts me to remove my card, and then it displays a message to insert a card to begin a new transaction."

"That's the loop structure of the program at work," I said. "Instead of the program just ending, it continues running—looping through that process over and over again."

I suggested to the class that we leave our restaurant advertising business behind us and write a program to display the numbers from 1 to 10 in the Output window. "This will be a bit of a tedious exercise," I said, "but I want to show you this method before I show you how the loop structure can make your coding faster and easier."

Exercise 6-4 Displaying the Numbers from 1 to 10 in the Output Window

In this exercise, we'll add code to our project to display the numbers 1 through 10 in the Output window.

1. Continue working with the project from Exercise 6-3.
2. Add a third Button control to your form. Name it btnNoLoop and change its caption to No Loop.
3. Double-click on the Button control to open the Visual Basic code window and place the following code in its Click event procedure.

```
Private Sub btnNoLoop_Click(ByVal sender As System.Object, _
  ByVal e As System.EventArgs) Handles btnNoLoop.Click

Console.Writeline(1)
Console.Writeline(2)
Console.Writeline(3)
Console.Writeline(4)
Console.Writeline(5)
Console.Writeline(6)
Console.Writeline(7)
Console.Writeline(8)
Console.Writeline(9)
Console.Writeline(10)

End Sub
```

4. Save your program—you'll be modifying it in Exercise 6-5.
5. Run the program, and click on the NoLoop Button control to trigger its Click event. The code that you have just placed in the Click event procedure of the NoLoop Button control will execute. You should see the numbers 1

through 10 displayed in the Output window. Your Output window should look similar to the illustration shown here.

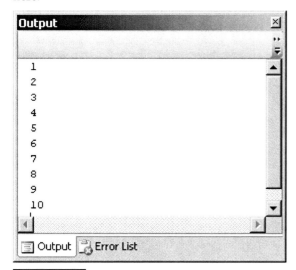

Discussion

Everyone agreed that nothing fancy was going on with this code. I guess by now, coding was becoming old hat to them. All we did was execute ten separate WriteLine methods of the Console object. I then asked each of them to modify their program to output the numbers 1 through 10,000 in the Output window. After their initial shock wore off (and after they realized I was joking), Joe chimed in.

"Well," Joe said, "I guess if we follow the same technique we used to display the numbers from 1 to 10 in the Output window, instead of writing 10 lines of code we're going to have to write 10,000. There must be an easier way!"

"You're right, Joe, there is," I answered. "Instead of writing 10,000 lines of code, we'll use a Visual Basic loop structure to repeat the Console.WriteLine method 10,000 times."

"But the number we need to display must change each time," Dave said, after thinking about that for a minute. "How can we handle that?"

"Good question, Dave," I said. "We'll use something called a counter variable to increment the value we display in the Output window by 1 each time the WriteLine method executes."

I explained that we would cover both the loop structure and variables in much more detail a little later on in the course. For now, we were going to take a quick look at the potential of loops in our programs. I then distributed this exercise for the class to complete.

Exercise 6-5 Displaying Numbers from 1 to 10---The Loop Structure

In this exercise, we'll add code to our project to display the numbers 1 through 10 in the Output window using a Visual Basic loop.

1. Continue working with the project from Exercise 6-4.
2. Add a fourth Button control to your form. Name it btnLoop and change its caption to Loop.
3. Double-click on the Button control to open the Visual Basic code window and place the following code in its Click event procedure.

```
Private Sub btnLoop_Click(ByVal sender As System.Object, _
    ByVal e As System.EventArgs) Handles btnLoop.Click

Dim intCounter As Integer          'Declare the counter variable


For intCounter = 1 To 10            'Loop structure begins here
    Console.Writeline(intCounter)
Next intCounter                     'Loop structure ends here

End Sub
```

4. Save your program.

5. Run the program, and click on the Loop Button control to trigger its Click event. The code that you have just placed in the Click event procedure of the Loop Button control will execute. You should see the numbers 1 through 10 displayed in the Output window (just as in Exercise 6-5).

Discussion

I ran the program myself on my classroom project, and the numbers 1 through 10 appeared in the Output window. Then, before anyone had a chance to say anything, I changed the number 10 to 10000 on the line of code reading.

For intCounter = 1 to 10

I ran the program again, and then clicked the Loop button. On my 700 megahertz classroom PC, the program displayed the numbers from 1 to 10000 in the Visual Basic Output window in about five seconds. I invited everyone to do the same.

"That's the beauty of the loop structure," I said, waiting while they changed their own code. "All I needed to do was change one line of code, and I changed the numbers displayed in the Output window dramatically. Imagine doing that with separate Console.Write statements!"

"That is amazing," Joe said. "Can you explain the code?"

"Sure thing, Joe. The first thing we did was to declare a variable," I said, as I displayed this line of code on the classroom projector.

Dim intCounter As Integer 'Declare the counter variable

"We'll discuss variables, exactly what they are and how to declare them, a little later in the course," I said. "For now, think of a variable as a placeholder in the computer's memory, where we can store data and sometimes addresses to objects. When we declare a variable, as we did here, we tell Visual Basic to create a variable with that name and to place it in the computer's memory. Once we declare the variable, we then implement the Visual Basic loop structure by using this statement."

For intCounter=1To10 'Loop structure begins here

"A For...Next loop," I said, "is a loop structure that causes the code within the body of the loop to be executed a definite number of times. There are also other Visual Basic loop structures that will execute code an indefinite number of times—indefinite, that is, at the time the programmer writes the code."

"Why would we want to do that?" Ward asked.

"Think back to our ATM example," I said. "The programmer who wrote that code has no idea how many customers will use the ATM in a given day. A definite type loop, the kind that we wrote here, doesn't make sense there."

"What part of this code is actually the loop structure?" Peter asked. "Is it the code between the For line and the Next line?"

"You hit the nail on the head, Peter," I answered. "The loop structure consists of the four lines of code beginning with the word For and ending with the line beginning with the word Next. Everything in between those two lines is called the body of the loop. Those statements—in this case, just a single line of code—are executed the number of times specified by the For line—in this case, a total of 10,000 times."

"How do we know the loop will execute 10,000 times?" Ward asked. "Is that what the 1 To 10000 tells Visual Basic?"

"That's right," I replied. "Those numbers are called the start and end parameters of the For...Next loop, and affect how many times the loop is executed. We'll learn more about the For...Next loop in the upcoming weeks."

"I'm not exactly clear how the numbers are being printed," Barbara said, smiling. "When I first saw this code, I thought we would print the word 'intCounter' in the Output window 10,000 times. Now I realize, at least I think so, that we are actually printing the value of the variable intCounter in the Output window."

"That's right, Barbara," I said, "Each time the code within the body of the loop executes, this statement prints the current value of the variable intCounter in the Output window."

Console.Writeline(intCounter)

"But how does the value of the variable change?" Lou asked. "I don't see any code that is adding to its value."

"Each time the body of the loop is executed," I said, "the value of the variable intCounter is automatically incremented by 1. That's what the Next statement does."

"So it's automatic, then," Dave said.

"Right, Dave," I agreed. "The first time the loop is executed, the value of intCounter is equal to 1, the second time 2, and so on. Ultimately, when the value of intCounter reaches 10,001 the loop ends, since that value exceeds the end parameter specified on the For line."

While I could see that my students understood what had happened with the loop, they weren't totally comfortable. I joked that our treatment of the loop structure today, though perhaps exhausting, wasn't exhaustive.

"Don't worry if you are not entirely clear about this," I said. "We'll talk about loops in much more detail in a few weeks."

I asked if there were any other questions, and Chuck said that he was still a little uncertain about events and when they occur.

"Your question, Chuck, is perfectly timed," I said. "For the remainder of today's class, we're going to be looking at techniques that can give us a behind the scenes look at the programs we write. In fact, I have an exercise prepared to show you a technique I use to visualize exactly when events occur."

In this exercise, you'll use two new Visual Basic statements to inform you when an event procedure has been triggered.

Exercise 6-6 Viewing Events as They Take Place

In this exercise, you'll create a new Windows application, and use a new Visual Basic statement to let you know when an event has been triggered.

1. Start a new Windows application.
2. Add two Button controls to your form. There's no need to change their Name or Text properties for this exercise.
3. Double-click on the first Button control to open the Visual Basic code window and place the following code in its Click event procedure.

```
Private Sub Button1_Click(ByVal sender As System.Object, _
   ByVal e As System.EventArgs) Handles Button1.Click

MessageBox.Show("Button1 Click Event has been triggered")

End Sub
```

4. We'll use another technique for the second Button control. Double-click on the second Button control, and place the following code in its Click event procedure.

```
Private Sub Button2_Click(ByVal sender As Object, _
   ByVal e As System.EventArgs) Handles Button2.Click

Debug.WriteLine ("Button2 Click Event has been triggered")

End Sub
```

5. Run the program, and click on the first Button control. When you do, a Visual Basic message box will display a message telling you that the Click event procedure for Button1 has been triggered. You'll need to click OK to make the message box go away.

6. Click on the second Button control. When you do, you should see a message appear in the Debug window indicating that the Click event for Button2 has been triggered. (You will need to click on Debug-Windows-Immediate, or press Ctrl+G to see the Debug (or Immediate) window.)

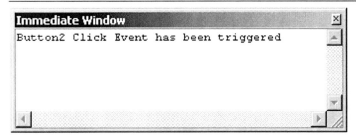

Discussion

I explained that the two techniques that we had employed in this exercise (the MessageBox.Show statement and the WriteLine method of the Debug object) are extremely useful whenever you are not sure of the exact timing of a Visual Basic event.

"Visual Basic programmers use one of these techniques quite often," I said, "to create what we call event viewers to clear up in our minds exactly when a Visual Basic event occurs. By placing these 'sentries,' as I call them, into an event procedure, you'll know exactly when the corresponding event is triggered."

"How does the Debug.WriteLine statement differ from the Console.WriteLine method we used earlier?" Mary asked.

"For our purposes, Mary, both are virtually identical," I answered.

"Do you have a preference for which one of these you use?" Linda asked. "MessageBox.Show, Console, or Debug objects?"

"As you can see, the MessageBox.Show technique tends to interrupt the program flow a little bit more," I replied. "The MessageBox.Show function is primarily a tool to communicate with the user of your program, whereas the WriteLine method of the Debug object is strictly a programmer tool. Also, it wouldn't be a great thing for you to code a MessageBox.Show function like this in your program, and to forget to take it out when you distributed your program to a client or a customer. Debug statements are not compiled into your executable—Visual Basic automatically removes them."

"Sounds like that's a good reason to opt for the Debug technique," Ward said.

There were no other questions, and so I suggested that we turn our attention to the Visual Basic Debugger.

The Visual Basic Debugger

"In one of our classes several weeks back," I said, "when we first examined the IDE, we looked at the Debug menu, and I promised you that we would look at the Debug menu in greater detail. Today's the day."

"Isn't the Debugger a tool for correcting errors in our program?" Steve asked. "We haven't written much code at all. Aren't we a bit too early for this?"

"No, I don't think we're too early at all, Steve," I said. "Just as the event viewer we wrote in our last exercise can be used to discover what's happening behind the scenes of our program, the Visual Basic Debugger's collection of tools can also be used to give us a picture of what's going on behind the scenes of a perfectly healthy program, not just a program that has errors."

"What's the benefit of that?" Mary asked.

"Many courses and books treat the Debugger as an afterthought," I said, "touting it as a tool to uncover problems in programs after they've been written. I believe the Debugger is much more. I think you'll find it to be an invaluable learning tool and one that you'll use frequently as you progress in your Visual Basic career. Whenever you run a program—even one that 'works'—consider using the Debugging techniques that you'll learn today to gain a fuller appreciation for how your program really works."

The Debug/Immediate Window

"The Debugger isn't just one tool," I continued, "but rather a collection of tools. We have already used the WriteLine methods of the Console object as a rudimentary debugging tool, enabling us to see the value of a variable as our program was running. And in the last exercise, we used the WriteLine method again, but this time with the Debug object to display a message to the Visual Basic Output window while our program was running. I'd like to introduce you to methods for pausing your running program."

Pausing a Visual Basic Program

"Why would we want to pause our program?" Rhonda asked.

"One reason is that if we pause a running Visual Basic program," I answered, "we can then view the values of properties and variables in the program."

I could see that some members of the class were pondering that possibility, so I asked everyone to rerun the code to display the numbers from 1 to 10,000 in their Output window.

"Notice," I said, as I ran the program myself, "that while our program is running, there isn't much of anything that we can do to interact with it. A long running loop like this is getting all of the attention of the computer. We can't minimize, maximize, resize, or move the form. We can't even click the Close button of the form to stop the program. Neither can we click the Control menu icon and stop the program that way. About the only thing we can do is to click Debug | Stop Debugging from the Visual Basic menu bar."

"What's happening with this program?" Chuck asked.

"Falling rock behavior?" Dave said.

"More like a runaway train," Linda said to some chuckles from her classmates.

"When we placed that loop structure code in the Button control's Click event procedure," I said, "we told Visual Basic to execute the body of the loop 10,000 times. Nothing else—not a request to move the form, minimize, maximize, even close it—will be able to stop Visual Basic before it reaches the End Sub statement in that event procedure."

"I guess I didn't realize that," Dave said. "So what you're saying is that when an event procedure begins, it ignores other events occurring in the program until that event procedure ends?"

"That's just about it, Dave," I said. "Let's try another experiment."

I asked everyone to start up their program, then to click the Loop button.

"Now fire up the Windows calculator," I said. I gave them a few moments to set this up, and I did the same on my classroom PC. "Are you able to run the Windows calculator at the same time your program is running that loop?"

"That worked," Rhonda said. "My loop is executing, and at the same time I'm able to work with the calculator. I also fired up Word at the same time. Why is it that we can run another Windows program, but we can't seem to get the attention of our own program?"

"The answer is preemptive multitasking," I said.

"I remember that," Barbara said. "If I recall, Windows 95 and above are preemptive multitasking operating systems, meaning that no single program—like ours—can monopolize the CPU. And I guess that's why when our program is busy counting from 1 to 10,000, Windows still allows us to start up the calculator."

"Still, Windows allows our program to monopolize itself?" Valerie said, smiling.

"That's right," I replied, "and that can be a real problem."

I suggested that quite often there are programs we write where we want the code in an event procedure to be interruptible by the code in another event procedure.

"Such as?" Jack asked.

"Suppose," I said, "you design a program that has two Button controls. Perhaps one button initiates a long running loop process that will take many minutes—perhaps hours—to complete. Maybe the other button, when clicked, permits the user to view sales invoices and obtain the results immediately. What if the user clicks the first button, and then has to wait hours for that event procedure to end before being able to click that second button?"

"You mean the user wouldn't be able to click another button either?" Blaine asked.

"That's right," I said. "Visual Basic will wait until the event procedure in that first Button control wraps up unless…"

"Come on, now," Linda said, "we're all waiting."

"Unless we code a DoEvents statement into the body of our loop," I said. "DoEvents tells Visual Basic to check for pending events within the program, even before the event procedure wraps up."

I asked everyone to make the following change to their loop code from Exercise 6-5.

```
Private Sub btnLoop_Click(ByVal sender As System.Object, _
    ByVal e As System.EventArgs) Handles btnLoop.Click

Dim intCounter As Integer

For intCounter = 1 To 10000
    Console.Writeline(intCounter)
    Application.DoEvents()
Next intCounter

End Sub
```

"DoEvents," I said, "is a method of the Visual Basic Application object. Run your program, click the Loop button, and see if you can't get its attention."

"That did the trick," Rose said, after a moment. "Now I can minimize, maximize, resize, and move the form. DoEvents certainly has made a difference!"

"Placing a DoEvents statement within the body of the loop is something you should always do," I said. "DoEvents instructs your program to check the Windows message queue for pending events. Perhaps most importantly, from a debugging point of view, it also enables us to pause our program by clicking the Break button."

"Break button?" Valerie said. "Where's that located on the toolbar?"

"You should see it on your Standard toolbar," I said. "It looks like this."

II

The Break Button

"Unlike the Stop Debugging menu item," I said, "which simply stops your program cold, the Break button only pauses your program, allowing you to restart it by clicking on the Start button (which becomes the Continue button when the program is paused)."

I asked everyone to run their loop program, and then to pause it shortly thereafter by clicking the Break button. I did the same.

"Look at the title bar," I said, "it should indicate that you are now in (Debugging) mode."

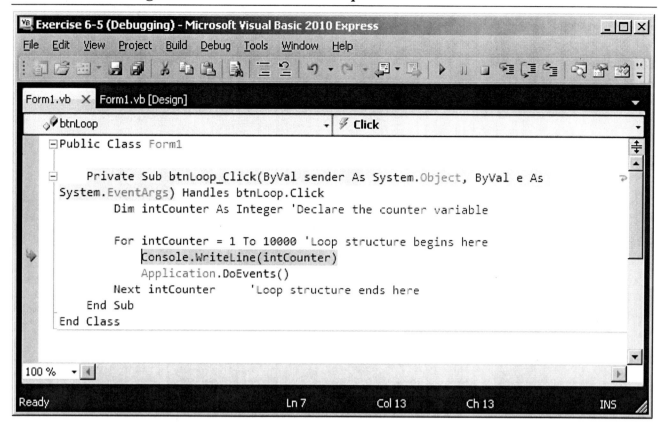

Displaying Values in the Code Window

"While the program is paused in this way," I said, "Visual Basic allows you to view the value of a variable or property in the code window, just by placing your mouse pointer over the code referencing either one."

I invited everyone in the class to view the value of the variable intCounter while their program was paused.

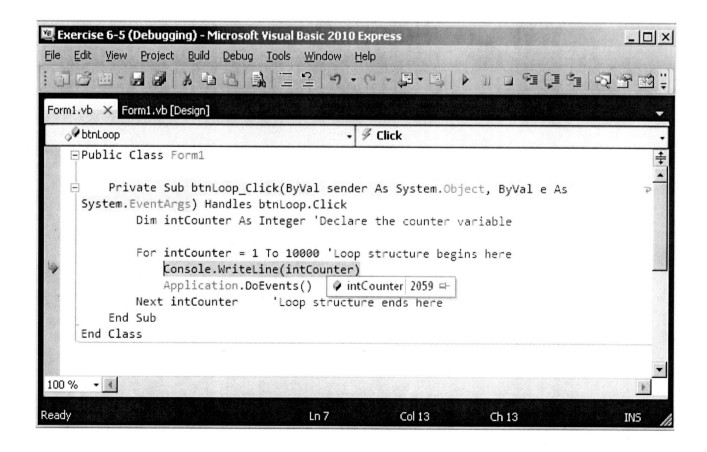

"Here you can see that I stopped the application when the variable was 4955," I said.

The Immediate Window

"In addition to viewing the values of variables and properties in the code window while your program is paused," I said, "you can also type Visual Basic commands and statements into the Immediate window. This gives you the ability to interrogate your program while it is paused and even to execute commands to see how they work prior to placing them into event procedures. For instance, after you've paused your program, you can type this command into the Immediate window."

Debug.Print intCounter

"This command will display the current value of the variable intCounter in the Immediate window," I said. "You sometimes see the same command abbreviated like this."

? intCounter

"Both commands work in exactly the same way," I said, "and for viewing the values of properties and variables, nothing is easier than moving the mouse pointer over them in the code window. You probably won't fully appreciate the value of the Command/Immediate window until one morning at 3:00A.M. when you're in the midst of trying to get some troublesome code to work properly. Then you'll find that being able to pause the program and use the Immediate window like this can be vitally important."

"I tried to type something into the Immediate window," Ward said, "but Visual Basic won't let me."

A quick trip to Ward's PC revealed that he had forgotten to pause the program before trying to type into the Immediate window. Unless the program is paused, you won't be able to type into the Immediate window.

"Are you saying that once the program has been paused," Rhonda said, "you can start it again, even though you've changed the value of a property or a variable?"

"That's right," I said. "You can type anything into the Immediate window while the program is paused and your program can then be restarted. I should also mention that it's possible to change your code in the code window while the program is paused and still restart the program—although Visual Basic will warn you that your code has changed."

"Do you do that often?" asked Valerie. "I mean, change your code and then restart?"

"Once in a while," I confessed, "I may pause the program—realize that the code isn't quite right, and rather than stop the program and correct it, I'll change it right there, and just continue running it. Most times Visual Basic will accept the change without complaining. If by chance you change something in the code that causes Visual Basic to balk at restarting, it will let you know that with a message."

The Stop Statement

"We've seen that you can pause a running program by clicking the Break button or by selecting Debug | Break from the Visual Basic menu bar," I continued. "And I believe I mentioned that there is also a keyboard method to pause your program, and that is to press the Break key on your keyboard. I also want to show you that there's a Visual Basic statement you can insert into your code that will pause your program when it is executed: the Visual Basic Stop statement."

I asked everyone to make the following change to the loop program.

```
Private Sub btnLoop_Click(ByVal sender As System.Object, _
    ByVal e As System.EventArgs) Handles btnLoop.Click

Dim intCounter As Integer

For intCounter = 1 To 10000
    If intCounter = 500 Then Stop
    Console.Writeline(intCounter)
    Application.DoEvents()
Next intCounter

End Sub
```

"With this change to the program" I said, "our program will pause as soon as the value of the variable intCounter is equal to 500. When the program pauses, Visual Basic will display the program's code window with the Stop statement highlighted and an arrow in the margin pointing to the paused line of code."

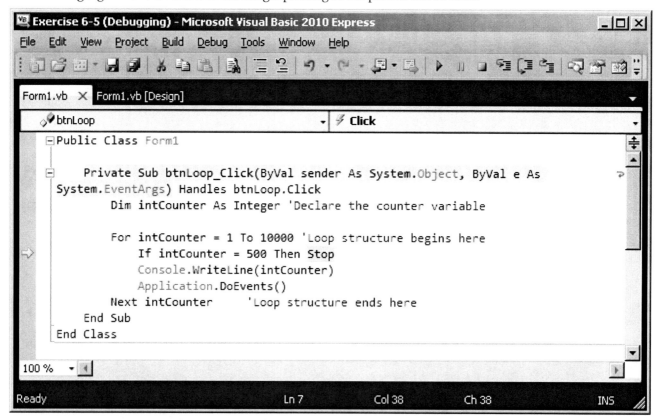

"And if we hold our mouse pointer over the value of intCounter in the code window," I said, "we'll see that the value of the variable is 500."

The Debug Menu

It was time to look at the Debug menu in a little more detail.

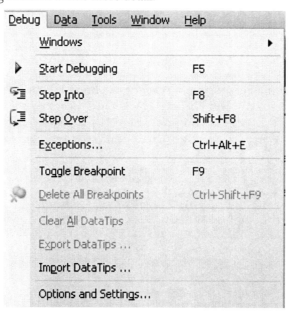

"The Debug menu," I said, "has several options that are invaluable in seeing behind the scenes of your program as well as in helping you to correct problems with your code. Let's look at some of those now."

Step Into

"I think the Step Into menu item is one of the most valuable debugging tools in all of Visual Basic," I said. "Step Into—or as I habitually call it, Step mode—allows you to view the execution of your code one line at a time. As you run your program in Step mode, the Visual Basic code window appears with the line of code that is about to be executed highlighted in yellow."

"I can see that would be valuable," Chuck said. "Kind of like watching something in slow motion."

"Exactly, Chuck," I said. I suggested that we rerun our loop program in Step mode by selecting Debug | Step Into (you can also just press the F8 function key). I did so myself, and when the form appeared, I clicked on the Loop button.. The Visual Basic code window then appeared.

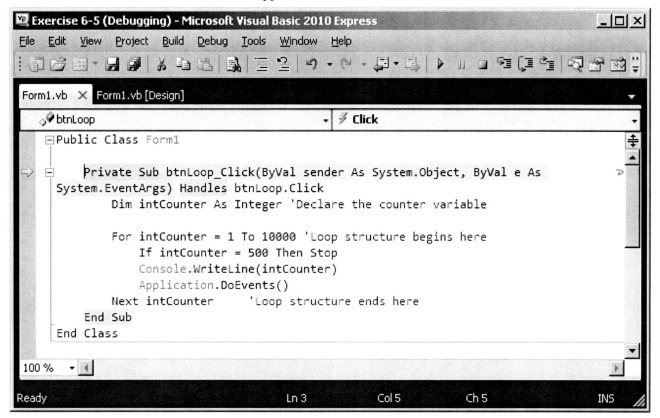

"What's going on?" Rhonda asked. "Why is the yellow line on the event procedure header for the Click event of btnLoop?

"Because we started the program in 'Step Mode'," I said, "when we clicked on the Loop button, Visual Basic is telling us that the first line of code it will execute is in the Click event procedure of the button."

"That makes perfect sense." Blaine said.

"The program is basically stopped here, is that right?" Dave asked, "With the line of code in yellow the one that is *about* to be executed? How do we execute it and move on to the next line?"

"Great question, Dave," I said. "To execute this line of code, either select Debug | Step Into one more time, or even easier, press the F8 function key again."

I did that, and we all saw how the next line of code in the btnLoop_Click event procedure was now highlighted in yellow.

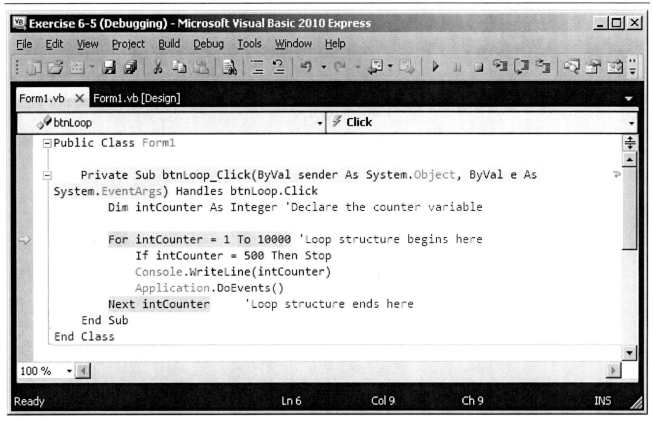

"I noticed that Step mode skipped right by the Dim statement." Barbara said. "Why is it telling us that the next line of code *about to be executed* is the For statement?"

"That's an excellent observation, Barbara" I said. "That's a quirk of in Visual Basic. Visual Basic doesn't bother to show us what it considers 'housekeeping' code—variable declarations. But don't worry, the declaration of the variable intCounter still occurred."

As we continued stepping through the program by pressing F8, the next four lines of code were executed one after the other. Again, I pointed out that in Step mode, the line of code that is highlighted is actually the next line of code that will be executed, not the line that was executed. Therefore, when Visual Basic paused on the line.

Console.Writeline(intCounter)

nothing had yet been displayed in the Output window. We then saw that after the line.

Next intCounter 'Loop structure ends here

was executed, the program jumped up to the If statement line, which is the first line of code in the body of the loop. We never saw this line of code.

For intCounter = 1 To 10000 'Loop structure begins here

executed again.

"I really expected that the program would jump back to the For intCounter line," Linda said.

"That's the line of code that initializes the loop," I said. "If you think about it, Visual Basic doesn't really need to execute that line of code again—it knows the start and end points for the loop control variable. When we cover loops in detail in a few weeks, why this happens may make more sense to you."

I sensed that everyone was enjoying the Debugger—I could barely get their attention as I started to cover the next item on the Debug menu.

Run To Cursor

"I think you've already seen," I continued, "that stepping through an entire Visual Basic program can be very tedious and time consuming. Setting a breakpoint can be a big help. Once you start a program in Step mode, you can always run it normally again just by pressing F5. Suppose you start in Step mode, but don't want to execute the program line by line, nor do you want to run it normally again. You might be wondering if there is something in between—and there is. What you can do is start the program in Step mode, then select a line of code in the event procedure that you want to execute up to by clicking on it with your mouse, then select Debug | Run To Cursor. This tells Visual Basic to execute the code normally up to that line in the code that you have selected. As soon as Visual Basic executes all of the lines of code up to that one, you're back in Step mode. I do this all the time by selecting the End Sub line in an event procedure, and then selecting Run To Cursor."

"I just did that," Kathy said, "and that worked beautifully. I can see that would be a big time saver."

> **NOTE: If you don't see the Run To Cursor item on your Debug menu, right-click your mouse in the code window—you'll see it there.**

Step Over

"Step Over is nearly identical to Step Into," I went on, "but it differs in the way that code is stepped through in a called subprocedure."

"What's that?" Rhonda asked. "What's a called subprocedure?"

I explained that we had not yet seen an example where the code in one event procedure can call or execute code in another procedure—a called subprocedure. But in advanced programming, it can happen quite frequently.

"Let's say you code in the Click event procedure of a Button control," I said, "which contains code to call and then execute code in another procedure called Smiley. If you want to step through the code in your event procedure, but not see the code in the Smiley Procedure line by line, select Step Over."

"Why would you skip over the code in Smiley?" Kate asked.

"It could be that the code in Smiley works flawlessly," I said, "and that you don't need to step through it to verify it. If the code in Smiley is voluminous, and it works fine, there would be no need to see it executed line by line."

No one seemed to have any trouble with Step Over—now on to Step Out.

Step Out

"If you are currently running your program in Step mode," I said, "Step Out tells Visual Basic to execute the remaining lines of code in the current event procedure normally. Once the event procedure runs to completion, your program is still in Step mode."

"In other words," Ward said, "you're telling Visual Basic to execute the code normally to the point of the End Sub statement and then go back to Step mode."

"I hadn't thought of it that way, Ward," I said, "but come to think of it, that's exactly right."

Set Next

"I don't know if you've noticed," I said, "but all of the Step commands we've studied so far have not affected the way our program executes—just whether or not the individual lines of code appear 'stepped' in the code window. However, Set Next Statement is an exception to that rule. Using Set Next, you can actually change the order in which the lines of code in your program execute, thereby allowing you to skip or event repeat lines of code in an event procedure."

> **NOTE: If you don't see the Set Next Statement item on your Debug menu, right-click your mouse in the code window—you'll see it there.**

"Can you explain why we would want to do that?" Rhonda asked. "I guess I don't understand."

"I can give you an example, Rhonda," I said. "Suppose you're working on a program that has been giving you a problem, and so you decide to run the program in Step mode. While you are running the program in Step mode, you begin to suspect one line of code in an event procedure as the cause of your problem, and you decide to delete it. Now, you could stop the program, delete the line of code, and then rerun the program to see if it works. However, this is a little clunky. Even better, while the program is still running in Step mode, you can test your theory that this line of code is really the problem by selecting the line of code after it with your mouse, then selecting Debug | Set Next Statement. The questionable line of code will be skipped, and if the program works correctly, you'll know that that line of code was the problem."

"And the great thing about that technique," Dave added, "is that if you're wrong, you haven't really altered the event procedure at all. There's nothing to undo."

"That's right, Dave" I agreed, "you haven't edited the event procedure at all. If it turns out you are correct, you can then safely delete that line of code."

Show Next

"Not surprisingly," I said, "it's easy to become confused while running your program in Step mode and not realize what line of code is next to be executed."

As you might imagine, this elicited quite a few laughs. "If you want to know the next Visual Basic line of code that will be executed in Step mode," I continued, "select Debug | Show Next Statement and Visual Basic will highlight it for you."

We had been working for quite a while and questions were becoming few and far between, a sure sign of fatigue. I called for a ten-minute break and told everyone that when we returned, we would wrap up our discussion of the Visual Basic Debugger.

The Locals Window

After we returned from break, I said that there are several windows in the Debugging environment which can be very useful when our program is paused.

"The Locals window," I said, "which can be accessed from the Visual Basic menu bar by selecting Debug | Windows | Locals, displays the values of just about everything in your program, including any variables that you declare."

I then started my Loop program, clicked the Break button, and brought up the Locals window.

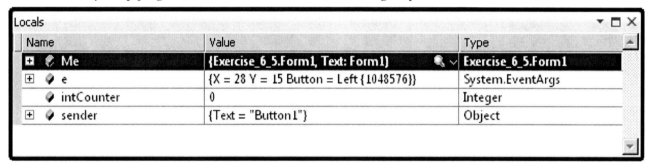

"As you can see," I said, "the Locals window will display the value of the variable intCounter— which is currently 1889—and in addition, if we were to click on the name Me with the + sign, we would be able to display the value of every property for the form."

The Me Window

"One of the more interesting, and dangerous, windows in the Debugger is the Me window," I said. "From this window it's possible to display and change the value of everything in your program and its environment. It may be some time before you understand half of what you see in there, and you must be very careful before changing anything. Still, from this window it is possible to change the value of every property and variable in your program— if you dare…" I then displayed the Me window by selecting 'Me' within the Locals window.

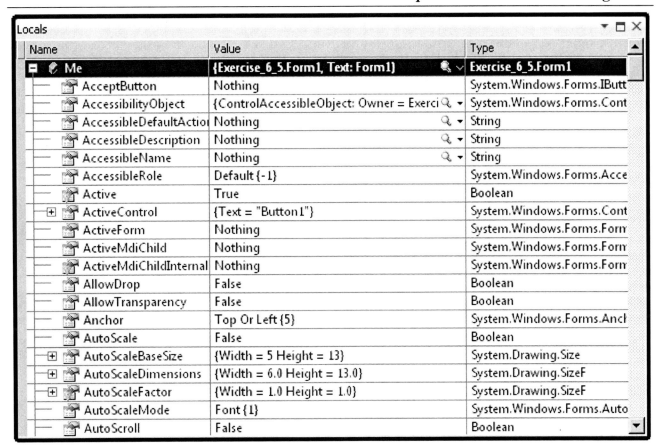

The Watch Window

"Unlike the Locals, Auto, and Me windows," I said, "which are pretty much preconfigured as to what they will display for you, you can configure the Watch window to show as much or as little of your program's properties and variables as you desire. Setting a watch, as we call it, is pretty easy. A watch can only be set when your program is paused. At that point, open your code window, select the variable for which you wish to set the watch, right-click, and select Instant Watch. A watch for that variable will be added to the Watch window. Now if you step through the program, the current value of that variable, and only that variable, will be displayed in the Watch window. You can do this for property values also, but for those, you need to enter them directly into the Watch window by selecting Debug | Windows | Watch from the Visual Basic menu bar, and typing their fully qualified name into the Name column of the Watch window."

"Fully qualified?" Steve asked. "What does fully qualified mean?"

"Fully qualified," I answered, "means that if you want to display the current value of the Form's Height property, that you type Me.Height into the Name column. Let me show you. To display the current value of the Loop button caption, you type Me.btnLoop.Text. The name of the current form is always addressed as 'Me'." I then set up a watch for the variable **intCounter**, the Form's height, and the caption of the Loop button, and displayed it on the classroom projector.

Breakpoints

"The final menu item I want to discuss today is Breakpoint," I said. "I know I've briefly mentioned this word and process earlier, but it bears repeating. When you set a breakpoint in the code window it behaves very much like coding a Stop statement in your program. A breakpoint is not code, but a marker set on a line of code. When you set a breakpoint in the code window, the line of code is marked in the margin with a red dot. When and if that line of code is executed, the program will pause, and the line of code will be highlighted in yellow."

"Is there a limit to the number of breakpoints you can set in your code?" Barbara asked.

"No," I said, "you can have as many breakpoints as you want set at one time."

"How do you set a breakpoint, again?" Peter asked.

"There are four ways to set a breakpoint," I answered. "First, click in the margin to the left of the line of the code on which you wish to set a breakpoint. This is by far the easiest method. Second, you can select a line of code in the code window on which you wish to set a breakpoint, and then press the F9 function key—a breakpoint will be set on that line of code. Third, you can select a line of code in the code window, right-click your mouse, and select Insert Breakpoint. Finally, you can select a line of code in the code window, and select Debug | New Breakpoint from the Visual Basic menu bar. A window will be displayed, and you'll be able to set the same kind of breakpoint there as you would if you used one of the other three methods. There are also some other features available that you may want to experiment with on your own."

"How can you turn a breakpoint off?" Rhonda asked.

"That's easy!" I said. "Breakpoints can be toggled off and on by pressing F9 or by reclicking in the left margin. You can also select Debug | Clear All Breakpoints from the Visual Basic menu bar and that will clear every breakpoint in your program in one fell swoop."

It had been a pretty exhausting day of code coverage, particularly the latter part of the class where we covered the topic of debugging in depth. Prior to dismissing class for the day, I asked my students to keep these debugging techniques foremost in their minds while writing their programs.

"You'd be surprised," I said, "at the number of people who call me or e-mail me for assistance, telling me their programs don't work. My first question to them is: have you run your program in Step mode? They hardly ever have, and without doing so, they have no real idea what the true source of the problem is. Nine times out of ten, after running their program in Step mode, they see what the problem is and solve it for themselves—which is a far better learning experience than having me do it for them."

Summary

In this chapter, we began by discussing the concepts of event-driven programs, comparing them to the older style procedural program. In an event-driven program, your program needs to do something only when an event occurs. Everything in between is handled by the operating system. We then took a look at the major events that we would be handling in the China Shop Project, such as the Load event of the Form, and the Click event of the Button controls.

We spent some time looking at the three major program structures in Visual Basic—the sequence structure, the selection structure, and the loop structure. We saw how Visual Basic code behaves like falling rock—which is the sequence structure. What that means is that program code will execute, one line after another, unless interrupted either by a selection structure (such as an If statement) or a loop structure (which repeats lines of code). Without selection structures or loop structures, the programs we write would be pretty unintelligent.

The last half of the chapter was devoted to looking at the tools that collectively make up the Visual Basic Debugger. As I mentioned, these tools are not merely intended to help you when your program is not working the way you believe it should. They can also be very useful for seeing the way your program behaves behind the scenes. One of the most valuable debugging tools is the use of Step mode, the Step Into command, which enables you to see the execution of your program line by line.

Chapter 7---Data

In this chapter, we're going to discuss the concept of data in a computer program. What that means is that you'll finally get an in-depth look at something we've used quite a lot already, variables. I'll also introduce you to constants, the different types of Visual Basic data, and the many operations that can be performed on that data.

Computer Data

"Data can be a very complex topic," I said, "but it's an extremely important one. Failure to understand data can lead to problems with your programs down the line. What you hear today may seem very theoretical to you, but it will be vital for your future programming career. Even if you don't see an immediate application for it, look at the information you receive today as something that you can tuck into your programming back pocket for future use."

Variables

"In the Visual Basic programs that we write," I said, "the data with which we work will come from three places. The first is the user, in the form of selections they make from controls that we place on a form. The second is from external sources, such as a disk file, database, or the Windows registry. Finally, we sometimes get data internally in the form of variables."

I continued by explaining that variables, as we had seen in some of the code we had written in last week's class, are placeholders in the computer's memory where we can temporarily store information.

"I'm a little confused as to why we would create a variable in the first place," Barbara said. "Isn't all of the data that we need entered by the user?"

"A good question, Barbara," I said, "and to a degree that's true. Most of the data programs need will be entered by the user, or come from a disk file or database. However, there are times when your program may need to create a variable to store the answer to a question that we ask the user, store the result of an calculation, or, as we saw in the code we wrote last week, keep track of a counter."

"You said that variables enable us to store information temporarily," Kate said. "Do you mean until our program ends?"

"Not necessarily, Kate," I replied. "Variables, depending upon how and where they are declared, have varying lifetimes. It may not be obvious, but no variable can live past the point where our program ends. Some variables exist for only as long as an event procedure runs, being 'born' when the event procedure is triggered, and 'dying' when the event procedure ends. Other variables live for as long as a form is loaded—and in a program that has more than one form, this is an important point to realize."

I asked everyone to consider a hypothetical program, which I hoped would illustrate the need for variables in a program. "Suppose," I said, "we write a Visual Basic program to add two numbers. The program contains a form with two text boxes, a label, and a Button control. We want the user to enter a number into each of the two text boxes, then click on the Button control, and have the sum of the numbers displayed in the label's caption."

I pointed out the flexibility of this program. "This hypothetical program marks a departure from the code examples we've seen so far in this course, where the outcome of the program was predetermined. Here, the result of the program—the sum of the two numbers—is determined by what the user enters into the text boxes."

"What does this have to do with variables?" Linda asked.

"Hold on, you'll see," I said, as I started a new Visual Basic Windows application, and quickly placed two text boxes, a label, and a Button control on the form. I brought up the Properties window for the Label and cleared its Text property. I then double-clicked on the Button control and entered this code into its Click event procedure.

```
Private Sub Button1_Click(ByVal sender As System.Object, _
    ByVal e As System.EventArgs) Handles Button1.Click

Dim intFirstNumber As Integer
Dim intSecondNumber As Integer
intFirstNumber = CInt(TextBox1.Text)
intSecondNumber = CInt(TextBox2.Text)
```

```
Label1.Text = Str(intFirstNumber + intSecondNumber)
End Sub
```

I ran the program and entered the number 1 into the first text box and the number 2 into the second. I clicked on the Button control and the results of the calculation—the number 3—were displayed in the Text property of the Label control.

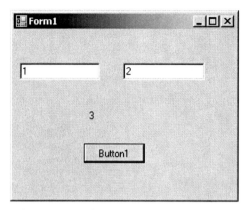

"I have absolutely no idea what that code means," Rhonda said, "but I love the program. I love its flexibility."

"At this point, Rhonda, I don't expect you to understand what's going on here," I said. "But by the end of today's class, I guarantee that you'll be comfortable with it."

"I think I can follow along with what's going on," Blaine said. "It looks like you're taking the Text properties of the two TextBox controls and assigning them to variables, then displaying the sum of the two variables in the Text property of the Label control. But what is CInt and Str?"

"Those are functions to perform data type conversion," I said. "As I mentioned when we started, an understanding of data in a Visual Basic program is very important—without those functions, this program would never run. Let me explain. The first two lines of code use the Visual Basic Dim statement—short for Dimension—to declare two Integer type variables called intFirstNumber and intSecondNumber into which we will store the two values that the user enters into the TextBox controls."

```
Dim intFirstNumber As Integer
Dim intSecondNumber As Integer
```

"The next two lines of code are a little more complicated," I said.

```
intFirstNumber = cInt(TextBox1.Text)
intSecondNumber = CInt(TextBox2.Text)
```

"The Text property of a TextBox control contains the value that the user enters into it. There's just one problem. Eventually, we want to perform a mathematical operation on that value, but the Text property of a TextBox isn't a numeric data type. It's something called a String, which is a character data type."

"Is that why you are assigning the value of the TextBox to an Integer variable?" Joe asked.

"That's excellent, Joe," I said, "That's exactly why. Unfortunately, we have one more problem. With Option Strict in place, we can't assign a String data type directly to an Integer data type. We must first convert the String data type to an Integer. That's why we used the CInt function with the value of the Text property of each TextBox as an argument, and then assigned that value to the Integer variable."

"So that's what CInt is," Linda said. "Convert-Integer?"

"That's a good way to think about it," I replied. "CInt is one of a series of functions that convert from one data type to another."

"What does Option Strict mean?" Chuck asked. "I don't recall you mentioning that before—did you?"

"I'm not sure that I have mentioned it before, Chuck," I said. "Option Strict is the default code option. It requires that all variables we use in code must first be explicitly declared, that any conversion from one data type to another not result in the loss of any data, and that in no case will Visual Basic convert from a String data type to a number and vice versa."

"What do you mean by loss of data?" Lou asked.

"You'll see in a moment or two," I answered, "that there are numeric data types that store whole numbers only—like Integer, and numeric data types that store numbers with fractional parts or decimals, such as the Single data type. If we were to store a value from a Single data type in an Integer data type, we'd lose the part to the right of the decimal point—and that would violate the Option Strict rule."

"Can we turn Option Strict off?" Mary asked.

"Yes, you can," I said, "by coding an Option Strict Off statement as the first line in the code window, like this…"

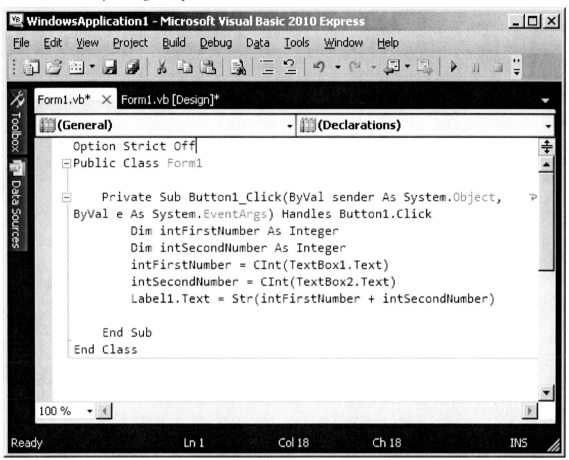

"…but that may not be the best idea. Option Strict in the long run will lead to less buggy code, and if you learn another language, such as C or Java, the habits you learn here in Visual Basic will be good ones to have."

"Didn't previous versions of Visual Basic have an Option Explicit statement?" Dave asked.

"That's right, Dave," I agreed, "and Visual Basic has one also. By default, both Option Strict and Option Explicit are on by default. Option Explicit requires that any variable that you use must first be declared. Never, ever, turn Option Explicit off—it will just lead to buggy code."

"If you turn Option Strict off, is Option Explicit still on?" Dave asked.

"Yes, it is," I said. "By default, both Option Strict and Option Explicit are on. If you turn off Option Strict, Option Explicit is still on. To turn off Option Explicit, you'll need to code an Option Explicit Off statement right after the Option Strict Off statement."

"What about that last line of code?" Valerie asked. "What's Str?"

Label1.Text = str(intFirstNumber + intSecondNumber)

"Str is the reverse of CInt," I said. "We first added the value of intFirstNumber and intSecondNumber, then took the result, and used the Str function to convert it to a string.

Then we assigned it to the Text property of the Label control. Since the Text property of the Label control is a String data type, we needed to convert it to a string prior to assigning the value to it."

How Do We Create a Variable?

"I think I understand what a variable is and what it's used for," Rhonda said. "But how do we create one? Is that what the line of code with 'Dim' does?"

"That's right, Rhonda," I said. "In Visual Basic, provided Option Strict or Option Explicit is turned on, you must formally announce to Visual Basic your intention to use a variable in your code by first declaring it. This declaration gives Visual Basic information it needs to name the variable and set up space in the computer's memory to hold it. Additionally, how and where you declare the variable will affect its scope and lifetime."

"Scope and lifetime?" Dave asked.

"Scope," I said, "refers to what parts of your Visual Basic program can see the variable. For instance, some programs that we write will have more than one form—and some may have other types of modules other than form modules called Standard modules. Will a variable declared in the Click event procedure of a Button control on Form1 be visible to a variable declared in the click event procedure of a CheckBox control on Form2? That's the scope issue, and we'll be discussing that today."

"What about lifetime?" Lou asked.

"Lifetime refers to how long a variable, once declared, lives," I said. "For instance, most variables that are declared in an event procedure live only for as long as the code in the event procedure is executing—and that's only until the End Sub line."

"Where else can you declare a variable other than an event procedure?" Peter asked.

"Besides event procedures," I answered, "you can declare variables in the Declarations section of your code window—which as we discussed last week is anywhere outside a procedure. Also, as we'll see in our last week of class, you can create your own custom procedures. These are procedures, much like event procedures, that are not triggered by an event, but which can be called by other code. In this class, we'll declare variables in all three places."

Variable Declaration

"In Visual Basic," I explained, "we can declare variables using six different Visual Basic declaration statements: Dim, Private, Public, Protected, Friend, and Shared. For the purposes of this course, we'll be discussing only the first three: Dim, Private, and Public. The other three pertain to Visual Basic project types that we aren't concerned about here."

"Can we use these declaration statements anywhere?" Dave asked.

"Perfect timing, Dave," I replied. "The answer is no. Within a procedure, both the event procedures for which we'll write the majority of our code and the custom procedures we'll write ourselves later on, only the Dim declaration statement may be used. Private and Public may not be used in a procedure—they can be used only in the Declarations section of the code window."

"What about the Dim statement?" Kathy asked. "Can that be used in the Declarations section?"

"Dim can be used in the Declarations section," I answered, "however, Microsoft recommends against doing so. Dim has the same affect as Private in the Declarations section, and so it's a good idea to use only Private and Public in the Declarations section. Here's a chart that summarizes where these declaration statements can and cannot be used."

Declaration Statement	Procedures?	Declarations Section?
Dim	Yes	Yes, but not advised
Private	No	Yes
Public	No	Yes

"I just tried to declare a variable below the Import statement at the top of my code window, and received a build error message," Jack said. "What did I do wrong?"

"It's a bit confusing," I noted, "but the Declarations section starts after the line that reads 'Public Class Form1'. Above that line is an area called the namespace, and we can't write code there, only code directives, such as the Import statements that you see there now, and the Option Strict and Option Explicit statements we discussed earlier."

I continued our discussion by making some general observations about the three different variable declaration statements:

- The scope of the variables declared with all three statements is complicated. Variables declared with the Dim statement in a procedure can only be seen by code within that procedure. The variables declared with the other two statements we'll discuss in detail a little later on.

- The lifetime of variables declared with all three statements is independent of the statement used to declare them. Their lifetime is entirely dependent upon where they are declared.

- Variables declared in a procedure cease to exist when the procedure ends. In other words, a variable declared in the Click event of a Button control "dies" when Visual Basic executes the End Sub statement of the Button control's event procedure.

- Variables declared in the General Declaration section of a form "die" when the form is unloaded or when the program ends.

"Now let's look at each declaration statement," I said, "and discuss each one in detail."

The Dim Statement

"We've seen it already, but here's the syntax for the Dim statement," I said, as I displayed the syntax on the classroom projector.

Dim variablename [As type]

"In case this is the first time you've seen the official Microsoft syntax for a statement," I said, "the words contained within brackets are optional. Therefore, 'As type' is an optional statement, but one which you should almost always include. Whenever possible, you should tell Visual Basic the exact data type of the variable you are declaring."

"Suppose you don't explicitly assign a variable type," Linda asked. "What happens then?"

"In that case," I answered, "Visual Basic sets the variable up as something called an Object data type, which is a horribly inefficient variable type. The bottom line: whenever possible, explicitly declare the data type."

"What are the rules for naming a variable?" Steve asked. "Can I name one just about anything I want?"

"Just about, Steve," I answered. "Here are the Visual Basic rules for naming variables:"

- Variable names must begin with a letter.

- Variable names must contain only alphabetic characters, decimal digits, and underscores.

- Variable names may not contain periods, commas, and other special characters.

- Variable names can be no longer than 255 characters.

- Variable names cannot have the same name as a Visual Basic statement, function, or command. For example, you can't name a variable 'Loop' or 'If'

- Variable names must be unique within their scope of declaration. For example, you can't declare two variables called intCounter in the same event procedure. Neither can you declare two variables called m_intCounter in the Declarations section of a form.

"My recommendations go a little further than the Microsoft recommendations," I said, "because I'm a stickler for readability. I want to be able to tell, from the name of the variable, its data type, its scope, and something about it. For that reason, I suggest that you name your variables using the following conventions:"

- The first three characters of the variable name should describe its data type. For instance, use int as the first three characters for an Integer data type variable. Some programmers use a single character, but three characters is much more descriptive.

- A variable declared in the Declarations section of a form should begin with the prefix "m_". Therefore, a variable called intCounter declared in the Declarations section of the form should be named m_intCounter. The m, which stands for module level, lets you know that the variable is declared at the module level.

- A variable declared as Public in the Declarations section of a Standard module (Standard modules are something we don't discuss in this class) should begin with the prefix "g_". Therefore, a variable called strUser declared in the Declarations section of a Standard module should be named g_strUser. The g, which stands for global, lets you know that the variable's scope is global to the project.

"Once you get beyond the prefix," I said, "the remainder of the variable name should be something meaningful, but not too lengthy. You have 255 characters to name your variable meaningfully, but remember this: the name that you assign your variable is the same name that you'll need to use when you refer to it in code. Long variable names can be a real pain to type, especially if you're not a quick typist. The ideal is to make your variable names as meaningful as possible with the fewest characters possible."

"Do you remember what you said earlier in the course about naming controls in mixed case?" Dave asked. "Does that apply to variables as well?"

"That's an excellent point, Dave" I said. "Just as I suggested last week that you should name Visual Basic controls in mixed case—for instance, btnOK for the OK button—name your variables in the same way. Then, as you type them into the code window, be sure to enter them in lowercase. Visual Basic should convert them to mixed case for you automatically. If the variable name doesn't change, you know something is wrong (most likely, you misspelled it)."

"Is the word 'As' required in a variable declaration?" Barbara asked.

"With Option Strict on," I said, "the As parameter is required. If we turn Option Strict off, we can choose not to declare an explicit data type, in which case the variable will be declared as a catchall Object data type. Take my advice: always use the As parameter, don't get lazy and not explicitly declare your variable's data type. Explicitly declaring the data type of a variable saves memory, and it can also prevent you from storing invalid data in a variable."

"What do you mean?" Ward asked.

"For instance, Ward," I said, "if we declare a variable as an Integer data type and then attempt to store a number with a decimal in that variable, Visual Basic won't allow it because of the variable's declared data type. If Visual Basic permitted that kind of operation, we would lose the decimal portion of the number—which, depending upon the program, could have catastrophic consequences."

"Let's get back to this Option Strict issue again," Chuck said. "You said with Option Strict off, we could declare a variable without an explicit data type and it would be created as what kind of data type?"

"Object," I answered quickly. "The Object data type is a chameleon data type, because it assumes the characteristic of the data that is stored in it."

"That doesn't sound so bad to me," Joe said.

"An Object data type consumes much more memory and can make your programs run slower," I said. "As I said earlier, always declare your variables with an explicit data type."

Declaring More than One Variable with one line of code

"While we're on the topic of variable declaration," Dave said, "can you declare more than one variable on the same line of code?"

"Yes," I said, "you can. In previous versions of Visual Basic, this was a problem. But with Visual Basic, this statement…"

Dim intPrice1, intPrice2, intPrice3 As Integer

"…will declare three variables, intPrice1, intPrice2, and intPrice3, all as Integer data types. Personally, for readability in this introductory course, I prefer that you declare each of your variables on a separate line of code like this…"

Dim intPrice1 As Integer
Dim intPrice2 As Integer
Dim intPrice3 As Integer

"…but with Visual Basic, you don't have to."

Variable Scope

"Variable scope," I said, "refers to what other parts of your Visual Basic program can see the variable. Another way to think about Scope is how far your variable can be seen from where it is declared. In the case of variables declared using the Dim statement, it's not very far. Since you should only use the Dim statement to declare a variable in a procedure, variables declared in a procedure using the Dim statement can only be seen in that procedure. Variables like this are said to have local scope. You might also hear them described as being local to the procedure in which they are declared."

"I'm a little confused," Rhonda said. "Is local scope a good thing or a bad thing?"

"That depends," I replied. "The rule of thumb is to declare your variables locally and then if they need to be seen outside the procedure, declare them in the Declarations section. For instance, suppose you write code in the Click event procedure of a Button control that performs some sort of calculation. In so doing, perhaps you store the result of that calculation in a variable you declared using the Dim statement in the Click event procedure. Is this variable local?"

"Yes, it is," Kate volunteered. "Code in another event procedure cannot see the value of the variable. Is that right?"

"Excellent, Kate," I answered. "You're absolutely right. In fact, not only can the value of that variable not be seen outside the procedure, when the Click event procedure ends—that is, when the End Sub is reached—the variable dies, and with it, the data that it contained."

I waited a minute before going on.

"Back to your question, Rhonda," I said. "Is a local variable a good thing or a bad thing? A local variable uses less of your program resources, which is a good thing, but if you need to have the value of that variable accessible from outside its procedure, well, that's."

"A bad thing!" Rhonda answered, finishing my sentence, and obviously understanding what I was getting at. "Okay, I think I'm beginning to understand. Declaring variables is more than just a matter of typing the word Dim."

"If you wanted to make the value of that variable visible to other procedures," Steve said, "how could you do it?"

"You can declare the variable in the Declarations section of the form," I said. "Then the variable and its data can be seen by every procedure contained within that form."

"Would you use Dim, Private, or Public for the declaration statement?" Mary asked.

"Remember, in theory we can use Dim in the Declarations section, but it's not recommended," I said. "So that leaves us with Private and Public. A variable declared as Private in the Declarations section can be seen by every procedure on the form, but not procedures on other forms. A variable declared as Public in the Declarations section can be seen by every procedure in every part of your Visual Basic project—that means every form and also every Standard module—something we won't be discussing in this class."

I waited a moment before continuing.

"Let me do a little demonstration to clear this up," I said. I started a new Windows application project, with a form containing a single Button control. I then placed the following code in the **Load** event procedure of the form.

Dim intDemo As Integer
intDemo = 22

"As you can see," I said, "I've declared intDemo as an Integer data type, and I've assigned the value of 22 to it. Because the variable is declared local to the Load event procedure, we would not expect it to be visible to any code outside of the event procedure. Let's prove that theory by placing code in the Click event procedure of the Button control to display the value of intDemo in a Visual Basic message box…"

```
Private Sub Button1_Click(ByVal sender As System.Object, _
  ByVal e As System.EventArgs) Handles Button1.Click

MessageBox.Show (intDemo)

End Sub
```

"My intention here is to display the value of the variable intDemo," I said, "but if I run this program now, we're not going to get very far."

I clicked the Start button and ran the program, but when I clicked on the Button control, the following error message was displayed on the classroom projector.

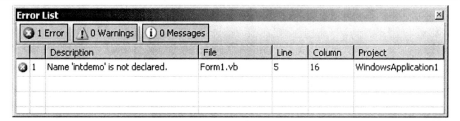

"Can anyone tell me what happened?" I asked innocently.

"You declared the variable intDemo in the Load Event procedure," Dave said, "and tried to refer to it in the Click event procedure of the Button control. You can't do that, because a variable declared in a procedure is local to that procedure and can't be seen outside of it. Besides, when the Load event procedure ended, the variable intDemo died—and with it, its value."

"Absolutely right, Dave," I said. "That's exactly what that build error is telling us. Now let's see what happens if we remove the declaration from the Load event procedure of the form. We'll leave the assignment of the value 22 in there, though, and declare the variable intDemo in the Declarations section of the form instead. Remember, the Declarations section begins after the line that reads 'Public Class'. For readability, we should place variable declaration statements after the 'Inherits' line…"

```
Public Class Form1
    Private intDemo as Integer
```

As before, I ran the program—this time with no error messages—and clicked on the Button control. This message box was displayed.

"Can you explain what's happening here?" Ward said, "I think I'm a bit lost."

"Changing the location of the declaration of the variable intDemo," I said, "from the form's Load event procedure to the Declarations section of the form changed its scope from local to what is known as Form level or sometimes Module level. What that means is that code in any event procedure on the form can see it—which is why we were able to assign a value of intDemo in the Load event procedure and displays its value in a message box in the Button1_Click event procedure."

I looked around the room and saw some uncertainty.

"Knowing where to declare your variables in order to make your program work the way you want is very important," I said. "But, and this is a big but, this knowledge doesn't happen overnight. It takes practice and experience, so don't worry if you're not totally understanding this."

"Thank goodness," Rhonda exclaimed out loud. "I thought it was me!"

I took a moment to assure Rhonda that everyone feels this way about variables the first time they see them.

The Private Statement

"Here's the syntax for the Private statement," I said as I displayed the syntax on the classroom projector. "Remember, the Private statement can only be used in the Declarations section of the form (or a Standard module)…"

Private variablename [As type]

"Notice that the syntax of the Private statement, except for the word 'Private' itself, is identical to that of the Dim statement," I said. "And not only is the syntax nearly identical, but the usage is too."

"Then what's the difference?" Linda asked.

"If you look at the chart I distributed earlier…"

Declaration Statement	Procedures?	Declarations Section?
Dim	Yes	Yes, but not advised
Private	No	Yes
Public	No	Yes

"…you'll see that the Private and Public statements can only be used in the Declarations section of the form."

"As far as scope for the Private variable," Dave said, "did you say that a variable declared using the Private statement in the Declarations section of the form can only be seen by procedures on the form? Is that right?"

"Right again, Dave," I said. No one had any more questions and so we moved on to the Public statement.

The Public Statement

I displayed the syntax for the Public statement on the classroom projector.

Public variablename [As type]

"Like the Private statement," I said, "the Public statement can only be used in the Declarations section of a form."

"What is the difference, then," asked Linda, "between the Private and Public statements?"

"In a single word, scope," I said. "A variable declared as Private in the Declarations section of a form is only visible to procedures on that form. However, a variable declared as Public in the Declarations section of a form is visible everywhere within the project. That may be hard for you to visualize right now since you haven't seen a project with more than one form. But believe me, in just about every Visual Basic project on which you'll work, you'll have more than one form."

No one seemed to having any problems with this material, and I took one final opportunity to summarize.

Where Should You Declare a Variable?

"We've seen that it's possible to declare variables in procedures and in the Declarations section of the form," I said, "so before we move on to a discussion of Visual Basic Data types, I just want to take this opportunity to give you some guidelines as to where to declare your variables. There are no hard and fast rules, but here are some guidelines:"

- Declare the variable with as limited a scope as necessary. Start by declaring the variable in the event procedure where you will use it. If that doesn't do the trick, expand the scope from there.

- If you know that a variable and its value will need to be accessed from more than one procedure on a form, declare the variable using the Private statement in the Declarations section of the form.

- If you know that a variable and its value will need to be accessed by a procedure on another form, declare the variable using the Public statement in the Declarations section of the form.

Must Variables Be Initialized?

Steve remarked that in other programming languages with which he was familiar, a variable is first declared and then its value needs to be initialized before it can be used in an expression. He wanted to know if that was true of Visual Basic.

I explained to the class that the term "initialization" means to assign an initial value to a variable after you declare it.

"Steve's right," I said. "In other programming languages, variables must be initialized before they can be used in an expression, but in Visual Basic it's not necessary. If you want, you can initialize your variables at the time you declare them. But it's not necessary. Visual Basic automatically initializes variables for you, based on their data type. For instance, variables declared as numeric data types, such as Integers and Longs, are initialized to 0. Variables declared as Strings are initialized to something called an empty string. There's a Visual Basic data type called Date, which is initialized to January 1, 0001 at 12:00 A.M. Visual Basic Boolean data types, which can hold either True or False values, are initialized to False."

Visual Basic Data Types

"It's now time," I said, "to take a closer look at the data types in Visual Basic. Data types follow the optional As statement in the variable declaration statements."

I reminded my students that if you don't explicitly declare a data type for your variable, the variable is implicitly declared as an Object, a data type that adapts itself to the actual data that is stored in it.

"The choice of a data type for your variable," I said, "can be crucial to the proper operation of your program. Each Visual Basic data type has unique memory requirements, along with capabilities and operations that you can perform on them."

I displayed this list of data types on the classroom projector:

- Boolean
- Byte
- Char
- Date
- Decimal
- Double
- Integer
- Long
- Short
- Single
- String

"For the next half hour or so we'll discuss all of these data types in detail. First, though, let's take a quick break so that we can tackle the subject fresh."

Numeric Data Types

After the break, I began to discuss the Visual Basic numeric data types. "Declare your variable as a numeric data type," I said, "when you know you will be using it to store a number which will later be used in a mathematical calculation."

"What about a telephone number or a Social Security number?" Ward asked. "Those both contain numbers, but are usually written with dashes in them."

"A String data type is a better choice for those two," I said, "Although they contain numbers, neither one of them is typically used in a mathematical calculation."

I continued by saying that Visual Basic has eight different numeric data types: Byte, Char, Decimal, Double, Integer, Long, Short, and Single.

"Typically I use Short, Integer, Long, Single, and Double in my work," I said. "Byte, Char, and Decimal are a bit specialized."

I then displayed this chart of the Visual Basic numeric data types on the classroom projector.

Data Type	Storage Size	Value Range
Byte	1 byte	0 to 255 (unsigned)
Char	2 bytes	0 to 65535 (unsigned)
Decimal	12 bytes	+/79,228,162,514,264,337,593,543,950,335 with no decimal point; +/-7.9228162514264337593543950335 with 28 places to the right of the decimal; smallest non-zero number is +/-0.0000000000000000000000000001

Double	8 bytes	-1.79769313486231E308 to -4.94065645841247E-324 for negative values; 4.94065645841247E-324 to 1.79769313486232E308 for positive values
Integer	4 bytes	-2,147,483,648 to 2,147,483,647
Long	8 bytes	-9,223,372,036,854,775,808 to 9,223,372,036,854,775,807
Short	2 bytes	-32,768 to 32,767
Single	4 bytes	-3.402823E38 to -1.401298E-45 for negative values; 1.401298E-45 to 3.402823E38 for positive values

I then continued with this explanation:

- Choose Byte, Char, Decimal, Integer, Short, and Long data types to store whole numbers (called integers), such as 23, 45, or 34470.

- Choose Decimal, Double, and Single data types to store numbers with fractions, such as 3.1416, 23.12, 45.22, or 357644.67.

"Now let's take a closer look at each of these," I said.

Byte

"The Byte data type can hold only whole, positive numbers; it can't be used to store a number with a fractional part. The size of the number that you can store in a Byte data type is not very large—from 0 to 255. Only use the Byte data type if you are certain that the number you will store in it is within that range, otherwise you will generate an error."

Char

"The Char data type, like the Byte data type, can hold only whole, positive numbers. It can store a number a little larger than the Byte data type—up to 65,535. Be certain that the number you will store in a variable of this type falls within that range, otherwise you will generate an error."

Short

"Next in line," I said, "in terms of storage capacity is the Short data type, also known as the Short Integer. Like the Byte and Char data types, the Short data type can store only a whole number. Unlike the Byte and Char data types, however, the Short data type can store a negative number. Its storage range is -32,768 to 32,767."

Integer

"Next up is the Integer data type," I said, "which is a larger version of the Short data type. Like all the numeric data types we've discussed so far, the Integer data type can store only whole numbers. Its storage range is pretty large: 2,147,483,648 to 2,147,483,647."

"What happens if you try to store a number with a fractional part in a variable declared as an integer?" Dave asked.

"With Option Strict on," I said, "Visual Basic won't even allow you to run the program."

"Can you give us some examples of when we would want to use the various data types?" Rose asked.

"Sure thing, Rose," I said. "We could use the Byte data type to easily store the number of students in this class. We could use Char to store the number of students on this campus. We could use a Short data type to store the temperature at the North Pole. Finally, we could use the Integer data type to store the number of people in the United States, but it wouldn't suffice to store the number of people in the world. That would require the Long data type, which we're about to examine."

"Does it hurt to declare all of our numeric variables as an Integer data type?" Linda asked.

"Declaring a variable larger than it needs to be is a waste of storage," I said. "As you can see from our chart, the Integer data type requires 4 bytes of storage. If you know that the values you'll be storing in a variable require the storage capacity of a Short data type, declare Short as the data type. This kind of attention to detail makes your program run faster, reduces its runtime requirements, and will be something that a prospective employer will be looking for when examining your sample code."

Long

"Next up is the Long data type," I said, "which is the largest version of the Integer data types. Like all the numeric data types we've discussed so far, the Long data type can store whole numbers only. Its storage range is huge: 9,223,372,036,854,775,808 to 9,223,372,036,854,775,807."

At this point I could see that Linda was beginning to look somewhat confused and was glancing back over her notes. Eventually she asked, "In the code where we counted from 1 to 10,000 using a For...Next loop, why did we declare the counter variable as Integer? Wouldn't it have been more efficient to declare it as Short?"

"That's a good point, Linda," I observed. "You're right in saying it would have been better to declare lngCounter as a Short or even a Char data type, both of which would handle whole numbers of 10,000 or less and which use less bytes to store the number than a Long. My excuse is that I've coded thousands of loops like this in my career, and I habitually code For...Next loops with the largest Integer data type I can. Because of that, it's easy to change the 10,000 to 1,000,000 without having to change the data type of our counter variable."

Linda was beginning to grow confident in her understanding of data types, and I could sense that she had another question.

"I know that the range for a Long data type is large," she said, "but I'm sure there are numbers in common ordinary life—such as the number of stars in the sky, for instance, that even the Large data type can't handle. What do we do then?"

"That's when we need to use either the Single or Double data type," I said.

Single

"The difference between the Single and Double data types, and the Integer data types that we've examined, is that both the Single and Double can store values that mathematicians call real numbers—that is, numbers with fractional parts. You may hear the Single and Double data types referred to as floating-point data types."

I explained that variables declared as Single data types require 4 bytes of RAM to hold them. Values for the single data type can range from -3.402823E38 to -1.401298E-45 for negative values and from 1.401298E-45 to 3.402823E38 for positive values.

"Unless you're fresh from a math class," I said, "you may have trouble reading that range, since they're expressed in a format known as scientific or exponential notation, which is a special notation used to represent very large numbers. In short, the number following the capital letter E tells you how many zeros follow the number in front of the capital letter E. For instance, the number 1.0E13 means that 13 zeros follow 1.0. That's a pretty big number, and looks like this is if we were to write it out."

10,000,000,000,000

"That number is read as '1 times 10 raised to the 13th power'. Trying to write out the range for the Single data type would be a good deal more difficult, since one end of the range has 38 zeros in it, and the other end has 45. We wouldn't have room to write the range on paper, so that's why we use exponential or scientific notation to represent the number."

"I guess any way you look at it, those are huge numbers," Kate said, laughing. "I'm not likely to think of a number that requires those values."

"Just remember," I said, "that if you need to store a value with a fractional part in a variable, you'll need to use one of these data types—most likely the Single."

Double

"Just as the Long data type is really a bigger version of the Integer," I said, "so the Double data type is a bigger version of the Single."

I explained that variables declared as Double data types require 8 bytes of RAM. Values for the Double can range from -1.79769313486232E308 to -4.94065645841247E-324 for negative values and from 4.94065645841247E-324 to 1.79769313486232E308 for positive values.

"If you take the upper limit for the Single data type," I said, "and add about 270 zeros to it, that will give a good estimate for the upper limit of the Double!"

I don't think there was anyone in the class who could think of a value that would exceed the range of the Double.

A moment later, Dave noted that both the Integer and Single data types require the same amount of RAM (4 bytes), yet the Single data type holds a much larger range of values.

"That's a good point," I said. "The two floating-point data types can store extraordinarily large values, but they do so at the expense of accuracy. If you need accuracy to the range of more than four places after the decimal point, you'll need to store the value in the Decimal data type—which gives you a lot more accuracy, but which requires more RAM to store the number."

Decimal

"The final numeric data type we'll discuss today is the Decimal," I said.

I explained that variables declared as Decimal data types consume 12 bytes of RAM. Values for the Decimal data type can range from +/-79,228,162,514,264,337,593,543,950,335 with no decimal point; +/-7.9228162514264337593543950335 with 28 places to the right of the decimal; and the smallest non-zero number is +/-0.0000000000000000000000000001

"The Decimal data type, which requires 12 bytes of RAM, has greater accuracy than either the Single or Double data types, but not quite the range. This data type should be chosen to store a value whenever accuracy is paramount, such as in financial calculations or scientific calculations."

Finished with our discussion of numeric data types, we then moved on to the String data type.

The String Data Type

"Choose the String data type," I said, "when you need to store text, such as a name, telephone number, or Social Security number. As I mentioned earlier, although a telephone number consists of numbers, these are not numbers that are typically used in a mathematical calculation, and so the String data type is more appropriate. Other common examples of values that should be stored as a String data type are ZIP codes, street numbers, and employee ID numbers."

"Previous versions of Visual Basic had two String data types, fixed length and variable length. Visual Basic has only variable length strings. A variable length string just means that the variable can hold as many characters as you assign to it via an assignment statement. There's no need to explicitly tell Visual Basic ahead of time how many characters the variable will hold." I displayed a string variable declaration on the classroom projector.

Dim strName as String

"How many bytes of RAM does a string variable require?" Chuck asked.

"It depends on the amount of characters that are stored in the variable," I said. "You might think that a string variable that contains the word 'Smiley' would consume 6 bytes of RAM. In actuality, it uses 22. All string variables require 10 bytes of overhead, plus two times the number of characters that are stored in it. Therefore, to store the word 'Smiley' in a string variable requires 22 bytes of RAM—10 + (2 times 6)."

"So if we were to store a single character in a string variable, it would use 12 bytes of RAM, is that right?" Rose asked.

"That's right Rose," I said.

"How large can a String data type be?" Blaine asked.

"A String data type can hold about 2 billion characters," I said. "That means in a single string variable, we could store the contents of any book ever written."

"Can you clarify for me how to assign a value to a string variable?" asked Ward. "Do we need to place the value within quotation marks?"

"That's a great question, Ward," I said, "and thanks for asking it. You're right, the assignment of a value to a string variable is different than assigning a number to a numeric variable. When assigning a value to a numeric variable, we don't put quotation marks around the value. When assigning a value to a string variable, we do. Here's an example of each."

I then displayed this example on the classroom projector.

```
Dim intDemo as Integer          'Declare an Integer Variable
Dim strDemo as String           'Declare a String Variable

intDemo = 22                    'Assign a value to the Integer variable
strDemo = "John Smiley"         'Assign a value to the String variable
```

"As you can see," I said, "when you assign a value to a string variable, you enclose the value within quotation marks. When assigning a value to a numeric variable, you must not enclose it within quotation marks."

"I just tried assigning a value to a string variable using an apostrophe around the value," Mary said, "but it won't work. We can't use an apostrophe?"

"I'm glad you tried that now," I said. "In Visual Basic, the apostrophe can only be used to designate a comment. Only quotation marks can serve as the delimiter around a string value."

No one had any other questions, and so we moved on to the remaining Visual Basic data types.

Other Data Types

"I hate to group the remaining data types into one big 'other' category," I said, "but that's exactly what they are. As a beginner, most of the variables that you will declare will either be Numeric data types or String data types. The variables we're about to discuss will be the kind you'll use as your sophistication and programming prowess increase."

Boolean

"Boolean data types," I said, "are sometimes called Yes/No data types. Boolean data types can have only two possible values: True or False."

I displayed this code on the classroom projector.

```
Dim blnMarried As Boolean       'Declare a Boolean Variable
Dim blnRetired As Boolean       'Declare a Boolean Variable

blnMarried = True               'Assign True
blnRetired = False              'Assign False
```

I explained that I had declared two Boolean variables, and then assigned the values True and False to the respective variables.

"What we've done here," I said, "is to declare two Boolean variables—one to represent someone's marital status, and the other to represent their retirement status. The Boolean variable is ideal to use when the value can only be a True/False or a Yes/No outcome."

I continued by pointing out that Visual Basic's treatment of Boolean variables is a little different than anything we've seen before.

"For instance," I said, "you can code an If statement to evaluate the value of a Boolean variable in this way…"

If blnMarried = True Then

"… or you can use this notation…"

If blnMarried Then

"In fact," I said, "those two statements are considered the same by Visual Basic."

"What happened to the word True in the second statement?" Barbara asked.

"You can do that with Boolean data types," I said. "If you omit the word True or False in the comparison statement, Visual Basic assumes True. In fact, with Boolean data types, instead of writing…"

If blnMarried = False Then

"…you can write this code."

If Not blnMarried Then

"That's cool," Bob said. "That's almost English-like."

"That's one of the great things about the Boolean data type," I said. "I think you'll agree omitting the True or False comparison makes the code a little easier to read. Again, this is something you can only do with the Boolean data type. By the way, we'll examine the Not keyword later in today's class."

Date

"Date data types are intended to hold dates," I said. "Choose this data type whenever you wish to store a date."

I explained that Date data types require 8 bytes of RAM, which makes them one of the most RAM-intensive data types we've examined. Valid values for the Date data type can range from January 1, 0001 to December 31, 9999.

"What's the advantage of using the Date data type over a String data type?" Steve asked. "Can't you store a date in a string variable?"

"It's true, you can store a date in a string variable," I said. "But the advantage of storing a date in a Date data type variable is that you get access to Visual Basic's built-in 'date arithmetic' and that means the ability to use an assortment of Visual Basic date functions. We had some experience last week with one of those functions when we worked with the WeekDay function against the return value of the Now function, which returns the current date as a Date data type. None of these Date functions can work on anything other than a Date data type—and that's why if you want to store a date in a variable, you should ensure that you store it as a Date data type."

Property Data Types

"I remember you saying that properties of the form and each one of the controls have a data type," Dave said. "In particular, you said that the Text property of a TextBox control is a String data type. How can we determine the data type of a form or a control's property?"

"That's a good question," I said. "Each property has its own data type, which is part of the object's definition, which is hidden away in the object itself. However, there is a way to find out the data type of an object's property, and that's to use the Visual Basic Object Browser."

I reminded the class that we had briefly discussed the Object Browser during our IDE overview a few weeks earlier. I displayed the Object Browser by selecting View | Object Browser from the Visual Basic menu bar.

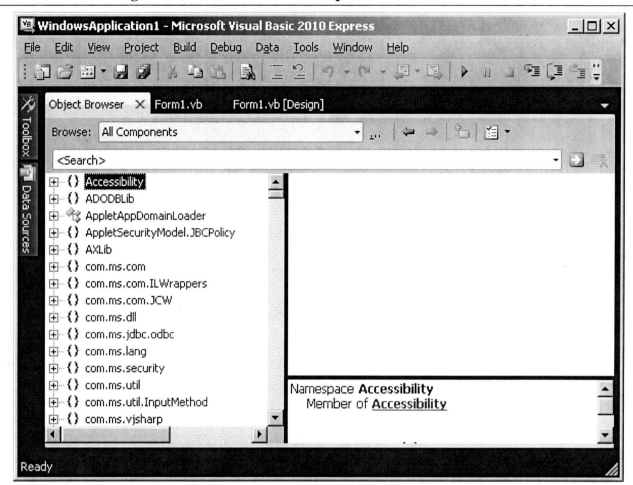

I pointed out that in Visual Basic, objects are members of object libraries. To find a property for an object using the Object Browser, type the name of an object in the Search Textbox at the top of the Object window. I did that, entering the word TextBox into the Search Textbox.

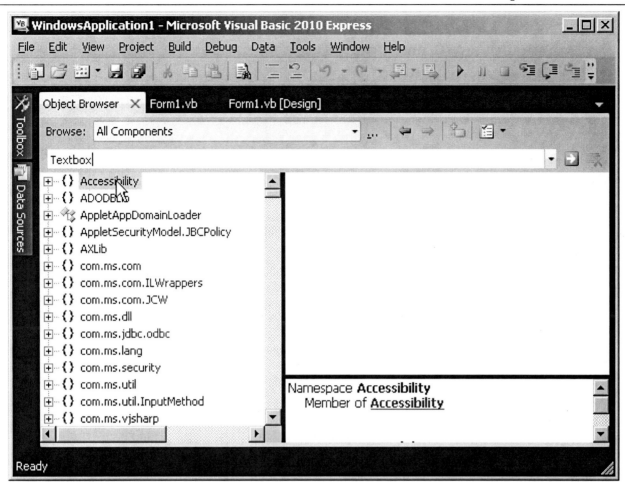

and then clicked the Green right arrow button. A window of results was returned.

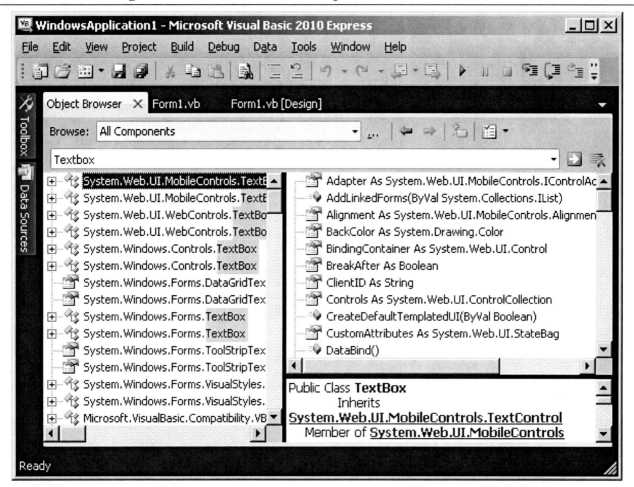

"As you can see," I said, "there are a number of instances of TextBox found in the Object Browser. The third is the definition of the TextBox class for a Windows Form---what we are interested in---which is where we'll find all of the properties, methods, and events of the TextBox control we place on a Windows Form."

I then selected the System.Windows.Controls.TextBox listed in the results window, and scrolled through the right pane, where the members (properties, methods, and events of the TextBox control) are listed, and found and selected the Text property.

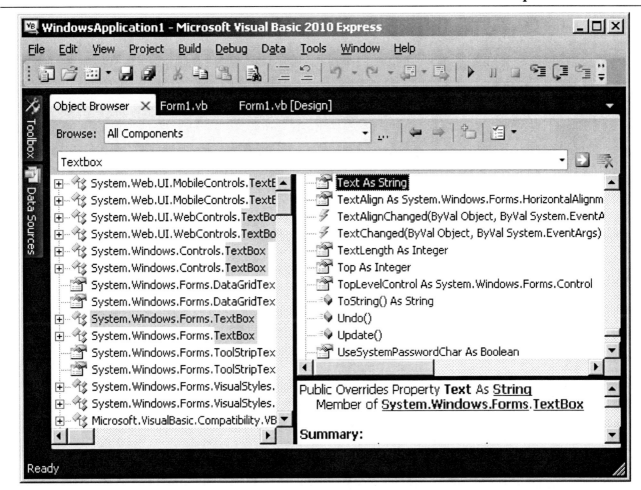

"Everything is in there," I said with a smile, "it's just a matter of being able to find it. I don't know whether you noticed, but the definition for the Text property is in the bottom pane of the Object Browser window. As you can see, the Text property of the TextBox control is a String data type."

I could see some of the students experimenting with the Object Browser. "Do we need to do this for each property we use?" Rhonda asked.

"I'm sorry, I didn't mean to imply that," I replied. "Knowing the data type of an object's property is helpful, but not essential. Besides, you should be able to find the same information somewhere in Visual Basic Help—but sometimes that is even more difficult to find. Some properties are fairly obvious from the Properties window. For instance, the Enabled property of a control is intuitively a Boolean data type, since only True and False appear as options for this property in the Properties window. However, other properties may not be so obvious, and knowing the data type of a property can save you headaches down the road."

Constants

"In addition to variables," I said, "there's one more Visual Basic entity for which you must choose a data type when you create it, and that's the Visual Basic Constant."

"Constant?" Linda asked. "That sounds like it should be the opposite of a variable."

"You're right, Linda," I said, "that's exactly how it sounds, but the constant is very much like a variable. A Visual Basic constant, like a variable, is a placeholder in the computer's memory that holds a value. Unlike a variable, however, you must assign a value to a constant when you declare it, and thereafter, the value of the constant can never change."

"How are constants declared?" Peter asked.

"You declare constants in a manner similar to a variable," I answered, "and as is the case with variables, if Option Strict is in effect, you must also declare a data type with its declaration. Constants can be declared anywhere you can declare a variable—that is, in a procedure or in the Declarations section of a form."

"What's the purpose of a constant?" Steve asked. "That is, when should you use one?"

I thought for a moment. "One good rule of thumb is this: whenever you find yourself declaring a variable, and assigning a value to it which never changes, it probably should be a constant. Also, if you make use of numeric literals—that is, numbers in your program—consider using a constant instead."

"Can you give us an example?" Linda asked.

"Sure thing, Linda," I replied. "For example, let's say you are writing a program to calculate payroll, and let's assume that there's a state tax rate equal to 1 percent of gross pay. Somewhere in your program, you are going to need to multiply the gross pay amount by 0.01, like this…"

sngGrossPayAmount * .01

"Now further suppose you perform this same calculation in several different places in your program, each time multiplying gross pay by the number 0.01. Let me ask this question: what happens to your program if the state tax rate changes from 1 percent to 2 percent?"

"Obviously," Dave said, "we would have to change the number we've been using from 0.01 to 0.02."

"That's right, Dave," I agreed, "and because we have that number hard-coded in several places in our program, we will need to through each and every line of code in our program looking for 0.01, and then changing it to 0.02."

"How can a constant help here?" Steve asked.

"Instead of using the number 0.01 in our calculations a multiple number of times," I answered, "we could declare a constant called STATETAXRATE, assign it the value of 0.01 and then use the constant in all of our calculations instead, like this."

sngGrossPayAmount * STATETAXRATE

"I see now," Rhonda said. "If the state tax rate changes, since we used the name of the constant—not the number 0.01 in our calculation—we only need to change the declaration statement for the constant to reflect the new value."

"That's perfect, Rhonda, " I said.

"Can we see an example of a constant declaration?" Barbara asked. I displayed this declaration of a constant on the classroom projector.

Const STATETAXRATE as Single = .01

"By convention," I said, "constants are named in all capital letters. This makes it pretty easy to identify constants in your code. Notice also that the value of the constant is specified when it is declared."

"I noticed," Ward said, "that the word 'constant' isn't spelled out in the declaration you displayed on the project—it's spelled C-O-N-S-T. Is that a mistake?"

"No, that's the correct spelling" I said, "I've seen quite a few programmers try to declare a constant by spelling the entire word, but that just generates an error."

"I see what you mean about a constant being very similar to a variable," Dave said. In fact, they don't seem very different at all. I guess the main difference is that a constant, once assigned a value, can never be changed."

"I have a question," Rhonda said. "In your example of the state tax rate, couldn't you have declared a variable, assigned it a value, and then used that variable in all of your calculations?"

"You've raised an interesting point," I said. "In fact, that's what a lot of programmers do, which is why I suggested that if you declare a variable, assign it a value, and it never changes, perhaps it should be a constant instead. But you should bear in mind that there are two big benefits to using constants. First, and perhaps most importantly, Visual Basic works with constants much more efficiently than variables. For a number of reasons, accessing a constant is faster than accessing a variable, and therefore your program will run faster. Secondly, the value of a constant can't be accidentally changed once it's been declared. This can prevent disastrous results in a program. The bottom line is: if you declare a variable, assign it a value, and there is no chance that the value of that variable will ever change, what you have there is a constant, and you should declare it as such."

Operations on Data

"Since you now all know something about Visual Basic's data types," I said, "now's the time to learn how to perform operations on that data. Let's start with arithmetic operations."

Arithmetic Operations

I explained that arithmetic operations are performed on data stored in numeric variables, numeric constants, or numeric properties.

"Now let's look at the various arithmetic operations available in Visual Basic."

The Addition Operator

"The addition operation (+) adds two expressions," I said, as I displayed this example of the addition operation on the classroom projector."

intValue1 + intValue2

"Notice that I didn't say that it adds two numbers. In Visual Basic, an expression can be a number, a variable, a constant, the value of a property, or any combination of these. As long as Visual Basic can evaluate the expression as a number, the addition operation will work."

"What do you mean by evaluate?" Kate asked.

"When Visual Basic evaluates an expression," I replied, "it examines the expression, substituting actual values for the variables, constants, and property values that it sees."

I took a moment to point out that Visual Basic performs operations on only a pair of operands at one time.

"What's an operand?" Ward asked.

"An operand is something that the operator operates on. There's an operand on either side of an arithmetic operator," I said. "No matter how many operators appear in an expression, Visual Basic performs an operation on just two operands at a time."

"That's a little surprising to me," Rhonda said. "Are you saying that no matter how fast my PC, it still performs arithmetic the way I was taught in school—one step at a time?"

"That's right, Rhonda," I said. I continued by explaining that the result of all Visual Basic arithmetic operations must either be assigned to a variable or become an expression in another Visual Basic statement, such as a MessageBox.Show statement. I then illustrated the use of variables with the operator with an example.

I placed a Button control onto a form and placed this code in its Click event procedure.

```
Private Sub Button1_Click(ByVal sender As System.Object, _
    ByVal e As System.EventArgs) Handles Button1.Click

Dim intValue1 As Integer = 13
Dim intValue2 As Integer = 3
Dim intResult As Integer

intResult = intValue1 + intValue2

MessageBox.Show (intResult)

End Sub
```

I then ran the program, clicked on the Button control, and the number 16 was displayed in a message box.

"This code," I said, "takes the value of the variable intValue1, adds it to the value of the variable intValue2, and then assigns the result to the variable intResult. The value of intResult is then displayed in a message box using the MessageBox.Show statement. We could streamline the code just a bit by eliminating the declaration of the variable intResult, and displaying the result of the operation directly in a message box…"

```
Private Sub Button1_Click(ByVal sender As System.Object, _
ByVal e As System.EventArgs) Handles Button1.Click
```

```
Dim intValue1 As Integer = 13
Dim intValue2 As Integer = 3

MessageBox.Show (intValue1 + intValue2)
End Sub
```

I reran the program and, once again, 16 was displayed in a message box.

"I know we *did* it," Kate said, "but are we *allowed* to do that?"

"Visual Basic permits it," I said. "In both cases, the addition operation is performed and the answer is displayed in the message box. The end result is the same."

"What method is best?" Barbara asked.

"Well," I replied, "if you use the expression directly, as we did in the second example, you save some memory in that you declare one less variable. On the other hand, you lose the answer."

"Lose the answer?" Peter asked.

"That's right," I said. "Since you're not storing the result in intResult, you no longer have the answer. If you need to display the result, or work with it somewhere else in your program, you'll need to use the first approach, which is to assign the value to a variable. Of course, this means that you use a tiny bit more memory, but it may be necessary. In the final analysis, the choice is yours, depending on the problem you are trying to solve!"

"In both of these examples," Linda said, "you first assigned values to variables and then performed the addition operation on the value of the variables. Is it possible to perform the addition on numeric literals?"

"Yes, you can," I said, as I displayed this code.

```
Private Sub Button1_Click(ByVal sender As System.Object, _
    ByVal e As System.EventArgs) Handles Button1.Click

MessageBox.Show (13 + 3)

End Sub
```

I ran the program and, once again, the number 16 appeared in a message box.

"What are the numeric literals that Linda was talking about?" Rhonda asked. "Are those the numbers in the MessageBox.Show statement?"

"Exactly, Rhonda," I replied. "Those are the numeric literals." I waited to see if there were any other questions before moving onto the Subtraction operator.

The Subtraction Operator

"As you may have guessed," I said, "the subtraction operator (-) works by subtracting two expressions. Look at this example."

```
Private Sub Button1_Click(ByVal sender As System.Object, _
    ByVal e As System.EventArgs) Handles Button1.Click

Dim intValue1 As Integer = 13
Dim intValue2 As Integer = 3

MessageBox.Show (intValue1 - intValue2)

End Sub
```

I then ran the program and clicked on the Button control. This time the number 10 was displayed in a message box.

The Multiplication Operator

"The multiplication operator (*) multiplies two expressions," I said.

"Now this is a little different than what I used in school," Mary said. "In school, we used the letter x to denote multiplication."

"I did as well," I said, "but the computer uses the asterisk instead. Except for the operator, everything works as you would expect."

```
Private Sub Button1_Click(ByVal sender As System.Object, _
    ByVal e As System.EventArgs) Handles Button1.Click

Dim intValue1 As Integer = 13
Dim intValue2 As Integer = 3

MessageBox.Show (intValue1 * intValue2)
End Sub
```

When I ran this program and clicked on the Button control, the number 39 was displayed in a message box.

The Integer Division Operator

"In Visual Basic," I said, "there are two division operations: integer division and floating-point division."

"Integers, those are the whole numbers, right?" Barbara asked.

"Right you are, Barbara," I said, "Integers are whole numbers, without fractional parts. When you perform integer division, the result is an answer that is a whole number."

"Is the answer rounded up or down?" Linda asked.

"No, there isn't any rounding," I said. "I call integer division 'guillotine' math—the fractional part of the answer is just chopped off."

"Does floating-point division return a result with a fraction?" Dave asked.

"That's right," I answered.

"Can you show us an example to clarify this a little bit?" Ward asked. "I'm afraid I'm missing something."

"Sure thing," I said. "If you use integer division, 7 divided by 2 returns a result of 3. If you use floating-point division, 7 divided by 2 returns a result of 3.5."

"Why use integer division in the first place?" Steve asked. "Shouldn't we be as accurate as possible?"

"Now, that's a very good question," I said. "However, sometimes we simply don't need the fraction. Prior to coding a division operation, you should ask yourself if the fractional part of the answer is significant. If the answer is no, then use integer division—which, by the way, is about 100 times faster than floating-point division."

"Wow, that is faster," Dave said. "What are the two operators for integer and floating-point division?"

I explained that using the back-slash (\) operator specifies integer division, whereas the forward-slash (/) specifies floating-point division.

"The following code illustrates the use of integer division," I said.

```
Private Sub Button1_Click(ByVal sender As System.Object, _
    ByVal e As System.EventArgs) Handles Button1.Click

Dim intValue1 As Integer = 7
Dim intValue2 As Integer = 2

MessageBox.Show (intValue1 \ intValue2)
End Sub
```

I ran the program, clicked on the Button control, and the number 3 was displayed in a message box.

"We all know that 7 divided by 2 is 3.5," I said, "but using the Visual Basic integer division operator, the answer is 3."

"I guess another way of describing integer division," Rose said, "is that the remainder is discarded."

"That's an excellent description of it," I agreed. "Keep that notion in mind, because in a few minutes, I'll be showing you a Visual Basic operation that retains the remainder and discards everything else!"

The Floating-Point Division Operator

"Floating-point division is the type of division we're all familiar with," I said. "The answer includes a fraction." I then displayed the following code illustrating the use of floating-point division operator (/).

```
Private Sub Button1_Click(ByVal sender As System.Object, _
   ByVal e As System.EventArgs) Handles Button1.Click

Dim intValue1 As Integer = 7
Dim intValue2 As Integer = 2

MessageBox.Show (intValue1 / intValue2)
End Sub
```

I ran the program and clicked on the Button control. This time, the number 3.5 was displayed in a message box.

The Mod Operator

"A few moments ago Rose mentioned the remainder that we lose when we perform integer division. You can think of the Mod operation as the reverse—it retains the remainder and discards the rest. For instance, 7 divided by 2 is 3, with a remainder of 1, but 7 Mod-ed by 2 is 1. It's that simple, really."

"What's the symbol for the Mod operation?" Ward asked.

"There's no special symbol as there are with the arithmetic operations," I said. "You actually use the word Mod. Let me show you."

```
Private Sub Button1_Click(ByVal sender As System.Object, _
   ByVal e As System.EventArgs) Handles Button1.Click

Dim intValue1 As Integer = 7
Dim intValue2 As Integer = 2

MessageBox.Show (intValue1 Mod intValue2)
End Sub
```

I ran the program and clicked on the Button control. The number 1 was displayed in a message box.

"I think I'm okay with the mechanics of the Mod operation," Rhonda said. "I just can't understand why you would ever want to use it. Can you give us an example?"

"The usefulness of the Mod operation," I said, "is not as obvious as some of the other arithmetic operators. One of the more useful characteristics of a Mod operation is that if the result of the Mod operation is 0, you know that the first expression is exactly divisible by the second expression. Another useful characteristic is that if you Mod a number by 2, if the result is 0, the number was even—if the result is 1, the number was odd."

"Oh, that's how you would do something like that," Steve said.

"That's right," I agreed, "if for some reason you asked the user to enter a number into a text box, you could use the Mod operation to tell them if the number was even or odd. Like this…"

I quickly created a new project, with a text box and Button control, and placed the following code into the Click event procedure of the Button control.

```
Private Sub Button1_Click(ByVal sender As System.Object, _
   ByVal e As System.EventArgs) Handles Button1.Click

If Val(TextBox1.Text) Mod 2 = 0 Then MessageBox.Show ("Number is even")
If Val(TextBox1.Text) Mod 2 = 1 Then MessageBox.Show ("Number is odd")
End Sub
```

I ran the program, entered the number 44 into the text box, clicked on the Button control, and a message box was displayed telling me the number was even. I then entered 43 into the text box, clicked on the Button control, and a message box was displayed telling me the number was odd.

"You're going to have to explain this to me," Ward said. "I think this went right over my head."

"Sure, Ward," I said. "The key to this program is this line of code."

If Val(TextBox1.Text) Mod 2 = 0 Then

"In the If statement," I said, "we first take the value of the Text property of the text box— whatever the user has entered—and execute the Val function against it. The Val function converts the String data type of the TextBox control to a number—something that the Mod operator is looking for. At that point, we Mod the value by 2. If the result of the Mod operation is 0, we know we have an even number, since dividing any even number by 2 results in no remainder. Then with this line of code…"

If Val(TextBox1.Text) Mod 2 = 1 Then MessageBox.Show ("Number is odd")

"…we check to see if the number is odd. An odd number that is Mod-ed by 2 will have a remainder."

"It can't be that easy," Ward said.

"It really is," I replied.

"Could we have used an Else statement here?" Dave asked.

"You've been reading ahead again, Dave," I said, smiling. "You're right, we could have used an Else statement like this…"

```
If Val(TextBox1.Text) Mod 2 = 0 Then
  MessageBox.Show ("Number is even")
Else
  MessageBox.Show ("Number is odd")
End If
```

"We'll learn more about the Else clause of an If statement next week," I promised. "We have one more arithmetic operator to discuss."

The Exponentiation Operator

"Math phobics beware," I said. "It's time to talk about exponentiation. The exponentiation operation ($\wedge$) raises a number to the power of the exponent. Take $2 \wedge 8$, for example. This notation means raise 2 to the power of 8, where 8 is the exponent. When you raise a number to the power of an exponent, you multiply that number by itself the number of times specified by the exponent. In this instance, that means you multiply 2 by itself 8 times, like this."

$2 * 2 * 2 * 2 * 2 * 2 * 2 * 2 = 256$

"The exponentiation operation is typically used in complex scientific and mathematical formulas. Fortunately, a lot of those are included in the Visual Basic language as ready-made functions. Let's see how we would code this in Visual Basic."

```
Private Sub Button1_Click(ByVal sender As System.Object, _
  ByVal e As System.EventArgs) Handles Button1.Click

Dim intValue1 As Integer = 2
Dim intValue2 As Integer = 8

MessageBox.Show (intValue1 ^ intValue2)

End Sub
```

I ran the program, clicked on the Button control, and received the expected answer of 256.

"Where is the character for the exponentiation operator located on the keyboard?" Rhonda asked.

"It appears on the key with the number 6," I said.

I asked if there were any questions, but no one had any. As promised, I gave the class a break, and told them that when they returned we would resume our coverage of data operations with something called the order of operations.

Order of Operations

"I mentioned earlier," I said, as we resumed after break, "that Visual Basic, when it evaluates an expression containing more than one operation, performs each operation one at a time. The natural question, then, is which operation Visual Basic performs first."

"That's right," Jack said. "If there's an expression that contains more than one operation, how does it decide?"

Rose said, "I would think that Visual Basic would perform the operations left to right in the expression. That's how I would do it."

"You may be right, Rose," I said, "that most people would evaluate an expression that way, but that's not the way Visual Basic performs the operations. Visual Basic follows a set of rules, known as the order of operations, that governs the order in which it performs these operations. A knowledge of the order of operations is crucial if you want your program to actually execute the way you intend."

I then displayed this code on the classroom projector. Before running it, I asked everyone in the class to perform the calculation mentally themselves.

```
Private Sub Button1_Click(ByVal sender As System.Object, _
    ByVal e As System.EventArgs) Handles Button1.Click

MessageBox.Show (3 + 6 + 9 / 3)

End Sub
```

I asked for, and received, a number of different responses. A couple of students suggested the answer was 12, a few said 6, and a number of students said that the answer would depend on exactly when the division operation was performed. Not wishing to keep them in suspense any longer, I ran the program, clicked on the Button control, and we saw the following message box.

"It looks as though Visual Basic performed the division first," Dave said.

"You're right, Dave," I said. "Visual Basic evaluated the expression into three separate operations."

1. 3 + 6

2. + 9

3. / 3

"Following the rules for the order of operations, Visual Basic actually performed the third operation, division, first," I said. "The order of operations is determined by the following rules:"

1. Operations in parentheses () are performed first.

2. Any exponentiation operations are performed next.

3. Any multiplication or division operations are performed next, from left to right in

the expression.

4. Finally, any addition or subtraction operations are performed, from left to right in

the expression.

"What does all that mean?" Rhonda asked.

"Here's what happens," I said. "When Visual Basic examines an expression, it looks to see if there are any operations within parentheses first. When it finds parentheses, it performs everything within the parentheses first.

Once all of the operations within parentheses are executed, Visual Basic then looks for any operations involving exponentiation, and if it finds any, performs them."

"Suppose there's more than one?" Lou asked.

"If there's more than one exponentiation operation," I answered, "Visual Basic performs them from left to right. Next, Visual Basic looks for operations involving multiplication or division, and performs them. If it finds more than one, it performs them from left to right. Finally, Visual Basic looks for operations involving addition or subtraction and performs them. Once again, it performs them starting at the left side of the expression and working its way to the right."

"Can you relate what you just said to the code example you showed us?" Kathy asked.

"Sure," I said. "Visual Basic first looked for parentheses in the expression. You've probably noticed that whenever we code a MessageBox.Show function there's a pair of parentheses around the expression that we want to appear in the message box. Since the entire expression appeared within parentheses, it had no impact on the evaluation of the expression. Visual Basic then looked for an exponentiation operator, but it found none. Next, it looked for multiplication or division operators. It found just the single division operator, which it then performed."

"So it actually performed the operation of 9 divided by 3 first," Valerie said. "No wonder the answer didn't agree with mine."

"After the division operation," I continued, "Visual Basic looked for any addition or subtraction operators. It found two, and performed these operations left to right, 3 plus 6 first, then the addition of 9 plus 3. I can show you how this all took place step by step; here are the results of the intermediate operations:"

1. Step 1 : 3 + 6 + 9 / 3

2. Step 2 : 3 + 6 + 3

3. Step 3 : 9 + 3

4. Step 4 : 12

I gave everyone a chance to take this in. "I hope this example shows you not only how Visual Basic evaluates an expression containing mathematical operators, but how important it is to compose the expressions you code carefully. For instance," I said, "suppose we had intended to calculate the average of 3 plus 6 plus 9 with this piece of code. We know that to calculate the average, we would add 3 plus 6 plus 9 and then divide by 3. If we were to bet our jobs on the answer that Visual Basic came up with we wouldn't have one very long!"

"You're right about that," Rose said, "but how could we code the expression to correctly computer the average of 3, 6, and 9?"

"One word," Jack suggested. "Parentheses."

That's right," I said, agreeing with Jack as I modified the code and displayed it on the classroom projector.

```
Private Sub Button1_Click(ByVal sender As System.Object, _
   ByVal e As System.EventArgs) Handles Button1.Click

MessageBox.Show ((3 + 6 + 9) / 3)

End Sub
```

Now when I ran the program and clicked on the Button control, the following message box appeared.

"This time," I said, "because we sandwiched the addition operations within a set of parentheses, Visual Basic performed both addition operations prior to the division—exactly what we wanted to happen. Step by step, it looks like this:"

1. Step 1 : (3 + 6 + 9) / 3

2. Step 2 : (9 + 9) /3

3. Step 3 : 18 / 3

4. Step 4 : 6

"Please excuse my dear Aunt Sally," I heard Linda mutter.

"What was that, Linda?" I asked.

"Please excuse my dear Aunt Sally," Linda repeated. "I learned that in ninth grade math class as a way to remember the order of operations. Parentheses-Exponentiation-Multiplication-Division-Addition-Subtraction."

"Absolutely right," I said, "I had forgotten all about that. That expression does summarize the order of operations perfectly."

Comparison Operators

"I was talking to a programmer friend of mine," Ward said, "and she mentioned something called comparison operators. Will you be covering those as well?"

"Yes, we will," I replied. "Just as arithmetic or mathematical operators compare two expressions to the left and right of the operator and return a result, comparison operators compare two expressions to the left and right of the operator and return a result. The difference here is that the result isn't a number, it's a value of True or False. Here are the six comparison operators."

Symbol	Explanation
=	Equal to
<>	Not equal to
>	Greater than
>=	Greater than or equal to
<	Less than
<=	Less than or equal to

"We'll only be discussing the most common comparison operator today: the equal sign (=)," I said.

"Isn't the equal sign also used to assign a value to a variable?" Barbara asked.

"You're right," I said. "The equal sign is used in two ways in Visual Basic. The first, as we've already seen, is where it's used to assign a value to a property or a variable, and as you'll see in a moment, it is also used as a comparison operator. For instance, here the equal sign is used to evaluate the truth of this statement."

If intValue = 22

"So the result of this code will either be True or False depending upon the current value of intValue?" Dave said.

"That's exactly right, Dave," I replied. "If the current value of intValue is 22, the result of this comparison will be True. If the value of intValue is anything other than 22, the result of this comparison will be False. This duality of the equal sign in Visual Basic is sometimes confusing for the beginner. Let me show you some code where the equal sign is used both ways in the same event procedure."

```
Private Sub Button1_Click(ByVal sender As System.Object, _
    ByVal e As System.EventArgs) Handles Button1.Click

Dim intValue As Integer
intValue = 22

If intValue = 22 Then
    MessageBox.Show ("The value of the variable is 22")
End If

End Sub
```

I ran the program, clicked on the Button control, and the following message box was displayed.

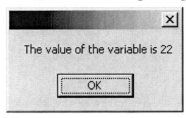

"In this example," I said, "since the value of the variable intValue is 22, Visual Basic evaluates the expression to True, and executes the line of code following the word Then in the If statement (we'll talk more about If statements next week!). Let's modify the program slightly so that you can actually see the return value of the comparison..."

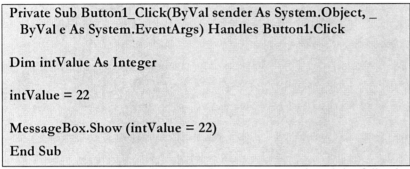

```
Private Sub Button1_Click(ByVal sender As System.Object, _
    ByVal e As System.EventArgs) Handles Button1.Click

Dim intValue As Integer

intValue = 22

MessageBox.Show (intValue = 22)

End Sub
```

I ran the program again, clicked on the Button control, and the following message box appeared.

"That's cool," Kate said. "We really did display the result of the comparison operation, didn't we?"

"Yes, we did, Kate," I replied, "likewise, if the value of intValue is not equal to 22, the result of the comparison operation would be False. Like this..." I modified the code slightly.

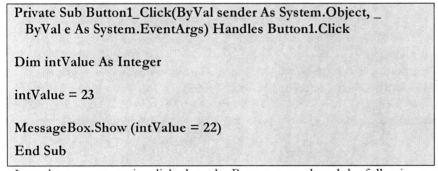

```
Private Sub Button1_Click(ByVal sender As System.Object, _
    ByVal e As System.EventArgs) Handles Button1.Click

Dim intValue As Integer

intValue = 23

MessageBox.Show (intValue = 22)

End Sub
```

I ran the program again, clicked on the Button control, and the following message box appeared.

Logical Operators

"So far," I said, "we've examined arithmetic operators and comparison operators. Now it's time to look at a set of operators that sometimes cause beginners' hearts to skip a beat: logical operators."

"Are those the And, Or, and Not operators?" Blaine asked.

"That's right, Blaine," I said. "In Visual Basic there are three logical operators: And, Or, and Not. Just like comparison operators, logical operators return a True or False value as the result of performing their operations on an expression. Logical operations can be confusing for the beginner, primarily because of the necessity to understand the truth or falseness of their expressions. Let's take a look at these operators individually."

The And Operator

"An And operation," I said, "returns a True value if the expressions on both sides of the And operator evaluate to True."

"Can you give us a real-world example to make this easier to understand?" Ward asked.

"I think so, Ward" I said, as I thought a moment. "On Wednesday morning, your best friend Melissa telephones you and invites you to lunch on Friday. You'd love to go, but you have two problems that prevent you from saying yes right away. First, you and your boss have not been on the best of terms lately, and you don't want to chance taking an extra long lunch on Friday— something which invariably happens when you go to lunch with Melissa. The only way you can envision going to lunch with your friend is if your boss happens to be out of the office on Friday."

"And the second problem?" Barbara asked. "You said there were two problems."

"The second problem," I said, "is that you're short of cash and it's your turn to pick up the tab for lunch. Luckily though, Friday happens to be payday and cash won't be a problem—provided the direct deposit of your paycheck goes through early Friday morning, something that is 50-50 at best. You decide to call your friend on Friday at 11:00 A.M. to let her know for sure."

I could see that some of the students were wondering what my heartfelt example had to do with the And operator. I explained that we can express our dilemma in the form of two expressions joined with the And operator in this way. "You can go to lunch with your friend Melissa if your boss is out of the office on Friday AND if the direct deposit of your paycheck gets into your bank account by 11:00 on Friday morning." I said.

"In other words, both expressions, the left expression 'Boss out of office?' and the right expression 'Money in account?' must both be true for the And operator to return a value of True."

Boss out of office AND Money in account

"So what happens?" Rhonda asked.

"On Friday morning," I said, "you arrive at the office. You're saddened to hear that your boss has called in to say she has the flu and won't be in at all that day."

"So the left expression, Boss out of office, is True," Dave said.

"That's right, Dave," I said. "We're halfway there. Our left expression evaluates to True. Now we have to wait on the direct deposit. The morning drags by as lunchtime gets closer and closer. For the moment, though, the And operation is returning a False value, since the right expression, Money in account, is still returning a False value. Remember, the And operation is True only if both the left and right expressions are True. Right now, only the left expression, Boss out of office, is True. Unfortunately, the last time you checked your balance, you found that your direct deposit still hasn't been made to your account, and $1.38 won't buy you and your friend Melissa much of a lunch."

"I wish we could see this graphically," Peter said.

"Actually, Peter," I said, "we can express this dilemma in the form of something called a truth table—here it is."

Expression 1	And	Expression 2	Statement
True	And	True	True
True	And	False	False
False	And	True	False
False	And	False	False

"A truth table," I said, "shows you the four possible outcomes for the And operation. As you can see, there's only one way for an And operation to return a True value, and that's if both Expression 1 (the left side) and Expression 2 (the right side) are True. On the other hand, there are three ways for the And operation to return a value of False."

"I don't like those odds," Kate said, laughing. "I don't think lunch looks too promising!"

"Can you rewrite the truth table in terms of the boss and the money?" Rhonda said. "I think that might help me visualize this."

I took a moment to work up this revised table and then displayed it on the classroom projector. The current situation is highlighted in bold.

Boss Out?	And	Money in Account?	Go to Lunch?
True	And	True	True
True	**And**	**False**	**False**
False	And	True	False
False	And	False	False

"That's better," Steve said. "This is beginning to make some sense to me now."

"Let's continue on with the story," I said. "As of 10:30, with no cash in the bank, lunch is a remote possibility. Just as you're about to call Melissa and tell her no, one last check of your bank balance shows that the direct deposit has made it, which means the right expression, Expression 2, is now True. Since both the left and right expressions evaluate to True, the entire And operation is True, and you and Melissa can now go off to lunch."

Boss Out?	And	Money in Account?	Go to Lunch?
True	**And**	**True**	**True**
True	And	False	False
False	And	True	False
False	And	False	False

"Can you give us an example of the use of the And operator in Visual Basic?" Dave asked. I thought for a moment, then quickly created a form with the now familiar single Button control and placed this code in its Click event procedure.

```
Private Sub Button1_Click(ByVal sender As System.Object, _
  ByVal e As System.EventArgs) Handles Button1.Click

Dim intValue As Integer = 13
Dim strName As String = "Smith"

If strName = "Smith" And intValue = 14 Then
  MessageBox.Show ("Both sides of the AND expression are True")
Else
  MessageBox.Show ("One or more sides of the AND expression are false")
End If

End Sub
```

I then ran the program, clicked on the Button control, and this message box appeared.

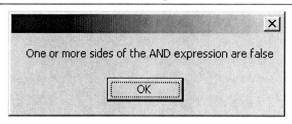

"In this expression," I said, "the left expression is True, since strName is equal to Smith, but the right expression is False, because the value of intValue is 13, not 14. Therefore, the And operation returns a value of False (consult the truth table to see this for yourself)."

I then changed the code to assign the value 14 to the variable intValue. When I reran the program, Visual Basic displayed this message box.

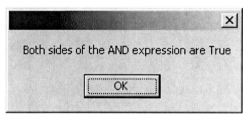

"Now the And operation returns a True value," I said, "because both the left and right expressions are True. True And True equals True."

The Or Operator

"I think if you're comfortable with the And operator," I said, "you won't have any trouble with the Or operator. An Or operation, just like the And operation, evaluates expressions to the left and right of the Or operator, returning a value of True or False. The difference are the rules for determining if the expression is True or False."

I displayed this truth table representing the Or operation.

Expression 1	Or	Expression 2	Statement
True	Or	True	True
True	Or	False	True
False	Or	True	True
False	Or	False	False

"Notice," I said, "that with the Or operation, as was the case with the And operation, we have four possibilities. In the case of the Or operation, however, three out of four results are True. In fact, with the Or operation, there is only one combination that returns a False value, and that's if both the left and right expressions are False."

"Can you give us another real-world example to illustrate the Or operation?" Linda asked. "Although I think it will be pretty hard for you to top that last one."

I thought for a moment. "Okay," I said, "let's try this one. It's Friday morning. While dressing for work, you receive a phone call from the host of an early morning radio show that is running a contest. He tells you that if the month of your birthday ends in the letter r or the last digit of your Social Security number is 4, you'll be the lucky winner of $10,000!"

"Sounds great to me!" Ward said.

"Let me get this straight," Rhonda said. "All you need to do to win the $10,000 is to have one of those conditions be True—is that right?"

"That's right, Rhonda," I said. "According to the rules of the contest, you'll win the $10,000 if either the left expression is True—month of your birthday ends in the letter r—or the right expression is True—the last digit of your Social Security number is 4. Unlike our lunch date dilemma, where we needed both expressions to be True to go to lunch with our friend, with an Or operation only one side of the expression needs to be True. How do you like your odds now, Kate?"

"I love 'em," she answered. "If that call were placed to me, I'd win the prize."

Kate wasn't alone—a quick poll of the class revealed that 4 out of the 18 students would win using the Or operation. And guess what—if the contest had called for the And operation, none of the students in the class would have won the cash!

I then displayed this truth table to reflect the radio contest. The three outcomes where the Or operation returns a True value are highlighted in bold.

Birthday Month Ends in r?	Or	Last Digit of Social Security is 4?	Win $10,000?
True	Or	True	**True**
True	Or	False	**True**
False	Or	True	**True**
False	Or	False	False

I then took the previous code example and modified it by changing the And operator to Or.

```
Private Sub Button1_Click(ByVal sender As System.Object, _
   ByVal e As System.EventArgs) Handles Button1.Click

Dim intValue As Integer = 13
Dim strName As String = "Smith"

If strName = "Smith" Or intValue = 14 Then
   MessageBox.Show ("One or more sides of the OR expression are True")
Else
   MessageBox.Show ("Both sides of the OR expression are False")
End If

End Sub
```

I ran the program, clicked on the Button Control, and this message box was displayed.

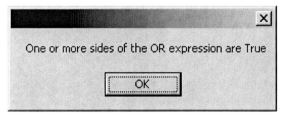

"Because the left expression is True," I said, "True is returned from the Or operation. If we were to change the value of strName from Smith to Smiley, the Or operation would return a False value." I did exactly that, changing the value of strName from 'Smith' to 'Smiley' and running the program again. When I clicked on the Button control, this message box was displayed.

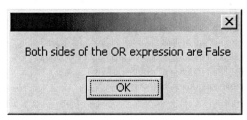

"The only way that an Or operation can return a False value," I said, "is if both the left and right expressions evaluate to False. That's the case here—intValue, with a value of 13, is not 14, and strValue, with a value of Smiley, is definitely not Smith."

"I just typed in some code and received an error message," Kathy said.

I took a quick walk to her PC, and saw that she had written the following code.

```
Private Sub Button1_Click(ByVal sender As System.Object, _
    ByVal e As System.EventArgs) Handles Button1.Click

Dim intValue As Integer = 13

If intValue = 13 Or 14 Then
    MessageBox.Show ("intValue is either 13 or 14")
End If

End Sub
```

"What did I do wrong?" she asked.

"I know what you wanted to do," I said, "but you confused Visual Basic. Your code was very much English-like, which is very tempting to do in Visual Basic, but you see, you don't really have two expressions on either side of the Or operator. Your left expression is intValue = 13, and your right expression is just the number 14. Remember, each expression must be able to be evaluated to a True or False value—your right expression can't be evaluated to a True or False value, so Visual Basic generated an error message."

"So how could I rewrite this?" she asked.

I displayed the correct code on the classroom projector.

```
Private Sub Button1_Click(ByVal sender As System.Object, _
    ByVal e As System.EventArgs) Handles Button1.Click

Dim intValue As Integer = 13

If intValue = 13 Or intValue = 14 Then
    MessageBox.Show ("intValue is either 13 or 14")
End If

End Sub
```

"Wow, that was simple," Kathy said. "Why didn't I think of that?"

"You did what a lot of beginners do, Kathy," I answered. "You wrote the code the way you ask the question in conversation. Unfortunately, as programmer-friendly as Visual Basic is, there are still some statements that can confuse it."

The Not Operator

"We have one more logical operator to discuss today," I continued, "and it's the Not operator. As opposed to the other logical operators, which operate on two expressions, the Not operator is called a unary operator because it operates on just a single expression."

"What does the Not operator do?" Steve asked.

"The Not operator is used as a negation," I replied. "It evaluates an expression, takes the True or False result, and then returns the opposite value. So if an expression evaluates to True, the Not operator returns False. If the expression evaluates to False, the Not operator returns True."

"Why in the world would you want to do something like that?" Rhonda asked.

"The Not operator can simplify your code," I said, "and make it easier to read and understand. Let me show you…"

I created a new Visual Basic project with a single Button control and placed this code in its Click event procedure.

```
Private Sub Button1_Click(ByVal sender As System.Object, _
    ByVal e As System.EventArgs) Handles Button1.Click

Dim intValue As Integer = 13

MessageBox.Show (intValue = 13)

End Sub
```

"Can anyone tell me what will happen when we run this code?" I asked. Dave suggested that a message box would be displayed with the word True in it.

"That's right," I said. "Since the value of intValue is 13, Visual Basic will evaluate the expression intValue = 13 as True."

I then ran the program and clicked on the Button control. As Dave had correctly predicted, a message box was displayed with the word True in it. I then changed the line of code that displays the message box to this.

MessageBox.Show (Not intValue = 13)

"Now what will happen?" I asked. Dave answered that he thought a message box with the word False would be displayed.

"Can you tell us why?" I replied.

"Because," he said, "the expression intValue = 13 will evaluate to True. Executing the Not operator on a True value gives us a False value."

"Excellent, Dave," I said, "Bill Gates himself couldn't have stated it better." I then ran the program, and clicked on the Button control. Dave was right; a message box was displayed with the word False in it. "Without the Not operator, to determine if a variable's value isn't a particular value would require some code that's very hard to read and understand, like this."

MessageBox.Show (intValue < 13 Or intValue > 13)

"Is that all there is to the Not operator, then?" Barbara asked.

"Basically, yes," I said. "I should point out that you can also use the Not operator with property values. I was about to give you a demonstration, but I just realized it's been a while since we've done an exercise, why don't we complete this one and you'll see what I mean."

I then distributed this exercise to the class.

Exercise 7-1 The Not Operator

In this exercise, you'll use the Not operator on a Visual Basic Boolean property—the Enabled property.

1. Start a new Windows application project.
2. Place a Button control and a Label control on the form, accepting the default names for both controls.
3. Double-click on the Button control to open the Visual Basic code window and place the following code in its Click event procedure.

```
Private Sub Button1_Click(ByVal sender As System.Object, _
  ByVal e As System.EventArgs) Handles Button1.Click

Label1.Visible = Not Label1.Visible

End Sub
```

4. Run the program, and click on the Button control. The Label control will disappear. Click on the Button control again and the label will become visible once more.

Discussion

"What happened?" Rhonda asked.

"By using the Not operator," I said, "we were able to create what amounts to a toggle switch in the Click event procedure of the Button control. Initially, the Label control was visible. When the Button control was clicked, we took the current value of the Visible property of the Label Control (either True or False) and executed the Not operation on it. If the Visible property was True, we set it equal to False, making the Label Control invisible. If the Visible property was False, the Not operation set it to True, making the Label Control visible again."

How Not to Use Not

After my explanation, everyone seemed content with their understanding of the Not operator, but before dismissing class for the day, I took a few moments to emphasize that the Not operator, as we had seen with the Or operator, should only be used with expressions that evaluate to a True or False.

"Here's a mistake that many beginners make with the Not operator," I said.

```
Private Sub Button1_Click(ByVal sender As System.Object, _
   ByVal e As System.EventArgs) Handles Button1.Click

Dim intValue As Integer

intValue = 10

If intValue Not 10 Then
   MessageBox.Show ("intValue is not equal to 10")
Else
   MessageBox.Show ("intValue is equal to 10")
End If

End Sub
```

I asked everyone to consider what this code was attempting to do.

"It looks to me," Rose said, "as if you are asking Visual Basic to determine if the value of the variable intValue is Not equal to 10. Since the value is 10, I would expect that we should see a message box indicating that intValue is equal to 10." I then ran the program, but instead of a message box appearing, I received an error message. "That's the same problem we had with the Or operator, isn't it?" Steve asked. "Exactly, Steve," I said, "we can't use the Not operator to determine if the value of intValue is not 10 because intValue isn't a Boolean variable. Instead, we need to use one of the comparison operators we learned about earlier, the inequality symbol <>, like this."

```
If intValue <> 10 Then
   MessageBox.Show ("intValue is not equal to 10")
Else
   MessageBox.Show ("intValue is equal to 10")
End If
```

I asked if there were any more questions. There were none, so I dismissed class for the day. I told everyone that next week we would take a more detailed look at Visual Basic selection structures in Visual Basic and, of course, apply that knowledge to the China Shop Project.

Summary

This was quite an exhaustive look at the use of data in Visual Basic. In this chapter, we learned about the importance of variables in Visual Basic. We learned when, where, and how to use variables, and about the different Visual Basic variable types that we can declare. In addition, we discovered how we can use a variety of operations to manipulate the data contained in those variables.

Variables are defined in memory to hold data or information. Each variable has a scope that determines what other parts of your program can see the variable, and a lifetime that determines when the variable dies. Some variables live for as long as your program runs, others live only for as long as an event procedure executes. We discussed the need to declare variables and decided that although it's theoretically possible not to declare a variable before using it (if Option Strict and Option Explicit are off) that isn't something a programmer should do. Declaring variables can be done using one of three statements:

- Dim. Used within a procedure, and its scope permits it to be seen only within that procedure.

- Private. Used in the General section of a module (Form, Standard, or Class), and its scope permits it to be seen only by procedures within that module.

- Public. Used in the General section of a module (Form, Standard, or Class), but unlike Private, its scope permits it to be seen in every procedure in every module in your program.

Visual Basic data types can be categorized in four broad ways:

- Boolean. True or False values only.

- Numeric. Numbers only.

- Date. Dates and times.

- String. A set of characters, treated as text. Strings can hold numbers, but these are not numbers that you can perform arithmetic on.

A constant is like a fixed variable and is declared using the Const keyword. Constants should be named in capital letters so they stand out in your code. Once a value is assigned to a constant, its value cannot be changed.

Finally, we took a look at arithmetic, comparison, and logical operators. Operators act on expressions and return a result. An example of a mathematical operator is the plus sign. We learned that multiple operators are treated in a defined order, called the order of operations: operations in parentheses are performed first, followed by exponentiation, then multiplication and division, and finally addition and subtraction.

An example of a comparison operator is the equal sign. An example of a logical operator is the word Not, which returns the opposite value of an expression that evaluates to True or False. An important point to remember is that the Not operator is not the same as the comparison operator <>, which means "is not equal to."

Hopefully, you should now be familiar, if not totally comfortable, with the ways we can manipulate data in Visual Basic programs. In the next chapter, we'll see how selection structures permit your program to make decisions.

Chapter 8---Selection Structures

In programming, one of the most important capabilities your program must have is the ability to adapt to conditions that are encountered during runtime. In this chapter, we'll continue to follow my Visual Basic class as we examine selection structures—specifically, the If statement and the Select...Case statement.

I arrived in the classroom a little later than usual and found a bit of a commotion.

"What's wrong?" I asked, noting that there was a group of people surrounding Rose and Jack.

"As you know," Jack said, "Rose and I are both engineers by trade and we work for the same company. Our company's biggest account is overseeing the construction of a new cruise ship in the United Kingdom. Anyway, it seems that construction is way ahead of schedule, and yesterday our supervisor told us that we're being called away to participate in the sea trials. So, you see, this will probably be our last class!"

"I'm disappointed," Rose said, "because I had hoped to finish the coding for the China Shop Project before we left, but there's no way we'll be near that point today."

I explained to both Rose and Jack that we would all be sorry not to have them present all the way through the project, but we hoped they would be able to return in time to see the final version of the China Shop Project implemented in Joe Bullina's store.

"As far as the China Shop Project," I said, "I have a surprise for you. By the end of today's class, we'll have coded a complete working prototype of the China Shop Project."

As the obvious shock of my last statement subsided, I began our eighth class.

Falling Rock Behavior

I began my presentation by reminding everyone of my analogy of the execution sequence of Visual Basic code to the behavior of falling rock.

"In the absence of other instructions," I said, "Visual Basic begins execution of the code in an event procedure from the first line of code and executes each line through to the End Sub statement without interruption."

I explained that although this behavior is fine in most circumstances, in some cases it isn't.

"There may be cases," I said, "where you need to perform a calculation, but the calculation varies depending on conditions that the program encounters at runtime. A program that is as inflexible as a rock dropped from your hand cannot possess this intelligent capability."

"In the China Shop Project, for example, we'll be calculating a total price for the customer's selection, but that price will vary based on the quantity selected by the user. Fortunately, Visual Basic gives us the ability to vary the way our program behaves based on conditions that it finds at runtime, such as which one of the radio buttons the user has selected to indicate his or her desired quantity of china. I know that we've already done some experimentation with this falling rock behavior, but I want to give you all a chance to work with a series of exercises which will give you the chance to observe this behavior a little more closely."

I then distributed this exercise to the class.

Exercise 8-1 Everything Entered into the Text Box is Displayed

In this exercise, we'll place a TextBox and a Button control on a form. We'll then place code in the Click event procedure of the Button control to display the contents of the Text property of the TextBox in the Output window. We'll see that whatever value we enter into the TextBox will be displayed in the Output window.

1. Start a new Windows application.
2. Place a TextBox and a Button control on the form. Accept the default names that Visual Basic assigns.
3. Double-click on the Button control and place the following code into its Click event procedure.

```
Private Sub Button1_Click(ByVal sender As Object, _
   ByVal e As System.EventArgs) Handles Button1.Click

Console.WriteLine (TextBox1.Text)
TextBox1.Text = ""
```

TextBox1.Focus()

End Sub

4. Save the project, as we'll be modifying it in Exercise 8-2.

5. Now run the program.

6. Enter some text into the text box and then click on the Button control. Whatever value you enter into the text box will be displayed in Visual Basic's Output window. The text box will then be cleared, ready for your next entry. Type some more text into the text box and click on the Button control. The new text entered in the text box will be displayed in the Output window as well.

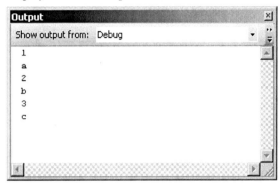

Discussion

I asked if there were any questions. "There are a couple of things I don't understand," Ward said. "What's the purpose behind assigning two quotation marks to the Text property of the TextBox, and what is going on with that Focus statement?"

"Let's take this from the top," I said. "The following line of code displays the contents of the TextBox in the Output window by printing the Text property of the TextBox control."

Console.WriteLine (TextBox1.Text)

"We've seen the WriteLine method of the Console object before, and I think everyone's okay with that. Now, Ward, here's the line of code you had a question about."

TextBox1.Text = ""

"What we're doing here," I said, "is clearing the contents of the TextBox control by setting its Text property equal to an empty string. This is similar to what we did ourselves in the Properties window before we ran the program, except that this time we're doing it in program code."

"Does that mean that all of the properties we can change in the Properties window at design-time can also be changed at runtime with code?" Steve asked.

"In general, that's true," I said, "but there are some exceptions."

"What about that next line of code?" Rhonda asked. "I don't understand what's going on there—what's focus?"

I displayed the line of code on the classroom projector.

TextBox1.Focus()

"Did you notice," I said, "that after you typed something into the text box and clicked on the Button control, that your cursor was automatically placed in the text box? That's what this line of code does. Without it, after we enter something into the text box and click on the Button control, focus would remain on the Button control. Since it's reasonable to believe that the user might want to enter more text into the text box, as a courtesy, we should execute the Focus method of the TextBox control to set the focus back to the text box. Now the user can just start typing into the text box without first having to TAB to it or click it with their mouse."

How Can We Improve upon This?

"If we want to ensure that the user enters something into the text box," I said, after waiting to see if anyone had any questions, "then this code has quite a few deficiencies. For instance, suppose the user fails to enter anything at all into the text box and just clicks on the Button control? The code will just blindly execute the WriteLine method of the Console object."

To show what I meant, I ran the program again and clicked several times on the Button control without entering anything into the text box. The empty strings in the Output window were obvious to everyone…

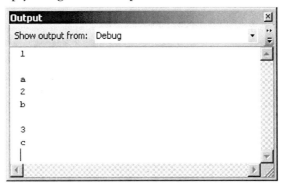

"Do we really want to display 'nothing' in the Output window?" I asked. "Probably not."

"How can we prevent it?" Peter asked.

"There are a couple of things we can do," I said. "We can disable the Button control until the user has made a valid entry in the text box, or we can place code in the Click event procedure of the Button control to check if the text box is 'empty' prior to executing the code to write to the Output window. If the text box is empty, we can display a message to the user informing them that they need to enter something into the text box."

"Which of those two alternatives is the best?" Jack asked.

"Both will achieve the purpose," I said, "but I think that the second alternative is probably the easier of the two, since all we need to do is code an If statement."

"You make that sound so simple!" Ward exclaimed, and he was right, so I apologized. Nothing is simple when you're a beginner, at least not until you've done it once or twice.

If…Then

"I know that we examined the If…Then statement very briefly a few weeks ago," I said. "Let's look at it in a little more detail now."

"Programmers," I continued, "use the If…Then statement to build some intelligence into their programs. The If…Then statement will conditionally execute one or more statements. Conditionally means that lines of code may or may not be executed, depending upon conditions found by your program at runtime."

"One thing that makes the If…Then statement a bit confusing to beginners is the fact that there are two ways to code it. The first method is the single-line style," I said, as I displayed the single-line style syntax on the classroom projector.

If some condition is true Then execute a statement

"The second method is known as the block form style." I said, as I displayed its syntax on the classroom projector.

If some condition is true Then
   execute a statement or statements
End If

"Regardless of the style," I said, "some condition is always evaluated. If it is True, a statement or statements following the word 'Then' are executed. These are sometimes called imperative statements. The difference between the single-line style and the block form style is the number of statements that can be executed if the condition is True. With the single-line style, only one line of code can be executed. With the block form style, one or more statements can be executed if the statement is True."

I waited to see if I was losing anyone before continuing.

"Notice that with the block form style, you must code an End If statement," I said. "Also, all imperative statements must appear after the word Then on a line or lines of their own. With the block form style, nothing can follow the word 'Then'. With the single-line style, only one imperative statement can be specified, and it must appear on the same line as the word 'Then'."

"So if you need to execute more than one imperative statement," Dave said, "you must use the block form method."

"Exactly, Dave," I said.

"This syntax is picky!" Rhonda said.

"At first it is, Rhonda," I said, "but after a while, you'll get pretty comfortable with it. In fact, what I tell many of my beginner students is rather than worrying whether to code the single-line style or the block form style, just code everything using the block form style—even where there is just a single imperative statement that you wish to execute if the condition is True."

"Can you do that?" Mary asked.

"Sure, you can," I said, "I know many Visual Basic programmers who never code a single line If statement—they use the block form all the time. In fact, many programmers think the block form is easier to read."

I gave them a moment to take that in.

"I notice that neither of these styles use Else," Steve commented.

"Actually," I said, "Else is a variation of the basic If...Then statement and we'll be looking at it shortly."

"In the syntax you just showed," Rhonda said, "what's a condition?"

"A condition is any Visual Basic expression that evaluates to a True or False value," I replied.

"I see," she said, nodding, "the same types of expressions we looked at last week with the comparison and logical operations."

"So you're saying that if a condition evaluates to True," Valerie said, "then all of the statements following the word Then are executed."

"That's right," I said, "but don't forget, there can be any number of statements executed if the condition is True. Typically, these statements appear as separate lines of code following the word Then."

"What if the condition evaluates to False?" Ward asked. "Does that mean that all of the statements following the word Then are bypassed?"

"Excellent, Ward," I said. "The only time the statements following the word Then are executed is if the condition evaluates to True. If the condition evaluates to False, they're all bypassed."

"I think this discussion would make more sense to me if you could give us an example," Rhonda said.

A good idea—I then created a new project with a single Button control and placed the following code into its Click event procedure.

```
Private Sub Button1_Click(ByVal sender As Object, _
  ByVal e As System.EventArgs) Handles Button1.Click

Dim intValue As Integer = 22

If intValue = 22 Then MessageBox.Show ("The value of intValue is 22")

End Sub
```

"This is an example of the single-line syntax," I said. "Notice that with the single-line syntax, there is just a single imperative statement following the word Then. This imperative statement appears on the same line following the word 'Then'. Also notice there is no End If statement required when using the single-line syntax."

I then ran the program, clicked on the Button control, and predictably, the message box appeared, displaying its message.

"You mentioned that some programmers use the block form style, even though it's not required for a single imperative statement," Dave said. "Could you show us that here?"

"And could you explain why we would want to do that again?" Ward asked.

"Sure, Ward," I said. "Some programmers believe that using the block form style even though it's not required to execute a single imperative statement enhances the readability of their code."

I changed the code, converting the single-line If statement to a block form If statement, and displayed it on the classroom projector.

```
Private Sub Button1_Click(ByVal sender As Object, _
    ByVal e As System.EventArgs) Handles Button1.Click

Dim intValue As Integer = 22

If intValue = 22 Then
    MessageBox.Show ("The value of intValue is 22")
End If

End Sub
```

I ran the program, clicked on the Button control, and received the same result.

"I understand much better now," Linda said, "and I think you're right. Using the block form style does seem to make the If statement stand out more. Is that also why you indented the code?"

"Yes," I replied. "Programmers routinely indent their code to make it more readable, particularly when they use If…Then statements. Of course, indenting has no effect on the execution of your code, although…"

"Although what?" Steve asked.

"Hiring managers look for good coding habits such as these when deciding among potential job candidates," I said.

"Are you saying that failing to indent your code can affect whether you are hired for a programming position?" Steve repeated.

"It could have a negative impact," I said, "in the same way that failing to properly comment your code can have an impact."

"Getting back to that code," I continued, "Suppose we were to change the assignment statement so that the value of intValue is 23, what will happen then?"

"Nothing," Peter answered. "We only have code in place to execute if the condition intValue = 22 is True."

"Strictly speaking," I said, "nothing appears to happen, but in fact, the condition is evaluated as False, and so the program skips to the line following the words End If, which in this case is the End Sub."

I continued by saying that if you need to execute more than one statement when the condition evaluates to True, you must use the block form syntax. To demonstrate the execution of more than one imperative statement with the block form, I quickly added a TextBox control to the project and modified the code in the Button control's Click event procedure to execute a second statement if the condition evaluates to True.

```
If intValue = 22 Then
    MessageBox.Show ("The value of intValue is 22")
    TextBox1.Focus()
End If
```

I ran the program, the message box was displayed, and focus was set to the text box. No one had any questions about the If statement, and so I suggested that we should turn our attention to using an If statement to handle the problem from Exercise 8-1 where the user enters 'nothing' into the text box and then clicks on the Button control.

Exercise 8-2 Using If…Then to Check for an Empty Text Box

In this exercise, we'll modify the code from Exercise 8-1, so that if the user makes no entry in the text box, a message box will be displayed instructing them that this is not permitted.

1. Continue working with the project from Exercise 8-1.
2. Modify the Click event procedure of the Button control so that it looks like this.

```
Private Sub Button1_Click(ByVal sender As Object, _
    ByVal e As System.EventArgs) Handles Button1.Click

If TextBox1.Text = "" Then
    MessageBox.Show("You must make an entry in the Textbox")
    TextBox1.Focus()
    Exit Sub
End If
```

```
Console.WriteLine(TextBox1.Text)
TextBox1.Text = ""
TextBox1.Focus()

End Sub
```

3. Save the project as we'll be modifying it in Exercise 8-3.

4. Now run the program.

5. Enter some text into the text box and then click on the Button control. As in the previous exercise, whatever text you enter into the text box will be displayed in the Output window.

6. Now, with the text box empty, click on the Button control. A message box will be displayed warning you that an empty entry is not allowed.

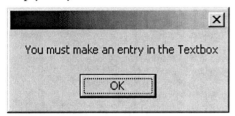

Discussion

"I think I understand what's going on here," Ward said, "but what is the purpose of the Exit Sub statement?"

"That's a good question," I said. "Let me answer your question by asking you one. If the user makes no entry in the text box, clicks on the Button control, and receives an error message, what should happen next?"

There was silence.

"Well," I said, "we've displayed the error message, and then set the focus back to the text box. Because of the 'falling rock' behavior of code execution, if we don't do something, the code following the words 'End If' will be executed—and we don't want that."

"So Exit Sub is a way to bypass the rest of the code in the event procedure?" Kathy asked.

"Exactly, Kathy," I said. "Exit Sub tells Visual Basic that we don't wish to execute any of the remaining code in the event procedure." I drew their attention again to the Exit Sub statement.

Exit Sub

"This line of code ensures that the rest of the code in the event procedure is not executed. It ends the execution of the code in the event procedure right there and then."

"Do you mean that nothing after the words Exit Sub is executed?" Barbara asked.

"That's right," I said. "Nothing. As soon as Visual Basic sees the Exit Sub statement, the event procedure is terminated. Do you see that without the Exit Sub statement we would execute the statements to display the contents of the text box in the Output window?"

"I see that," Rhonda said, "but couldn't we have placed the If statement after the code to display the text box contents in the Output window?"

"What's that expression about closing the barn door after the horse has gone?" I said. "If we placed the If statement after the WriteLine statement, we would display the contents of the empty text box in the Output window and then we would perform the If test to see if it was empty!"

After a moment or two, Rhonda readily agreed that this wouldn't make any sense at all. The If...Then statement was exactly where it belonged, at the beginning of the event procedure.

If...Then...Else

"I was thinking that there must be a more elegant way of writing this code," Dave said. "Isn't the use of an Exit statement such as Exit Sub frowned upon in some circles?"

"The use of Exit statements is sometimes frowned upon," I agreed, "but remember, the syntax is available in the language, so it's perfectly valid to use it. But you are right—there is a more eloquent way of writing this code, and it does eliminate the need to code an Exit Sub statement in the event procedure."

I continued by explaining that with the If...Then statement, we tell Visual Basic to execute one or more imperative statements if the condition evaluates to True, but we never specify what to do if the condition evaluates to False.

"The If...Then...Else statement," I said, "allows us to specify one or more imperative statements to execute if the condition evaluates to False."

I displayed the syntax for the If...Then...Else statement.

If some condition is true Then
    execute a statement or statements
ElseIf some other condition is true Then
    execute a statement or statements
Else
    execute a statement or statements
End If

"I've read about the Else statement," Dave said, "but I'm not familiar with the ElseIf statement."

"ElseIf is an optional statement," I said. "In reality, it's just like another If statement that is coded before the End If statement. You can have as many ElseIf statements as you need to test the condition or conditions you wish to evaluate—or you can have none at all."

"This looks like it can get pretty complicated," Ward said. "It's like we really have three variations on the If statement, don't we? How do you decide which one of the three to use?"

"You're right, Ward," I said. "There really are three 'flavors' of the If statement and the differences between them can be very subtle:"

- The first flavor, the simple If...Then statement (whether single-line or block form), specifies code to execute for a True condition, but no code for the False condition.

- The second flavor, the If...Then...Else statement, specifies code for both the True and False conditions.

- The third flavor, the ElseIf statement allows you to specify multiple True and False conditions.

I suggested that we take the code from Exercise 8-2, and modify it to include statements to execute if the condition is False.

Exercise 8-3 The If...Then...Else Statement

In this exercise, we'll modify the code from Exercise 8-2, using an Else statement to eliminate the need to code an Exit Sub statement.

1. Continue working with the project from Exercise 8-2.
2. Modify the Click event procedure of the Button control so that it looks like this.

```
Private Sub Button1_Click(ByVal sender As Object, _
   ByVal e As System.EventArgs) Handles Button1.Click

If TextBox1.Text = "" Then
   MessageBox.Show ("You must make an entry in the textbox")
Else
   Console.WriteLine (TextBox1.Text)
   TextBox1.Text = ""
End If

TextBox1.Focus()

End Sub
```

3. Save the project if you wish—we won't be modifying it any further.
4. Now run the program.
5. Notice how the behavior of the program hasn't changed, although the code to implement it has changed.

Discussion

"So the behavior of the program hasn't changed a bit here," Ward said, "although we did change the code."

"That's right," I said, "I would say the code is a bit more eloquent."

"How so?" Steve asked.

I asked everyone to compare the code from Exercise 8-2 with the code in this exercise. "We have one less line," Steve said. "Is that what makes it more eloquent?"

"That's part of it," I said, "but I think you would also have to agree that this code is much more readable now—it just flows better. Instead of having the somewhat cryptic Exit Sub statement, not only do we explicitly state what code will be executed if the condition is True, but also the code that will be executed if the condition is False. Nothing is left to the imagination."

"I notice also," Dave said, "that in the previous version of the code we repeated the line TextBox1.Focus twice; now that line of code is outside of the If…Then…Else structure. I presume that's because we set focus to the text box regardless of whether the condition evaluates to True or False?"

"An excellent observation, Dave" I said. "If we have code that is to be executed regardless of whether the condition is True or False, we just place it outside of the If…Then…Else structure."

Everyone seemed to understand what I was talking about.

If…Then…ElseIf

"Can you give us an example of code with an ElseIf statement?" Joe asked.

After thinking for a few moments, I said, "To make this all a little more understandable, let me use pseudocode to illustrate an ElseIf statement."

I saw some puzzled looks.

"I mentioned pseudocode very early on in the course," I said. "Pseudocode is just a tool that programmers use to express a complex problem, but instead of coding it up in a particular language, pseudocode let's us express the problem in English. Then, when we have it worked out to our satisfaction, we can translate the pseudocode into whatever language we happen to be working work. Remember, what you see here isn't Visual Basic code—so don't try to type it into a code window!"

I then displayed this pseudocode on the classroom projector.

```
There is an employee working for a company. According to the rules of company…

If the employee's age is 62 or greater Then
    he must be retired
ElseIf the employee's age is 61 Then
    he has 1 year until retirement
ElseIf the employee's age is 60 Then
    he has 2 years until retirement
ElseIf the employee's age is 59 Then
    he has 3 years until retirement
Else
    he has a really long time to go
End If
```

Note: Pseudocode is just a way of expressing a complex statement in English, prior to coding it in an actual programming language. This is not unlike the wording we used in our Requirements Statement.

I suggested that we try coding this pseudocode ourselves using Visual Basic, but I warned everyone that this code would be a bit unwieldy. "Using a series of ElseIf statements can be cumbersome," I said. "After we code up this pseudocode in this exercise, in Exercise 8-5 we'll see how we can streamline this code using another selection structure called the Select… Case statement."

Exercise 8-4 The If…Then…ElseIf Statement

In this exercise, we'll explore the If..Then..ElseIf statement.

1. Start a new Windows application.
2. Place a TextBox and a Button control on the form. Accept the default names that Visual Basic assigns.
3. Double-click on the Button control and place the following code into its Click event procedure.

```
Private Sub Button1_Click(ByVal sender As Object, _
  ByVal e As System.EventArgs) Handles Button1.Click

If TextBox1.Text = "" Then
  MessageBox.Show ("You must make an entry in the textbox")
ElseIf Val(TextBox1.Text) > 61 Then
  Console.WriteLine (TextBox1.Text & " - You must be retired")
ElseIf Val(TextBox1.Text) = 61 Then
  Console.WriteLine (TextBox1.Text & " - You have 1 year until retirement")
ElseIf Val(TextBox1.Text) = 60 Then
  Console.WriteLine (TextBox1.Text & " - You have 2 years until Retirement")
ElseIf Val(TextBox1.Text) = 59 Then
  Console.WriteLine (TextBox1.Text & " - You have 3 years until retirement")
Else
  Console.WriteLine (TextBox1.Text & " - You have a long time until retirement")
End If

TextBox1.Text = ""
TextBox1.Focus()

End Sub
```

4. Save the project—we'll be modifying it in Exercise 8-5.
5. Now run the program.
6. Type **62**, **61**, **60**, **59**, and **40** into the text box and click on the Button control after each entry. All of the various messages should be displayed in the Visual Basic Output window. If you try clicking the Button control without making an entry in the text box, you will receive an error message. Your output window should look like this.

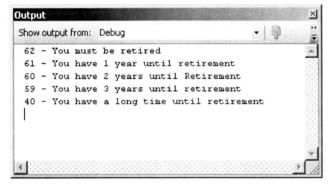

Discussion

There was probably more code in this exercise than in any of the others we had done so far, and several of my students became confused and lost their places. Fifteen minutes later, though, I was happy to see that everyone in the class had successfully completed it.

"I don't think we've ever written that much code," Rhonda said.

"I think you're right, Rhonda" I replied. "As you probably noticed, when you write code that tests for a variety of different conditions, your code can really 'balloon', but sometimes it just can't be helped. The code you've written for this exercise, though lengthy, is still pretty manageable. But suppose we had a requirement to print a different message for every age between 1 and 100?"

"That would really balloon the code," Mary said. "Is there an alternative to the ElseIf statement?"

"Yes, there is," I said, "and we'll get to that in a minute. But before we go there, I'd like to explain this code in just a bit more detail."

I displayed the first two lines of code from the exercise on the classroom projector.

```
If TextBox1.Text = "" Then
   MessageBox.Show ("You must make an entry in the textbox")
```

"What we're doing here," I said, "is checking to ensure that the user has made an entry in the text box, which of course is exactly what we did in the previous exercise. Now, the next line of code may look familiar to you."

```
ElseIf Val(TextBox1.Text) > 61 Then
```

"I see that we're using the Val function here," Linda said. "I seem to recall having discussed that before."

"That's right, Linda," I answered. "The Val function converts the String data type of the Text property of the TextBox into a Numeric data type. We're using it here to convert the user's entry in the text box to a number."

"I'm sure we've covered this before," Steve said, "but why is the Val function necessary?"

I reminded the class that each property has a data type of its own and the Text property is a String data type.

"It's not possible to perform numeric comparison on a string," Ward said. "Isn't that right? Is that why we had to use the Val function prior to comparing the Text property of the TextBox to the number 61?"

"Exactly right, Ward" I replied. "In order to perform any arithmetic or numeric comparisons on a String data type, we must first convert the string to a Numeric data type, and that's what the Val function did here."

"What is that funny character on the next line of code?" Chuck asked.

I explained that the next line of code uses the concatenation character, the ampersand (&)

```
Console.WriteLine (TextBox1.Text & " - You must be retired")
```

to join the string " -You must be retired" with the value of the Text property of the TextBox. Therefore, if the number 62 has been entered into the text box, the Output window then displays the following message: 62 -You must be retired.

"That's clever," Steve said. "So we're using the value of a property in the message—not a numeric literal."

"That's right, Steve," I said. "Using the value of the property, and then concatenating it to the message gives us a much more flexible and descriptive message. No matter what age the user enters into the text box, that age is displayed in the Output window, concatenated to an appropriate descriptive message."

"What about the rest of the code?" Rhonda asked. "Can you explain the rest?"

"Sure," I said. "After we convert the entry in the TextBox to a Numeric data type, we then compare it, using the greater-than comparison operator, to see if it is greater than 61. We learned last week that comparison operations return a True or a False value. If the number entered into the text box is greater than 61, a True value is returned, and we then display the user's age, joined with the string '- You must be 'retired' in the Visual Basic Output window."

"What if the user's age is not greater than 61?" Kate asked. "This is where I became confused."

"If the user's age is not greater than 61," I said, "the comparison operation returns False, and our code jumps right to the line beginning with ElseIf and executes it. Of course, the ElseIf line turns out to be another If statement which is then evaluated."

```
ElseIf Val(TextBox1.Text) = 61 Then
   Console.WriteLine (TextBox1.Text & " - You have 1 year until retirement")
```

"This code also converts the value in the Text property to a Numeric date type," I said, "and then determines if that value is equal to 61. If it is, we execute the imperative statement following the word Then, displaying an appropriate message in the Visual Basic Output window. If the entry in the text box is not equal to 61, we jump right to the next ElseIf statement to determine if the user's age is 60."

```
ElseIf Val(TextBox1.Text) = 60 Then
   Console.WriteLine (TextBox1.Text & " - You have 2 years until retirement")
```

"I'm okay with this," Linda said. "This is basically the same code we used to determine if the user's age is 61. If it is, we display a slightly different message in the Output window."

"That's right," I agreed, "and we can say the same thing about this section of code, which checks to see if the user's age is 59."

```
ElseIf Val(TextBox1.Text) = 59 Then
   Console.WriteLine (TextBox1.Text & " - You have 3 years until retirement")
```

"Now, can you imagine," I said, "if we had to write individual lines of code for every age from 59 on down to 1. Fortunately, we can take care of all of those possibilities with the simple Else statement."

```
Else
   Console.WriteLine (TextBox1.Text & " - You have a long time until retirement")
End If
```

"By using the Else statement here," I said, "we tell Visual Basic that all of the remaining ages fit into one big category and to display, in the Output window, a generic message about having a long time until retirement."

I asked if there were any questions. "We didn't discuss the two lines of code outside of the If…Then…Else structure," Rhonda said.

"Good point," I replied. "These two lines of code are executed regardless of the age that the user enters into the text box. They clear the contents of the text box, and set focus to it."

```
TextBox1.Text = ""
TextBox1.Focus()
```

"I just wanted to mention," Linda said, "that I ran this code in Step mode and it really made things very clear for me."

"That's a great point, Linda," I said. "Beginners should probably run every piece of code they write in Step mode to see what's going on behind the scenes of their program."

Select…Case

"Suppose we were asked to modify our program to do something like this?" I asked, displaying this modified pseudocode on the classroom projector.

There is an employee working for a company. According to the rules of company…

If the employee's age is 62 or greater Then
   he must be retired
ElseIf the employee's age is 61 Then
   he has 1 year until retirement
ElseIf the employee's age is 60 Then
   he has 2 years until retirement
ElseIf the employee's age is 59 Then
   he has 3 years until retirement
ElseIf the employee's age is between 50 and 59 Then
   he has a short time to go
ElseIf the employee's age is between 40 and 49 Then
   he has some time to go
ElseIf the employee's age is between 25 and 39 Then
   he has a pretty long time to go
ElseIf the employee's age is between 18 and 24 Then
   he has a really long time to go
Else he should be in school
End If

"That will complicate our program quite a bit," I said. "Are we up to an If…Then…Else statement with nine alternatives?"

"That's a lot of ElseIf statements," Ward said.

"The more alternatives we have in an If…Then…Else statement," I said, "the harder the program is to write, read, and modify, and the more likely it is that we'll make a mistake when we code it. Fortunately, there is an alternative to the If…Then…Else statement called the Select…Case statement, which can be a godsend when your program must evaluate many alternatives like this one."

I then displayed the syntax for the Select…Case statement on the classroom projector.

Select Case testexpression [Case expressionlist1 [statementblock-1]] [Case expressionlist2 [statementblock-2]]

.

.

[Case Else

[statementblock-n]]

End Select

"Rather than trying to dryly explain this syntax," I said, "let me display an example of the Select…Case statement on the classroom projector. This is the first statement in a Select…Case structure."

Select Case intValue

"The Select…Case statement begins with the words Select Case followed by what is called a test expression. You should be familiar with expressions by now. An expression is evaluated, and a result is returned. With the Select…Case statement, there is just a single test expression coded at the 'top' of the Select Case statement, and according to the rules for the Select…Case statement, the test expression must return either a number or a string. In this example, our test expression is actually a variable called intValue. Following that first line of code containing the test expression comes a series of Case statements. Here's the first one in our demo."

Case 1 MessageBox.Show ("intValue is equal to 1")

"This code tells Visual Basic to display a message if the value of the variable intValue is equal to 1. What makes the Select…Case structure so powerful is the ability to easily specify multiple conditions such as this one."

Case 2,3
  MessageBox.Show ("intValue is either 2 or 3")

"The comma in the Case statement," I said, "is read like an Or operator. And look how easily a range of values can be specified."

Case 4 to 8
  MessageBox.Show ("intValue is in the range 4 through 8")

"Or this way."

Case Is > 45
  MessageBox.Show ("intValue is greater than 45")

"Why is the word 'Is' in that code?" Linda asked.

"I originally wrote that as Case > 45," I said, "but Visual Basic inserted the word 'Is' for me. According to the rules of the Select Case Statement you are not permitted to repeat the name of the test expression in a Case expression. In other words, you can't repeat the word intValue anywhere in your Case expressions. I suspect Visual Basic uses the word 'Is' as a replacement for intValue. You can read the statement as Case intValue > 45, but you mustn't enter the code that way."

I paused before continuing.

"Finally, how about this code?" I continued.

Case 1 To 3,5,9 To 13, Is > 100
  MessageBox.Show ("Wow!")
  MessageBox.Show ("This is great!")

"Trying to do this type of multiple condition testing is very tedious with an If…Then…Else statement," I said, "but virtually a snap with the Select…Case statement."

"It looks to me," Rhonda said, "like the Select…Case statement is just perfect. Why bother using the If…Then…Else statement at all?"

"The Select…Case statement does have its limitations," I said. "Remember, with the Select…Case statement you are limited to a single test expression, which means you have to formulate your case expressions around that limitation."

"In the syntax you displayed on the projector," Dave said, "there was a Case Else statement. What does that do?"

"The Case Else statement is an optional catchall statement," I said, "just like an ElseIf. Basically, you use the Case Else statement to handle a case you can't anticipate. If the test expression doesn't fall into one of the preceding Case statements, the code in the Case Else statement is executed."

Case Else
   MessageBox.Show ("Nothing was True")

"Suppose you have several Case expressions that evaluate to True?" Barbara asked. "Are all the tests done or does Visual Basic stop after the first True one, like the If statement? For example, in the code you just showed us, there were two Case statements that would evaluate to True for a value of intValue equal to 1."

"That's a excellent question," I said. "In Visual Basic, if a Case expression evaluates to True, all of the remaining Case expressions are bypassed. Therefore, if you have more than one Case expression that can evaluate to True, the first one in the list is the one that will have its code executed. In the example I showed you, if intValue was equal to 1, only the first Case statement would be executed."

We had been working for a long time without a break. I suggested that we complete one more exercise before taking a break.

Exercise 8-5 The Select…Case Statement

In this exercise, we'll explore the Select…Case statement.

1. Continue working with the project from Exercise 8-4.
2. Modify the Click event procedure of the Button control so that it looks like this.

```
Private Sub Button1_Click(ByVal sender As Object, _
   ByVal e As System.EventArgs) Handles Button1.Click

If TextBox1.Text = "" Then
   MessageBox.Show "You must make an entry in the textbox"
   TextBox1.Focus()
Exit Sub
End If

Select Case Val(TextBox1.Text)
   Case Is > 61
      Console.WriteLine (TextBox1.Text & " - You must be retired")
   Case 61
      Console.WriteLine (TextBox1.Text & " - You have 1 year until retirement")
   Case 60
      Console.WriteLine (TextBox1.Text & " - You have 2 years until retirement")
   Case 59
      Console.WriteLine (TextBox1.Text & " - You have 3 years until retirement")
   Case 50 To 58
      Console.WriteLine (TextBox1.Text & " - You have a short time to go")
   Case 40 To 49
      Console.WriteLine (TextBox1.Text & " - You have some time to go")
   Case 25 To 39
      Console.WriteLine (TextBox1.Text & " - You have a pretty long time to go")
   Case 18 To 24
      Console.WriteLine (TextBox1.Text & " - You have a long time to go")
   Case Else
      Console.WriteLine (TextBox1.Text & " - You should be in school")
End Select

TextBox1.Text = ""
TextBox1.Focus()
```

End Sub

3. Save the project if you wish—we won't be modifying it.

4. Now run the project.

5. As was the case with Exercise 8-4, enter a number of different retirement ages into the text box and watch as various retirement messages are displayed in the Visual Basic Output window.

Discussion

"Most programmers find the Select…Case statement to be pretty straightforward," I said.

"I noticed that we included the test for an empty TextBox outside the Select…Case statement," Bob said. "Couldn't we have included that test within the Select…Case statement?"

"Unfortunately not," I said, as I displayed the code on the classroom projector.

If TextBox1.Text = "" Then
   MessageBox.Show "You must make an entry in the textbox"
   Exit Sub
End If

"Do you remember that I said that we could specify only a single test expression in the Select Case statement? That means we can't specify a test expression for both an empty text box and a specific value in the text box. Since we coded the test expression like this."

Select Case Val(TextBox1.Text)

"…we needed a separate If…Then test for an empty text box. Notice also, that, as we did before, we converted the String data type of the Text property of the TextBox to a Numeric value using the Val function. This first Case…"

Case Is > 61

"…is checking to see if the entry in the Textbox is greater than 61. This line of code…"

Case 61

"…checks whether the value entered into the text box is 61. The next few lines of code perform the same check for the ages 60 and 59. This line of code…"

Case 50 To 58

"…illustrates how easy it is to check for a range of values entered into the text box using the Select…Case structure. This next series of Case statements operates in the same manner, the only thing that changes is the message displayed. Finally," I said, "here's the catchall Else case."

Case Else
   Console.WriteLine (TextBox1.Text & " - You should be in school")

"If none of the other Case expressions evaluates to True," I said, " the message '- You should be in school' is displayed in the Output window."

"So the presumption here," Linda said, "is that if we get this far in the code, the user's age is less than 18?"

"That's right." I said. "Now before you say it, Linda, I know we could have coded a Case expression to handle this, like this, for example."

Case Is < 18

"But I wanted to give everyone a chance to work with the Case Else statement. Finally, beginners frequently forget this all-important line—the End Select statement!"

End Select

"We can't forget the End Select statement," I said, "since it marks the end of the Select Case structure. When a Case expression evaluates to True and its statement or statements are executed, code execution resumes with the line of code following the End Select statement."

I concluded by asking everyone to look at the two lines of code after the End Select statement. Since it's outside of the Select…Case structure, this code is executed regardless of the evaluation of the individual Case expressions.

TextBox1.Text = ""
TextBox1.Focus()

I asked if there were any questions. There were none, and so I told everyone to take a well-earned break.

"When we return from break," I said, "we'll begin coding the China Shop Project."

The China Shop Project

"We now know enough about Visual Basic," I said, "to put some basic code structures into our project, and to begin to code the China Shop project. It won't have all the bells and whistles that our Requirements Statement is asking for, but it should at least produce a usable quote."

"Let's take a moment to review where we are with the project," I continued, "since it's been a couple of weeks since we last worked with it. Our user interface is basically in place now. The menu must be added, of course, but that will come toward the end of this course. When we start the program, the list box is loaded with the three brands of china that the China Shop sells. Clicking the radio buttons and check boxes triggers the default behavior of these controls, but at this point, nothing more. Clicking the Calculate and Reset buttons also has no effect on the program."

"How far do you think we'll get with the program today?" Rhonda asked.

"I think we'll have time to write code for the Click event procedures of both the Calculate and Reset Button controls," I said.

"You mean we'll actually be to the point of calculating a price today?" Ward asked.

"I think so," I replied. "First, though, we need to place some code in the Click event procedures of our RadioButton controls."

I reminded everyone that to calculate a sales quote for the China Shop application, our program needs three pieces of information: a brand of china, the user's selection of a quantity, and his or her selection of one or more china items.

"I think it will make our job of calculating a price a little easier," I said, "if we store the customer's quantity selection in a form-level variable, and then use that value later on in our computations. To do that, we'll place code in the Click event procedures of the four RadioButton controls."

Exercise 8-6 Coding the Click Event Procedures of the Four RadioButton Controls

In this exercise, you'll code the Click event procedures of the four RadioButton controls.

1. Load up the China Shop Project.
2. Place the following code in the Declarations section of the form. Place the following code in the Declarations section of the form. Place it right after the Public Class Main statement. This statement will declare a form-level variable called m_intQuantity.

```
Private m_intQuantity as Integer
```

3. Place the following code into the Click event procedure of the rad1 RadioButton.

```
Private Sub rad1_Click (ByVal sender As Object, _
   ByVal e As System.EventArgs) Handles rad1.Click

m_intQuantity = 1

End Sub
```

4. Place the following code into the Click event procedure of the rad2 RadioButton.

```
Private Sub rad2_Click (ByVal sender As Object, _
   ByVal e As System.EventArgs) Handles rad2.Click

m_intQuantity = 2

End Sub
```

5. Place the following code into the Click event procedure of the rad4 RadioButton.

```
Private Sub rad4_Click(ByVal sender As Object, _
```

```
  ByVal e As System.EventArgs) Handles rad4.Click
m_intQuantity = 4
End Sub
```

6. Place the following code into the Click event procedure of the rad8 RadioButton.

```
Private Sub rad8_Click(ByVal sender As Object, _
  ByVal e As System.EventArgs) Handles rad8.Click
m_intQuantity = 8
End Sub
```

7. Save the China Shop Project.
8. The addition of this code will have no obvious impact on your program, but you should run the program anyway to ensure that it still runs without errors.

Discussion

"I was able to complete this exercise," Rhonda said, "but I must confess I'm not absolutely sure what's going on here."

"I suspect you're not the only who feels that way," I said. "What we've done is place code into the Click event procedures of each one of the radio buttons. Whenever they are clicked, the value of m_intQuantity is set equal to the quantity that they represent. For instance, when rad8 is clicked, that indicates the user is selecting a quantity of 8 for their china purchase, so we set the value of m_intQuantity equal to 8."

"I'm okay with that," Steve said, "but why did we declare the variable in the Declarations section of the form? Why not within the Click event procedures of the RadioButton controls?"

"A variable declared in the Click event procedure of the RadioButton would live only for as long as the Click event procedure." I said. "As soon as the code in the Click event procedure finished executing, the variable would die, and along with it, its value."

"And a form-level variable stays around for as long as the form is loaded," Dave said, "plus since it's a form-level variable, the value can be seen by all of the code on the form."

"That's right!" I said. "Once we have the customer's desired quantity stored in the variable m_intQuantity, that value can be seen by all of the event procedures on the form. Later on we'll see that fact becomes very important to the Click event procedure of the btnCalculate Button control."

"I just wanted to let everyone know," Kate said, "that if you run your program in Step mode, you'll get a beautiful view of the assignment of the variable being made whenever one of the radio buttons is clicked."

Kate's point was excellent. Although the code we had just added to the China Shop Project had no obvious impact on the program, we could see its impact behind the scenes by running our program in Step mode.

"That's a great point, Kate," I said "By running the program in Step mode, we'll be able to see the assignment of values to m_intQuantity as they take place. You can also, if you wish, place breakpoints on the code in the RadioButton control's event procedures which will cause the program to enter Break mode when those lines of code are encountered."

"I didn't realize how much," Barbara said, "Step mode and breakpoints could help me understand what is actually going on in the program, I think I'll use it all of the time now."

I reminded everyone that part of our requirements for the China Shop Project was to provide a Complete Place Setting check box, which when selected would automatically select the check boxes of all of the individual china items.

Exercise 8-7 Coding the Click Event Procedure for the chkCompletePlaceSetting CheckBox

In this exercise, you'll code the Click Event procedure of the chkCompletePlaceSetting CheckBox.

1. Continue working with the China Shop Project (or load it up if you have closed it).
2. Place the following code into the Click event procedure of the chkCompletePlaceSetting CheckBox.

Private Sub chkCompletePlaceSetting_Click(ByVal sender As Object, _

```
ByVal e As System.EventArgs) Handles chkCompletePlaceSetting.Click
If chkCompletePlaceSetting.Checked = True Then
  chkPlate.Checked = True
  chkButterPlate.Checked = True
  chkSoupBowl.Checked = True
  chkCup.Checked = True
  chkSaucer.Checked = True
Else
  chkPlate.Checked = False
  chkButterPlate.Checked = False
  chkSoupBowl.Checked = False
  chkCup.Checked = False
  chkSaucer.Checked = False
End If

End Sub
```

3. Save the China Shop Project.

4. Run the program and click on the Complete Place Setting check box. All of the china items (except for the platter) will automatically be selected.

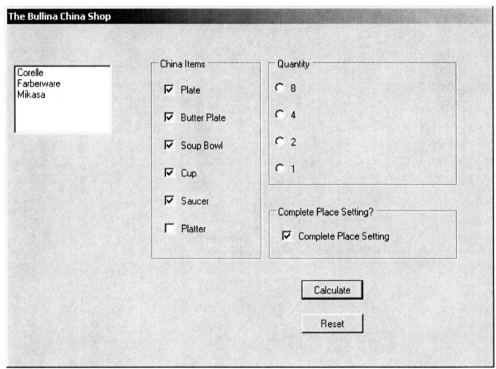

5. Click on the Complete Place Setting check box again. This time all of the china items (except for the platter) will automatically be deselected.

Discussion

I scanned the room for obvious signs of difficulty, but found none—most of my students seemed to be pretty proud of themselves, and I found more than one clicking on the Compete Place Setting check box over and over again.

"I had no trouble doing the exercise," Linda said, "but I am a little confused as to when exactly the Click event procedure of the CheckBox takes place. Does it take place before or after the check mark appears or disappears in the check box?"

"That's a good question," I said. "The Click event procedure of the CheckBox takes place after the check mark appears or disappears. That's why we're able to use the Checked property of the CheckBox to determine if we should check or uncheck the other check boxes. Let's take a closer look at the code now…"

I continued by explaining that the first thing we do in this code is to determine what the current state of the Complete Place Setting's check box is. We used the Checked property to determine if there's a check mark in the check box.

If chkCompletePlaceSetting.Checked = True Then

"The Checked property is a Boolean property," I said, "and if it's equal to True, that tells us that the customer has just placed a check mark in the Complete Place Setting check box. That means we should now place check marks in the five check boxes representing the items that comprise a complete place setting (that is, all of the items except for the platter), by setting their Checked properties to True."

chkPlate.Checked = True
chkButterPlate.Checked = True
chkSoupBowl.Checked = True
chkCup.Checked = True
chkSaucer.Checked = True

"At this point," I continued, "we could check to see if the Checked property of the Complete Place Setting check box is False with another If…Then statement, but since the Checked property of the check box is a Boolean value, if it's not True it must be…"

"False," Ward said, taking the words right out of my mouth.

"That's right, Ward," I agreed, "if the Checked property's value isn't True, it must be False. So we can handle that eventuality with an Else statement, using it to set the Checked properties of each of the five check boxes comprising a complete place setting to False."

Else
  chkPlate.Checked = False
  chkButterPlate.Checked = False
  chkSoupBowl.Checked = False
  chkCup.Checked = False
  chkSaucer.Checked = False

"I've got to tell you," Rhonda said, "I think this is really neat. If the rest of the programming of the China Shop Program turns out to be this much fun, I think I'm hooked on programming."

Since there were no more questions about this event procedure, I told everyone that it was now time to move on to the 'bread and butter' of the program, the Click event procedure of the Calculate Button control.

Exercise 8-8 Coding the Click Event Procedure of the Calculate Button

In this exercise, you'll code the Click Event procedure of the btnCalculate Button control.

1. Continue working with the China Shop Project (or load it up if you have closed it).
2. Place the following code into the Click event procedure of the btnCalculate Button control.

```
Private Sub btnCalculate_Click (ByVal sender As System.Object, _
   ByVal e As System.EventArgs) Handles btnCalculate.Click

'Declare our variables
Dim sngTotalPrice As Single
Dim sngButterPlatePrice As Single
Dim sngCupPrice As Single
Dim sngPlatePrice As Single
Dim sngPlatterPrice As Single
Dim sngSaucerPrice As Single
Dim sngSoupBowlPrice As Single

'Has the customer selected a brand of china?
If lstBrands.Text = "" Then
   MessageBox.Show("You must select a China brand")
   Exit Sub
End If

'Has the customer selected one or more china items?
```

```
If chkPlate.Checked = False And _
  chkButterPlate.Checked = False And _
  chkSoupBowl.Checked = False And _
  chkCup.Checked = False And _
  chkSaucer.Checked = False And _
  chkPlatter.Checked = False Then
    MessageBox.Show("You must select one or more china items")
    Exit Sub
End If

'Has the customer selected a quantity?
If rad8.Checked = False And _
  rad4.Checked = False And _
  rad2.Checked = False And _
  rad1.Checked = False Then
    MessageBox.Show("You must select a quantity")
    Exit Sub
End If

'If the customer has selected a platter
'warn them that there is only 1 permitted per sales quotation

If chkPlatter.Checked = True And m_intQuantity > 1 Then
  MessageBox.Show("Customer is limited to 1 platter per order." & _
  chr(13) & "Adjusting price accordingly")
End If

'All the pieces are here, let's calculate a price
'Assign prices to each item

Select Case lstBrands.Text
  Case "Mikasa"
    If chkPlate.Checked = True Then
      sngPlatePrice = 25
    End If
    If chkButterPlate.Checked = True Then
      sngButterPlatePrice = 10
    End If
    If chkSoupBowl.Checked = True Then
      sngSoupBowlPrice = 10
    End If
    If chkCup.Checked = True Then
      sngCupPrice = 5
    End If
    If chkSaucer.Checked = True Then
      sngSaucerPrice = 5
    End If
    If chkPlatter.Checked = True Then
      sngPlatterPrice = 50
    End If
  Case "Farberware"
    If chkPlate.Checked = True Then
      sngPlatePrice = 10
    End If
    If chkButterPlate.Checked = True Then
      sngButterPlatePrice = 3
    End If
    If chkSoupBowl.Checked = True Then
      sngSoupBowlPrice = 5
```

```
      End If
      If chkCup.Checked = True Then
        sngCupPrice = 3
      End If
      If chkSaucer.Checked = True Then
        sngSaucerPrice = 3
      End If
      If chkPlatter.Checked = True Then
        sngPlatterPrice = 13
      End If
    Case "Corelle"
      If chkPlate.Checked = True Then
        sngPlatePrice = 4
      End If
      If chkButterPlate.Checked = True Then
        sngButterPlatePrice = 1
      End If
      If chkSoupBowl.Checked = True Then
        sngSoupBowlPrice = 2
      End If
      If chkCup.Checked = True Then
        sngCupPrice = 1
      End If
      If chkSaucer.Checked = True Then
        sngSaucerPrice = 1
      End If
      If chkPlatter.Checked = True Then
        sngPlatterPrice = 5
      End If
  End Select

  'Add the prices together and multiply by the quantity to calculate a grand total
  sngTotalPrice = (((sngPlatePrice + sngButterPlatePrice + _
                  sngSoupBowlPrice + sngCupPrice + sngSaucerPrice) _
                  * m_intQuantity) + sngPlatterPrice)

  'If the price is greater than 0, display the price and make the label visible
  If sngTotalPrice > 0 Then
    lblPrice.text = "The price of your order is $" & sngTotalPrice
    lblPrice.Visible = True
  End If

End Sub
```

3. Save the China Shop Project.

4. Run the program. Select *Mikasa* as your choice of china brand, **2** for quantity, and select **Plate**, **Butter Plate**, and **Soup Bowl** as your china items. If you now click on the Calculate button, a calculated price of **$90** should be displayed.

The Bullina China Shop

Corelle
Farberware
Mikasa

China Items
☑ Plate
☑ Butter Plate
☑ Soup Bowl
☐ Cup
☐ Saucer
☐ Platter

Quantity
○ 8
○ 4
⊙ 2
○ 1

Complete Place Setting?
☐ Complete Place Setting

The price of your order is $90

Calculate

Reset

Discussion

It took about 15 minutes for everyone to complete this exercise. As I had warned the class, there was a lot of typing to do, and more than one student made typos entering the code. But when they were all finished, I could sense their feeling of accomplishment. In essence, their version of the China Shop Program was complete—it was now calculating a price quotation for a mythical customer.

"I just noticed something," Dave said, "shouldn't we be calculating a discount for a Complete Price Setting? I selected everything except a Platter for the Mikasa brand, and with a quantity of 1, the program displayed a total of $55, when it should be $50."

"Good point Dave," I said, "That calculation can be a bit tricky, and so I thought we would hold off on that until we discuss Arrays and File Operations—don't worry we will get to it."

"I won't let you forget," Dave said smiling.

Let's take a good look at this code now," I said, as I attempted to pry them away from their efforts running the program. "The first thing we did here was to declare local variables that we use in the price calculation. It's good programming practice to declare variables at the 'top' of an event procedure. Also, as a courtesy to other programmers who may read your code, it's a good idea to insert comments, like the ones we have used here, to indicate exactly what is going on in the program."

```
'Declare our variables
Dim sngTotalPrice As Single
Dim sngButterPlatePrice As Single
Dim sngCupPrice As Single
Dim sngPlatePrice As Single
Dim sngPlatterPrice As Single
Dim sngSaucerPrice As Single
Dim sngSoupBowlPrice As Single
```

"What exactly are these variables used for?" Chuck asked.

"The methodology we'll use to calculate a total price," I said, "requires that we first calculate a subtotal price for each item of china that the customer desires. These variables represent the prices of each china item, and the variable sngTotalPrice is the variable that will store the grand total."

"That makes a lot of sense to me," Rhonda said. "What are those If…Then statements used for?"

"Before we can calculate a price," I said, "we need to ensure that the customer has provided us with the following three pieces of information:"

- A brand of china

- One or more china items

- A quantity

"We use three If…Then statements to ensure we have everything we need to calculate a sales quotation." I said. "This first section of code ensures that the customer has made a selection in the list box by checking the Text property of the ListBox. If the Text property is empty, we know that no brand has been selected, and we display a message to the user and then bypass the rest of the code by executing the Exit Sub statement."

```
'Has the customer selected a brand of china?
If lstBrands.Text = "" Then
   MessageBox.Show("You must select a China brand")
Exit Sub
End If
```

"I'm still a little confused," Valerie said. "How does a value get stored in the Text property of the ListBox?"

"When the customer makes a selection of an item in the list box by clicking on it, the Text property of the ListBox is automatically set to the name of the item that the customer has selected."

"I see," Valerie said, "so if the customer selects Mikasa in the list box, the Text property of the ListBox is then assigned the value Mikasa?"

"I just saw that," Ward said excitedly. "When I ran the program in Step mode and used the Immediate window to display the Text property of the ListBox."

"Great," I said, "now you're getting the idea."

"So if the customer has made no selection at all in the list box," Blain said, "the Text property of the ListBox will contain an empty string."

"Exactly," I answered. "Now let's examine the code to determine if the customer has made at least one selection of a china item."

```
'Has the customer selected one or more china items?
If chkPlate.Checked = False And _
   chkButterPlate.Checked = False And _
   chkSoupBowl.Checked = False And _
   chkCup.Checked = False And _
   chkSaucer.Checked = False And _
  chkPlatter.Checked = False Then
    MessageBox.Show("You must select one or more china items")
    Exit Sub
End If
```

"This code," I said, "checks the Checked property of each one of our CheckBox controls to ensure that the customer has selected at least one item. Notice the use of the And operator here, and notice also how we used the line continuation character to make the code more readable—otherwise we would have had one gigantic line of code."

"The And operator," Barbara said, "requires that for the entire statement to be considered True, every expression must be True also?"

"That's right, Barbara," I said, "that means that if the customer hasn't selected at least one item of china, the If…Then statement evaluates to True. We then display a warning message to the customer and exit the Click event procedure using the Exit Sub statement."

I then displayed the code that ensures that the customer has selected a quantity.

```
'Has the customer selected a quantity?
If rad8.Checked = False And _
   rad4.Checked = False And _
```

```
      rad2.Checked = False And _
      rad1.Checked = False Then
      MessageBox.Show("You must select a quantity")
      Exit Sub
End If
```

"Again, we use the And operator here," I said. "If the Checked property of all four RadioButtons is False, we know that the customer has not made a quantity selection."

I waited to see if anyone was confused before continuing. "At this point, provided the customer has made a selection of a china brand, one or more items, and a quantity, we now have all the ingredients we need to calculate a price—but there's one more section of code we need to execute before we get to the actual price calculation."

```
'If the customer has selected a platter
'warn them that there is only 1 permitted per sales quotation
If chkPlatter.Checked = True And m_intQuantity > 1 Then
   MessageBox.Show("Customer is limited to 1 platter per order." & _
   chr(13) & "Adjusting price accordingly")
End If
```

"You may remember," I said, "that Joe Bullina has a policy of permitting the customer to purchase just one platter. As you'll see shortly, we can handle the special problem that restriction poses in our calculation pretty easily, but we really should tell the customer about the limitation and that's what this code does. We check to see if the Platter check box is checked, and also if the customer's selected quantity is greater than 1. If it is, we display a message to the user."

"What's going on with chr(13) in the message box?" Barbara asked.

"If you want to display more than one line in a message box," I said, "you need to concatenate the ASCII character for a line feed to the first line of your message—that's what we're doing here. As a result, the message looks a little more readable."

I quickly ran the program, selected Mikasa as my brand, Platter as an item, and a quantity of 4. I then clicked the Calculate button and the following message box was displayed on the classroom projector.

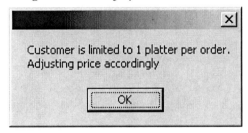

"How did you decide what to do in your code after this?" Rhonda exclaimed. "This is the part of programming that really confuses me! How did you ever come up with that formula to calculate the price?"

"Let me first state that there are probably several ways to calculate the price," I said. "What I did was come up with my own algorithm to do it."

"What's an algorithm?" Steve asked.

"An algorithm is just a step-by-step methodology to solve a problem," I said. "My children are learning algorithms in school now, but instead of calling them algorithms, they call them word problems. But regardless what you call them, an algorithm is just a way of coming up with a method or formula to solve a problem. And what I do is develop the algorithm using paper and pencil first."

"Paper and pencil?" Steve asked, obviously surprised.

"That's right," I said. "Once your algorithm works on paper, the hardest part is really out of the way and you can then translate the algorithm into Visual Basic code."

"You make it sound so easy," Ward said. "What's the algorithm at work here?"

"Let me take you through my original thought process," I replied, "which began with a statement of the problem. What is it that we need to do?"

"Calculate a price," Ward answered.

"That's good, Ward," I said. "Now, can you tell me how we calculate a price?"

"Once we know that the customer has selected a brand, one or more items, and a quantity, we determine the brand of china that the customer has selected, determine the quantity the customer has selected, and then, for each item of china the customer has selected, multiply the unit price by the quantity," Ward replied after thinking for a moment.

"That sounds like a great algorithm to me!" I said. "I can tell you, Ward, that you're right on with this algorithm."

"It can't be that easy," Barbara said.

"All algorithms aren't this easy," I said, "but as simple as this price calculation is, without coming up with an algorithm in a methodical way, it's very possible to mess it up. Ordinarily, what we would do now is sit down once again with pencil and paper, and test the algorithm using some simulations. For instance, the customer selects the Mikasa brand, selects a plate, butter plate, and soup bowl, and a quantity of 2—calculate the price. We would then ensure that the algorithm calculates the correct price, which in this case is $90."

"What do we do now?" Joe asked.

"We translate Ward's algorithm into Visual Basic terms now," I said. "First, how do we know what brand the customer has selected?"

"By examining the ListBox," Linda said.

"Good," I said, "but not just the ListBox—what property of the ListBox?"

"The Text property of the ListBox," Steve answered.

"Excellent," I said. "And how do we know what quantity the customer has selected?"

"By determining which of the four radio buttons have been selected," Kathy said.

"Not quite, Kathy," I said, "do you remember what we did earlier in the Click event procedures of each one of the RadioButtons?"

"That's right," Dave said, "we determined the customer's quantity by checking the value of the variable m_intQuantity, which is updated whenever one of the RadioButtons is clicked."

"Great, Dave," I said. "Now what about the china items? How can we determine which items the customer has selected?"

"By examining the CheckBox controls," Ward answered. "If the check box has a check mark in it—I mean, if the Checked property is equal to True—that means the customer wants that item to be included in their price quotation."

"Everything you've all said is excellent," I said. "I guess the most difficult part of this is how to determine the unit price for the individual items of china." While the class was pondering this, I displayed this code on the classroom projector.

```
'All the pieces are here, let's calculate a price
'Assign prices to each item
Select Case lstBrands.Text
  Case "Mikasa"
    If chkPlate.Checked = True Then
      sngPlatePrice = 25
    End If
    If chkButterPlate.Checked = True Then
      sngButterPlatePrice = 10
    End If
    If chkSoupBowl.Checked = True Then
      sngSoupBowlPrice = 10
    End If
    If chkCup.Checked = True Then
      sngCupPrice = 5
    End If
    If chkSaucer.Checked = True Then
      sngSaucerPrice = 5
    End If
```

```
    If chkPlatter.Checked = True Then
      sngPlatterPrice = 50
    End If
  Case "Farberware"
    If chkPlate.Checked = True Then
      sngPlatePrice = 10
    End If
    If chkButterPlate.Checked = True Then
      sngButterPlatePrice = 3
    End If
    If chkSoupBowl.Checked = True Then
      sngSoupBowlPrice = 5
    End If
    If chkCup.Checked = True Then
      sngCupPrice = 3
    End If
    If chkSaucer.Checked = True Then
      sngSaucerPrice = 3
    End If
    If chkPlatter.Checked = True Then
      sngPlatterPrice = 13
    End If
  Case "Corelle"
    If chkPlate.Checked = True Then
      sngPlatePrice = 4
    End If
    If chkButterPlate.Checked = True Then
      sngButterPlatePrice = 1
    End If
    If chkSoupBowl.Checked = True Then
      sngSoupBowlPrice = 2
    End If
    If chkCup.Checked = True Then
      sngCupPrice = 1
    End If
    If chkSaucer.Checked = True Then
      sngSaucerPrice = 1
    End If
    If chkPlatter.Checked = True Then
      sngPlatterPrice = 5
    End If
End Select
```

"Can anyone explain what's going on in this section of code?" I asked. "It looks to me," Dave said, "that we are using a Select...Case statement to determine the brand of china that the customer selected. Within the Select...Case structure, we appear to be checking each CheckBox Checked property to determine what items the customer has selected. If the customer has selected the item, we are then assigning a price, unique to that item and brand, to one of the variables we declared earlier."

"An excellent analysis, Dave," I said. "That's exactly what we are doing."

I continued by explaining that at the very top of the event procedure, we had declared six variables to store prices for each of the individual items of china.

"For instance," I said, "sngPlatePrice is the variable that we use to hold the price for a plate, sngSoupBowlPrice is the variable that we use to hold the price for a soup bowl, and so on."

"Didn't we promise Mr. Bullina that we would look up prices from a text file?" Linda asked.

"That's a good point," I replied, "and you're right. The way we've 'hard-coded' these prices into our program is a bad idea in a commercial program, but as they say, you need to crawl before you can walk. For now, this will be fine—in the upcoming weeks, we'll make good on our promise by modifying our program to read unit prices from an external disk file." I waited a moment before continuing.

"Let's examine that hypothetical scenario we went through a moment ago," I said. "A customer selects Mikasa for the brand, a quantity of 2, and selects a plate, butter plate, and soup bowl. What will be the values of the individual variables in this event procedure?"

"Let's see," Linda said, without a moment of hesitation, "sngPlatePrice will be equal to 25, sngSoupBowlPrice will be equal to 10, and sngButterPlatePrice will equal 10, sngCupPrice will equal."

She hesitated.

"Excellent so far," I said. "But why the hesitation?"

"I'm not sure what the value of sngCupPrice will be, since our mythical customer hasn't selected it," she said.

"No need to worry," I assured here. "Since we declared sngCupPrice as a Single type variable, it was automatically initialized with a value of 0. Since our mythical customer hasn't selected a cup, a value is never assigned to sngCupPrice—it retains its initial value of 0."

"In that case," she continued, "sngCupPrice is 0, sngSaucerPrice is 0, and sngPlatterPrice is 0."

"At this point," I said, "we now have values for each of the six variables that will comprise the grand total, which brings us to this code."

```
'Add the prices together and multiply by the quantity to calculate a grand total
sngTotalPrice = (((sngPlatePrice + sngButterPlatePrice + _
          sngSoupBowlPrice + sngCupPrice + sngSaucerPrice) _
          * m_intQuantity) + sngPlatterPrice)
```

"Any idea what is happening here?" I asked.

"It looks like we're taking the value of all the variables, except for the variable representing the platter, and adding them together. Then we're multiplying that sum by the value of the variable m_intQuantity, which is the customer's selected quantity. Then we're adding the price of the platter variable to calculate the total price and assigning that value to the variable sngTotalPrice," Barbara said.

"A wonderful explanation, Barbara!" I said. "I couldn't have said it any better myself."

"I don't understand why the price of the platter is not multiplied by m_intQuantity," Rhonda said.

"That's because of the limit of one platter per customer," I replied. "We never want to multiply the unit price of the platter by more than 1."

"That's right," Rhonda said. I waited a moment, but there were no more questions. Everyone seemed to understand the calculation of the sales quotation—not a simple undertaking—but we still had one more piece of code in the event procedure to discuss.

```
'If the price is greater than 0, display the price and make the label visible
If sngTotalPrice > 0 Then
    lblPrice.text = "The price of your order is $" & sngTotalPrice
    lblPrice.Visible = True
End If
```

"This is the code that displays the sales quotation," I said.

I reminded everyone that earlier in the course we had decided to make the Label control invisible until it was time to display the price. "For that reason," I said, "we use an If...Then statement to determine if the value of the variable sngTotalPrice is greater than 0. If it is, we then assign the value of the variable sngTotalPrice to the Text property of the Label control and then we make the Label control visible. If the value of sngTotalPrice is 0, the Label control remains invisible."

No one had any questions, and so it was time to complete the final exercise of the day.

Exercise 8-9 Coding the Click Event Procedure of the Reset Button

In this exercise, you'll code the Click event procedure of the btnReset Button control.

1. Continue working with the China Shop Project (or load it up if you have closed it).

2. Place the following code into the Click event procedure of the btnReset Button control.

```
Private Sub btnReset_Click(ByVal sender As Object, _
    ByVal e As System.EventArgs) Handles btnReset.Click

lstBrands.SelectedIndex = -1
chkPlate.Checked = False
chkButterPlate.Checked = False
chkSoupBowl.Checked = False
chkCup.Checked = False
chkSaucer.Checked = False
chkPlatter.Checked = False
rad8.Checked = False
rad4.Checked = False
rad2.Checked = False
rad1.Checked = False
chkCompletePlaceSetting.Checked = False
lblPrice.Visible = False

End Sub
```

3. Save the China Shop Project.

4. Run the program. Select a brand of china, a quantity, and some items. Click the Calculate button to display a price. Now click the Reset button, and all the selections should be cleared.

Discussion

"This is probably the only line of code that caused you some hesitation," I said. "This line of code deselects the selected brand in the list box by setting the SelectedIndex property of the ListBox to -1."

lstBrands.SelectedIndex = -1

I explained that the SelectedIndex property of the ListBox contains the number of the item selected in the list box.

"The first item in the list box is number 0," I said, "the second item is 1 and so on. Setting this property to -1 deselects every item in the list box. This next section of code deselects all of the china items by setting the Checked properties of each of their CheckBoxes to False."

chkPlate.Checked = False
chkButterPlate.Checked = False
chkSoupBowl.Checked = False
chkCup.Checked = False
chkSaucer.Checked = False
chkPlatter.Checked = False

"And this code deselects each RadioButton," I said, "once again by setting their Checked properties to False."

rad8.Checked = False
rad4.Checked = False
rad2.Checked = False
rad1.Checked = False

"Next we remove the check mark in the Complete Place Setting check box," I continued.

chkCompletePlaceSetting.Checked = False

"And finally, the lblPrice label is made invisible again."

lblPrice.Visible = False

No one had any questions, nor was there any more material to cover in today's class.

"Our prototype is essentially complete," I said, "Now comes the moment of truth when we have to unveil our work to the customer!"

Reviewing the Prototype

"Just in time!" Joe Bullina exclaimed, as he walked into the classroom with a smile on his face. As I had known we would be finishing up coding the prototype today, I had arranged for Joe Bullina to pay us another surprise visit. All of my students seemed very excited about showing off their prototypes, so after he exchanged 'hellos' with everyone, I sat Joe down in front of my computer and ran the application for him. Joe spent a few moments interacting with the interface, selecting various options and watching, sometimes in amazement, at the way the program calculated prices. Meanwhile, everyone in the class crowded behind him in dead silence.

"I'm simply overwhelmed," Joe finally said. "This program is fantastic!"

I felt as if everyone let out a big sigh of relief—there's always some anticipation when you show the user your prototype for the first time. Joe then spent about half an hour reviewing the prototypes made by the students (at least those who weren't too shy to share them with him).

"So when can I have this installed in the China Shop?" Joe asked.

"Not for a few weeks yet," I said. "You see, it's still not finished!"

"It looks great!" Joe exclaimed. "It seems to do everything I want. What else is left to do?"

"What you are looking at, Joe," Linda said, "is just a prototype of the application. We have designed it just to show you how things will look in the final version, but there are still some enhancements that need to be made."

"What kind of enhancements?" Joe asked.

"Well, for one thing," Ward began, "with this version of the program, you can't change the prices of your china items."

"And we haven't put a menu in place yet either" Barbara added.

"That's right," said Joe, "I remember those details from the Requirements Statement. Well, in that case, I'll leave you to get on with it! Let me know how things are going, won't you, John?"

I assured Joe that we would keep him up to date on the project and thanked him for coming in to see us.

"Well, there you have it!" I exclaimed, when I got back from showing Joe out of the classroom. "I think it's safe to say that Joe liked what he saw, and that he's given us the green light to continue."

"Did you notice how excited he was when he saw the prototype?" Kate added.

"Yes," said Linda, "he really was excited. In fact, I thought he might have taken the program with him back to the China Shop today if we hadn't stopped him."

"You're probably right, Linda," I said. "We're lucky we have a written Requirements Statement that stopped him from rushing ahead with a program that's only partially complete. The value of the Requirements Statement isn't only to ensure that everyone agrees on what needs to appear in the program, but also to keep everyone on the right track as the project progresses!"

With that final statement, I dismissed class, telling them on their way out that next week we would begin the real job of turning our prototype into a production-ready application.

Summary

In this chapter, we examined selection structures and how they are used to vary the way a program behaves based on conditions found at runtime. We saw that there are several types of selection structures, and how each is best utilized.

We've also come to a significant point in our project: the working prototype. This is a very important stage in the development process, because all the key working parts of the program are now in place. From this point onward, we'll be adding functionality and code to turn our prototype into a professional-level program. Let's take a look at what this chapter taught us.

Remember the falling rock? We've seen how we can use selection structures to change this behavior, starting with the plain If...Then statement. If a condition evaluates to True, the imperative statement or statements following the word "Then" are executed. The If...Then statement can be expanded to include alternative instructions for a False condition as well, using the Else keyword, and even further with a set of ElseIf keywords.

After a number of ElseIf's, your code will begin to look cumbersome. At this point, it's more elegant to use the Select Case structure. Always remember to include the End Select (or, in the case of If…Then statements, the End If line); otherwise, Visual Basic will complain that it doesn't know where your statement ends. You'll get a compile error when you try to run the program.

Chapter 9---Loops

In this chapter, we'll discuss the various types of loop structure available in Visual Basic. As you'll see, loop processing can give your program tremendous power.

Why Loops?

"A few weeks ago we took a brief look at loops," I said. "In today's class, we'll examine the loop structures available in Visual Basic in much more detail."

I continued by explaining that a loop allows the programmer to repeat the execution of a section of code without having to type lines of code over and over again.

"The ability to have parts of your program repeat," I said, "can give it enormous power to do many types of operations that would otherwise be impossible."

"Can you give us an example?" Mary asked.

"Sure, Mary," I said, "in a few weeks, we'll use Visual Basic to read records from an external disk file. The thing about reading records from an external file (or even a database) is that you don't know ahead of time how many records you'll be reading. The Visual Basic loop structure makes it possible to read every record in the file with just a few lines of code, whether there are millions of records or just one."

"Are there different types of loops in Visual Basic?" Dave asked. "I know there are in other languages."

"You're right, Dave," I said, "there are several different types of loop structures available in Visual Basic. Some types of loops are designed to execute code a definite number of times. That's the type of loop we examined a few weeks ago when we displayed the numbers from 1 to 10,000 in the Visual Basic Output window."

"Wasn't that a For…Next loop?" Linda asked.

"Right you are, Linda," I said. "The For…Next loop is a 'definite' type of loop. Other Visual Basic loop structures are less definite in nature, which means that when you write your code, you can't be sure how many times the loop will need to be executed. These types of loops are dependent upon a test condition to reach their end point. Let's take, for instance, the example of reading that external disk file again. If we need to read all of the records from the disk file into our computer program, we most likely do not know ahead of time how many records are in that file— in fact, the file could be empty! This type of programming problem requires an 'indefinite' type of loop called a Do…Loop to read all of the records in the file, regardless of how many records are in it."

I suggested that before we examine the Do…Loop structure, we quickly revisit the For…Next loop we had seen a couple of weeks earlier.

The For...Next Loop

I displayed the syntax for the For…Next loop on my classroom projector.

For counter = Start To End [Step increment] statements Next counter

"As I mentioned earlier," I said, "the For...Next loop is a loop structure that is executed a predetermined number of times as determined by the Start and End parameters in the first line of the loop structure. Let's take a look at the For…Next loop we coded a few weeks ago."

```
Private Sub btnLoop_Click(ByVal sender As System.Object, _
    ByVal e As System.EventArgs) Handles btnLoop.Click

Dim intCounter As Integer          'Declare the Loop Control variable

For intCounter = 1 To 10           'Loop structure begins here
    Console.Writeline(intCounter)
Next intCounter                    'Loop structure ends here

End Sub
```

"Most beginners believe that the first step in coding a For...Next loop is the first line of the loop structure, the For line," I said. "However, notice that prior to that line, we first need to declare a numeric variable, called a counter or

Loop Control variable. Its name reveals its function—it's absolutely necessary to the proper control of the For…Next loop. Without it, the loop simply won't run."

Dim intCounter As Integer

"The Loop Control variable is just an ordinary variable," I said, "and it should be declared as a Numeric data type—Integer or Long is fine. You can name the Loop Control variable anything you want, but typically, I name mine intCounter or lngCounter to reflect its use in the program. This next line of code…"

For intCounter = 1 To 10

"…is the first statement in a For…Next loop. It provides Visual Basic with the information it needs to set up the loop. First off, it identifies the Loop Control variable, intCounter, and specifies the Start parameter as 1 and the End parameter as 10. In doing so, it also initializes the value of intCounter to 1."

"Does this mean that the loop will execute 10 times?" Peter asked.

"Yes, that's exactly what it means!" I said.

I then brought up the code window, placed a breakpoint on the For statement, and ran the program. When I clicked on the Button control named Loop, my code window looked like this.

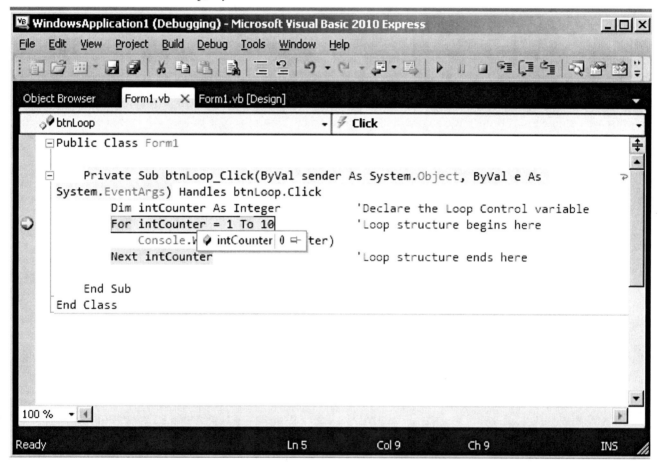

"Notice the value for the variable intCounter," I said as I placed my mouse pointer over the word ***intCounter*** in the code window. "Visual Basic displays the current value of the variable intCounter as 0. When the For line is executed for the first time, the value of ***intCounter*** will change to 1."

I pressed F8 until the line of code beginning with the word For was executed. Then I held my mouse pointer over the word ***intCounter*** again.

"Notice," I said, "that the value of ***intCounter*** is now 1, indicating that the Loop Control variable has been initialized by the For…Next loop."

I continued to run the program in Step mode by pressing F8. The value of the Loop Control variable was incremented by 1 each time the loop was executed.

"What statement is it that actually increments intCounter?" Kate asked.

"It's the Next statement," I said. "Next marks the end of the loop structure. Between the line beginning with the word For and the line beginning with the word Next is what is known as the body of the loop. With a For...Next loop, before any of the code inside the body of the loop is executed, the value of the Loop Control variable is compared to the End parameter. As long as the value of the Loop Control variable has not exceeded the value of the End parameter, the code inside the body of the loop will be executed. As soon as the value of the Loop Control variable is greater than the value of the End parameter, the loop ends, and the statement following the Next statement is executed."

"In the syntax you displayed on the projector," Barbara said, "you show a Step parameter. Why didn't we code one in your example?"

"Good question, Barbara," I said. "The Step parameter is optional, and if you don't specify one, Visual Basic presumes the Step parameter is a positive 1."

"What exactly does the Step parameter do?" Lou asked.

"It tells Visual Basic by how much to increment or decrement the Loop Control variable after each iteration or repetition of the loop," I explained. "We could also have coded our For statement like this."

For intCounter = 1 To 10 Step 1

Variations on the For...Next Theme

I pointed out that our For...Next loop was a pretty "vanilla" version of what the For...Next loop can do.

"What do you mean by vanilla?" Bob asked.

"By that I mean that you can use the Start, End, and Step parameters to create some very interesting code," I answered. "For instance, if you give your Step parameter a negative value, the value of the Loop Control variable will decrease instead of increase. And the Start parameter doesn't need to be 1, it can be any number—in fact, it doesn't even have to be a positive number."

I explained that you can simulate real-world situations more accurately if you get a little creative with the parameters of a For...Next loop.

"For instance," I said, "suppose you own a hotel, and the floors in the hotel are numbered from 2 to 20. Let's further pretend that your hotel has three elevators. Elevator #1 stops at all the floors, Elevator #2 stops only at the even-numbered floors and Elevator #3 stops only at the odd-numbered floors. Now suppose we want to write a program using a For...Next loop that displays, in the Visual Basic Output window, the floor numbers at which Elevator #1 stops. Here's an exercise to do exactly that."

Exercise 9-1 A More Complex For...Next Loop

In this exercise, you'll code a For...Next loop to display the floors at which Elevator #1 stops.

1. Start a new Windows application.
2. Place a Button control on the form and change its caption to "Elevator #1" by changing its Text property.
3. Double-click on the Button control and place the following code into its Click event procedure.

```
Private Sub Button1_Click(ByVal sender As System.Object, _
  ByVal e As System.EventArgs) Handles Button1.Click

Dim intCounter As Integer

For intCounter = 2 To 20
  Console.Writeline(intCounter)
Next intCounter

End Sub
```

4. Save the project, as we'll be modifying it in Exercise 9-2.
5. Run the program and click on the Button control. Your Output window should look like this.

Discussion

"Where's the first floor of the hotel?" Kathy asked.

"Remember, the floors are numbered from 2 to 20," Mary said.

"Oh, that's right," Kathy said, "and the fact that our Start parameter began with 2 is why the Output window started with number 2?"

"That's right, Kathy," I replied. "Now let's get to work on Elevator #2—that's the elevator that stops only at the even-numbered floors of the hotel. Do you have any ideas on how we should code a For...Next loop to display only the even-numbered floors where Elevator #2 stops?"

After a minute or so, Dave suggested that a For...Next loop with a Start parameter of 2, an End parameter of 20 and a Step parameter of 2, would do the trick.

"Excellent job, Dave," I said, as I distributed this exercise for the class to complete.

Exercise 9-2 Modifying the For...Next Loop to Handle Even Floors

In this exercise, you'll code a For…Next loop to display the even-numbered floors at which Elevator #2 stops.

1. Continue working with the project from Exercise 9-1.
2. Place a second Button control on the form and change its caption to "Elevator #2" by changing its Text property.
3. Double-click on the Button control and place the following code into its Click event procedure.

```
Private Sub Button2_Click(ByVal sender As System.Object, _
   ByVal e As System.EventArgs) Handles Button2.Click

Dim intCounter As Integer

For intCounter = 2 To 20 Step 2
   Console.Writeline(intCounter)
Next intCounter

End Sub
```

4. Save the project, as we'll be modifying it in Exercise 9-3.
5. Run the program and click the Elevator #2 button. Your Output window should look like this.

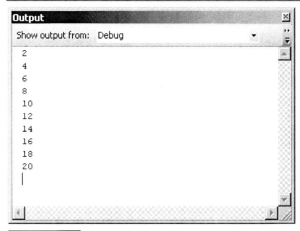

Discussion

"Well done, Dave," Rhonda said, obviously impressed.

"What about Elevator #3, the one that stops only at odd-numbered floors?" I asked. "How should we code that?"

Linda suggested that a For...Next loop with a Start parameter of 3, an End parameter of 20 and a Step parameter of 2 would be the way to go.

"Shouldn't the Start parameter be 1?" Rhonda asked.

"Don't forget, Rhonda," I said, "the hotel has no first floor—the first odd-numbered floor is 3." I then distributed this exercise for the class to complete.

Exercise 9-3 Modifying the For...Next Loop to Handle Odd Floors

In this exercise, you'll code a For...Next loop to display the odd-numbered floors at which Elevator #3 stops.

1. Continue working with the project from Exercise 9-2.
2. Place a third Button control on the form and change its caption to "Elevator #3" by changing its Text property.
3. Double-click on the Button control and place the following code into its Click event procedure.

```
Private Sub Button3_Click(ByVal sender As System.Object, _
   ByVal e As System.EventArgs) Handles Button3.Click

Dim intCounter As Integer

For intCounter = 3 To 20 Step 2
   Console.Writeline(intCounter)
Next intCounter

End Sub
```

4. Save the project, as we'll be modifying it in Exercise 9-4.
5. Run the program and click the Elevator #3 button. Your Output window should look like this.

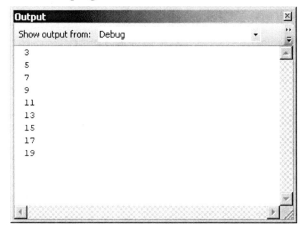

Discussion

"Why not use an End parameter of 19?" Barbara asked.

"That would also work," I said. "This code may be a little more readable in that the End parameter happens to be the top floor of the hotel."

I continued by saying that all three of the loop's parameters (Start, End, and Step) could be expressed not as numerical literals, as we had in the exercises, but also as variables or constants. I then distributed this exercise to demonstrate my point.

Exercise 9-4 Modifying the For...Next Loop to Work with Constants

In this exercise, you'll code a For...Next loop to display the floors at which Elevator #1 stops, but instead of using numeric literals for the Start, End, and Step parameters, you'll use constants.

1. Continue working with the project from Exercise 9-3.
2. Place a fourth Button control on the form and change its caption to "Elevator #1—Constants" by changing its Text property.
3. Double-click on the Button control and place the following code into its Click event procedure.

```vb
Private Sub Button4_Click(ByVal sender As System.Object, _
    ByVal e As System.EventArgs) Handles Button4.Click

Const BOTTOM_FLOOR As Integer = 2
Const TOP_FLOOR As Integer = 20
Dim intCounter As Integer

For intCounter = BOTTOM_FLOOR To TOP_FLOOR
    Console.Writeline(intCounter)
Next intCounter

End Sub
```

4. Save the project, as we'll be modifying it in Exercise 9-5.
5. Run the program and click the Elevator #1 button—Constants. Your Output window should look like this.

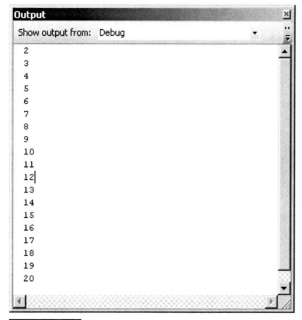

Discussion

"Does everyone see what we're doing here?" I asked. "The names BOTTOM_FLOOR and TOP_FLOOR are constants that you have declared," Linda said, "and you are using them in place of numeric literals for the Start, End, and Step parameters in the For...Next loop."

"That's excellent," I said. "Does everyone see how using constants like this can make your code a lot more readable? Now let's suppose that we want to display all the floors of the hotel backwards. That's no big deal with a For...Next loop, but we'll have to be careful."

I then distributed this exercise for the class to complete.

Exercise 9-5 Displaying the Floors Backwards

In this exercise, you'll code a For…Next loop to display the floors of the hotel backwards. But beware—this code has a bug in it and won't behave properly.

1. Continue working with the project from Exercise 9-4.
2. Place a fifth Button control on the form and change its caption to "Floors—backwards" by changing its Text property.
3. Double-click on the Button control and place the following code into its Click event procedure.

```
Private Sub Button5_Click(ByVal sender As System.Object, _
   ByVal e As System.EventArgs) Handles Button5.Click

Dim intCounter As Integer

For intCounter = 20 To 2
    Console.Writeline(intCounter)
Next intCounter

End Sub
```

4. Save the project, as we'll be correcting it in Exercise 9-6.
5. Run the program and click the Floors button—backward. Unfortunately, nothing will happen.

Discussion

"What happened?" Rhonda asked. "Nothing seems to be happening." Rhonda was correct. Nothing appeared to be happening, at least nothing was displayed in the Output window. We decided to set a breakpoint in the Click event procedure to see what was really happening. We ran the program, clicked on the Button control named Floors, and immediately the program was placed in Break mode. Pressing function key F8, we saw the For line of our For…Next loop executed—and then the program immediately jumped to the End Sub line, ending the event procedure.

"Can anyone tell me what happened?" I asked.

No one had an immediate solution, but then Barbara said, "I think, since the Start parameter of the Loop Control variable—20—was already greater than the End parameter—2—at the beginning of the loop, the body of the loop never executed. The loop was immediately exited."

"That's excellent, Barbara," I said. "That's exactly what happened."

"I would have thought that Visual Basic would have executed the body of the loop at least once," said Dave.

"Not with a For…Next loop, Dave," I answered. "However, there are some types of Visual Basic loops where that is the case—that is, the body of the loop is executed at least once—but not with a For…Next loop. In the For…Next loop, the Loop Control variable is compared to the End parameter before the body of the loop is ever executed. In a few moments, we'll examine another type of Visual Basic loop structure that executes the body of the loop first and then determines whether the loop should terminate."

"So how can we make this loop count backwards?" Rhonda asked. "What do we need to change?"

"We need to specify a Step parameter with a negative number," I said, "to make the loop count backwards. In our case, -1."

I then distributed this exercise for the class to complete.

Exercise 9-6 Displaying the Floors Backwards Correctly

In this exercise, you'll correct the code from Exercise 9-5, so that the floors of our hotel are correctly displayed backwards.

1. Continue working with the project from Exercise 9-5.
2. Change the For line of code in the click event procedure of the fifth Button control (Button5) to look like this.

```
For intCounter = 20 To 2 Step -1
```

3. Save the project if you wish—we won't be modifying it any further.
4. Run the program and click the Floors button—backward. Your Output window should look like this.

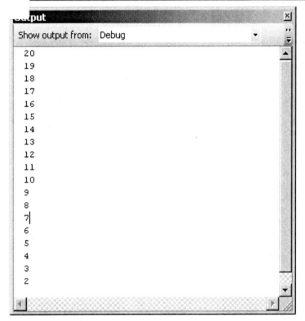

Discussion

"Remember to be very careful when you compose the For line in a For...Next loop," I said. "If you want to make the loop count backwards, you'll need to specify a negative number for the Step parameter."

There were no more questions, and so I suggested we take a break.

"When we return from break," I said, "we'll examine the indefinite kinds of Visual Basic loops—the Do...Loop family."

Do...Loops

Resuming after break, I began a discussion of what I term the Visual Basic indefinite loops, the family of Do...Loops.

"The Do…Loop is a bit confusing at first," I said, "because it has two syntaxes, with two variations on each."

I then displayed this syntax for the Do...Loop on the classroom projector.

Do [[While | Until] condition]
　[statements]
　[Exit Do]
　[statements]
Loop

"You can also use this syntax," I said.

Do
　[statements]
　[Exit Do]
　[statements]
Loop [[While | Until] condition]

"This looks really confusing to me," Joe said.

"The Do...Loop appears confusing because there are four variations of it," I said. "Just like the For...Next loop, the Do...Loop structure permits you to repetitively execute a section of code. But as you'll see, the end point for the Do...Loop is not nearly as definite as for the For...Next loop."

"How so?" Mary asked.

"In the For...Next loop," I continued, "we designate a definite End parameter for the Loop Control variable. With a Do...Loop, there's no built-in Loop Control variable. You need to specify a condition in the Loop Control (that line that begins with the word Do) that is tested each time the loop is executed. Quite a few beginners forget that fact, and manage to code something called an endless or infinite loop."

"What kinds of conditions can you specify in the Do loop?" Ward asked. "Any expression or condition that evaluates to a True or False value," I said, "just like the comparison operations we saw last week." I warned the students that just about everyone manages to code an endless loop once or twice in their programming career.

"Coding an endless loop in a For...Next loop is next to impossible," I said, "because the Loop Control variable is automatically incremented, and eventually, its value will exceed the End parameter of the For statement. But the Do...Loop is a different story. It's the programmer's responsibility to ensure that the loop eventually comes to an end."

"Are we going to discuss all four variations of the Do...Loop?" Dave asked. "Yes, we are," I replied. "Each variation has its own advantages and peculiarities, and I think it's important to understand all four variations."

Do While...Loop

I suggested that we begin with the Do While...Loop. I displayed its syntax on the classroom projector.

Do While condition
   statements
   Exit Do
   statements
Loop

"I call this the Do While...Loop," I said, "because the first line of the structure begins with the words Do While, and the last line contains just the single word Loop. Everything else in between is considered the body of the loop."

"How long will the body of the loop be executed?" Steve asked.

"As long as the condition specified evaluates to True," I said. "What this means is that the body of the loop is not guaranteed to execute even one time—the condition could immediately evaluate to False. Before the body of the loop is executed for the first time, the condition is evaluated. If the condition evaluates to False immediately, the body of the loop is bypassed. It's important to take this behavior into consideration when you code your loop. As you'll see in a few moments, there's a variation of this loop in which the body of the loop is always executed at least once."

"Don't you want every loop you code to execute at least once?" Rhonda asked.

"Not necessarily," I answered. "For instance, suppose you are using a loop to read records from a file. If the file is empty—which can happen—you wouldn't want to execute the code to read a record. If you did, your program would bomb."

"That makes sense," Rhonda said.

At this point, I suggested that we complete an exercise to illustrate the Do While...Loop.

Exercise 9-7 The Do...While Loop

In this exercise, you'll code a Do While...Loop to display numbers in the Visual Basic Output window.

1. Start a new Windows application.
2. Place a Button control on the form and change its caption to "DoWhile...Loop" by changing its Text property.
3. Double-click on the Button control and place the following code into its Click event procedure.

```
Private Sub Button1_Click(ByVal sender As System.Object, _
    ByVal e As System.EventArgs) Handles Button1.Click

Dim intValue As Integer = 1

Do While intValue < 5
    Console.WriteLine (intValue)
    intValue = intValue + 1
Loop

End Sub
```

4. Save the project, as we'll be modifying it in Exercise 9-8.
5. Run the program and then click the Do While...Loop button. Your Output window should look like this.

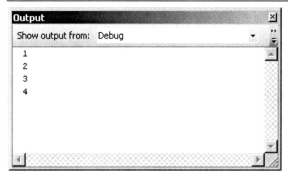

"One of the nice things about working with the Do While...Loop," I told everyone, "is that it is somewhat intuitive. Here we're telling Visual Basic, while the value of intValue is less than 5..."

Do While intValue < 5

"...to display the value of intValue in the Output window..."

Console.WriteLine (intValue)

"Of course, the important thing to bear in mind here is that we needed to explicitly initialize, outside the body of the loop, the value of intValue to 1..."

Dim intValue As Integer = 1

"...and then increment the value of intValue by 1 as the last line of code in the body of the loop."

"The variable intValue," Dave said, "reminds me of the Loop Control variable from the For...Next loop."

"You're right about that, Dave," I said. "With the Do...Loop varieties, there is no formal Loop Control variable as there is in a For...Next loop. In effect, we have to create our own."

"How important is it to increment the value of intValue inside of the loop?" Kathy asked.

"Vitally important," I said. "Many beginners make one of two mistakes: they either initialize the value of intValue inside the body of the loop, or they increment the value of intValue outside the loop. If you initialize the value of intValue within the body of the loop, guess what? Each time the body of the loop is executed, intValue is reset to 1. And if you increment the value of intValue outside the body of the loop, then the Do condition never becomes False—in either case, an endless loop occurs."

There was a momentary silence, and then Joe had a question.

"Why didn't the number 5 display in the Output window?" he asked. "Why did it stop at 4?"

"Unlike the For...Next loop," I said, "which ends when the value of the Loop Control variable exceeds that of the End parameter, with the Do...Loop, the loop ended as soon as the value of intValue reached 5. That was, after all, the condition we specified: continue the loop while the value of intValue is less than 5. As soon as intValue reached 5, the loop ended."

"You had said that Do...Loops were more of an indefinite variety of loops," Linda said. "This loop seemed pretty definite to me. Can you give us an example of an indefinite loop?"

"I sure can," I said. "How about a loop that runs until the user tells the program to stop?"

I then distributed this exercise for the class to complete.

Exercise 9-8 An Indefinite Version of the Do...While Loop

In this exercise, we'll create a loop structure that displays numbers in the Output window. However, the numbers will only be displayed for as long as the user chooses to continue.

1. Continue working with the project from Exercise 9-7.
2. Place a second Button control on the form and change its caption to "Indefinite Do While...Loop" by changing its Text property.
3. Double-click on the Button control and place the following code into its Click event procedure.

```
Private Sub Button2_Click(ByVal sender As System.Object, _
   ByVal e As System.EventArgs) Handles Button2.Click

Dim intValue As Integer = 1
```

```
Dim strContinue As String = "YES"

Do While UCASE(strContinue) = "YES"
  Console.WriteLine (intValue)
  intValue = intValue + 1
  strContinue = InputBox  ("Should I continue?", "The Indefinite Loop", "Yes")
Loop

MessageBox.Show ("All Done!")

End Sub
```

4. Save the project if you wish, although we won't be modifying it again.
5. Run the program and click the Do While...Loop button. The program will display the number in the Output window and then ask you if you want to continue.

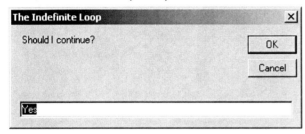

6. Answer yes by clicking OK. The number 2 will then be displayed in the Output window, followed by the same question. Numbers will continue to be displayed in the Visual Basic Output window as long as you click OK.
7. Type No or click Cancel. A goodbye message will be displayed..

Discussion

"This code is an example of the indefinite type of Do...Loop," I explained. "We wrote this code because we had no idea how many numbers the user would want displayed in the Output window. We needed a way for the loop to continue indefinitely, but still with a way to be ended. That's the beauty of the Do...Loop—in this case, as soon as the condition evaluates to False, the loop ends."

I continued by saying that, as we had done in the previous exercise, the first thing we did here was to declare the variables we would use in the event procedure.

"Remember," I said, "with a Do...Loop there is no built-in Loop Control variable, so in order for the loop to eventually end, we need to declare a variable of our own which will be used in a condition test to see if the loop should be terminated. That's the function of the variable strContinue here, a variable whose value will be determined by the user—although as you can see, we initially declare its value as YES."

Dim strContinue As String = "YES"

"Thereafter, the user's response to the question 'Should I continue?' will be stored in this variable."

"What's the significance of initializing the variable to the value YES?" Kate asked. "Is that important?"

"It's vitally important," I said. "The initial value of strContinue is tied to the condition we're testing in the Do...Loop. We're telling Visual Basic to execute the loop while the value of strContinue is YES. If we didn't initialize the value of strContinue to YES, the body of the loop would never execute—not even once—since the condition would immediately evaluate to False."

I waited a moment before continuing.

"Let's take a look at the first line of the Do...Loop statement," I said.

Do While UCASE(strContinue) = "YES"

"What is UCASE?" Linda asked.

"UCASE is a function that takes a string value and returns the string converted to uppercase characters," I said. "For instance, the string j-o-h-n would be returned as J-O-H-N. In this way, however the user enters the word 'yes' in response to our question, ultimately their response is converted to the word 'YES' in uppercase letters. That makes our comparison much easier."

"How so?" Chuck asked.

"Did you realize," I answered, "that the user can type the word 'yes' in eight different ways?"

"What do you mean, eight different ways?" asked Barbara.

"Each letter of the word 'yes' can be entered by a user in either uppercase or lowercase," I explained. "And while it's nice to believe that the user would enter 'YES' in all capital letters if we asked them to, in reality, some users mix and match case as they're typing values. If you were to write out all the possible combinations of the word 'yes' you would find there are eight different ways of writing it:"

YES yES
YEs yEs
YeS yeS
Yes yes

"Converting the user's response to all uppercase," I said, "means that we only need to perform the comparison one way. The alternative would be to write code that looks like this."

```
Do While (strContinue) = "YES" Or (strContinue) = "YEs" Or _
  (strContinue) = "YeS" Or (strContinue) = "Yes" Or _
  (strContinue) = "yES" Or (strContinue) = "yEs" Or _
  (strContinue) = "yeS" or (strContinue) = 'yes'
```

"That makes sense," Ward said.

"These next two lines of code I think we've seen before," I continued.

```
Console.WriteLine (intValue)
intValue = intValue + 1
```

"Here we're displaying the value of intValue in the Output window, and then incrementing its value by 1. Incrementing the value of intValue by 1 is not nearly as important in this exercise as it was before, since it's really the value of strContinue that determines if and when the loop ends. I know this next line of code is new to you."

```
strContinue = InputBox("Should I continue?", "The Indefinite Loop", "Yes")
```

"What's going on here?" Barbara asked. "Is InputBox another function?"

"That's right, Barbara," I said. "InputBox is a function that permits you to obtain a response from the user of your program. In some ways, it should remind you of the MessageBox.Show function. The difference is that the user's response is returned to you, and in our case, we store the user's response in the variable called strContinue."

"It looks like the InputBox function is accepting three arguments," Dave said. "Can you explain them?"

"Be glad to, Dave," I said, as I ran the program to display the input box on the classroom projector.

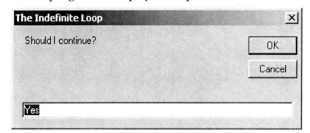

"The input box has a title bar, a prompt, two buttons named OK and Cancel, and, as we've already seen, a text box, in this case with the word Yes already in it."

"What's the syntax for the InputBox function?" Dave asked.

"The InputBox function has seven arguments in all," I said, "only three of which we are concerned with, and only one of which is mandatory. That's the first argument, the Prompt argument ("Should I continue?"). The next is the

Title argument, and it specifies a title for the input box ("The Indefinite Loop"). The third argument, Default, specifies a default response to be included in the text box. In our case, we preloaded the text box with the word Yes. It's a good idea to specify, as a Default argument, the value that most users are likely to want to type into the text box. That way, the user only needs to click OK if that's their response."

"So this loop continues until the user answers No?" Ward asked.

"Not exactly," I said. "The loop continues until the user enters something other than Yes or its variations in the text box portion of the input box—or until they click Cancel."

Prior to moving on, I repeated that one of the biggest mistakes beginners make with the Do...Loop family is to forget to include code within the body of the loop that enables the loop to end.

"Because the condition being tested in our loop is strContinue equal to YES," I said, "if we failed to give the user the opportunity to change the value of strContinue, we would have wound up with an endless loop."

Do...Loop While

"When we began our discussion of the Do…Loop earlier," I said, "I mentioned that there are four variations of the Do...Loop structure. With the Do While...Loop, the first line begins with the words Do While and the last line contains just the single word Loop. We're about to discuss the cousin of the Do While…Loop, which I call Do…Loop While, because the first line of this variation begins with the word Do, and the last line begins with the words Loop While."

"Is the location of the word While significant?" Linda asked.

"Great deduction, Linda," I said. "In the first Do…Loop structure we examined, with the line containing the word While appearing as the first line of the loop structure, the test condition is evaluated prior to the body of the loop ever executing once. With this loop structure, since the word While appears as the last line of the loop structure, the body of the loop is guaranteed to execute at least once."

I suggested that we complete an exercise in which we would code one more Do While...Loop and then change it to the Do...Loop While variation.

Exercise 9-9 The Do...Loop While versus the Do While...Loop

In this exercise, we'll place two Button controls on the form. We'll then place code in the Click event procedure of Button1 that implements a Do While...Loop structure, while in the Click event procedure of Button2, we'll place code that implements a Do...Loop While structure. A word of warning—this exercise is intended to highlight the differences between the two loop types in terms of when the test condition is evaluated. When you run the program and click the first button, nothing will appear to happen—that's intentional. When you click the second button, the number 5 will be displayed in the Output window, and then the loop will end.

1. Start a new Windows application.
2. Place two Button controls on the form. Change the name of the first Button control to Do While…Loop and the second Button control to Do…Loop While by changing their Text properties.
3. Double-click on the first Button control and place the following code into its Click event procedure.

```
Private Sub Button1_Click(ByVal sender As System.Object, _
   ByVal e As System.EventArgs) Handles Button1.Click

Dim intValue As Integer = 5

Do While intValue < 5
   Console.WriteLine (intValue)
Loop

End Sub
```

4. Double-click on the second Button control and place the following code into its Click event procedure.

```
Private Sub Button2_Click(ByVal sender As System.Object, _
   ByVal e As System.EventArgs) Handles Button2.Click

Dim intValue As Integer = 5
```

```
Do                                      'Body of loop executes once
   Console.WriteLine (intValue)
Loop While intValue < 5                 'intValue is not < 5--loop ends

End Sub
```

5. Save the project if you wish, although we won't be modifying it again.
6. Run the program and click the Do While...Loop button. Oops! Nothing appears in the Output window.
7. Click the Do...Loop While button. The number 5 should appear in the Output window.

Discussion

"Can anyone tell me what's going on here?" I asked.

"For both Button controls," Dave said, "the value of intValue was initialized to 5, and both loops specified that the body of the loop should execute only while the value of intValue was less than 5. Button2 displayed the number 5 in the Output window because the test condition was evaluated at the end of the loop structure, after the body of the loop had already been executed. The test condition for Button1 was evaluated at the beginning of the loop, before the body of the loop had a chance to be executed."

"That's an excellent analysis, Dave" I said. "You're right, the test condition in Button1 was evaluated at the beginning until variations of the Do...Loop. Since the test condition evaluated immediately to False, the body of the loop was never executed. For Button2, the test condition was evaluated after the body of the loop had already been executed."

I asked if there were any questions about the Do While family of loops. There were none, and so we moved on to the Do Until variations of the Do...Loop.

Do Until...Loop

"It looks to me as though the difference between the Do While...Loop structures and the two Do Until...Loop structures may be largely a matter of semantics," Linda suggested.

"You're quite right, Linda," I said. "It's a matter of how the test condition is expressed. In a Do While loop, the body of the loop is executed while the test condition evaluates to True. As soon as the test condition evaluates to False, the loop ends. With the Do Until loop, the body of the loop is executed until the test condition evaluates to True. As long as the test condition evaluates to False, the loop continues to run. I should point out that any test condition you can express with a Do While loop can also be expressed with a Do Until loop. Here's some simple pseudocode to illustrate the differences between the two families of loops. First, the Do While loop..."

Do While the temperature in the room is less than 72 degrees
  Run Heater
Loop

"...and then the Do Until loop..."

Do Until the temperature in the room is greater than or equal to 72 degrees
  Run Heater
Loop

I pointed out that that the location of the word Until is just as significant in the Do Until loops as the word While is in the Do While family.

"The location of the word Until," I said, "impacts when the test condition is evaluated—either before the body of the loop is executed or after the body of the loop has been executed once."

I suggested that we complete this exercise to see the difference between the two loop families.

Exercise 9-10 The Do...Until Loop Structure

In this exercise, we'll use a Do Until...Loop structure to display the numbers 1 through 4 in the Visual Basic Output window.

1. Start a new Windows application.
2. Place a Button control on the form and change its caption to "Do Until...Loop" by changing its Text property.
3. Double-click on the Button control and place the following code into its Click event procedure.

```
Private Sub Button1_Click(ByVal sender As System.Object, _
  ByVal e As System.EventArgs) Handles Button1.Click

Dim intValue As Integer = 1

Do Until intValue >= 5
    Console.WriteLine (intValue)
    intValue = intValue + 1
Loop

End Sub
```

4. Save the project, as we'll be modifying it in Exercise 9-11.

5. Run the program and then click the Do Until...Loop button. Your Output window should display the numbers 1 through 4.

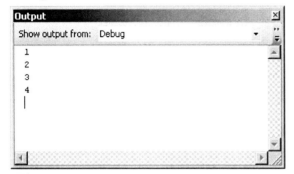

Discussion

"Basically what you've done here," Mary said, "is get the same result that we saw in Exercise 9-7—except we used the Do Until loop—is that right?"

"Exactly, Mary," I said. "As I mentioned, any test condition that can be expressed using a Do While loop can also be expressed using a Do Until loop—although you'll probably find them to be the converse of one another."

"Converse?" Chuck said. "Do you mean the opposite?"

"That's right, Chuck," I answered. "Let's take a look at the first line of the Do While loop from Exercise 9-7…"

Do While intValue < 5

"…and the first line of the Do Until loop from Exercise 9-10…"

Do Until intValue >= 5

"Less than 5 and greater than or equal to 5 are the converse of one another."

"So which structure should we use?" Blaine asked.

"The choice is yours, Blaine," I answered. "Frequently, it comes down to which syntax is more readable."

Do...Loop Until

"We have one more variation of the Do Until family to discuss," I said, "and that's the Do...Loop Until structure. The Do...Loop Until is very similar to the Do...Loop While we examined earlier. Because of the location of the word Until, the body of a Do…Loop Until will be executed at least once, something that is not guaranteed by the Do Until...Loop. Here's an exercise to illustrate the Do…Loop Until structure."

Exercise 9-11 The Do...Loop Until

In this exercise, we'll see how the Do…Loop Until structure executes the body of the loop at least once.

1. Start a new Windows application.

2. Place a Button control on the form and change its caption to "Do…Loop Until" by changing its Text property.

3. Double-click on the Button control and place the following code into its Click Event procedure.

```
Private Sub Button1_Click(ByVal sender As System.Object, _
  ByVal e As System.EventArgs) Handles Button1.Click
```

```
Dim intValue As Integer = 5

Do                                'Body of loop executes once
   Console.WriteLine (intValue)
Loop Until intValue >= 5          'intValue is >=5--loop ends

End Sub
```

4. Save the project if you wish—we won't be modifying it any further.
5. Run the program.
6. Click on the Button control. The number 5 will be displayed in the Output window.

Discussion

"Can anyone tell me the difference between this program and the one from the previous exercise?" I asked.

"I think I can," Ward said. "In this program, even though the value of intValue was already 5, the body of the loop still executed, because of the location of the Until statement. That's why the number 5 was displayed in the Output window. "

"You're right on the mark, Ward," I said.

We had been working for a long time and had now finished our treatment of loops. Ordinarily, I would have dismissed class for the day, but I elected to take a quick break instead.

"When you return," I said, "I'll have a surprise for you."

Mr. Bullina Sends a Surprise

When my students returned from break, a couple of them immediately asked about the surprise.

"Joe Bullina had pictures taken of the three china brand patterns he sells in the China Shop," I said, "and had them converted into graphics files. A disk containing the three files arrived at my home yesterday, and I brought them here with me this morning. I've placed the three files, Corelle.gif, Farberware.gif, and Mikasa.gif, in your \VBFiles\China subdirectory."

"Wow, does that mean we'll be displaying those images in the PictureBox control?" Rhonda asked.

"Yes, that's right," I answered. "In fact, here's an exercise to do exactly that."

I then distributed this exercise to the class.

Exercise 9-12 Loading an Image into the PictureBox Control

In this exercise, we'll modify the China Shop Project to load graphic files into the Image property of the PictureBox control when a china brand in the list box is selected. We'll place code in the SelectedIndexChanged event procedure of the lstBrands ListBox to do this.

1. Load up the China Shop Project.
2. Ensure that the following three files have been copied into your \VBFiles\China subdirectory: Corelle.gif, Farberware.gif, and Mikasa.gif. (These files are available on my Web site at http://www.johnsmiley.com/downloads/chinagraphics.zip.)
3. In the SelectedIndexChanged event procedure of the lstBrands ListBox, place the following code.

```
Private Sub lstBrands_SelectedIndexChanged (ByVal sender As System.Object, _
   ByVal e As System.EventArgs) Handles lstBrands.SelectedIndexChanged

If lstBrands.SelectedIndex = -1 Then Exit Sub

picChina.Image = Image.FromFile("C:\VBFiles\China\" & lstBrands.Text & ".gif")

End Sub
```

4. Save the China Shop Project.
5. Run the program. Select each one of the brands of china in the list box. When you do, you should see the corresponding china pattern appear in the picture box.

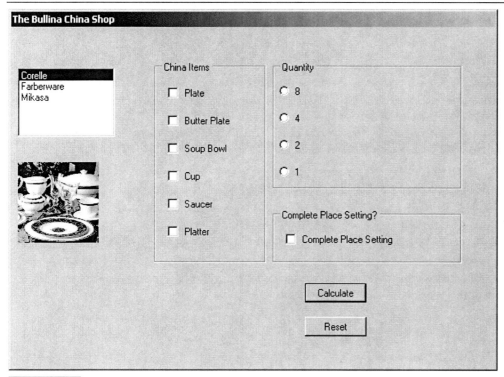

Discussion

"I think the customers will really love these graphics," Kathy said.

"I agree," I said. "I think it adds a great touch to the program. Let's review the code we've just written to see how we managed to get the graphics into the picture box. Here's what happens. When the customer selects a brand of china in the list box, their selection is stored in the Text property of the ListBox control. We then use that Text property to determine the appropriate graphic file to load into the Image property of the PictureBox control. That's what this line of code does."

picChina.Image = Image.FromFile("C:\VBFiles\China\" & lstBrands.Text & ".gif")

"It's important to note here," I continued, "that in order for this process to work, the name of the graphics file for the individual china brand must match the name of the brand that is selected in the list box. As long as that is the case, we can use the FromFile method of the Image object to load the graphics file into the Image property of the PictureBox control. The graphic file will then be displayed in what, prior to that, is an empty picture box. We use the ampersand character to join the name of the Text property of the ListBox control to the directory path of the China Shop. We then join the file extension for the graphics file, .gif, to the end of that string."

I could see that several people were confused.

"For instance," I said, "if the customer selects Mikasa as their brand, the Text property of the ListBox control contains Mikasa. Let's translate this line of code as Visual Basic would."

picChina.Image = Image.FromFile("C:\VBFiles\China\" & "Mikasa" & ".gif")

This becomes.

picChina.Image = Image.FromFile("C:\VBFiles\China\Mikasa" & ".gif")

which becomes.

picChina.Image = Image.FromFile("C:\VBFiles\China\Mikasa.gif")

"Did that help?" I asked.

I could see that it had.

"What's the purpose of the FromFile method of the Image object?" Ward asked. "What is the Image object?"

"The Image object is one of a series of Visual Basic system objects," I said. "Its function is to convert the name of a graphics file into a format that the Image property can understand—that's what the FromFile method does."

"What does the line of code before we actually set the Image property of the PictureBox control do?" Dave asked, indicating this line of code.

If lstBrands.ListIndex = -1 Then Exit Sub

"Good question," I said. "Before loading the Image property of the PictureBox control, we need to account for the possibility that the SelectedIndexChanged event of the ListBox control could be triggered with no china brand selected. Our program will bomb if we attempt to execute the Image.FromFile method with nothing in the Text property of the PictureBox control. That's why we check to see if the ListIndex property of the ListBox control is -1. If it is, that means that no brand has been selected, so we need to exit the event procedure using the Exit Sub statement."

"How can the SelectedIndexChanged event of the ListBox control be triggered when no item in the list box has been selected?" Barbara asked.

"Another good question," I said. "Do you remember earlier in the course I said that an event can be triggered in three ways? One way is by an action on the part of the user, such as clicking on an item in the list box. Another way is by the operating system, such as the Tick event procedure of the Timer control, and, finally, the third way is through Visual Basic code. It turns out that the following code that we placed in the Click event procedure of the btnReset Button control will trigger the SelectedIndexChanged event of the ListBox."

lstBrands.ListIndex = -1

"If an item in the ListBox has been selected," I explained, "then setting the ListIndex property to -1 will trigger the SelectedIndexChanged event of the ListBox—which in turn will execute this code. That's why we need to check to see if the ListIndex property is -1 before trying to load an image into the picture box."

I invited everyone to run the China Shop Program in Step mode. I did also, and when we clicked the Reset button, as I predicted, the SelectedIndexChanged event of the ListBox control was triggered.

"We have one extra line of code that we need to add to the Click event procedure of the btnReset Button control," I said. "That will be the final exercise of the day."

Exercise 9-13 The btnReset Button Revisited

In this exercise, we'll modify the Click event procedure of the btnReset Button control to clear the Image property of the PictureBox control.

1. Load up the China Shop Project (if it's not already loaded).
2. Add this line of code to the **end** of the Click event procedure of the btnReset Button control.

picChina.Image = Nothing

3. Save the China Shop Project.
4. Run the program. Make a selection of a china brand, one or more items, and a quantity.
5. Now click Reset. In addition to the other controls being cleared, the image will be cleared from the picture box as well.

Discussion

The line of code we added simply clears out any images displayed in the picture box by setting the Image property to Nothing, a special Visual Basic value, when the Reset button is clicked. I waited for questions, but there were none.

It had been a long class. I could see that everyone was feeling proud of the product they were producing week by week. In addition, I could also see that they were pretty worn out; it had been an intense session. Prior to dismissing class, I told everyone that in our next class, we would be doing quite a bit of work with strings.

Summary

In this chapter, we discussed how loop processing can make your programming life a lot easier and make your programs extremely powerful. There are several types of loop statements. Here's a reminder of some of the different loop structures we discussed:

- For…Next loops These loops execute a definite number of times. The number of times that the loop runs is determined by the Start, End, and Step parameters set in the For line of the Loop control.

- Do…While loops These loops execute an indefinite number of times, determined by a test condition. The Do…While loop continues to run while a specified condition is True.

- Do…Until loops These loops execute an indefinite number of times, determined by a test condition. The Do…Until loop continues to run until a specified condition becomes True.

We have also modified the China Shop Project so that the appropriate graphic image is loaded into the frame to display an image of each type of china.

In the next chapter, we'll take a look at strings and how to manipulate them.

Chapter 10---String Manipulation

In the last chapter, we examined loop structures which, when combined with selection structures, allow us to write extremely powerful programs with display-making capabilities. In this chapter, you'll follow my class as we turn our attention to working with strings and manipulating them. A knowledge of string manipulation has two benefits. First, many programming problems (particularly those involving the use of external disk files) require a familiarity with strings, and the types of operations that can be performed upon them. Secondly, working with the string manipulation functions in this chapter gives you a chance to work with program algorithms, which will strengthen your programming abilities. By the end of this chapter, you'll be familiar with some string manipulation operations that can be performed with Visual Basic, and you'll also be a better programmer.

What Exactly Is a String?

I began our tenth class by telling everyone that I had great news.

"I received e-mail from Rose and Jack yesterday," I said, "and they told me that they had arrived safely in the United Kingdom, and hoped to wrap up their work in time to get back for the implementation of the China Shop Project at the end of our course. They told me to be sure to pass their best wishes on to everyone."

I continued by saying that in today's class, we would be taking a close look at the String data type.

"The String data type," I said, "as we learned earlier in the course, is one of the many Visual Basic data types. But the String data type, since it's comprised of a series of characters, sometimes poses interesting challenges and also interesting possibilities."

"Such as?" Linda asked.

"Let me give you an example," I said. "A few years back I had a client who had a file of names and addresses. We'll see later on in the course that string data contained in a disk file is 'sandwiched' between quotation marks and separated by commas—and that was the case here. Unfortunately, the name field consisted of a first and last name, and the address field consisted of a street, city, state, and zip code. Plus, some of the names contained a middle initial."

"Is that a problem?" Ward asked.

"Not necessarily," I said, "but unfortunately, in this case, my client needed to take this data and produce mailing labels for a marketing campaign he was performing. Mailing labels require the street to be on one line, and the city, state, and zip code to be on another. Plus, to be eligible for a discounted rate at the post office, he needed to sort the mail by zip code. To make a long story short, the format of the address data was such that he couldn't use it—until he called me."

"What did you do for him?" Kate asked.

"Using the techniques you'll learn today," I replied, "I was able to extract the street, city, and zip code from the address field in the data file, and produce the mailing labels in the correct format, sorted so that he was able to get the discount."

"I see," Rhonda said. "Are strings found only in external disk files?"

"No," I said. "To refresh your memory, a string is just a series of characters, and in addition to being found in external disk files, variables can be declared as strings. You'll also find that certain Visual Basic properties, such as the Text property of a TextBox, are String data types. Being able to work with string data and knowing how to manipulate it is so important in my opinion that we'll be spending our entire class session today on the topic. Not only is working with strings important for itself, but the process of working with strings can really strengthen your programming skills. By the end of today's class, I dare say you'll be amazed at some of the algorithms we come up with to manipulate string data."

String Concatenation

"We've already spent some time working with arithmetic that can be performed on Numeric data types," I said. "Today, you'll also see that it's possible to perform similar arithmetic on strings."

"String arithmetic!" Rhonda exclaimed.

"That's right," I said. "One type of string arithmetic is called string concatenation, and you've already had a chance to see it in action. Concatenation is defined in Webster's Dictionary as 'to link together in a series or chain.' In Visual Basic, concatenation means to join two strings together—much like railroad cars are coupled to one another."

"We've already used concatenation in the China Shop Project, haven't we?" Valerie asked.

"That's right, we used concatenation in the Click event procedure of the Calculate Button control," I said as I displayed this code on the classroom projector.

```
If sngTotalPrice > 0 Then
    lblPrice.text = "The price of your order is $" & sngTotalPrice
    lblPrice.Visible = True
End If
```

"You need to be careful when using concatenation," I said. "If you are browsing through Help, you may discover that Visual Basic has two operators that can perform string concatenation: the plus (+) operator and the ampersand (&) operator, which we've used here. Microsoft recommends using the & operator instead of the + operator—and there's good reason to avoid the + operator."

"Why is that?" Joe asked.

"The + operator works fine when concatenating one string to another," I said, "but it falls short when concatenating a String data type to a non-String data type, such as a number or a date. The & operator is much more forgiving of the data types it is asked to join, whereas the + operator works only with string data. What this means is that if you try to concatenate a string with something other than a string, the + operator can cause your program to bomb."

"So the rule of thumb is not to use the + operator?" Linda asked.

"That's the Microsoft recommendation," I said. "Use the & operator instead. Now let's see the concatenation operation in action."

I then created a new project with a single Button control and entered the following code in its Click event procedure.

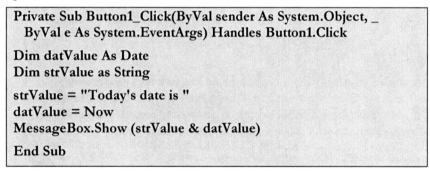

```
Private Sub Button1_Click(ByVal sender As System.Object, _
    ByVal e As System.EventArgs) Handles Button1.Click

Dim datValue As Date
Dim strValue as String

strValue = "Today's date is "
datValue = Now
MessageBox.Show (strValue & datValue)

End Sub
```

I ran the program, and clicked the button. The following message box was displayed on the classroom projector.

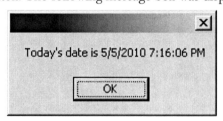

"Does everyone what's happening?" I asked. "The & operator allowed us to concatenate a String data type with a Date data type, resulting in this informative message."

"That's cool," Kathy said, "I had no idea you could do something like that."

"Can you give us another example of string concatenation?" Blaine asked.

"I think so," I answered. "Let's say you have two TextBox controls on a form. One TextBox is designed to allow the user to enter their first name, and the other for the user to enter their last name. Suppose you then wanted to display their full name in the Visual Basic Output window—could you do that?"

"I don't think I would even know where to start with that one!" exclaimed Kate.

"That's okay, Kate," I answered. "I happen to have an exercise here that will lead you through the process." I then distributed this exercise for the class to complete.

Exercise 10-1 Concatenating Strings

In this exercise, you'll use string concatenation to join the contents of two text boxes and display the result in the Visual Basic Output window.

1. Start a new Windows application.
2. Place a Button control on the form and accept the default name that Visual Basic assigns.
3. Place two TextBox controls on the form, and change the Name property of the first TextBox to txtFirstName and the Name property of the second TextBox to txtLastName.
4. Double-click on the Button control, and place the following code in its Click event procedure.

```
Private Sub Button1_Click(ByVal sender As System.Object, _
   ByVal e As System.EventArgs) Handles Button1.Click

If txtFirstName.Text = "" Then
   MessageBox.Show("First name must be entered")
   txtFirstName.Focus()
   Exit Sub
ElseIf txtLastName.Text = "" Then
   MessageBox.Show("Last name must be entered")
   txtLastName.Focus()
   Exit Sub
End If

Console.WriteLine ("Your full name is " & txtFirstName.Text & txtLastName.Text)

End Sub
```

5. Save the project—we'll be modifying it in Exercise 10-2.
6. Run the program. Enter your first name in the first text box and your last name in the second text box.
7. Click the button. The program will display your full name in the Visual Basic Output window. But wait, there's something wrong! What is it?

Discussion

"I see the problem," Ward said excitedly. "There's no space between the first and last name. It all ran together."

"Absolutely right," I said, as I ran the program myself, and displayed the Output window on the classroom projector.

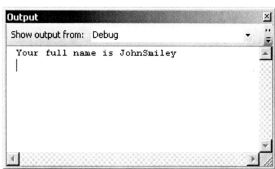

I explained that the code we had written contained a common error that many beginners make when performing string concatenation for the first time—failing to realize that the space is a legitimate character.

"Before I discuss how to correct this error, though," I said, "let me make sure that everyone understands what's happening here. First, notice how we use an If...Then...Else statement to determine if either the first name or last name text boxes are empty..."

If txtFirstName.Text = "" Then

"When you are soliciting input from a user," I said, "especially when it's via a text box, this type of data validation is extremely important. It's important to try to anticipate the kinds of mistakes that a user will make, such as forgetting to make an entry in one or both of the text boxes and then clicking the button."

"The double quotation marks," Blaine said. "Is that how we check for an empty text box?"

"Yes, it's one way," I said. "Here, we are checking the TextBox for an empty string, and we do that by comparing the Text property to a pair of quotation marks with no space in between. If the Text property of either txtFirstName or txtLastName is empty, we display a warning message to the user (always make it pleasant!). Then, as a courtesy to the user, we set the focus back to the empty text box using the Focus method. Finally, we bypass the rest of the code in the Click event procedure by using the Exit Sub statement."

> **Note: Beginners frequently make the mistake of putting a space between the two quotation marks when testing for an empty text box. There is no space between them. In a similar way, in order to clear a text box beginners will often select the Text property in the Properties window, and then press the SPACEBAR. This sets the Text property to a space.**

I continued by examining these two lines of code.

Console.WriteLine ("Your full name is " & txtFirstName.Text & txtLastName.Text)

"These two lines of code perform the string concatenation," I said. "Notice our use of the ampersand (&) operator. Unfortunately, it's this line of code that also contains the mistake I alluded to earlier."

I continued by pointing out that this code contains two ampersand (&) operators.

"There are actually two separate string concatenations taking place here," I said. "First, the string literal 'Your full name is' is concatenated with the Text property of the txtFirstName TextBox. Then that joined string is concatenated with the Text property of the txtLastName TextBox. By the way, just like the numeric operations that we discussed last week, if there are multiple string operators in an expression, the operations are performed left to right."

I waited for questions, but no one had any.

"Finally," I said, "provided that the user has made an entry in both text boxes, we display the entire joined string in the Visual Basic Output window. Most beginners, I would bet, would expect that if we enter **_John_** in the first text box and **_Smiley_** in the second, that this sentence will be displayed in the Output window."

Your full name is John Smiley

"Instead, this sentence is displayed."

Your full name is JohnSmiley

"And there's no doubt," I said, "that's not what we intended to do here. However, computer programs do exactly what we tell them to do, and in this case, unfortunately, what we intended is not what we told the program to do."

"What do you mean?" Steve asked.

I asked everyone to count the total number of spaces in the sentence that was displayed in the Visual Basic Output window.

"There is a total of four spaces," I said.

- One space between the words "Your" and "Full"
- One space between the words "Full" and "Name"
- One space between the words "Name" and "is"
- One space between the words "is" and "JohnSmiley"

"Now count the number of spaces in the sentence we wanted to display," I said. "You should count a total of five spaces."

- One space between the words "Your" and "Full"
- One space between the words "Full" and "Name"
- One space between the words "Name" and "is"
- One space between the words "is" and "John"
- One space between the words "John" and "Smiley"

"Can anyone tell me what's missing?" I asked.

"The space between the words 'John' and 'Smiley,'" Peter said. "But how can we insert a space between them?"

"That's the trick," I said. "How to insert a space between the user's first and last names. There are actually several techniques to do that, and we'll learn one right now in this exercise."

Exercise 10-2 Correcting the String Concatenation

In this exercise, you'll correct the code from Exercise 10-1 to properly include a space between the user's first and last names.

1. Continue working with the project from Exercise 10-1.
2. Modify the Click event procedure of the Button control so that it looks like this.

```
Private Sub Button1_Click(ByVal sender As System.Object, _
  ByVal e As System.EventArgs) Handles Button1.Click

If txtFirstName.Text = "" Then
  MessageBox.Show("First name must be entered")
  txtFirstName.Focus()
  Exit Sub
ElseIf txtLastName.Text = "" Then
  MessageBox.Show("Last name must be entered")
  txtLastName.Focus()
  Exit Sub
End If

Console.WriteLine("Your full name is " & txtFirstName.Text & " " & txtLastName.Text)

End Sub
```

3. Save the project if you wish, although we won't be modifying it any further.
4. Run the program. Enter your first name in the first text box and your last name in the second text box.
5. Click the button. The program will display your full name in the Output window, this time with a space between your first and last name.

Discussion

I ran the program myself, and the following screen was displayed on the classroom projector.

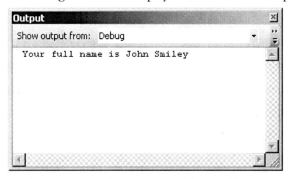

"That's better," Rhonda said. "Now there's a space between your first and last name."

"Can anyone tell me the difference between this code and the code from the previous exercise?" I asked.

"In this exercise," Kate said, "there were actually three string concatenations that were performed and one of them was the concatenation of a space between the first and last names."

Console.WriteLine("Your full name is " & txtFirstName.Text & " " & txtLastName.Text)

"That's excellent, Kate!" I exclaimed.

I sensed that my students were beginning to feel pretty confident with string concatenation.

Breaking Strings Apart

"Okay," I said, "now that we've joined strings together, let's examine techniques for taking strings apart."

"Is that how you solved that problem you told us about with the mailing labels?" Ward asked.

"That's exactly right, Ward," I said, "I did that using the techniques which I'm about to show you here."

I suggested that we now complete an exercise in which we would enter a full name into a text box, and ask Visual Basic to separate the first and last name portions.

Exercise 10-3 Pulling Strings Apart

In this exercise, you'll reverse the process of Exercises 10-1 and 10-2, but taking the user's full name and pulling apart the first name and last name portions.

1. Start a new Windows application.
2. Place a Button control on the form and accept the default name that Visual Basic assigns.
3. Place a TextBox on the form, and change its Name property to txtFullName.
4. Double-click on the Button control, and place the following code into its Click event procedure.

```
Private Sub Button1_Click(ByVal sender As System.Object, _
  ByVal e As System.EventArgs) Handles Button1.Click

Dim intLengthOfString As Integer
Dim intWheresTheSpace As Integer
Dim strFullName As String
Dim strFirstName As String
Dim strLastName As String

If txtFullName.Text = "" Then
  MessageBox.Show ("Your full name must be entered")
  txtFullName.Focus()
  Exit Sub
End If

strFullName = txtFullName.Text
intLengthOfString = Len(strFullName)
intWheresTheSpace = InStr(strFullName, " ")

If intWheresTheSpace = 0 Then
  MessageBox.Show ("Please enter your full name with a space" & _
    Chr(13) & "between your first name and last name")
  txtFullName.Focus()
  Exit Sub
End If

strFirstName = strFullName.Substring(0, intWheresTheSpace - 1)
strLastName = strFullName.Substring(intWheresTheSpace)


Console.WriteLine ("Your first name is: " & strFirstName)
Console.WriteLine ("Your last name is: " & strLastName)

End Sub
```

5. Save the project if you wish, although we won't be modifying it any further.
6. Run the program. Enter your full name (no middle initials, please!) into the text box.
7. Click the button. The program will display your first name and last name in the Visual Basic Output window.

Discussion

I immediately ran the program myself, entering my full name into the text box, and the following was displayed in the Visual Basic Output window.

"I don't know about anyone else," Rhonda said, "but I'm pretty confused about this exercise."

"This exercise illustrates what I call the blindfold nature of programming," I said.

"Blindfold nature of programming?" Valerie asked.

"That's right," I said. "My full name, including the space between my first and last name, contains a total of 11 characters. Linda's full name contains a total of 16 characters."

"And your point is?" Linda asked.

"My point is that it's impossible to know ahead of time the exact construction of the full name that the user will enter into the text box," I answered. "That's what I mean by the blindfold nature of programming. We have to devise a technique, an algorithm, that allows us to deduce the first name and the last name from any entry made in the text box."

"Wow, that's not easy," Blaine said. "I know you wrote the code to do that, but how would we go about doing something like that?"

"The first step in developing that algorithm," I said, "is to take an inventory of the things we do know, even before the user makes an entry in the text box."

"Such as?" Joe said.

"The full name," Dave suggested. "We know that the user will enter their full name into the text box and then click the button."

"Good," I said. "The full name is a definite given. Now, can anyone describe the characteristics of what we call a full name?"

This seemed to stymie everyone a bit.

"How about this?" I said. "A full name is two words separated by a space."

I think the simplicity of the definition startled everyone.

"I hadn't thought about it that way," Mary said, "but you're right. If you look at the full name, it does contain a space in it. And to the left of the space is the first name, to the right of the space is the last name!"

"Excellent, Mary," I said, "and that's exactly how I came up with my algorithm. The rest was pretty easy—finding Visual Basic code to isolate the word to the left of the space and the word to the right of the space. Now granted, I know it wouldn't be that easy for you yet, but it will be once you're more familiar with the syntax of the language."

I continued by explaining that this process of examining what you do know, what you don't know, and then determining how to solve a problem is called developing an algorithm.

"Developing an algorithm to solve a problem may be the single most difficult thing to do in all of programming," I told them. "Syntax can be looked up in a Help file, and there are many sources of information on techniques. Unfortunately, though, in many cases, there's not much Help to show you how to develop an algorithm to solve a problem. Sometimes it just takes lots of experiments until you get it right. There is good news, however. Most of the really hard algorithms have already been developed for us."

"Where can we find these algorithms?" Rhonda asked.

"Online help, Visual Basic books, Visual Basic magazines, the Internet," I replied. "You really can't read too much! Some of the topics and techniques you come across may seem difficult at first, but the more contact you have with new ideas and programming techniques, the stronger your skills will become."

"Can you explain the algorithm you used to solve this problem?" Valerie said. "And may I ask where you found it?"

"This particular algorithm I developed on my own," I said, "and it probably took me several hours to get it to work. But as I recall, it was loads of fun working it out."

I then displayed this algorithm on the classroom projector.

Problem: The user has entered his or her full name into a text box. Determine the user's first name and last name.

Things I Know:

1. The user will type his or her full name into the txtFullName text box.

2. The user's first name begins in position 1 of the txtFullName text box.

3. There is a space between the first and last name in the full name text box.

4. The first character of the last name appears one character after the space.

The Scenario:
The user types John Smiley into the txtFullName text box.

The Algorithm:

1. Determine the number of characters or the length of the full name (11 characters).

2. Determine the position of the space character (position 5). To the left of the space character is the first name.

3. Determine the length of the first name, which is equal to the location of the space less 1 (5 − 1 = 4).

4. To the right of the space character is the last name. The length of the last name is the length of the full name less the position where the space was located (11 − 5 = 6).

"That's really cryptic," Steve said.

"If you think this is cryptic, Steve," I said, "let me ask you this question. During break last week, I heard you telling Kathy what a big fan of crossword puzzles and cryptograms you are. How would you describe your methodology to solve a crossword puzzle or a cryptogram to someone who never worked on one before?"

"I see what you mean," Steve said. "It would be pretty difficult to sit down and describe that process on a piece of paper."

"Just give this a chance and be patient with yourself," I said. "If you don't understand it the first time through, don't worry—it will come."

I waited a moment for more questions before continuing.

"As you can see from the algorithm I displayed on the projector," I said, "the first thing I do when developing an algorithm is to write down the things I know—such as the fact that the user will enter their full name into the text box, there will be a space between the first and last names, and so on. Notice how I worked with a concrete example, my own name. Working with a concrete example makes developing and solving the problem much easier. Something else I do, which I didn't show on the projector, is to draw my user interface on a sheet of paper. I also draw boxes on the paper to represent variables and properties, and I place values in the boxes to depict their values. For instance, while developing this algorithm, I drew a box on a sheet of paper to represent the text box, then entered my full name in it. I then took a minute to observe the characteristics of the full name that I listed in my algorithm, and eventually I developed the full algorithm that you see here."

"I think you left out a few hours of pain and suffering here," Linda said jokingly.

"Not really," I said. "Once you get involved in the process of developing an algorithm, it really can be a lot of fun. I think most programmers enjoy solving puzzles, and that's all an algorithm is anyway. I'll acknowledge, however, that understanding and working with someone else's algorithm can be difficult at first."

"So it's okay if we don't perfectly understand what you've done here?" Kate asked.

"That's right," I said. "And if you feel overwhelmed with the notion of an algorithm, just relax. As we proceed through the rest of the course, I'll be introducing you to most of the common algorithms that you'll need to be productive programmers."

It was now time to explain the code in the exercise in detail.

"The first thing we did, as usual," I said, "was to declare the variables we will need in the event procedure."

Dim intLengthOfString As Integer
Dim intWheresTheSpace As Integer
Dim strFullName As String
Dim strFirstName As String
Dim strLastName As String

"We'll discuss these variables as we encounter them in the rest of the code," I said.

I continued by saying that, after declaring these variables, we then check to ensure that the user has entered something into the text box.

If txtFullName.Text = "" Then
    MessageBox.Show ("Your full name must be entered")
    txtFullName.Focus()
    Exit Sub
End If

"At this point," I said, "we aren't testing for what we consider a valid full name—which would contain a space in it. The test for a valid full name is a little more complicated, and we'll get to that in a moment. For now, we just want to make sure that the text box isn't empty. If the text box is empty, we display a message to the user and set the focus back to the text box."

So far, so good. No one seemed to be having any problems.

"Now," I said, "if the user has entered something into the text box, the next thing we do is take the Text property of the txtFullName TextBox and assign it to the variable strFullName."

strFullName = txtFullName.Text

Dave said, "I noticed when I was completing the exercise that we use this variable in several string operations within the event procedure. Could we have worked with the Text property directly instead?"

"That's an excellent question," I said. "The rule of thumb is that if you need to refer to the value of a property several times within a procedure—in an expression, for instance—it's better to first assign the value of the property to a variable, and then use the variable in the expression instead."

"Why is that?" Blaine asked.

"Obtaining the value of a variable is faster than obtaining the value of a property," I said. "When you take the Visual Basic Objects course here at the university, you'll learn that any time you set or retrieve the value of a property, there's some overhead involved that isn't there when you work with a variable. Therefore, working with variables is faster than working with properties."

The Len Function

I continued by explaining that once we assigned the Text property of txtFullName to the variable strFullName, we then used the Len function to determine the number of characters or the length of strFullName.

intLengthOfString = Len(strFullName)

"By the way," I said, "this satisfies the first step of our algorithm, which is to determine the length of the full name that the user enters into the text box."

"Have we seen this function before?" Kate asked.

"No, we haven't," I answered. "The Len function returns a value equal to the length of the string specified as its argument. Here, we then take this return value and assign it to the variable intLengthOfString which we'll use later in the algorithm."

"I like your descriptive variable name," Rhonda said. "It makes the code much easier to follow."

"No doubt, the choice of variable names is important," I said. "Let's presume that the user has entered 'John Smiley' into the text box. Can anyone tell me what the value of the variable intLengthOfString will be?"

"Eleven," Mary said.

"Absolutely correct," I said. I began to discuss the next line of code.

The InStr Function

intWheresTheSpace = InStr(strFullName, " ")

> **Alert: Notice that there's a space between the quotation marks in the second argument of the InStr function.**

"This line of code," I said, "fulfills the second step of our algorithm, which is to determine the location of the space character in the full name that the user entered into the text box. This is easy in Visual Basic because of the InStr function, which returns a value equal to the position of one string within another. In other words, the InStr function searches for one string within another string, and then tells you where its starting position is. Here we're using it to search for a space character, " ", within the string strFullName. In the case of 'John Smiley,' the space character is at position 5. We then take the return value of the InStr function and assign it to the variable intWheresTheSpace."

"I'm still a little confused," Ward said. "Maybe this will help," I said, as I showed Ward the Help file listing for the InStr function.

InStr([start,]String1, String2[, compare])

"I'm afraid that doesn't help much," Ward said, smiling. "It looks like there are four arguments—not the two used in our code."

"Good point, Ward," I said. "The InStr function is a Visual Basic function that has optional arguments. Only two arguments, the string to search for, String2, and the string to be searched, String1, are required. The Start and Compare arguments are optional."

I explained that the first argument, Start, is optional and is used to specify the starting position in the string to be searched, String1. By default, the InStr function begins searching from the beginning of String1. However, if you wanted to start searching from a different character position 2, you would specify a value for the Start argument."

"Why would you want to do that?" Linda asked.

"Strings can be very long," I said, "billions of characters in length. If you were searching through an extremely long string, specifying a Start parameter can save you a lot of time."

"That makes sense," Joe said.

I continued by explaining that the second argument, String1, is the string to be searched.

"This argument is required," I said. "In our code, String1 is the variable strFullName, which contains the value of the Text property of txtFullName. The third argument, String2, the string to search for, is also required, and in our case is the space character."

"And we tell Visual Basic that by specifying a pair of quotation marks with a space in between," Ward said. "I think I understand the InStr function much better now."

"Let's not forget the fourth and final argument, Compare," I said, "Compare is an optional argument that specifies the type of comparison InStr should perform while searching for String2 within String1. There are two possible values for the Compare argument: 0 (binary) or 1 (textual). Binary is the default. By the way, a quirk of the InStr function is such that if you specify a Compare argument, you must also specify the Start argument."

"I'm almost afraid to ask what the differences between the two are," Joe said.

"It's no big deal, Joe," I said. "A binary comparison is a case-sensitive search and a textual comparison is case-insensitive. By default, the comparison type for the InStr function is binary, which means that Visual Basic will only consider String2 found in String1 if the match is exact, counting case."

"Come again?" Steve asked.

"For instance," I said, "with a binary comparison, the uppercase letter A is considered different than the lowercase letter a. Do you remember our discussion of the ASCII code earlier in the class? These two characters A and a have different ASCII values, and with a binary comparison, are considered different characters. However, with a textual comparison, the letter A and the letter a are considered to match."

"I have a question," Kathy said. "Suppose String2 is found in String1 more than once? What will be the return value of InStr?"

"That's a good question, Kathy," I said. "If the string you are searching contains more than one instance of the string you are searching for, InStr stops after finding the first occurrence. In other words, only the location of the first instance of the string is returned. This is important to remember if you attempt to use the InStr function to search for more than one occurrence of a string within another string."

"How can we get around that limitation?" Dave asked.

"One way would be to use loop processing," I said. "We can use a loop structure to vary the Start parameter of the InStr function. We'll see this a little later on in today's class."

"What's the return value of InStr if String2 isn't found in String1?" Chuck asked.

"The return value will be 0," I replied, "and that's the reason we wrote the next line of code in the exercise. We can use a return value of 0 from the InStr function to determine if the user entered a space in the text box."

```
If intWheresTheSpace = 0 Then
    MessageBox.Show ("Please enter your full name with a space" _
      Chr(13) & "between your first name and last name")
    txtFullName.Focus()
    Exit Sub
End If
```

"What we do," I said, "is check the value of the variable intWheresTheSpace. If it's 0, we know that the InStr function did not find a space in the variable strFullName. And since the value of that variable is equal to the Text property of txtFullName, a 0 indicates the user did not enter what we consider a valid full name into the text box. If that's the case, we display a message box with a warning message and exit the event procedure. By the way, note the way we concatenate the ASCII character 13 between the two pieces of the message we wish to display in the message box. This causes the message in the message box to be neatly formatted on two lines."

As a demonstration of this code, I ran the program, entered my name into the text box, omitting the space between my first and last name, and then clicked the button. The following message box was displayed.

"Okay," I said. "Let's review where we are so far. We now have the user's full name stored in the variable strFullName. We also know the position, within that variable, of the space character. Those are the two pieces of information that we absolutely must have in order to extract the first and last names."

"Can you explain to us again," Rhonda asked, "how the extraction is performed?"

"Sure," I said. "We know that the first name portion of the full name entered into the text box lies to the left of the space character. We also know that the first character of the first name starts at position 1. Armed with these facts, we can deduce that the length of the first name is equal to the location of the space character less 1—or to express it another way, the value of the variable intWheresTheSpace less 1. Therefore, if the user entered John Smiley into the text box, the length of the first name is 4, since the value of intWheresTheSpace is equal to 5."

I paused to look for signs of confusion before continuing.

"Knowing the length of the first name," I said, "takes care of step 3 of our algorithm and also allows us to extract the first name from the strFullName variable. We do that by using the Visual Basic Substring method."

The Substring Function

I explained that the Visual Basic Substring method returns a string of characters from another string.

"There are two variants of the Substring method of the String object," I said. "Both variants operate on a String object and return a string. The first variant uses two arguments. The first argument is the zero-based **starting position** within the String to 'extract' and the second argument is the **number of characters** within the String to extract. Here's the code that 'extracts' the First name from strFullname. Notice that our starting position is zero based---it's 0, which is the first character in the String. For the second argument, we use the value of the variable intWheresTheSpace -1 which is 4."

strFirstName = strFullName.Substring(0, intWheresTheSpace -1)

I saw a bit of confusion in the faces of my students, so I quickly displayed a translation of the Visual Basic SubString method on the classroom projector.

strFirstName = strFullName.Substring(0, 4)

"The SubString method is zero based," I said, "in other words, it considers the first position in the string it's searching through to be position 0. "

I gave everyone a chance to think about this.

"Zero based numbering is something you find in languages such as C, C++ and C#," I said, "Early versions of Visual Basic tried to make things easier on programmers by making everything begin with 1. It's just something you'll have to get used to. We'll also need to remember this a little bit later in our code—but you'll see that in a minute."

"I think the zero based issue confuses me a bit," Kate said, "but I think I see what's going on. strFirstName is now equal to positions 0, 1, 2 and 3 of the strFullName. Is that correct?"

"Exactly, Kate," I said. "I couldn't have said it better myself."

I waited a moment for questions before moving on.

"And now, the final step in the puzzle is to extract the last name portion from the full name. In a way, this is a little easier than extracting the first name. I mentioned earlier that the Substring method has two variants. One variant allows us to supply just the zero-based starting position within the String to extract---the Substring method then extracts and returns from that point to the end of the String."

"In other words," Dave picked up quickly, "we don't need to worry about calculating the length of the Last Name?"

"That's right Dave," I said, "although you could always make things harder on yourself by supplying both the starting position of the Last Name in the strFullname, and its length."

"No need to do that if we don't need to, is there?" Linda said.

"Absolutely right," I said. "Let's take a look at the Substring method that returns the Last Name. Here it is."

strLastName = strFullName.Substring(intWheresTheSpace)

"In our simple exercise," I said, "my Last Name starts in position 6---but since the Substring method is zero based, it's really position 5. The value of intWheresTheSpace is 5."

"And that's all we need to provide, is that correct?" Barbara asked. "Just the starting position---without a second argument, the Substring method returns the rest of the string from that location?"

"That's right Barbara," I said.

I then displayed this Visual Basic translation on the classroom projector.

strLastName = strFullName.Substring(5)

"So when this code executes," Kate said, "the value Smiley is assigned to the variable strLastName."

"Right again, Kate," I said. "We now have both pieces of the puzzle, the first name and the last name! The next two lines of code just display the values of the variables strFirstName and strLastName in a Visual Basic Message Box."

Console.WriteLine ("Your first name is: " & strFirstName)
Console.WriteLine ("Your last name is: " & strLastName)

I asked if there were any questions.

"I think I understand what we've done," Barbara said, "but until I've had a chance to work with these functions myself, I'm going to be a little uncomfortable with them."

"That's true of most of what you'll learn in this course," I said. "The more practice you have, the better you'll be with your coding. That's why I'm so glad you all have the chance to work on the China Shop Project."

We had been working for some time, and so I asked the class to take a break. When we returned from break, I told my students that we were far from finished with our look at strings.

"Earlier," I said, "I was asked if the InStr function can be used to locate more than one occurrence of a string within another string, and I said no, but I did mention that there is another technique we can use. In the following exercise, I'll give you a chance to see that technique in action as you write own version of a Search and Replace function."

Exercise 10-4 Your Own Search and Replace---the Hard Way

In this exercise, you'll use the Mid function to create your own Search and Replace program.

1. Start a new Windows application.
2. Place a Button control and four TextBox controls on the form and accept the default names that Visual Basic assigns.
3. Change the Text property of the form to "Search and Replace."
4. Change the name of the first TextBox control to txtSource, and place a label control next to it. Change the Text property of the Label control to "Source.:
5. Change the name of the second TextBox control to txtSearchFor, and place a label control next to it. Change the Text property of the Label control to "Search For:."
6. Change the name of the third TextBox control to txtReplaceWith, and place a label control next to it. Change the Text property of the Label control to "Replace With:."
7. Change the name of the fourth TextBox control to txtTarget, and set its ReadOnly property to True. Place a label control next to it. Change the Text property of the Label control to "Target:."
8. Change the MaxLength properties of both txtSearchFor and txtReplaceWith to 1. This will ensure that only one character can be entered into either text box.
9. Change the Text property of the Button control to OK. Your form should now look similar to this.

10. Double-click on the Button control, and place the following code into its Click event procedure.

```
Private Sub Button1_Click(ByVal sender As System.Object, _
   ByVal e As System.EventArgs) Handles Button1.Click

Dim intLengthOfSource As Integer
Dim intLengthOfSearchFor As Integer
Dim intCounter As Integer
Dim strSource As String
Dim strSearchFor As String
Dim strReplaceWith As String
Dim strPiece As String
Dim strTarget As String

If txtSource.Text = "" Then
   MessageBox.Show ("A String to be searched must be entered")
```

```
      txtSource.Focus()
      Exit Sub
    ElseIf txtSearchFor.Text = "" Then
      MessageBox.Show ("A search character must be entered")
      txtSearchFor.Focus()
      Exit Sub
    ElseIf txtReplaceWith.Text = "" Then
      MessageBox.Show ("A replacement character must be entered")
      txtReplaceWith.Focus()
      Exit Sub
    End If

    strSource = txtSource.Text
    strSearchFor = txtSearchFor.Text
    strReplaceWith = txtReplaceWith.Text
    intLengthOfSource = Len(strSource)
    intLengthOfSearchFor = Len(strSearchFor)

    For intCounter = 0 To intLengthOfSource - 1 Step intLengthOfSearchFor
      strPiece = strSource.Substring(intCounter, intLengthOfSearchFor)
      If strPiece = strSearchFor Then
        strTarget = strTarget + strReplaceWith
      Else
        strTarget = strTarget + strPiece
      End If
    Next intCounter

    txtTarget.Text = strTarget

  End Sub
```

11. Save the project—you'll be modifying it in Exercise 10-5.
12. Run the program.
13. Type the word **Titanic** into the Source text box.
14. Enter the character **t** into the Search For text box.
15. Enter the character ***** into the Replace With text box.
16. Click the button. What is displayed in the Target text box? Your form should look like this.

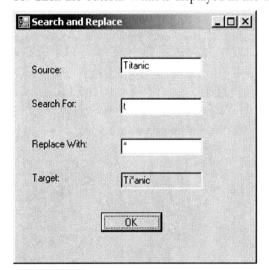

Discussion

"I thought Exercise 10-3 was confusing," Rhonda said, "but this one was much worse!"

"There's no doubt that this exercise is more complicated than the previous one," I said, "but I think after we've had a chance to go through the code step by step, you'll all understand what's going on in the program. You'll also have a real appreciation for how the Search and Replace functions in other programs work—but you'll see later on there's an easier way to do this than we used here."

"Do you mean this is how the Search and Replace function works in Microsoft Word?" Joe asked.

"Not far from it," I said. "I don't want to mislead you, though, this code has a lot of holes in it. I didn't ask you to set the MaxLength properties of the two TextBoxes to 1 for nothing—this code works best when it's asked to search for a single character and to replace it with a single character. Feel free to see how this code behaves with more than one character to search for, and more than one character to replace if you wish. But the important thing about this exercise isn't so much writing a perfect Search and Replace algorithm, but to see the power that the ability to manipulate strings can give your program."

I continued by saying that, once again, this code illustrates the blindfold nature of programming.

"Just as we saw in the previous exercise," I said, "there are pieces of data that we don't know when we write the program, and pieces of data that only become known to our program when the program runs. Unfortunately, just about everything in this exercise amounts to an unknown at the time we code it. We have absolutely no idea what string the user will enter into the first text box to designate the string to search through, what character (or characters) the user will enter into the second text box to designate the characters they wish to search for, and what character (or characters) the user will enter into the third text box to designate the characters they wish to replace."

"That's right," Linda said, "at least in the previous exercise, we knew the format that the user would be entering into the text box—a full name, with the first and last names separated by a space. Here, we're totally in the dark."

"That's right, Linda," I said. "Now, who can tell me what the first step in solving a problem like this should be?"

"I bet I can guess," Kate said. "Develop an algorithm!"

"Right you are, Kate," I said as I displayed this algorithm on the classroom projector.

Problem: Search for a character within a string and replace that character, when found, with a replacement character.

Things I Know:

1. The user will enter a string to search through in a text box. It can be any length.
2. The user will enter a single character to search for in a second text box.
3. The user will enter a character to replace with the found character in a third text box.

The Scenario:

1. The user types **Titanic** into the txtSource text box.
2. The user types **t** into the txtSearchFor text box.
3. The user types ***** into the txtReplaceWith text box.

The Algorithm:

1. Determine the number of characters or the length of the source string (7 characters).
2. Determine the length of the search string (1 character).
3. Use the Mid function to move through the source string in increments of the length of the search string (1) looking for the search string until the end of the source string is reached.
4. If the search string is found in the source string, replace it with the replacement string.
5. If the search string is not found, continue searching with the next character in the string.

I waited a moment, saw obvious looks of confusion, and then suggested that we begin with a discussion of the code.

"As usual," I said, "the first thing we did was to declare the variables we will need in the event procedure."

I displayed the first two variable declarations on the classroom projector.

Dim intLengthOfSource As Integer
Dim intLengthOfSearchFor As Integer

"These two variables, similar to the ones we used in the previous exercise, will be used to hold the length of the Text properties of the txtSource and txtSearchFor TextBoxes," I said. "intLengthOfSource represents the length of the string to be searched and intLengthOfSearchFor represents the length of the string to search for—as we'll see in a moment, these values will be important as we move through the source string. The next variable declaration you probably recognize from last week—it's a Loop control variable, and we'll be using it within a For...Next loop."

Dim intCounter As Integer

"One of the reasons the code in this exercise is more difficult to follow than the code in the previous exercise is that we needed to use a Loop structure in order to examine the source string character by character."

I continued on by explaining that the next three variable declarations hold the Text properties of the three TextBoxes on our form.

"Remember," I said, "it's best to work with variable values instead of property values in our code."

Dim strSource As String
Dim strSearchFor As String
Dim strReplaceWith As String

"What's that next variable declaration?" Steve asked. "strPiece?"

Dim strPiece As String

"Do you remember how, in the previous exercise, we assigned the return value of the Substring method to a variable?" I asked. "We're using this variable, strPiece, in a similar way. Finally, strTarget is the variable we'll use to assign the replacement string to."

Dim strTarget As String

Everyone seemed to be pretty comfortable with this next section of code. It was the same type of text box validation that we had performed in Exercise 10-3.

```
If txtSource.Text = "" Then
   MessageBox.Show ("A String to be searched must be entered")
   txtSource.Focus()
   Exit Sub
ElseIf txtSearchFor.Text = "" Then
   MessageBox.Show ("A search character must be entered")
   txtSearchFor.Focus()
   Exit Sub
ElseIf txtReplaceWith.Text = "" Then
   MessageBox.Show ("A replacement character must be entered")
   txtReplaceWith.Focus()
   Exit Sub
End If
```

"We want to be sure," I said, "that the user has entered something into all three text boxes. The If...ElseIf statement is ideal for checking that the user has."

"I meant to ask you this while I was completing the exercise," Barbara said, "and I think I heard you mention it a few minutes ago. Why did we set the MaxLength property to 1?"

"The MaxLength property of the TextBox is used to restrict the number of characters that can be entered into a text box," I replied. "We wanted to restrict the replacement string to 1 character, and the MaxLength property is the best way to do that."

I then explained that, after checking to ensure we have all of the information we need from the user, we then assign the Text property of each TextBox to the three variables we declared for that purpose.

```
strSource = txtSource.Text
strSearchFor = txtSearchFor.Text
strReplaceWith = txtReplaceWith.Text
```

"Our algorithm indicates that we need to determine the length of the strSource and strSearchFor strings, and we do that with the next two lines of code which uses the Visual Basic Len function."

intLengthOfSource = Len(strSource)
intLengthOfSearchFor = Len(strSearchFor)

"Before we examine the next section of code," I said, "which can be confusing, I want to try to reproduce for you the methodology I followed when I was trying to develop this algorithm on paper."

I asked everyone to take out a piece of paper and a pencil or pen, and look away from their monitors for a few minutes.

"Okay now," I said. "Follow along with me and let's see what happens."

1. Write the source string on a sheet of paper. In our case, it's Titanic.

2. Using your pen or pencil, advance through the source string, examining each character one at a time.

3. As you advance through the characters in the source string, mark each character you examine with an arrow.

4. If the character you examine in the source string does not match your search string (t), write the examined character underneath the source string.

5. If the character you examine in the source string matches the search character (t), write the replacement string character (*) underneath the source string.

"This process is a repetitive one; and that's just perfect for a Visual Basic loop," I said.

I performed this process myself. Here's an illustration of what I did on the classroom whiteboard.

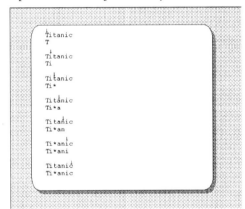

"Starting at the first character of the source string," I said, "and moving one character at a time to the right until we reach the end of the string is something that we can simulate in code using a Visual Basic loop structure. And the examination of each character in the source string can be done by using the Visual Basic Substring method. Let's continue looking at that code now. Here's the first line of the Loop structure."

For intCounter = 0 To intLengthOfSource - 1 Step intLengthOfSearchFor

"Using the For...Next loop structure allows us to have a definite start and stop point for our loop. Remember, we know where we want to start our search (the first character in the string) and where we want to stop our search (the last character in the string). The Start and End parameters of the For...Next loop structure are perfect for that. Because of the Zero-based nature of the Visual Basic Substring Method, the Start parameter will be 0, and the End parameter is the value of the variable intLengthOfSource -1."

"Why did we specify the Step parameter as the length of the search string?" Dave asked. "Why not just make it 1?"

"You're right, Dave," I said. "We could have done that, and the code would still have worked fine, since the replacement string is only one character in length. Looking down the road, however, which is something programmers should always do, we may need to enhance the capability of this program to search for a string that is longer than just one character—and that's why the Step parameter is coded using the value of the variable intLengthOfSearchFor. If you want to experiment using replacement strings longer than one character, remember to set the MaxLength property of txtSearchFor and txtReplaceWith back to their default values of 0, which permits any number of characters to be entered into the text box."

"What's going on with this next line of code?" Lou asked. "This is the one that really confused me."

"This line of code," I answered, "allows us to move through our string, character by character, just like we did using pen or pencil on paper."

strPiece = strSource.Substring(intCounter, intLengthOfSearchFor)

"That's why it's in the body of the loop. During each iteration of the loop, this line uses the Visual Basic Substring method to progressively extract the characters in the source string, in this case one by one, and then stores the return value in the variable strPiece."

"I know you covered this earlier," Barbara said, "but can you go over the syntax of the Substring method again?"

"There are two variants of the Substring method of the String object, I said. "Both variants operate on a String object and return a string. The first variant uses two arguments. The first argument is the zero-based starting position within the String to 'extract' and the second argument is the number of characters within the String to extract. Provided all of these arguments are valid, a character or characters will be returned. Let's examine what Visual Basic does with this statement the first time through the loop."

strPiece = strSource.Substring(intCounter, intLengthOfSearchFor)

I displayed the translation of this code on the classroom projector.

strPiece = "Titanic"(0, 1)

"Okay, that makes more sense," Rhonda said. "strSource is easy, that's just the string to search. intCounter is the Loop control variable, which is equal to 0 the first time through the loop, and intLengthOfSearchFor is 1 because that's the length of the string we're searching for."

"That's a great analysis," I said. "Now, what about the second time through the loop?"

"Each time the loop is executed," Dave said, "the value of intCounter is incremented by 1, so the start argument of the Substring method will also be incremented by 1."

"Absolutely correct," I said.

I then displayed the translation of the Mid method through the next five iterations of the loop.

strPiece = "Titanic"(1, 1)
strPiece = "Titanic"(2, 1)
strPiece = "Titanic"(3, 1)
strPiece = "Titanic"(4, 1)
strPiece = "Titanic"(5, 1)

"As you can see," I said, "each iteration through the loop results in a different character being extracted and assigned to the variable strPiece. In essence, what we've done with the For loop is simulate the action of the pen and paper process of examining the source string character by character."

I paused a moment before continuing.

"Now what about simulating the replacement process?," I continued. "Remember that, if the character we examine is not the character we are looking for, using pen and paper, we just write that character under the source string. If the character happens to be the one we are looking for, we write the replacement character under the source string. This next section of code is critical."

If strPiece = strSearchFor Then

"If this statement evaluates to True," I said, "then we know we've found the character or characters that we're looking for. If so, we concatenate the current value of strTarget with the replacement character or characters, which is stored in the variable strReplaceWith…"

strTarget = strTarget + strReplaceWith

"…If the statement evaluates to False, we know we haven't found the character we're looking for. Therefore, we concatenate the current value of strTarget with the character we just examined, which is stored in the variable strPiece…"

Else
    strTarget = strTarget + strPiece
End If

"Finally," I said, "when our For Loop has finished, we take the value of the variable strTarget, and assign it to the Text property of txtTarget."

txtTarget.Text = strTarget

I looked around the room for signs of confusion, but it appeared that everyone, amazingly enough, was okay with the explanation.

"I noticed when I ran the program," Dave said, "that only the lowercase t was replaced in the source string. I suppose we could make the code replace both the lowercase t and the uppercase t as well, couldn't we?"

"Yes, we could," I said. "There's a method of the String object called ToUpper. It takes a string, and 'upper cases' every character in the String. If we 'upper case' the string we are searching for, along with the string we are searching, it effectively makes the search case insensitive."

"So what do we do?" Rhonda asked.

"To make this code case-insensitive all we need to do is change one line of code, and that's within the body of our loop," I explained. "Change your code to use the ToUpper() method of the String object so that it looks like this."

```
For intCounter = 0 To intLengthOfSource - 1 Step intLengthOfSearchFor
    strPiece = strSource.Substring(intCounter, intLengthOfSearchFor)
    If strPiece.ToUpper = strSearchFor.ToUpper Then
        strTarget = strTarget + strReplaceWith
    Else
        strTarget = strTarget + strPiece
    End If
Next intCounter
```

I ran the program again.

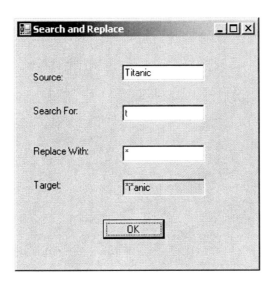

The Replace Function

"That did the trick," I said. "Every t, regardless of case, has been replaced with an asterisk. Now I'd like you to complete an exercise using the Visual Basic Replace function, which will streamline the code you just wrote and make your Search and Replace program a lot more powerful."

Exercise 10-5 Your Own Search and Replace---the Easy Way---Using the Replace Function

In this exercise, you'll take the code you wrote in Exercise 10-4, and modify it to use the Visual Basic Replace function.

1. Continue working with the project from Exercise 10-4.
2. Place a second Button control on the form and accept the default name that Visual Basic assigns.
3. Change the Text property of the first Button control to "The Easy Way".
4. Change the Text property of the second Button control to "Replace Function".
5. Double-click on the Button control, and place the following code into its Click event procedure.

```
Private Sub Button2_Click(ByVal sender As System.Object, _
  ByVal e As System.EventArgs) Handles Button2.Click

Dim strTarget As String

If txtSource.Text = "" Then
  MessageBox.Show ("A String to be searched must be entered")
  txtSource.Focus()
  Exit Sub
ElseIf txtSearchFor.Text = "" Then
  MessageBox.Show ("A search character must be entered")
  txtSearchFor.Focus()
  Exit Sub
ElseIf txtReplaceWith.Text = "" Then
  MessageBox.Show ("A replacement character must be entered")
  txtReplaceWith.Focus()
  Exit Sub
End If

strTarget = Replace(txtSource.Text, txtSearchFor.Text, txtReplaceWith.Text)
txtTarget.Text = strTarget

End Sub
```

6. Save the project, although we won't be modifying it any further.
7. Run the program.
8. Type the word Titanic into the Source text box.
9. Enter the character t into the Search For text box.
10. Enter the character * into the Replace With text box.
11. Click the second button. You should get the same results as when you clicked on the first button.

Discussion

"Wow, what a difference that Replace function makes," Steve said. "We've cut the code in the procedure in half. Why didn't we use the Replace function the first time?"

"We wouldn't have learned as much about algorithms," I said, "if we had done it the easy way the first time."

"How does the Replace function work?" Rhonda asked.

"The Replace function requires three arguments," I said, "although a total of six are possible. The first argument is the string containing characters to be replaced, the second argument is the string to be searched for, and the third argument is the replacement string. Optionally, the fourth argument is the starting position to begin the search. If this argument is omitted, the value is presumed to be 1, which means the search begins at the beginning of the string. The fifth argument, also optional, is count, which specifies the number of substitutions to perform. If count is omitted, count is presumed to be -1, which means that all possible substitutions are made. Finally, the sixth argument, also optional, is a Compare argument. If omitted, the comparison is based on the Option Compare statement in effect, which is generally a binary comparison—which means the substitution is case-sensitive."

strTarget = Replace(txtSource.Text, txtSearchFor.Text, txtReplaceWith.Text)

"I notice," Steve said, "that this time around we didn't assign the value of the Text properties of the txtSource, txtSearchFor, and txtReplaceWith TextBoxes to variables—instead we used the property values directly in the Replace function. Didn't you say it's more efficient to store those property values in a variable, and then use the variables in an expression?"

"In general that's true, Steve, particularly when using the Text properties within a loop," I replied. "However, in this exercise, we were using the Text properties in an expression just once—not many times within a loop—so there was no efficiency to be gained by assigning the values of the properties to a variable. You see how not doing so streamlined the code quite a bit."

It had been another intensive class. As I began to dismiss the students for the day, Rhonda said, "I'm a little disappointed that we haven't touched the China Shop Project today."

"This is the last week that we won't work on it," I said. "Next week, we'll learn how to read from and write data to a disk file in Visual Basic, and then we'll be modifying the China Shop Project to load china brands and inventory prices from a disk file into our program."

Summary

- In this chapter, we examined string operations in detail. In particular, we saw that:

- A string is a series of characters.

- String concatenation allows you to join strings together in a meaningful way.

- There is a series of string functions that can be used to break strings apart.

- You can use Visual Basic functions and statements to locate characters in strings (called substrings), and to extract those characters and in some cases change them.

Strings are an integral part of programming in Visual Basic and having a sound working knowledge of how to manipulate them will stand you in good stead for future programming. In the next chapter, we'll be considering how to send and retrieve data to and from disk files, and how to print information using Visual Basic.

Chapter 11---File Operations

The ability to read data from and write to disk files is an important programming skill. In this chapter, you'll follow my class as they learn how to perform these disk operations.

Disk File Operations

I began by informing everyone that the topic for today's class would be disk file operations.

"I thought that disk file operations had pretty much gone the way of the dinosaur," Dave said. "I hardly ever see file operations mentioned anywhere in the books that I pick up. Everything seems to point you in the direction of using databases."

"Your observations are right on the mark," I said. "Disk file operations from within Visual Basic may be one of its biggest secrets. More advanced programmers choose to use databases to store data from their programs. Database operations are beyond the level of this introductory course, but disk file operations are a perfect fit for the beginner programmer. Besides, the skills you learn today as we read from and write to files will not be wasted. They'll form an important foundation when you graduate to database processing. Let's take a look at disk file operations now."

I continued by explaining that working with disk files, though not as prevalent as it once was, is still a viable way of saving data from within your program.

"You can also read data from a disk file into your program," I said. "Don't forget, part of our China Shop Requirements Statement indicates that we will read inventory data into our program from a disk file—specifically, data that we will use to load china brands into the lstBrands ListBox, and the inventory pricing data necessary to calculate a sales quotation. Right now, that pricing data is included in the actual code of our program—that's known as hard coding. After today's class, the China Shop Project will read the brands of china from a disk file directly into the lstBrands ListBox!"

"Are disk file operations like this done much in the real world?" Kathy asked.

"That's a hard question to answer," I said. "Perhaps not so much for newer applications, which tend to rely on interacting with modern databases such as Microsoft Access, Microsoft SQL Server, or Oracle. However, I believe there's a huge inventory of existing DOS Basic programs that were written long before the advent of modern database packages. Some of these programs are still running today, and still reading and writing disk files. In fact, it's not uncommon to have a student or two enroll in one of my classes because of a desire or need to convert one of these programs into Visual Basic. You never know when you might be hired to convert one of these old programs to Visual Basic, and an understanding of disk file operations can mean the difference between getting the job and losing it to someone else."

Writing Data to a Disk File

"What types of operations can you perform on a disk file?" Valerie asked.

"Writing data to and reading data from a file are the two basic operations," I suggested after thinking for a moment.

"Shouldn't we also add append to that list?" Dave asked.

"Good point, Dave," I said.

"Append?" Blaine asked.

"Append means to write to the end of an already existing file," I said. "We'll examine that operation in a few minutes. But before we look at append, let's first examine writing data to a disk file. Writing data to a disk file isn't difficult, but it does require that we perform three steps, in this order:"

1. Open the file to which you want to write data by creating a Visual Basic **StreamWriter** object.

2. Write data to that file using either the **Write** or **WriteLine** method of the **StreamWriter** object.

3. After you are done writing data, close the file you have opened using the **Close** method of the **StreamWriter** object.

"That doesn't seem very difficult at all," Joe said. "It sounds as if everything is done using the StreamWriter Object. Is that all we need to do to write data to a file?"

"The process isn't very difficult," I said. "Probably the most complicated part is learning the syntax to create the StreamWriter object. Let's examine that first."

The StreamWriter Object

"Have we created objects before?" Linda asked.

"Not quite like this," I said, "Throughout the course, we've been working with objects---such as the Console object---and we've created a String object to store text values. But the StreamWriter Class gives us a chance to create a very powerful Visual Basic object that is designed to permit us to write to, and read from, our computer's hard disk drive."

"As I recall," Dave said, "a class is a template or blueprint for an object. One class can spawn many objects, is that right?"

"Right on the mark Dave," I said, "the .NET Framework defines the StreamWriter class, and we create objects of the class to give us the functionality to write a file to our computer's disk drive. Probably the most important part of that process is how we create the object, and it's really pretty simple. We create an instance of an object by executing the Visual Basic New statement. The new statement executes the code in the class's Constructor, which is a special method that is executed when Visual Basic sees the new statement. It's the **New** statement that really gives birth to the object. Let me show you. But before I do, I should also mention that using the StreamWriter object requires us to code an Imports statement in our class---here it is…"

Imports System.IO

"The StreamWriter object is part of the System.IO namespace," I said, "so we need to tell Visual Basic to include that namespace into our program prior to working with the StreamWriter object. As you'll see shortly when you complete an exercise to create a file of your own, you just add this Imports statement at the very top of your Code Window."

I then displayed the syntax for the creation of the StreamWriter object on the classroom projector.

Dim sw As New StreamWriter("C:\VBFILES\PRACTICE\GRADES.TXT")

"Uh-oh, you're not going to display our grades, are you?" Blaine said jokingly, referring to the name of file.

"Don't worry," I said, "everyone in this class is well on their way to earning an A. The file you see referenced here contains the grades from a class I taught in the summer semester here at the university, but the names have been changed to protect the innocent!"

I continued by explaining that this statement was instructing Visual Basic to open a file named GRADES.TXT, located in the subdirectory C:\VBFILES\PRACTICE for Output mode. Once opened, the file thereafter would be referenced by the name of the StreamWriter object, which we called sw.

"So sw is the name of the StreamWriter object?" Dave asked.

"That's right Dave," I said. "We could have called it anything we wanted to—but once we create the StreamWriter object, we need to refer to it by that name throughout the rest of our code."

"Where's the Constructor?" Kate asked.

"The Constructor follows the word New," I said. "Constructors are methods that are named with the same name as the Class, so the StreamWriter Constructor is the word StreamWriter along with the information included within the parentheses---which in this case is the path and file name of the file we wish to open for output."

"How does Visual Basic know we want to write data to this file?" Ward asked, "as opposed to reading data from it?"

"Because we're using the StreamWriter object," I answered. "If we had opened the file using the StreamReader object, Visual Basic would know that we are working with the file for input. Since we're using the StreamWriter object, Visual Basic knows that we want to work with the file for some kind of output action."

"What's an output action?" Rhonda asked.

"Output means that we'll be writing text to the file," I said.

"Suppose the file already exists?" Linda asked. "Will it be overwritten and its previous contents lost?"

"That is the case with this particular form of the Constructor," I said, "It's possible to create a StreamWriter object and open the file in Append mode, using another form of the Constructor, once again specifying a file name, but this time telling Visual Basic that if the file already exists, we want to open the file and append any data we write to it at the end of the file. Here's the alternate form of the Constructor..."

Dim sw As New StreamWriter("C:\VBFILES\PRACTICE\GRADES..TXT", True)

"Do you see the difference?" I asked. "This form of the Constructor uses the Boolean value true after the path and file name."

"How many forms of the StreamWriter Constructor are there?" Linda asked.

"There are seven," I said, "but in this course, we'll use these two---one to open a file for output, and one to open a file for append. Does everyone understand the difference between the two?"

It appeared everyone did.

"How exactly do we write data to the file?" Barbara asked. "Is that part of the StreamWriter Constructor?"

"No, it's not," I answered. "although we use the same object---the StreamWriter object. Writing data to a file requires that we execute either the Write or WriteLine method of the StreamWriter object. Before I discuss it, though, I'd like to quickly review disk files."

"Isn't WriteLine the same statement we use to direct output to the Visual Basic Output window?" Linda asked.

"That's a good observation, Linda," I replied. "The name of the statement is the same, and its function is similar. In one case we direct output to the Visual Basic Output window, in the other case we direct output to a disk file. This is an example of what is known in the world of objects as **Polymorphism**—that is, more than one command (in this case Visual Basic methods) that have the same name and perform a similar function, but are used with two different objects. As you'll see, knowing how to direct output to the Visual Basic Output window makes learning how to direct output to a disk file a little easier."

I continued by explaining that there are many types of disk files that can be found on a PC, but the type in which we are specifically interested are called data files.

"A typical data file contains records," I said, "and each record in the file contains one or more fields of data. A field is a single piece of information. For instance, we have data files here at the University that contain information about its students. Each record is comprised of fields representing the student's name, address, telephone number, and other pertinent information. This collection of fields electronically describes a student. Usually, but not always, the records in a data file are stored in what is known as a comma delimited fashion."

"What does that mean?" Blaine asked.

"That means that fields are separated with a comma, and each record ends with a carriage return and line feed character, thereby ensuring that each record begins on a new line," I answered.

> **NOTE: If you are familiar with PC databases, the concept of a data file is similar, although data files are a little more simplistic.**

The WriteLine Method

"The WriteLine method," I continued, "allows you to write fields of data as discrete pieces of data which another program, such as one written in Visual Basic, can then read. In some languages, creating a comma delimited record is a bit easier than it is in Visual Basic In Visual Basic, we need to place the comma between the fields ourselves. Take a look at this code."

Dim sw As New StreamWriter("C:\VBFILES\PRACTICE\DEMO1.TXT")
sw.WriteLine("John Smith" + "," + 100)
sw.WriteLine ("Joe Jones" + "," + 99)
sw.Close()

"This code consists of the StreamWriter Constructor method," I said, "along with the execution of two WriteLine methods and a Close method. Since the WriteLine and Close methods are methods of the StreamWriter object we created on the first line of code, we need to preface them with the name of the object---in this case 'sw'---although we could have called it anything we wanted to."

I gave everyone a chance to take this in before continuing.

"Again, the StreamWriter Constructor opens a file called Demo1.TXT for output in the \VBFILES\PRACTICE folder. We'll talk about the Close method in a few minutes. The first WriteLine method writes the string 'John Smith' followed by a comma, and then the number 100, to our output file. Notice that 'John Smith' appears within quotation marks in the WriteLine method—that's because it is what is known as a String literal, and that's the convention for String Literals. The same with the comma—it also is a string literal. The number 100 is a numeric literal---and the convention for a numeric literal is NOT to use quotation marks. Notice also how we concatenated the comma between 'John Smith' and 100---as I mentioned a few minutes ago, unlike other programming languages, Visual Basic will not do this for us. After the first WriteLine method is executed, a new line is begun and the string 'Joe Jones' will be written to the file, followed by a comma and then the number 99. This process will be repeated as long as WriteLine methods are executed. When the file is closed, an invisible End Of File marker (sometimes called an EOF) is placed after the end of the last record, marking the end of the file."

> **NOTE: You could also have written 100 as a String Literal to the output file—but it's a good habit to get into when referring to Numeric Literals NOT to use quotation marks.**

There were no further questions, so I created a new Visual Basic project and placed the code in a Button control. I then ran the program and clicked on the button.

"Nothing obvious has happened," I said, "but we can use Notepad to view the file we just created."

I then opened the file using Notepad, and this screenshot was displayed on the classroom projector.

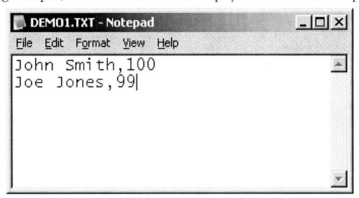

"That's cool," Chuck said.

"Chuck's right," Ward said, "this is a very powerful feature."

"What would happen if we didn't place quotation marks around the names or the commas?" Steve asked.

"Visual Basic would be horribly confused," I said, "In the case of the names, it would try to interpret them as variable names---which haven't been declared. In the case of the comma, it would have no idea what you are trying to do."

The Write Method

"What's the difference between the Write and WriteLine methods?" Barbara asked.

"The WriteLine method appends a new line character at the end of the data it writes," I said, "the Write method does not. Therefore, if you execute the Write method, if you then execute a Write or WriteLine method, the new data will be on the same 'line' as the previous data. For instance, we could have coded the previous example to look like this and still produce the same output file..."

```
Dim sw As New StreamWriter("C:\VBFILES\PRACTICE\DEMO.TXT")
sw.Write("John Smith")
sw.Write(",")
sw.WriteLine(100)
sw.Write ("Joe Jones")
sw.Write (",")
sw.WriteLine (99)
sw.Close()
```

"That makes sense," Blaine said.

The Close Method

"I have a question, but not directly about the WriteLine method," Barbara said. "You said that an invisible End Of File marker is placed at the end of the file when you close the file. Can you elaborate on that a little bit?"

The End Of File marker," I said. "is an invisible mark that is automatically placed at the end of a file whenever a file opened for output or append is closed. How does a file get closed? By coding the Close method of the StreamWriter object we previously opened."

sw.Close()

"I must caution you," I continued, "to be careful with your use of the Close() method. Programmers sometimes accidentally close files they are still working on. Closing an open file is the last operation you should perform on your file. If you forget to close a file that you have opened for Output or Append mode, the possibility exists that all or some of the data you have written using the Write or WriteLine methods will be lost."

"Wow, that's severe," Steve said.

"Very severe," I agreed. "I can assure you, if you make that mistake once, you won't forget to close a file ever again."

I then told the class a story about a COBOL program I wrote many years ago that was intended to write output records to a mainframe disk file.

"This program," I said, "ran for hours and hours, and after it finished, I anxiously reviewed the contents of the output file, only to find that it was empty. After scouring through my code for several days trying to determine what was wrong, making minor modifications, and then running and rerunning the program, I suddenly realized that my program had no Close method! With no Close method, the data that my program had been writing to the output disk file was never saved. Needless to say, I have never forgotten to code a Close method since!"

"So other programming languages besides Visual Basic have Close methods?" Rhonda asked.

"Goodness, yes!" I said. "Just about everything that we're learning in this course applies equally to the other major programming languages such as C, C++, C# and Java. All of the fundamentals, such as selection structures, loops, string manipulation, and file operations, are available in other programming languages too----although not exactly the same way."

"That's great news," Steve said. "Does that mean that after this course I can apply what I've learned here to C#, C++ and Java?"

"That's right, Steve," I said. "In fact, some of the syntax—particularly with C#—is even identical. Some of the particulars of the languages might vary a little bit, but you'll find that the basics are the same. For instance, every language has an If statement---but I'm afraid I'm digressing a bit too much here."

"I have a pretty far-fetched question," Joe said. "Is there any way to see the EOF marker in a file?"

"That's not far-fetched at all, Joe" I said. "Curiosity is the sign of a great programmer. Unfortunately, with the tools available here in the classroom, we can't see the EOF marker. Notepad won't show it to us, although there may be some high-tech editors that will show you the EOF. Just remember that the EOF is really nothing special. It's just an invisible character that the Operating System uses to mark where a file ends."

There were no more questions.

"What we need now is to complete an exercise that will give you an opportunity to create a disk file of your own," I said, "and here it is."

Exercise 11-1 Create an Output Disk File

In this exercise, you'll use Visual Basic to create a disk file containing the names and grades of fictional Visual Basic students.

1. Start a new Windows Forms Application.
2. Place two text boxes on the form.
3. Change the Name properties of the two text boxes to txtName and txtGrade, respectively.
4. Place a Button control on the form and accept the default name that Visual Basic assigns.
5. Double-click on the Button control, and place the following code into its Click event procedure.

```
Private Sub Button1_Click(ByVal sender As System.Object, ByVal e
  As System.EventArgs) Handles Button1.Click
```

```
  If (txtName.Text = "") Then
    MessageBox.Show("Name must be entered")
    txtName.Focus()
    Exit Sub
  ElseIf (txtGrade.Text = "") Then
    MessageBox.Show("Grade must be entered")
    txtGrade.Focus()
    Exit Sub
End If

Dim sw As New StreamWriter("C:\VBFILES\PRACTICE\EX11-1.TXT", True)
sw.WriteLine(txtName.Text.ToUpper() + "," + txtGrade.Text)
sw.Close()
txtName.Text = ""
txtGrade.Text = ""
txtName.Focus()
End Sub
```

CAUTION: Do not include a space between the quotation marks in the 'if' statements.

6. Place this line of code at the top of the Code window.

Imports System.IO

7. Save the project—we'll be modifying it in Exercise 11-2.

8. Run the program.

9. Type **Barry** in the first text box and the number **95** in the second, then click the button. The record will be written to the file EX11-1.TXT in the \VBFILES\PRACTICE subdirectory of your hard disk.

10. Using the following table, enter the remaining five names and grades into your disk file. Don't forget to click the button after each entry.

STUDENT	GRADE
Barry	95
Al	70
Tim	100
John	85
Mary	84
Sue	65

11. Stop your program and then use Notepad to view the file. It should look like this.

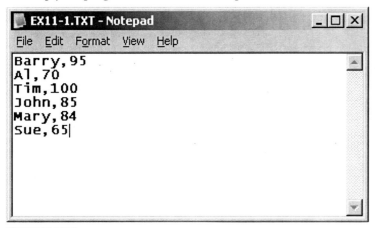

Discussion

There were no major problems with this exercise—in fact, I think everyone had a great time coding it.

"I have a couple of questions," Linda said. "First, you must remember that I'm a DOS user at heart. Anyway, while I was entering the information into the text boxes, out of habit I pressed the ENTER key and of course, nothing happened. The new record was added to the file only when I clicked the button. I was hoping there is a way that pressing the ENTER key would trigger the Click event of the Button control."

"That's a good idea," Rhonda said. "That would make data entry easier. I seem to recall discussing something like that a few weeks ago."

"You're right, Rhonda," I said. "You can designate the Button control in the AcceptButton property of the form, in which case, pressing the ENTER key does trigger the Click event of the Button control. That would produce the behavior that Linda is looking for."

"Okay, second question," Linda said. "I'm sure I must have done something wrong, but when I ran the program and began to type the student's name into the first text box, I noticed that the focus wasn't on the text box, but was on the button instead."

"You must have placed the Button control on the form before your text boxes," I said. "The initial TAB order of your controls is determined by the order in which you place the controls on the form. The exercise was written in such a way that you should have placed the text boxes on the form first, then the Button control. When you started your program, the focus should have been on the first text box you placed on the form."

"Say no more," Linda said. "That's exactly what I did. Without thinking, I placed the Button control on my form first—then placed the TextBox controls. So that's why the Button control received the focus first."

"That's right," I said. "Don't forget, you can always change the TAB order of your controls by selecting View | Tab Order from the Visual Basic menu bar."

"Essentially, we are closing the file after each record is written to the file, isn't that right?" Barbara asked. "That's not exactly the technique you used in the earlier example when you opened a file, wrote two records to it, and then closed it."

"That's a very good question," I said. "As you've seen here, writing data to a disk file is relatively easy, but it does require that we give some thought as to how we want to code it. In this exercise, each time the user wants to add a new record to the file, he or she enters information into the two text boxes, and then clicks the button. This action triggers the Click event procedure of the Button control, in which we open the file via the StreamWriter Constructor, write a record to it, and then close it. We could have written the code in such a way that when the program first begins, we open the file and then close the file when the program ends, leaving it open in the interim for the user to add as many records to the file as they want. That would be a viable alternative to the method we've chosen here. We would have placed the code to open the file in the Load event procedure of the form—and the code to close the file in the Unload event of the form."

After pausing for a moment I continued.

"Personally, I'm not a big fan of that technique," I said. "I like to open and close the file---or StreamWriter object---in the same event procedure in which the records are being written. With the other technique, there's always the possibility that the user will start the program, enter some records, and then, for whatever reason, not end the program immediately—thereby leaving the file opened. What happens if there's a power failure or the computer is accidentally turned off? All of their work could be lost if the file is never closed properly."

That explanation satisfied Barbara, and so I suggested that we take a closer look at the code.

"This first section of code," I said, "performs validation on the txtName and txtGrade text boxes, the same type of validation that we performed on the text boxes in the exercises we did last week and the week before."

```
If (txtName.Text = "") Then
  MessageBox.Show("Name must be entered")
  txtName.Focus()
  Exit Sub
ElseIf (txtGrade.Text = "") Then
  MessageBox.Show("Grade must be entered")
  txtGrade.Focus()
  Exit Sub
End If
```

"When writing data to a disk file, validation is very important. Disk files are by their nature, permanent, and the output written by your program to that disk file may become input used by another program. The last thing we want to do is write incomplete or inaccurate data to a disk file."

"If you don't mention GIGO here," Kate said, "you'll be the first computer teacher I've had who hasn't."

"GIGO?" Rhonda asked. "What is that?"

"GIGO," I said, "stands for Garbage In, Garbage Out. Basically what that means is that if you allow bad data to get into a file, sooner or later that data will be output somewhere—usually in the form of a report—with potentially embarrassing results."

I continued by explaining that this next line of code creates a StreamWriter object that opens the file EX11-1.TXT for Append mode in the \VBFILES\PRACTICE subdirectory.

Dim sw As New StreamWriter("C:\VBFILES\PRACTICE\EX11-1.TXT", True)

"The StreamWriter object can open a file for ordinary Output mode," I said, "or for Append mode, which is designated by the Boolean value true following the path and name of the file we wish to open."

"Why did we choose Append mode and not Output mode here?" Steve asked.

"We chose Append, and not Output, because of the way in which we're writing data to the file," I said. "Each time the button is clicked, we create a StreamWriter object, open the file, write the record, and then close the file. If we accepted the ordinary Output mode here, we would overwrite the existing contents of the file each time we clicked the button. Append mode tells Visual Basic that we want to open the file, and if it already exists, add records to the existing records already there."

Bob said, "I'm confused by the next line of code after the StreamWriter constructor statement."

"That would be the WriteLine method of the StreamWriter object," I said as I displayed it on the classroom projector.

sw.WriteLine(txtName.Text.ToUpper() + "," + txtGrade.Text)

"This looks confusing," I said, "but let's break it down, and I think you'll find it pretty straightforward. This is the line of code that writes the record to the file. The syntax is the name of our StreamWriter object—sw—followed by a period, followed by the word WriteLine, followed, in parentheses, by one or more expressions representing the fields that we want to write in the record. In this instance, we're writing to the file the text properties of both text boxes—separated by a comma."

"That's not what's confusing me," Bob said. "I'm confused by the ToUpper method. Why are we using that here?"

"We discussed the ToUpper method briefly two weeks ago in our class on String manipulation," I said. "The ToUpper method returns the uppercase of a string. Here we are using it to convert the name that the user enters into the txtName text box to uppercase."

"Is that something we need to do?" Kate asked.

"Converting text to uppercase like this, so that the text is capitalized in the disk file, is a matter of personal preference," I replied. "I like the consistency it provides, in that all the names in the disk file will be in the same format. Besides, I don't want names that are all in lowercase letters—which is the way some users would enter them. When those names are eventually output somewhere—and they will be—they'll look horribly sloppy."

I paused before continuing.

"This line of code may be the most crucial line of code in the program—it closes the StreamWriter object, which in turn closes the file, ensuring that anything written to it has been saved..."

sw.Close()

"Finally," I said, "this section of code clears the entries in the text boxes and sets the focus to the first text box. This is just a courtesy to the user."

txtName.Text = ""
txtGrade.Text = ""
txtName.Focus()

"Should there be a space between those quotation marks?" Mary asked.

"No, there shouldn't be a space," I said. "We want to clear the text boxes. If you include a space between the quotation marks, you'll enter a single space character into the TextBox controls, which will confuse our validation code. What you want to code here is two quotation marks with nothing in between."

I asked if there were any more questions about writing data to a disk file. There were none, and so it was time for a break. After that, we could discuss reading data from a disk file—a process that is just a bit more complicated that writing data to one.

The StreamReader Object

"The basic process of reading data from a disk file is the same as writing data," I said, after we resumed from a fifteen minute break. "Again, it requires three steps:"

1. Open the file from which you want to read data by creating a Visual Basic **StreamReader** object.

2. Read data from that file using the **ReadLine** method of the Visual Basic **StreamReader** object.

3. After you are done reading data, close the file you have opened using the **Close** method of the **StreamReader** object.

"Is the process to create a StreamReader object similar to that of creating a StreamWriter object?" Kathy asked.

"It's very similar," I said, "take a look."

Dim sr As New StreamReader("C:\VBFILES\PRACTICE\EX11-1.TXT")

"Visual Basic knows that we intend to open the file for input---bringing the information into program memory," I said, "because we are using the StreamReader object to open the file."

"And the Close method is the same too?" Ward asked.

"That's right, Ward," I said. "except that we're using the Close method of the StreamReader object, not the StreamWriter object. In fact, the only basic thing we'll do differently to read data from a disk file instead of writing data is to code a ReadLine method instead of a either a Write or WriteLine method. However, as you'll see shortly, we'll need to do so within the context of a loop, and we will run into a small complication."

The ReadLine Method

"You can think of the ReadLine method of the StreamReader object," I said, "as the reverse of the WriteLine method of the StreamWriter object we learned about earlier. The WriteLine method writes data to a disk file and the ReadLine method reads data from a disk file."

"I understand where the data goes when we write to a file," Ward said, "it goes to the file specified in the StreamWriter object's Constructor method. But where does the data from the file go to when we read it?"

"That's a wonderful question Ward," I said, "The data goes into one or more variables---and as we'll see in a few minutes, with comma delimited records, it goes into an Array. In its simplest form, with just one 'field' to a line in a file, we need to declare a string variable to hold the value we read, then execute the ReadLine method from within a while loop that continues to execute until we get to that magical End Of File marker. Presuming we had a file called THREESTOOGES.TXT that contained the names of the original Three Stooges---Moe, Larry and Curly---with each name on a separate line…"

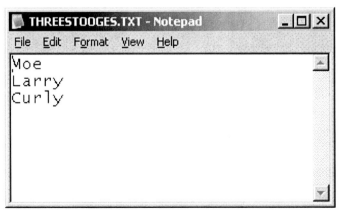

"We could use this code to read each of the names, and to display them in an Output Window. "

```
Dim sr As New StreamReader("C:\VBFILES\PRACTICE\THREESTOOGES.TXT")
Dim line As String

Do
  line = sr.ReadLine()
  If line Is Nothing Then Exit Do
  Console.WriteLine(line)
Loop

sr.Close()
```

I took a minute to create the text file, then quickly created a new a Visual Basic Windows Forms Application with a button. Placing this code in the Click event procedure of a button control, I clicked on the button, and the names of the original Three Stooges were displayed in the Output window.

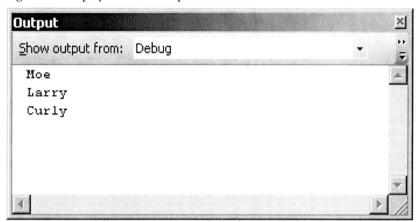

"As you can see," I said, "the ReadLine method of the StreamReader object retrieves one line at a time from the file opened by the StreamReader. When first opened, an invisible line marker points to the first line of the file. Each time we execute the ReadLine method, the value of the line is returned and placed in the String variable line---again, we could declare this variable with any name we want. As we execute the ReadLine method, the line pointer advances through the file. When the last line of the file has been read using the ReadLine method, the line pointer is advanced to the so-called End of File marker. We can detect that End Of File marker in our code by checking to see if the value of the line variable is 'Nothing'---if the return value of the ReadLine method is 'Nothing', we know that we have reached the end of the file, and we exit our DO loop with the Exit Do statement."

I gave everyone a chance to absorb this.

"Can you go over that code again Professor?" Linda said, "I don't think I understand what is happening."

"Sure thing Linda," I said. "This line opens a StreamReader object for input."

Dim sr As New StreamReader("C:\VBFILES\PRACTICE\THREESTOOGES.TXT")

"This line of code declares a String variable to store the value of the line we will read from our input file---the return value of the ReadLine method is a String---so we need a variable in which to store it..."

Dim line As String

"These next few lines of code," I said, "look complicated, but what we're doing is setting up an endless Do loop...."

Do

"...Within the body of the loop we execute the ReadLine method, whose return value is a line from our Input File..."

line = sr.ReadLine()

"...We test the value of the line variable to see if we have reached the End Of File marker. We know that we have if the value of line is Nothing, in which case we exit the Loop by executing the Exit Do statement..."

If line Is Nothing Then Exit Do

"Presuming we haven't read the End Of File marker from the input file, we then execute this line of code which writes the value of the variable line to the Console, and the Loop continues..."

Console.WriteLine(line)
Loop

"When we the Loop finally ends because we have reached the End of File marker, we close the StreamReader, and along with it, our Input file…"

sr.Close()

"I don't think we've seen that Exit Do syntax before," Linda said. "Is that a new one to us?"

"I believe you're right Linda," I said, "It's something that's quite useful if you have a Loop construction like this, whose termination is dependent upon something like an End-Of-File marker. With a Do…Loop, the responsibility for ending the loop is up to the programmer---and the only way to do that is to code a Test condition of some kind within the body of the loop, and to execute the ExitDo statement to exit the body of the loop."

After a minute of silence, Dave had a question.

"From what you've shown us here, it looks like the ReadLine method of the StreamReader object can only read one line at a time," he said, "What happens if the line contains more than one field, such as a comma delimited file we created in Exercise 11-1."

"That's a great observation, Dave," I said. "and you're right. If we have a comma delimited file, the entire line of the file will be read into a single String variable."

"Does that mean we would need to use some of the String Manipulation techniques we learned two weeks ago to separate or 'parse' the fields?" Dave asked.

"That's something we'll be covering when we learn about Arrays in two weeks," I said. "For now, why don't we take this opportunity to practice what we've just learned with an exercise of our own."

I then distributed this exercise for the class to complete.

Exercise 11-2 Reading Records from a Disk File

In this exercise, you'll read the records you wrote to the disk file in Exercise 11-1, and display their information in the Visual Basic Output window.

1. Continue working with the project from Exercise 11-1.
2. Place a second Button control on the form and accept the default name that Visual Basic assigns.
3. Double-click on the Button control and place the following code into its Click event procedure.

```
Private Sub Button2_Click(ByVal sender As System.Object, ByVal e
    As System.EventArgs) Handles Button2.Click

    Dim line As String
    Dim sr As New StreamReader("C:\VBFILES\PRACTICE\EX11-1.TXT")

    Do
        line = sr.ReadLine()
        If line Is Nothing Then Exit Do
        Console.WriteLine(line)
    Loop
    sr.Close()

End Sub
```

4. Save the project, although you won't be modifying it any further.
5. Before you run the program, use Notepad to ensure that you have only the six correctly formatted records in the file. Blank lines and empty lines at the end of your file will cause your program to bomb. Now run the program.
6. Click the second button. The program will display, in the Visual Basic Output window, the six records you wrote to the disk file \VBFILES\PRACTICE\EX11-1.TXT in Exercise 11-1.

Discussion

Only two people had a problem with the exercise---both Blaine and Linda had accidentally modified the input text file while looking at it, and inserted a blank line at the end which caused the program to bomb (exactly why we'll learn a bit later on in the course.)

Beyond that, no one seemed to have any problems with the exercise. I ran the program myself, clicked the second button, and displayed the Visual Basic Output window for all to see.

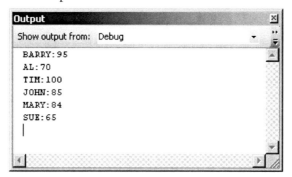

"That was really pretty easy," Ward said. "I'm more impressed than ever. Believe me, I'll be able to use this. However, I'm afraid I don't understand a thing that's going on the in the program—can you explain it?"

"I can understand that Ward," I said, "I'll be glad to explain the code---let's take a look at it now. As usual, the first we do is declare any variables we need in our program. The first one, a String variable called line, is used to store the contents of each line as it is read from our input file via the ReadLine method of the StreamReader object…"

Dim line As String

The next line of code uses the StreamReader Constructor to open the file EX11-1.TXT for Input mode in the \VBFILES\PRACTICE subdirectory."

Dim sr As New StreamReader("C:\VBFILES\PRACTICE\EX11-1.TXT")

"With these lines of code," I continued, "we set up a loop to read each line in the input file, checking the value of the variable line for the special Visual Basic value of 'Nothing', which indicates we have reached the End-Of-File marker."

Do
**   line = sr.ReadLine()**
**   If line Is Nothing Then Exit Do**
**   Console.WriteLine(line)**
Loop

"Why do we need to set up an endless loop?" Steve asked. "We know there are six records in the file."

"That's true," I said. "At this moment in time the file contains six records, but the number of records in a disk file will vary. The Do…Loop structure is a perfect tool to enable us to read an unknown number of records in a file."

"What happens to the value of the variable line when the next record is read?" Rhonda asked.

"The value is overwritten," I said. "That's why we immediately display the value of the line variable in the Visual Basic Output window."

I paused before continuing to see if there were any questions. There were none, and I went on, "And finally, this line of code closes the StreamReader object, and along with it, the opened file."

sr.Close()

There were no more questions, so I suggested that we use our newly acquired file processing skills to modify the China Shop Project to load the brands of China in the lstBrands ListBox from a disk file. I reminded everyone that currently we had the following lines of code in the Load event procedure of the China Shop form.

lstBrands.Items.Add("Corelle")   **'Add Corelle**
lstBrands.Items.Add("Farberware")   **'Add Farberwarre**
lstBrands.Items.Add("Mikasa")   **'Add Mikasa**

"There's nothing wrong with this code," I said, "except for the fact that if the China Shop decides to sell an additional brand of china, we would have to modify the program code itself. With the change to the program we're about to make, changing, adding, or deleting brands of china to be sold will be a simple matter of just updating a text file using Notepad."

I then distributed this exercise for the class to complete.

Exercise 11-3 Reading Data into the lstBrands ListBox

In this exercise, you'll modify the China Shop Project to read brands of china from a text file, and load them into the lstBrands ListBox.

1. Load up the China Shop Project.
2. Place this line of code at the top of the Code window, above the line of code that denotes the Class header for the form.

Imports System.IO

3. Use Notepad to create a file called BRANDS.TXT containing the following three records. Be careful NOT to insert any blank lines at the end of the file.

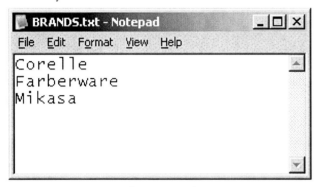

4. Save this file in the \VBFILES\CHINA subdirectory.
5. Find the Load procedure of Main, and modify it so that it looks like this.

```
Private Sub Main_Load(ByVal sender As System.Object, ByVal e
    As System.EventArgs) Handles MyBase.Load

    Dim strBrand As String
    Dim sr As New StreamReader("C:\VBFILES\CHINA\BRANDS.TXT")

    Do
        strBrand = sr.ReadLine()
        If strBrand Is Nothing Then Exit Do
            lstBrands.Items.Add(strBrand)
    Loop

    sr.Close()
End Sub
```

6. Save the China Shop Project by clicking on the Save icon on the Visual Basic toolbar.
7. Run the program. Three items should appear in the List Box, this time loaded from the disk file instead of within code.

Discussion

There were just a few problems in completing the exercise. One student placed quotation marks around the china brand names in their disk file---which meant quotation marks appeared around the brands in the lstBrands Listbox when the program started up. Another student inserted several blank lines at the end of their disk file, which resulted in blank items appearing in the lstBrands ListBox. Still another student saved their file in the wrong location. As a result, when he ran his version of the China Shop Project, the program bombed because it couldn't find the file.

All in all, though, once we made our way through these problems, everyone was very happy with the result.

Linda asked, "Is the code we see here pretty much a blueprint for reading any kind of file?"

"Any kind of text file with just one field," I said. "Remember, I promised to show you a technique that will allow you to read files where the line contains comma delimited fields---this data file contained just one 'field' per line, so it's a pretty simplistic example—but it did give you a chance to practice. I should tell you that Visual Basic can also read something called a Binary file. Binary files are files such as graphics files---files that don't have much meaning in the types of programs that we write. Binary files require a different technique---and Reader---to read. But for files that contain text data, with a single field on each line, basically we declare a String variable, create a loop to read the records until the EOF is reached, do 'something' with the data we have read, and then close the file via the close method of the StreamReader object when we encounter the EOF."

Everyone in the class seemed to be having a great time running and rerunning the China Shop Project. It was all I could do to get their attention as I began to explain the code.

"We started by declaring a single String variable," I said. "to store the contents of the lines in the file as we read them."

dim strBrand As String

"This line of code creates a StreamReader object called 'sr', which in turn opens the file BRANDS.TXT for Input."

Dim sr As New StreamReader("C:\VBFILES\CHINA\BRANDS.TXT")

"Between the Do and Loop statements, we set up a loop to read each line in the input file, checking the value of the variable line for the special Visual Basic value of 'Nothing', which indicates we have reached the End-Of-File marker."

```
Do
    line = sr.ReadLine()
    If line Is Nothing Then Exit Do
    lstBrands.Items.Add(strBrand)
Loop
```

"Remember, Nothing refers to the End Of File marker for the file opened with the StreamReader object. If the ReadLine method does not return that special character, undoubtedly the most important line of code is then executed---this one, which uses the Add method of the ListBox control to load the value of the variable strBrand into the List Box."

lstBrands.Items.Add(strBrand)

"Finally, this line of code closes the file."

sr.Close()

I asked if there were any questions, but there were none. I looked up at the clock and realized that we were done for the day.

"It's been a fun and enjoyable class," I said. "We continue to make good progress with the China Shop Project, and next week we'll learn how we can give our programs a professional and polished look by adding menus to them."

Summary

You now know how to use disk files to read and write simple data to and from files. Specifically, in this chapter, you learned that:

- You can read from and write to disk files.

- The StreamWriter or StreamReader Constructor defines the file from which you want to read data and the file to which you want to write data.

- ASCII delimited files contain a record per line, with fields separated by commas.

- Close methods---not surprisingly!---close a file that you've been either reading from or writing to.

- The ReadLine method is used to read data from a file.

- The WriteLine statement is used to write data to a file.

You learned the simple GIGO principle, which in this case amounts to always make sure that the data you write to a file is in the correct format. If you think you're working with one kind of data, but you're actually getting another, you will get strange and unusable results—and worse yet, the program reading the file may bomb.

In the next chapter, we will continue to enhance our China Shop Project's interface by adding some neat, functional menu choices that let the user adapt the interface to their own requirements.

Chapter 12---Finishing the User Interface

In this chapter, we'll finish building the user interface of the China Shop Project. By the end of this chapter it will begin to look and behave like a high-powered Visual Basic program. Follow my class as we learn how to create a Visual Basic menu structure for the China Shop Project.

Where Are We Now?

I began the class by asking everyone to tell me where they thought we stood with the China Shop Project. After a few minutes, the consensus was that the China Shop Project was functional, but fell short of the Requirements Statement we had developed during our first two weeks of the course. In comparing the Requirements Statement to the current state of the program, we noted the following deficiencies:

1. There is no menu structure.

2. There is no way for the user to turn the display of the system date and time on or off.

3. Since there is no way for the user to turn off or turn on the display of the system date and time, this preference is not being saved to the Windows Registry.

4. There is no way for the customer to change the colors of the form.

5. Since the color of the main form cannot be changed, the user's color preference is not being saved to the Windows Registry.

6. Although we are reading china brands from a disk file, inventory china prices are still hard coded and not being read from a disk file.

7. There is no way to gracefully exit the program, and doing so should require the user to enter a password.

"During today's class," I said, "we'll take care of the deficiencies numbered 1, 2, 4 and 7. We'll handle number 6 next week when we discuss arrays. Numbers 3 and 5 will be corrected in our last class. Today, let's discuss how to develop a Visual Basic menu."

Drop-Down Menus

"In Visual Basic," I said, "there are two types of menus: drop-down menus and pop-up menus, also called context menus. If you hear the term 'menu' used by itself, it usually means a drop-down menu."

In order to demonstrate exactly what I meant by a drop-down menu, I asked everyone to click on the Project menu. I did the same and my classroom projector looked like this.

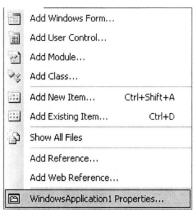

"A drop-down menu is just a standard Windows menu," I said. "A pop-up, or context menu, however, is something some of you may <u>not</u> be familiar with."

As an example of a pop-up menu, I asked everyone to open up the Visual Basic code window and to right-click their mouse within the code window. I did the same and the following pop-up or context menu was displayed.

"In Windows," I said, "a right-click of the mouse displays a pop-up menu, also called a context menu, and sometimes called a shortcut menu. The term 'context menu' applies because the particular pop-up menu displayed varies depending on where the user right-clicks their mouse."

"So if I right-click on the form," Ward said, "the pop-up menu I see will be different from the one I see if I right-click in the code window?"

"That's right," Rhonda said, turning to Ward. "When I right-click on the form, I do see a different pop-up menu."

"Also," I said, "you'll see a different pop-up menu if you right-click when your mouse pointer is over a control on the form." As a demonstration, I placed a control on my form and then right-clicked my mouse.

"Will we learn how to create pop-up menus?" Barbara asked.

"Not in this class," I said. "Today we'll be concentrating just on adding a drop-down menu to the China Shop Project. Adding pop-up menus isn't that difficult, but it is a bit more complex than a drop-down menu."

A First Look at the MenuStrip Control

"So far," I said, "whenever we have wanted to add a visual control to our user interface, we have gone to the toolbox to find it. And that's no different with creating a menu in Visual Basic— although I should tell you that prior versions of Visual Basic did not have a control for a menu in the toolbox the way Visual Basic does."

I then selected the Visual Basic MenuStrip control in the toolbox.

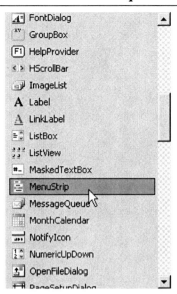

"If we double-click the MenuStrip control in the Visual Basic toolbox," I said, "the icon for the control is placed in the Visual Basic Component Tray, and the menu itself appears at the top of the form." I then double-clicked the MenuStrip control, and that's exactly what happened.

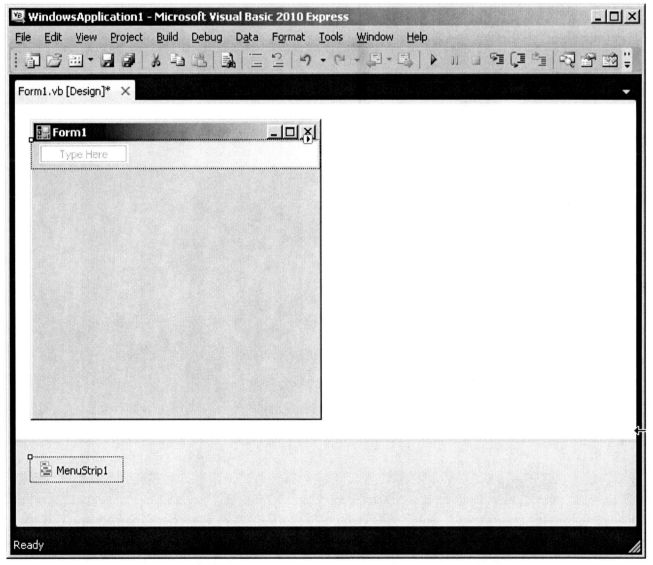

"I remember the Component Tray," Linda said. "Isn't that where the Timer and ColorDialog Controls went when we selected them for the China Shop Project?"

"That's right, Linda," I said. "Both the Timer and ColorDialog Controls went into the Component Tray—and that's also where an icon representing the MenuStrip control goes. However, the menu itself also appears at the top of the form."

"Is that what Type Here is?" Peter asked. "The menu?"

"That's right, Peter," I said. "By default, the one and only menu item of the MenuStrip control is an item captioned 'Type Here'—but we'll see how to change that in a moment."

"What do we do now?" Mary asked.

"Well," I said, "unfortunately, adding new menu items isn't nearly as easy as it should be, but if you follow my simple steps, everything will be fine. First off, there are two types of menu items that can be added to the menu: top-level menu items and submenu menu items. Top-level menu items appear at the top of the form, and submenu items appear under top-level menu items. As a demonstration, let's design a typical menu bar for a Windows program, with top-level menu items consisting of <u>F</u>ile, <u>E</u>dit, and <u>V</u>iew, along with some submenu items under File. Our first step is to change the displayed caption of our one and only menu item, currently captioned 'Type Here'. That's easy to do---all we need to do is select the menu item itself on the form and type over the text."

I did so, typing the word 'File' over 'Type here'…

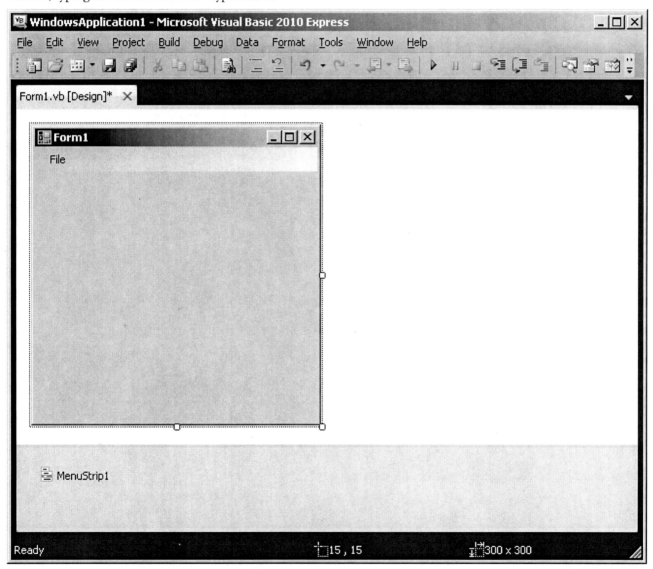

"If the MenuStrip control is a control like all other controls," Dave said, "does that mean it has Properties?"

"Dave, you read my mind," I said, "not only does the MenuStrip control show up in the Properties window, but all of the individual menu items we'll add will also show up. Let's first take a look at the menu item we just added--- File…"

I then brought up the Visual Basic Properties window (you can do this by pressing the F4 function key or selecting View | Properties window from the Visual Basic menu bar). I selected FileToolStripMenuItem in the Object list box of the Properties window.

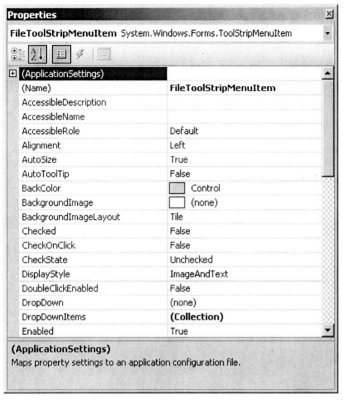

"Notice that the first menu item on the form is named FileToolStripMenuItem. When we code the China Shop Project, we'll give each menu item a meaningful name, just as we did with all of our other controls. Ordinarily, menu controls are named with the prefix 'mnu', followed by a meaningful description. Let's name this first menu item mnuFile---we can easily change the name in the Properties window."

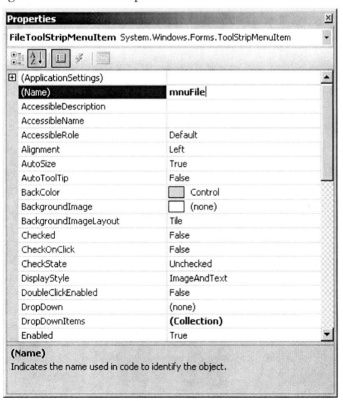

"In the same way," I continued, "if we wanted to, we can change the displayed caption of the menu item. If you remember our discussion of hot keys or access keys from earlier in the course, in order to make the File menu item accessible via the ALT-F key combination, we should change its Text property to &File."

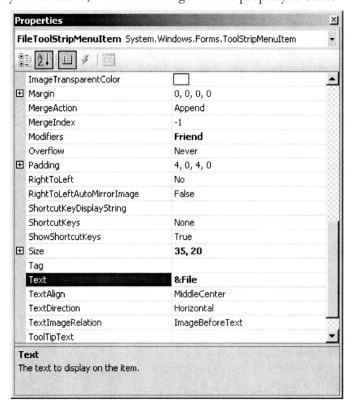

"If we take a look at our form now," I said, "we'll see that changing the Text property of the menu item has had an immediate effect on the menu on our form---notice the underline under the letter 'F.'"

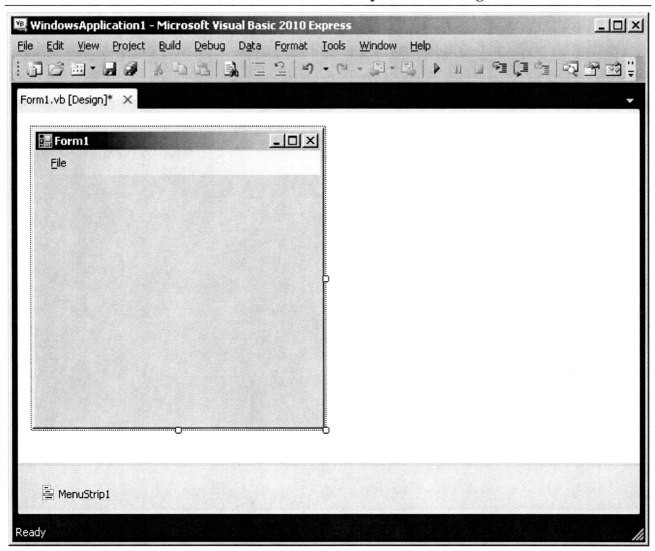

Adding Top-Level Menu Items

"Suppose we want to add another top-level menu item?" Valerie asked. "Is that difficult."

"This is where some confusion can come in," I said. "To add a top-level menu item, click the first menu item on the form. When you do, a new menu item will appear to the <u>right</u> and also below the menu item you clicked, both with 'Type Here' as the displayed caption."

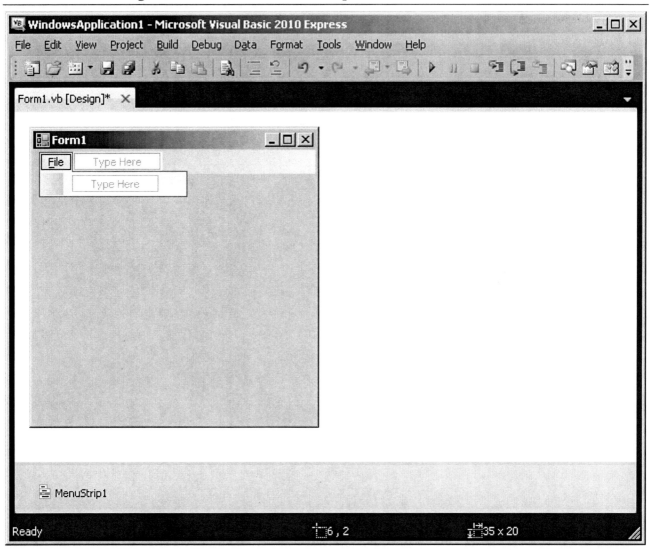

"You now have two choices," I continued, "if you want to create a top-level menu item, type the caption for the menu item into the 'Type Here' area to the right. If you want to create a submenu, type the caption for the menu item into the 'Type Here' area underneath. For instance, we want to create a menu item called Edit to the right of File. We do that by typing &Edit into the menu item to the right---we can take care of the access key right away."

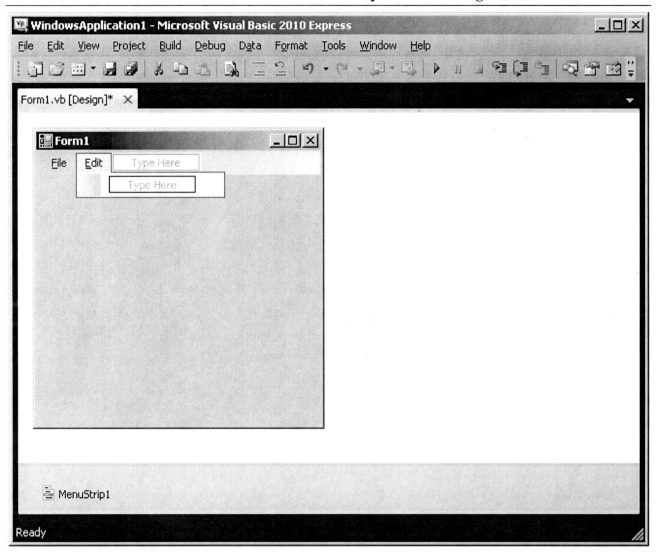

"We seem to be starting the process all over again," Dave said. "Once again, we have a menu item to the right of the existing one, and also underneath."

"That's right, Dave," I said. "We have one final top-level menu item to add, and that's for <u>View</u>. We'll do that by typing &View into the menu item caption."

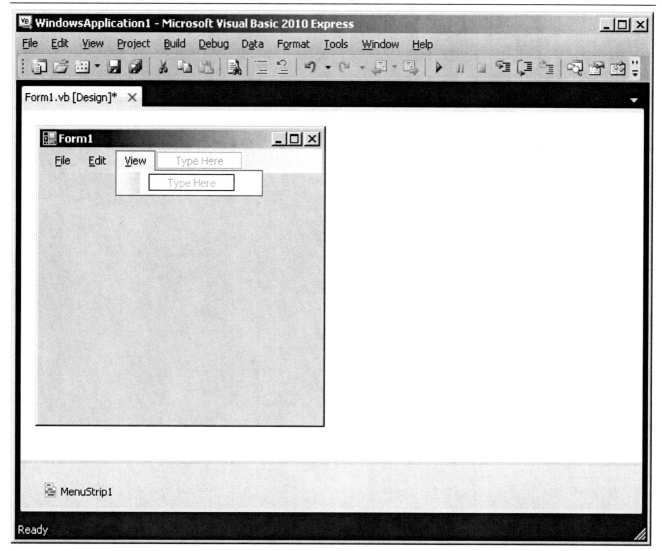

"Now what?" Rhonda said. "Don't we want to create a submenu under File? How do we get rid of that menu item to the right of View?"

"Actually, it's not really there," I said. "If you click on the form itself, all you'll see are the three top-level menu items."

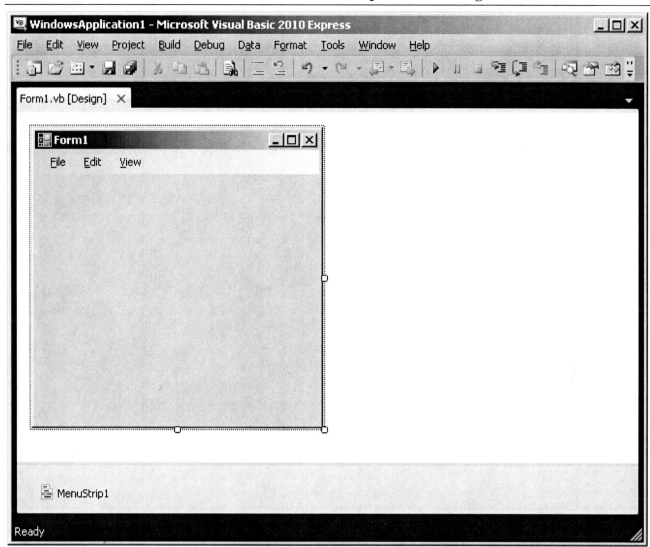

Adding Submenu Items

"I see what you mean. This is a little confusing," Barbara said.

"Don't worry," I said. "After you create a menu or two, you'll feel pretty comfortable with it. Now, to create the submenu under File, we just click on the File menu item, and once again, you'll see the now familiar menu item to the right, and the menu item underneath."

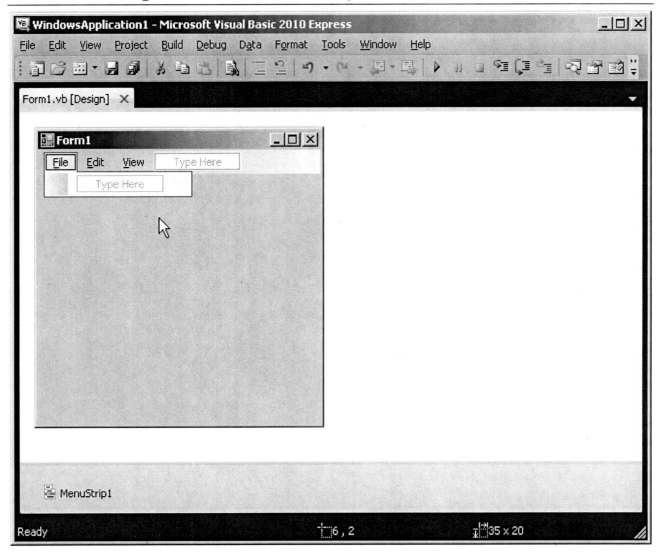

"I bet we work with the menu item underneath this time, don't we?" Rhonda asked.

"That's right, Rhonda," I said. "To create a submenu of File, that's the one we need to work with. We'll keep things simple here, by creating just two submenu items, called <u>New</u> and <u>Exit</u>. To create the New submenu item, we'll type &New into the Type Here area of the menu item."

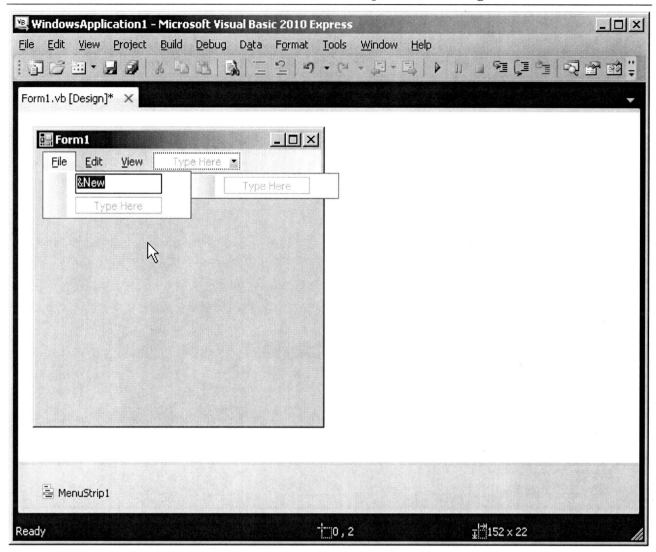

"Something that you'll almost certainly find confusing," I said, "is that as soon as you click on the form, the New submenu will seem to disappear. That's because it's a submenu, and in fact, the only time we'll be able to see it is when we run the program."

I then ran the program, clicked on the File menu item, and the New submenu appeared.

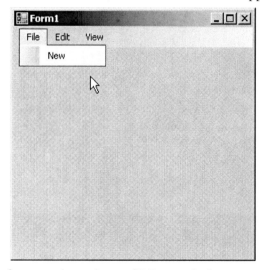

"Is it possible to create a submenu from another submenu?" Dave asked.

"Good question, Dave," I replied. "You can create menu structures that are six levels deep—that is, a menu with five submenu levels. To create a submenu from a submenu, you need to first select the submenu. As we've seen already, this will then create two new menu items, one underneath and one to the right. It's the menu item to the right that we want to work with. That's the submenu of the submenu."

> **NOTE: To create a submenu from another submenu, first select the submenu, which will create two menu items beneath and to the right of the existing menu item. Type into the menu item on the right to create the submenu's submenu.**

"Not to overstate the obvious," Linda said, "but when you ran the program and clicked on New, nothing happened. What do we need to do to make something happen when we click on a menu item?"

"It's pretty simple, really," I said, "we need to place some code in the Click event procedure of the menu item. But before I show you that, first we need to add the Exit submenu. All we need to do is type E&xit for the submenu's caption."

"Why does the ampersand go in front of the letter x and not the letter E?" Joe asked.

"We want to make the access key combination ALT-X," I said, "which is the Microsoft convention for the Exit submenu. If we had specified a caption of &Exit, we would have specified an access key combination of ALT-E."

"Of course," Joe said, "that makes perfect sense. The ampersand goes in front of the letter to be designated as the access key."

I then typed the caption for the Exit submenu as E&xit.

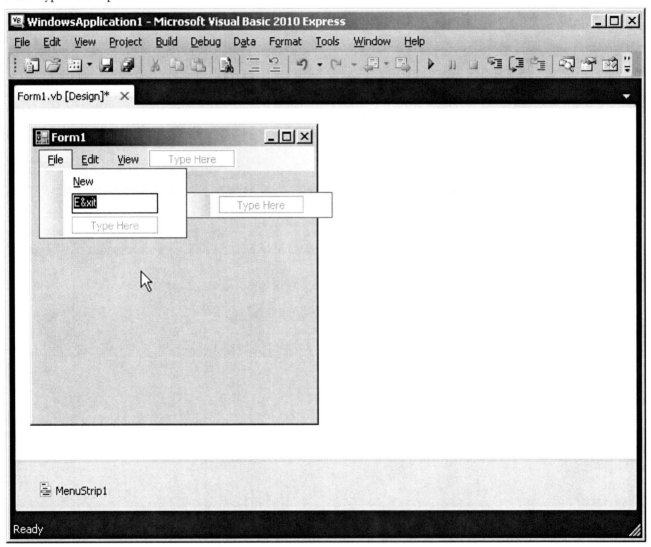

"Should we add a separator bar between File and Exit?" Dave asked.

"A separator bar?" Lou asked.

"Good point, Dave," I said. "A separator bar is the horizontal line that is sometimes placed between menu items— it's used to compartmentalize common menu items. For instance, earlier when we looked at the Visual Basic Project menu item, there was a separator bar between Add New Class and Add New Item. Typically, on a File menu, the Exit menu is separated from the other commands with a separator bar."

"How do we create a separator bar?" Kathy asked. "Do we place a dash or hyphen for the caption?"

"That's a good guess, Kathy," I replied. "In fact, that's how we did it in previous versions of Visual Basic. But in Visual Basic, we right-click on a submenu item to bring up this shortcut menu. It's important to note that the Separator bar will be inserted ABOVE the selected menu item, so if we want to insert a Separator bar between New and Exit, we need to select the Exit submenu…"

I then right-clicked on the Exit submenu item to bring up this shortcut menu.

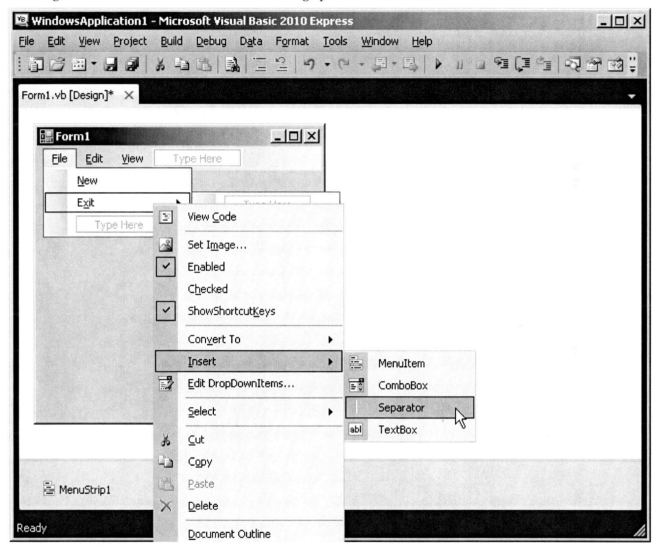

"If we select Insert Separator," I said, "we'll insert a separator bar above the Exit submenu."

I did exactly that.

"Although we can see the Separator bar in Design mode," I said, "we can see it much better if we run the program, and select File from the menu bar."

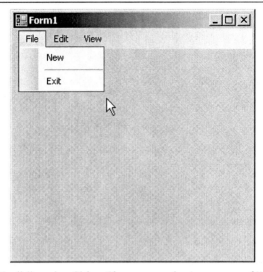

"That's great," Barbara said. "Will building the China Shop menu be just as easy?"

"Almost," I said. "The China Shop menu bar does have a few more submenus to contend with."

Deleting Menu Items

"Suppose you make a mistake while creating the menu structure?" Dave asked.

"It's fairly easy to correct any mistakes you might make," I said. "If you want to delete a menu item, just select it, then right-click your mouse and select Delete."

Inserting Menu Items

"If you forget a menu item and want to insert a new one, Visual Basic will permit you to insert a top-level menu item to the left of an existing top-level item, or to insert a submenu item above an existing submenu item. Just select the menu item you want to insert above or to the left, right-click your mouse and select Insert-Menu Item."

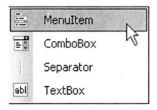

"Is it time to work on the China Shop menu?" Chuck asked.

"Not quite Chuck," I replied, "First I want to discuss just a few properties of the menu items."

MenuItem Properties

"Let's look at some of the MenuItem properties in turn." I said.

The Name Property

"Each menu item is an object just like any other object in Visual Basic," I said, "and therefore must have a unique Name property, used to identify it to Visual Basic. As with other controls in Visual Basic, it is possible to write code that manipulates the menu item's properties, so you need to establish a sound naming convention for your menu items. Microsoft conventions suggest that menu item names should begin with the prefix 'mnu'. Of course, as with other controls, the rest of the name should convey the meaning and use of the menu item. By convention, for example, the name for the top-level menu item File is mnuFile."

"What about submenu names?" Dave asked. "How should they be named?"

"Microsoft recommends including the name of the parent menu item in the submenu's name," I answered. "For example, the submenu Exit of the top-level menu File is commonly named mnuFileExit."

The Text Property

"Each menu item in a drop-down menu has a Text property," I continued. "The Text property, as we have seen, identifies the menu item to the user."

The Checked Property

"The Checked property of the menu item," I said, "permits us to display a submenu item with a check mark next to it. This property is not valid for a top-level menu. You frequently see this property used to remind the user of the options they have selected in their program. For instance, in the Microsoft Word View menu, if the user has chosen to display the Word ruler, a check mark appears next to that menu item."

CAUTION: The Checked property is not valid for a top-level menu.

I then opened Microsoft Word, displayed it on the classroom projector, and directed the class' attention to the View menu.

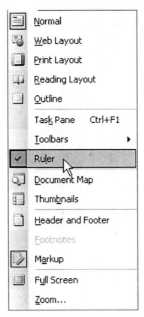

"Because I have chosen to display the Ruler in Word," I said, "that menu item has a check mark next to it. By default, the Checked property of a menu item is False, which means no check mark appears. If the value of the

Checked property is set to True, a check mark appears. We'll use this property in the China Shop Project to let the user know which date and time display preference they have chosen and is in effect."

The ShortcutKeys Property

"What's the ShortcutKeys property?" Mary asked. "When I clicked on it in the Properties window, a dialog box appeared."

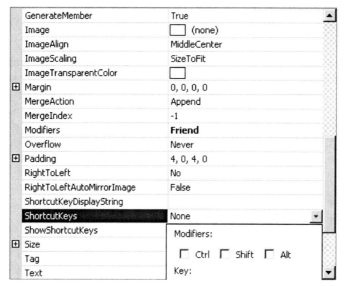

"That's right, Mary," I said. "A shortcut key, not to be confused with an access key, allows you to press a key or series of keys to trigger the Click event procedure of that menu item. The keys and key combinations that you see in the property's dialog box are the only keys permitted to be designated as shortcut keys. You can select virtually any combination of a letter with the Control key, the shift key, the Alternate key, and combinations thereof---however, the only thing you can't do is designate the same shortcut key for two different menu items."

CAUTION: Two menu items may <u>not</u> have the same shortcut key.

"How is a shortcut key different from an access key?" Steve asked.

"A shortcut key," I replied, "no matter how many levels deep within the menu structure, can be used to trigger the Click event procedure of that menu item. An access key, on the other hand, only works with visible menu items—it won't work with hidden submenus."

"Just out of curiosity," Dave said, "how many levels of submenus can we have?"

"You can have a total of five submenus nested from the top-level menu item," I replied, "or if you want to think of it in this way, a total of six menu levels."

Menu Item Events

"I believe you said there is only one event procedure associated with the menu items, the Click event procedure," Barbara said. "Is there only one Click event procedure for the entire menu or does each menu item have its own one?"

"Good question," I said. "Every menu item reacts to its own Click event, therefore each menu item, top-level or submenu, has its own Click event procedure."

"How and where do we place the code for the Click event procedure?" Rhonda asked.

"There are two ways to add the code to the Click event procedure," I said. "Probably the easiest way is to double click on the menu item in Design mode. That will open the code window for the Click event procedure of that particular menu item. You can also find the event procedure for the menu item by opening the code window as you normally would and then selecting it using the object list box and procedure list box of the code window. We'll see how that works in just a few minutes."

There were no more questions about the menu control, and so, after a short break, I suggested that at this point it would be a good idea for everyone to begin coding the menu for the China Shop Project.

Exercise 12-1 Create the Menu for the China Shop Project

In this exercise, you'll create the menu for the China Shop Project.

1. Load the China Shop Project.
2. Select the MenuStrip control in the Visual Basic toolbox and double-click it to place it on the Visual Basic System Tray. An initial menu item captioned "Type Here" should also appear on your form.

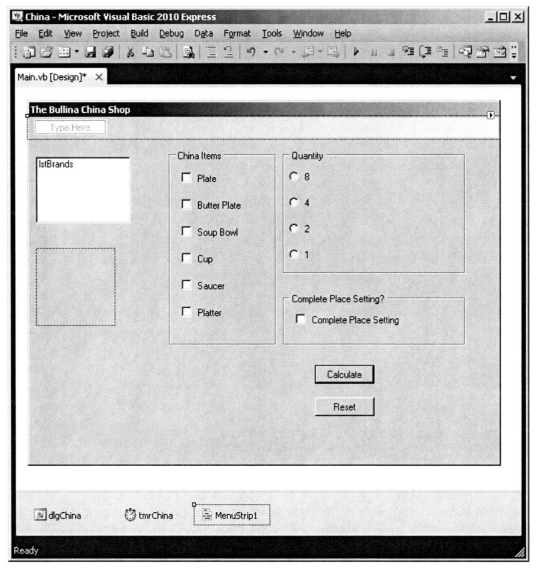

3. Replace "Type Here" with **&File** to change the Text property of this menu item. This will designate the letter F as the access key for this menu item. Your form (and its menu) should look like this.

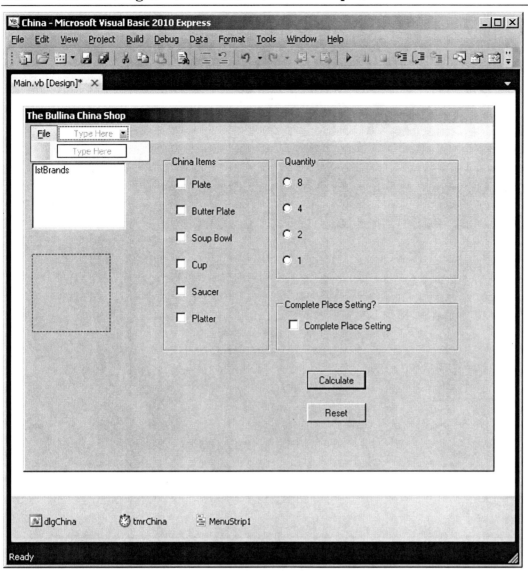

4. Display the Properties window for this menu item, and change its Name property (most likely named FileToolStripMenuItem) to mnuFile.

> **CAUTION: Because of the way that multiple menu items appear on the form when designing a menu, be very careful when changing the names of your menu items to ensure that you are changing the correct control. Verify this by checking its Text property.**

5. The next menu item we want to add is the Exit submenu under File. Click underneath the File menu item, and Replace "Type Here" with **E&xit** to change the Text property of this menu item. This will designate the letter x as the access key for this menu item.

6. Display the Properties window for this menu item, and change its Name property to **mnuFileExit.** Double-check the Text property of this menu item (it should read "E&xit") to be sure you are changing the Name property of the correct item.

7. We now want to insert a Separator Bar ABOVE the Exit menu Item. Select the Exit menu item and right-click your mouse to bring up the shortcut menu.

8. Select Insert Separator to insert a separator bar above it, between File and Exit.

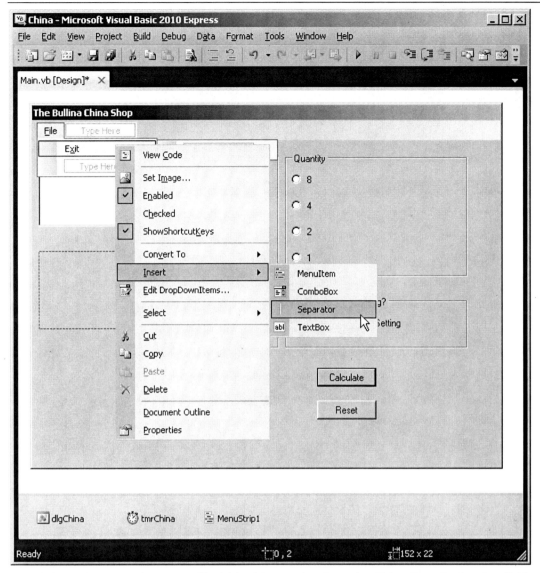

9. This is the last menu item we will add in this exercise. Save the China Shop Project by clicking the Save icon on the toolbar.

10. Run the program. You should have a menu with one top-level menu called File. If you click on the File menu item, you should see the Exit submenu.

11. You might also want to experiment with the access keys. At this point, clicking on the menu items doesn't do anything—but don't worry, we'll get to that in just a few moments.

Discussion

Prior to the exercise, I had decided to break the process of creating the China Shop menu into two separate exercises so that I could better check on everyone's progress. There were several minor problems, but mainly it was just a matter of getting accustomed to working with the MenuStrip control and the menu items. With no major problems, we moved on to the next exercise.

Exercise 12-2 Completing the China Shop Menu

In this exercise, you'll complete the China Shop menu.

1. If the China Shop program is still running, stop it now.

2. We now want to add a second top-level menu called Preferences. To do that, click on the existing top-level menu item called File. Two menu items will appear, to the right and below File.

3. Select the menu item to the right of File, and replace "Type Here" with **&Preferences** to change the Text property of this menu item. This will designate the letter P as the access key for this menu item.

4. Display the Properties window for this menu item, and change its Name property to **mnuPreferences**. Double-check the Text property of this menu item (it should read "Preferences") to be sure you are changing the Name

property of the correct item.

5. Select the menu item beneath the Preferences menu item to create the first submenu item under Preferences (you may need to click on the Preference menu item to see it) and replace "Type Here" with **Date and Time On**. Your form (and its menu) should look like this.

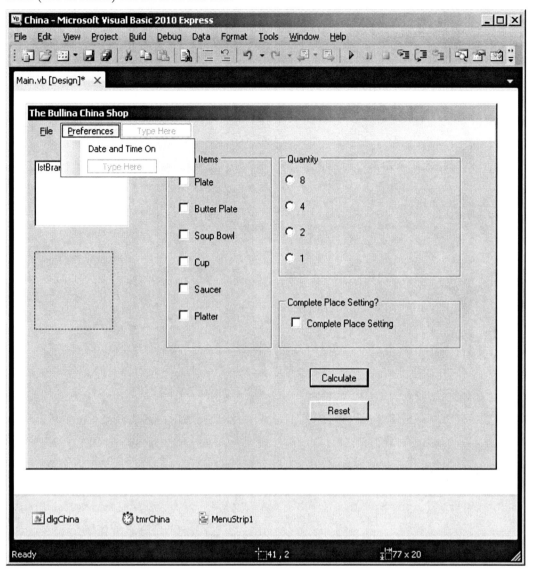

6. Display the Properties window for this menu item, and change its Name property to **mnuPreferencesDateAndTimeOn**. Double-check the Text property of this menu item (it should read "Date and Time On") to be sure you are changing the Name property of the correct item.

7. On your own, complete the remainder of the menu using the following table as your guide. Included in the table are the menu items we've already completed. Note that both Custom and Default are submenus of a submenu (Custom is a submenu of Colors which is a submenu of Preferences). Be careful with these—remember, to make a submenu from a submenu, click on the submenu and two new menu items will appear, one beneath and one to the right. The menu item to the right is the submenu of the submenu.

Caption (Text Property)	Name	Submenu?	Parent
&File	mnuFile	No	
- (Separator Bar)	mnuDash1	No	
E&Xit	mnuFileExit	Yes	mnuFile
&Preferences	mnuPreferences	No	

Date and Time On	mnuPreferencesDateAndTimeOn	Yes	mnuPreferences
Date and Time Off	mnuPreferencesDateAndTimeOff	Yes	mnuPreferences
&Colors	mnuPreferencesColors	Yes	mnuPreferences
Custom	mnuColorsCustom	Yes	mnuPreferencesColors
Default	mnuColorsDefault	Yes	mnuPreferencesColors

8. When you have finished, your form (and its menu) should look like this.

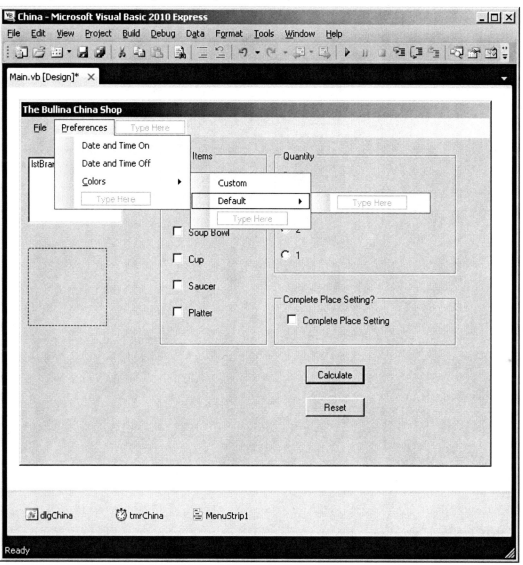

9. If anything is wrong, you can adjust the properties of any of the menu items using the Properties window. If you need to delete or insert menu items, you can do that also.

10. Check the Properties window to determine if you have any extra menu items on your form. This can easily happen while you are placing menu items on your form. If you do, select them with your mouse, right-click and select Delete to delete them.

11. Save the China Shop Project by clicking the Save icon on the toolbar.

12. Run the program to verify the menu structure. At runtime, your form (and its menu) should look like this.

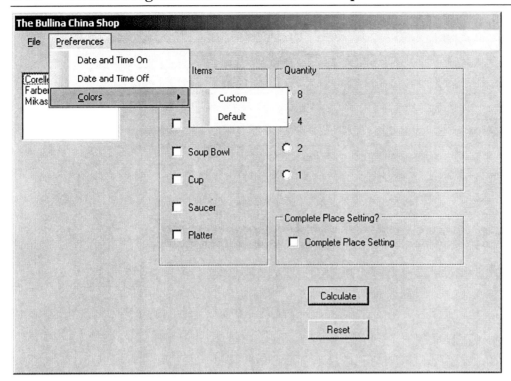

13. Remember, at this point, if you click on the menu items, nothing appears to happen, but it won't be long before we add code to the menu items to take care of that.

Discussion

The class had a few problems creating the menu structure. Creating menus with Visual Basic is not nearly as easy as it was with earlier versions, but once the students overcame their fear of hurting something, and started creating their menus with a little bit more confidence, the exercise proceeded smoothly. It's relatively easy to fix things that go wrong when creating menus. You can bring up the Properties window to change Text and Name properties, select existing menu items to delete them, and insert new menu items between them.

Rhonda discovered that there's no easy way to designate a menu item as a submenu item once it's on the form. She accidentally created each of her menu items as top-level menu items. To correct the problem, she needed to delete the menu items, then repeat some steps, but she soon corrected the problem. It was now time to move on to placing code in the Click event procedures of the menu items to make them functional.

Coding the Menu Item Controls

It had been a pretty busy morning, and I asked everyone to take a ten-minute break. When my students returned, I told them that we would spend the remainder of the class completing a series of exercises in which we would place code in the Click event procedures of the menu items. I could tell they were excited at the prospect.

"Before we start to code the Click event procedures for our menu items," I said, "we need to declare two Form-level variables."

"We've already declared a form-level variable if I remember correctly," Kate said.

"That's right, Kate" I said. "We added a form-level variable called m_intQuantity to the Declarations section of our form a few weeks ago."

NOTE: m_intQuantity was declared in Chapter 8, Exercise 8-6.

"Remember, a module-level variable is one that can be seen from any procedure on our form. Now we need to declare two additional module-level variables: one to store the user's color preference and the other to store the user's date and time display preference."

Exercise 12-3 Declare Two Form-Level Variables

In this exercise, you'll declare two form-level variables in the Declarations section of the form module.

1. If the China Shop Project is running, stop it now.
2. Place the following code in the Declarations section of the form, right after the form-level variable declaration of

the variable m_intQuantity. When you are done, you should have all three variables declared, right above the Public Sub New procedure.

Private m_intQuantity as Integer
Private m_intBackColor As Integer
Private m_blnDateDisplay As Boolean

3. Save the China Shop Project by clicking the Save icon on the toolbar.

Discussion

No one seemed to have any problems completing the exercise.

"I know we've covered this," Ward said, "but what does the m prefix signify?"

"The m prefix signifies that this is a variable declared in the Declarations section of a form," I said.

There were no more questions, so I continued, "We'll see shortly how these variables are used, but first, let's code the Click event procedure of the Exit menu item."

I then distributed the following exercise.

Exercise 12-4 Add Code to the Click Event Procedure of mnuFileExit

In this exercise, you'll add code to the Click event procedure of the menu item mnuFileExit.

1. If the China Shop Project is still running, stop it now.
2. We want to place code in the Click event procedure of mnuFileExit. There are two ways to do this. In Design mode, you can select the form's File | Exit menu item, then double-click on it, and the Visual Basic code window for the Click event procedure of mnuFileExit will open. You can also simply open the Visual Basic code window and, using the Class Name and Method Name list boxes, select the Click event procedure of mnuFileExit that way. Depending on which method you use, the Procedure header for the event procedure will be slightly different, but for our purposes, this won't be a problem. If you use the first method, the procedure header will read "Private." Using the second method, the procedure header will read "Protected."
3. Place the following code in the Click event procedure of mnuFileExit.

```
Private Sub mnuFileExit_Click(ByVal sender As Object, _
   ByVal e As System.EventArgs) Handles mnuFileExit.Click

Dim strResponse As String

strResponse = InputBox ("Enter a password in order to exit the program",  "Exit the Program?")

If strResponse = "061883" Then
   MessageBox.Show("Thank you for using the China Shop Program!")
   Me.Close()
Else
   MessageBox.Show("The password is not correct!")
End If

End Sub
```

4. Save the China Shop Project by clicking the Save icon on the toolbar.
5. Run the program and select File | Exit from the China Shop's menu. A dialog box will be displayed prompting you for a password.

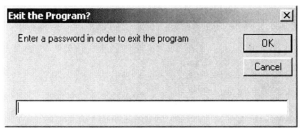

6. Enter an incorrect password; this can be anything except 061883. A message will be displayed telling you that the password is incorrect.

7. Enter the correct password, 061883, and a message will be displayed thanking you for using the China Shop program. Click the OK button, and the program will then end.

Discussion

In contrast to the last few exercises, there were quite a few questions at the conclusion of this one.

"In this exercise," I said, "we placed code in the Click event procedure of the Exit submenu which will prompt the user for a password and, provided the correct password is entered, end the program. Prompting for a password is a good idea, particularly in a kiosk-style application, where invariably a user will either accidentally or intentionally try to exit the program."

I continued by explaining that there were two new Visual Basic statements introduced in this code, the Close statement and the InputBox function.

"Let's examine the InputBox function first," I said. "The InputBox function is similar to a MessageBox.Show function in that it displays a dialog box containing an OK and a Cancel button. Unlike the MessageBox.Show function, which is used only to display a message, the InputBox function has the ability to accept a response from the user via the text box located right in the middle of the dialog box. The user's entry in the text box is then returned to the event procedure that called it via a return value, and that return value can be stored in a variable—which is exactly what we did here."

"Is that why we declared the variable strResponse?" Ward asked.

Dim strResponse As String

"Yes," I replied, "we declared that variable because we wanted to store the user's response in a variable so that we could examine it later." I continued by saying that this is the line of code that triggers the display of the input box.

strResponse = InputBox ("Enter a password in order to exit the program", "Exit the Program?")

"The InputBox function can accept up to seven arguments. We used just two of them here. The first argument is the Prompt argument, which specifies the value prompt that is displayed in the dialog box. The second argument is the Title argument, and that specifies the caption for the Title bar to be displayed in the InputBox dialog box."

"What happens after the user makes an entry in the text box and clicks OK?" Blaine asked.

"At that point," I answered, "whatever entry the user makes is returned via the InputBox function's return value to the variable strResponse. We then use an If statement to determine if the password the user has entered is correct."

```
If strResponse = "061883" Then
   MessageBox.Show("Thank you for using the China Shop Program!")
   Me.Close()
Else
   MessageBox.Show("The password is not correct!")
End If

End Sub
```

"Here we're looking for the value 061883 as the correct password," I said. "If the value of strResponse is equal to that value, we display a message thanking the user for using the China Shop program and then use the Close statement to close the China Shop form. If, however, the password the user entered is incorrect, we display a message telling the user they have entered an incorrect password, the event procedure ends, and the program continues running."

"What does Me refer to?" Rhonda asked.

"Me means the current form," I said. "It's a frequently used shortcut referring to the current form. I used it here so you would become familiar with it. I can guarantee that you'll see Me sometime in the future when you're reading code other programmers have written. Programmers love shortcuts, and Me is shorter and quicker to type than an actual form name."

"Does closing the China Shop form end the program?" Linda asked.

"Good point, Linda," I said. "We don't discuss multiple form projects in this class, but in any Visual Basic program, when the last open form in a Visual Basic project is closed, the program ends."

I concluded our discussion of the InputBox function by stating that it does have some disadvantages.

- You can only use the InputBox function to accept a single piece of information from the user. For instance, you can ask the user to provide their name using an input box, but you cannot use it to accept both their name and age at the same time.

- You cannot perform validation on the entry the user makes in the text box until the user presses the ENTER key and their entry is stored in the variable you have declared to hold the return value of the function. This is in contrast to the validation capability that exists by using the KeyPress event of the TextBox control.

- There is no PasswordChar property of the InputBox as there is with the TextBox control. The PasswordChar property of the TextBox control allows you to echo back a character, such as an asterisk, while the user is making an entry in the text box. The InputBox has no such capability.

- The InputBox is limited to an OK and a Cancel button, unlike the MessageBox.Show function which has the capability to display a wider range of buttons.

"What's a PasswordChar property?" Chuck asked.

"The PasswordChar property allows you to mask the user's entry into a TextBox control," I said. "For instance, you can set the PasswordChar property of a TextBox control to an asterisk—that way, anything the user enters into a text box will be displayed as an asterisk. The problem with an input box is that it doesn't support that property. If you ask the user to enter a password, as we did here, anyone looking over the user's shoulder will be able to see the password entered into the input box."

"What's the alternative to using the InputBox function?" Dave asked.

"You could add another form to your project, and use it to simulate the behavior of an input box by placing a text box on it along with button. With your own form, you can overcome the deficiencies of the InputBox. As you can imagine, some programmers simply don't bother. It's easier to use the InputBox function."

I asked if there were any other questions.

"Isn't embedding the password in the code like this a bad idea?" Linda asked. "Suppose Mr. Bullina wants to change the password after we've installed the program in the China Shop?"

"You're right, Linda," I said. "Embedding the password in our code like this isn't the greatest idea, but for now, I want to keep things as simple as possible. We could certainly think of alternatives to this approach, such as creating another disk file containing the password for the China Shop, but that would be one more file for the China Shop staff to manage. Let's agree to look at this as a future enhancement—perhaps in our database course. I'm sure Mr. Bullina will want us to review how the program is working after a few months of operation as part of Phase 6 of the SDLC."

"What's the significance of the password?" Rhonda asked. "Does 061883 mean anything?"

"A little mystery is a good thing," I said, smiling.

I then distributed this exercise for the class to complete.

Exercise 12-5 Add Code to the Tick Event Procedure of tmrChina

In this exercise, you'll add code to the Tick event procedure of the Timer control.

1. If the China Shop Project is still running, stop it now.

2. We want to place code in the Tick event procedure of tmrChina. Using the technique of your choice, place the following code into its Tick event procedure.

```
Private Sub tmrChina_Tick(ByVal sender As Object, _
  ByVal e As System.EventArgs) Handles tmrChina.Tick
```

lblDateAndTime.Text = CStr(Now)

End Sub

3. Save the China Shop Project by clicking the Save icon on the toolbar.

4. Run the program. The date and time should be displayed in the Label control's caption in the upper-right portion of the China Shop form.

Discussion

I ran the program myself and, sure enough, the date and time were now displayed.

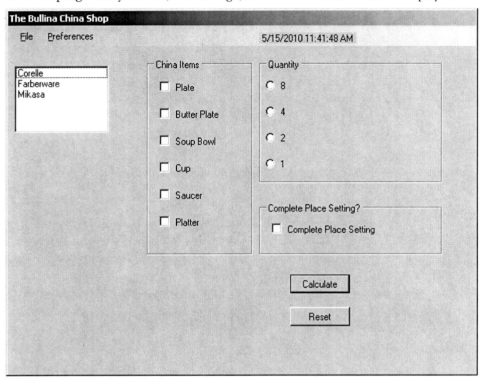

"I don't see a date and time," Ward said.

I took a quick walk over to Ward's workstation and we discovered that while the Interval property of the Timer control was properly set at 1000, the Enabled property of the Timer control was set to False.

"By default," I said, "the Interval property of the Timer control is 0, which means that the Tick event is never triggered. When we placed the Timer control on the form, we set it to 1000, which equates to 1000 milliseconds, which is one second. The Timer control's Enabled property must also be set to True in order for its Tick event procedure to be triggered."

"Can you explain this code?" Lou asked.

"Sure," I replied. "This single line of code takes the value of the system variable Now, which is your PC's date and time, and assigns it to the Text property of the Label control lblDateAndTime. Now returns a date type return value, so we must use the CStr function to convert that value to a String prior to assigning it to the Text property of the Label control."

lblDateAndTime.Text = CStr(Now)

"What makes the date and time display change?" Steve said.

"Because we set the Interval property of the Timer control to 1000," I said, "the Tick event is triggered every second. Each time it's triggered, the code in the Tick event procedure executes, assigning the current value of Now—the current date and time—to the label's Text property."

I waited for questions, but there were none.

"Now that we have the date and time displayed," I said, "let's add code to the menu items that determine whether the user wants the date and time to be displayed."

Exercise 12-6 The Click Event Procedure of mnuPreferencesDateAndTimeOff

In this exercise, you'll place code in the Click event procedure of mnuPreferencesDateAndTimeOff to disable the display of the date and time in the lblDateAndTime Label control.

1. If the China Shop Project is still running, stop it now.
2. We want to place code in the Click event procedure of mnuPreferencesDateAndTimeOff. Using the technique of your choice, place the following code into its Click event procedure.

Private Sub mnuPreferencesDateAndTimeOff_Click (ByVal sender As Object, _
  ByVal e As System.EventArgs) Handles mnuPreferencesDateAndTimeOff.Click

mnuPreferencesDateAndTimeOff.Checked = True
mnuPreferencesDateAndTimeOn.Checked = False
tmrChina.Enabled = False
lblDateAndTime.Visible = False
m_blnDateDisplay = False

End Sub

3. Save the China Shop Project by clicking the Save icon on the toolbar.
4. Run the program. Select Preferences | Date And Time Off from the menu. When you do so, the date and time will no longer be displayed on the form. In addition, a check mark will be displayed next to the menu item in the Preferences menu. Unfortunately, at this time, selecting Preferences | Date And Time On will not redisplay the date and time (not until you complete the next exercise anyway!).

Discussion

Many of the students seemed truly impressed with the bells and whistles we were adding to the China Shop Project. We had only one problem with the exercise. Several students accidentally placed the code into the mnuPreferencesDateAndTimeOn Click event procedure instead of mnuPreferencesDateAndTimeOff. A quick cut and paste operation took care of that problem.

I ran the program myself and selected Date And Time Off from the Preferences menu. As promised, there was no longer a date and time display, but perhaps most impressive to everyone was the check mark next to Date And Time Off alerting the user to that fact.

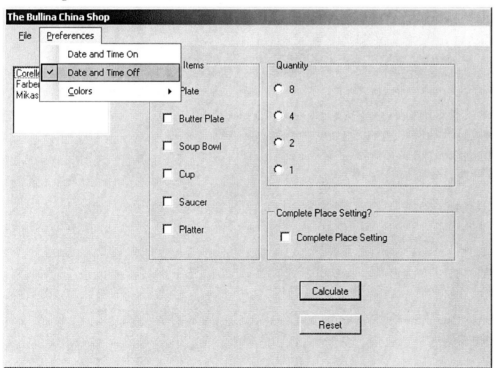

"Let me explain this code," I said. "The first thing we did here was to update the Checked properties of mnuPreferencesDateAndTimeOff and mnuPreferencesDateAndTimeOn. Remember, if the Checked property of a menu item is set to True, that menu item will have a check mark displayed next to its caption. When the user decides they do not want the date and time displayed, it makes sense to place a check mark next to the Date And Time Off menu item to remind them of that fact. Conversely, we also remove the check mark from the Date And Time On menu item by setting its Checked property to False."

mnuPreferencesDateAndTimeOff.Checked = True
mnuPreferencesDateAndTimeOn.Checked = False

"Most importantly, we also need to stop the display of the date and time," I said. "There are a number of ways we could do this. For instance, we could have made the Label control that is used to display the date and time invisible. We could also have disabled the Timer control or set its Interval property to 0. The most thorough way, from my point of view, is to disable the Timer control and also make the Label control invisible."

tmrChina.Enabled = False
lblDateAndTime.Visible = False

"By setting the Enabled property of the Timer control to False," I said, "we stop the Tick event from triggering, which prevents the code in the event procedure from executing. Now, if that's all we had done, something—the last date and time displayed—would still be visible in the label's caption. For that reason, we also had to make the Label control invisible by setting its Visible property to False."

"Why didn't we just make the Label control invisible and not worry about the Timer control?" Steve asked.

"It wouldn't be a great use of our system resources to have the Tick event triggering unnecessarily every second," I replied.

"What about the update of the variable m_blnDateDisplay?" Mary asked.

"You're right, Mary," I said. "We set the form-level variable m_ blnDateDisplay to False."

m_blnDateDisplay = False

"We'll see the importance of this variable later," I said. "We'll use this variable when the China Shop is loaded to determine the initial setting of the date and time display, and we'll also use it when we save the user's preferences to the Windows Registry." I waited for more questions, but there were none. "Now let's code the Click event procedure for mnuPreferencesDateAndTimeOn."

Exercise 12-7 Coding mnuPreferencesDateAndTimeOn's Click Event Procedure

In this exercise, you'll place code in the Click event procedure of mnuPreferencesDateAndTimeOn to enable the display of the date and time in the lblDateAndTime Label control.

1. If the China Shop Project is still running, stop it now.
2. We want to place code in the Click event procedure of mnuPreferencesDateAndTimeOn. Using the technique of your choice, place the following code into its Click event procedure.

```
Private Sub mnuPreferencesDateAndTimeOn_Click (ByVal sender As Object, _
    ByVal e As System.EventArgs) Handles mnuPreferencesDateAndTimeOn.Click

mnuPreferencesDateAndTimeOff.Checked = False
mnuPreferencesDateAndTimeOn.Checked = True
tmrChina.Enabled = True
lblDateAndTime.Visible = True
m_blnDateDisplay = True

End Sub
```

3. Save the China Shop Project by clicking the Save icon on the toolbar.
4. Run the program and select Preferences | Date And Time Off from the menu to turn off the display of the date and time.
5. Now select Preferences | Date And Time On. When you do, the date and time will be displayed again. In addition, a check mark will be displayed next to the Date And Time On menu item.

Discussion

Again, everyone seemed to be pretty impressed with the progress they were making enhancing the user interface.

"I'm confused!" Rhonda said. "When we started the program, why was the date and time still being displayed? At the end of the previous exercise, we had turned it off. Why didn't the program remember that?"

"In short," I answered, "because we haven't built that functionality into the program yet. Eventually, we'll save the value of the variable m_blnDateDisplay to the Windows Registry, and then read that value when our program starts up. Until then, our program isn't smart enough to remember the user's preferred settings from one running of the program to the next, but I guarantee we'll take care of that in our last class. For now though, our program will start with the date and time displayed." Rhonda and the rest of the class seemed satisfied with that explanation. "This code is very similar to the code that turns off the display of the date and time," I continued. "As we did with the code in the mnuPreferencesDateAndTimeOff Click event procedure, we update both the Checked properties of mnuPreferencesDateAndTimeOff and mnuPreferencesDateAndTimeOn. This time, however, we place a check mark next to the Date And Time On caption and remove the check mark from the Date And Time Off menu item."

mnuPreferencesDateAndTimeOff.Checked = False
mnuPreferencesDateAndTimeOn.Checked = True

"We had previously turned off the display of the date and time by disabling the Timer control and making the lblDateAndTime Label control invisible, so we reverse those actions with this code," I explained.

tmrChina.Enabled = True
lblDateAndTime.Visible = True

"Finally, we set the form-level variable m_blnDateDisplay to True."

m_blnDateDisplay = True

I asked if there were any questions about the menu items pertaining to the date and time display. There were none, so we began to discuss changing colors of the form. I distributed the following exercise.

Exercise 12-8 The Click Event Procedure of mnuColorsCustom

In this exercise, you'll modify the Click event procedure of the mnuColorsCustom menu item to display the ColorDialog box and to change the BackColor property of the form to match the user's selection.

1. If the China Shop Project is still running, stop it now.
2. We want to place code in the Click event procedure of mnuColorsCustom. Using the technique of your choice, place the following code into its Click event procedure.

```
Private Sub mnuColorsCustom_Click (ByVal sender As System.Object, _
   ByVal e As System.EventArgs) Handles mnuColorsCustom.Click

dlgChina.ShowDialog()
Me.BackColor = dlgChina.Color
m_intBackColor = dlgChina.Color.ToARGB

End Sub
```

3. Save the China Shop Project by clicking the Save icon on the toolbar.
4. Run the program. Select Preferences | Colors | Custom from the menu, and the ColorDialog box will be displayed. Select a color and click OK. The background color of the form will change.

Discussion

I immediately ran the program myself and selected Preferences | Colors | Custom from the main menu. The following dialog box was displayed.

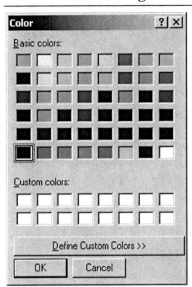

I selected one of the colors from the ColorDialog box and the color of the form changed. "Let's take a look at this code," I said. "This line of code is all it takes to display the ColorDialog box of our ColorDialog Control."

dlgChina.ShowDialog()

"The ShowDialog method of the ColorDialog Control displays the ColorDialog box," I explained. "Once the user has made a selection of a color and clicked OK, that color selection is stored as a Visual Basic Color object referenced in the ColorDialog Control's Color property."

"Color object?" Linda asked.

"That's right, Linda," I said. "In Visual Basic, Color is a special object—much like Date is a special data type. It can make working with colors a little tricky, but stick with me, you'll be fine. Once we have the Color object stored in the Color property of the ColorDialog box, all we need to do is set the BackColor property of our form equal to that Color object, like this."

Me.BackColor = dlgChina.Color

"There's that Me reference again," Rhonda said. "That just means the current form, is that right?"

"That's right, Rhonda," I replied.

Dave asked, "Can we presume from the fact that we directly assigned the Color property of the ColorDialog Control to the form's BackColor property that the BackColor property of the form is also a Color object?"

"Excellent analysis, Dave," I said, "and you're right. If the BackColor property of the form was not a Color object data type, we would have had to perform a data conversion—which in fact is what we do with this line of code."

m_intBackColor = dlgChina.Color.ToARGB

"Here we're setting the form-level variable m_intBackColor equal to the new value of the BackColor property of the form. But because ultimately we will store this value in the Windows Registry—which doesn't support Color object types—we first need to convert the Color object data type to an Integer. We can do that by using the ToARGB function of the Color Object. In fact, any Visual Basic object that is of the Color family supports this function."

"This is beginning to sound suspiciously like inheritance in C++ and Java," Dave said.

"Right again, Dave," I said. "Visual Basic is much more object-oriented than its predecessors. In fact, later on in the course you'll see that we'll create a Color object of our own and use its derived FromARGB method to set the BackColor property of the form equal to the user's preferred color as found in the Windows Registry—but more on that later."

"So at this point, if we change the color of the form, stop the program, and then run it again, will the color will go back to that drab gray color?" Ward asked.

"That's right," I said. "The user's preferred color won't be seen at startup until we save the color in the Windows Registry—via the m_intBackColor variable—and then write code to read that value when the program starts up."

"What happens if the user clicks the Cancel button instead of the OK button?" Joe asked. "I just did that and my form turned black."

"That's an excellent point, Joe," I said. "Unfortunately, the default value of the Color object of the ColorDialog Control is black. So if the user displays the ColorDialog box, but instead of making a selection of a color, they click on the Cancel button, the BackColor of the form is set to the default color of the ColorDialog Control, which is black."

"Is there anything we can do about this?" Mary asked. "Is there a way to determine if the user clicked Cancel instead of OK?"

"As a matter of fact there is, Mary," I said. "The ShowDialog method of the ColorDialog Control is actually a function. In Visual Basic—and other programming languages as well—a function returns a value. It just so happens that the return value of the ShowDialog method is a signal to let the programmer know if the user clicked OK or Cancel. If the user clicks OK, the return value will be 1. If the user clicks Cancel, the return value will be 2."

"So all we have to do," Dave said, "is use an If statement to determine what the return value of the ShowDialog function is."

"That's right, Dave," I replied, "and if it's a value of 2, we can bypass the rest of the code that ordinarily would be used to change the color of the form."

"Did you say 1 or 2 means the user clicked the Cancel button?" Linda asked. "That's hard to remember."

"We're fortunate in that instead of looking for these hard to remember values, we can instead refer to those values through the use of something called an enum—which is short for enumerated list," I answered. "All of the return values of the dialog boxes in Visual Basic are part of this enumerated list, so we can look for the return value DialogBox.Cancel instead."

"That is easier, isn't it?" Ward said. "I'm all for that! So what should our code look like to handle this problem with the Cancel button?"

"I just happen to have an exercise that will lead you through it," I said. I then distributed this exercise for the class to complete to handle the Cancel button problem.

Exercise 12-9 Correct the Click Event Procedure of mnuColorsCustom to Handle the Cancel Button

In this exercise, you'll modify the Click event procedure of the mnuColorsCustom menu item to display the ColorDialog box—and to handle the Cancel button problem.

1. If the China Shop Project is still running, stop it now.
2. Modify the code in the Click event procedure of mnuColorsCustom so that it looks like this.

```
Private Sub mnuColorsCustom_Click (ByVal sender As System.Object, _
  ByVal e As System.EventArgs) Handles mnuColorsCustom.Click

Dim intRetValue as Integer

intRetValue = dlgChina.ShowDialog()

If intRetValue = DialogResult.Cancel Then
  Exit Sub
End If

Me.BackColor = dlgChina.Color
m_intBackColor = dlgChina.Color.ToARGB

End Sub
```

3. Save the China Shop Project by clicking the Save icon on the toolbar.
4. Run the program. Select Preferences | Colors | Custom from the menu and the ColorDialog box will be displayed. Instead of selecting a color, click Cancel instead. No change to the form should occur. Now select Preferences | Colors | Custom again. This time select a color and click OK. The background color of the form will change.

Discussion

"That's much better," Ward said, obviously impressed with his coding prowess. "One little If statement did it. I'm beginning to get the hang of this."

"You're right, Ward," I said. "One little If statement can make all the difference in the world. Actually, we needed to first add a declaration of an Integer variable to hold the return value of the ShowDialog method."

Dim intRetValue as Integer

"Once we did that, this If statement, looking for the Cancel value of the DialogResult enum family, enabled us to bypass the rest of the code in the procedure via an Exit Sub statement."

If intRetValue = DialogResult.Cancel Then
  Exit Sub
End If

"My only question," Dave asked, "is what happened to the return value of the ShowDialog method the first time we ran this code. Can it be ignored?"

"Good question, Dave," I said, "and an equally good conclusion on your part. That's exactly what happened. It's up to the programmer to handle any return values from the methods we call. In Exercise 12-8, we simply chose to ignore it. However, in this exercise, it was vitally important."

I waited to see if there were any other questions before continuing. "We have one more menu item for which we need to write code," I said, "the Colors | Default menu item, which will change the color of the form back to its default color."

Exercise 12-10 The Click Event Procedure of mnuColorsDefault

The Click Event Procedure of mnuColorsDefault

1. If the China Shop Project is still running, stop it now.
2. We want to place code in the Click event procedure of mnuColorsDefault. Using the technique of your choice, place the following code into its Click event procedure.

```
Private Sub mnuColorsDefault_Click (ByVal sender As Object, _
  ByVal e As System.EventArgs) Handles mnuColorsDefault.Click

Me.BackColor = System.Drawing.SystemColors.Control
m_intBackColor = System.Drawing.SystemColors.Control.ToARGB

End Sub
```

3. Save the China Shop Project by clicking the Save icon on the toolbar.
4. Run the program. Select Preferences | Colors | Custom and change the color of the form to something other than its default gray color.
5. Now select Preferences | Colors | Default. When you do, the background color of the form will change back to its default gray color.

Discussion

Again, everyone seemed to be excited about the enhancements they were making to the user interface of the China Shop Project. In effect, our menu was now complete. I explained that all it took to change the color of the form back to its default value was two lines of code.

Me.BackColor = System.Drawing.SystemColors.Control
m_intBackColor = System.Drawing.SystemColors.Control.ToARGB

"By now we're all familiar with Me.BackColor," Rhonda said. "But what are we assigning to it?"

"Good question, Rhonda," I said, "and maybe the answer to that can best be demonstrated if we stop the program and display the BackColor property of the form." I did exactly that and displayed this screenshot on the classroom projector.

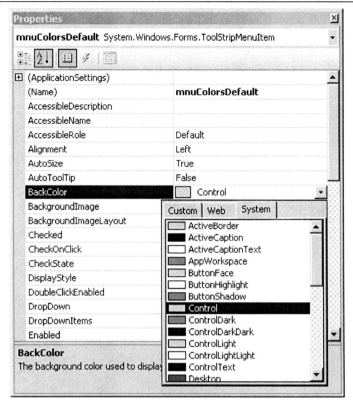

"Notice that the default property value for the BackColor property of the form is something called Control," I said. "Ultimately, this is a value that is determined by the user's selection of a color scheme in the Windows Control Panel. By specifying Control as the default value of the form, we ensure that if the user selects another color scheme, the color of the form will always change accordingly."

"Is that what Control means at the end of that assignment statement?" Dave asked.

"That's right, Dave" I said. "This line of code tells Visual Basic to assign the BackColor of the form based on the user's color preference in the Control Panel."

Me.BackColor = System.Drawing.SystemColors.Control

"Unfortunately, at least for beginners, that entire string is a bit difficult to fathom, but basically we're using a Visual Basic object hierarchy based on the Drawing object of the Visual Basic System object to do it. And, as we did when we changed the BackColor of the form to a custom color, we also need to update the form-level variable m_intBackColor."

m_intBackColor = System.Drawing.SystemColors.Control.ToARGB

"And we used the ToARGB function to convert the Color object to an Integer data type, is that right?" Kate asked.
"That's perfect, Kate," I said.

I continued by explaining that we would eventually make use of this form-level variable to load the user's preferred color when we load the China Shop form. At this point, there were no more questions, and so we took a break.

"When you come back from the break, we'll spend a few minutes discussing Visual Basic's MessageBox.Show function," I said.

More on the MessageBox.Show Method

After the break, I started my discussion of the Show method of the MessageBox method by saying that although we had used it quite a bit throughout the course, we really had only scratched the surface of what it can do.

"For instance, every Message Box that we've displayed so far has had only one button. We can actually display as many as three buttons with the MessageBox.Show method and use the return value of the MessageBox.Show method to determine which button the user clicked."

The Return Value of the MessageBox.Show Method

"I thought all the MessageBox.Show method could do was display a message and an OK button," said Barbara.

"No, the Message Box can display as many as three buttons and a title," I replied. "The Show Method of the MessageBox object has as many as 21 variations in its signature---number and types of arguments---but here's the one we're going to be concentrating on in the next few minutes."

MessageBox.Show (text, [, caption] [, buttons] [, icon] [,default])

"Only the text argument is required," I explained. "that's the argument that is used to display a message to the user. The caption, which is an optional argument, appears in the title bar of the Message Box window. Also optional, the buttons and icon arguments provide some additional niceties for the Message Box." I then suggested that we complete a few exercises to practice the MessageBox.Show method.

Exercise 12-11 Using the MessageBox.Show Method

In this exercise, you'll create a new Windows Forms Application, add a Button control to your form, and write code using the MessageBox.Show method to display a simple Message Box.

1. Start a new Windows Forms Application project.
2. Add a Button control to your form.
3. Place the following code in its Click event procedure.

```
Private Sub Button1_Click(ByVal sender As System.Object, ByVal e
    As System.EventArgs) Handles Button1.Click

    MessageBox.Show("I love Visual Basic Express")

End Sub
```

4. Run the program and click the button. You should see the following Message Box.

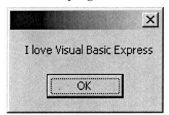

5. Notice that by default there is 'nothing' in the title bar of the Message Box---that's a little awkward. Let's correct that by modifying the code to look like this by specifying a value for the caption argument.

```
Private Sub Button2_Click(ByVal sender As System.Object, ByVal e
    As System.EventArgs) Handles Button1.Click

    MessageBox.Show("I love Visual Basic Express", "Programming is fun")

End Sub
```

6. Save your program.
7. Run the program and click the button. You should see the following Message Box---this time with a more descriptive title bar.

Discussion

"Does everyone see the effect of coding the caption argument?" I asked. "Now we have a title bar of our own choosing---not an empty one. Now let's move onto the buttons argument, which is a bit more complicated."

The Buttons Argument of the MessageBox.Show Method

I continued by explaining that the buttons argument is actually an enumeration called MessageBoxButtons, much like the DialogResult enumeration we saw earlier with the ShowDialog method.

"It's really very easy," I said, "the Show method of the MessageBox object is capability of displaying six different button appearances----all we need to do is specify the enumeration value equating to the buttons we wish to display in the Message Box as the buttons argument to the MessageBox.Show method."

I then displayed this table on the classroom project with the possible enumeration values for the MessageBoxButtons enumeration.

MessageBoxButtons Enum Constant	Description
AbortRetryIgnore	The Message Box contains Abort, Retry, and Ignore buttons
OK	The Message Box contains an OK Button
OKCancel	The Message Box contains OK and Cancel buttons
RetryCancel	The Message Box contains Retry and Cancel buttons
YesNoCancel	The Message Box contains Yes, No, and Cancel buttons
YesNo	The Message Box contains Yes and No buttons

"You'll see in a minute," I said, "how easy this is to work with."

The Icon Argument of the MessageBox.Show Method

"In a similar way," I said, "the icon argument is an enumeration called MessageBoxIcon. There are a bunch of different icons that you can display in a Message Box, and displaying an icon for the Message Box is simply a matter of specifying its enumeration value for the icon argument of the MessageBox.Show method."

I then displayed this table on the classroom projector.

MessageBoxIcon Enum Constant	Description
Asterisk	The Message Box contains a symbol consisting of a lowercase letter i in a circle.
Error	The Message Box contains a symbol consisting of a white X in a circle with a red background.
Exclamation	The Message Box contains a symbol consisting of an exclamation point in a triangle with a yellow background.
Hand	The Message Box contains a symbol consisting of a white X in a circle with a red background
Information	The Message Box contains a symbol consisting of a lowercase letter I in a circle
None	The Message Box contains no symbols
Question	The Message Box contains a symbol consisting of a question mark in a circle.
Stop	The Message Box contains a symbol consisting of a white X in a circle with a red background.
Warning	The Message Box contains a symbol consisting of an exclamation point in a triangle with a

	yellow background.

> **NOTE: Microsoft discourages the use of the Question Mark message icon. In its own words, the question-mark message icon is no longer recommended because it does not clearly represent a specific type of message and because the phrasing of a message as a question could apply to any message type. In addition, users can confuse the message symbol question mark with Help information. Therefore, do not use this question mark message symbol in your message boxes. The system continues to support its inclusion only for backward compatibility.**

"Something I barely mentioned," I said, "is the fact that when you display a series of buttons, you can specify one button to be the default. In other words, it's already 'preselected' with focus when the Message Box is displayed. It's a good idea to do this for cases where there's an obvious choice that the user will make a majority of the time. I should also mention that it's advised that in a Message Box with an OK and Cancel button, you make the Cancel button the default button. That way, if the user accidentally hits the ENTER key, the worst thing that will happen is that they will cancel any action that they might have taken. Not surprisingly, setting the default button in a Message Box is as simple as specifying the value DefaultButton enum as the default argument of the Show method of the MessageBox object."

I then displayed this table of MessageBoxDefaultButton enum values on the classroom projector.

MessageBoxDefaultButton Enum Constant	Description
MessageBoxDefaultButton.Button1	The first button in the Message Box is the default button.
MessageBoxDefaultButton.Button2	The second button in the Message Box is the default button.
MessageBoxDefaultButton.Button3	The third button in the Message Box is the default button.

I thought a practical exercise of all of the arguments was in order, and so I posed this question.

"Suppose," I said, "you wanted to display a Message Box that has Abort, Retry, and Ignore buttons, with a Stop Message icon, where the second button is the default button?"

Dave volunteered the code, and I displayed it on the classroom project for his approval.

```
MessageBox.Show("I love Visual Basic Express", _
            "Programming is fun", _
            MessageBoxButtons.AbortRetryIgnore, MessageBoxIcon.Stop, _
            MessageBoxDefaultButton.Button2)
```

After receiving his go-ahead, I reran the program, and the following screenshot was displayed on the classroom projector.

"Absolutely perfect," I said.

"Wow, that's amazingly easy," Mary said.

"Why is it that even though we displayed three buttons," Dave said, "we didn't have to set up a variable to handle the return value?"

"That's an excellent question," I said. "In Visual Basic, you have the option of discarding the return value when you call a method. If you want to do 'something' with the return value, that's up to you. Here's an exercise to work with the return values of the MessageBox.Show method."

Exercise 12-12 Using the Return Value from the MessageBox.Show Method

In this exercise, you'll create a new Windows Forms Application, add a Button control to your form, and write code to see how you can use the return value that is generated from the MessageBox.Show method when you display more than one button.

1. Start a new Windows Forms Application project.
2. Add a Button control to your form.
3. Place the following code in its Click event procedure.

```
Private Sub Button1_Click(ByVal sender As System.Object, ByVal e
    As System.EventArgs) Handles Button1.Click

    Dim RetValue As DialogResult

    RetValue = MessageBox.Show("I love Visual Basic Express", _
                "Programming is fun", _
                MessageBoxButtons.AbortRetryIgnore, MessageBoxIcon.Stop)

    Select Case RetValue
        Case DialogResult.Abort
            MessageBox.Show("You clicked the Abort button")
        Case DialogResult.Retry
            MessageBox.Show("You clicked the Retry button")
        Case DialogResult.Ignore
            MessageBox.Show("You clicked the Ignore button")
    End Select
End Sub
```

4. Run the program and click on the Abort button. You should see a Message Box informing you that you clicked Abort.

5. Do the same for the Retry and Ignore buttons.

Discussion

"That was great," Ward said. "I had no idea the MessageBox.Show method was this powerful."

"Is DialogResult the same enum we saw earlier with the ColorDialog box?" Linda asked.

"It's the same one," I said. I waited a minute or two to see if any of my students were having problems---they weren't.

"What will we be doing next week, then?" Joe asked.

"Next week," I said, "we'll examine some of the common errors Visual Basic programmers make in their programs, as well as learning how to gracefully deal with errors that our users may introduce. This process, called Exception Handling, is a feature of more sophisticated programming, so of course we'll want to incorporate it. Then the next week, in our last week of class, we'll discuss using the Windows Registry to save user preferences, and wrap up our course by looking at some code optimization techniques and delivering our program to Joe Bullina at the China Shop.

No one seemed to have any questions dealing with the MessageBox.Show method, and there were no other questions. I dismissed class for the day.

Summary

In this chapter, we spent some time enhancing the visual interface of our China Shop Project. In the process, we discussed creating drop-down menus. We also learned more about the MessageBox.Show method, and saw how we can adapt it to fit a particular function.

Specifically, we covered:

- Using the Visual Basic to construct drop-down menu items

- Adding captions, names, and shortcuts to the menu items that we built

- How to create customized message boxes using the MessageBox.Show method

The user interface is an important part of your application. A user likes to feel that the application knows what it's doing. Even if you think you will be the only person to use your program, you'll find it's a lot nicer to have something that behaves like a well-polished application at your fingertips—even more so if you know that you've created it yourself!

In the next chapter, we're going to take a look at arrays. You'll see how they can help you in your programming by enabling you to solve problems that might otherwise be impossible.

Chapter 13---Arrays

In this chapter, we'll see how array processing can make long, tedious programming chores easier to handle.

I began our thirteenth class by telling my students that the entirety of today's class would be devoted to the topic of arrays.

"Are variable arrays similar to regular variables?" Rhonda asked.

"Yes, they are, Rhonda," I replied. "A variable is a single piece of data stored in the computer's memory and given a name. A variable array is a collection of variables of the same data type stored in the computer's memory, each having the same name, and each possessing a unique number called a subscript which is used to identify them. Individual members of an array are called elements of the array."

> **NOTE: You sometimes see the terms subscript and index used interchangeably.**

Why Arrays?

"In the world of programming,' I continued, "solutions to certain kinds of programming problems lend themselves quite nicely to the use of variable arrays, which we'll refer to as arrays from this point forward."

"What kinds of problems?" Chuck asked.

"In general, Chuck," I said, "problems where there is need to manipulate large amounts of data, but the data isn't really unique as much as it is multiple instances of the same data. For example, suppose you are a meteorologist, and you want to write a program to deal with 365 days' worth of high temperature readings. You could declare and store the reading in variables called intHigh1 through intHigh365, but that would require 365 individual declaration statements, 365 assignment statements, and so on. An array is a much better choice to store these 365 readings. An array declaration to hold 365 members or elements requires just a single declaration statement."

I waited to see if I had lost anyone, but everyone seemed okay so far.

"Let me give you another example," I said. "Last Wednesday evening I gave a midterm examination to my Database Administration class. I only have six students in the class, and I'd like to calculate the overall class average for the midterm. Does anyone have any ideas as to how we could write a program to calculate the average?"

"I guess one approach would be to create a form on which we place six text boxes and a button," Rhonda suggested. "We could then enter the grades for the six students into each of the six text boxes, and when we click the button, we could display the average of the six grades in a message box or a Label control."

"That's not a bad idea, Rhonda," I said. "For reasons you'll see later, I term your method the brute force method. Now suppose I told you that my Database Administration class really has 150 students. Does that change your approach to solving the problem?"

"I think we need to find a better approach," Rhonda replied. "I really don't think we want to place 150 text boxes on a form!"

"You're right, and that better approach is to use an array," I said. "However, before we start to discuss arrays in detail, let's program your solution to the problem first. In order to understand how tedious programming would be without arrays, it's a good idea to see the brute force method in action."

I then distributed this exercise to the class for them to complete.

Exercise 13-1 Brute Force: Life Without Arrays

In this exercise, you'll write code to calculate the class average of six midterm examinations.

1. Start a new Windows application project.
2. Place six TextBox controls on the form.
3. Change the Name property of the six text boxes to **txtGrade1, txtGrade2, txtGrade3, txtGrade4, txtGrade5** and **txtGrade6**.
4. Clear the Text property of the six text boxes.
5. Add a Button control to your form.
6. Place the following code in its Click event procedure.

```
Private Sub Button1_Click(ByVal sender As System.Object, _
    ByVal e As System.EventArgs) Handles Button1.Click

Dim sngAverage As Single
Dim intGrade1 As Integer
Dim intGrade2 As Integer
Dim intGrade3 As Integer
Dim intGrade4 As Integer
Dim intGrade5 As Integer
Dim intGrade6 As Integer

If txtGrade1.Text = "" Or txtGrade2.Text = "" Or _
    txtGrade3.Text = "" Or txtGrade4.Text = "" Or _
    txtGrade5.Text = "" Or txtGrade6.Text = "" Then
    MessageBox.Show ("You must fill in all 6 grades")
    Exit Sub
End If

intGrade1 = cInt(txtGrade1.Text)
intGrade2 = cInt(txtGrade2.Text)
intGrade3 = cInt(txtGrade3.Text)
intGrade4 = cInt(txtGrade4.Text)
intGrade5 = cInt(txtGrade5.Text)
intGrade6 = cInt(txtGrade6.Text)

sngAverage = (intGrade1 + intGrade2 + intGrade3 + _
            intGrade4 + intGrade5 + intGrade6) / 6

Console.WriteLine ("The class average is " & sngAverage)

End Sub
```

7. Save your program, although you won't be modifying it any further.
8. Run the program.
9. Enter the following grades into the six text boxes: **90, 91, 80, 77, 100, 44**.
10. Now click the button. The average 80.33334 will be displayed in the Visual Basic Output window.

Discussion

Everyone agreed that the code in this exercise did what every good program must do—it worked. Beyond that, it had been an extremely tedious exercise to code.

"Let's take a look at the code from the exercise now," I said. "As usual, the first thing we do is declare any variables that we will need to use in the event procedure."

```
Dim sngAverage As Single
Dim intGrade1 As Integer
Dim intGrade2 As Integer
Dim intGrade3 As Integer
Dim intGrade4 As Integer
Dim intGrade5 As Integer
Dim intGrade6 As Integer
```

"I mentioned earlier in the course that it's more efficient to perform arithmetic operations on variables, not properties. That's why we declared six Integer variables to hold the numbers entered into the six text boxes. In addition, we also declared a variable of a Single data type to hold the result of our calculation."

"Single, that's a data type with a fractional part, isn't it?" Blaine asked.

"That's right, Blaine," I answered. "We want to calculate the class average as precisely as possible, so we need to declare a variable that can handle fractions." I explained that in the next section of code, we do the same type of validation we've been performing on text boxes throughout the course to ensure that something has been entered into each text box.

```
If txtGrade1.Text = "" Or txtGrade2.Text = "" Or _
   txtGrade3.Text = "" Or txtGrade4.Text = "" Or _
   txtGrade5.Text = "" Or txtGrade6.Text = "" Then
   MessageBox.Show ("You must fill in all 6 grades")
Exit Sub
End If
```

"This next section of code converts the String data type of the Text property of each text box to an integer, and then assigns that value to a variable," I explained.

```
intGrade1 = cInt(txtGrade1.Text)
intGrade2 = cInt(txtGrade2.Text)
intGrade3 = cInt(txtGrade3.Text)
intGrade4 = cInt(txtGrade4.Text)
intGrade5 = cInt(txtGrade5.Text)
intGrade6 = cInt(txtGrade6.Text)
```

"Here's the most important piece of code," I continued, "the calculation of the class average. The class average is calculated by adding the values of the six variables together and then dividing by 6. The result of that calculation is stored in the variable sngAverage. Take note of the parentheses around the addition operations—that's because of the order of operations. Without parentheses, intGrade6 would be divided by the number 6 first, and that value then added to the other intGrade variables. That would result in an erroneous average calculation."

```
sngAverage = (intGrade1 + intGrade2 + intGrade3 + _
             intGrade4 + intGrade5 + intGrade6) / 6
```

"Finally, we display the results in the Visual Basic Output window, concatenating the value of the variable sngAverage to the message 'The class average is'," I added.

```
Console.WriteLine ("The class average is " & sngAverage)
```

I scanned the room for signs of confusion, but no one seemed to be having any trouble understanding what we had just done.

"I think you're all pretty comfortable with this code," I said. "There's really nothing here we haven't seen before."

I then made this startling suggestion: "I'd like you all to modify this code to calculate the class average for a class with 500 students."

"I know you're kidding," Joe said.

"Well, I am...and then again I'm not. Suppose we really needed to be able to calculate the average for a class with 500 students. Could we do it?" I asked.

Everyone agreed that modifying the code in this exercise to calculate the class average for 500 students would be a nightmare.

"We would need 500 text boxes and 500 variables to store the values of the Text property," Kate said. "A form can't hold that many text boxes, can it."

"We can't fit that many text boxes on a single form," Barbara insisted.

"Plus we would need to change the Name property of 500 text boxes and clear the Text property of 500 text boxes," Chuck added.

What's an Array?

"All of your points are excellent ones," I said. "Now you're seeing the type of problem that lends itself to array processing. An array can make this problem much easier to solve."

"Did you say that an array is a separate data type, like Integer or Single?" Peter asked.

"Many beginners make the mistake of thinking of an array as a separate data type," I said, "but arrays are just a special implementation of one of the other data type—there are Integer arrays, String arrays and even Date arrays."

"I'm still a little confused as to exactly what an array is," Rhonda said. "Is there any way you can make it clearer?"

"In the past," I said, "most of my students have found my analogy of an array to a hotel to be pretty useful. Just about everyone has stayed in a hotel or motel. Think of a regular variable as a storage location in the computer's memory consisting of just a single floor. An array, on the other hand, is a storage location in the computer's memory having more than just a single floor—plus, each floor has a floor number."

"Like a hotel," Joe said.

"Just like a hotel," I said. "I'm not much of an artist, but here's a graphic depiction of what I mean."

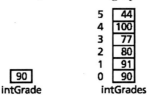

"This drawing is an attempt to illustrate the previous example with six midterm grades," I said. "On the left, we have an ordinary Integer variable called intGrade. On the right, we have an array of Integer variables called intGrades. As you can see, the variable on the left can hold only one value at one time and it contains the first midterm grade. The array on the right contains all six midterm grades."

"What are those numbers to the left of the grades in the array?" Barbara asked.

"In keeping with our hotel analogy, those are the floor numbers, or in computer terms, the array subscripts. A subscript uniquely identifies the element within the array—each element has one, and they cannot be repeated."

"Why does the first element begin with zero?" Ward asked.

"Let me guess, that's the basement?" Rhonda said, obviously joking.

"In a way, Rhonda, you're right," I replied. "In the computer world, many things begin with the number 0 instead of 1, and an array is no different. By default, the first element of an array begins with the number 0. The bottom element is technically called the lower bound of the array and the top element is called the upper bound of the array."

Declaring an Array

"How do you declare an array?" Steve asked. "Is it different from declaring an ordinary variable?"

"Declaring an array isn't much different from declaring an ordinary variable," I continued. "You just need to let Visual Basic know up front how many elements the array will contain.

Here's the array declaration for intGrades."

Dim intGrades(5) As Integer

"What's that number in the parentheses?" Ward asked. "Is that the number of elements in the array?"

"No," I replied, "that's what most beginners think at first. The number in parentheses is the upper bound, or top floor, of the array. Arrays are numbered beginning from 0. That means with a lower bound of 0, and an upper bound of 5, there will be a total of 6 elements in this array."

"Can it be changed?" Linda asked.

"Yes, it can," I said. "The number in parentheses represents the initial upper bound of the array. It can be changed by using the ReDim statement like this."

ReDim intGrades(25)

"Not only that, but if you are unsure as to what size the array should be initially, you can leave the size parameter empty, like this."

Dim intGrades() as Integer

"How is it possible that you wouldn't know the size of your array ahead of time?" Mary asked. "One good example is the midterm grade project we're working with now," I replied. "For instance, although we have an enrollment of 50 students in the class, some students may be sick on the day of the midterm, so the actual number of students taking the examination may be less than 50. So you see, it wouldn't be until runtime that we know the exact number of students who took the midterm—and therefore the size of the array."

"What do we do then?" Steve asked.

"We have several choices," I said. "We can size the array large enough to handle the worst case scenario—in the case of the midterm grade program, 50 elements. The problem with that is you don't always have enough information to make a ballpark estimate. For instance, you might be asked to write a program that reads records in a file, and there can be anywhere from one to billions of records in the file. Declaring the initial size of the array to several billion is a waste of memory and can lead to some real problems."

"So what can we do then?" Peter asked.

"In most cases," I said, "the better choice is to declare the array with no initial size and then use the Visual Basic ReDim statement to resize the array whenever you need to add another element to it. We'll do this later on in the China Shop Project. An array of this type is called a dynamic array, in that its size changes dynamically as the program is running. An array whose size is known ahead of time and which never changes is called a static array."

Referring to Elements of an Array

As there were no more questions about declaring arrays, it was time to move on to the subject of working with them in code.

"How do we assign values to an array element?" Steve asked. "And how can we retrieve the value from one of the elements?"

"It's similar to working with an ordinary variable," I said. "The difference is that we reference the subscript of the element within parentheses. For example, if we had an array called intGrades, we would use this code to refer to the array element containing a subscript of 2 in the intGrades array."

intGrades(2)

"By the way," I cautioned, "the array element with a subscript equal to 2 is actually the third element in the array. Since array numbering starts with 0, the first element has a subscript of 0, the second element a subscript of 1, and the third element a subscript of 2."

"Are values assigned to an array element the same way?" Steve asked. "That is, using the subscript number within parentheses?"

"That's right, Steve," I replied. "Again, just reference the subscript of the array within parentheses. For instance, you can use this syntax to assign the value 80 to subscript 2 of the array intGrades."

intGrades(2) = 80

Kathy asked, "What happens if we declare a static array and try to refer to an element that doesn't exist?"

"You'll receive an error message that looks something like this," I answered. I wrote this code.

Dim intArray(10) as Integer
intArray(11) = 44

I then placed it in a Button control and ran the program, and an IndexOutOfRangeException message was displayed.

"I'm afraid I don't see what the problem is here," Lou said. "The size of the array is 11, and you just assigned a value to the 11th element."

"The problem is I tried to assign a value to the 12th element." I answered. "Subscript 11 is actually the 12th element of the array, and we sized it only for 11 elements. This array has a lower bound of 0 and an upper bound of 10. Subscript 11 does not exist."

"That's confusing, isn't it?" Peter said.

> **CAUTION: Previous versions of Visual Basic permitted you to alter the lower bound of the array by setting Option Base 1 in the Declarations section of your form. Visual Basic does not have this capability.**

"I agree, Peter," I said, "this can be confusing. Just remember that the upper bound of the array—the top floor of our hotel—is actually 1 less than its size."

I pointed out that you are not restricted to using numeric literals when referring to the subscripts of an array.

"You can use any expression within the parentheses, as long as the expression evaluates to a valid subscript number." I explained. "For instance, provided the value of a variable intCounter is a valid subscript number, this is a valid assignment statement."

intGrades(intCounter) = 80

"You'll see this will come in handy a little later on," I said.

I waited for questions, but there were no more. I think everyone, for the moment anyway, felt comfortable declaring and working with arrays.

"I have a exercise for you to do which will give you a chance to use an array to perform the same average calculation we did in the last exercise."

Exercise 13-2 Our First Look at Arrays

In this exercise, you'll create your first array.

1. Start a new Windows application project.
2. Add a Button control to your form.
3. Place the following code into its Click event procedure.

```
Private Sub Button1_Click(ByVal sender As System.Object, _
   ByVal e As System.EventArgs) Handles Button1.Click

Dim intGrades(5) As Integer
Dim intCounter As Integer
Dim intTotal As Integer
Dim sngAverage As Single

intGrades(0) = 90
intGrades(1) = 91
intGrades(2) = 80
intGrades(3) = 77
intGrades(4) = 100
intGrades(5) = 44

For intCounter = 0 To 5
  Console.WriteLine (intGrades(intCounter))
  intTotal = intTotal + intGrades(intCounter)
Next

sngAverage = CSng(intTotal / intCounter)

Console.WriteLine ("The class average is " & sngAverage)

End Sub
```

4. Save your program, although you won't be modifying it any further.
5. Run the program.
6. Now click the button. The numbers 90, 91, 80, 77, 100, and 44 will be displayed in the Visual Basic Output window, along with the average 80.33334.

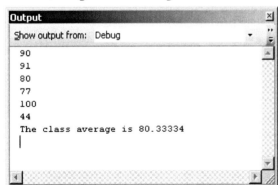

Discussion

"This is certainly a lot more streamlined than the other code," Ward said, "but I'm not quite sure I understand what's happening. Can you explain the code?"

"Sure thing, Ward," I said. "As usual, we declare any variables that we will need to use in the event procedure. This first line of code declares a static array called intGrades consisting of six elements, where the lower bound is 0 and the upper bound is 5."

Dim intGrades(5) As Integer

"We now declare our ordinary variables. intCounter is a Loop Control variable, and intTotal and sngAverage are both used to calculate the class average," I explained.

Dim intCounter As Integer
Dim intTotal As Integer
Dim sngAverage As Single

"The next six lines of code load the six elements of the intGrades array," I said.

intGrades(0) = 90
intGrades(1) = 91
intGrades(2) = 80
intGrades(3) = 77
intGrades(4) = 100
intGrades(5) = 44

"At this point," I continued, "our array now has six elements loaded. We then use a For...Next loop to display each element of the array in the Visual Basic Output window, and to add their values to the variable intTotal."

For intCounter = 0 To 5
  Console.WriteLine (intGrades(intCounter))
  intTotal = intTotal + intGrades(intCounter)
Next

"Within the body of the loop, we use the WriteLine method of the Console object to display the value of each the array element," I explained. "Notice that the Loop Control variable is used, within parentheses, to specify the subscript of the array element we want to display in the Output window."

Console.WriteLine (intGrades(intCounter))

"After we have displayed the value of the array element in the Output window, we then add it to the value of the variable intTotal," I continued. "intTotal thus maintains a running total of the array elements we have displayed in the Output window."

intTotal = intTotal + intGrades(intCounter)

"The first time the body of the loop is executed." I said, "the value of intCounter is 0, and this statement is interpreted by Visual Basic like this."

intTotal = intTotal + intGrades(0)

"This statement can also be interpreted like this."

intTotal = 0 + 90

"The second time through the loop," I continued, "the value of intCounter is 1, and this statement is interpreted by Visual Basic like this…"

intTotal = intTotal + intGrades(1)

"…or this."

intTotal = 90 + 91

I then explained that this process was repeated until all the elements of the array had been processed.

"This line of code calculates the average once the loop processing has ended," I explained. "Remember that intTotal is the running total of all the scores, and intCounter is a Loop Control variable that counts the number of grades. We use the CSng function which returns a Single data type from the division of the two Integer values."

sngAverage = CSng(intTotal / intCounter)

"This line of code prints the class average on the form."

Console.WriteLine ("The class average is " & sngAverage)

"Something is bothering me," Dave said. "The calculation of the class average works, but I don't quite understand why. The class average is equal to the sum of the grades divided by the number of grades entered, in this case, 6. Isn't the value of intCounter at the end of the loop equal to 5?"

"That's a good question," I said, "but you're forgetting about the behavior of the For…Next loop. After the iteration of the loop where the final grade is printed, the Next statement causes the value of intCounter to be incremented by 1. At that point, its value becomes 6. The For statement then compares the value of intCounter—6—to the end parameter of the loop, which is 5, and because 6 is greater, the loop ends."

That seemed to satisfy Dave.

"There's another way to load the elements of an array," I said, "in addition to the technique we just saw, and that's to load them when the array is declared. Here's an exercise to demonstrate that technique."

Exercise 13-3 Loading Array Elements at Declaration Time

1. Start a new Windows application project.
2. Add a Button control to your form.
3. Place the following code into its Click event procedure.

```
Private Sub Button1_Click(ByVal sender As Object, _
    ByVal e As System.EventArgs)

Dim intGrades() As Integer = {90, 91, 80, 77, 44, 100}
Dim intCounter As Integer
Dim intTotal As Integer
Dim sngAverage As Single

For intCounter = 0 To 5
    Console.WriteLine(intGrades(intCounter))
    intTotal = intTotal + intGrades(intCounter)
Next

sngAverage = CSng(intTotal / intCounter)

Console.WriteLine("The class average is " & sngAverage)

End Sub
```

4. Save your program, although you won't be modifying it any further.
5. Run the program.
6. Now click the button. The numbers 90, 91, 80, 77, 100, and 44 will be displayed in the Visual Basic Output window, along with the average 80.33334.

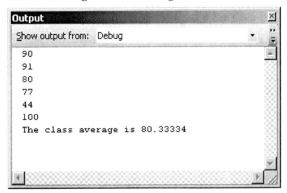

Discussion

"Assigning values to the array when you declare it streamlines the process of adding elements to our array," I explained.

I continued by saying that the code in this exercise was virtually identical to the code from the previous exercise, with the exception of the way we declared and loaded the array elements.

"The array is declared and loaded in a single Visual Basic statement, the Dim statement," I explained.

Dim intGrades() As Integer = {90, 91, 80, 77, 44, 100}

We had been working for some time, so I suggested that we take a break.

"When we resume after break, we'll look at dynamic arrays," I told them.

Dynamic Arrays

"I mentioned earlier that in addition to the static arrays we've just been looking at, there's another type of array called a dynamic array," I said. "In Visual Basic, 'dynamic' means that the number of elements in the array can change. The size—and therefore the upper bound—of a dynamic array can change while the program is running."

"Why would you declare a dynamic array? Don't you always know the size of your array ahead of time? Why would we change its size while the program is running?" Ward asked.

"Let's re-examine our problem of calculating the average of 50 grades," I replied. "Remember, just because we have 50 enrolled students doesn't mean that all 50 students will show up for the midterm examination. The dynamic array is the perfect way to handle this situation."

"Is there a special way to declare a dynamic array?" Linda asked.

"You can declare the dynamic array with an initial size, like this," I said…

Dim intGrades(50)

"…and then later use the ReDim statement to resize the array if necessary."

ReDim intGrades(55)

"You can also use this dynamic array declaration with empty parentheses."

Dim intGrades()

"How many elements are there in this array?" Kate asked.

"Right now, none," I replied. "With this type of dynamic array, no operation can be performed on it until the ReDim statement is executed to give it an actual size, like this."

ReDim intGrades(5)

"With a dynamic array," I continued, "you can use the ReDim statement as many times as necessary within your program."

"What happens to the data already present in an array when you use the ReDim statement?" Linda asked.

"That's an excellent question," I replied. "Ordinarily, if you use the ReDim statement, any data already present in the array will be lost. There is, however, an optional parameter of the ReDim statement called Preserve that permits any data already present in the array to be saved."

ReDim Preserve intGrades(5)

I continued our discussion of dynamic arrays by saying that they are extremely handy for file processing.

"In fact," I said, "we'll use array processing to read inventory prices into our China Shop Project to calculate the customer's sales quotation. I have an exercise here which will illustrate the use of array processing in reading data from a disk file."

Exercise 13-4 Add Elements to an Array from a Disk File

In this exercise, you'll load elements into a dynamic array using a disk file as its source.

1. Use Notepad to create a file called GRADES.TXT in your \VBFiles\Practice subdirectory that contains the data you see in the following screenshot. Notice that the file contains six records and each record contains a single numeric value representing a midterm grade.

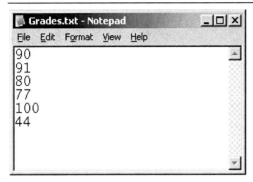

2. Start a new Windows application project.

3. Add a Button control to your form.

4. Place the following code into its Click event procedure.

```
Private Sub Button1_Click(ByVal sender As System.Object, _
    ByVal e As System.EventArgs) Handles Button1.Click

    Dim intGrades() As Integer
    Dim intCounter As Integer
    Dim intTotal As Integer
    Dim sngAverage As Single
    Dim line As String
    Dim sr As New StreamReader("C:\VBFILES\PRACTICE\GRADES.TXT")

    Do
        line = sr.ReadLine()
        If line Is Nothing Then Exit Do
        ReDim Preserve intGrades(intCounter)
        intGrades(intCounter) = line
        intCounter = intCounter + 1
    Loop
    sr.Close()

    For intCounter = 0 To (intGrades.Length - 1)
        Console.WriteLine(intGrades(intCounter))
        intTotal = intTotal + intGrades(intCounter)
    Next

    sngAverage = CSng(intTotal / intCounter)
    Console.WriteLine("The class average is " & sngAverage)
End Sub
```

5. Place this line of code following the last using statement at the top of the Code window, above the line of code that denotes the Class header for the form.

Imports System.IO

6. Save your program, although you won't be modifying it any further.

7. Run the program.

8. Now click the button. The numbers 90, 91, 80, 77, 100, and 44 will be displayed in the Visual Basic Output window, along with the average 80.33334.

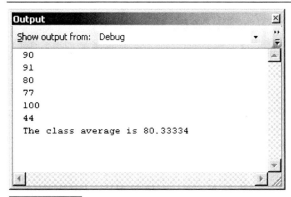

```
90
91
80
77
100
44
The class average is 80.33334
```

Discussion

I ran the program myself, and the midterm grades and the class average were displayed in the Visual Basic Output window.

"Different program, same result," I said. "You may recognize some of this code from one of our previous exercises on file processing. The difference between this program and the program from Exercise 13-3 is that here we read the six grades from a disk file, and instead of storing the grades in six variables with different names, we stored them as elements of one array."

I continued by explaining that as usual, the first thing we do is declare the variables that we will need to use in our event procedure.

"Notice the empty parentheses following the name of the array," I said, "which indicates to Visual Basic that intGrades is a dynamic array."

Dim intGrades() As Integer

"The next four lines of code," I continued, "declare the same variables that we've used in the last few exercises. intCounter is a Loop Control variable. intTotal is a variable that will be used to store the sum of the values in our array, and sngAverage is a variable that will be used to store the calculated class average. As we saw two weeks ago, line is a variable that is used to store the line we read from our text file."

Dim intCounter As Integer
Dim intTotal As Integer
Dim sngAverage As Single
Dim line As String

I paused before continuing. "This next line of code creates a StreamReader object, and at the same time opens the disk file GRADES.TXT for input," I explained.

Dim sr As New StreamReader("C:\VBFILES\PRACTICE\GRADES.TXT")

"This next section of code," I stated, "sets up a Do...Loop structure that reads each record in the disk file into the variable line, which in turns stores that value as an element of the intGrades dynamic array."

Do
    line = sr.ReadLine()
    If line Is Nothing Then Exit Do
    ReDim Preserve intGrades(intCounter)
    intGrades(intCounter) = line
    intCounter = intCounter + 1
Loop

"These statements," I said, "are similar to the code we saw in one of our previous exercises dealing with disk files. Remember that the ReadLine statement reads a field from a record in our open file into a variable. Here, the field is being read into a variable called line..."

line = sr.ReadLine()

"If the variable line contains the EOF marker we exit the loop..."

If line Is Nothing Then Exit Do

"...otherwise, we then execute this line of code..."

ReDim Preserve intGrades(intCounter)

"…and then read the value of the variable line into an element of the intGrades array…"

intGrades(intCounter) = line

"…the subscript of the element determined by the current value of the variable intCounter."

"That's clever," Valerie said. "So that's how we increment the values of the subscripts."

"In fact, Valerie," I replied "it's this next statement that increments the value of intCounter by 1."

intCounter = intCounter + 1

"To summarize," I said, "within the body of the loop we read the single field from the current record of our open file, determine if it's the invisible EOF marker, if not, then ReDim or redeclare the size of our array, then copy the value of the line field from the line variable into an element of our array, and then increment the value of the variable intCounter by 1."

"I know you mentioned this, but what's the purpose of word 'Preserve' again?" Ward asked.

"We use Preserve," I said, "because we don't want to lose any data already present in the array. After each iteration of the loop, there's already data in the array. If we executed the ReDim statement with no Preserve keyword, we would wipe out the data already in there."

I wasn't sure I was getting through to Ward, and so I tried it this way.

"Since we initially declared the array intGrades as a dynamic array with no initial size value, we need to use the ReDim statement to resize the array each time the body of the loop is executed," I explained. "Each time the body of the loop is executed, we use the ReDim statement to increase the array's upper bound by one. What makes this tricky is that divergence I pointed out earlier between the array's Size parameter and its upper bound, which is its highest subscript value or highest 'floor' if you are still following the hotel analogy. We will use the value intCounter to keep track of the current subscript value, which begins with 0."

Everyone seemed to be following the discussion. Just to be sure, I displayed this sketch on the classroom projector to illustrate how our dynamic array expands each time the body of the loop is executed.

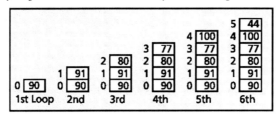

I was a little surprised, but everyone seemed to be following this.

"We've seen this next line of code before," I continued. "All it does is close the file we opened earlier."

sr.Close()

"The following section of code uses a For…Next loop to display each grade in the Visual Basic Output window and also keep a running total of the grades."

```
For intCounter = 0 To (intGrades.Length - 1)
    Console.WriteLine(intGrades(intCounter))
    intTotal = intTotal + intGrades(intCounter)
Next
```

"Length attribute?" Linda asked. "What's that?"

"Do you remember a few minutes ago I mentioned that in Visual Basic, Arrays are actually objects?" I asked. "As a byproduct of that, each Array that we declare has a Length attribute, which tells us exactly how many elements are in the Array. By specifying that the For loop should continue to execute while the value of the row Loop Control variable is less than the Length attribute of the Array, we ensure that we access each and every element of the Array. However, since Arrays are zero-based, we first need to subtract 1 from the actual Length."

"And we know what the Start parameter of the For…Next loop should be," Linda said, "because the lower bound of the array—or the lowest subscript number—is always 0, is that right?"

"That's excellent, Linda," I said. "You're absolutely right, the lower bound is always 0. That's why the Start parameter of our For...Next loop is 0. In this case, with a six element array, Visual Basic will interpret this line of code..."

For intCounter = 0 To (intGrades.Length - 1)

"...as..."

For intCounter = 0 To (6 – 1)

"...as..."

For intCounter = 0 To 5

"We've seen the rest of the code before, so I won't waste time discussing it," I added.

I was just about to start my discussion of multidimensional arrays, but then realized that before doing so, I needed to discuss how to deal with comma delimited files—something we would need to know how to do in order to complete the China Shop project.

Before doing so, however, I suggested that we take a fifteen minute break.

Comma Delimited Files

"Next up," I said, "is how to deal with the problem of comma delimited data in our Input file."

"I'm not so sure I understand what the problem is," Rhonda said. "Can't we use the same technique we just learned to read a file whose lines contain more than one 'field'?"

"We can use the same technique Rhonda," I said, 'but the problem is that the data we read will all be stored into a single variable. Suppose we had a file that stored the names and addresses of some customers that looked like this..."

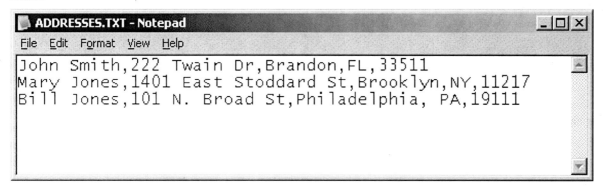

```
ADDRESSES.TXT - Notepad
File  Edit  Format  View  Help
John Smith,222 Twain Dr,Brandon,FL,33511
Mary Jones,1401 East Stoddard St,Brooklyn,NY,11217
Bill Jones,101 N. Broad St,Philadelphia, PA,19111
```

"As you can see, there are 3 lines, each one having 5 fields, representing the Customer's Name, Street, City, State and Zip Code. If we use the same technique we used before our break to read data from this file, each line will be stored in a single String variable."

"I think I see what you mean," Rhonda said.

"I guess at that point we could use some of the techniques we used two weeks ago to parse the line into parts?" Dave volunteered.

"What does Dave mean by Parse?" Rhonda shot back.

"Parsing means to break apart Rhonda," I answered, "That's the technique we used with the Substring function two weeks ago."

"Wow, what a mess that can be," Ward said, "you mean we need to go through the entire line looking for commas?"

"No, there is an easier way," I said. "Fortunately, the Visual Basic String object has a method called Split which is quite clever. It takes a String, and given a delimiter value or values, scans the String, and breaks it up based on the delimiters."

"Where does it place the result?" Steve asked.

"Into an Array," I said. "where each element of the Array is a parsed element."

"So in the example you displayed on the projector," Dave said, "A five element Array would be created. John Smith would appear as one element of the Array, 222 Twain Dr another element, Brandon a third, FL the fourth, and 33511 the fifth and final element."

"Absolutely correct," I said. "You hit the nail on the head. This can be pretty cumbersome to talk about---why don't I give you a chance to read the file you created in Exercise 12-1, using the Split method to place each of the two fields---Name and Grade---into separate Array elements. Code this exercise up, and then I'll take some time to explain what you've done."

Exercise 13-5 Reading Comma Delimited Records from a Disk File

In this exercise, you'll read the records you wrote to the disk file in Exercise 11-1, and display their information in the Visual Basic Output window.

1. Start a new Windows application project.
2. Add a Button control to your form.
3. Place the following code into its Click event procedure.

```
Private Sub Button1_Click(ByVal sender As System.Object,
   ByVal e As System.EventArgs) Handles Button1.Click

   Dim line As String
   Dim fields() As String
   Dim delimiter As Char = ","
   Dim sr As New StreamReader("C:\VBFILES\PRACTICE\EX11-1.TXT")

   Do
      line = sr.ReadLine()
      If line Is Nothing Then Exit Do
      fields = line.Split(delimiter)
      Console.WriteLine(fields(0) + ":" + fields(1))
   Loop

   sr.Close()
End Sub
```

4. Place this line of code following the last using statement at the top of the Code window, above the line of code that denotes the Class header for the form.

Imports System.IO

5. Save the project, although you won't be modifying it any further.
6. Before you run the program, use Notepad to ensure that you have only the six correctly formatted records in the file. Blank lines and empty lines at the end of your file will cause your program to bomb. Now run the program.
7. Click the button. The program will display, in the Visual Basic Output window, the six records you wrote to the disk file \VBFILES\PRACTICE\EX11-1.TXT in Exercise 11-1.

Discussion

Only two people had a problem with the exercise---both Blaine and Linda had accidentally modified the input text file while looking at it, and inserted a blank line at the end which caused the program to bomb (exactly why we'll learn a bit later on in the course.)

Beyond that, no one seemed to have any problems with the exercise. I ran the program myself, clicked the second button, and displayed the Visual Basic Output window for all to see.

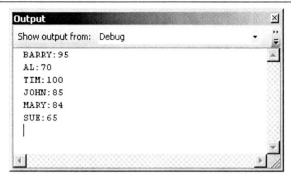

"That was really pretty easy," Ward said. "I'm more impressed than ever. Believe me, I'll be able to use this. However, I'm afraid I don't understand a thing that's going on the in the program—can you explain it"

"I can understand that Ward," I said, "I'll be glad to explain the code---let's take a look at it now. As usual, the first we do is declare any variables we need in our program. The first one, a String variable called line, is used to store the contents of each line as it is read from our input file via the ReadLine method of the StreamReader object…"

Dim line As String

As I mentioned, the Split method of the String object examines a String for one or more delimiters (such as a comma) and when it finds them, 'splits' the string and returns the results into a variable number of Array elements. For that reason, we need to declare an Array, which I have called fields…"

Dim fields() As String

"Notice how we haven't given the Array a size declaration," I said, "since it's unknown---it will be the Split method that loads the elements of the Array, and until the Split method is executed, it's size is unknown. We also need to declare a variable, and initialize it with the delimiter we are looking for in the String that is to be split. I declared a char variable, called delimiter and initialized it with a comma…"

Dim delimiter As Char = ","

"I should mention," I continued, "that it's possible to look for more than one delimiter in the search string---to do so, you declare a char Array and initialize it with the multiple delimiters you are looking for, like this…"

Dim delimiters() As Char = {" ", ",", ".", ":", "\t"}

The next line of code uses the StreamReader Constructor to open the file EX12-1.TXT for Input mode in the \VBFILES\PRACTICE subdirectory."

Dim sr As New StreamReader("C:\VBFILES\PRACTICE\EX11-1.TXT")

"Now we set up a loop, using the ReadLine method to read each line in the input file, checking for the invisible End Of File marker…"

Do
  line = sr.ReadLine()
  If line Is Nothing Then Exit Do

"Why do we need to do that?" Steve asked. "We know there are six records in the file."

"That's true," I said. "At this moment in time the file contains six records, but the number of records in a disk file will vary. The While structure is a perfect tool to enable us to read an unknown number of records in a file. All we need to do is tell Visual Basic to begin reading the records in the file and continue to read them until it reaches the EOF marker, or null character. Because Visual Basic can detect the invisible End Of File marker, we code our loop in such a way that it continues to read records from the opened disk file until it encounters the EOF."

I paused a moment before continuing.

"This line of code is new…."

fields = line.Split(delimiter)

"…it's the execution of the Split method of a String object, the String object in this instance is the String variable line, which contains the line we have just read from our input file. Notice that the Split method requires just a single argument—the delimiter variable that we declared and initialized with a comma. There are actually six variants of the Split method, accepting different numbers and types of arguments. For instance, if your delimiter isn't a single character, but instead is a String such as '00', you would need to declare a String variable instead. Notice how the return value of the Split method is assigned to our String Array called fields---when this line of code executes, the Array fields will have elements that we can access. For now, we display each of them---there are two---in the Visual Basic Output window, separated by a colon(:) using this statement"

Console.WriteLine(fields(0) + ":" + fields(1))

"What happens to the values of the variables---line and fields---when the next record is read?" Rhonda asked.

"The values are overwritten," I said. "That's why we immediately display them in the Visual Basic Output window."

I paused before continuing to see if there were any questions. There were none, and I went on, "And finally, this line of code closes the StreamReader object, and along with it, the opened file."

sr.Close()

No one seemed to have any big problems understanding what we had just done---I was a bit surprised, but with no questions from the class, it was time to move on.

Array Dimensions

Having seen how to work with comma delimited files, it was now time to begin my discussion of multidimensional arrays.

"All the arrays we've seen so far have been one-dimensional arrays," I explained.

"Dare I ask the difference?" said Kathy tentatively.

"Well, the comma delimited file we just worked with can be used as an illustration," I said. "Let's use Notepad to see the difference. In Notepad, one-dimensional arrays appear as a single column of data. Two-dimensional arrays appear as rows and columns of data. For instance." I said, as I displayed this file on the classroom projector.

"This is a two-dimensional text file," I explained. "This file contains not only the original midterm grades we worked with earlier today, but two other grades as well—the final examination and research paper grade."

"So you mean that the first column of numbers are midterm scores, the second column the final examination, and the third column the research paper?" Ward asked.

"That's right," I replied. "And each row represents a record for one student. This data can be represented using a single two-dimensional array, something you'll see in a little while. We could use three separate one-dimensional arrays to represent the data, with each column of numbers assigned to a one-dimensional array. In fact, that's a technique we'll use later on today in the China Shop Project."

"You mentioned the word 'multidimensional' a moment ago," Joe said. "Does that mean you can have more than two dimensions in an array?"

"Yes, you can have more than two dimensions in an array," I answered. "You can easily create three or four dimensional arrays. In fact, Visual Basic allows you to declare an array with up to 60 dimensions—but trying to envision that is another thing again!"

I then explained that Visual Basic gives you the ability to represent any real-world object with an array. However, anything more than a three-dimensional array is pretty difficult for most people to visualize.

"What kind of real-world object would you represent with a three-dimensional array?" Kathy asked.

"One classic example," I said, "is the owner of a farm who decides to use an array to keep track of where his crops are. He plants crops in fields (one dimension), and in a field, he plants crops in rows (second dimension) and columns (third dimension). Imagine a farm that consists of 10 separate fields where each field is made up of 100 rows and columns. A three-dimensional array is perfect to represent this."

"Is there a limitation to how large an array can be?" Steve asked.

"In theory, no," I said, "but there is a practical limitation in terms of your PC's memory limit. Multidimensional arrays, in particular, can tax the memory of your PC. Adding dimensions to an array will geometrically increase the storage requirements for the array."

I could see that some of my students were getting tense.

"Don't worry," I told everyone, "we'll restrict our discussion today to two-dimensional arrays. Just remember that everything you learn about two-dimensional arrays can be applied to an array with three or more dimensions."

I continued by explaining that the declaration for a multidimensional array is slightly different from the declaration for a one-dimensional array.

"With a multidimensional array, you need to declare a size for each dimension of the array," I explained. "Here's the declaration for the file we just viewed in Notepad that contains a midterm, final examination, and research grade for six students."

Dim intGrade(5, 2) As Integer

"When Visual Basic sees a comma in a variable declaration like this," I said, "right away it knows that it is dealing with the declaration for a two-dimensional array. The more numbers separated by commas, the more the dimensions in the array. In this instance, the first dimension has a size of 6— lowest subscript is 0, highest is 5. The second dimension has a size of 3—lowest subscript is 0, highest is 2. To calculate the total number of elements in an array, you multiply the two size figures. In this case, we have 18 elements or test scores in the array, since 3 multiplied by 6 is 18."

"How do we refer to individual elements within a multidimensional array?" Peter asked.

"Good question, Peter," I said. "One-dimensional arrays are referenced by using a single subscript. Two-dimensional array elements are referenced by using two subscripts. For example, to refer to the research paper grade for the second student, we would use this notation."

intGrades(1,2)

"The first number refers to the first dimension (or row) representing students," I said. "Subscript 1 is student number 2. The second number refers to the second dimension (or column) representing the test. Subscript 2 is the third test score, which happens to be the research paper."

I looked for signs of confusion, but happily there were none. I suggested that now would be a great time for an exercise for everyone to get their feet wet with a two-dimensional array.

Exercise 13-6 A Two-Dimensional Static Array

In this exercise, you'll have an opportunity to work with a two-dimensional array.

1. Start a new Windows application project.
2. Add a Button control to your form.
3. Place the following code into its Click event procedure.

```
Private Sub Button1_Click(ByVal sender As System.Object, _
  ByVal e As System.EventArgs) Handles Button1.Click

  Dim intGrades(5, 2) As Integer

  intGrades(0, 0) = 90
  intGrades(0, 1) = 40
  intGrades(0, 2) = 70

  intGrades(1, 0) = 91
  intGrades(1, 1) = 66
  intGrades(1, 2) = 95

  intGrades(2, 0) = 80
  intGrades(2, 1) = 82
```

```
intGrades(2, 2) = 84

intGrades(3, 0) = 77
intGrades(3, 1) = 55
intGrades(3, 2) = 44

intGrades(4, 0) = 100
intGrades(4, 1) = 99
intGrades(4, 2) = 78

intGrades(5, 0) = 44
intGrades(5, 1) = 33
intGrades(5, 2) = 78

For intRow = 0 To (intGrades.GetLength(0) - 1)
  For intCol = 0 To (intGrades.GetLength(1) - 1)
    Console.Write(intGrades(intRow, intCol) & " ")
  Next intCol
  Console.WriteLine()
Next intRow
```

End Sub

4. Place this line of code following the last using statement at the top of the Code window, above the line of code that denotes the Class header for the form.

Imports System.IO

5. Save your program, although you won't be modifying it any further.
6. Run the program.
7. Now click the button. The grades from the file will be displayed in the Visual Basic Output window.

Discussion

I immediately ran the program myself and the following screen was displayed on the classroom projector.

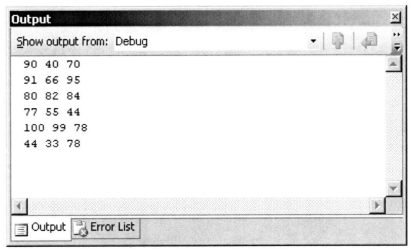

"As you can see," I said, "what we've done is write code to load the three quiz grades for six students into a two-dimensional Array and then display them in the Visual Basic console."

"This is pretty impressive," Rhonda said. "Although I must confess, I'm not real clear with how you did this."

"Don't worry, Rhonda," I said, "I'll be glad to explain it."

"That first line of code, is that the declaration for the two-dimensional Array?" Peter asked.

"Yes it is, Peter," I replied. "Here we are declaring a two-dimensional Array, and the numbers within the parentheses indicate the size of each dimension. Remember, by convention, in a two-dimensional Array, the row is specified first, followed by the column."

Dim intGrades(5, 2) As Integer

"Once we've declared the Array," I said, "this next section of code initializes each element of the Array, here, one line of code at a time."

```
intGrades(0, 0) = 90
intGrades(0, 1) = 40
intGrades(0, 2) = 70

intGrades(1, 0) = 91
intGrades(1, 1) = 66
intGrades(1, 2) = 95

intGrades(2, 0) = 80
intGrades(2, 1) = 82
intGrades(2, 2) = 84

intGrades(3, 0) = 77
intGrades(3, 1) = 55
intGrades(3, 2) = 44

intGrades(4, 0) = 100
intGrades(4, 1) = 99
intGrades(4, 2) = 78

intGrades(5, 0) = 44
intGrades(5, 1) = 33
intGrades(5, 2) = 78
```

"It's possible to initialize the elements of a two-dimensional Array the same way we initialized the elements of the one-dimensional Array in Exercise 13-3, like this."

```
Dim intGrades(,) As Integer = {{90, 40, 70}, _
                               {91, 66, 95}, _
                               {80, 82, 84}, _
                               {77, 55, 44}, _
                               {100, 99, 78}, _
                               {44, 33, 78}}
```

"Some students find this syntax confusing, so I'll leave it up to you to determine which syntax you prefer to use. Now, with our two-dimensional Array loaded with values, what remains is to navigate through the 18 elements of the Array and display them on the Visual Basic console. This next section of code is similar to the code you saw in Exercise 13-4, but because we are dealing with an Array that has not just one dimension but two, the technique is more complex, requiring us to use something called nested For loops."

```
For intRow = 0 To (intGrades.GetLength(0) - 1)
  For intCol = 0 To (intGrades.GetLength(1) - 1)
    Console.Write(intGrades(intRow, intCol) & " ")   Next intCol
  Console.WriteLine()
Next intRow
```

"This is where I got totally lost when I did the exercise," Kate said. "You say this is a nested For loop? I think I've heard some programmers at work use that term. It sounds very complicated."

"Nested For loops can be intimidating, Kate," I said, "but if you just remember that a nested For loop is nothing more than a loop whose body itself contains a For loop, I think you'll be OK."

I paused a moment to give everyone in the class to take in what I had just said.

"A nested For loop is a For loop that contains another For loop in its body," I repeated. "The first For loop structure is called the outer loop, and the For loop that appears in its body is called the inner loop. If you check the code, you'll see that each For loop has its own unique Loop Control variable. I've named the Loop Control variable of the outer loop row, and the Loop Control variable of the inner loop col. This is because the outer loop is intended to process the columns in the two-dimensional Array, and the inner loop is intended to process the rows. Think of these For loops almost like a mouse pointer that is directing a screen cursor to various positions within the Array."

"This is confusing," Rhonda chimed in. "I keep trying to visualize what's going on with the code but..."

"I think if you take it a step at a time, you'll be fine," I said. "And that's exactly what we're going to be doing in a minute. Notice that the outer loop has a body consisting of three lines of code: another For loop, a **Write()** method, and a **WriteLine()** method. The inner loop has a body consisting of just one line of code: the **Write()** method."

"Isn't the **WriteLine()** method part of the body of the inner loop?" Barbara asked.

"No, it's not," I said. "The inner loop—the one that uses col as the Loop Control variable—has just one line of code in it, the **Write()** method."

I paused for a moment before continuing.

"You'll see in a minute," I said, "as we step through this code, that the body of the inner loop will be executed a total of 18 times, while the body of the outer loop will be executed just six times."

"Is that because there are six rows of data in the Array?" Dave asked.

"Exactly, Dave," I said.

"But there are only three columns in the Array," Blaine said, "Why would the inner loop be executed 18 times? Shouldn't it be executed just three times?"

"That's a good question, Blaine," I responded. "The inner loop is executed three times, but each time the outer loop is executed, which is six times, the inner loop is once again executed three times. Six multiplied by three is 18—that's the total number of times the inner loop is executed."

"It also happens to be the number of elements in the Array," Dave said.

I saw a great deal of confusion on the faces of my students.

"Don't worry if you feel a little overwhelmed by this right now," I said. "I think this will all make a lot more sense to you in a few moments. Let's get back to the body of the inner loop now. Amazingly, it consists of just this single line of code."

Console.Write(intGrades(intRow, intCol) & " ")

"This line of code will be executed a total 18 times," I explained, "which, as Dave pointed out, is the total number of elements, or quiz grades, in our two-dimensional Array. Using nested For loops, the values of the two Loop Control variables, intRow and intCol, are varied to point to each element in the Array and displayed in the Visual Basic Console."

For intRow = 0 To (intGrades.GetLength(0) - 1)
**   For intCol = 0 To (intGrades.GetLength(1) - 1)**

"Again, the first loop is known as the outer loop," I continued, "and we use it to move through the rows in the Array. We initialize its Loop Control variable, intRow, to 0, and for its termination point, we use the GetLength attribute of the intGrades Array."

"GetLength?" Mary asked. "Didn't we use the Length attribute in the other exercise?"

"That's right, Mary," I answered. "The Length attribute returns the length of a one-dimensional Array. When you are dealing with a multidimensional Array, we need to use the GetLength attribute, which permits us to specify, as an argument, the Array dimension whose length we wish to return. Specifying zero as an argument returns the length of the row dimension, which is six. Specifying one as an argument returns the length of the column dimension, which is three. Ultimately, Visual Basic interprets this line of code."

For intRow = 0 To (intGrades.GetLength(0) - 1)

"…to look like this."

For intRow = 0 To 5

"That means that the outer loop is executed six times, is that right?" Chuck asked.

"Exactly right, Chuck," I said. "Now let's take a closer look at the inner loop, which is used to process the columns in the Array."

For intCol = 0 To (intGrades.GetLength(1) - 1)

"I want you to notice the GetLength attribute as we use it here. We used the GetLength attribute in the outer loop also, and in that case, it returned a value equal to the number of rows in the Array. In this case, we're asking Visual

Basic to return the Length attribute for the second dimension of the of the Array, and that's why we used the number one as an argument here. Ultimately, Visual Basic interprets this code to look like this."

For intRow = 0 To 2

"And that's why the inner loop is executed three times?" Chuck asked.

"That's right, Chuck," I said.

"Maybe this will help," I said, "to give you an appreciation for the sequence of code execution." I then displayed this table on the classroom projector.

Again, I emphasized that the body of the loop is executed 18 times and we verified that by running the code in Step mode. Here I've illustrated some of the results we saw.

Statement	intRow	intCol	intGrades	Value of intGrades
For intRow = 0 to 5	0	0	0,0	
For intCol = 0 to 2	0	0	0,0	
intGrade(0,1)	0	0	0,0	90
Next intCol	0	1	0,1	
intGrade(0,2)	0	1	0,1	40
Next intCol	0	2	0,2	
intGrade(0,3)	0	2	0,2	70
Next intCol	0	2	0,2	
Next intRow	1	2	1,2	
For intCol = 0 to 2	1	0	1,0	
intGrade(1,0)	1	0	1,0	91

"This table shows the statements that are being executed," I said, "as well as the values of the row and col Loop Control variables, the Array element that is being pointed to by the value of row and col, the value of that Array element, and the result of the execution of the statement."

We spent the next few minutes going over the table.

"I hope that helped," I said, as I scanned the faces of my students for signs of confusion.

"Yes, it did," Ward said. "I have just one question: why did we use the **Write()** method in the body of the inner loop to print the values of the individual elements of the Array and not the **WriteLine()** method?"

"The **Write()** method doesn't generate a new line character," I said. "If we had used the **WriteLine()** method, we would have had a single column of values displayed in the Visual Basic console, with each value appearing on a line by itself. Instead, we executed the **Write()** method, which tells Visual Basic to display a value in the Visual Basic console but not to generate a new line character. As a result, the cursor in the Visual Basic console remains on the same line. We did execute the **WriteLine()** method, but only at the end of each row, as the last statement in the body of the inner loop."

We took a few minutes to run the program in Step mode to see how the code in this section was processing. I asked if there were any questions, but there were none. I told everyone that if they were still confused by the code they saw here, they weren't alone. Working with multidimensional arrays requires patience and practice, and the more you work with them, the more comfortable you'll become.

"My only question," Kathy said, "is when should we use an array."

"You need experience to determine when your program can benefit from an array," I explained. "I frequently tell my students that beginner programmers find it hard to believe they'll ever use an array and experienced programmers are always looking for an excuse to use them."

It was now time for a break. I told everyone that when they returned, we would modify the China Shop Project to incorporate some array processing of our own.

Modifying the China Shop Project to Include Arrays

"In our last two exercises of the day," I said, "we'll modify the China Shop Project to incorporate array processing."

I then distributed this exercise for the class to complete.

Exercise 13-7 Modify the China Shop Project to Load an Array

In this exercise, you'll modify the China Shop Project to read inventory prices into six one-dimensional arrays for later processing.

1. Use Notepad to create a file called PRICES.TXT in your \VBFiles\China directory that contains the data you see in the following screenshot. Notice that the file contains three records. Each record contains one text field representing a china brand, and seven numeric fields representing prices for items applicable to that brand, in this order: Plate, Butter Plate, Soup Bowl, Cup, Saucer, Platter, Complete Place Setting Discount. All fields are separated by commas.

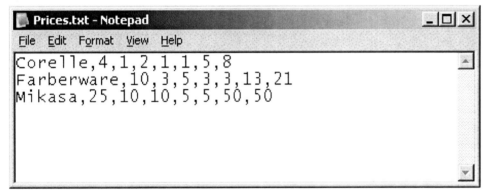

2. Load the China Shop Project.
3. Place this line of code at the top of the Code window.

Imports System.IO

4. You need to declare several form-level dynamic arrays in the Declarations section of the form. Since these are dynamic arrays, don't forget to add the closing parentheses. You should see that you have <u>three</u> variables already declared there: m_intQuantity, m_intBackColor, and m_blnDateDisplay. Add the following seven dynamic array declarations *after* m_blnDateDisplay.

```
Private m_sngBowlPrice() As Single
Private m_sngButterPlatePrice() As Single
Private m_sngCupPrice() As Single
Private m_sngPlatePrice() As Single
Private m_sngPlatterPrice() As Single
Private m_sngSaucerPrice() As Single
Private m_sngCompletePrice() As Single
```

5. Find the Load procedure of the form, delete the current lines of code that add the china brands to the lstBrands ListBox, and replace it with the following code. Be careful—the Input statements are not in alphabetical order. They appear in the order in which the prices are stored in the PRICES.TXT file, which is the same order in which they appear on the China Shop form.

```
Private Sub Main_Load(ByVal sender As System.Object, _
    ByVal e As System.EventArgs) Handles MyBase.Load

    Dim line As String
    Dim fields() As String
    Dim delimiter As Char = ","
    Dim intCounter As Integer
```

```
Dim sr As New StreamReader("C:\VBFILES\CHINA\PRICES.TXT")
Do
  line = sr.ReadLine()
  If line Is Nothing Then Exit Do

  ReDim Preserve m_sngBowlPrice(intCounter)
  ReDim Preserve m_sngButterPlatePrice(intCounter)
  ReDim Preserve m_sngCupPrice(intCounter)
  ReDim Preserve m_sngPlatePrice(intCounter)
  ReDim Preserve m_sngPlatterPrice(intCounter)
  ReDim Preserve m_sngSaucerPrice(intCounter)
  ReDim Preserve m_sngCompletePrice(intCounter)

  fields = line.Split(delimiter)
  lstBrands.Items.Add(fields(0))
  m_sngPlatePrice(intCounter) = fields(1)
  m_sngButterPlatePrice(intCounter) = fields(2)
  m_sngBowlPrice(intCounter) = fields(3)
  m_sngCupPrice(intCounter) = fields(4)
  m_sngSaucerPrice(intCounter) = fields(5)
  m_sngPlatterPrice(intCounter) = fields(6)
  m_sngCompletePrice(intCounter) = fields(7)

  intCounter = intCounter + 1
Loop
sr.Close()
End Sub
```

6. Save the China Shop Project by clicking the Save icon on the Visual Basic toolbar.

7. Run the program. At this point, you won't notice any obvious differences in the program, although now the items in the lstBrands ListBox are being loaded from the PRICES.TXT file instead of BRANDS.TXT, and your seven dynamic arrays have been loaded with values. You still need to change the code in the Click event procedure of the btnCalculate Button control to utilize the prices loaded in your array to calculate the customer's sales quotation. We'll do that in the next exercise.

Discussion

"The purpose of this exercise was to eliminate the hard coding of the china inventory prices into our program and to load them into arrays for later processing. In the next exercise, we'll modify the code in the Click event procedure of btnCalculate to read prices from those arrays," I said.

"I understand why we're loading the prices from a file, but why load them into an array, why not just an ordinary variable?" Rhonda asked.

"Loading prices into a dynamic array provides the most flexibility for our program," I replied. "This allows the China Shop to offer another brand of china for sale without us having to change any of our code—all we would need to do is add another line to PRICES.TXT. Believe me, this can make you very popular with a client who doesn't want to pay more money to have you come in and make a change to a program just to be able to see another brand of china. To offer another brand of china for sale, all someone at China Shop must do is another line to the PRICES.TXT file reflecting the brand of china and its item prices."

"I noticed that we are no longer reading the BRANDS.TXT file and that it appears we are loading the ListBox by using the PRICES.TXT file," Linda commented.

"That's right, Linda," I said. "It doesn't make sense to maintain two files when one will do the job, so we'll no longer be needing the BRANDS.TXT file. Our program will read the brand of china from the first field of the PRICES.TXT file and load the brand into the ListBox using the value for that field."

"Can you explain what's going on with the arrays?" Joe asked.

"Sure thing, Joe," I said. "Our code reads the data from the file into seven separate one-dimensional arrays. Each array represents a different china item—like cup or plate—and each element in the array represents the price for a brand of china for that item. Element 0 is the brand associated with the first record in the file—in this case Corelle—Element 1 the second brand, Farberware, and Element 2, Mikasa."

"Why didn't we use one two-dimensional arrays here instead of seven one-dimensional arrays?" Dave asked.

"We could have used a two-dimensional array here Dave," I answered, "but for beginners, arrays are difficult enough to deal with. Taxing you with additional demands of a two-dimensional array doesn't make a lot of sense to me when a one-dimensional array will do. Besides, if you want, you can always convert the code to use a single two-dimensional array later."

I waited for questions, but there were none, so I began to explain the code in the exercise.

"The first thing we did was to use Notepad to create the PRICES.TXT file," I said. "This is the file that the China Shop staff will modify when they want to update inventory prices. Let's review the format of this file one more time."

I explained that there is a line or a record for each brand of china in the China Shop's inventory—a total of three lines in all.

"There are a total of eight fields," I said, "one character field and seven numeric fields. The first field in the record is a character field consisting of the name of the china brand, followed by the seven numeric fields representing the price for a plate, butter plate, bowl, cup, saucer, and platter of that brand. The final field represents the discounted complete place setting price. Remember that the seven numeric fields will be loaded into separate arrays. The string field will be used to populate the lstBrands ListBox. And a big caution here: we decided to have the order of the prices in the file be the same order as they appear in the form—and this has significant importance to the order of our Input statements that we coded. The Input statements must match the order of the fields in the file, otherwise our prices will be off."

"I had forgotten about that discount price," Linda said. "I almost did myself," I said, "because we haven't calculated a discounted price in the code we've written so far, but we did promise Joe Bullina we would calculate the discount." Again I paused for questions, but there were none. "After creating the file PRICES.TXT," I added, "we then declared seven form-level dynamic arrays in the Declarations section of the form module."

```
Private m_sngBowlPrice() As Single
Private m_sngButterPlatePrice() As Single
Private m_sngCupPrice() As Single
Private m_sngPlatePrice() As Single
Private m_sngPlatterPrice() As Single
Private m_sngSaucerPrice() As Single
Private m_sngCompletePrice() As Single
```

"I noticed that some of you almost forgot to code that empty set of parentheses at the end of the declaration," I continued. "The empty parentheses tells Visual Basic that it is dealing with a dynamic array."

"Why did we declare the dynamic arrays at the form module level?" Dave asked. "Aren't all of the calculations using those variables performed in the Click event procedure of btnCalculate—in which case they could be declared there?"

"You raise a good point," I said. "The reason I asked you to declare them at the form level is that I can foresee the possibility that we might want to access the values in these arrays from another event procedure sometime in the future. In fact, during our last week of class, we'll do exactly that."

I suggested that we then look at the revised code in the Load Event procedure.

"As usual," I began, "the first thing we do is declare any variables that we'll need to use in the procedure—in our case, that's four variables, all of which we've seen before. line is the variable into which we read the line from our text file, fields is a Dynamic String Array into which the comma delimited fields of the line variable are placed, and delimiter is the variable that contains the delimiter value to be used with the Split method...."

```
Dim line As String
Dim fields() As String
Dim delimiter As Char = ","
```

"...and intCounter is a Loop Control variable which we'll use to specify the subscript numbers of the elements we load to our arrays."

Dim intCounter As Integer

"This line of code declares a StreamReader object and opens the file PRICES.TXT for input," I said.

Dim sr As New StreamReader("C:\VBFILES\CHINA\PRICES.TXT")

I explained that the next lines of code initiates a Do Loop that will repeat until the invisible EOF marker of PRICES.TXT is encountered—the ReadLine method reads a line from our PRICES.TXT file into the variable line.

Do
  line = sr.ReadLine()
  If line Is Nothing Then Exit Do

"Within the body of the loop," I continued, "we coded seven ReDim Preserve statements."

ReDim Preserve m_sngBowlPrice(intCounter)
ReDim Preserve m_sngButterPlatePrice(intCounter)
ReDim Preserve m_sngCupPrice(intCounter)
ReDim Preserve m_sngPlatePrice(intCounter)
ReDim Preserve m_sngPlatterPrice(intCounter)
ReDim Preserve m_sngSaucerPrice(intCounter)
ReDim Preserve m_sngCompletePrice(intCounter)

I reminded everyone that the ReDim statement redeclares the size of our dynamic arrays by adjusting its upper bound.

"Since we declared these arrays with no initial size," I said, "each time the body of the loop executes we need to execute the ReDim statement to increase its size by 1. This is why we take the current value of intCounter and add 1 to it."

"And Preserve ensures that we don't lose any data we already have in the arrays, is that right?" Linda asked.

"That's right, Linda," I said. "Now, the next line of code uses the Split method to load all of the comma delimited fields from the variable line into the fields Dynamic Array---because we have 8 'fields' on each line of our input file, our fields array will have 8 elements, numbered 0 through 7.

fields = line.Split(delimiter)

"Because we know that the Brand name of the China pattern is the first 'field' in our input file, we can use this syntax to add the brand to our listbox…"

lstBrands.Items.Add(fields(0))

"Similarly," I continued, "because we know the 'order' of the remaining fields in the input file, we can then execute these lines of code to load the prices of the 7 individual price arrays…"

m_sngPlatePrice(intCounter) = fields(1)
m_sngButterPlatePrice(intCounter) = fields(2)
m_sngBowlPrice(intCounter) = fields(3)
m_sngCupPrice(intCounter) = fields(4)
m_sngSaucerPrice(intCounter) = fields(5)
m_sngPlatterPrice(intCounter) = fields(6)
m_sngCompletePrice(intCounter) = fields(7)

"The next line of code increments the counter variable intCounter by 1," I explained, "and marks the end of the loop."

  intCounter = intCounter + 1
Loop

"And finally, this line of code closes the PRICES.TXT file."

sr.Close()

No one seemed to have any major problems with the exercise, and I sensed some anticipation of the next exercise to come. I also noticed a few students using the Immediate window to display the values of various elements of their arrays and I praised them for it. I then announced that in our final exercise of the day, we would modify the code in the Click event procedure of the btnCalculate Button control to calculate a sales quotation for our customer using the values in those arrays. I then distributed this exercise for the class to complete.

Exercise 13-8 Calculating Prices Based on Our Arrays

In this exercise, you'll modify the code in the Click event procedure of btnCalculate to use the values of the dynamic arrays to calculate the customer's sales quotation.

1. Continue working with the China Shop Project.
2. Delete the existing code in the Click event procedure of btnCalculate, and **_replace_** it with the code shown here.

```
Private Sub btnCalculate_Click (ByVal sender As System.Object, _
  ByVal e As System.EventArgs) Handles btnCalculate.Click

Dim sngTotalPrice As Single
Dim sngButterPlatePrice As Single
Dim sngCupPrice As Single
Dim sngPlatePrice As Single
Dim sngPlatterPrice As Single
Dim sngSaucerPrice As Single
Dim sngSoupBowlPrice As Single
Dim sngCompletePrice As Single
Dim intCounter As Integer

'Has the customer selected a brand of china?
If lstBrands.Text = "" Then
  MessageBox.Show("You must select a China brand")
  Exit Sub
End If

'Has the customer selected one or more china items?
If chkPlate.Checked = False And _
  chkButterPlate.Checked = False And _
  chkSoupBowl.Checked = False And _
  chkCup.Checked = False And _
  chkSaucer.Checked = False And _
  chkPlatter.Checked = False Then
  MessageBox.Show("You must select one or more china items")
  Exit Sub
End If

'Has the customer selected a quantity?
If rad8.Checked = False And _
  rad4.Checked = False And _
  rad2.Checked = False And _
  rad1.Checked = False Then
  MessageBox.Show("You must select a quantity")
  Exit Sub
End If

'If the customer has selected a platter
'warn them that there is only 1 permitted
'per sales quotation

If chkPlatter.Checked = True And m_intQuantity > 1 Then
  MessageBox.Show("Customer is limited to 1 platter per order." & Chr(13) & _
        "Adjusting price accordingly")
End If

'All the pieces are here, let's calculate a price
'Calculate subtotal prices by item
intCounter = lstBrands.SelectedIndex
sngSoupBowlPrice = m_sngBowlPrice(intCounter) * chkSoupBowl.CheckState
sngButterPlatePrice = m_sngButterPlatePrice(intCounter) * chkButterPlate.CheckState
sngCompletePrice = m_sngCompletePrice(intCounter)
```

```
sngCupPrice = m_sngCupPrice(intCounter) * chkCup.CheckState
sngPlatePrice = m_sngPlatePrice(intCounter) * chkPlate.CheckState
sngPlatterPrice = m_sngPlatterPrice(intCounter) * chkPlatter.CheckState
sngSaucerPrice = m_sngSaucerPrice(intCounter) * chkSaucer.CheckState

If chkSoupBowl.Checked And chkButterPlate.Checked And _
  chkCup.Checked And chkPlate.Checked And _
  chkSaucer.Checked Then
  MessageBox.Show("Price includes a Complete Place Setting Discount")
  sngTotalPrice = (sngCompletePrice * m_intQuantity) + sngPlatterPrice
Else
  sngTotalPrice = (((sngSoupBowlPrice + sngButterPlatePrice + _
                    sngCupPrice + sngPlatePrice + sngSaucerPrice) * _
                    m_intQuantity) + sngPlatterPrice)
End If

'If the price is greater than 0, display the price and make the label visible

If sngTotalPrice > 0 Then
  lblPrice.Text = "The price of your order is "& Format(sngTotalPrice, "$##,###.00")
  lblPrice.Visible = True
End If

End Sub
```

3. Save the China Shop Project by clicking the Save icon on the Visual Basic toolbar.
4. Run the program. Select Mikasa as your choice of china brand, select 2 for quantity, and select Plate, Butter Plate, and Soup Bowl as your china items. Then click the Calculate button. A calculated price of $90 should be displayed.

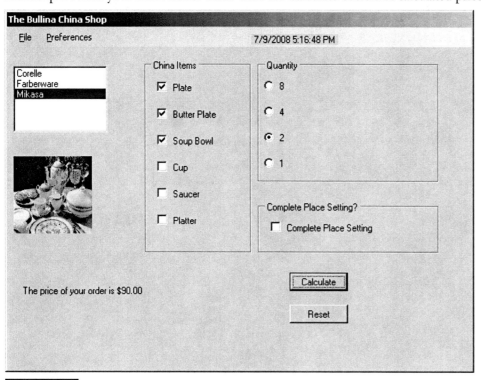

Discussion

The final exercise of the day was not without its difficulties. The code was pretty tedious to enter, and because some of the code remained the same and some of it needed to be changed, it became confusing at times. However, all in all, the exercise went pretty smoothly and after about fifteen minutes, everyone had completed it.

"The purpose of this exercise," I said, "was to remove the hard-coded prices that had been written into the program and instead use the price values in the dynamic arrays which we created and loaded in the previous exercise. As was the case in the first version of the code in btnCalculate, we'll calculate subtotal values for one of the items of china selected by the customer and then add them together to arrive at a grand total sales quotation. Obviously, what will complicate the code here is the fact that we're now looking up prices for the items in the various arrays, plus we are also now calculating a discount for a complete place setting. Let's look at the code now, much of which is identical to what was in the first version of this code before we modified it."

I continued by explaining that, as usual, the first thing we did was to declare the variables we will need to use in the event procedure.

```
Dim sngTotalPrice As Single
Dim sngButterPlatePrice As Single
Dim sngCupPrice As Single
Dim sngPlatePrice As Single
Dim sngPlatterPrice As Single
Dim sngSaucerPrice As Single
Dim sngSoupBowlPrice As Single
Dim sngCompletePrice As Single
Dim intCounter As Integer
```

"Only sngCompletePrice and intCounter are new variable declarations," I explained. "The other variables remain the same from the first version of this code. The variable sngCompletePrice is required because we are now calculating a complete place setting discount. It will store the subtotal value for a complete place setting, if the program determines that one has been selected by the customer. intCounter is a variable we will use to identify the subscript of the element we want to access in one of the appropriate price arrays. The value of intCounter will be equal to the SelectedIndex property of the lstBrands ListBox. For instance, if the customer selects Corelle as their brand of china, the value of SelectedIndex will be 0, and we'll assign 0 to the value of intCounter as well. That value will be used as the subscript to access the items in each of the seven dynamic arrays."

I paused to see if I was losing anyone, but my students seemed to be following along fine.

"Since each of our seven arrays has three different elements," I continued, "one for each brand of china, we absolutely need to know the brand the customer has selected in order to access the correct price in each of the arrays. The elements in our array are numbered 0, 1, and 2, where 0 is equal to Corelle, 1 is Farberware, and 2 is Mikasa. That is also the same order that these brands appear in the list box—in fact, that sequence is by design, since both the list box items and the arrays were loaded from the same records in the PRICES.TXT disk file. The bottom line is that we can use the SelectedIndex property of the ListBox to access elements in the seven arrays, because the SelectedIndex property is equal to 0 when the customer selects Corelle, 1 when Farberware is selected, and 2 when it's Mikasa."

"Would this code work even if the records in the file weren't sorted alphabetically?" Linda asked.

"Yes, it would," I replied, "since both the list box and the arrays are loaded from the same file, PRICES.TXT. The only thing that could cause us a problem here is if the records were not sorted alphabetically and the Sorted property of the ListBox was set to True. In that case, the SelectedIndex property and the element number in each of arrays would not match, and we would wind up accessing the wrong values in each of the arrays."

I waited for questions, but I think everyone was satisfied with my explanation.

"The next few lines of code haven't changed since the first version of this code, so I won't discuss those again in detail," I said, referring to the code to check that the customer has selected a brand of china, one or more items of china, and a quantity.

"This line of code assigns the value of the SelectedIndex property to the variable intCounter," I explained, "and that's to enable the proper access of the elements in each of the price arrays."

```
intCounter = lstBrands.SelectedIndex
```

"This next section of code," I continued, "looks pretty complicated, but it isn't really. What we're doing here is calculating the individual subtotal prices for each item of china. We take the price of the item in the array and multiply it by the CheckState property of its respective CheckBox. If the check box is selected, its CheckState property is 1. If it's not checked, its CheckState property is 0. Let's look at the calculation for the soup bowl subtotal."

```
sngSoupBowlPrice = m_sngBowlPrice(intCounter) * chkSoupBowl.CheckState
```

"Let's pretend that the customer has selected Mikasa as their brand of china," I said. "In this case, the SelectedIndex property of the lstBrands ListBox is equal to 2. This means that we assign the number 2 to the value of the variable intCounter. We then use that value of intCounter to access the element of m_sngBowlPrice whose subscript is 2. It turns out its value is equal to 10."

"How do you know that?" Ward asked.

"That's the price that is found in the PRICES.TXT for a Mikasa soup bowl," I replied. "It's also the value that we've recorded in our documentation as being the price for the Mikasa soup bowl."

"What's going on with the CheckState property?" Linda asked.

"We go through the motions of looking up the price for each item of china," I said, "regardless of whether the customer actually selected it. However, once we look up the price, we then multiply it by the value of CheckState for the respective check box. If the customer has selected the check box, CheckState will be equal to 1. If not, CheckState will be equal to 0. Suppose the customer has indicated a desire to purchase the soup bowl by selecting the Soup Bowl check box. The CheckState property of chkSoupBowl will be equal to 1, and the price of the soup bowl—10—is then multiplied by 1 giving us 10. Therefore, the value of sngBowlPrice will be set to 10. If the customer has decided not to purchase a soup bowl, then the CheckState property of chkSoupBowl will be 0. Anything multiplied by 0 is 0 and so the value of sngBowlPrice will be set to 0. We then perform this same calculation for the remaining six subtotal variables: sngButterPlatePrice, sngCompletePrice, sngCupPrice, sngPlatePrice, sngPlatterPrice, and sngSaucerPrice."

```
sngButterPlatePrice = m_sngButterPlatePrice(intCounter) * chkButterPlate.CheckState
sngCompletePrice = m_sngCompletePrice(intCounter)
sngCupPrice = m_sngCupPrice(intCounter) * chkCup.CheckState
sngPlatePrice = m_sngPlatePrice(intCounter) * chkPlate.CheckState
sngPlatterPrice = m_sngPlatterPrice(intCounter) * chkPlatter.CheckState
sngSaucerPrice = m_sngSaucerPrice(intCounter) * chkSaucer.CheckState
```

"I noticed, that the calculation for sngCompletePrice is different from the others," Kate said.

"Good observation, Kate," I responded. "Although there is a check box to indicate a complete place setting, we don't multiply the CheckState property of its CheckBox by the price in the m_sngCompletePrice array. Instead, we use an If test to determine if the complete place setting discount price should be used in the calculation of the grand total."

I could see some of my students were confused and I asked them to hold on. "In this version of the code," I said, "we use an If...Else statement to determine if the Plate, Butter Plate, Soup Bowl, Cup, and Saucer check boxes have been selected."

```
If chkSoupBowl.Checked And chkButterPlate.Checked And _
    chkCup.Checked And chkPlate.Checked And _
    chkSaucer.Checked Then
  MessageBox.Show("Price includes a Complete Place Setting Discount")
```

"Because there is a discount for a Complete Place Setting selection, we have two different price calculations that can be performed here."

```
sngTotalPrice = (sngCompletePrice * m_intQuantity) + sngPlatterPrice
```

"As you can see, we take the value of sngCompletePrice, multiply it by the value of m_intQuantity, which contains the customer's selected quantity, and then add the value of sngPlatterPrice to that value."

I reminded the class that if the customer had not made a selection of a platter, the value of sngPlatterPrice would be 0. "Does everyone understand what is going on here?" I asked. There were mostly nods, but I thought posing another example would be a good idea.

"Suppose," I said, "the customer selects the Mikasa brand, a quantity of 4, and checks the Complete Place Setting check box. However, they don't want a platter. Let's take this a step at a time, by replacing the sngCompletePrice variable with its value, which for Mikasa is 50. Since the customer has not selected a platter, the value for sngPlatterPrice is 0. So the line of code that performs the price calculation really looks like this."

```
sngTotalPrice = (50 * 4) + 0
```

"Taking this a step further, the calculation looks like this," I said.

```
sngTotalPrice = (200) + 0
```

"So the calculated price for a Mikasa complete place setting, quantity of 4, without a platter is $200," I announced.

I then ran the program and displayed the results on the classroom projector. Several students asked me to run the program in Step mode, which I thought was a great idea. I explained that the discounted complete place setting calculation is slightly simpler than the alternative, where we add all of the subtotal prices together to arrive at a grand total.

```
sngTotalPrice = (((sngSoupBowlPrice + sngButterPlatePrice + _
            sngCupPrice + sngPlatePrice + sngSaucerPrice) * _
            m_intQuantity) + sngPlatterPrice)
```

This code was identical to the calculation we had performed in the first version of the Click event procedure of btnCalculate, so I did not discuss it.

"Finally," I said, "this code is nearly identical to the previous version of the code, with the exception of the line of code containing the Visual Basic Format function."

```
If sngTotalPrice > 0 Then
    lblPrice.Text = "The price of your order is"& Format(sngTotalPrice, "$##,###.00")
    lblPrice.Visible = True
End If
```

"What we've done here is improve upon the display of the price quotation," I explained, "by using the Visual Basic Format function to display a currency format. For more information on the Format function, you can consult Visual Basic Help."

"I may be wrong about this," Kate said, "but I think we're just about ready to deliver this program to the China Shop."

"Just about, Kate," I agreed. "We don't have very much left to do. In fact, some time this week, I'd like to contact Joe Bullina to schedule a delivery date and time for the program!"

"What will we be doing next week, then?" Joe asked.

"Next week we'll examine Exception Handling in Visual Basic," I answered. "Then, in our last week of class, we'll discuss using the Windows Registry to save user preferences, and finally wrap up by looking at some code optimization techniques."

I dismissed class for the day and told everyone that during the evening I would be placing a shore-to-ship call to Rose and Jack to see how they were coming along with the ocean tests on their company's new ocean liner. Would they make it back for the delivery of the China Shop Project?

Summary

In this chapter, I suspect you learned just about everything you've always wanted to know about array processing, and more. In particular we learned about the various types of arrays, both static and dynamic, and also about array dimensions. Arrays are a frequent source of confusion for new programmers, and I hope our coverage of them will make your future work with them easier.

Specifically, we saw:

- Why arrays are useful in making our code easier to write and use.

- Different types of arrays: static, dynamic, one- and two-dimensional.

- How arrays can reduce the amount of hard-coding we have in our China Shop Project. This means that when prices change we don't need to change the Visual Basic Code, we only need to amend the prices stored in the disk file.

In the next chapter, we'll explore some of the common errors that can occur in Visual Basic programming, and look at how to make allowances for problems that might occur when our programs run.

Chapter 14---Exception Handling

In this chapter, you'll follow my university class as I show them how to avoid some of the mistakes that beginner programmers commonly make. I'll also show you how to detect and handle the errors that slip through your fingers.

Common Beginner Errors

I began our fourteenth class by telling everyone that my shore-to-ship call to Jack and Rose had gone well and that they had informed me they would be back in time for next Saturday's final class. Both would be returning to the United States on the maiden voyage of the ocean liner that they had helped engineer.

"Talk about following through with the SDLC!" Dave exclaimed. "They helped design the ship, now they're participating in the implementation, feedback, and maintenance phases."

"That's a great point, Dave," I said. "We'll be doing the same thing next week when we deliver the China Shop Project to Joe Bullina."

I began by explaining that as a programming teacher, it's always tempting to show my students examples of bad code early on in a class in an effort to show them what not to do. However, after many years of teaching, I have learned that there's a big danger in illustrating bad code or code that contains errors too early in the class.

"I always wait until we've established a strong foundation in good coding techniques," I said, "before discussing the types of errors you can make which can ruin your programming reputation. We'll be spending today's class examining the common errors that beginners make and then finish up by writing code to protect the China Shop Project from those same errors."

Referring to an Element Outside the Array Bounds

"Let's start by examining one of the more frequent runtime errors that occurs when working with arrays," I said, "and that's when we try to access an array element that is outside of the array's defined boundaries. Let's take a look at this code in which we have declared an array called **grades** that has six elements."

```
Private Sub Button1_Click(ByVal sender As System.Object,
ByVal e As System.EventArgs) Handles Button1.Click

    Dim grades(5) As Integer

    grades(0) = 82
    grades(1) = 90
    grades(2) = 64
    grades(3) = 80
    grades(4) = 95
    grades(5) = 75
    grades(6) = 44

End Sub
```

"I don't see anything wrong with this code," Rhonda said. "Is there a problem with it?"

"Yes, there is," I said. "We declared the Array to have an upper bound of 5...

Dim grades(5) as Integer

"...that means it has six elements. However, the last subscript value that we can legally refer to is 5---in our code, we're trying to refer to element number 6, which would be the seventh element in the Array. The problem is, we declared the Array to have just six elements..."

grades(6) = 44

"I understand now," Rhonda said. "And you say this won't be detected as an error until we run the program?"

"Unfortunately not, Rhonda," I said. "The compiler isn't smart enough to alert us to the problem. It won't be until runtime that this error becomes evident."

I then placed this code in the click event procedure of a button control, and clicked on the run button---and as I predicted, there were no error messages.

"Let's see what happens now when we click on the button," I said.

I did so, and the following Error message was displayed.

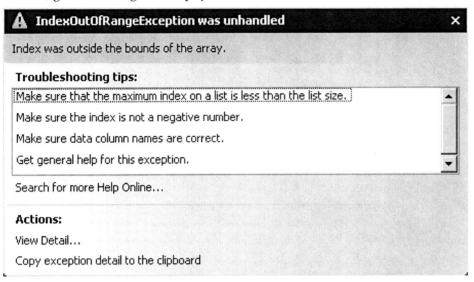

> **NOTE: If you are following along with me, Visual Basic will display the above message as a transparent window, and direct you, via a pointer, to the line of code causing the problem.**

"Basically," I said, "Visual Basic is telling us that we are trying to reference an Array element that does not exist."

There were no questions and so I continued.

Forgetting to Increment a Counter Variable

"This is one of the most common errors I see: forgetting to increment a counter variable," I continued, and went on to explain that many of the programming tasks we had examined during the course depended heavily upon declaring, incrementing, and examining a counter variable somewhere within a program.

"Counter variables," I explained, "are variables that you declare to do exactly that: count something. For example, last week in Exercise 13-4 we wrote code that added elements to an array from a disk file."

I gave everyone a chance to refer back to that exercise.

"In that exercise," I said, "in order to calculate the class average, we had to know the number of student grades that were in the file. To keep track of that number, we declared a variable called intCounter. Had we forgotten to increment this counter variable, a number of problems could result."

I displayed the code from Exercise 13-4 on the classroom projector.

```
Private Sub Button1_Click(ByVal sender As System.Object, _
    ByVal e As System.EventArgs) Handles Button1.Click

    Dim intGrades() As Integer
    Dim intCounter As Integer
    Dim intTotal As Integer
    Dim sngAverage As Single
    Dim line As String
    Dim sr As New StreamReader("C:\VBFILES\PRACTICE\GRADES.TXT")

    Do
        line = sr.ReadLine()
        If line Is Nothing Then Exit Do
        ReDim Preserve intGrades(intCounter)
        intGrades(intCounter) = line
        intCounter = intCounter + 1
    Loop
```

```
sr.Close()

For intCounter = 0 To (intGrades.Length - 1)
    Console.WriteLine(intGrades(intCounter))
    intTotal = intTotal + intGrades(intCounter)
Next

sngAverage = CSng(intTotal / intCounter)
Console.WriteLine("The class average is " & sngAverage)
End Sub
```

and pointed out the line of code where we incremented the counter variable.

```
intCounter = intCounter + 1
```

"Notice the code to increment the counter variable," I said. "I can't tell you the number of times that beginners forget to declare and increment a counter variable."

Forgetting to Add to an Accumulator

"An accumulator," I said, "is not much different from a counter variable. A counter variable is used to count the instances of something, like the number of tests taken or given or the number of employees in a company. An accumulator variable is a little different in that it is declared to hold the sum of something, such as the total value of all of the test grades or the total value of all salaries in a company."

Barbara said, "At work, I've heard accumulator variables referred to as data buckets by some of the programmers."

"That term brings back some memories of programming in COBOL," I chuckled. "Back then, we called our accumulator variables data buckets as well."

"Have we worked with accumulator variables in the class?" Rhonda asked.

"Yes, we have, Rhonda," I said, "Last week, we wrote code to sum the individual midterm grades, placed that value in an accumulator variable called intTotal, then divided that value by the number of tests taken, and displayed the result in the Visual Basic Output window. In that code, every time the user entered another grade, we added that grade to the accumulator value. If we had forgotten to add the grade to the accumulator variable, we would have displayed an incorrect average on the form, most likely 0."

"And there goes our reputation!" Rhonda said.

"That's right, Rhonda," I agreed. "It doesn't take many mistakes to tarnish it."

I displayed the code on the classroom projector and highlighted the area of code where we added the grade to the accumulator variable.

```
intTotal = intTotal + intGrades(intCounter)
```

"Forgetting to add a value to the accumulator variable is a very common type of Visual Basic error," I explained.

"What kind of error would this generate?" Ward asked.

"The program would run," I said, "but most likely the program would display an average of 0, something bound to greatly upset the professor of the class."

Not providing a way for a while structure to end

"Another type of runtime error that is common for beginners," I said, "is to code a While loop and forget to provide a way for it to end. A few weeks ago, we wrote this code in Exercise 9-7 to display the floor numbers of a hotel."

```
Private Sub Button1_Click(ByVal sender As System.Object,
    ByVal e As System.EventArgs) Handles Button1.Click

Dim intValue As Integer = 1

Do While intValue < 5
    Console.WriteLine (intValue)
    intValue = intValue + 1
Loop
```

```
End Sub
```

"Beginners," I continued, "frequently forget that in a While loop, it's important to include somewhere within the body of the loop code that enables the loop to eventually end. Otherwise, we have what is known as an endless loop. In the case of this code, we told Visual Basic to continue executing the loop while the value of the counter variable is less than 5. Since we initialized the counter variable to 1, if we didn't place some code in the body of the loop to do something to cause the value of the counter variable to become 5 or greater, the loop would never end. What we did, of course, was write this line of code that increments the value of the counter variable every time the body of the loop is executed."

```
intValue = intValue + 1
```

"What happens if we forget this code?" Joe asked.

"We'd create a program that would display the number 2 indefinitely in the Console Window—in other words, an infinite loop," I replied, as I displayed this code on the classroom projector.

```
Private Sub Button1_Click(ByVal sender As System.Object,
    ByVal e As System.EventArgs) Handles Button1.Click

Dim intValue As Integer = 1

Do While intValue < 5
    Console.WriteLine (intValue)
Loop

End Sub
```

I then ran the program, clicked on the button, The number 1 continued to display on the Visual Basic console. Because the program wouldn't stop, I had to stop it using the End button on the Visual Basic Toolbar.

"So that's an infinite loop," Rhonda said, "and all because we forgot one little line of code."

Failing to include the Imports IO.Sys statement

"The next series of errors we'll be discussing all deal with file operations," I continued. "The first one is probably the most common error I see when trying to diagnose students' inabilities to work with files, and that's to fail to include the Imports statement for IO.SYS. Without it, you simply don't have access to any of the File Operations capabilities in Visual Basic. Just to remind you, this statement needs to be at the top of your code window."

```
Imports System.IO
```

"I know I've been guilty of that one many times already," Rhonda said.

"I'm sure you're not the only one Rhonda," I said, with a smile on my face.

Trying to Open a File For Reading That Does Not Exist

"The next error," I continued, "is a very common one for beginners to make: trying to open a file for Read operations when the file does not exist. Last week, in Exercise 13-5, we wrote code to read comma delimited records from a disk file in our practice directory, and placed that code in the Click event procedure of a Button control."

I displayed the code from Exercise 13-5 on the classroom projector…

```
Private Sub Button1_Click(ByVal sender As System.Object,
    ByVal e As System.EventArgs) Handles Button1.Click

Dim line As String
Dim fields() As String
Dim delimiter As Char = ","
Dim sr As New StreamReader("C:\VBFILES\PRACTICE\EX11-1.TXT")

Do
    line = sr.ReadLine()
    If line Is Nothing Then Exit Do
    fields = line.Split(delimiter)
    Console.WriteLine(fields(0) + ":" + fields(1))
```

> **Loop**
>
> **sr.Close()**
> **End Sub**

...and pointed out the line of code where we attempted to open the disk file via the creation of a StreamReader object...

Dim sr As New StreamReader("C:\VBFILES\PRACTICE\EX11-1.TXT")

"What happens if the file doesn't exist??" Rhonda asked.

"Let's see," I suggested.

I then <u>temporarily</u> renamed the file from my classroom PC, ran the program, and clicked on the button control. The following screenshot was displayed on the classroom projector.

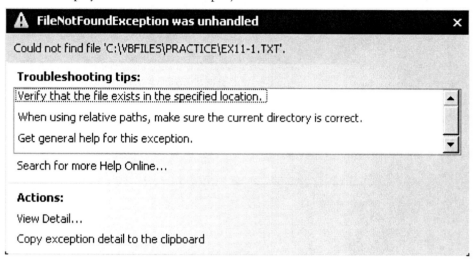

"A FileNotFoundException is generated when you try to open a file for Reading that doesn't exist," I explained. "By the way, if the folder you specified doesn't exist, you will receive this error."

I then changed our code to refer to a folder name that didn't exist on my classroom PC, ran the program, and clicked on the button control. This screenshot was displayed.

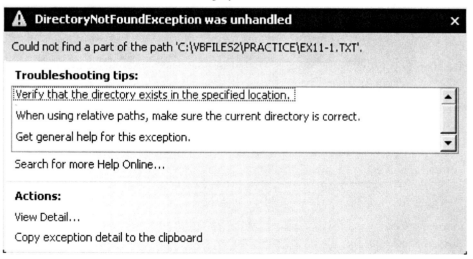

"How could a file be missing?" Ward asked. "Where would it go?"

"Accidents happen," I replied, "A user could delete the file by accident, or they could move it, possibly while renaming the folder it's contained in. They might even rename it. In some more complicated applications, files are created by other programs, and if those programs don't run, the required files aren't created. As a result, when the program goes looking for the file, it can't find it."

"Is this something we'll need to concern ourselves with for the China Shop project?" Steve asked. "since we're now reading a file to obtain the latest prices of China?"

"Yes it is Steve," I said. "We'll be doing that a little later on today."

Forgetting to Close a File

"I know we covered this a few weeks back, but suppose you forget to close a disk file? Does that cause problems?" Rhonda asked.

"Forgetting to close a file is another typical error for the beginner," I said. "Forgetting to close a file can have some potentially disastrous results for your program, especially if you are writing records to a file."

I reminded everyone that we had used the Write method to write records to a disk file during our class on file processing.

"It may surprise you to know," I said, "that just because you execute a Write method, that does not mean the data is immediately written to the open file. The operating system typically buffers write requests."

"Buffers write requests?" Kate said. "What exactly does that mean?"

"It means that the Operating System, in an effort to speed up overall program performance, writes records in batches," I explained. "For instance, suppose you are writing several thousand records to a disk file. Rather than writing this data one record at a time, the Operating System may choose to write ten records at a time, or twenty, perhaps even hundreds in one single operation. What that means is that the records you think you are writing to your open file are actually being stored in a buffer in the computer's memory, waiting to be physically written to the disk."

"Now where does the problem come in?" Mary asked.

"The problem, Mary," I said, "is that if your program comes to an abrupt halt without executing a Close method, there may be records sitting in the buffer that haven't been written to the disk yet."

"And those records are lost," Dave said.

"That's right, Dave," I replied.

"So you won't lose all of the data you've written," Linda said, "just some of it."

"That's always a possibility," I said. "Although I must say in my experience it rarely happens that you lose data—but again, it's always a possibility. The bottom line is that the only way to ensure it doesn't happen is to execute the Close method of the StreamWriter object."

We had been working for some time, and I suggested it would be a good time to take a break. I told my students that when we returned we would be looking at the more subtle types of errors that beginners make—errors that can really drive you crazy.

Reading Too Many or Too Few Fields from a Disk File

"Another frustrating type of problem," I continued, "is when you read records from a file and get the data into your program, only to discover that it doesn't seem to be in the right place."

"Right place?" Rhonda asked. "What do you mean?"

"For instance," I answered, "let's say you have a file with three fields in each record. You write code to open the file, read the data into three variables, and then perform some kind of processing. Somehow, it appears that the data from field 1 is in the variable declared for field 2. And then sometimes the data from field 1 appears in the variable declared for field 3. I term this 'skewed' data."

"That happened to me last week when I was working on the code for the China Shop Project," Kate said. "I finally figured out that I forgot to account for one of the elements of the array that the Split method creates for us."

"You hit the nail right on the head there, Kate," I said. "The Split method creates an array with an element for each 'field' in the input record. You need to account for each of those elements, which usually means taking the value in the array element and copying it to an variable."

"Do you think you could show us an example of this?" Steve asked. "I'm still not sure I understand the problem you're describing."

I thought for a moment and then gave the class this scenario.

"Suppose we have a file called CITIES.TXT, which contains ten records, and each record contains three fields—City, State, and Zip Code. That gives us a total of 30 fields in the file."

I took a minute to create the file in Notepad, saving it as CITIES.TXT in the \VBFiles\Practice folder.

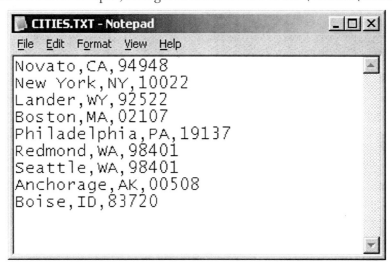

"We can use this code," I continued, "to read the data from the CITIES.TXT file and display that data in the Visual Basic Output window."

```
Private Sub Button1_Click(ByVal sender As System.Object, ByVal e As System.EventArgs)
Handles Button1.Click

  Dim line As String
  Dim fields() As String
  Dim delimiter As Char = ","
  Dim strCity As String
  Dim strState As String
  Dim strZipCode As String

  Dim sr As New StreamReader("C:\VBFILES\PRACTICE\CITIES.TXT")
  Do
    line = sr.ReadLine()
    If line Is Nothing Then Exit Do
    fields = line.Split(delimiter)
    strCity = fields(0)
    strState = fields(1)
    strZipCode = fields(2)
    Console.WriteLine(strCity & "," & strState & "," & strZipCode)
  Loop

  sr.Close()
End Sub
```

I quickly created a project, placed the above code in the Click event procedure of a Button control and ran the program. The following results were displayed in the Visual Basic Output window.

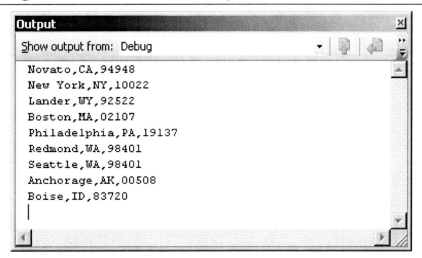

"In an ideal world," I said, "we open the file, declare a variable for each field in the record, and then code a separate assignment statement for each field in the record within a While...Loop. This sounds simple enough, but suppose that someone makes an innocent mistake, such as typing an extra comma in a comma delimited file."

"With large files," I said, "things like this can happen quite often---and it's almost like looking for a needle in a haystack."

"If someone does that, won't the program just bomb?" Kathy asked.

"Unfortunately not," I said, "most likely we'll read some data into the wrong variables."

"I'm not sure I understand what you mean," Mary said, "Can you show us?"

"Sure thing Mary," I said, "suppose someone places an 'extra comma' between the State field and the Zip Code field in our first line."

I modified the CITIES.TXT file using Notepad and displayed it on the classroom projector.

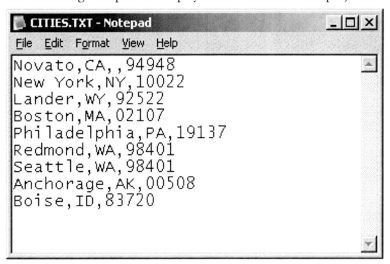

"Any guesses as to what will happen when we run our program against this file?" I asked.

"I think that instead of displaying 9 lines in the Visual Basic Output window, we'll display 10 instead," Blaine said.

"I think the program will bomb," Steve suggested.

"My guess is that the program will still display 9 records," Ward said, "but the data will be in the wrong place."

"Let's see," I said as I ran the program with the modified CITIES.TXT file. The following output appeared in the Visual Basic Output Window.

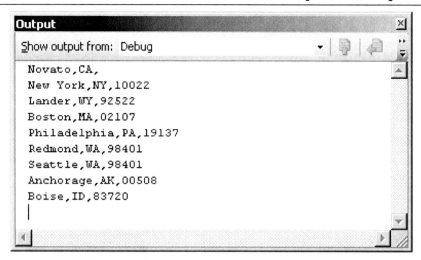

"Well, the program didn't bomb," Rhonda said.

"Looks like we 'lost' the Zip Code for the first line in the file," Dave said. "I presume that when the Split function parsed that first line in the file, it created a 4 element array, not the 3 element array we were expecting. As a result, a null value was assigned to the line of code designated to assign a value to strZipCode---and since we didn't anticipate needing to deal with the fourth element of the fields array, the real value of the Zip Code was simply bypassed."

"Absolutely correct Dave," I said, "I couldn't have said it better myself."

"Unfortunately," I said, "for this kind of error, there isn't much you can do, Comma delimited files are prone to errors like this. Fortunately, in the real world of programming, it's usually well-tested programs that produce large comma delimited files in the first place, which can reduce the possibility of errors like this."

Division by Zero

I continued by stating that in the computer world, another common type of error is division by zero, which in most programming languages is a big no-no.

"What's 12 divided by 1?" I asked.

"12," Mary replied.

"Now what about 12 divided by 1/2?" I continued.

After a moment's hesitation, Dave answered, "24."

"Correct," I said.

There were some puzzled faces.

"I know I've caught you math-phobics on that one," I said. "A number, divided by a number smaller than 1, always results in an answer larger than the original number."

"I believe in using math terms," Ward said. "You mean to say that when we divide by a number by another number smaller than 1, we take the reciprocal of that number and multiply by it. In other words, 12 divided by 1/2 becomes 12 multiplied by 2."

I then displayed the following chart on the board.

Number 1 (Dividend)	Number 2 (Divisor)	Answers
12	1	12
12	1/2	24
12	1/3	36
12	1/4	48
12	1/10	120

| 12 | 1/100 | 1,200 |
| 12 | 1/1000 | 12,000 |

I continued by telling my students that as the divisor approaches 0, the answer becomes larger and larger. In fact, it becomes an infinite number, which is impossible to represent in a computer. "For that reason," I continued, "dividing a number by 0 in your computer program causes most programs to bomb." I then created a new Windows application with a text box and placed the following line of code in the Click event procedure of a Button control.

Console.WriteLine (12 / Val(TextBox1.Text))

"Because the Text property of a TextBox is a string," I said, "we must convert the string to a number prior to dividing it into 12. Now let's run the program."

I ran the program, entered the number 0 into the text box, and clicked the button. The following was displayed in the Visual Basic Output window.

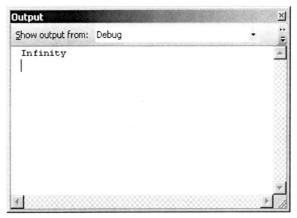

"Visual Basic displays the result as the special value Infinity," I said. "This is Visual Basic's attempt to resolve the division by 0 problem, and it's certainly better than having your program bomb. But I need to point out that the type of division operation we performed here was floating point division. Suppose we decided to perform integer division instead."

I then modified the code to look like this.

Console.WriteLine (12 \ CLng(TextBox1.Text))

ran the program, entered the number 0 into the text box, and clicked the button. The following error message was displayed on the classroom projector.

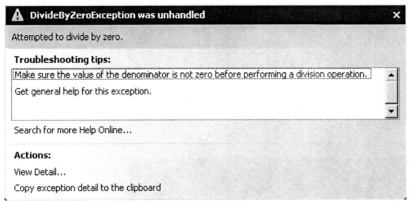

"It's a lot harder to get this division by 0 error in Visual Basic," I said, "but it is possible. In this case, performing integer division with a divisor of 0 got through Visual Basic's defenses, and we caused the program to bomb. By the way, behind the scenes, we created an Err object with a Number property of 11, which is the Error number for division by 0."

I waited for a moment before continuing.

"This particular error is more likely to occur when you use a property whose value is 0, or an uninitialized variable value in a division operation. For instance, this code will also cause the same division by zero error."

```
Dim lngValue As Long
Console.WriteLine (12 \ lngValue)
```

"As you can see," I explained, "the value of lngValue here has never been assigned a value. By default, its value is 0, and when used as the divisor in an integer division operation, causes the program to bomb."

I went on to explain that most beginners aren't aware of the problems with division by 0, and their immediate response most likely would be that they would never intentionally divide by 0.

"That's what I was going to say," Ward said. "However, I can see from the examples you've shown us that it's an error that can show up in many different ways."

"This would seem to be something that you could prevent with an If statement," Barbara suggested.

I agreed, explaining that all of the runtime errors we had examined could be detected by a program pretty easily by using If...Then...Else statements.

"However," I said, "these errors can be detected and handled even easier by using Exception Handling routines. That's what we'll examine when we return from break."

Exception Handling

After break, I told everyone that we spent the first part of our class intentionally creating errors to cause our programs to bomb. During the last half of our class, we would be examining ways of gracefully handling those errors in such a way that our programs just don't stop in midstream.

"Nothing can ruin your reputation faster," I said, "than having a customer spread the word that he or she loves your programs, except for the fact that they bomb once in a while."

I explained that it isn't always possible to code a program that will never encounter an error. For instance, you might write a program that reads data from a disk file, the name and location of which is specified by the user at runtime.

"Suppose the customer informs your program that the file is located on a disk in the disk drive, but forgets to insert the disk?" I said. "I do this quite frequently myself. Believe it or not, something simple like this can cause your program to bomb, since when your code attempts to open the file, the file is not there."

"That generates an error?" Ward asked. "In Microsoft Word, a warning message is displayed."

"That's exactly the point, Ward," I replied. "The programmer who wrote that piece of the Microsoft Word program implemented some form of Exception Handling, intercepting the error that is triggered, and substituting in its place a more user-friendly message. Most importantly, though, Microsoft Word continues running instead of coming to a halt—which is what our Visual Basic program will do."

"Can we do something like that in our programs?" Barbara asked. "I mean, intercept those nasty error messages we saw earlier and replace them with messages of our own?"

"Yes, we can," I said. "It's actually pretty easy to write code to react to Visual Basic error messages and replace them with more soothing messages that appear as warnings instead. Let's begin our look at Visual Basic Exception Handling by completing an exercise in which we intentionally cause a division by 0 error."

I then distributed this exercise to the class.

Exercise 14-1 Intentionally Generate an Error

In this exercise, you'll intentionally generate a division by 0 error. But don't worry—in the next exercise, you'll implement Exception Handling to gracefully handle it.

1. Start a new Windows application project.
2. Add a Button control to your form.
3. Place the following code in its Click event procedure.

```
Private Sub Button1_Click(ByVal sender As System.Object, _
   ByVal e As System.EventArgs) Handles Button1.Click

Dim lngValue As Long
```

Console.WriteLine (12 \ lngValue)

End Sub

4. Save your program—you'll be modifying it in Exercise 14-2.
5. Run the program and click the button. The program will bomb and display this error message.

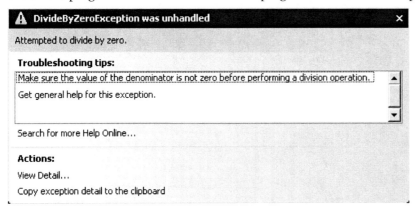

Discussion

There weren't any questions about the exercise. Everyone understood what had happened. Our program had divided the number 12 by the uninitialized variable lngValue (which therefore had a value of 0) and the program had simply bombed. As you can see, a program that terminates abnormally can be pretty nasty."

"So will we be able to prevent this type of problem?" Kate asked.

"There's nothing we can do to prevent this kind of error, " I said. Instead, we'll concentrate on intercepting Visual Basic exceptions so that when they do occur, the program doesn't come to a grinding halt."

Visual Basic Exceptions

"Is a Visual Basic exception the same as a Visual Basic error?" Steve asked. "I think you've used both terms in the last few minutes."

"The Visual Basic language," I said, "prefers to call its errors 'exceptions.' In fact, when a Visual Basic runtime error occurs, an Exception object is created. Once the Exception object is created, we have access to its attributes, which can provide us information about the exception."

"The Exception object is an object that we don't have to create ourselves?" Kate asked.

"That's right, Kate," I said. "When the runtime error is generated, Visual Basic automatically creates the Exception object for us."

"What can we do when a Visual Basic runtime error occurs?" Ward asked.

Ignore the Exception

"One thing we can do is to ignore the error," I said.

"What's that?" Ward asked.

"We can ignore the error," I said, "and just let the program bomb. This is an alternative that many Visual Basic programmers choose."

"Is it OK to ignore exceptions?" Mary asked.

"No, it's not Mary," I said. "It's foolish to ignore an exception that you suspect may occur, and you should do your best to anticipate them and react to them. As you gain experience in Visual Basic, you'll see that most of the code you write won't trigger exceptions. You'll also learn the kind of code that is likely to trigger an exception."

"Such as prompting a user to give us a number we then use in division!" Valerie asked.

"That's right, Valerie," I said. "Also, code that opens external files or databases is the kind of code that can trigger runtime exceptions. The point is, not every piece of code you write needs to be written to handle exceptions. The code that experience and testing has revealed is capable of triggering a runtime exception is the code that needs to include Exception Handling code, and that means coding a Try-Catch-Finally block."

Handle the Exception with Try-Catch-Finally Blocks

"Try-Catch-Finally block?" Kate asked. "Is that what you just said?"

"That's right, Kate," I replied. "A Try-Catch-Finally block. The idea is to try the code in the Try block that may cause an exception and then use the Catch block to specify the code that should execute if an exception occurs."

"So that's the reason it's called a Try block?" Mary asked.

"That's the reason, Mary," I said.

"What about the Finally block?" Steve asked.

"The Finally block specifies code that is to be executed whether an exception occurs or not," I said. "Usually, this is code that performs some kind of housekeeping function such as closing files---or thanking the user for using our program."

"Are you going to show us an example of the Try-Catch block?" Rhonda asked.

"Even better," I said, "I'm going to give you a chance to work with them on your own by modifying the code from Exercise 14-1 to include exception handling."

I then distributed this exercise for the class to complete.

Exercise 14-2 Try-Catch-Finally Block

In this exercise, you'll modify the program from Exercise 14-1 to use Try-Catch-Finally blocks to deal with the Division by Zero exception that resulted in Exercise 14-1.

1. Continue working with the project from Exercise 14-1.
2. Add a second Button control and place the following code in its Click event procedure.

```
Private Sub Button2_Click(ByVal sender As System.Object, _
    ByVal e As System.EventArgs) Handles Button2.Click

Dim lngCounter As Long

Try
    Console.Writeline(12 \ lngCounter)
    Catch When Err.Number = 11
        MessageBox.Show("You may not divide by zero")
    Catch When Err.Number <> 11
        MessageBox.Show(Err.Number & Chr(13) & Err.Description)
    Finally
        MessageBox.Show ("Try-Catch-Finally is an essential part of every program")
End Try

End Sub
```

3. Save your program, although you won't be modifying it any further.

4. Run the program and click the button. As before, the program will display a customized error message and continue to run. It will also display a second message box—did you see it?

Discussion

I immediately ran the program, and we saw two Message Boxes displayed. The first informed us about the division by 0 error.

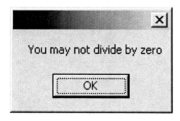

This was the *second* Message Box.

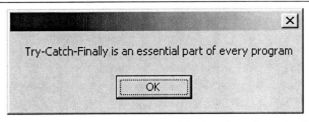

"Let me explain what's going on here," I said. "We used a Try block to intercept the Division by Zero Exception before it caused our program to come to an abrupt halt. The code in the Try block is the code we warn Visual Basic **may** cause a runtime exception."

Try
 Console.WriteLine(12 \ lngCounter)

"..Following the word Try is the line or lines of code we believe may have a problem, followed by one or more Catch statements which are to be executed if there is an error."

Catch When Err.Number = 11

"What is Err?" Steve asked.

"Err is the Error object," I said, "and it is created whenever a Visual Basic runtime error occurs. Because it's an object, just like a form or a control, we have access to its properties, and we can display these values in a message box---in this case, we're examining its Number property---and reacting to it.. If it's equal to 11---the number equating to a Division by Zero Exception---we display a user friendly error message to the user…"

Catch When Err.Number = 11
 MessageBox.Show("You may not divide by zero")

"If the Number property is anything but 11, we know we have an Exception that was generated by something other than a Division by Zero Exception, and we just display the value of the Number property and Description in a Message Box."

Catch When Err.Number <> 11
 MessageBox.Show(Err.Number & Chr(13) & Err.Description)

"The thing to bear in mind here," I continued, "is that we will never reach this part of our code unless some exception has been generated in our program."

"Is the Err object created only if we code a Try-Catch-Finally block handler?" Joe asked.

"That's a good question, Joe," I answered. "Regardless of whether we code Exception handling procedures or not, the Err object is still created. It's up to us to use it if we wish."

"I think I'm a little confused here," Linda said. "Can we run this program in Step mode?"

"An excellent idea," I said, and I did as Linda requested. In "slow motion" we saw that as soon as the line of code to perform division by 0 was executed, Visual Basic immediately jumped to the code in the Catch block.

"I don't recall seeing the When keyword before," Linda said. "Is that part of the Catch syntax?"

"That's right, Linda," I said. "That's the syntax to use to implement your 'Catch' logic."

"That finally Catch statement," Dave said, "That's the code that's executed regardless of whether an Exception is generated. Is that right?"

"That's perfect Dave," I replied. "In this instance, regardless of whether or not we trigger a Division by Zero Exception in our code, the Finally block will be executed. Finally designates the code that is to be executed just before the Try…End Try structure completes. It's something you may or may not want to code---it depends on the situation."

I waited for questions before continuing.

"I should also show you this alternate form of code," I said, "although it requires us to instantiate an instance of the Err object—something you'll learn about in the Objects class."

Private Sub Button2_Click(ByVal sender As System.Object, _

```
    ByVal e As System.EventArgs) Handles Button2.Click
Dim lngCounter As Long
Try
    Console.Writeline(12 \ lngCounter)
  Catch F as DivideByZeroException
    MessageBox.Show("You may not divide by zero")
  Catch When Err.Number <> 11
    MessageBox.Show(Err.Number & Chr(13) & Err.Description)
  Finally
    MessageBox.Show ("Try and catch is preferred by many
programmers")
End Try

End Sub
```

"Does everyone see the difference?" I asked as I displayed this line of code on the classroom projector.. "It's in the section of code that checks for a Division by Zero Exception. Instead of checking for the Number property equal to 11, within the Catch clause, we instantiate a special object called DivideByZeroException, and call it 'F'."

Catch F as DivideByZeroException

"What happens," I continued, "is that if a Division by Zero Exception has occurred, this clause will be executed, and the MessageBox.Show method will be executed."

"So what we're saying is to explicitly catch a DivideByZeroException?" Barbara asked.

"That's right," I said. "In fact, I don't know if you noticed as I was entering this code in the code window, but a bunch of different Exception type objects appeared in the AutoList members window as I typed the phrase 'Catch F as...'"

"I think I'll stick with checking for the Number property of the Err object," Chuck said. "I think this is a bit confusing."

"And I think I prefer this new method," Rhonda said. "What's your preference?"

"Either one is fine with me," I said.. "I've used both of them. In fact, we're about to code an Exception Handler in the China Shop Project.---can you guess which one we'll use?"

Rhonda had one more question---"How do we determine the various Err Numbers?"

"You can find a list of them in Visual Basic help," I said, "as far as the Exception objects we just lightly touched upon, as I mentioned, within the Code window when you type 'Catch F as...' you'll see a list of all of them. You can also use the Object Browser to display them."

There were no more questions, so it was time to turn our attention to Exception Handling in the China Shop Project.

Exception Handling in the China Shop Project

"We'll code an Exception Handler in just one procedure of our China Shop Project, the Load event procedure of the form," I said. "Can anyone tell me why it would be a good idea to code an Exception Handler in that procedure?"

"The disk file access, I would think," Chuck answered.

"Right you are," I said. "Any time you have a procedure that operates on disk files, you should code an Exception Handler."

I explained that the most likely error to occur in the Load event procedure of the form would be if the input file PRICES.TXT was missing.

"There's really nothing we can do if this happens," I explained, "beyond displaying a user-friendly warning message to the China Shop staff member and ending the program. The important point to remember is that message will prevent the program from bombing and destroying our reputation."

I explained to the class that in the final exercise of the day, we would simulate the problem of the missing PRICES.TXT file by using Windows Explorer to rename it, and then run the program to see the impact of a missing input file.

"At that point," I said, "we'll add Exception handling code to more gracefully deal with the problem."

I then distributed the final exercise of the day to my students.

Exercise 14-3 Code an Exception Handler in the Load Event Procedure

In this exercise, we'll temporarily rename the file PRICES.TXT to PRICES.BAK in the Load event procedure of the China Shop form. We'll run the program, which will cause it to bomb. We'll then code an Exception Handler to deal with the missing file, and run the program, observing the behavior of the Exception Handler. Finally, we'll rename PRICES.BAK to PRICES.TXT.

1. Load the China Shop Project.
2. Use Windows Explorer to rename PRICES.TXT to PRICES.BAK (PRICES.TXT should be in your \VBFiles\China folder).
3. Run the program. The file that the Load event procedure requires is missing so the program will bomb with the following message.

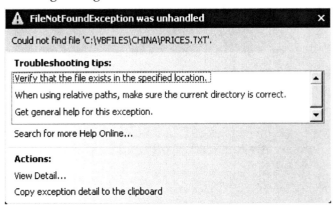

4. Stop the program.
5. Change the code in the Load event procedure of the form so that it looks like this.

```
Private Sub Main_Load(ByVal sender As System.Object, _
  ByVal e As System.EventArgs) Handles MyBase.Load

  Dim line As String
  Dim fields() As String
  Dim delimiter As Char = ","
  Dim intCounter As Integer

  Try
    Dim sr As New StreamReader("C:\VBFILES\CHINA\PRICES.TXT")

  Do
    line = sr.ReadLine()
    If line Is Nothing Then Exit Do

    ReDim Preserve m_sngBowlPrice(intCounter)
    ReDim Preserve m_sngButterPlatePrice(intCounter)
    ReDim Preserve m_sngCupPrice(intCounter)
    ReDim Preserve m_sngPlatePrice(intCounter)
    ReDim Preserve m_sngPlatterPrice(intCounter)
    ReDim Preserve m_sngSaucerPrice(intCounter)
    ReDim Preserve m_sngCompletePrice(intCounter)

    fields = line.Split(delimiter)
    lstBrands.Items.Add(fields(0))
    m_sngPlatePrice(intCounter) = fields(1)
    m_sngButterPlatePrice(intCounter) = fields(2)
```

```
        m_sngBowlPrice(intCounter) = fields(3)
        m_sngCupPrice(intCounter) = fields(4)
        m_sngSaucerPrice(intCounter) = fields(5)
        m_sngPlatterPrice(intCounter) = fields(6)
        m_sngCompletePrice(intCounter) = fields(7)

        intCounter = intCounter + 1
      Loop

      sr.Close()


      Catch F As FileNotFoundException
        MessageBox.Show("A file required by the China Shop program is missing." & _
                Chr(13) & "Please ensure that PRICES.TXT" & _
                Chr(13) & "is in The China Shop directory on " & _
                "the computer's hard drive", _
                "Bullina China Shop")
      Me.Close()

      Catch ex As Exception
        MessageBox.Show("An unexpected error has occurred." & _
                Chr(13) & ex.Message, _
                "Bullina China Shop")
      Me.Close()
    End Try

End Sub
```

6. Click the Save icon on the toolbar to save the China Shop Project.

7. Run the program. This time, instead of bombing with a Visual Basic error, the program will display a user-friendly message indicating that the input file cannot be found.

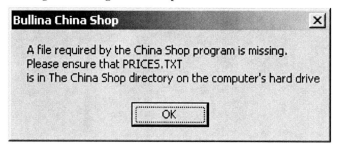

8. Click OK in the message box. The program will gracefully end.

9. Use Windows Explorer to rename PRICES.BAK to PRICES.TXT.

10. Run the program to ensure that it's once again finding the PRICES.TXT file properly.

Discussion

"I think I understand what's going on here," Rhonda said, "but can you explain the code in the Exception Handler?"

"I'd be glad to," I said. "We began by enclosing 'most' of the code we already had in the Load event procedure within a Try...End Try block. Notice how we included the declaration of the StreamReader within the Try block---if we didn't do that, if the file can't be found, the program would bomb, but not trigger our Exception Handler..."

```
Try
  Dim sr As New StreamReader("C:\VBFILES\CHINA\PRICES.TXT")
```

"I noticed that," Kate said. "I noticed that you chose to declare Exception objects within the Catch clauses---instead of using the Number property of the Err object?"

"That's right Kate," I said, "Visual Basic is a true Object Oriented language---we should probably get used to dealing with objects. Let's examine those Catch clauses more carefully. The first one is meant to handle or 'trap' the FileNotFoundException that was generated when we renamed the PRICES.TXT file..."

```
Catch F As FileNotFoundException
   MessageBox.Show("A file required by the China Shop program is missing." & _
                   Chr(13) & "Please ensure that PRICES.TXT" & _
                   Chr(13) & "is in The China Shop directory on " & _
                   "the computer's hard drive", _
                   "Bullina China Shop")
   Me.Close()
```

"I know the syntax for the Catch clause is a little foreign to you," I continued, "but you'll get used to it in no time. Here we've created an instance of the FileNotFoundException and called it 'F'. At that point, if this Exception is triggered, we display a Message Box with a user friendly error message. Notice, by the way, that we are concatenating ASCII values of 13 to our display message---this enables the Message Box to neatly display multiple lines. Also, we are now using the title parameter of the MessageBox.Show method to display a title bar in our Message Box."

Linda said, "I see that if we couldn't find the input file, we execute the Close method of the Form---using the keyword 'Me'. Doesn't that end the program?"

"Yes it does Linda," I said, "without valid prices, we can't provide a quote and after displaying an error message, we really have little choice but to end the program."

I paused a moment before continuing.

"This second Catch clause basically is a catchall," I said. "If the FileNotFoundException is not triggered, any other exception that is triggered will cause this Catch clause to execute. Notice how we create an instance of the Exception object. This is the 'grandfather' of all Exception objects. In fact, the FileNotFoundException object is also an Exception object. That's why it's important that this Catch clause appears after any specific Exception clauses you code."

```
Catch ex As Exception
   MessageBox.Show("An unexpected error has occurred." & _
                   Chr(13) & ex.Message, _
                   "Bullina China Shop")
   Me.Close()
```

"So if we code this clause ahead of the FileNotFoundException clause," Joe asked, " the code in this clause would be executed?"

"That's right Joe," I replied. "this really should be the last Catch clause to appear in the Try-Catch block. And don't forget—if no exceptions are generated, no Catch clauses at all are executed."

"I noticed there's no Finally clause," Rhonda said.

"That's right Rhonda," I said. "there's nothing we need to do at the end of Try-Catch block. If we encounter no exceptions, the Main Event procedure ends and our form is displayed. If an exception is triggered, we display an error message and end the program. "

There were no other questions.

"Next week will be a bittersweet class for us," I continued, "as we finish up the China Shop Project—and our course. Don't forget, if you wish, you can travel to the China Shop with me and participate in the installation of the program."

NOTE: Be sure to rename PRICES.BAK to PRICES.TXT in your China Shop folder.

Summary

This chapter was designed to show you the various types of errors that all programmers— especially beginners—can make in their programs. We've actually covered two different types of errors here: mistakes made by programmers, such as forgetting to open or close a file, and errors that are not the result of a programming mistake—such as a missing, renamed, or moved file.

We learned that you can't always code for every eventuality. You could put Exception Handlers in every procedure of your program, trying to intercept every error that you think of. That's one extreme. We learned that you should definitely code an Exception Handler in when you're working with disk files.

And now a word or two of advice. Everyone makes mistakes when they start programming. Never let this discourage you. When you first learn something new, it's a strange and awkward experience as you become familiar with it. But it's also an exciting time. Never let the frustrations of learning something new thwart that excitement. As time goes by, experience will help you make less mistakes.

In the final chapter of this book, we're going to complete the China Shop Project. Among the enhancements we'll add is some code that makes it easier for the user to save and retrieve their customized settings (their chosen background color, for example).

Chapter 15---Customizing Your Program

In this, our final chapter, we'll follow my class as we complete the China Shop Project, and then deliver and install the program at the Bullina China Shop.

"When will we be delivering the program?" Ward asked.

"I have some pretty exciting news," I said. "At the end of last week's class, I told you that we would be delivering the program to the China Shop today. I figured that as many of us as cared to would drive over to the China Shop and install the program, however, during the week, Joe Bullina called me. This is obviously a man who likes to do things big. He told me he's planning on having a huge ribbon cutting ceremony in honor of the program, and he's hired a caterer and a band!"

From the looks on everyone's faces, it was obvious to me they would all be making the trip to the China Shop.

"Gee, it's a shame," Mary said, "but it doesn't look like Rose and Jack will make it after all. I don't see either one of their cars in the parking lot. Has anyone heard from them?"

"They called me two nights ago from their ship somewhere in the middle of the Atlantic," I replied. "They told me the trip had been pretty smooth, but the weather was frigid. They said they had spoken to the captain, who assured them they would be arriving in New York harbor early this morning, a few hours ahead of schedule. I expect them to be here before the end of class."

"That's great news," Linda said. "It will be great to have them back in the fold. So will the delivery and installation of the China Shop Project to Joe Bullina just about wrap up the SDLC?"

"That will take us into the Implementation phase," I said, "which is Phase 5 of the SDLC. We'll begin the Implementation phase today and conclude during the course of the week with some training we'll provide to Joe Bullina and his staff. Phase 6 of the SDLC, the Audit and Maintenance phase, will begin today as well as we observe the China Shop Project in the China Shop."

I waited for more questions.

"So what will we be covering today?" Rhonda said. "I half expected that we would meet here, then drive over to the China Shop."

"We still have some material to cover, Rhonda," I said. "In today's class we'll be examining how to customize and fine-tune your program, plus there are still a few items on our Requirements Statement that we have not yet implemented."

"What's that?" Blaine asked.

"We aren't saving the user's preferences for color selection or date/time preference display," I said. "We'll be writing those preferences to the Windows Registry, which is what we'll discuss now. Then in the last part of class, we'll discuss streamlining our code."

Writing to the Windows Registry

"I always thought that writing to the Windows Registry was a dangerous thing," Kate said.

"Me too," Kathy agreed. "Can't you corrupt the Windows Registry like that?"

I explained that the Windows Registry is a database that the Windows operating system uses to store and track information necessary for the operation of your computer.

"The horror stories you've heard have probably been about people who directly edited their Registry," I said, "But reading from and writing to the Windows Registry from within Visual Basic is perfectly safe—provided you use the methods provided by Visual Basic to do so. However, for those of you who still feel a bit squeamish about it, I'm going to show you how to back up your Windows Registry prior to working with it."

I continued by explaining that the benefits of using the Windows Registry to store information for later use in your program are immeasurable.

"What types of information can we record in the Registry?" Kate asked.

"I use the Windows Registry to store small pieces of information that must be maintained from one session of the program to another," I replied.

"Such as?" Kate asked.

"For instance," I replied, "some programs—such as Visual Basic—use the Registry to record the windows, their size and location that are open when the program is exited. Another example is Microsoft Word. I bet many of you have noticed that Word records the last few files that you accessed."

"So that information is stored in the Windows Registry?" Blaine asked.

"That's right, Blaine," I said. "All sorts of things like that are stored in the Windows Registry to give a customized look and feel to the program. Does anyone remember what we said we'd use the Windows Registry for in the China Shop Project?"

"I think we said we would store information about the user's preference for colors, and the date and time display," Blaine answered.

Registry Keys and Subkeys

"Where are these values stored?" Dave asked. "Is there a special location in the Windows Registry for our values?"

"That's an excellent question Dave," I said, "and you're right. Within the Windows Registry is a section that, by convention, is available for our use. Before I describe it, I should tell you that the Windows Registry is divided into sections called keys, and subsections of these keys are called subkeys. By convention, programmers may write data about a software program in a section----or subkey---called Software, which is located within the CurrentUser subkey of the Windows Registry."

I saw some obvious signs of confusion in the eyes of my students.

"Don't concern yourself too much with the terms," I said, "essentially these sections, or subkeys, are the same as subfolders on your hard drive. For our China Shop program, we'll be writing data to the Startup subkey, within the BullinaChina subkey, within the Software subkey, within the CurrentUser key of the Windows Registry."

"That's a mouth full," Ward said.

"Graphically Ward," I said, "that would look something like this."

Registry\CurrentUser\Software\BullinaChina\Startup

I gave everyone a moment to ponder this.

"Does that mean that each user has their own copy of these values?" Dave asked.

"That's right Dave," I said, "on a PC in which multiple users log in, each user has their own copy of their Registry values. In the case of the China Shop, I suspect each morning the same user of the China Shop PC will be logging in and starting up our program."

"In the case of the China Shop," Dave continued, "what happens if the subkey section doesn't exist prior to our trying to write to it?"

"Before we write to the Registry," I said, "we first need to locate and open the subkey that we wish to write to. If it doesn't exist, we'll then create the subkey in the Registry. If it already exists, we simply write to it. Here's a preview of the code that we will use to determine if the Startup subkey for our China Shop application exists. First, we create an instance of a RegistryKey object, and then execute its OpenSubKey method…"

dim key as RegistryKey = Registry.CurrentUser.OpenSubKey("Software\\BullinaChina\\Startup", true);

"What does the true argument refer to?" Steve wondered.

"True means we can write a value to the subkey," I said, "If we wanted to open the subkey Registry entry just to read the value, we can either specify false for a value, or not refer to it all like this."

dim key as RegistryKey = Registry.CurrentUser.OpenSubKey("Software\\BullinaChina\\Startup")

I paused a moment before continuing.

"If the return value of the OpenSubKey method is 'Nothing', that tells us the key does not exist and we then use the CreateSubKey method to create it…"

If key Is Nothing Then key = Registry.CurrentUser.CreateSubKey("Software\\BullinaChina\\Startup")

"That doesn't look too bad," Rhonda said. "I'm surprised that I can understand it so easily."

Using SetValue to write to the Windows Registry

"That's right, Rhonda" I said. "I think you'll find that working with the Windows Registry with Visual Basic is surprisingly simple. Once you know that the Registry subkey exists---or that you've created it---saving information to the Registry subkey and retrieving it from the Registry subkey is amazingly easy. Two Visual Basic statements allow us to easily do this. The GetValue method of the Registry key object reads data from the subkey, and the SetValue method of the Registry key object writes data to the subkey. Let's take a look at the SetValue method first."

I then displayed the syntax for the SetValue method on the classroom projector.

key.SetValue(Name, Value)

"That seems simple enough," Dave said, "it looks like all we need to do is name the value we wish to save, and then specify the value."

"That's right Dave," I said, "the hard work has already been done when we either execute the OpenSubKey or CreateSubKey methods of the RegistryKey object. Both of those methods return a 'reference' to the appropriate Windows subkey in the Windows Registry. With that reference set, executing the SetValue method of the Registry key object creates an entry in the Registry with that value."

"It would be nice if we could see a visual representation of what this is doing," Ward said.

"Well do that a little later on in the class, Ward," I answered, "and it will certainly clear things up for us."

"Is there anything magical about the name we choose for the value?" Barbara asked.

"Not at all Barbara," I said. "For instance, we'll store the user's preferred color in the Registry within the Startup subkey with a name of BackColor."

"So we can name these sections, or subkeys, anything that we want?" Linda asked.

"Yes, you can," I answered, "but of course, as with anything you name in a Visual Basic program, be sure you pick something that's meaningful."

I continued by explaining that once you've decided what to call your Registry entry—that is, you've come up a names for the setting—the rest is easy.

"At that point," I continued, "all you need to do is execute the SetValue method, specifying the name for the value, and then the value itself. I should mention here that Visual Basic stores the value you save in the Registry as a string— which, as we'll see, will have ramifications later on."

I then displayed this example of the SetValue method on the classroom projector.

key.SetValue("Left", "50")

"Many applications," I said, "keep track of the locations of Windows that are opened within it by saying the Left and Top Properties in the Windows Registry. Provided that we have executed the OpenSubKey method of a Registry Key object to return a reference to a subkey in the Windows Registry, this code will create a subkey entry with the value 50 in the Windows Registry with the Name Left."

I told the class that, at this point, our logical step is to complete an exercise in which we would write an entry to the Windows Registry.

"You mentioned that some of us might want to back up the Windows Registry before we write to it," Rhonda said. "Are you going to show us how to do that?"

"You're right," I said, "I almost forgot. Here's an exercise that will lead you through that process."

Exercise 15-1 Backing Up the Windows Registry

In this exercise, you'll learn how to back up the Windows Registry to a file on your PC.

1. Click the Windows Start button.
2. Click Run.
3. Type regedit into the text box and click OK.

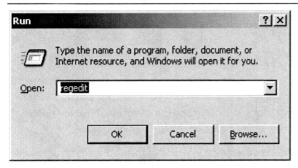

4. The Windows Registry Editor will appear.

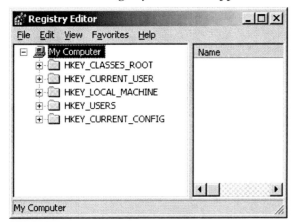

5. Select File | Export from the menu.

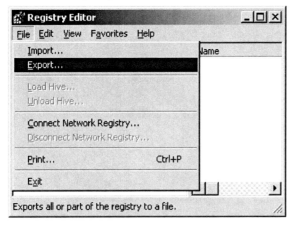

6. A dialog box will appear asking you to specify the name for the Registry backup. I usually name my Registry backup files according to the date I backed them up. For instance, since today is July 12, 2008, let's name the Registry backup 20080712. The extension .reg will automatically be added to the file.

7. Click Save and a backup of the Registry will be saved for you.

Discussion

"Backing up the Registry, as you can see, is pretty easy," I explained. "Restoring the Registry, if you need to do that, is a little more complicated, and I'm not going to get into that here. The important thing is that if you are at all squeamish about working with the Registry, you now have peace of mind if you have a backup. By the way, it's a good idea to keep that Registry backup somewhere other than your hard drive. If your hard drive should fail, your Registry backup will go with it."

"Are you saying it isn't necessary to back up the Windows Registry?" Linda asked.

"Experts will tell you that you should periodically back up the Windows Registry," I said, "and I agree with that. What I'm saying is that nothing you do from within your Visual Basic program can harm the Registry."

Everyone in the class seemed content that they knew how to back up the Registry.

"In our next exercise," I continued, "we'll use the SetValue method to save the user's preferences for color and date and time display in the China Shop program to the Windows Registry—then, in a later exercise, we'll read that entry."

Exercise 15-2 Write to the Windows Registry

In this exercise, we'll place code in the China Shop Project to write the user's preferences for color and date and time display to the Windows Registry.

1. Load the China Shop Project.
2. In order to be able to work with the Windows Registry, we need to include an Imports statement, much as we did prior to working with files in Exercise 11-1. Therefore, place this line of code at the top of the Code window, after the Imports statement for System.IO.

Imports Microsoft.Win32

3. We already have code in the mnuColorsCustom_Click event procedure. Modify it so that it looks like this.

Private Sub mnuColorsCustom_Click (ByVal sender As System.Object, _

```
        ByVal e As System.EventArgs) Handles mnuColorsCustom.Click

    Dim intRetValue As Integer
    Dim key As RegistryKey

    intRetValue = dlgChina.ShowDialog()
    If intRetValue = DialogResult.Cancel Then
        Exit Sub
    End If

    Me.BackColor = dlgChina.Color
    m_intBackColor = dlgChina.Color.ToArgb

    key = Registry.CurrentUser.OpenSubKey("Software\\BullinaChina\\Startup", True)

    If key Is Nothing Then
        key = Registry.CurrentUser.CreateSubKey("Software\\BullinaChina\\Startup")
    End If

    key.SetValue("BACKCOLOR", m_intBackColor)
    key.Close()
End Sub
```

4 We already have code in the mnuColorsDefault_Click event procedure. Modify it so that it looks like this.

```
Private Sub mnuColorsDefault_Click (ByVal sender As Object, _
        ByVal e As System.EventArgs) Handles mnuColorsDefault.Click

    Dim key As RegistryKey

    Me.BackColor = System.Drawing.SystemColors.Control
    m_intBackColor = System.Drawing.SystemColors.Control.ToArgb

    key = Registry.CurrentUser.OpenSubKey("Software\\BullinaChina\\Startup", True)

    If key Is Nothing Then
        key = Registry.CurrentUser.CreateSubKey("Software\\BullinaChina\\Startup")
    End If

    key.SetValue("BACKCOLOR", m_intBackColor)
    key.Close()
End Sub
```

5 We already have code in the mnuPreferencesDateAndTimeOff_Click event procedure. Modify it so that it looks like this.

```
Private Sub mnuPreferencesDateAndTimeOff_Click (ByVal sender As Object, _
        ByVal e As System.EventArgs) Handles mnuPreferencesDateAndTimeOff.Click

    Dim key As RegistryKey

    mnuPreferencesDateAndTimeOff.Checked = True
    mnuPreferencesDateAndTimeOn.Checked = False
    tmrChina.Enabled = False
    lblDateAndTime.Visible = False
    m_blnDateDisplay = False

    key = Registry.CurrentUser.OpenSubKey("Software\\BullinaChina\\Startup", True)

    If key Is Nothing Then
        key = Registry.CurrentUser.CreateSubKey("Software\\BullinaChina\\Startup")
    End If

    key.SetValue("DATEDISPLAY", m_blnDateDisplay)
    key.Close()
End Sub
```

6 We already have code in the mnuPreferencesDateAndTimeOn_Click event procedure. Modify it so that it looks like this.

```
Private Sub mnuPreferencesDateAndTimeOn_Click (ByVal sender As Object, _
  ByVal e As System.EventArgs) Handles mnuPreferencesDateAndTimeOn.Click

  Dim key As RegistryKey

  mnuPreferencesDateAndTimeOff.Checked = False
  mnuPreferencesDateAndTimeOn.Checked = True
  tmrChina.Enabled = True
  lblDateAndTime.Visible = True
  m_blnDateDisplay = True

  key = Registry.CurrentUser.OpenSubKey("Software\\BullinaChina\\Startup", True)

  If key Is Nothing Then
    key = Registry.CurrentUser.CreateSubKey("Software\\BullinaChina\\Startup")
  End If

  key.SetValue("DATEDISPLAY", m_blnDateDisplay)
  key.Close()
End Sub
```

7 Save the China Shop Project by clicking the Save icon on the toolbar.

8 Run the program.

9 Select Preferences | Colors | Custom from the menu bar. When the ColorDialog box appears, select your favorite color, and then click OK. The background color of the form will change. Behind the scenes, the String value of that selected color will be written to the Windows Registry.

10. Select Preferences | Date And Time Off to toggle the display of the date and time off. Behind the scenes, the string "False" will be written to the Windows Registry.

11. End the program by selecting File | Exit from the menu bar. Don't forget to enter the correct password (061883)!

12. Now run the China Shop Project again. Did the program remember the changes you made to the color of the form and the date and time display?

Discussion

"Something's wrong," Rhonda said. "It doesn't appear as though my settings were saved. After I started the China Shop Project again, my colors were still the default, and the date and time is still being displayed."

"Actually, Rhonda, you haven't done anything wrong." I said. "At this point, the program won't remember the changes the user makes to the color and date and time selections. Can anyone tell me why?"

"That's easy," Dave said. "We haven't written any code yet to read those preferences from the Windows Registry when the China Shop Project starts up."

"That's excellent, Dave," I said.

"I entirely forgot about the GetValue method you mentioned earlier," Ward said. "That's the method we need to execute in order to read values from the Registry."

"That's right, Ward," I said. "We need to write code that executes when the China Shop Project starts up which will read the values we just saved to the Windows Registry, and set the user's preferences accordingly. We'll be doing that shortly. But before we do that, let's take a quick look at the code we wrote that saved the user's preferences to the Windows Registry. I want to make sure everyone understands what is happening here."

I suggested that we examine the Click event procedure of mnuColorsCustom.

"Most of this is code I've already gone over," I said. "All we're doing is creating an instance of a RegistryKey object, then executing its OpenSubKey method for the Registry subkey we wish to write to."

key = Registry.CurrentUser.OpenSubKey("Software\\BullinaChina\\Startup", true)

"…We check to see if we have received a null reference to the subkey. If we have, that means the subkey does not yet exist, in which case we execute the CreateSubKey method of the RegistryKey object to create one…"

If key Is Nothing Then
  key = Registry.CurrentUser.CreateSubKey("Software\\BullinaChina\\Startup")
End If

"Really," I continued "it's only the first time that the China Shop program is run by a specific user on a specific PC with this code in it that the subkey shouldn't exist. Thereafter, each time the user of the program changes their preferred color, the subkey should exist."

"I notice," Dave said, "that we didn't specify a true value for the CreateSubKey method of the RegistryKey object."

"Good observation Dave," I said, "by default, when we execute the CreateSubKey method, the subkey is opened with write permission."

I paused a moment before continuing.

"Finally," I said, "we then write the current value of m_intBackColor to the BACKCOLOR value of the Startup subkey."

"Here are the new lines of code in the event procedure," I said.

key.SetValue("BACKCOLOR", m_intBackColor)

"...I didn't mention this before, but it's a good idea to close the subkey after we've written to it. The Windows Registry, as we saw when we backed it up, is a data file like the ones we worked two weeks ago, and it's a good idea to graceful close the subkey."

key.Close()

"Is there a way to verify that this setting was actually saved in the Registry?" Steve asked.

Using RegEdit

"Somehow I knew you'd ask that," I said. "It's a logical question—how do we really know the value was written to the Registry—and for that matter, what does a Registry entry look like? We can verify, and see, the Registry entries by using the Registry Editor again. Remember, that's how we backed up the Registry a few minutes ago. This time we'll use it to search for the Registry entries we just made."

I then clicked Start | Run and entered regedit in the Run box, which brought up the Registry Editor.

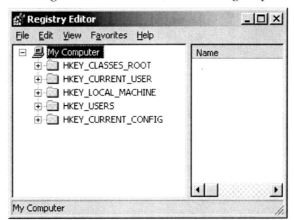

"Once the Registry Editor appears," I said, "we need to find the entries we just wrote to the Registry. Navigating through the Registry can be very tedious, and of course, you never want to change any of the values you see there. The fastest—and safest—method for finding a particular entry in the Windows Registry is to access the Find command. We can do this in two ways, either by selected Edit | Find from the Registry Editor's menu bar or by pressing CTRL-F."

I selected CTRL-F to display the Find dialog box.

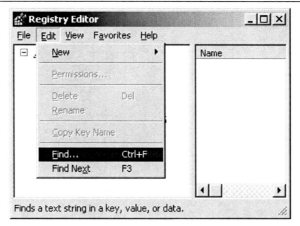

"Once the Find dialog box appears," I said, "we can enter a search term. Searching for AppName is the easiest way to find the entries we just made."

I then typed **BULLINACHINA** in the Find What box.

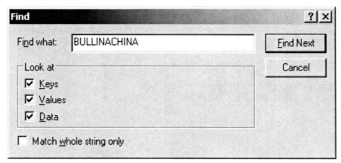

After a delay of many seconds, the following screen was displayed.

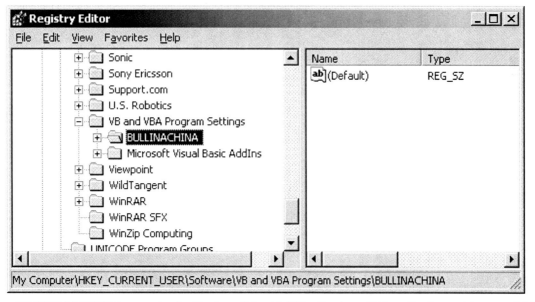

"There's our BULLINACHINA entry in the Registry," I said. "The Registry Editor displays subkeys as folders. Notice the plus sign—that means we can expand the folder to see what's inside." I then expanded the BULLINACHINA folder and the STARTUP folder was revealed.

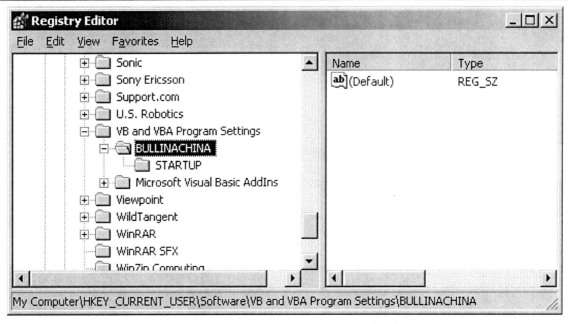

Finally, after expanding the STARTUP folder, we were able to see that both of our entries, BACKCOLOR and DATEDISPLAY, had been stored in the Windows Registry.

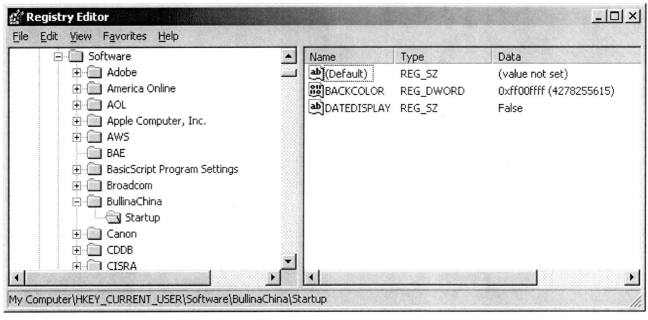

"As you can see," I said, "in the right window pane are our two keys: BACKCOLOR and DATEDISPLAY. If we double-click on the BACKCOLOR key, a dialog box will appear with its value, which equates to the color selection I made just a few moments ago."

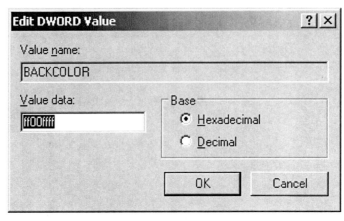

"Remember, this number is stored in the Registry as a string. If we double-click on the DateDisplay key, a dialog box will appear with its value—False—which indicates to our program that the user does not want the date and time displayed."

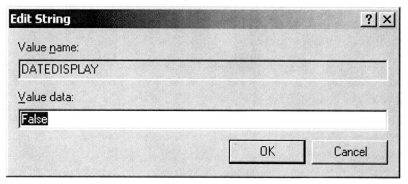

"Can we change the values we see here using the Registry Editor?" Mary asked.

"Yes, we can," I said, "but I wouldn't advise it. You can also delete keys you see in the Registry Editor. Just remember, changing values or deleting keys here is not a smart idea."

I gave everyone a chance to use the Registry Editor. After a few minutes, it seemed like everyone was ready to move on. No one seemed to have any major problems, except for one student who had named their subkey CHINA instead of BULLINACHINA.

"So that's the Windows Registry," Ward said. "I always thought it was this big, mysterious, hidden thing."

"Don't underestimate it," I said nervously. "We've just seen a part of it. And it is hidden— with good reason."

We continued our discussion of the code we had written by examining the code for the mnuColorsDefault_Click event procedure.

"This code," I explained, "is very similar to the code in the Click event procedure of mnuColorsCustom. In fact, the code to write the value of the default color to the Registry is identical to that of the code found in the Click event procedure of mnuColorsCustom."

key.SetValue("BACKCOLOR", m_intBackColor)

"So the code to save to the Registry is the same whether the user selects a custom color or a default color?" Rhonda asked.

"That's right, Rhonda," I answered.

I waited for more questions, but there were none.

"Let's look at the code to save the user's preferences for the date and time display," I continued, "by examining the code in mnuPreferencesDateAndTimeOff. This code is very similar to the code we saw in the other two menu item Click event procedures. Basically, we set the value a form-level variable, and then use the SetValue method to save that value to the Windows Registry. We're using the same subkey in the Windows Registry, Startup---what's different is the name we give to the value, in this case DATEDISPLAY…"

key = Registry.CurrentUser.OpenSubKey("Software\\BullinaChina\\Startup", true)

If key Is Nothing Then
  key = Registry.CurrentUser.CreateSubKey("Software\\BullinaChina\\Startup")
End If

key.SetValue("DATEDISPLAY", m_blnDateDisplay)
key.Close()

"Here's the code for mnuPreferencesDateAndTimeOn," I explained. "The code to write to the Windows Registry is identical."

key = Registry.CurrentUser.OpenSubKey("Software\\BullinaChina\\Startup", true)

If key Is Nothing Then
  key = Registry.CurrentUser.CreateSubKey("Software\\BullinaChina\\Startup")
End If

key.SetValue("DATEDISPLAY", m_blnDateDisplay)
key.Close();

I asked the class if there were any questions about writing data to the Windows Registry. No one had any, and so we moved on to a discussion of reading data from the Registry.

Reading from the Windows Registry

"We just saw how relatively easy it is to write to the Windows Registry," I said. "I think you'll find it's nearly as easy to read from the Registry using the corresponding GetValue method. We'll just have to deal with the issue of the values in the Registry being String data."

"Suppose you try to read from the Registry, and the subkey isn't found, what happens?" Ward asked. "I would think that would be likely in the early stages of a program's use."

"You're right about that, Ward," I agreed. "Even before the user has a chance to make selections which are saved in the Registry, our China Shop Project will be attempting to read those values from the Registry. What will happen when they're not there?"

"Just a guess," Dave volunteered. "A Visual Basic error is triggered?"

"Not quite Dave," I said, "As was the case for the code we wrote when writing to the Windows Registry, we'll first try to open the subkey to see if it exists---if it doesn't, the OpenSubKey method will return a null value, and we'll then take that opportunity to create the subkey. Only if the subkey exists, and the Startup value we are looking for is present, will we attempt to either set the user's preference for a Date/Time display or color selection. You'll see that in just a minute."

"What does the syntax for the GetValue method look like?" Ward asked.

I then displayed the syntax of the GetValue method on the classroom projector.

key.GetValue("BACKCOLOR")

"This is the syntax for the GetValue method," I said, "as you can see, it's pretty simple---having opened the appropriate subkey using the OpenSubKey method, we then specify the name of the value we are looking for as the single argument to the GetValue method."

> **NOTE: There is a version of the GetValue method in which it accepts two arguments. The first is the name of the value to be retrieved, and the second is a default value in the event it's not found. You can experiment with this on your own.**

"…One more thing---you'll need to assign the return value of the GetValue method to a variable of an appropriate type. The return value will be a String data type---but in the case of the China Shop Project, we'll be using the return value to update a Color Data Type—in the instance of the Form's BackColor property---and a Boolean Data Type—in order to specify the user's preference for the display of the Date and Time. That will complicate things just a bit, as you'll see when you do the following exercise to modify the Load event procedure of the China Shop form."

There were no more questions, and so I gave my students this exercise to complete.

Exercise 15-3 Reading from the Windows Registry

In this exercise, we'll place code in the Load event procedure of the form to read the entries we wrote to the Registry in Exercise 15-2.

1. Load the China Shop Project.
2. Find the Load event procedure of the form. Modify it so that it looks like this.

```
Private Sub Main_Load(ByVal sender As System.Object, _
   ByVal e As System.EventArgs) Handles MyBase.Load

   Dim line As String
   Dim fields() As String
   Dim delimiter As Char = ","
   Dim intCounter As Integer
   Dim key As RegistryKey              'New declaration

   Try
      Dim sr As New StreamReader("C:\VBFILES\CHINA\PRICES.TXT")

      Do
         line = sr.ReadLine()
```

```
        If line Is Nothing Then Exit Do
        ReDim Preserve m_sngBowlPrice(intCounter)
        ReDim Preserve m_sngButterPlatePrice(intCounter)
        ReDim Preserve m_sngCupPrice(intCounter)
        ReDim Preserve m_sngPlatePrice(intCounter)
        ReDim Preserve m_sngPlatterPrice(intCounter)
        ReDim Preserve m_sngSaucerPrice(intCounter)
        ReDim Preserve m_sngCompletePrice(intCounter)

        fields = line.Split(delimiter)
        lstBrands.Items.Add(fields(0))
        m_sngPlatePrice(intCounter) = fields(1)
        m_sngButterPlatePrice(intCounter) = fields(2)
        m_sngBowlPrice(intCounter) = fields(3)
        m_sngCupPrice(intCounter) = fields(4)
        m_sngSaucerPrice(intCounter) = fields(5)
        m_sngPlatterPrice(intCounter) = fields(6)
        m_sngCompletePrice(intCounter) = fields(7)

        intCounter = intCounter + 1
    Loop

    sr.Close()

Catch F As FileNotFoundException
    MessageBox.Show("A file required by the China Shop program is missing." & _
            Chr(13) & "Please ensure that PRICES.TXT" & _
            Chr(13) & "is in The China Shop directory on " & _
            "the computer's hard drive", _
            "Bullina China Shop")
    Me.Close()
Catch ex As Exception
    MessageBox.Show("An unexpected error has occurred." & _
            Chr(13) & ex.Message, _
            "Bullina China Shop")
    Me.Close()
End Try

' New Registry Reading code here

key = Registry.CurrentUser.OpenSubKey("Software\\BullinaChina\\StartUp")
If key Is Nothing Then
    key = Registry.CurrentUser.CreateSubKey("Software\\BullinaChina\\StartUp")
End If

If key.GetValue("DATEDISPLAY") Then
    m_blnDateDisplay = Convert.ToBoolean(key.GetValue("DATEDISPLAY"))
End If

If m_blnDateDisplay Then
    mnuPreferencesDateAndTimeOn.PerformClick()
Else
    mnuPreferencesDateAndTimeOff.PerformClick()
End If

If key.GetValue("BACKCOLOR") Then
    m_intBackColor = Convert.ToInt32(key.GetValue("BACKCOLOR"))
    Me.BackColor = Color.FromArgb(m_intBackColor)
End If
End Sub
```

3. Click the Save icon on the toolbar to save the China Shop Project.

4. Run the program. When the program starts up, the changes you made in Exercise 15-2 to the form's background color and to the date and time display will be restored.

Discussion

"This looks and feels like a Windows program now," Linda said, obviously proud of herself.

"Congratulations, everyone," I said excitedly, "this completes the China Shop Project! At this point, we have fulfilled all of the requirements we agreed to in our written Requirements Statement with Joe Bullina."

"So we're done?" Rhonda asked. "Just about," I said. "In the second half of today's class we'll optimize our code a bit—but as far as Joe Bullina is concerned, it's time for him to pop the champagne! Let's take a look at the code in the Load event procedure."

"Really, not much of it has changed," Blaine said.

"That's right, Blaine," I said. "Just a few lines of code are necessary to read our Registry entries and to update the form accordingly. These lines of code create a RegistryKey object, and then use the GetValue method to locate the DATEDISPLAY key in the Windows Registry."

```
key = Registry.CurrentUser.OpenSubKey("Software\\BullinaChina\\StartUp")

If key Is Nothing Then
    key = Registry.CurrentUser.CreateSubKey("Software\\BullinaChina\\StartUp")
End If

If key.GetValue("DATEDISPLAY") Then
    m_blnDateDisplay = Convert.ToBoolean(key.GetValue("DATEDISPLAY"))
End If
```

"Notice," I said, "that because the value of DateDisplay is stored as a string in the Windows Registry, and m_blnDateDisplay is declared as a Boolean data type, we need to convert the return value of the GetValue method to a Boolean data type using the Convert.ToBoolean method of the Convert class."

"So that's what the line of code is doing," Kate said. "I wasn't sure what was going on there."

"That's an odd construct for the If statement and the GetValue for DATEDISPLAY?" Ward pondered. "What are you saying there?"

"We're checking to see if there is a key value for DATEDISPLAY," I said. "If the value doesn't exist, then the return value of the GetValue method would be Nothing. VB doesn't have an explicit way to check for 'Something'---this is the way to do it."

I continued by explaining that once we read the value of the DateDisplay key from the Windows Registry, its value, after we convert it to a Boolean data type, is then assigned to the m_blnDateDisplay form-level variable.

Linda said, "In and of itself, that doesn't impact the display of the data and time on the form?"

"That's right, Linda," I said. "At this point, we've read the value for the user's preference for date and time from the Windows Registry—now we have to act on that preference. That's what this next Section of code does."

```
If m_blnDateDisplay Then
    mnuPreferencesDateAndTimeOn.PerformClick()
Else
    mnuPreferencesDateAndTimeOff.PerformClick()
End If
```

"This code really confused me," Ward said. "What's going on here?"

"We're checking the value of the variable m_blnDateDisplay for a True value," I explained. "If the value is equal to True, that means the user prefers to see the date and time displayed on the form. Now, it so happens that we already have code in the Click event procedure of mnuPreferencesDateAndTimeOn that we can 'borrow' by simulating the click of that menu item by executing its PerformClick method."

"Borrow?" Rhonda asked. "What do you mean by that?"

I replied, "You've probably heard the phrase 'Don't reinvent the wheel.' If the user wants to see the date and time displayed, we need to do a number of different things. We need to make the label control in which the date and time appears visible. We need to enable our Timer control. And then we need to set a checkmark on one menu item—Date And Time On—and remove a checkmark from another menu item—Date And Time Off."

"You're right," Dave said, "I forgot all that. And that's exactly what the code in the Click event procedure of mnuPreferencesDateAndTimeOn does. So are you saying that since that event procedure has instructions to perform those methods, executing its PerformClick method will execute that code?"

"Exactly right, Dave," I said. "As I said, why reinvent the wheel? We already have code written to perform those methods. Rather than type it all over again here in the Load event procedure, all we need to do is execute it from there."

"I don't see the words True or False in the If statement," Barbara said. "Are they implied somehow?"

"That's right, Barbara," I replied. "When using Boolean variables in an expression like this, there's no need to code the 'equal to True' part of the expression—the comparison to True is implied. The longer version of the code would look like this."

If m_blnDateDisplay = true Then

"I think using the comparison to True is a little more readable," Ward said.

"That's your choice," I responded. "I wanted you to see this style, because you'll see it a lot in other programmers' code. How readable it is depends on their selection of a meaningful variable name. In this instance, someone else reading our code would know they are working with a Boolean data type because of the 'bln' prefix."

I waited for a moment before continuing.

"In the same way," I said, "if the user's preference is that we not display a date and time, then we execute the code in the Click event procedure of mnuPreferencesDateAndTimeOff by executing its PerformClick method.

"Again, to avoid reinventing the wheel," Rhonda said.

"That's right," I replied. "By the way, borrowing code like this is something you should do whenever possible. Not only does it save you typing, it eliminates the possibility of making a mistake when repeating the code. Plus—and this is a big plus—if you need to change the code executed when the user decides on a preference, you only need to change it in one place."

"I can see that as a big advantage," Ward said. "Let's finish up our review of this code by looking at the code to read the user's preferred color from the Registry, and to then modify the BackColor property of our Form."

If key.GetValue("BACKCOLOR") Then
    m_intBackColor = Convert.ToInt32(key.GetValue("BACKCOLOR"))
    Me.BackColor = Color.FromArgb(m_intBackColor)
End If

"You may recall," I said, "that when we stored the user's preferred color in the Windows Registry, we first converted the color to a long integer, then stored the String value of that number in the Windows Registry. Likewise, when we read the value from the Registry, since the value is a string, we need to convert it back to an integer. That's why we execute the ToInt32 method of the Convert class against it prior to assigning it to the variable m_intBackColor."

m_intBackColor = Convert.ToInt32(key.GetValue("BACKCOLOR"))

"…This line of code takes the numeric value of m_intBackColor, and uses the FromARGB of the Color object variable to convert it to a special Color object, then assigns that value to the BackColor property of our form."

Me.BackColor = Color.FromArgb(m_intBackColor)

After a few seconds, Ward said, "I hear what you're saying, but it's going to take a while for that to sink in."

I explained to Ward, and the rest of the class, that of all the things they would learn in the world of Visual Basic programming, probably no single topic would be as confusing—at least initially—as objects.

I asked if there were any more questions, but there were none.

"Again, I want to congratulate all of you for completing your first programming application," I said. "The China Shop Project is now functionally complete, although we will be enhancing it just a bit after break. After that, we'll give the program a thorough test before heading off to the China Shop to deliver and install it."

"When is Joe Bullina expecting us?" Kathy asked.

"Around 3:00 P.M." I said as I checked the classroom clock. "It's 12:30 now. Why don't we take a quick break, and when we return, we'll discuss some optimization techniques. Then we'll pack up and head off to the China Shop."

As my students vanished in the direction of the vending machines, I took a quick peek out the windows of the classroom toward the parking lot. No sign of Rose and Jack yet.

Optimizing Visual Basic Code

No sooner did I turn around from the window that I discovered that the classroom was full again. Apparently everyone was so excited at the prospect of delivering the China Shop Project to Joe Bullina that they had quickly returned from break. After checking the parking lot one more time for Rose and Jack, I excused myself for a minute and gave Joe Bullina a call to confirm that we were on schedule to arrive at the China Shop at 3:00.

"Our final topic for today—and for the course," I said upon returning to the classroom, "is to see if there is any way to optimize the code we wrote."

"What exactly is meant by code optimization anyway?" Bob asked. "I've heard that term quite a bit."

"There are two types of code optimization," I said. "Optimization to make your code more readable—which means it's easier to understand, maintain, and modify—and optimization to make your program run more quickly and efficiently."

User-Written Procedures

"Virtually all of the code that we've written in the China Shop Project," I continued, "with the exception of some form-level variables, has been placed in an event procedure. We know that event procedures are executed when the event they are associated with is triggered in the Windows environment. For instance, if the user clicks a button, the Click event procedure of that Button control is executed, along with any code that has been placed within it. In Exercise 15-3, we saw how we can execute the code in one event procedure from another by triggering an event from another procedure. It's also possible to write procedures of our own, sometimes called a user-written procedure."

"Are you talking about creating our own event procedures?" Bob asked.

"No, not an event procedure," I said. "Event procedures are procedures that are triggered when an event takes place. I'm talking about creating procedures that are not associated with a particular event."

"How is their code executed then, if the procedure isn't triggered by an event?" Joe asked.

"We call it ourselves from another procedure," I answered.

"Why bother writing your own procedures?" Linda asked. "Are they really necessary? Can't we do everything we need in our programs by writing code in event procedures?"

"You could probably get away without writing your own procedures," I said. "After all, we've done a pretty good job with the China Shop Project and we haven't written one of our own—yet. Nevertheless, writing your own procedures is something that experienced programmers do all the time. They can make your code neater and more readable, and the real payback comes in reducing the amount of duplicated code."

"In other words," Linda added, "the payback comes in not reinventing the wheel."

"That's right, Linda," I said. "In the last exercise, we all saw how we might have been inclined to write the same code in the Load event procedure that was already present in the Click event procedures of mnuPreferencesDateAndTimeOn and mnuPreferencesDateAndTimeOff."

"But we didn't duplicate it," Linda said. "We triggered their respective Click events to execute their code."

"That's right," I said. "But the next logical step would be to take any code that we execute from multiple locations within our program and place it in a single procedure of its own—one that we create ourselves."

"Such as the code in the Click event procedures of those menu items?" Linda asked.

"Yes, the code in those Click event procedures would be good candidates to put into a procedure of its own," I replied. "I should mention that another reason to write your own procedures is modularity. Modularity means that the code in a procedure, either an event procedure or one you write of your own, should perform one function, and one function only. Module code is easier to read, understand, and maintain. And because main functions are broken into modules, making changes to them is easier—all of the code is in a single place. Of course, like anything, modularity can be taken to an extreme. But if you find that you have code in a procedure that is performing a million different functions, that's a good reason to take that code and place it in a procedure of its own."

"Can you give us an example of modularity?" Kate asked.

"I think so, Kate," I said. "Consider the Load event procedure of the China Shop form. Right now, an argument could be made that we have code in this event procedure which is performing more than one function. We're reading the Windows Registry, opening a disk file, loading the lstBrands list box, and loading the elements of an array. That sounds like four functions to me."

"So are you saying that we should take the code in the Load event procedure," Dave asked, "and turn it into four separate user-written procedures?"

"A software engineer would suggest that," I said. "The thing to remember is that our China Shop Project runs perfectly fine as is—we don't need to make a single change to it. But if we take a little time right now to optimize our code, if we ever need to change the China Shop Project, our program will be much easier to modify."

"Where do we place the procedures that we write ourselves?" Barbara asked.

"The procedures that we'll write today will all go in the Declarations section of our form," I replied. "If we had more than one form in our project, and more than one form needed to access the code in our procedure, it would make sense to place them in the Declarations section of what is called a standard module."

There were no more questions and so I suggested that at this point we should examine, in detail, how to write our own procedures.

Writing Our Own Procedures

"There are actually two types of procedures," I said, "subprocedures and functions. A subprocedure is a procedure that executes, but does not return a value to the program that calls it. A function executes, but does return a value."

"Like the MessageBox.Show function that returns a value equal to the button the user clicks?" Ward asked.

"That's right, Ward," I said. "That's a good example of a function. We can write functions of our own just like that, although in the China Shop Project, we'll only work with subprocedures."

I waited for questions before continuing.

"I have an exercise for you to complete which I hope will show you just how easy it is to create and write your own subprocedures," I said. "After that, we'll add a subprocedure the China Shop Project."

I then distributed this exercise to my class.

Exercise 15-4 Creating Your Own Subprocedure

In this exercise, you'll learn how to create a subprocedure of your own.

1. Start a new Windows application project.
2. Add a Button control to your form.
3. To add a subprocedure to your project, you need to code the procedure in an open portion of your form module—you cannot insert the code within an existing procedure. A good place to insert your procedure is at the top of the Code window, after the lines that read Public Class and Inherits System.Windows.Forms.Form.
4. You will now create a subprocedure of your own called DisplayAnswer. Open the Code window and type the following line of code.

Public Sub DisplayAnswer()

5. As soon as you press the ENTER key, Visual Basic will insert an End Sub statement for you. Your code should now look like this.

Public Sub DisplayAnswer()

End Sub

6. Now fill in the rest of the subprocedure, so that it looks like this.

Public Sub DisplayAnswer()

Dim intX As Integer = 9
Dim intY As Integer = 13

MessageBox.Show (intX + intY)

End Sub

7. Insert this code into the Click event procedure of the Button control.

```
Private Sub Button1_Click(ByVal sender As System.Object, _
   ByVal e As System.EventArgs) Handles Button1.Click

Call DisplayAnswer()

End Sub
```

8. Save your program—you'll be modifying it in Exercise 15-5.

9. Run the program and click the button. The number 22 will be displayed in a message box.

Discussion

"Congratulations!" I said. "You've all just written your first subprocedure."

"Is that all there is to it?" Rhonda asked. "I thought it would be much more complicated than this."

"Rhonda's right," I said, "this wasn't bad at all. All we needed to do was code a procedure header—the first line of the procedure—write the code, and then call the procedure from somewhere else in our program."

"When we named and defined the procedure," Mary asked, "why did we place an empty set of parentheses after the procedure name?"

"That empty set of parentheses tells Visual Basic that our procedure has no arguments," I explained. "That tells Visual Basic we won't be passing it any qualifying arguments when we call it. In other words, we just want the code to run exactly as it stands."

I asked if anyone had any problems completing the exercise.

"When I first created the procedure," Valerie said, "I misspelled its name, and when I called it, I received an error message saying that the procedure I was calling wasn't found. It was easy enough to figure out what went wrong and fix it."

"I think I mentioned this tip earlier," I said, "but if I didn't, here goes again. Define all of your procedure names in mixed case, as we did here. Then when you reference the procedure name in your code, type it in lowercase. If Visual Basic doesn't change the name of the procedure to mixed case for you, you know that something's wrong somewhere. Either you misspelled the procedure name, or the procedure isn't named with the name you think it is."

"That's right, I remember you saying that." Valerie commented. "I should have noticed when I coded the Call statement that the procedure name wasn't changed to mixed case. I typed it in lowercase and it stayed that way."

"Do we need to use the keyword Call when we call our procedures?" Kate asked.

"No," I replied, "using keyword Call is optional, although I prefer to use it. It alerts me—and others reading my code—that the procedure I'm calling is a user-written procedure. We could just as easily have coded the call of the procedure like this."

DisplayAnswer()

"What about naming conventions for the procedures we write?" Barbara asked.

"That's a good question, Barbara," I said. "Here are some Microsoft recommendations for naming procedures." I then displayed these Microsoft recommendations on the classroom projector:

- The procedure name should use mixed case and be as long as necessary to describe its purpose.

- For frequently used or long terms, standard abbreviations are recommended to help keep name lengths reasonable.

"How is a function different from a procedure?" Joe asked. "And how do we code one in Visual Basic?"

"The difference is that a function returns a value," I answered. "There is a bit of a trick in passing the return value back to the code calling it. In Visual Basic, we set the function name equal to the return value, usually as the last line of code in the function. I'd like to give you all an opportunity to code up a function of your own—a slight variation on the DisplayAnswer subprocedure we just coded."

I then distributed this exercise to the class for them to complete.

Exercise 15-5 Creating Your Own Function

In this exercise, you'll learn how to create a function of your own.

1. Continue working with the project from Exercise 15-4.
2. Add a second Button control to your form.
3. Adding a function to your project is no different than adding a subprocedure. You need to code the function in an open portion of your form module— you cannot insert the code within an existing procedure. A good place to insert your function is at the top of the Code window, after the line that reads Public Class, right above the Load event procedure.
4. You will now create a function of your own called FDisplayAnswer. Open the Code window and type the following line of code.

Public Function FDisplayAnswer() As Integer

5. As soon as you hit the ENTER key, Visual Basic will insert an End Function statement for you. Your code should now look like this.

Public Sub FDisplayAnswer()

End Function

6. Now fill in the rest of the function, so that it looks like this.

Public Function FDisplayAnswer() As Integer

Dim intX As Integer = 5
Dim intY As Integer = 7

FDisplayAnswer = intX + intY

End Function

7. Insert this code into the Click event procedure of the second Button control.

Private Sub Button2_Click(ByVal sender As System.Object, _
 ByVal e As System.EventArgs) Handles Button2.Click

Dim intRetValue As Integer

intRetValue = FDisplayAnswer()

MessageBox.Show(intRetValue)

End Sub

8. Save your program, although you won't be modifying it any further.
9. Run the program and click the second button. The number 12 will be displayed in a message box.

Discussion

"Congratulations!" I said. "You've all just written your first function."

"I see that a function is similar to a procedure," Kate said. "There were two differences that I saw in the definition itself. First, the function header contains an 'As' clause. I presume that's the data type of the return value?"

"That's right, Kate," I agreed. "Since a function returns a value, we need to include the data type of the return value in the function header. What else did you notice was different?"

"The way the return value is passed back to the calling code," Steve chimed in.

"That's right, Steve," I said, "the return value is passed back to the calling code by assigning a value to the function name with this line of code."

FDisplayAnswer = intX + intY

"The call to the function is a bit different also, isn't it?" Chuck asked.

"Yes, it is," I agreed. "Because a function returns a value, when we call a function, we need to expect a return value. That means either assigning the return value to a variable or using it in an expression. In this exercise, we declared a variable called intRetValue…"

Dim intRetValue As Integer

"…and then assigned the return value of our function call to it using this line of code."

intRetValue = FDisplayAnswer()

"Finally, with this line of code we display the return value in a message box."

MessageBox.Show(intRetValue)

It appeared that everyone was following along. I waited a moment and then asked if there were any questions. There were none. I glanced at the classroom clock. It was about 1:30, and I was conscious that I had promised Joe Bullina we'd make it to the China Shop by 3:00. I was just about to start talking again when I became aware of a distraction in the classroom.

"Rose and Jack," I said, as I saw the happy couple come into the classroom.

"Welcome back. It's great to see you. We were getting worried that you wouldn't make it."

"You didn't tell anyone about our surprise, did you?" Rose asked, smiling.

"No, I didn't," I replied. "You swore me to secrecy—and I must say I keep a secret better than anyone I know."

"What secret?" Rhonda asked excitedly.

"The strangest thing happened on our cruise from London to New York," Jack said. "We were eating a late dinner on Thursday night. It was about 11:40, just short of midnight, when this incredible urge came over us…"

"Well, what happened?" Blaine asked

"We made our way to the bridge of the ship," Rose explained, "looking for the captain. He wasn't there, and so we asked the first officer to get him out of his cabin."

"Go on," Lou said excitedly, "this is getting interesting. Don't tell me you noticed something on the horizon?"

"The first officer found the captain," Jack said, "and after he came to the bridge, something caught his eye, and he ordered the engines scaled back to half speed. And then…"

"And then what?" Mary asked anxiously.

"He married us," Rose replied. "Right there on the bridge of the ship."

"I didn't think sea captains still did that," Ward said.

"So that's the big surprise!" Valerie said. "Congratulations. And I'm so glad you decided to spend your honeymoon in the China Shop with all of us. You two are really dedicated!"

"Professor Smiley has been keeping us apprised of the developments with the China Shop Project," Rose explained. "And of course, we took our laptops along with us on the voyage. In fact, we're both right about where the rest of the class is. I don't think we've missed a beat."

"Well, Rose and Jack," I said, "I'm glad that you're both back with us today. With the two of you back in the fold again, we can put a nice close to the project we all started sixteen weeks ago. How about if we make a few enhancements to the China Shop Project before we deliver it?"

Subprocedures in the China Shop Project

"What kind of enhancements will we be making?" Rose asked.

"I thought it would be a good idea," I said, "if we move some of the code we've already written into separate subprocedures. This will make our code more modular, which will make it easier to read, follow, and modify in the future if we need to."

I then distributed the final exercise of the course to my students to complete.

Exercise 15-6 Coding the China Shop Project Subprocedures

In this exercise, you'll take the code in the Load event procedure of the form and place it into two separate procedures called ReadTheRegistry and ReadPrices.

1. Load the China Shop Project.
2. You will now create a subprocedure called ReadTheRegistry. Open the Code window and type the following line of code.

Public Sub ReadTheRegistry()

3. As soon as you hit the ENTER key, Visual Basic will insert an End Sub statement for you. Your code should now look like this.

Public Sub ReadTheRegistry()

End Sub

4. Now fill in the rest of the subprocedure, so that it looks like the following code. You may recognize this as some of the code that currently exists in the Load event procedure of the form. Don't worry about that for now. You'll erase this code from the Load event procedure shortly.

```
Public Sub ReadTheRegistry()
  Dim key As RegistryKey
  key = Registry.CurrentUser.OpenSubKey("Software\\BullinaChina\\StartUp")
  If key Is Nothing Then
     key = Registry.CurrentUser.CreateSubKey("Software\\BullinaChina\\StartUp")
  End If
  If key.GetValue("DATEDISPLAY") Then
     m_blnDateDisplay = Convert.ToBoolean(key.GetValue("DATEDISPLAY"))
  End If
  If m_blnDateDisplay Then
     mnuPreferencesDateAndTimeOn.PerformClick()
  Else
     mnuPreferencesDateAndTimeOff.PerformClick()
  End If
  If key.GetValue("BACKCOLOR") Then
     m_intBackColor = Convert.ToInt32(key.GetValue("BACKCOLOR"))
     Me.BackColor = Color.FromArgb(m_intBackColor)
  End If
End Sub
```

5. You will now create a subprocedure called ReadPrices. Type the following line of code after the ReadTheRegistry subprocedure.

Public Sub ReadPrices()

6. As soon as you hit the ENTER key, Visual Basic will insert an End Sub statement for you. Your code should now look like this.

Public Sub ReadPrices()

End Sub

7. Now fill in the rest of the subprocedure, so that it looks like the following code. You may recognize this as some of the code that currently exists in the Load event procedure of the form. Don't worry about that for now. You'll erase this code from the Load event procedure shortly.

```
Public Sub ReadPrices()
  Dim line As String
  Dim fields() As String
  Dim delimiter As Char = ","
  Dim intCounter As Integer
  Try
    Dim sr As New StreamReader("C:\VBFILES\CHINA\PRICES.TXT")
    Do
       line = sr.ReadLine()
       If line Is Nothing Then Exit Do
```

```
        ReDim Preserve m_sngBowlPrice(intCounter)
        ReDim Preserve m_sngButterPlatePrice(intCounter)
        ReDim Preserve m_sngCupPrice(intCounter)
        ReDim Preserve m_sngPlatePrice(intCounter)
        ReDim Preserve m_sngPlatterPrice(intCounter)
        ReDim Preserve m_sngSaucerPrice(intCounter)
        ReDim Preserve m_sngCompletePrice(intCounter)

        fields = line.Split(delimiter)
        lstBrands.Items.Add(fields(0))
        m_sngPlatePrice(intCounter) = fields(1)
        m_sngButterPlatePrice(intCounter) = fields(2)
        m_sngBowlPrice(intCounter) = fields(3)
        m_sngCupPrice(intCounter) = fields(4)
        m_sngSaucerPrice(intCounter) = fields(5)
        m_sngPlatterPrice(intCounter) = fields(6)
        m_sngCompletePrice(intCounter) = fields(7)

        intCounter = intCounter + 1
      Loop

      sr.Close()

    Catch F As FileNotFoundException
      MessageBox.Show("A file required by the China Shop program is missing." & _
              Chr(13) & "Please ensure that PRICES.TXT" & _
              Chr(13) & "is in The China Shop directory on " & _
              "the computer's hard drive", _
              "Bullina China Shop")
      Me.Close()
    Catch ex As Exception
      MessageBox.Show("An unexpected error has occurred." & _
              Chr(13) & ex.Message, _
              "Bullina China Shop")
      Me.Close()
    End Try

End Sub
```

8. All of the code in the Load event procedure of the form has been moved to the two subprocedures we just coded. Modify the code in the Load event procedure so that it looks like this.

```
Private Sub Main_Load(ByVal sender As System.Object, _
  ByVal e As System.EventArgs) Handles MyBase.Load

Call ReadTheRegistry()

Call ReadPrices()

End Sub
```

9. Click the Save icon on the toolbar to save the China Shop Project.

10. Run the program. Verify that the program behaves as it did before (it should, we haven't changed any code, just moved it). In particular, make sure that the list box of china items is loaded at startup, along with the user's preferences for color and date and time display. You should also verify that the Exception Handler, now in ReadPrices, works if the PRICES.TXT file is missing.

Discussion

"All we really did in this exercise," I explained, "was to take code out of the Load event procedure of the China Shop form and place it into two subprocedures of our own—ReadTheRegistry and ReadPrices."

"Now tell me why we did this again?" Rhonda asked.

"For a couple of reasons," I said. "The first was readability. I'm sure you would agree that the code in the Load event procedure is a lot easier to read and understand than it was before. We took the cumbersome code we had there before and placed it in two separate subprocedures. And that brings us to the second reason—modularity. We now have a subprocedure devoted to doing one function, reading the Registry. And a second subprocedure devoted to reading prices into an array from the PRICES.TXT file. Modularity makes modifying programs much easier. For instance, if we later decide to store another value in the Windows Registry, we know where all of the code in our program that reads the Registry is located—it's in the ReadTheRegistry subprocedure."

Dave said, "Also, if we ever need to read the Registry to obtain the user's current preferences, all we need to do is call the ReadTheRegistry subprocedure from anywhere within the program."

"That's a great point, Dave," I said.

"Should we write a subprocedure to write to the Registry also?" Jack asked.

"We certainly could do that, Jack," I said, once again glancing at the classroom clock. "But right now, I think everyone is eager to get to the China Shop. Let's consider doing that during our Feedback and Maintenance phase. I'm sure we'll be doing some fine tuning of the program anyway. And now, for the last time in this course, are there any questions?"

No one had any—there seemed to be great anticipation among my students.

"I want to thank everyone for an excellent class," I said, "I can't remember ever enjoying a class more, and I can't think of a better group of people to have spent four months of Saturdays with than you folks."

"Don't get sentimental on us now," Linda said. "You know we'll all be back next semester to take your Intermediate Visual Basic course. Besides, we still have some work to do. Shouldn't we be heading over to the China Shop now?"

"Absolutely," I replied, "We don't want to keep Joe Bullina waiting."

Testing Our Program

"How are we going to work this?" Dave asked. "Counting yours, we have nineteen different versions of the China Shop Project. And since you encouraged us to be creative, we don't have nineteen carbon copies of the program either—each person's version is different. Which one are we going to install in the China Shop?"

"When I spoke to Joe Bullina earlier in the week," I explained, "I told him exactly that myself, Dave. I guess because he's in a customer service business, he's reluctant to hurt anyone's feelings— in short, he doesn't want to be the one to pick the version of the program to be installed in the China Shop. And of course, neither do I. Joe asked that prior to arriving at the China Shop today, we find a way to pick one of the program versions as the one to be installed in the China Shop. So here's what I'm going to ask you to do. I want you all to spend the next ten minutes or so testing your programs and making any fine-tuning adjustments you deem necessary. Then I'd like you to take a quick walk around the classroom observing your classmates' programs. On my desk I have a ballot form where you can vote for what you consider to be the top three programs. The program that receives the most first-place votes will be the program that we install at the China Shop. And just so you don't feel compelled to vote for me, I'm removing my version of the program from eligibility. This is your project, and one of you deserves to have the place of honor in the China Shop."

"Can you give us some guidelines on testing our programs?" Linda asked.

"Sure thing, Linda," I said. "At a minimum, the program must properly calculate a sales quotation. You all have the Requirements Statement with the price matrix included, so run through some pricing scenarios to ensure that the program is working. You also want to make sure the program has the flexibility to dynamically change prices and even brands of china offered by updating the PRICES.TXT file."

"I would think that most of the real bugs have been discovered by now," Valerie commented.

"I'm not sure we can say that with 100 percent certainty," I said. "There's always the possibility that something might have slipped through. However, I think I can say with a great deal of confidence that this program is bug free. Obviously, the more complicated the program, the less certain you will feel."

"Should we test each and every price combination?" Rhonda asked. "That's a lot of testing."

"You're right, Rhonda," I said. "There are many possible price combinations here, but I don't ordinarily test each and every one. I do something called scenario testing. I write down several representative scenarios on a piece of paper and test them. For instance, customer John Smith comes into the China Shop and selects a brand of Mikasa, a platter, a plate, and a cup, with a quantity of two each. I then calculate the sales quotation manually and then run the program to see if the program's calculated price matches the one I worked out on paper."

"I did something similar to that," Chuck said, "except that I used Microsoft Excel to develop a worksheet of possible scenarios. Then I ran my program and tested as many possibilities as I could."

"That's a good idea, Chuck," I agreed.

My students then spent the next fifteen minutes or so testing their programs one last time, carefully reviewing their classmates' projects, and voting for what they considered to be the top three projects. As I collected their ballots and tallied the totals, I asked everyone in the class to give me a disk with a copy of their project as well.

"Class is officially dismissed for today," I said as I gave everyone a copy of a map to the China Shop. "I'll see you all at the China Shop—and please drive safely."

I called Dave aside. Dave had volunteered to coordinate the installation of the program on the China Shop's PC. I handed him the disk of the project that had received the most first-place votes.

"The way I drive," I said, "I'm sure I'll wind up being the last one to arrive at the China Shop. Would you mind installing this project?"

"I'd be glad to," Dave said, as he glanced at the student's name on the disk and smiled. "I'll take care of this. See you there."

We Meet at the Bullina China Shop

No sooner was I out the classroom door than a former student of mine stopped me in the hallway with a Java problem. Half an hour later, I was finally on my way. As I am not the world's fastest driver, I arrived nearly an hour late at the China Shop.

When I arrived, I could tell from the lack of available parking places in the China Shop parking lot that a lot of fanfare was taking place inside. As I walked through the door, my eyes and ears were met with an incredible amount of activity. The place was packed with staff, students, and customers. A buffet table of simply delicious-looking food was set up in the middle of the China Shop, and balloons and streamers hung from the ceiling.

Joe Bullina caught sight of me.

"John, this program is wonderful," he said excitedly. "I can't believe what a great job your students did with this. Everyone simply loves the program. The customers love it. The sales staff loves it. I love it. Here, have a sandwich!"

Amid the hullabaloo, I glanced toward the middle of the China Shop and there, on a kiosk in the middle of the sales floor, was a computer running the China Shop Project. And there stood Rhonda in front of the computer, training the sales staff with all the confidence of an accomplished, experienced programmer.

"Joe, I've got to tell you that you really know how to celebrate the computer age!" I said.

"For the last ten minutes Rhonda's been proudly demonstrating her version of the China Shop Project to the sales staff," Joe explained. "She really did a wonderful job with her program. My sales staff seems mesmerized by her program—they haven't moved from their seats."

Joe shouted across the room. "Come on, Midge, give the customers a chance to use the new program."

I wandered over to the kiosk and caught Rhonda's eye.

"I'm so honored—flabbergasted, really—that the class voted for my version of the program," she said. "To say that this has made my week is an understatement. More like my year. I'm just so overwhelmed that someone like me with absolutely no programming background could write a program like this. And I've got to tell you, I felt like I asked so many stupid questions during the course..."

"You know what I always say, Rhonda," I said, interrupting her, "the only stupid question is the one you don't ask. Your questions were always good ones, and they were probably questions that many of the other students were dying to ask but didn't have the nerve to."

"Really?" Rhonda said. "That's nice of you to say. I've got to tell you—I really enjoyed this course very much. You know, you should consider taking those notes of yours and writing a Visual Basic book—I bet it would be a best seller."

"Maybe I'll do that someday," I told her, "if I ever get a minute."

Joe Bullina caught my eye and pointed out a lively couple who were coming over to the kiosk.

"I met this couple about an hour ago," he said, directing his attention to the man and woman who must have been in their eighties. "I'm not sure if they came in for the free food or because of the Computer Celebration Sale. This is Rita and Gil."

Joe explained to me that when he told Rita and Gil that the China Shop would be implementing a new computer system within the hour they had insisted on being the first customers to use it.

"John and his programming class developed this program," Joe said as he uprooted Midge from in front of the computer, and pulled over two chairs for Rita and Gil.

"Our son is also a computer teacher," Rita said as she sat down on one of the two chairs.

"And he's very good," Gil added.

"Let me say I'm extremely honored to have you be the first customers to use our new computer system," Joe said proudly.

Rita looked up at us and proclaimed, "Gil has promised to buy me new china for our anniversary. Sixty-six happy years on November 23rd."

"Congratulations!" Joe said. Gil sat down on a chair beside Rita and the two of them began to use the system.

"Gil," Linda said, "you seem to be pretty good with that mouse. Have you used a PC before?"

"I used computers for many years while I was still working," Gil explained, "but I've been retired for over twenty years. Back then we didn't have personal computers—everything was mainframes. However, I've gotten pretty good with them during my retirement."

"Those two look very familiar to me," Linda whispered in my ear. "Have we seen them at the university?"

"I don't think so," I told her. "I've had seniors in some of my computer classes, but definitely not these two. But you're right, they do look very familiar to me."

I took out a notepad and made some notes of Rita and Gil's first session with the China Shop Project. While they worked at the kiosk, I chatted with some of the other students from the class, as I continued to observe them. After a few minutes, Rita and Gil rose from their chairs and made their way to the counter at the front of the store.

"The China Shop Project worked as designed," I told my assembled class. "The customers— Rita and Gil—used the program to make selections of china, received a sales quotation, and after making a decision, they walked to the counter and purchased their china."

As I finished speaking, another customer took his place in front of the kiosk. Linda, sensing that he was having some difficulty using the program, came over to assist him. I heard Linda ask his name (Bill, I believe). As Linda proceeded to assist him, I gathered as many of my students as I could gather around the kiosk. Some of them were still eating the sandwiches that Joe Bullina had provided for us. By now, there was a quite a crowd gathered around Linda and the man with the thick head of black hair using the program.

"I want to thank Dave for installing Rhonda's version of the China Shop Project on the kiosk PC," I said. "Installing the program on the kiosk PC began Phase 5 of the SDLC, the Implementation phase. Installation, fine tuning, and training are all part of this phase."

Joe Bullina was standing next to me, and I turned to him and said that Phase 5 of the SDLC likely would last for at least the next week.

"Pairs of students have volunteered to be on site to make observations and assist with any problems that may come up," I explained. "And I should tell you they volunteered even before they knew what kind of party you throw. Part of what they'll be doing is showing your sales staff how to update your inventory prices."

"It's comforting to know they'll be here," he said. "I think I'll need to order more sandwiches! By the way, what are those notes you're taking?"

"Even though we're now in the midst of Phase 5 of the SDLC," I replied, "we can proceed concurrently with Phase 6, which is feedback and maintenance."

"Feedback and maintenance?" Joe asked.

"We want to make sure that the program is behaving according to the Requirements Statement we gave you when we agreed to write the program," I explained. "A big part of this phase is observing the program to see how it's being used and how well it's being received by your customers—those observations are in my notes."

"And don't forget to record how it's being admired," Joe Bullina added proudly.

"I have to agree that positive feedback is a wonderful thing," I said, smiling.

"What about maintenance?" Joe asked. "What's involved in that?"

"The maintenance phase handles any changes to the program that are necessitated by governmental regulations, changes in your business rules, or just changes that you decide you want to make to the program," I replied.

"After seeing the great work you've done on the project," he said, "I'm sure I'll have more work for your class."

"Sadly, though," I said, "today marks the end of our introductory Visual Basic course—any changes you need will have to be done by another class. However, many of these students will be signed up for my intermediate programming course starting in five weeks."

Joe seemed happy with the idea of having that class enhance the program, and I watched him walk to the counter with customer Bill, who was making a surprise purchase of china for his daughter.

"That fellow looks very familiar to me also," Linda said. "What is it about this place? Maybe Joe Bullina should rename it Déjà Vu. By the way, can I see your notes from Rita and Gil's session at the kiosk?"

"Here they are," I said, as I handed Linda my notes. "Based on my initial observations, I think I already know what our first change to the program will be. We've got to make the font size larger for our customers over the age of 40!" Linda began to read my observations:

1. Rita sits down at the computer.

2. Rita wants Mikasa china, so she clicks on Mikasa in the list box. The Mikasa pattern appears in the Image control.

3. Rita wants a complete place setting, so she clicks on the Complete Place Setting check box. Five check marks appear for the china items comprising a complete place setting.

4. Rita clicks the Calculate button.

5. A message box displays a warning that she has not yet picked a quantity. The bell that sounds when the message box displays startles her.

6. Rita clicks OK to make the message box go away.

7. Rita selects a quantity of 8 by clicking the option button labeled 8.

8. Rita clicks Calculate.

9. A message box displays a message that the calculated price reflects a discount for a complete place setting. I think both Rita and Gil are puzzled as to what this message means. Rita clicks OK to make the message box go away.

10. The order price of $400 is displayed in the lower left corner of the form.

11. Gil takes over and clicks the Reset button. All of the controls are reset.

12. Gil is having trouble seeing the display, so he changes the color from the default gray to cyan by using the main menu of the form. A larger font here would be a good idea.

13. Gil believes they are running late for a movie they want to see. He turns the display of the date and time on using the form's menu. Now he knows they are late!

14. Gil thinks the price of Mikasa is too expensive and clicks on Farberware in the list box.

15. Gil doesn't think they need a complete place setting. He selects the plate, cup, saucer, and a platter.

16. Gil thinks they only need four of each. He clicks the option button labeled 4.

17. Gil only wants one platter, but is confused because there is no place to specify a quantity for just the platter.

18. Gil clicks the Calculate button.

19. A message box is displayed saying that he is limited to a quantity of one platter. He clicks OK to make the message box go away.

20. The order price of $77 is displayed in the lower left corner of the form.

21. They get up to go to the counter to make their purchase.

"Interesting observations," Linda said.

"Joe," I said, turning to Joe Bullina for a final time, "on behalf of everyone in the class, I want to thank you for the wonderful opportunity you've given us to work on a first-rate project. I'm sure we'll be in touch."

I shouted across the room to my assembled class, "I've got to take off now. Everyone please be mindful of your coverage schedules and, if you have any problems, you all know where to find me. I hope to see you in five weeks."

Summary

Congratulations! You've finished the class, and completed and implemented the China Shop Project. I hope you felt the same excitement my students did at delivering and installing the China Shop Project—because you were a big part of it also. But please don't let this be the end of your learning.

At this point, you should feel confident enough to tackle a variety of Visual Basic programs. I hope that by following along with my introductory computer programming class, you've seen how real-world applications are developed.

That's not to say that all projects go as smoothly as this one did, nor does every client meet us on implementation day with sandwiches, balloons, and streamers. You can expect your share of mistakes, misinterpretations, and misunderstandings along the way. Nevertheless, it's always exciting, and if you love it as I do, it's always fun.

As I close, I just want to give you a few words of advice. First, remember that in programming there's rarely a single "correct" solution. Secondly, always be your own best friend. Inevitably, while trying to work through a solution, there will be frustrating moments. Never doubt yourself, and never get down on yourself.

Finally, remember that there is always more to learn. The world of programming is an endless series of free learning seminars. All you need to do is open up a manual, read a help file, surf the Internet, or even pick up a copy of your favorite programming book, and you are well on your way. You can never know it all, let alone master it all. But always try to move in that direction. Good luck and I hope to see you in another Visual Basic class some day!

Index

CPSIA information can be obtained at www.ICGtesting.com
Printed in the USA
BVOW051255170212

283193BV00001B/18/P